APPLETON-CENTURY-CROFTS SOCIOLOGY SERIES

Edited by John F. Cuber

THE SOCIOLOGY OF SOCIAL PROBLEMS

The SOCIOLOGY of SOCIAL PROBLEMS

by
Paul B. Horton
WESTERN MICHIGAN COLLEGE

and
Gerald R. Leslie
PURDUE UNIVERSITY

New York

APPLETON-CENTURY-CROFTS, INC.

Copyright, © 1955 by

APPLETON-CENTURY-CROFTS, INC.

All rights reserved. This book, or parts thereof, must not be reproduced in any form without permission of the publishers.

5126-4

Library of Congress Card Number:
55-9166

PRINTED IN THE UNITED STATES OF AMERICA

Preface

A TEXTBOOK should do at least two things. First, it should present both a body of data and interpretations of those data adequate to meet the reasonably critical demands of professional colleagues and, second, it should present the information in such a fashion as to stimulate and challenge the students who will use it.

Built upon the assumption that modern social science provides the tools to permit significant, systematic, and consistent interpretation of social problems data, this book employs three separate, but related, frames of reference that have proved more than ordinarily useful. Social change and resulting social disorganization, the emergence of value-conflicts, and the influences of personal deviation are brought to bear upon each problem. This is no "omnium gatherum" of facts and varying interpretations of those facts, nor is it a narrowly particularistic interpretation.

Part I includes a chapter on the nature and definition of social problems, a chapter on logical and statistical problems involved in the interpretation of facts, and a chapter which outlines the three frames of reference. Part II comprises the major part of the book and consists of a series of chapters devoted to various social problems. Each chapter contains a body of the most relevant data bearing upon the problem and interprets these data in terms of each of the three approaches. Through such practical application, the concepts of social disorganization, value-conflicts, and personal deviation are continuously rendered more meaningful. In Part III, two chapters integrate and re-examine the fully developed concepts. A final chapter projects the completed picture of social problems a short distance into the future and explores briefly the possibilities there.

Most of those who use the book will be lower division students with quite limited training in sociology. The book has been written with these students in mind. It strives to be readable and interesting, and yet sociologically sophisticated. It avoids the use of unnecessary technical jargon but seeks to provide a thorough understanding of basic sociological concepts. It assumes that a textbook need be neither a "students' book" nor an "instructors' book," but may adequately meet the needs of both.

The intellectual and personal debts contracted by the authors in the preparation of the manuscript can only be acknowledged in general. The various footnotes and bibliographic references contained in the text suggest major sources of intellectual obligation. Deep personal gratitude is due to Dr. John F. Cuber who encouraged and assisted us at each step of the way; to the various members of our respective Departments of Sociology who assisted in many different ways; and to our wives, for assistance far beyond the call of duty.

The manuscript remains, however, the sole responsibility of the authors. The organization of the book and the separate chapters were worked out with full and complete collaboration, criticism, discussion, and suggestions among ourselves. In the actual writing, Horton prepared Chs. 1, 3, 5, 6, 8, 10, 12, 13, 15, 17, 19, and 22, and Leslie prepared Chs. 2, 4, 7, 9, 11, 14, 16, 18, 20, and 21.

P. B. H.

G. R. L.

Contents

Part III

CONCLUSIONS

Illustrations

Tables

Part I

ORIENTATION TO THE STUDY OF SOCIAL PROBLEMS

CHAPTER I

Why Study Social Problems?

A group of whites and Negroes stand watching a mechanical cotton picker bring economic, social, and psychic chaos to their lives. A lonely girl permits herself to be picked up by a man. The member of a religious or racial minority turns away in dejection from an employment office, denied again a job because of creed or skin color. A public-health report sums up in cold statistics the story of emaciated and scarred bodies ravaged by tuberculosis and syphilis in an overcrowded urban slum or a disintegrating rural area. A juvenile delinquent, raised in an "exclusive" neighborhood, has his thieving or hoodlumism "covered up" by his parents on a promise "not to do it again." A flood rips through homes, factories, and eroding farm land in one of the country's great river valleys. The sun turns a sickly green at noon during a Kansas dust storm, and the people try to wash the earth out of their mouths and keep it from their lungs. And the finest examples of young manhood leave their home to "save the world for Democracy." [1]

THESE are the personal symptoms of social problems. Their consequences in financial cost and emotional insecurity reach into every home and dislocate the life of every community. This year we shall spend at least $15 billion on social welfare measures, admit 140,000 new patients to mental hospitals, imprison 70,000 new criminals, and pay a national crime bill some four or five times as great as the cost of operating all the nation's schools, colleges, and universities. We cannot escape the conclusion that social problems affect all of us, and that is reason enough for wanting to know something about them. What are they? Why do they exist? Who is responsible for them? How much do they cost? What can be done about them?

To ask these questions takes but a short paragraph; to answer them would require a library with half its shelves filled with books not yet written. Even the first question, What are the social problems?, is much more complicated than it appears.

[1] Alfred McLung Lee and Elizabeth Briant Lee, *Social Problems in America* (New York, Henry Holt & Company, Inc., 1949), p. 3.

3

DEFINITION OF A SOCIAL PROBLEM

Whenever people begin to say, "Isn't it awful! Why don't they do something about it?", we have a social problem. A formal definition might read, "*A social problem is a condition affecting a significant number of people in ways considered undesirable, and about which it is felt something can be done through collective social action.*" This definition has four distinct ideas: (1) a condition affecting a significant number of people; (2) in ways considered undesirable; (3) and about which it is felt something can be done; (4) through collective social action. Each of these four ideas needs to be examined in detail.

1. *"A condition affecting a significant number of people ..."*

One's pet peeves are not social problems unless they also disturb a good many other people. How many people? There is no figure to state how many people must be affected before a condition qualifies as a social problem. But when a condition affects enough people so that a number of them take notice and begin to talk and write about it, a social problem exists. One way of measuring public concern with a condition, for example, is to count the number (and length) of magazine articles devoted to it each year, as listed in the periodical index. When numerous articles are appearing, it is clear that the condition has attracted widespread concern and has become a social problem.

2. *"in ways considered undesirable ..."*

Child labor was no social problem as long as most people considered child labor beneficial. Only when a considerable number of people decided that child labor was harmful and began saying, "Isn't it awful!"—only then did child labor become a social problem. A social problem involves, therefore, a *value-judgment,* a decision that the condition is "*bad.*" A particular person's value-judgment may define a condition either as an undesirable situation requiring change or as a proper and acceptable part of the society. During the Reformation period, such instruments of torture as the stake, rack, and thumbscrew were accepted by both Protestant and Catholic as proper means of defending the faith. Consequently, neither Catholic nor Protestant considered religious intolerance or persecution as a social problem. Neither objected to the *use* of the thumbscrew; to each the problem lay merely in the fact that the "wrong" people were being thumbscrewed. In other words, the values of the period approved the use of torture in suppressing heresy, while values differed as to which heresies should be suppressed. The values of Reformation man, therefore, defined the problem not as the achievement of religious tolerance but as the suppression of dissent. The values held by most of us today would define the problem as exactly the opposite.

These examples show how *values may define any condition as a social problem or prevent designation of any particular condition as a problem.* Suicide, drunkenness, narcotic addiction, homosexuality, starvation, kissing on Sunday, beating one's children, not beating one's children—any of these may be defined as a social problem by the values of the society or may be defined as acceptable and nonproblematic. No condition, no matter how dramatic or shocking to someone else, is a social problem *unless and until* the values of a considerable number of people within the society define it as a problem.

3. "and about which it is felt something can be done ..."

Everybody talked about the weather, but nobody did anything about it until very recently. Conditions that cannot be changed or escaped must be accepted, usually with the aid of a supporting set of rationalizations. In much of the world, until very recently, famine was not a social problem because of the belief that famine was nature's inescapable way of removing surplus population. Flood control became a social problem only when we discovered that floods could be prevented; prior to that time, floods were simply a misfortune to be endured and survived. Now that we may possibly exercise some control over the weather through cloud-seeding, the weather is becoming a social problem, and debate has already arisen over who owns the clouds in the sky and who may say where rain shall fall.

The nature of a problem also changes as techniques of treatment are developed. For centuries, the mental illness problem was purely one of protecting the sane and disposing of the mentally ill; only recently (and to a lesser degree than might be imagined) has the problem become one of treating and curing the mentally ill. This is due not to any hardheartedness of our ancestors, but to their lack of any means of treatment for mental illness.

A condition is a problem when *it is believed* something can be done about it. It is *the belief* in the possibility of treatment that causes people to consider it a problem. Whether this belief is correct can often be determined only by trial. Meanwhile the *hope* of treatment is sufficient to lead people to consider a condition a problem and seek to do something about it.

4. "through collective social action."

If a local butcher short-weights his customers or some lunatic dumps arsenic into a water reservoir, this is not a *social* problem, since a simple police action will dispose of it. No general public discussion, crystallization of value-judgments, exploration of alternatives, determination of treatment, or organization of pressure is needed before the situation can be dealt with. Social problems are confined to those situations which are so complex that public concern, discussion, opinion formation, and pressure are needed if a treatment is to be sought.

Social problems are, therefore, *social in origin* ("a condition affecting a significant number of people..."); *social in definition* ("in ways considered undesirable..."); and *social in treatment* ("and about which it is felt something can be done through collective social action").

FALLACIES ABOUT SOCIAL PROBLEMS

Although most people have a certain amount of knowledge about social problems, much of this "knowledge" is unorganized, frequently contradictory, and often incorrect. A listing of some of the widespread fallacies about social problems will reveal how superficial and unreliable is much of this popular "knowledge."

1. *That People Agree on What Are the Social Problems*

Although many people may agree that housing, poverty, and unemployment are social problems in America, there are many others who emphatically disagree. Important real-estate spokesmen have insisted that there has been no real housing shortage. Some religious sects claim that poverty is spiritually beneficial, while some well-to-do folk argue that poverty is good for people (other people, that is). An occasional employer is heard to remark that a moderate amount of unemployment (three or four million) is a good thing, for it encourages "troublesome" workers to be quiet and work harder. Most people agree that race relations are a social problem in America. To some the problem is how to complete the emancipation of the Negro, whereas to others the problem is how to put him back in his "place." To a rather small but eloquent minority, cigarette smoking is a major social problem and moral issue. Although there may be considerable agreement upon some problems, this agreement is never complete; on other problems there may be very little agreement as to their nature or indeed if they exist.

2. *That Social Problems Are Natural and Inevitable*

To attribute a problem to "natural law" is a delightfully simple way to dispose of it and avoid doing anything about it. The "natural law" cited usually turns out to be an a priori assumption that has emerged from the depths of an armchair rather than the result of scientific research. The "natural law" of self-interest, that is, that people work hard only for private gain, is easily disproved by data from dozens of other cultures, and even in our society would hardly explain the motivation of Florence Nightingale, Thomas Edison, or "Flagpole" Kelley; yet this "law" is often invoked to sanction the status quo. The "natural law of the survival of the fittest," borrowed from zoology where it has some truth, can easily be shown to be quite inoperative in human society, where man-made customs and institutions interfere with the survival process; yet this may be cited as a "natural law of society" to sanction the success of the successful and to discourage sympathy for the unfortunate.

It will be seen in following chapters that social problems are not products of natural law or physical inevitability. In only one sense are social problems inevitable—namely, that *certain social arrangements make certain outcomes inevitable.* But this is a totally different kind of inevitability, because it is somewhat under human control.

3. *That Social Problems Are Abnormal*

Problems are sometimes discussed as though they were unexpected, freakish, unexplainable things which pop up where they have no business being, like sand in a fruit salad. Thus, the slum problem may be discussed as though the slum were an "abnormal" or "substandard" part of our city, with failure to recognize that the slum is just as "natural" and "normal" a product of urban ecological processes as are the business district, the parks and monuments, and the attractive new suburban developments. Such problems as mental illness, alcoholism, and drug addiction are often discussed purely in terms of personal abnormality, with disregard of the fact that the same traditions and social pressures which make a person competitive, ambitious, and hard-working also produce the insecurities and anxieties which may lead to mental illness, alcoholism, or drug addiction. Our high divorce rate is usually described, with much wringing of hands, as a symptom of social breakdown; it is much more accurately viewed as a perfectly logical expression of the high value our society now places on individualism and marital happiness. In short, *social problems are the logical, understandable, and inevitable products of present social values and practices.*

4. *That Social Problems Are Caused by Bad People*

This is probably the most widespread fallacy of all. In many ways we are conditioned to analyze problems in terms of a simple good-bad dichotomy. Our nursery tales are filled with fair young princes decapitating fiery dragons or evil witches, whereupon all dangers cease and joy reigns forever. Most of our novels and practically all of our movies avoid

offending any group by presenting all problems as simple contests between the good people and the bad people, and with the defeat of the
bad people the matter is happily ended. <u>Our religious training has, in
the past, encouraged us to impute evil motives to those who do things we
consider evil.</u> To all this conditioning is added the fact that among the
people involved in social problems, we constantly see some doing "bad"
things—being selfish, brutal, exploitative, lazy, and shiftless. It is easy to
jump to the conclusion that the problem exists *because* some people are
selfish, shiftless, or lazy. When we observe that a drunkard is unemployed,
our conditioning leads us to assume that he is unemployed because he
drinks, not that he drinks because he is unemployed. Although either
possibility may be true, our conditioning prepares us to assume one
explanation and fail even to consider the other.

This makes the average person's study of social problems an elaborate
game of "I spy," a search for the villain instead of a search for insight.
To many people, "doing something" about a social problem means finding
and punishing the "bad" people. The chapters to follow will try to show
how *each problem is a product of existing social institutions and practices
and not primarily a product of willful wickedness.* We shall see how the
"evil" conduct of the persons involved is more properly viewed as a
symptom of the problem and *not its cause.* We shall also see how merely
punishing the "bad" people, although it may relieve our feelings, will
have very little permanent effect upon the problem.

5. *That Problems Are Created by Talking About Them*

This belief takes the form of the suggestion that it is not entirely decent,
gentlemanly, or "American" to talk about things like slums, poverty,
inadequate medical care, or racial discrimination because ignorant and
irresponsible people may become dangerously inflamed. To talk about
such things is to "stir up trouble," "foment class hatred," and so on.
Such a belief is, of course, completely undemocratic and therefore
"un-American," for it assumes that the common people cannot be trusted
to use responsible judgment, whereas democracy is based upon the belief
that the common people can be trusted to make wise decisions most of
the time.

This fear that talk is dangerous exaggerates the excitability of our
people. Most people are more interested in movies and television come-
dians than they are in social issues. If one doubts this, let him try promoting a local forum or discussion group! Reformers have always found
the task of arousing people exasperatingly difficult. Only when the problem deeply affects *them,* or sharply threatens *their* cherished values, are
most people enough concerned even to listen, let alone do anything
about it.

It is true that talking about a problem may lead to a greater public awareness of it, and this may be what some people fear. But to imagine people will tell one another about a nonexistent problem until they have manufactured a myth is to exaggerate people's readiness to borrow trouble.

6. That All People Would Like to See the Problem Solved

The belief that everyone would like to solve the problem, disagreeing only on methods, is a naive illusion. The fact is that for every problem, there are some *people who do not want the problem solved.* During the war, this writer once talked to a women's group about racial discrimination and they nodded sympathetic agreement with each remark; but during the tea which followed, a number were overheard exchanging lamentations because Negro cleaning women were demanding as much money as white workers received! Whatever their professed ideals might be, these women did not wish to surrender their genteel exploitation of Negroes. Certain southwestern farm operators who employ "wet-backs" [2] at very low wages have no interest in doing anything about the "wet-back" problem and strive to prevent effective enforcement of the immigration laws. "Full employment," with plenty of well-paid jobs for everyone, would cause many of us much distress; under such conditions, employers have difficulty in finding good workmen, middle-class housewives cannot get good, cheap cleaning women, and we are annoyed to find stores understaffed, repair work poorly done, and good "service" difficult to obtain.

Plenty of well-paid, pleasant jobs for all would mean that the dirty unpleasant work simply wouldn't get done.[3] Ending residential segregation of Negroes would greatly reduce the income from much housing into which Negroes are now crowded at fantastically high rentals; the owners (some white and some Negro) of this very profitable housing have no interest in reducing residential discrimination. Slum housing, however wretched, is often a highly profitable investment;[4] is it surprising that its

[2] "Wet-backs" are Mexicans who illegally cross the border, generally crossing the river at night, to work as seasonal farm labor. Some farm operators employ them at low wages and may even cheat them of their small earnings by reporting them to the government for deportation after the operators are through with them for the season.

[3] This situation was to a limited extent true during World War II. It would have been even more true had it not been for the Negroes, whom we forced to do most of the dirty, unpleasant jobs by excluding them from most of the nice ones.

[4] Slum property normally earns a rental income far higher than its sale value would justify or, conversely, slum property sells at a price far lower than its rental value would justify. This is due largely to the high risk involved in slum property ownership. Slum property is highly inflammable but often uninsurable, and almost never insurable at a figure that represents its rental earning power. Furthermore, much slum

owners should be disinterested in slum clearance? The big conventions that put so much money in the cash registers of a city's hotels, restaurants, and stores are more likely to visit a city in which high-class prostitution, exciting floor shows, "honest" gambling, and after-hour taverns are readily available. A too-determined enforcement of the laws governing prostitution, gambling, entertainment, and tavern closing hours would, in any major city in America, likely meet the strenuous opposition of powerful sections of the business community and of many local citizens of all classes who enjoy these attractions.

For any social problem one might mention, a sizable array of groups can be found who do not desire its solution. Either their values do not define it as a problem or a solution would prove costly to them in money, status, power, sentiment, or something else they treasure.

7. That Problems Will Solve Themselves

A central element of the American ethos is a general expectation of progress. Although the formal theory of automatic and inevitable social progress has taken quite a beating in the carnage of recent decades, most Americans nevertheless seem to accept it piecemeal, if not *in toto*. Most discussions of any problem are sprinkled with such sage observations as, "Of course, it's improving, and . . . ," or "It's not as bad as it used to be, and. . . ." These statements are sometimes descriptively true, yet behind them often lurks the unspoken suggestion that such progress comes about naturally with the passing of time, like the growth of a tree or the melting of an iceberg. From this position, it is but a short step to the faith that only patience is needed, for time will solve all problems. And this provides a beautiful rationalization for inactivity; it enables one to make a very creditable display of sympathetic feeling for the unfortunates without requiring the sacrifice of a penny of money or an hour of time. It enables one to be both humanitarian and thrifty.

A belief that problems improve if left alone is based on this theory of automatic, inevitable progress, a theory which no social scientist accepts today. To apply it to social problems is naive and unsound. Although some problems (for example, the assimilation of the immigrants) may grow less pressing as time passes, others (crime, traffic, housing) seem to grow more serious. To expect problems to solve themselves will remain a forlorn hope.

---

housing would either be condemned or would require costly repairs if the health and safety laws were enforced. Slum housing, then, is a highly profitable investment, as long as it doesn't burn down and the local officials can be dissuaded from tearing it down.

8. *That "Getting the Facts" Will Solve the Problem*

No problem can be treated intelligently without first "getting the facts" about it, but "getting the facts" is no guarantee that people will interpret those facts in the same way. Facts in themselves mean nothing and lead nowhere. Facts must be *interpreted* before they have meaning. Does the fact that a manager gets $100,000 a year and his workers $4000 mean the manager is getting too much, or too little? Does the fact that many respectable citizens gamble mean that the laws against it should be repealed so their gambling will be legal, or enforced so their gambling will be discouraged? It is clear that *a fact has meaning only as it is interpreted according to one's values.* When people have the same values, fact-gathering may help resolve their disagreements. When people have differing values, fact-gathering cannot possibly resolve their disagreements; it only enables each individual to defend his values more convincingly. Since nearly all social problems involve conflicting value-judgments, it is useless to hope that fact-gathering will solve them. It is difficult enough for people to agree upon *means* when they share the same ends or goals; when their goals differ, agreement on means is impossible.

The process of "getting the facts" does, however, have certain utility. Carefully collected facts can demolish the rationalizations through which some people evade the problem. Statements such as "There is no real poverty in America," or "Everyone who really needs medical care can get it in America," can be answered only with facts. And large masses of carefully collected and fully digested facts are needed before people (who agree upon values and objectives) can work out any practical modes of treatment. Facts are exceedingly important, but we need a clear understanding of what *can* and what *cannot* be accomplished by fact-gathering.

9. *That Problems Can Be "Cured" Without Institutional Changes*

Many folk are like the fat man who wants to reduce without giving up any of the things he likes to eat. We would like to solve social problems if we could do so without changing anything. Social scientists are invited to produce some quick, painless social panacea that will solve the problem without anyone's sacrifice of money, power, or sentiment. This is impossible. A complete solution of nearly any problem would require sweeping changes in present institutions and practices. To "cure" the problem of poverty would require such extensive changes in our educational, economic, and governmental institutions as to make some of them unrecognizable. To "solve" the housing problem would probably require either a drastic reduction of building costs through new materials and processes or large government subsidies for housing; either "solution" would involve major institutional changes and exact costly penalties from many vested interest groups. Problems are painful, but so are "solutions"; and then the "solutions" create still new problems to be solved.

Since the genuine solution of social problems nearly always involves sweeping institutional changes, and these are costly and difficult to promote, it is unrealistic to expect that these problems will be solved easily or quickly. Institutional changes come slowly, and therefore basic solutions of social problems will come slowly, if at all. Meanwhile, however, considerable *amelioration* or "improvement" may be possible. Although we shall not eliminate poverty or unemployment in the near future, we have already developed moderately successful programs for reducing the personal suffering involved. We shall not eliminate crime, but we may develop more effective techniques of reforming criminals. There is no prospect of eliminating mental illness, but there are excellent prospects for greater success in curing mentally ill persons. Although a generally acceptable solution to most problems in the near future is not possible, considerable success in reducing the personal suffering and social waste of social problems *is* possible. Upon this realistic distinction any practical proposal must be founded.

ATTITUDES TOWARD SOCIAL PROBLEMS

One's attitudes and values determine the meanings that he finds in the facts he observes. A study of some widespread attitudes toward social problems may help to show why people react to facts so differently.

1. Indifference

Possibly the most widespread attitude is that of unconcern. Few of us become much agitated over anything which does not involve our own welfare. There is never time enough for all the things we want to do, and there are many diversions more entertaining than boning up on the present status of the migrant labor problem. Pressures of home, family, friends, job, hobbies, and so on keep us so busy that in idle moments we crave amusement and relaxation, not social surveys and research studies. General interest in a problem is likely to develop only when people sense a serious threat to their welfare or a particularly shocking denial of their values.

2. Fatalistic Resignation

Another attitude is the passive acceptance of misfortune. Countless millions have endured great suffering and even starvation with a calm, stoical resignation. If one believes the way to meet misfortune is to endure it quietly, he does not attempt to "solve" the problem. In fact, there *is* no problem—nothing that we should "do something" about—if one believes misfortune is simply an inescapable fate one must endure. It is not that these people *refuse* to do anything about problems; it is rather that the thought of trying to do something would not even occur to them, just as it would not occur to most of us to react to a sore thumb by chopping it off.

3. Cynicism

To the confirmed cynic, all talk about social problems is a waste of time; the "unfortunates aren't worth getting excited over," and the "do-gooders" are "a bunch of hypocrites secretly grinding their own axes." The cynic believes that people are really a sorry lot, that all people are motivated purely by self-interest and other ignoble motives, and those who are not completely repulsive are either amiable scoundrels or pious frauds. The cynic's pet phrases are, "So what! They like it that way," "Everybody has an angle," "They wouldn't take care of it if they had it," "They are too dumb to know any better," and so on. Since those in trouble are not worth saving, and their "saviors" cannot be trusted, why not just let each person "stew in his own juice"?

4. Religious Retribution

This attitude views problems as God's punishment for man's sin. If there be drought, flood, war, pestilence, depression, high prices, low prices, or any other calamity, some proclaim it as God's punishment of sinful man.[5] If this is true, the solution for social problems is to be found not in social policy or institutional changes, but in penitence, righteousness, and prayer.

The questions of God's intervention in human affairs and of the functions of penitence and prayer are in the field of philosophy and religion, not sociology. These are questions for which there are no scientific techniques for seeking an answer. In the study of social problems, however, sociologists find it more successful to analyze them in terms of social rather than supernatural causation. Furthermore, we now have enough facts about social problems to realize that the theory of religious retribution scarcely does justice to God. It would cast Him in the role of one who uses a punishment that is both unjust and ineffectual. The sacrifices of war, depression, and other problems are never equally divided; there is no evidence that only the "wicked" suffer. Neither is there evidence

---

[5] Sometimes this attitude is even applied to distressed individuals, and the unemployed or those in poverty are seen as being individually punished for their sin. A few generations ago both physical and mental illness were also considered as divine punishments for sin, although this view is no longer widely held in our society.

that those who suffer through being poor, ill, unemployed, or shot at generally become more godly, righteous, or noble as a result. Instead, there is some evidence that those who endure insecurity and hardship are likely to become selfish, callous, and insensitive. The modern conception of God as a wise, just, and loving Father is not compatible with the theory of religious retribution, but is entirely compatible with the theory that social problems result from imperfectly harmonized social institutions.

5. Sentimentalism

The sentimentalist, unlike all four of those above, is not trying to run away from the problem but is most anxious to do something about it. The sentimentalist is deeply moved, saying, "Oh, those poor, poor, people; let's do something quick!" The sentimentalist does not see distressed persons as symptoms of the institutional imperfections of society; he sees them only as suffering individuals who need help as quickly and directly as possible. The sentimentalist is so absorbed in distributing baskets to the poor and in finding a generous physician to sew up poor old Widow Brown's rupture that he never stops to wonder whether it might be possible to reduce the number of people who must depend on basket-handing and medical generosity. The sentimentalist often idealizes the distressed, endowing them with a nobility few possess. Upon eventually discovering that the distressed are not saints but ordinary folk, and are often greedy, shiftless, and "ungrateful," the sentimentalist may become a cynic.

But one should not too severely criticize the sentimentalists. Although their indiscriminate basket-handing doubtless encourages some people to become professional relief clients, there is little evidence to support the accusation that they do more harm than good. And the sentimentalist approach was the forerunner of the social-scientific approach; out of earlier efforts to "do good" and the discovery that these efforts often failed, there came a realization that more knowledge was needed. This led to a more careful study of social problems. The sentimentalist approach to organized social work is now largely abandoned, with professionally-trained social workers increasingly replacing the well-intentioned amateurs of the past.

6. Social-Scientific Attitude

This is the attitude of the social scientist and the professionally-equipped social worker. Although there may be deep sympathy for distressed persons, it is recognized that sympathy is not enough; it must be joined by expert knowledge and professional insight. Like all science, the social-scientific attitude toward social problems begins by asking, What is the problem? What are the relevant facts concerning it? What are the various value-judgments involved? What are the alternative possibilities for treatment and what is involved in each? Which policies are most likely to produce "desirable" results, as measured by the most widely held values?

This is the most difficult approach of all. Whereas all the foregoing attitudes provide simple, definite answers, the social-scientific approach has none ready-made. These must emerge from the painstaking, objective study of the problem in a field where objectivity is extremely difficult to maintain. Not many can succeed in maintaining it.

OBJECTIVES FOR OUR STUDY

1. Awareness

First of all, students should become aware of the main social problems. Have you ever visited a place and then been surprised at how often you heard or read about that place thereafter? The place had been mentioned just as frequently before you visited it, but you never noticed these comments until you were acquainted with it; thereafter you noticed each reference because it tied up with something you knew about. In a similar manner, an awareness of a particular problem causes us to notice things we would otherwise overlook. We notice each reference to it in the newspaper, possibly take time to read a magazine article, or prick up our ears when it enters the conversation. In this way we may constantly increase our knowledge about a problem and the validity of our judgments concerning it.

2. Factual Knowledge

All intelligent analysis must rest upon facts. To "discuss" a social problem accomplishes little unless someone in the group knows what he is talking about. Although fact-gathering will not automatically solve any problem, it is entirely impossible to analyze a problem intelligently until large masses of facts have been collected, organized, and interpreted.

3. Understanding of the Sociology of Social Problems

This means to have a general understanding of why and how problems develop, of how people are affected by them, and what is involved in dealing with them. These general understandings become a frame of reference within which data may be catalogued and problems studied. If one has a thorough understanding of the sociology of social problems, then data on any particular problem can be rather quickly organized and the problem can be analyzed intelligently. These general understandings help one decide which data are significant and which are trivial; they help one to interpret new data correctly and mentally fit it in place so that he keeps his thinking up to date. The data in this text will soon be obsolete, and the complexion of many problems may change considerably within a few years; yet if the student understands the *sociology* of social problems, he will not find it hard to interpret new data and understand new developments.

4. Relation of Theory and Practice

To poke fun at "theory" and "theorists" is as American as hot dogs. Our frontier values, which rated skill with axe and mule team above skill with Latin verbs and metaphysical propositions, are mirrored in the present pride of the average man in being "a practical man, not a theorist."

The naiveté of this anti-intellectual bias is evident when one recalls that in social policy, as in most other fields, theory and practice are inseparable. Every "practical" policy flows from some theory of causation, and every theory carries some implications for control or treatment. One who tries to separate them merely reveals his ignorance of their relation, and most self-styled "practical" men are simply unaware of the theories that underlie their action. For example, the person who says, "Criminals should be punished, not coddled; give them nice long sentences on the rock pile and they would think twice before doing it again," probably imagines that he is speaking "practical common sense," untouched by "mere theory." In truth, however, this man is subscribing to a number of theories. He is applying the 4000-year-old theory that man is a hedonistic creature, determining his actions on a basis of simple pleasure-pain calculations, so that if we make the consequences sufficiently painful, he will refrain from the act. He is also using the theory that man is a purely rational being whose actions are determined not by habit, or training, or emotion, but by coldly rational and logical calculation. Still other theories about the existence of free will, the efficacy of punishment, and the processes of learning are assumed. Hundreds of pages would be needed merely to state the theories underlying this man's innocent remark, and thousands of books have been written to explain and debate them. Of all this, our "practical" man knows nothing; he merely "knows" that he has "the answer."

The practical man who imagines he is unmoved by theoretical considerations is, in fact, slave to the theories of some dead economist or philosopher. His stout denial of theoretical contamination only reveals his ignorance of the theories which guide his thinking. Both the "conservative" and the "liberal" support economic policies equally derived from economic theory; their main theoretical difference is that whereas one prefers policies based on the theories of classical economists like Smith,

Ricardo, and Carver, the other supports programs based on the newer theories of Veblen, Keynes, and Slichter.

It is, of course, quite true that some scholarly folk become so immersed in theoretical abstractions that they seem innocently unaware of the realities surrounding them. It is from such persons that the stereotype of the impractical theorist probably was drawn.[6] Sound theory is tested by successful application. Not until it is shown that a theory works can we know whether the theory is sound. Vague theorizing or failure to test the theory at every possible point have no place in science, and persons guilty of these errors deserve no defense.

It is equally true that practice divorced from theory is not always practical; it may be merely guesswork, sanctified by precedent. One does not become a "practical" man merely by announcing himself as one. The genuinely practical man, in the field of social policy, is one who knows and understands the theoretical underpinning of his recommendations, who knows how they have worked out elsewhere, and has some factual basis for predicting their effectiveness.

To help the student gain a clear picture of the relation of theory to practice is one of the objectives of this book. To recognize that sound theory is established by successful applications; that no policy is any sounder than the theory from which it flows; that only when one thoroughly understands the theories involved is he qualified to select a practical course of action; that much "practical common sense" is nothing more than guesswork and folklore—to recognize these is to clear one's mind of a clutter of myth and misconception that obstructs clear thinking.

5. *A Sense of Perspective*

Some people find the study of social problems most upsetting. Just as many people are frightened by all the diseases they find listed in a medical textbook, some students are disturbed at the great amount of implied

---

[6] It is important to remember that the stereotype of the impractical college professor grew up at a time when the college curriculum was largely composed of pure science, classical studies, ancient languages, and other content quite remote from everyday life. Today the emphasis is quite different, and it is likely that the modern professor of Political Science, History, or American Literature has at least as practical and realistic an understanding of our social world as has the average physician, engineer, or businessman.

It is also interesting to note that the businessman is rated as "practical" if his business prospers, a physician if his patients survive, and a mechanic if he can fix a car so it runs. A teacher, however, rarely is so classed merely because he can teach well; to be a "practical" man the teacher must also show that he can run a business, treat a stomach-ache, and overhaul his car. It may be that the teacher would be successful in business about as often as the businessman would be successful in teaching. Yet no matter how well a teacher can teach, many people (including some who failed as teachers themselves) will continue to consider him a childish, impractical theorist.

criticism of our society in a social problems course. For some others, the awareness of social imperfections may become almost an obsession. They become so impressed with the suffering, frustration, and waste of a problem-ridden society that they fail to see this in relation to the more encouraging aspects of the total picture. A sense of perspective is necessary if we are to see a problem without exaggeration or distortion.

Present problems should be seen against a background of past realities, not of a mythical past. The popular complaint that "Things aren't what they used to be" overlooks the fact that they never were! The past was rarely the tranquil, problem-free pastoral scene we sometimes imagine. History books rarely give full details on past problems, and today we are simply unaware of how sharp and bitter they may have been. Most people will probably be amazed to hear that in earlier periods of American history, government was far more corrupt, vote frauds more common, war profiteering far more flagrant, grafting more widespread, business methods less scrupulous, minorities more often mistreated, drunkenness more commonplace, church memberships proportionately less numerous, labor violence more unrestrained, employers incomparably more ruthless, newspaper bias more pronounced, police less efficient and more brutal, and wife beating and cruelty to children more common than they are in America today. Those who lament that public morality is declining and society is racing to destruction need something more than cries of alarm to prove their case. In fact, some modern problems (for example, newspaper bias, "influence peddling" in government, truth in advertising) have become problems because our values now define as undesirable certain behavior which earlier generations accepted without question. A century ago, it was taken for granted that a senator had a personal financial interest in any legislation he sponsored (and he often did). Today, such a revelation usually brings electoral defeat, if not worse, to any senator who is thus compromised. In a very real sense, some modern problems have arisen because our standards of public morality are "higher" than those of our predecessors. This is scarcely a reason for despair.

This text will strive to place each problem in a reasonable perspective, presenting it in its setting of past history, present trends, future prospects, and mitigating circumstances. In this way, the student may be helped to develop an attitude of realistic analysis that avoids the twin extremes of naive evasion and morbid exaggeration.

6. Appreciation of the Proper Role of the Expert

Americans distrust "experts." We want no one telling us what to do. We readily array the "common sense" of a "plain, practical American" against the "theories" of some "long-hair expert."

Although in a democracy every person is equally entitled to hold his own opinion, it does not follow that those opinions are equally valuable. If we want a useful opinion on why our head throbs or our car stalls, we ask an appropriate expert. But when we wonder why Susie has grown disobedient or how to reduce sex crimes, we disdain to ask the expert and confidently announce our own opinions, perhaps after "discussing" the question with others who know no more about it than we do.

Many of these contradictions may stem from failure to distinguish between *questions of knowledge* and *questions of value.* In matters of knowledge there are right and wrong answers, whereas in matters of value there are no right and wrong answers, merely differing preferences. In matters of value the layman and the experts are equals, each equally entitled to his preferences. But in matters of knowledge the layman and the expert are *not* equals, and for the layman to debate a matter of knowledge with the expert is futile and presumptuous. To illustrate, the question of whether leisure should be used in viewing paintings or prizefights is a matter of value, and all are entitled to their tastes; but the question of whether an alleged Van Gogh is authentic is a question upon which expert knowledge is needed while lay opinions are not worth much.

Stated in its simplest terms, *the function of the scientific expert is not to tell people what they should want, but to tell them how best to get what they want.* When experts are *agreed* upon the futility of one policy or the soundness of another, it is sheer stupidity for the layman to disagree. Although it is quite possible that all the experts are wrong, it is so much more probable that the layman is wrong that he would be wiser to keep his silence. When the experts are disagreed among themselves, then it is stupid for the layman to consider any answer as positive and final. To illustrate, since the experts in criminology are agreed that criminal behavior is learned and not inborn, the layman who talks of a "criminal instinct" or a "born criminal" simply reveals his ignorance. Since these same experts are not entirely certain as to what measures will most successfully reduce crime, the layman who confidently prescribes a particular treatment simply makes a fool of himself.

In the field of social problems, the function of the expert is to provide accurate descriptions and analyses of social problems and show laymen what consequences will follow each proposed treatment. It is scarcely his task to tell people what kind of a society they should want, but to show them how to get the kind of society they want, if possible. Since people often want contradictory things (for example, cheap labor and prosperity), it is also the function of the social scientist to show laymen [7] wherein their values are incompatible, and where they must compromise

[7] With regard to social problems, the term *laymen* refers to everyone except social scientists. Workers, farmers, businessmen, and government administrators are all laymen where social problems are concerned, just as the sociologist is a layman in the field of farm technology or medical diagnosis.

or choose between them. More simply, to say to the laymen, "If you do this, here is what happens"—this is the function of the social scientist.[8] The task of the student is to learn how to recognize an expert when he sees one, and how to guide his own thinking by expert knowledge rather than by folklore and guesswork.

7. Personal Orientation

In the course of his study of social problems, the student will probably develop a personal reaction to them. Each student will have some attitude towards social problems, perhaps one of the "attitudes" discussed a few pages earlier. Many students take a course in social problems not from any consuming curiosity, but because the course is required, or comes at a convenient hour, or the instructor is popular, or some other reason. No particular interest, sympathetic or otherwise, is necessarily implied. Yet these students nevertheless find themselves developing attitudes toward the subjects they study. To some, social problems remain a subject to be completed, a course to be passed, and not vital situations dramatically and tragically affecting the lives of human beings. To some, the study of social problems may be a depressing recital of miseries and woes, whereas to others it may be a catalog of suggestions and encouragement. A great many students may find that the continual emphasis upon the institutional setting of social problems fills them with a vast sense of futility—what can one person do? If a problem grows from the ponderous movement of impersonal social trends and forces, what use for one person to try to stem the course of social change?

Granted it is true that one person cannot do much, students who feel impelled to "do something" should remember that they are never alone. Changes in social policy grow from changes in the thinking of large numbers of people. Although a single person does relatively little to affect that change, each person is an indispensable part of that change merely by being on one side rather than the other. As a famous clergyman has noted, one may avoid a depressing sense of personal helplessness by asking, "Am I part of the problem or part of the answer?" [9] Are you one of those whose ignorance, indifference, prejudice, and self-interest are roadblocks in the path of intelligent social policy? Or are you one whose sympathetic interest, realistic knowledge, and open-minded receptivity place you on the side of those seeking to promote intelligent social policy?

[8] There are some social scientists who feel that the social scientist should also tell people what they *ought* to do, but they are in the minority. All would agree, however, that the scientist is also a citizen and that he may share in any movements he wishes. Here, however, he acts as a private citizen pursuing his own values, not as a scientific spokesman expressing the conclusions of science.

[9] Harry Emerson Fosdick, "Are We Part of the Problem or of the Answer?" *National Education Association Journal,* 36 (December, 1947), pp. 621-622.

Even though one may accomplish very little by himself, the knowledge that he is on the "right" side is a powerful antidote for despair.

PLAN OF THIS BOOK

This introduction is followed by a chapter presenting the three common approaches used by sociologists in studying social problems and showing how each will be used in this text. This is followed by a chapter discussing the puzzling question of how to know when to believe what you read or hear.

Part II consists of a number of chapters, each exploring a social problem in some detail. For each problem, a considerable body of factual data will be presented, the problem will be analyzed according to each of the three approaches, and the probable consequences of alternative modes of treatment will be explored.

Part III attempts a reappraisal of the three approaches and of the special contributions of each to a more complete understanding of social problems. A final chapter will indulge in the fascinating but hazardous pastime of attempting to predict the future development of social problems in America and the general lines of treatment which American society will employ.

SUMMARY

This introductory chapter attempts to give some impression of the nature and scope of social problems and to arouse some interest in them. Social problems are defined as conditions affecting many people in ways thought harmful, but avoidable through social action. Contrary to widespread but fallacious belief, (1) people do not agree upon which conditions are problems; (2) problems are not natural or inevitable; (3) problems are not abnormal, but are normal results of our social arrangements; (4) problems arise from social arrangements, not from "bad" people, and the "badness" of the people involved should usually be viewed as symptoms or results rather than causes of the problem; (5) problems are genuine and are not illusions created by wild talk; (6) many people do not really want certain problems solved; (7) most problems do not solve themselves or die out as time passes; (8) "getting the facts" will rarely solve a problem because people hold different values and want different outcomes; (9) problems cannot be thoroughly solved without major changes in present social institutions and practices.

Different persons hold different attitudes toward social problems in general. Some are *indifferent* and disinterested. Some are *fatalistically resigned,* accepting social problems as unavoidable scourges to be endured with patience. Some are *cynical* in their belief that the victims of problems are not worth helping and that the reformers are corrupt and venal.

Some consider social problems as *religious retribution,* as divine punishment for man's misdeeds. All four of these attitudes discourage any attempt at treatment. The *sentimentalist* wants to "do something" but is guided by emotion rather than scientific knowledge, and his efforts are often wasted. The *social-scientific* attitude attempts to apply scientific technique to the analysis of a problem so that effective social policies may be developed.

Through the study of social problems the student may develop: (1) *awareness* of present problems; (2) accurate *factual knowledge* about some of them; (3) some *understanding of the sociology of social problems,* of the general way in which problems develop; (4) an intelligent understanding of the *relation of theory and practice* whereby all theory is tested by practical application while all practical policy is based on sound theory; (5) *a sense of perspective* so that a problem is seen in proper relation to the past and present society without distortion or exaggeration; (6) an *appreciation of the proper role of the expert* respecting social problems, with some skill in locating and using expert knowledge and opinion; and (7) *a personal orientation* that is intellectually and emotionally satisfying to the student.

SUGGESTED READINGS

CUBER, John F., *Sociology: A Synopsis of Principles,* 3rd ed. (New York, Appleton-Century-Crofts, Inc., 1955), Chs. 2 and 3. A general discussion of the sociological frame of reference. Although not directly addressed to social problems, its treatment of causality, case materials, and objectivity will be helpful in studying social problems.

NORDSKOG, John Eric, McDONAGH, Edward C., and VINCENT, Melvin J., *Analyzing Social Problems* (New York, The Dryden Press, 1950), Ch. 1. A collection of essays defining social problems and discussing the sociological approaches to their study.

Statistical Abstract of the United States (Published annually by the U. S. Department of Commerce), and

The World Almanac and Book of Facts (Published annually by the *New York World-Telegram and Sun*). These two books are not "readings," but are sources of statistical and factual information. They are the most easily accessible sources for data on practically any subject. Every student should thumb through these books in order to know what kinds of information can be found in them.

STEINBECK, John, *The Grapes of Wrath* (New York, Viking Press, Inc., 1939; Garden City, N. Y., The Sun-Dial Press, 1941; New York, Bantam Books, 1945), Ch. 5. A famous and highly controversial "social problem" novel dealing with the "Okies," the marginal Southern farmers whom drought and farm mechanization displaced and converted into migrant farm workers during the 1930's. Chapter 5 raises and gives an answer to the perennial question, Who is to blame?

QUESTIONS AND PROJECTS

1. List a number of modern conditions which we consider to be social problems, but which the values of an earlier period would not have defined as problems. List some, not problems to us, that would have been considered problems in our earlier period.

2. Have there been any continuous problems throughout recorded history? If so, what values, continuously held, define these conditions as problems?

3. Of the problems listed as chapter titles in the Table of Contents of this textbook, which would probably *not* be social problems in the Soviet Union? Why?

4. State some current public controversies that continue largely because of lack of knowledge with which to settle the issue. State some which exist largely because of disagreements upon values. Which group is the larger?

5. Do any social problems arise from our lack of ability to control the factors producing the situation?

6. What "harm," if any, has been done by the sentimentalist approach to social problems? What "good" has it done?

7. What difference does it make whether social problems are viewed as abnormal or as normal aspects of social organization?

8. What is meant by the suggestion that the "bad" people involved in social problems are more symptomatic than causative?

9. In what sense are social problems inevitable?

10. What kind of controversies can be solved by determining the relevant facts? What kind cannot be solved by fact-finding? Why?

11. Does an "awareness" of social problems, and a recognition that their origin lies in our social structure make one a less "loyal" citizen?

12. Is it possible to be "practical" without also being "theoretical"? Can one be "theoretical" without being "practical"?

13. What is meant by a "sense of perspective" on social problems?

14. Read Chapter 5 of John Steinbeck's *The Grapes of Wrath*. Who or what is "to blame" for the situation? Why doesn't Pa fulfill his threat to "shoot the man who's starving" him? What significant insights into the sociology of social problems does this chapter illustrate?

CHAPTER 2

Approaches to the Study of
Social Problems

An Indian Tsar commanded to gather together all the blind men, and when they were collected, he commanded to show them his Elephants. The blind men went to the stables, and began to feel of the Elephants.

One felt of the leg; another, of the tail; a third of the rump; a fourth, of the belly, a fifth, of the back; a sixth, of the ears; a seventh, of the tusks; an eighth, of the trunk.

The Tsar called the blind men to him, and asked them; "What are my Elephants like?"

And one blind man said; "Thy Elephants are like pillars." This blind man had felt of the legs.

The second blind man said; "They are like brooms." This one had felt of the tail.

The third said; "They are like wood." This one had felt of the rump.

The one who had felt of the belly said; "Elephants are like lumps of earth."

The one who had felt of the side said; "They are a wall."

The one who had felt of the back said; "They are like a hill."

The one who had felt of the ears said; "They are like a handkerchief."

The one who had felt of the head said; "They are like a mortar."

The one who had felt of the tusks said; "They are like horns."

The one who had felt of the trunk said; "They are like a stout rope."

And all the blind men began to dispute and quarrel.[1]

WE MAY smile at the confusion and inaccuracy occasioned by the narrowness of the blind men's "point of view." Structurally, the elephant *is* somewhat like a pillar, *and* like a wall, *and* like a rope. Yet we can sympathize with anyone who must depend for his understanding of the pachyderm upon the observations of these men. An elephant is a large and complex organism with many different features. Social problems, like the elephant, are complex phenomena!

[1] Leo Nikolaievich Tolstoi, "The Tsar and the Elephants," in *The Great Fables of All Nations,* selected by Manuel Komroff (New York, Tudor Publishing Company, Dial Press, Inc., 1928), pp. 439-440.

THE COMPLEXITY OF SOCIAL PROBLEMS

The average layman is apt to think of social problems as relatively clear-cut, uncomplicated conditions which need to be remedied. Nothing could be further from the truth. For example, the individual "criminal" who robs filling stations, burglarizes homes, hijacks trucks, or swindles widows out of their life savings is only one part of the crime picture. The tenement district that requires "double" police protection, the police officials who occasionally are "silent partners" in crime, and the "honest" merchant who has two prices for each article of merchandise are also parts of the crime problem. Then there is the corporation that sells millions of dollars worth of stock, pays fabulous salaries to its officers, and goes into bankruptcy before going into production. Many persons in the United States today feel there is much that is criminal in such situations; other powerful groups deny that there is anything ethically, morally, or legally amiss. Reformatories and prisons become known as "schools for crime," taking in clumsy first-offenders and turning out crafty, hardened criminals. Yet many prison officials and much of the general public believe that the criminal must be "punished." Later on in this book two full chapters will be devoted to various aspects of the crime problem. For now, the above paragraph is probably enough to illustrate that *social problems must be approached from many different points of view*.

A SOCIOLOGICAL FRAME OF REFERENCE

Students who have taken courses in sociology will be familiar with the sociological point of view. For beginning students, and as a refresher for the others, it may be well to point up certain basic aspects of the sociological frame of reference.

Constant Change

Culture, or the social heritage, is in a constant state of change. Some cultures change faster than others, just as certain aspects of a given culture change faster than other aspects of that culture. Thus, for the past two thousand years Western European culture has changed much faster than Chinese culture. Chinese culture has never been static, however, and during the past century its rate of change has been greatly accelerated. Similarly, it is something of a truism that our technology has changed much faster than the comparable nonmaterial aspects of culture—institutions, customs, and traditions. Both the fact of unending culture change and the differential rate of culture change have important bearing on the study of social problems.

Cultural Relativity

The principle of "cultural relativity" is another important phase of the sociological frame of reference. Briefly, this principle recognizes that any one of several cultural practices may satisfy the needs of a given society. To illustrate, all societies have some sort of marriage system. But not all societies have monogamy, the marriage system which permits one to have only one mate at a time. Polygyny, or the practice of taking multiple wives, and polyandry, the taking of multiple husbands, may work as well in societies that sanction them as does monogamy in our society. This does not necessarily mean that polygyny or polyandry would work in *this* society, but it does imply that there is nothing "natural" or "inherent" about monogamy. So it is in all other aspects of culture. Definitions of the propriety of given behavior patterns arise within the culture and vary markedly from one culture to another.

VARIABILITY IN MARRIAGE FORMS

MONOGAMY   POLYGYNY   POLYANDRY

FIG. 2-1

Learned Behavior

It must also be recognized that personality, or behavior, derives largely from the society and culture in which the individual lives. Whether one is sad or joyful at the death of a loved one depends on how death is defined by the culture. Whether grief is expressed through weeping, or through smiling and the wearing of certain apparel, is similarly defined. In one society boys are taught to be aggressive and domineering, whereas in another society men are supposed to be shy and dependent. In the United States, middle-class boys achieve by excelling in school the same prestige that "street-corner" boys gain by stealing tires. Biologically, the human species is everywhere and always the same, but human *behavior* varies strikingly from culture to culture and from time to time.

In the study of social problems, one frequently encounters the argument that proposed changes are undesirable *because* they are "contrary to human nature" or to the customary ways of doing things. They supposedly will not work because they are new or different or "radical." The student who understands the above principles will require more satisfactory evidence than such a priori statements before either accepting or rejecting proposed solutions to social problems.

Approaches to the Study of Social Problems

Because of the tremendous number and the involved nature of social problems, no single approach to their study has proved wholly satisfactory. There are at least three relatively distinct approaches that have proved useful in the study of various problem situations. These three approaches are (1) the social-disorganization approach, (2) the personal-deviation approach, and (3) the conflict-of-values approach. Each of these approaches will be employed in examining the specific social problems treated in Part II of this book.

THE SOCIAL-DISORGANIZATION APPROACH

One of the major bonds holding a society together is the system of values shared by its members. At the most abstract level, there is likely to be loyalty to broad principles such as democracy, freedom, a faith in education, and monogamy. Through actual experience and usage these broad principles are translated into a vast network of customary and expected behaviors. Thus, in practice a society's monogamous values, in addition to specifying the number of mates one may have, might also require that people marry as soon as they are old enough to do so, that once married they should stay married, that wives should be subservient to their husbands, that they should have many children, and that the children should respect and obey their parents. From the most general principles to the minute details of everyday life, behavior is regulated and controlled. Occasionally, special enforcement agencies such as the police must step in, but more often the informal pressures of public opinion and the expectations of friends and associates are sufficient. Enforcement in any direct sense is usually unnecessary, for people regard the customary ways of doing things as being the only "right" and "natural" ways. They behave according to the "rules" of the society partly because it never occurs to them to do otherwise and partly because they tend to be distrustful of that which is new or different. The resulting order and regularity in human relationships is termed *social organization*.

Not always, though, do the rules function efficiently. They are especially vulnerable to breakdown under the influence of social change in other aspects of the society. People try to adjust to the new conditions by adhering to the time-honored ways, but instead of satisfaction they reap frustration and unhappiness. The order and predictability of former days are replaced by confusion and chaos. This is the condition of *social disorganization*. To illustrate, note once again the kind of monogamous mores recounted in the previous paragraph. This might well be a description of the American pattern of colonial days. Marriages were permanent, stable, and productive unions. The hard task of farming was aided by the ready manner in which men, women, and children adapted to the roles laid out for them. But conditions have changed considerably since colonial days. Farming as a way of life has largely given way to urban living and mass-production industries. The family has not disappeared but there are marked evidences of disorganization within it. Divorce rates have soared, personal unhappiness presumably is even more widespread, many women want careers *as well as* marriage, family size has dwindled, and childlessness is common. People want to be successful in marriage, but many of the old rules which governed relationships between men and women—which kept women in the home, and which ensured large families—seem to have broken down. Many private and public agencies now are concerned with the "disorganization" of the family. They see *a problem* about which something needs to be done. Proposals ranging from the advocacy of "free love" to demands for stricter divorce laws are frequently made. Changes in the basic conditions of life have caused a breakdown of the traditional rules and have resulted in widespread personal unhappiness.

The uprooting of established customs by the force of social change, widespread dissatisfaction with existing conditions, and clamor for solutions are major factors in social problems. By analyzing the changes from the breakdown of the original rules to the current proposals for solution an attempt at understanding can be made. Very specifically, in employing the *social-disorganization approach* to social problems, here are some of the questions we ask:

What are the traditional rules?
What forces have changed the situation?
Which of the rules have broken down?
Which groups are dissatisfied? What solutions do they propose?
What new rules or definitions may emerge from the situation?

THE PERSONAL-DEVIATION APPROACH

1. Deviation from Accepted Norms

The same basic learning processes that mold most people according to the accepted patterns in their social groups also produce substantial numbers of deviants—persons who do not fit into the generally accepted patterns. Some Southern whites, for example, condemn the segregation of Negroes, occasional physicians favor a system of public health insurance, and some wealthy men vote for laws which increase their own taxes. In each instance, such people violate the mores of their own groups and seemingly act contrary to their own best interests. Not all of these people are otherwise maladjusted, but many of those whose deviancy does extend into other areas are deeply involved in the issues to which their deviation "sensitizes" them. They are among the first to insist that a problem exists, they are among the most ardent adherents to various proposed solutions, and they rise to do battle with those who oppose them. Many of them are motivated by the extreme personality needs that are termed *neurotic*. They are frightened, anxious, insecure people whose interests in particular problem situations are secondary to the satisfaction of their own neurotic needs.

2. Deviation in Terms of Accepted Norms

In some cases of personal deviation, cultural factors appear to play a major role. Deviants are generally thought to be emotionally or socially maladjusted people—and many of them are. But many persons considered deviant by majority standards may not have rejected the values and demands of their associates. They may be deviant precisely because they are well adjusted to the demands of *their* associates! Certainly, part of the criminality common in slum areas of our large cities is of this sort. Though such behavior is negatively defined by the larger culture, it may be accepted and even expected *in that area*. The slum youth may develop a deviant life organization by moving up from *petit* larceny gangs to hijacking or some other of the "rackets" as naturally as the middle-class boy moves up from kindergarten to the practice of law or medicine. Though the slum youth frequently knows his pattern to be disapproved by outsiders, they *are* outsiders. Their disapproval may arouse none of the guilt and none of the motivation for change generally assumed to be present in lawbreakers. Wherever there exist *subcultures* whose values conflict with those of the larger culture, we may expect to find such patterns of deviant life organization. These subcultures are many, in the modern scene, and their deviant patterns produce deviant personalities that are part and parcel of social problem situations.

3. Inability to Adhere to Accepted Norms

Not all deviants are clearly engaged either in violating accepted standards or in adhering to the generally disapproved standards of deviant subcultures. Several classes of persons are deviant specifically in that they are incapable of adhering consistently to the required set of standards. "Deficiency" or "inadequacy" is the problem. The existence of large numbers of persons who are seriously deficient or inadequate is itself a social problem. Since their incapacity is not likely to be questioned, the mentally deficient are perhaps the best single example of such deviant groups. Many other groups, however, seem to have little power to alter their deviant patterns. The mentally ill, narcotic addicts, alcoholics, and even some confirmed gamblers appear not to have the willful control over their behavior that is presumed to be a characteristic of normal men.

Each of the three types of personal deviation described above is an important factor in the analysis of social problems. Here are the questions we ask in employing the *personal-deviation approach:*

What deviant persons and groups are involved?
What personal and/or cultural factors account for their deviancy?
How does the fact of their deviancy help create the problem?
How does their deviation affect the way they see the problem?
What alternatives are there for dealing with the deviants?

THE CONFLICT-OF-VALUES APPROACH

A society's values are its estimates of worth; its preferences, its likes and dislikes. The society takes its character from these values whether they be monogamy, democracy, and practicality, or whether they be some other set such as polyandry, theocracy, and other-worldliness. Modern societies, moreover, are characterized by diversity and heterogeneity. Consequently, rather than having *a* set of values they have *many* sets of values—which results in the likelihood of disagreement over value-questions. Whenever any group decides that some action is or is not desirable, it is likely to be opposed by other groups with conflicting values. Groups with one set of values will claim that inadequate housing, racial segregation, and "witch-hunting" are social problems, and groups with different values will say they are not. Moreover, people who agree, for example, that inadequate housing is a problem, will disagree on how to deal with the problem. Values are involved in the origin, definition, and solution of social problems. The late Richard C. Fuller, who was instrumental in developing the value-conflict approach, proposed a regular series of stages which problems pass through in the process of being defined and solved.[2]

[2] Richard C. Fuller and Richard R. Myers, "The Natural History of a Social Problem," *American Sociological Review,* 6 (June, 1941), pp. 320-328.

Awareness

As indicated in Chapter 1, before any condition becomes a social problem, people must become aware that the condition is undesirable and that
something can be done about it. Typically, conditions that are eventually
defined as problems are at first regarded as inevitable or even desirable.
At first there are no important conflicts of values. Under the impact of
social change, a few people begin to raise questions, to challenge, and to
debate. Agitation develops for something to be done. Gradually, the
awareness first experienced by a few persons or groups, spreads to large
segments of the society. In this developing awareness, the social problem
(not necessarily the condition defined as the problem) comes into existence.

Policy Determination

As the problem awareness gradually spreads through the society, the
conflicts of values become increasingly sharp and bitter. Solutions and
means of achieving those solutions are discussed. Agreement comes first
with regard to what solutions are possible and desirable, and means of
achieving those solutions are debated and argued. Poverty, for example,
was at first defined by many groups as natural, inevitable, and even desirable. Eventually, most groups agreed that at least the more serious consequences of poverty should be eliminated. The question then became one
of *how* they should be eliminated. We have not progressed much beyond
that point even today. Some groups advocate slum clearance, others
would settle for the establishment of clinics to provide free medical care,
while still others hold out for minimum wage laws. *The emphasis in the
policy-determination stage shifts from what should be done to how do we
do it.*

Reform

As basic solutions and policies for achieving them are decided upon,
the problem becomes one of *action*. The remaining questions of policy are
likely to be those that lie in the province of the experts or specialists entrusted to carry out the will of the people. If slum clearance is to be the
answer, procedures must be formulated for acquiring the slums and relo-
cating the people who live there. Details of construction have to be
worked out. Then, conditions and arrangements for the rent, lease, or sale
of the new buildings are required. These are all "technical" problems
which the conflicting interest groups generally leave to the experts to
work out. *This is the stage of implementation rather than the stage of
decision.*

The general logic of this "natural history" of social problems is simple enough. Awareness must precede effective discussion of possible solutions, and the debate is apt finally to crystallize into action. It is important to remember, however, that this is only a general pattern and an ideal one at that. Most actual problems will vary from it in greater or lesser degree. In some instances, for example, there are latent or even active conflicts already present in the developing problem area. In other instances, there may never develop a general awareness of the problem, especially if it is a local one. In still other instances, legislatures, government agencies, and the like may attempt to regulate conditions that are not yet defined as problems by the public at large. The stages of awareness, policy determination, and reform may be scrambled in order, or even too confused to define clearly. The natural history is a tool for analyzing social problems, not the analysis itself.

Here are the questions we ask in employing the *conflict-of-values approach:*

What are the values which are in conflict?
How "deep" is the value-conflict?
Which values are more consistent with other values such as "democracy" and "freedom"?
What value-sacrifices would each solution require?
Are some problems insoluble now, because of irreconcilable conflicts?

THE ANALYSIS OF SOCIAL PROBLEMS

Part II of this book analyzes each of a series of current social problems in considerable detail. In each case, the attempt has been to marshal and present the most relevant facts bearing upon the origin and development of the problem, upon its present status as indicated by the findings of scientific research, and upon the various possible lines of future development. These data, when considered in the light of our three approaches, provide a basis for evaluating the already proposed and yet-to-be-proposed solutions to various aspects of problem situations. Rather than advocate given types of solutions, we have maintained the role of analysts who foresee and predict certain outcomes when this or that policy is followed. It is consistent with the position of the social science analyst to say, "*If* these are your values, *then* this is the solution which will work," or that "This solution which you propose is not consistent with your other basic values," but he generally does not, *as a scientist,* adopt the role of value-advocate.

At our present state of knowledge, it is entirely reasonable to expect that there will be more adequate data available on some problems than on others and that, consequently, more precise and more rounded analyses will be possible in some situations than in others.

Each problem in Part II is analyzed (1) in terms of its relation to social change and social disorganization, (2) in terms of the deviant behavior patterns involved, and (3) in terms of the conflicts of values among different social groups.

SUMMARY

Social problems are not clear-cut, uncomplicated, readily corrected situations, but are complex phenomena difficult to subject to objective analysis. The task of analysis requires that a frame of reference be adopted. Three major approaches—social disorganization, personal deviation, and conflicts of values—are used in this book.

The term *social organization* refers to all the organized and customary ways of doing things in a society, and is characterized by order, stability, and predictability of behavior. *Social disorganization,* a product of social change, occurs when the customary ways of doing things break down or are no longer adequate. The resulting confusion and disorder are major elements to be considered in analyzing social problems. Analysis begins with a description of the original behavior patterns, traces their breakdown under the influence of social change, and finally moves to consideration of current proposals for dealing with the situation.

Patterns of social organization and social disorganization have their individual or personal counterparts. The deviant behavior of individuals is also a factor in social problems. Such deviancy cannot be accounted for solely in terms of institutional maladjustments but must be explained in the context of personality development. In some instances deviant behavior is learned as part of the subculture in which the person participates, whereas in others it can be explained only in terms of the unique experiences of the individual. This uniqueness results from the facts that experiences are never identical, that certain experiences are likely to be crucial ones, that experiences occur in different sequences, and that the individual's interpretations of experiences vary.

Modern societies are characterized by a great deal of disagreement over basic values. People disagree over which conditions should be regarded as social problems, over whether anything can be done about undesirable conditions, and over which of the available solutions should be tried.

SUGGESTED READINGS

BROWN, Lawrence G., *Social Pathology* (New York, Appleton-Century-Crofts, Inc., 1942). An excellent, thorough analysis of the development of personal deviation. Details the influences of heredity, culture, and the unique experiences of the person.

ELLIOTT, Mabel A., and MERRILL, Francis E., *Social Disorganization,* rev. ed. (New York, Harper and Brothers, 1941). A long-established textbook in the field of social problems. Interprets a wide range of problems in terms of the social disorganization approach.

FULLER, Richard C., "The Problem of Teaching Social Problems," *American Journal of Sociology*, 44 (November, 1938), pp. 415-435. The original formulation of the "conflict-of-values" approach to social problems.

FULLER, Richard C., and MYERS, Richard R., "The Natural History of a Social Problem," *American Sociological Review*, 6 (June, 1941), pp. 320-328. A fuller exposition of the "natural-history" concept of social problems outlined in this chapter.

LEMERT, Edwin, *Social Pathology* (New York, McGraw-Hill Book Company, Inc., 1951). An excellent book on social and personal deviation. For the student with some background in sociology.

OGBURN, William F., *Social Change* (New York, Viking Press, Inc., 1922). An early major treatise stressing the appearance of social disorganization through the process of social change.

QUESTIONS AND PROJECTS

1. Evaluate the statement that "in most cases it is more accurate to speak of *social problem areas* rather than of *the* race problem or *the* crime problem."

2. What constitutes "human nature" depends upon the values of one's society as well as upon biology. Explain.

3. What is meant by the term *cultural relativity?* How is knowledge of the principle of cultural relativity apt to influence one's thinking on social problems?

4. How does the breakdown of customs and traditional behavior patterns help to create social problems?

5. Explain how variability in cultural standards may result in the development of personal deviation. How may the unique experiences of a particular individual result in personal deviation even when the social environment seems quite favorable?

6. Define the term *values.* How does the multiplicity of values in modern society affect the solution of social problems?

7. Talk to two or three people of the same generation as your grandparents about what family life was like when they were young and what it is like today. Pick out from their discussions what "rules" governing family life seem to have broken down and compare their interpretations of modern family life with your own. Explain how both social disorganization and reorganization occur through social change.

8. Read Margaret Mead's *Sex and Temperament in Three Primitive Societies* and relate its contents and point of view to the learned nature of human behavior discussed in this chapter. How do you explain the personality differences found among members of these three societies? Relate the principle involved to personality development in modern American culture.

CHAPTER 3

The Interpretation of Data

THIS is the only social-problems book most students will ever read, even those who actually read this one. Whatever is "learned" about social problems after completing this course will come largely through what is read in newspapers and magazines, heard on the radio, seen on television, and picked up in casual conversations. From these sources one rarely gets an authoritative, objective, and comprehensive analysis of a social problem. Instead he gets bits of gossip, sensational incidents, offhand guesses, wild charges, and various kinds of propaganda. The extent to which one remains intelligently informed about his social world will be largely measured by how skillfully he mentally catalogues and interprets these bits and pieces of social data which come his way. *If this textbook has any enduring value for students, it lies mainly in helping them develop skills in collecting and interpreting the scattered social data which they will continually encounter.*

A certain amount of the social data—the "facts," incidents, charges and countercharges, and so on—which one finds in popular sources is simply untrue. Much more consists of half-truths, distortions, and exaggerations. And all data need to be related to other data before they have meaning. Therefore, we need to know (1) whether to accept a report as true, and (2) what difference it makes even if it is true.

THE TECHNIQUE OF SUCCESSFUL LYING, AS PRACTICED BY TALENTED LIARS

Most people have heard about the laws of libel and slander and have a comfortable feeling that "they wouldn't dare say those things if they weren't true." Along with this is the folk belief that "where there's smoke there must be fire," a statement fairly true in a folk society but not necessarily true in a mass society wherein propaganda is a fine art. There are many ways to plant a lie without running afoul of the laws of libel and slander. A good way to learn how to recognize truth is to discover how liars go about their business. If we know the tricks of the skillful liar, we may be able to detect his half-truths and falsehoods.

1. Lie *About a Group*

A group cannot sue for libel or slander. A person can sue and under certain circumstances a corporation or organization can sue or prosecute, but an unorganized group of people cannot sue one who slanders them. To charge that "John Jones is a robber" would invite a libel suit. But to charge "the bankers are a bunch of robbers," or "the labor leaders are a bunch of communists," or "the Jews are a bunch of subversives," is perfectly legal in most states. No particular *person* or *organization* has been slandered, so no one can bring a legal action. (Three states now have "group libel" laws, but in the other forty-five there is still an open season.)

2. Lie *About a Dead Man*

He is in no position to sue you. Neither can his heirs. The death of a public figure often brings forth a rash of scandalous tales, whose publication during his lifetime would have invited libel suits. Some of these may be true; many are half-truths or falsehoods.

3. *Imply Guilt by Association*

This is a modern version of the ancient technique of lying by implication. To say "John Jones is a communist" would invite libel suits, but to say "John Jones, who so often follows the Communist party line" is quite safe. (Since the Communist party line has changed and veered so often, there is probably *nobody* who has *not* been in agreement with communists at some time or other.)

Another way to do this is to bracket one's name with that of several widely distrusted persons. If we say "Joe Doaks, Adolf Hitler, and Joseph Stalin all believed in . . . ," everyone gets the idea that Joe Doaks is not to be trusted. To see just how effectively this device of bracketing names together will color the impression one receives, try comparing the two following hypothetical statements:

Senator Taft, General MacArthur, ex-President Hoover, and many distinguished Americans were highly critical of President Truman's foreign policy.

Senator Taft, Joseph Stalin, Andrei Vishinsky, and America's enemies throughout the world were highly critical of President Truman's foreign policy.

Another technique is to get the victim before the camera lens along with some disreputable character. If this fails, it is easy with scissors and paste pot to concoct a composite photograph which seems to show the victim surrounded by scalawags. A misleading picture can be worth 10,000 misleading words. Partly by this means, suspicions of sympathy for communism were successfully fastened onto one of the most conservative members of the United States Senate, and this single picture was given much credit for his defeat.[1]

In those instances where two persons are in close *personal* association over some period of time, there is good reason to suspect that they may have had similar ideas. But a purely *verbal* association, in which two people happen to have been on the same side of a particular question at a particular moment, is a very different matter. Consider this syllogism: [2]

> The Pope believes in child-labor laws.
> Stalin believes in child-labor laws.
> Therefore, the Pope is a Communist.
> (or)
> Therefore, Stalin is a Catholic.

The syllogism works either way. By this weird sort of "logic" one can prove anyone guilty of practically anything.

4. Impute Motives, Purposes, or Consequences

This is another way to lie by implication. To charge specific *actions* may be dangerous; it is too easy to prove or disprove such charges. Instead, one can be charged with *wishing* to bring about some despicable end. The charge "Mr. Jones strangled a worker" is too easily checked to be safe unless true; to say "Mr. Jones wants to starve us workers into submission" is libel-proof, since who can prove in court what Mr. Jones "wants"? So instead of hearing public charges that "Joe Brown is a communist," we are more likely to hear that "Joe Brown has aided the communist cause by . . ." or "Joe Brown expressed the communist viewpoint in saying. . . ." Such statements are libel-proof ways of implying that Joe Brown is a communist. *Such inferences may, of course, be entirely true.* The important thing to note is that the mere fact that such statements do not produce libel suits is no *proof* that the charges are true.

5. Use Weasel Words

A weasel is a small animal that can wiggle through a tiny opening. Weasel words are shrewdly chosen qualifying words that make a state-

---

[1] *Time* magazine reported, "[Senator] Tyding was up for re-election to a seat he had held since 1926. Franklin Roosevelt in 1938 vainly tried to beat Tydings on the ground that he was too conservative. [Senator] McCarthy, by accusing Tydings of sympathy for Communism, succeeded where Roosevelt had failed. The campaign against Tydings included a faked photograph showing Tydings and Communist Earl Browder cheek by jowl. . . . The Tydings defeat made Joe [McCarthy] a power. If he could successfully smear one of the most conservative and best entrenched Senators, was any man safe from his furious onslaught?" (*Time* [October 22, 1951], pp. 21-22.) For a reproduction of this picture, see *Time* [March 20, 1951], p. 61.

[2] Stuart Chase, "Guilt by Association," *New York Times,* October 14, 1951.

ment highly misleading, yet allow the speaker to defend himself by pointing out the technical accuracy of his statement. Thus he wiggles out of being caught lying.

Weasel words are often found in patent-medicine advertising. Federal laws prevent claims that a remedy will "cure" an illness unless they are scientifically established. So the vendor must find some way to assure purchasers that it will cure their ills without actually *saying* that it will. He does this by using weasel words which few people will notice or understand, but which will legally protect him. Thus an advertisement may read, "If you have nagging backache, dizzy spells, tiredness, indigestion, insomnia, etc., due to nonorganic and nonsystemic bile deficiency, _____ pills will bring you positive relief." The phrase "due to nonorganic and nonsystemic bile deficiency . . ." provides the legal protection; it also excludes most of the real cases of bile deficiency and reveals the pills as remedy for a practically nonexistent illness. A well-known mouthwash promises to prevent bad breath "due to local mouth conditions." Among people who brush their teeth, bad breath is rarely due to local mouth conditions, but people who don't know this may be deceived into believing this mouthwash can cure *their* bad breath.

Radio and television announcers who deliver the commercials have developed a definite technique known as the "throw-away." This consists of sliding over the weasel words and emphasizing the others, so the weasel words will not be noticed or remembered. For example: "If *you* suffer from *nagging back-ache* due to functional disorders, *try so-and-so!*"

This technique of using weasel words is regularly used by highly reputable persons and organizations. After a much publicized gasoline economy run, in which different makes of automobiles were matched for economy over an 840-mile course, four different automobile makers published advertisements claiming to have "won" the contest. The dramatic headlines read, "_____ Beats All-Time Record," "_____ Wins Again in Economy Run," "Three _____'s Finished 1st, 2nd, and 3rd in Actual Miles Per Gallon," and "1951 _____ Wins Sweepstakes in Economy Run." How could there be four winners? Many things which seem impossible at the finish line become possible at the advertising copy writer's desk! The first car covered the most miles per gallon, and its advertisement was free from double-talk. The second headline was preceded by a line of small type saying, "Among 26 cars entered in standard classifications . . . ," thereby excluding all the more economical cars that beat it. The third headline was followed by small type explaining that it won over all (unnamed) cars in "Class C." The fourth advertisement explained in small type that its car won by setting a new record of "66.484 ton-miles per gallon."

Since most people are accustomed to take advertising claims with a grain of salt, this contest on the copy writers' boards may mislead very few people. It is in fields of social policy that this technique may so mislead people as to make accurate description of social issues very difficult. As an example, a newspaper column by a certain well-known and highly respected columnist is so misleading as to suggest intentional intellectual dishonesty. After discussing how farmers and workers have improved their incomes in the 1941-1950 period, he adds: [3]

Now let us consider the people who get the earnings of capital, who are the objects of constant attack by politicians and others. The yield of their stocks rose from the 1941 level only nine per cent. Compare that nine per cent with the 115 per cent increase in wages.

Do you see any "jokers" in this statement? It seems to say that while workers more than doubled their incomes, the incomes of stockholders scarcely increased at all. But such a conclusion would be completely untrue. The weasel word that provides the built-in misrepresentation is the term *yield,* a term which very few people understand. The yield of a stock is computed by dividing the annual dividend by the current market value of the stock. A stock paying high dividends will ordinarily have a high market value, and a stock paying low dividends will ordinarily have a low market value, with both stocks having about the same yield. When the dividends rise, the stock's market value rises, and the yield remains about the same. The truth in this instance is that in 1950, most stocks paid dividends a great deal higher than they did in 1941, but the yield was about the same because the market value of the stock had also increased—a development which made few stockholders unhappy! We are not concerned here with the question of whether stockholders were getting too little or too much; our concern is with the manner in which a columnist who must have known what he was doing apparently sought to mislead and deceive his readers.

There is no way to detect weasel words. Sometimes the qualifying phrases are so obvious that the suspicions of the critical reader are instantly aroused. But in other cases some special knowledge of the technical terms is needed. In the above case, only one familiar with the technical vocabulary of finance would realize that the writer was misleading his unsuspecting readers. It would seem that in interpreting data, while an awareness of the rules is helpful, there is no substitute for an intimate and thorough knowledge of the subject.

6. Quote Out of Context

The Bible says, "Let him who stole steal"—clearly a subversive doctrine. Of course, if St. Paul's statement is quoted in full, "Let him who stole steal no more" (Ephesians, 4:28), the meaning is somewhat changed. By

[3] Syndicated newspaper column, March 17, 1951.

leaving out part of a sentence, or omitting the sentences that precede or follow it, the most innocent remark can be made to sound most damning indeed! For example, in attempting to depict a famous historian as having communist sympathies, a well-known senator quoted him as saying, "I happen to believe that the Communist party should be granted the freedom of political action and that communists should be allowed to teach in universities," but the senator did not quote the rest of the sentence—"so long as they do not disqualify themselves by intellectual distortion in the classroom." [4] By omitting the qualifying words that one has attached to his statement, an unscrupulous critic can attribute to his victim a damaging position he does not actually hold.

Sometimes two separate phrases or sentences are glued together and quoted as a single statement. One supposed "quotation" from Owen Lattimore's writings, cited against him before the McCarran Committee, turned out to be two separate sentences *eleven pages apart,* joined and quoted as a single statement.[5] With scissors and paste pot, a man can be made to say practically anything!

Equally common is the practice of ignoring the *time* context of one's words or action. During World War II, Charles Lindbergh was attacked and his Americanism questioned because he had accepted a Nazi decoration, although he had received this decoration several years earlier while on a semiofficial *secret mission for our government.* Unjustified attacks were also made against the patriotism of many business executives whose firms had exchanged technical information with German firms *before the war.*

It is currently fashionable in some circles to question the loyalty and "Americanism" of those who made friendly remarks about Russia back when she was our ally. Government employees who entertained Russian guests when we were allies, even if only officially, may be challenged to "explain" their "communist associations" today. By examining a man's *past* words and actions in the light of *present* knowledge and social attitudes, it is easy to depict practically anyone as either a traitor or a fool. As Sir Winston Churchill, certainly not a pro-communist, writes in his memoirs,[6]

It is easy, after the Germans are beaten, to condemn those who did their best to hearten the Russian military effort and to keep in harmonious contact with our great ally, who had suffered so frightfully. What would have happened if we had quarrelled with Russia while the Germans still had almost three hundred divisions on the fighting front? Our hopeful assumptions [that Russia would be reasonable] were soon to be falsified. Still, they were the only ones possible at the time.

[4] *New York Times,* November 2, 1952, p. 84.

[5] Elmer Davis, *But We Were Born Free* (Indianapolis, The Bobbs-Merrill Company, 1952), p. 165.

[6] Sir Winston Churchill, *The Second World War, Volume Six, Triumph and Tragedy* (Boston, Houghton Mifflin Company, 1953), p. 402.

7. Become a Congressman

By this means your opportunities for libel-free lying are greatly magnified. This does *not* imply that most congressmen are liars; on the contrary, the average senator or representative probably compares most favorably with the voters who elect him. But the congressman has an *opportunity* for wild lying such as no ordinary citizen enjoys. Congressmen enjoy "Congressional immunity" which means (among other things) that they cannot be sued for libel or slander because of anything they say in Congress or in committee. This limitation is necessary in order to protect a congressman from being sued everytime he opens his mouth or being blackmailed into silence by threats of lawsuits. A few congressmen have abused this privilege and have even become notorious for the grave personal accusations they make with little or no real evidence to support them. The accused persons have absolutely no recourse except to proclaim their innocence and hope that their denial will get as wide publicity as the accusation—but it rarely does.

Once a congressman has made his accusation in Congress or in a committee hearing, it then becomes a part of the *Congressional Record* and can be freely reprinted by anybody without fear of libel suits. Consequently, if one wishes to give wide publicity to libel-proof charges against some person or group, he may get a friendly congressman to insert them in the *Congressional Record;* then they can be repeated and reprinted at will and in perfect legal safety.

8. Become a Witness Before a Congressional Committee

Persons whom one accuses cannot sue him for anything he says when giving testimony before a Congressional committee. These committee proceedings then become public records, with "Congressional immunity," and can be reprinted at will. Although the witness may be prosecuted for perjury if he lies, this action must be brought *by the committee, not by the injured victim.* Committees rarely prosecute a "friendly" witness, that is, one who tells them what they want to hear. So the fact that grave charges against persons or groups are made before Congressional committees and never effectively refuted, or the accuser ever brought to trial, does *not* prove that the charges are true. They may be true, half-true, or completely false.

Most Congressional committee work is serious business, in which congressmen conscientiously seek to collect the facts needed to frame effective legislation and discharge their other proper duties. But the power to do this can also be perverted to serve partisan political purposes, pursue a private vendetta, or confuse and distort issues. When this is attempted, truth and "fair play" are likely to take a beating.

9. Repeat the Lie at Every Opportunity

Hitler argued that the bigger and more preposterous the lie, the more firmly will it be believed, *if it is repeated often enough.* Sometimes it seems as though Hitler were right. An American business executive sadly concedes: [7]

Tell a big lie to millions of people, tell it over and over without bothering about facts or logic, without regard to how preposterous or ridiculous or vicious it sounds at first, and pretty soon it acquires the status of fact with those unhappy people who are not in a position to check the facts.

Pretty soon even the injured and slandered parties, who know better, are panicked into fighting the big lie or negotiating over it, just as if it were the truth.

CRITERIA OF RELIABILITY IN INTERPRETING DATA

It is clear that many reports cannot be accepted as true. Some are willful falsehoods, some are unintentional errors, and some are products of neurotic, irresponsible people who are emotionally unable to distinguish between facts and wishful thinking. Are there any tests or rule-of-thumb ways of evaluating reports and estimating their reliability?

1. Authorship—Who Said It?

Who makes the charge or reports the disturbing facts?

a. Is He an Authority on the Subject Involved? Some people become "authorities" on government, foreign affairs, or practically anything, not through professional training, but through the ingenuity of their press agents. A continuous parade of "diet specialists" collect lecture fees and book royalties without displaying either scientific training or professional experience in dietetics. The counseling field is cluttered with thousands of self-anointed "psychologists," [8] "counselors," and human-relations "experts" who have no professional training in these fields. [9] It is a profitable racket, as long as there are people who do not inquire whether the "authority" is a reputable professional person or a pious fraud.

Many people without college degrees have become recognized authorities through private study and experience, such as Edison, Steffannson, and others. The question is: "Experience makes one an expert in what?" The obvious answer is, "Experience makes one an authority in the matter

---

[7] Philip D. Read, quoted in *The Progressive*, 15 (October, 1951), p. 8. (Mr. Read is Chairman of the Board of Directors of the General Electric Company.)

[8] At present, anyone who can spell the word can call himself a "psychologist" and collect fees for his "services," a situation which the reputable psychologists are most anxious to correct through appropriate legislation.

[9] See Mrs. Lee R. Steiner, *Where Do People Take Their Troubles?* (New York, International Universities Press, 1945).

in which he is experienced; in unrelated fields he is not an authority." To repeat such an obvious truth seems unnecessary, were it not that this fact is so often overlooked. A successful businessman has learned much about the conduct of a business, but his business experience has not necessarily qualified him as an authority on diet, teaching methods, or race relations. The college professor of physics is unlikely to be an authority on the cultural patterning of personality or on the state of competition within the oil industry.

We must also distinguish between "familiarity with" and "knowledge about" phenomena. A bank cashier who has handled millions of dollars does not thereby become an authority on government finance or banking legislation. The girls who pack pills in a pharmaceutical house have some familiarity with many drugs but have no thorough understanding of their nature or use. A foreman who has bossed many Negro workmen may imagine that he "understands Negroes," when all he really may have learned is how to handle a certain class of Negroes in a particular situation. This may not stop him from speaking confidently on all phases of Negro life. A superficial familiarity with a subject does not make one an authoritative philosopher thereupon.

b. What Is the Author's Known Bias? Is the author known to be a liberal, a moderate, or a conservative? Is he an atheist, an agnostic, or a believer? In which faith? *All persons have biases,* but some control them better than others. In interpreting an author's statements, it is helpful to know what his biases are and to note how deeply they color his judgments.

c. Is the Author Emotionally Stable? This is exceedingly important. Most of the very violent diatribes against government, against business, against the church, and so on, are the products of neurotic, paranoid, or otherwise maladjusted personalities. Most extremists, both right-wing and left-wing, are maladjusted persons whose bitter attacks stem from their inner emotional problems rather than from the realities of the situations they fret about.[10] Unfortunately, it is not always easy to detect a neurotic upon brief acquaintance. Many neurotics are brilliant, engaging people who speak and write convincingly. But when one has a reputation for instability—for taking extreme positions, for rapidly changing his story, for changing sides and causes frequently, his claims may be discounted accordingly.

2. Sponsorship—Who Publishes, Distributes, or Sponsors It?

The law generally requires that the publisher of printed material be identified. Reputable publications do not ordinarily publish grave charges

[10] See Harold D. Lasswell, *Psychopathology and Politics* (Chicago, University of Chicago Press, 1930); also C. S. Bluemel, *War, Politics, and Insanity* (Denver, The World Press, Inc., 1950).

or shocking reports without making some investigation. An article in the *New York Times* or the *Christian Science Monitor* will be widely accepted by discriminating readers, since these newspapers enjoy an excellent reputation for objectivity, whereas certain other papers are notorious for distorting the news to make it fit the editorial policy.[11] Labor newspapers and trade journals clearly reflect the biases and vested interests of their respective groups; this means that while the *facts* they present will generally be true, the *selection* and *interpretation of* these facts reveals the bias of the publishers.

Sometimes the real sponsor hides behind an apparent, phony sponsor. Certain "labor papers," published by groups of employers, stockholders, or others sympathetic with their interests, have been printed to look like a labor newspaper, so as to be able to criticize union policies more effectively. One used the terminology of unionism in promoting the interests of investors.[12] In political campaigns, it is a common practice for, say, the Democrats to help elect their candidate Joe Doaks by organizing a "Republicans for Joe Doaks Committee." If possible, some disgruntled Republicans are rounded up for this committee; if not, a purely paper committee is set up as a means of confusing the Republican voters. (The Republicans, of course, sometimes use the same tactic by setting up a "Democrats for Pete Zilch Committee.")

Sometimes organizations with similar names have opposing purposes. The *National Education Association* is an organization of educators, whereas the *American Education Association* contains few, if any, teachers and seeks mainly to cut school costs and combat what it views as "radicalism" in the schools. The *American Civil Liberties Union* is composed of people seeking to protect the constitutional rights of all citizens regardless of race, religion, or political belief, whereas the *American Civil Rights Congress* was an organization exploiting civil-liberties issues in order to promote communist propaganda. Both communist and fascist organizations invariably hide behind extremely patriotic-sounding titles. All organized pressure groups choose impressive titles, dripping with noble words, so it becomes clear that the title of an organization tells little about its purposes. One must know something of the membership and purposes of a sponsoring organization before one can correctly evaluate its publicity.

3. Vested Interest—Whose Axe Is Showing?

The vested interest of a spokesman can often be seen peeking between the lines of his arguments. In many attacks upon the "frills" of education

---

[11] See Milton Mayer, "How to Read the *Chicago Tribune*," *Harper's*, 198 (April, 1949), pp. 24-35.

[12] Cf. *New York Times Magazine*, November 23, 1952, p. 31.

the desire to cut school costs is easy to sense, while the vested interests of wealthy persons who oppose the "welfare state" are as obvious as are the vested interests of low-income people who favor it. Of course, it is possible to collect and state facts with complete honesty despite one's vested interest. But in evaluating data we must never forget that one's selection of data to present and the interpretation one gives are almost inevitably affected by one's vested interest.

4. Factual Content—How Specific Is the Author?

Is the report based on established facts or does it consist largely of unproved assumptions, imputed motives, and undocumented accusations? Are the "facts" really facts upon which all qualified observers would agree, or are his "facts" really assumptions and accusations stated as if they were facts? Sometimes a number of people who share the same viewpoint will quote one another's opinions and accusations back and forth until they become accepted as facts. Most "crime waves" and narcotic drug scares are in this category. One person announces a crime wave, the next expresses alarm over the "crime wave," a third asks what to do about "the widely-recognized crime wave," and so on until many people accept this "crime wave" as fact.

Is the report filled with vague, sweeping phrases such as "the government honeycombed with subversives," "the thousands of loafers on the public payroll," "all that business profiteering while our boys were dying," "the Jews getting control of everything," and the like? All such statements are worthless unless accompanied by sufficiently exact, detailed, and complete factual data to justify them.

5. Verifiability—Can It Be Checked?

Unless one is not only a liar but also a fool, he will be careful about the accuracy of statements which can easily be checked by his audience. A statement that "wages (or profits) doubled last year" could be quite easily checked against the statistics; the statement that "workers today are a bunch of loafers who don't work like they used to" cannot be checked easily or accurately; since both the machinery and the product have changed, it is difficult to make an exact comparison between present and earlier productivity.

The more easily a statement can be checked, the *more likely* it is to be reliable. There is no guarantee that it will always be true, however. One may make an unintentional error or simply be careless about checking his facts. Or one may simply lie in the belief that the truth will never catch up with the lie. Yet the general rule is that reliability will vary directly with verifiability.

6. Relevancy—Do the Data Support the Conclusions?

When confronted by a distressing lack of evidence to prove one's case, an ancient dodge is to prove a different case. A lot of irrelevant evidence can be cited as though it supported the original conclusion. For example, the maker of a well-known mouthwash wishes to promote it as a cold preventative. Since the cold germ has not been isolated and therefor there is no evidence that his mouthwash kills the cold germ, he simply advertises how many millions of other germs his mouthwash kills. Or suppose one wishes to convict the school of responsibility for juvenile delinquency. He has no evidence showing that the methods of the school really promote delinquency, so he cites lots of statistics documenting the *increase* in delinquency, and many hearers will forget that he presented no evidence that the school is responsible. Or suppose he wishes to convict the local relief office of wasting the taxpayers' money. All the evidence shows that the local office is administering the welfare laws efficiently, so he accuses the relief clients of being a bunch of worthless bums—lazy, drunken, and syphilitic—and he may convince many people that the local relief officials are horribly incompetent. Fortunately, the test of relevancy can be applied quite easily, merely by asking, How directly are the data related to the conclusions drawn therefrom?

7. Style—Is the Style Descriptive or Propagandistic?

a. Are the familiar propaganda devices used? Material that employs the standard propaganda devices *may* nevertheless be truthful and accurate, but is still under suspicion until its exact purposes and content are established. The standard propaganda devices include: [13]

1. *Name-calling*—giving an idea (or person) a bad name, so it will be rejected without examining the evidence—"socialized medicine," "slave labor act," "rich man's tax law," "communistic idea."
2. *Glittering generality*—associating an idea with noble sounding words with no exact meaning—"The American Way," "sancity of the home," "the future of America," "patriotic support," "sound program."
3. *Testimonial*—linking a loved or hated person with an idea— "The Jeffersonian principle of . . .", "Washington would be shocked at . . .", "Russia will be happy if . . .", "Our boys overseas pray that . . .", etc.
4. *Plain folks*—making one's ideas look like those "of the people." "Your plain Yankee horse sense tells you . . .", "The simple faith of my mother tells me that . . .", "I'm just a simple farm boy, not a corporation lawyer, and . . ."
5. *Card-stacking*—using only those selected facts, true or false, which support one's case. Supporting facts are emphasized, and damaging facts ignored.
6. *Band-wagon*—"Everybody's doing it", "Every thinking person now realizes that . . .", "Join the rising tide of protest against . . .", "Unite with that great army of patriotic Americans who . . ."

[13] Adapted from Institute for Propaganda Analysis, *The Fine Art of Propaganda* (New York, Harcourt, Brace & Company, Inc., 1939), pp. 23-24.

b. Is the style accusatorial and conspiratorial? Does the material abound in cloak-and-dagger suspense, with a dark plot on every page, and a subversive or a traitor or a blood-sucking capitalist behind every bush? If so, it is probably the work of a crackpot. Dependable, reliable reporting is usually written in sober, precise, and cautious language, and any writing which departs from this should be very critically examined. Of course, a skillful propagandist addressing well-educated minds will assume a dignified style. So while a melodramatic style suggests unreliability, a sedate style is no guarantee of positive reliability.

c. Is the style factually informative or platitudinous and tautological? A platitude is a statement of a truth so obvious as to be inane, such as "Our future lies before us," "The home is the cradle of civilization," or "The race belongs to the swift." Many a speaking reputation, political career, or churchman's eminence rests on ability to recite old platitudes so eloquently that they sound original and profound. A tautology is a needless repetition of the same idea in other words, such as "audible to the ear," or "visible to the eye." Attributed to Calvin Coolidge are the statements that "When there are not enough jobs for everybody, unemployment results," and "The cure for unemployment is work." Skillfully tautological writing sounds impressive but is devoid of meaning.

d. Is the statement cluttered with meaningless words and mystical expressions? Father Divine reassures his followers that they "can speak the words into 'tangibilization' or outer expression 'visibilated'," [14] and the Prophet Jones tells Father Divine, "I know that the chassis of your divine mind has been lubricated with divine lubrimentality." [15] A well-known promoter of diet fads and dubious food products suddenly recalled in middle age that he recovered from an ordinarily fatal childhood illness after eating "green vegetables *saturated with the earthy elements*" (italics ours).[16] Enigmatic and unprecise prose of this sort is the hallmark of dubious promotions.

8. Consistency—Does It Agree with Other Known Facts?

This is perhaps the most useful test of all, *providing one knows the other facts* about the matter. Some knowledge of the scientific facts about race should render one immune to most racial propaganda. Some who express alarm over the rising death rates from cancer and heart disease might be less disturbed if they realized that these increases are largely statistical illusions produced by the decline of other death rates. As stated before, there is no substitute for knowledge in interpreting data.

[14] Quoted in Hadley Cantril, *The Psychology of Social Movements* (New York, John Wiley & Sons, Inc., 1941), p. 128.

[15] Quoted in *Life* (September 28, 1953), p. 106.

[16] See Spencer Klaw, "Gayelord Hauser, The Blackstrap King," *Reporter*, 4 (March 20, 1951), pp. 31-34. See also *Consumer Reports*, 16 (February, 1951), p. 86.

9. Plausibility—Does the Story Sound Reasonable?

The writer recently inspected a book describing how FBI agents, police officers, the courts, various state and federal agencies, and the American Medical Association all conspired to persecute, beat up, maim, and nearly kill a poor soul who was merely trying to bring a great medical discovery to the American people.[17] It is very unlikely that such an array of reputable persons and agencies would act in such a manner, especially since many of them had nothing to gain. It is much more plausible to assume that this lurid tale is the work of irresponsible people whose veracity and judgment cannot be trusted. Many people firmly believe in spiritualism and it is impossible to prove scientifically that there is no communication between the living and the dead. But when the "spirits" which the mediums summon insist on appearing only in darkened rooms in prepared quarters and are preoccupied with sighs and groans and tooting trumpets, with trivial recollections and missing odds and ends of trash, but never locate any historically important missing documents or have anything of importance to say, which is more plausible—to accept spiritualism at face value, or to conclude that it probably is a pious fraud?

THE INTERPRETATION OF STATISTICAL DATA

Disraeli once observed that there are three grades of liars—plain liars, d_____ liars, and statisticians. This unkind remark springs from the fact that it is possible to manipulate statistics in such a way as to support whatever point of view one wishes. But simply to dismiss statistics as misleading and confusing is pointless, for statistics mislead and confuse only when one does not know how to interpret them. There are elaborate statistical formulas for determining the significance and reliability of a statistic, but this text is concerned only with some simpler tests which the student can apply.

1. The Use of Averages

One might say that the average income of his former college classmates is $25,000 a year. He might also say it is $5000. Both figures are approximately true. The divergence between them stems from the fact that there is more than one kind of average. One could divide last year's baby crop into the number of married women and find that the average housewife had .132 of a baby last year, showing that there are some measurements where an average is meaningless. One could compute the average height

---

[17] See Albert Q. Wahl and others, *The Birth of a Science* (Lutheran Research Society, 1949). In view of the preceding discussion of sponsorship, it is interesting to note that this organization is in no way affiliated with the Lutheran Church.

of river vessels in order to determine how high above the river to build a bridge, thereby showing that for some purposes an average is useless. An average, like a post-hole-digger, is useful only when properly employed.

There are three "averages" in standard use, each an absolutely genuine "average." They are computed differently and have different uses. The most common one is the *arithmetic mean*, found by adding all the values and dividing the sum by the number of cases. For most people, this is the only average they know of, and this is the one usually meant when simply identified as "the average." Quite different is the "mode," which is that value appearing most frequently and, therefore, is descriptive of the largest number of cases. The "median" is the mid-point in the series of cases, with half the cases above and half below this figure. Figure 3-1 shows how these averages differ in stating the "average" family income in the United States. All are genuine averages, but the mean is misleading in this case because so many families are below this average. Both the mode and the median would more accurately describe how the typical family lives and would be more satisfactory for most purposes. If one is seeking material for propaganda, he picks whichever average best suits his purposes. Whenever a frequency distribution approaches the "normal" or bell-shaped curve, the three averages are the same; when the distribution is *skewed*, or lopsided, the averages differ. The more strongly skewed the distribution, the less satisfactory will the mean be as a picture of the "typical" case. Whenever there are a number of extreme cases in the series, one knows in advance that the mean will be a misleading average.

2. Importance of the Base

Each year many more women are murdered at home by their husbands than are slain on the street by sexual psychopaths, but this does not prove that women would be safer if they slept on the sidewalks, since the number of women at home vastly exceeds the number of unescorted women on dark streets at night. To be comparable, two statistics must have a comparable base. All statistics have some starting point in time or some universe of data on which they are based. A percentage, for example, has no meaning by itself—it is a percentage *of* something. An advertiser's claim that "79 per cent prefer El Faggo cigarettes," has no real meaning as it stands; 79 per cent *of whom* prefer El Faggo *over what?* The fact that women drivers are involved in fewer accidents than men, in proportion to their numbers, is inconclusive; it is not the *number* of women drivers, but the proportion and type of *driving* done by women that is the base against which the percentage of accidents involving women should be compared.

Percentage comparisons can also be misleading when drawn on a

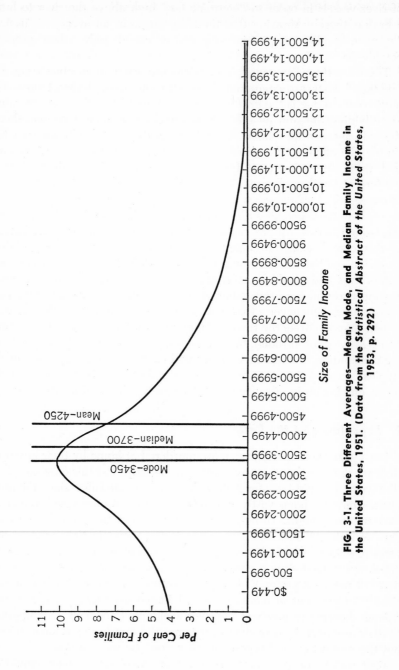

FIG. 3-1. Three Different Averages—Mean, Mode, and Median Family Income in the United States, 1951. (Data from the Statistical Abstract of the United States, 1953, p. 292)

very small base. Occasionally one sees a "research" project in which the data consist of only a small handful of cases, yet these have been fully analyzed in terms of percentages and other statistical procedures. A percentage based on two or three dozen cases or informants is not worth much—the base is too small. The same holds true when computing percentage of increase or decrease. The writer knows of a storekeeper who at the close of a year's business showed a net profit of $1.71 for the year; the following year he did little better, clearing $42.34. Since a well-run store of this size was earning about $10,000 a year, to claim that this storekeeper increased his profits by 2476 per cent would be true, but most misleading. A percentage of change may be very misleading if the starting point is near zero.

TABLE 3-1. Effects Upon Different Incomes of Adding 10 Per Cent to 1951 Income Tax Rates

Income Before Taxes	A Taxes at 1951 Rates	B Taxes if Rates Increased 10 Per Cent	C Per Cent of Increase in Taxes Paid	D Income Left After Taxes	E Per Cent Decrease in Income After Paying Taxes
$ 2500	$ 51	$ 76	50	$ 2424	2
25,000	8536	10,736	26	14,264	13
250,000	195,066	219,766	13	30,234	45
2,500,000	2,247,566	2,477,266	11	22,734	91

Table 3-1 shows what may happen when a constant percentage is computed on bases of differing size. Suppose that tax revenues were to be increased by adding ten percentage points to the income tax rates on all size incomes. Although such a proposal might have the appearance of "justice," it is clear that it would not impose equal sacrifice upon all groups. Notice particularly how the same set of facts can be used to support opposite conclusions. If one wishes to make this look unfair to the poor man, one will cite the percentages in Column C, which show that the "little fellow" has his taxes increased proportionately more than the wealthy person. If one wishes to make this look unfair to the rich man (as it obviously would be), one will cite the percentages in Column E, showing how much this tax rate change would reduce the income he had left after taxes. Probably no one has proposed exactly this tax schedule; it is cited purely to illustrate how percentages can be used and misused. Much of the demogoguery in tax debates has made just such use of percentages to buttress anguished cries of outrage at such "injustice."

Statistics are often used to measure changes from a *base year* that provides a starting point for comparison with the present. An objective scientist attempts to select a normal or typical year for the base year, such as 1926 for a pre-depression year, or 1939 for a prewar year. A propagandist selects a base year that is particularly favorable to the case he is trying to make. Depending upon which year is picked as a starting point, it is often possible to make a set of figures support either of two opposite conclusions. In Table 3-2 are detailed data on wages and prices, while Table 3-3 demonstrates how those data can be used to show (*a*) how wages have not kept up with prices, or (*b*) how wages have advanced more than prices. The trick is merely in picking the starting

TABLE 3-2. Which Rose Faster—Wages or Prices?

Consumer price index and average weekly earnings in manufacturing industry, 1939 to June, 1948

Date	Price Index	Weekly Earnings	Date	Price Index	Weekly Earnings
1939	100.0	$23.86	1947		
1945			Jan.	153.3	$47.10
Jan.	127.1	47.50	Feb.	153.2	47.29
April	127.1	47.12	March	156.3	47.72
July	129.4	45.12	April	156.2	47.50
Oct.	128.9	41.02	May	156.0	48.44
1946			June	157.1	49.33
Jan.	129.9	41.15	July	158.4	48.98
Feb.	129.6	40.55	Aug.	160.3	49.17
March	130.2	42.14	Sept.	163.8	50.47
April	131.1	42.88	Oct.	163.8	51.05
May	131.7	42.51	Nov.	164.9	51.29
June	133.3	43.31	Dec.	167.0	52.69
July	141.2	43.38	1948		
Aug.	144.1	44.99	Jan.	168.8	52.07
Sept.	145.9	45.39	Feb.	167.5	51.75
Oct.	148.6	45.73	March	166.9	52.06
Nov.	152.2	45.79	April	169.3	51.79
Dec.	153.3	46.96	May	170.5	51.86
			June	171.7	52.85

Federal Reserve Bulletin, various dates.

TABLE 3-3. Comparative Price and Wage Changes, as of June, 1948, Based upon Different Base Periods

Year and Month Chosen as Base Period	Price Index from Base Period to June, 1948	Wage Index from Base Period to June, 1948	Wages Ahead of Prices in June, 1948 by:	Prices Ahead of Wages on June, 1948, by:
1939 = 100	171.7	221.3	23%	———
Jan., 1945 = 100 .	134.6	111.3	———	12%
June, 1946 = 100.	128.8	122.0	———	11%
July, 1946 = 100	121.6	121.8	⅙ of 1%	———

Computed from data in Table 3-2.

point and measuring only the changes thereafter. Thus, if the starting point is the year of 1939 or the month of July, 1946, it can be shown that wage increases have kept nicely ahead of price rises, whereas if January, 1945, is selected as a base month, one finds wages falling 12 per cent behind prices.[18]

Whenever index numbers are used, or percentage comparisons for two different periods are presented, the base year or starting point must be critically examined. Is it a relatively normal year or a highly abnormal one? Is the base period long enough so that seasonal or annual variations are evened out? Frequently a base period of several years is used in order to get a base which is not distorted by peculiarities of a single year.[19]

3. Opinion Measurement

A complete study of the art of opinion measurement would fill several volumes. Since public-opinion polls are often cited in debates about social problems, students should be able to recognize the more obvious of the pitfalls that may destroy the accuracy of opinion measurement.

a. Sampling errors probably have ruined more opinion polls than any other error. First, the sample must be *adequate,* that is, large enough to be reliable. A few dozen cases are practically useless; several hundred are better, several thousand better yet. In the second place, the sample must be *representative,* that is, it must represent all classes of the population accurately. For example, a representative sample of the student body of a college must have the same percentage of freshmen, of sophomores, of juniors, and of seniors as there are in the entire student body. One does not get a representative sample by standing on a street corner and quizzing passers-by, because not all groups use that particular street. A student sample collected in fraternity houses and campus hangouts would underrepresent both the more studious students and the less prosperous ones. An alumni sample picked from alumni mailing lists probably is overloaded with the more successful alumni, who are more easily located than are the class failures. The telephone book, a popular source for sample-building, includes few names of the very poor. An *uncontrolled* sample, such as street-corner passers-by or those who mail in a ballot

---

[18] The problem of accurately comparing wage and price changes is complicated by still other difficulties. *Which* prices shall be included in the price index? Which wages shall be used—wages of *all* wage earners, of *factory* wage earners, or only of *manufacturing production* workers (the one given above)? Shall it be *gross* hourly wages, weekly wages, or "take-home" pay? In deciding which to use, beautiful opportunities for "card-stacking" are presented.

[19] E.g., the "parity price" formula used to determine federal price supports for farm products is based on a five-year period, 1910-1914. The Bureau of Labor Consumer Price Index was based on prices of selected items for the 1935-1939 period until 1953. Since 1953, the Consumer Price Index has been based on 1947-1949 prices.

printed in a newspaper, may be so far from representative that it is not worth much. The first step, therefore, in evaluating any opinion research, is to take a long hard look at the sample.

b. A second common error, often intentional, lies in *"loading" the questions,* wording them in such a way as to get a desired response. This is done deliberately when the "research" is intended as support for propaganda and it may also be an unintentional result of carelessness or ignorance. In both instances an inaccurate measure is the result. Shortly before the United States entered World War II, one group was polling people on the question, "Should U.S. stay out of this foreign war?" while another group was asking, "Would our active participation in this war be preferable to a Nazi domination of Europe?" (approximate quotations). Each question drew an overwhelming majority of "yes" responses, for each was worded so as to invite a "yes" response.

c. Limiting of responses. If responses are to be tabulated, the informants must select one of a series of prepared answers. It may be that these answers are "loaded," or so few answers offered that some persons can find none which suits them. If this happens, the findings of the survey are not valid.

The highly reputable opinion-measurement concerns, such as the Gallup Poll, the Fortune Survey, or the National Opinion Research Center, generally avoid these errors, but "opinion surveys" made by less competent or reputable agencies should be very carefully examined for possible error.

4. Association and Causation

A favorite method of hunting for "causes" is to hunt for statistical associations. Association or correlations [20] have been found between drinking and unemployment, broken homes and juvenile delinquency, smoking and school failures, and hundreds of others. What does "association" mean?

The first step in evaluating a claimed association (assuming that the statistics themselves appear to be accurate) is to contrast the association with the total universe from which it is drawn. For example, suppose that 50 per cent of the unemployed are "drinkers." This tells us nothing until we know how many of the general population are "drinkers." If 50 per cent of the general population also drink, then there is no real association between drinking and unemployment; whereas if considerably fewer (or

[20] A statistical association is a relationship between two pairs of categories, such as drinker-nondrinker and employed-unemployed. A correlation is a statistical measure of degree of association between two sets of quantitative variables, such as amount of education and amount of annual income.

more) of the general population are "drinkers," then an association exists. *We have a genuine association only when the factor we are studying appears much more (or less) often in the observed group than in the general population.* Delinquency is associated with broken homes only if delinquents come from broken homes more often than nondelinquents. Suppose that 50 per cent of the delinquents came from broken homes. If only 25 per cent of *all* children live in broken homes, then there is an association, since the broken homes are contributing more than their share; but if 50 per cent of all children live in broken homes, then there is no association, since the broken homes are contributing exactly their proportionate share.

This step of contrasting the association with the total universe is one which students often have difficulty in grasping, so some further illustrations are needed. The examples in Table 3-4 may clarify the central point, namely, that a genuine association exists only when two things appear together either more frequently or less frequently than would be normally expected.

TABLE 3-4. When Does a Percentage Indicate a Statistical Association?

If:	We Need to Know:	Before Trying to Decide:
50% of the college girls drink	what per cent of all girls of college age drink	whether college girls drink any more or less than average
25% of fatal accidents involve drinking drivers	what per cent of all cars are driven by drinking drivers	whether drinking drivers contribute more or less than their share of accidents
50% of all cancer victims have a relative or ancestor who had cancer	what per cent of all people also have a relative or ancestor who has had cancer	whether those with cancerous relatives are more likely than average to contract cancer
75% of the delinquent children have fathers who do not go to church	what per cent of all children have fathers who do not go to church	whether paternal church-going is associated with delinquency rates
10% of the relief clients are illiterate	what per cent of all people of similar age are illiterate	whether illiteracy is associated with relief status
20% of the penitentiary inmates are mentally retarded	what per cent of all people of similar age are mentally retarded	whether mental retardation is associated with criminal status
10% of the convicted criminals are foreign-born	what per cent of all persons of similar ages are foreign-born	whether the foreign-born contribute more or less than their share of convicts
40% of the former college athletes die of heart diseases	what per cent of all men die of heart diseases	whether there is any association between athletic activity and heart disease

Above percentages are hypothetical, not authoritative.

If a genuine association is found, the next question is to settle the matter of causation. Which is cause and which is effect? Whenever two factors are associated, there are at least four possibilities:

1. *A* causes *B*.
2. *B* causes *A*.
3. Both *A* and *B* are caused by *C*.
4. *A* and *B* are independent and the "association" is accidental.

To be more specific, consider the well-established association between smoking and poor grades in elementary school. The possibilities include:

1. Smoking among small boys causes poor grades. (It upsets digestion, interferes with mental concentration, and has other ill effects.)
2. Poor grades cause smoking. (Boys who get failing grades smoke to show off, to rebuild ego, and express defiance of school authorities.)
3. Both are caused by a third factor. (Boys who hate school are likely to smoke to express defiance, and get poor grades because they are disinterested; in the lower social class, both early smoking and a disinterest in school are part of the class culture.)
4. They may be independent variables. (Some boys get poor grades because of limited intelligence and smoke because the gang does.)

This case shows how a statistical association never identifies the cause; it merely states that two factors move together, without telling why. The difficult question of determining *what causes what* is only begun, once a valid association is established.

A coefficient of correlation is a particular kind of measure of association used when associating two or more quantitative variables. For example, if height and weight of a group of people show a coefficient of correlation of $+.80$, this would mean that in most cases the taller persons are heavier than the short persons. This is called *positive* correlation, for both variables rise or fall together. In *negative* or *inverse* correlation, the two variables move in opposite directions. For example, as people get older, their hearing usually fades; age and hearing acuity, therefore, would show a negative coefficient of correlation, written with a minus sign preceding the coefficient.

How much does a coefficient of correlation mean? A coefficient of less than $\pm.20$ (either positive or negative) is so low as to have scarcely any significance. Those between $\pm.20$ and $\pm.40$ are worthy of slight significance; between $\pm.40$ and $\pm.60$ deserve moderate significance; between $\pm.60$ and $\pm.80$ receive considerable significance; those between $\pm.80$ and ±1.00 are deserving of great significance. But even a very high correlation between two variables never proves that one causes the other; it only suggests that one *may* be the cause of the other and that further study is needed to settle the point.

DEFINITION OF TERMS

The terms *liberal, conservative, radical,* and *reactionary* arise frequently in any discussion of social problems. Since these terms are used in several ways in public discussion, it is necessary to define them.

As used in this textbook, these terms represent four points along a continuum, with "radical" at one end and "reactionary" at the other, and with "liberal" and "conservative" respectively a little to the left or right of center. The conservative is one who considers the existing society, or the status quo, to be relatively satisfactory and wishes to preserve it without any great change. The liberal agrees that the existing society is fairly satisfactory, but thinks that quite a number of "improvements" can and should be made. Both agree that *some* "improvements" are desirable, but disagree upon *how much* "improving" is needed. Present American conservatives and liberals agree in supporting a private enterprise system with *some* public ownership and *some* government controls, although the liberals favor *more* public ownership and control than do the conservatives. Both approve government expenditure for welfare purposes, but liberals favor further increases in these services, while conservatives hesitate to expand government functions or expenditures. At present, most American liberals favor increased government expenditures for health services, federal aid to education, and conservation of natural resources, and favor federal control of public lands and public development of multiple-purpose river development authorities (like TVA), whereas most conservatives have far less enthusiasm for these ideas.

Radicals and reactionaries share an intense dislike for the status quo, but disagree in their recommendations. The reactionary (or extreme "right-winger") wishes to return to an earlier, and presumably better, pattern of social organization. Most American reactionaries would like to return to about the sort of relationship between government, business, and labor which existed during the Coolidge, or perhaps the McKinley, administration. Labor unions, the Social Security System, civil rights legislation, most government welfare services, and practically all other liberal programs are viewed as abominations. The reactionary hates the liberals, distrusts the conservatives, considers the Eisenhower administration almost as "bad" as the Roosevelt and Truman administrations, and finds much to admire in fascism.

The radical (or extreme "leftist") considers the status quo basically repulsive and wishes to replace it with a new, fundamentally different society. He dismisses the conservatives as irrelevant and hates the liberals for trying to improve or patch up the society he wishes to overthrow. Since he wishes to replace and not to reform the society, the policies he is "for" at any given moment are likely to be expedient bits of propaganda rather than genuine objectives. The American radical in the recent past was likely to be either a communist, a "fellow-traveler," or a "parlor pink." At present, radicalism in America has been forced "underground" to a degree which makes it difficult to locate and define clearly.

Although these terms may have other acceptable definitions, this is the way these terms are used in this volume.

SUMMARY

Data (facts) lead nowhere by themselves; they are quite motionless. Data must be *interpreted* before they have meaning. The first problem is to be reasonably certain whether the data are *true*. The popular faith that "they couldn't say those things if there weren't some truth in them" underestimates both the skill of an accomplished liar and the unintentional distortion inherent in one's frame of reference. Those who wish to falsify the truth are likely to:

1. Lie about a group.
2. Lie about a dead man.
3. Impute guilt-by-association.
4. Impute wicked motives, purposes, or consequences.
5. Use weasel words.
6. Quote out of context.
7. Find a friendly congressman.
8. Find a friendly witness before a Congressional committee.
9. Repeat the lie until it becomes accepted as fact.

How is authoritative fact to be recognized when it is found? Among the useful tests for reliability are:

1. Authorship—who said it?
   a. What is his training and competence?
   b. What is his bias?
   c. Is he emotionally stable?
2. Sponsorship—who publishes, distributes, or promotes it?
3. Vested interest—whose checkbook is showing?
4. Factual content—how specific is it?
5. Verifiability—can it be checked and verified?
6. Relevancy—do the data support the conclusions?
7. Style—is it descriptive or propagandistic?
8. Consistency—does it agree with other known facts?
9. Plausibility—does the whole story sound reasonable?

In interpreting statistical data, there is great danger of following truthful statistics to false conclusions. In the use of averages, the *mean* will always be misleading if based on a lopsided rather than a "normal" distribution, whereas the *mode* or *median* will usually give a more nearly typical picture.

Statistics are no more reliable than the base upon which they are computed. The base year for index numbers, the area, the group, or the sample may be chosen to give a true picture, or may be chosen so as to conceal the true picture of the facts. Often no single statistic will give the whole picture, so several must be used.

Public-opinion measurement can be used either to measure opinion or to manufacture and distort opinion. Intentional or unintentional distortion may be suspected whenever the sample is too small to be adequate, or too carelessly controlled to be accurately *representative* of all groups and classes of people. The wording of the questions may be loaded, or the informant be forced to choose between loaded responses, and the findings accordingly worthless.

Associations and correlations are most useful in suggesting hypotheses and indicating *possible* causes. But an association is significant only when it occurs more often than chance would indicate; therefore, every claimed association between two factors must be checked by asking how often these two factors normally occur together. When it is found that two factors *do* occur together more often (or less often) than can be accounted for by chance, it still remains to be shown whether either causes the other. Neither association nor correlation proves anything beyond the possibility of causation.

It is no easy adventure upon which the student is invited. The interpretation of data is the most difficult task in social science. It requires a degree of objectivity which not all students are willing or able to develop; it demands an awareness of the common pitfalls such as those described in this chapter; it requires an accumulation of factual knowledge—a lot of plain, unvarnished, unspectacular, painstakingly-acquired facts—without which no intellectual tricks or short-cuts will bring that practical understanding of social issues which students presumably desire. Although the study of social problems should never be dull, neither will it be easy; and the most difficult task of all will be to recognize the truth when one has found it.

SUGGESTED READINGS

DUNHAM, Barrows, *Man Against Myth* (Boston, Little, Brown & Company, 1947). A critical examination of some of the major myths and intellectual clichés of our time.

EVANS, Bergen, *The Natural History of Nonsense* (New York, Alfred A. Knopf, Inc., 1946). A highly entertaining account of many popular myths and superstitions, which the author demolishes with a rare blend of wit and science.

YOUNG, Pauline V., *Scientific Social Surveys and Research* (New York, Prentice-Hall, Inc., 1949). An authoritative textbook in research methods in the social sciences.

AUDIO-VISUAL AIDS

Whispers (Teaching Film Custodians, Inc., 25 West 43rd, New York), 10
   minutes, sound, black and white. Local interest groups to whom a suggested
   civic improvement threatens financial loss organize a whispering campaign
   that defeats the proposal and ruins the reputation of its sponsor.

QUESTIONS AND PROJECTS

1. Why not pass a law to prevent the telling of falsehoods and the stating
of unjust accusations?

2. Are there any methods, direct or indirect, of telling a lie other than
the ones listed in this chapter?

3. How new are these methods of telling lies? Does any group or party
monopolize them?

4. Do the people who tell and imply these lies believe them themselves?
Is most such lying intentional or unintentional?

5. Under what circumstances, if any, is one justified in inferring "guilt"
from association?

6. If Congressional immunity gives a congressman an opportunity for
reckless lying, why not abolish Congressional immunity, and hold congressmen
accountable under the laws of libel and slander like anyone else?

7. What should be one's first move in reading a serious book or article?

8. Is it safe to assume that any speaker or writer who "takes sides"
strongly has a vested interest to defend?

9. What are the three statistical averages? Which, if any, is the most true
or genuine? Which gives the best picture of the "typical" case? Which may give
the most nontypical picture?

10. What is a representative sample? In building a representative sample of
the student body, what characteristics would need to be checked?

11. What does an association or correlation tell about causes?

CHAPTER 4

Interest and Pressure Groups in Modern Society

THE National Association of Manufacturers said: . . . If you have a good witness to defend Taft-Hartley or know a good witness, please wire us at once. Also wire both House and Senate Labor Committees at once for permission to testify.

Unless this is done, the revision of Taft-Hartley will be undertaken against a background of union-inspired testimony, and the future labor-management law will not be to the liking of business.[1]

The C.I.O. leader prepared a 15,000-word statement for the House labor committee suggesting removal of practically all major provisions of the present law. "There will be some," said Reuther, "who will say that the substantial amendments we have proposed amount to actual repeal. To this soft indictment we plead guilty." [2]

It [The Chamber of Commerce] urged local firms to participate in the I G H A T movement. The letters stand for—"I'm Gonna Holler About Taxes." This was initiated by Quaker Oats and International Harvester with assistance from Sears, Roebuck & Company.[3]

A year ago the Aluminum Co. of Canada, Ltd. offered to sell the U. S. 200,000 tons of aluminum over a three-year period at a cent lower than domestic prices, but the R.F.C. rejected the proposal after U. S. producers protested.[4]

The National School Boards Association adopted yesterday a resolution urging that adequate instruction be given in the nation's public schools concerning the United Nations and UNESCO including criticism when warranted.[5]

For a while . . . it looked as if the P.T.A. had a shoo-in proposal. Then the city's Christian Scientists roused themselves in protest. Fluoridation, they in-

[1] *Indianapolis Star*, February 15, 1953.
[2] *Lafayette Journal and Courier*, March 12, 1953.
[3] *Indianapolis Star*, February 15, 1953.
[4] Reprinted from *Time;* copyright Time Inc. 1952.
[5] *Indianapolis Star*, February 15, 1953.

sisted, meant enforced medication. . . . Seattle's Christian Scientists were joined by the Washington State Council Against Fluoridation and a group called the National Nutrition League, Inc. Arrayed against them were the District Dental Society, the Trustees of the King County Medical Society, and a formidable list of other organizations.[6]

Re your brief reference to Governor Adlai E. Stevenson's veto message concerning the notorious anti-cat measure (a bird lover's bill "to prohibit cats from running at large" in Illinois): I wish to state that The American Feline Society, Inc. played no small part in this legislative battle which could have conceivably cost the lives of 5 million of Illinois cats . . .[7]

Each of the above quotations portrays action taken by a special kind of modern group—the pressure group. How many pressure groups are there in the United States? Nobody knows. What *is* known is that the number is tremendously large and constantly increasing.

PRESSURE GROUPS

Pressure groups exist to do just what the name implies, to apply pressure wherever necessary in order to gain their ends. Pressure groups operate largely in the field of practical "power politics." They work for the passage of legislation favorable to themselves, to combat unfavorable legislation, and they attempt to influence the administration of laws already in existence. Accordingly, they seek the election of particular political candidates, they attempt to influence the appointment of public officials, they conduct "lobby" operations in state and national capitals, and they conduct extensive "educational" campaigns designed to influence public opinion. Pressure groups are deeply involved in all extensive conflicts of interests in the contemporary scene.

Pressure groups are a natural consequence of the advantages of organization in modern society. In any complex social system, organized power is the most effective power. Few individuals possess enough power to attain their goals unaided, and even those few persons who do have such power become still more powerful when they band together. The existence of pressure groups is as natural in one area of life as it is in any other. The efficient conduct of religious, educational, civic, and business affairs requires pressure groups. Pressure groups operate within the society's largest enterprises and in its most specialized and isolated conflicts. The present chapter focuses on the operation of pressure groups in a crucial segment of American culture—the economic system.

[6] Reprinted from *Time;* copyright Time Inc. 1952.
[7] Robert Lothar Kendell, President, The American Feline Society, Inc., in *Time,* February 18, 1952, by permission.

The Special Character of Pressure Groups

Pressure groups, regardless of where they are found, tend to be characterized by (1) money, organization, and power, and (2) the employment of propaganda.

1. *Money, Organization, and Power.* The rapid growth of pressure groups in recent decades springs directly from the recognition that organized and financially powerful minority groups can often further their interests at the expense of larger unorganized majorities. The explanation for this situation is quite simple. Organization makes possible the massing of capital, especially if the organized interests are moneyed interests to begin with, and the possession of capital enables one to exert great power over public opinion and eventually over the legislative processes themselves. The possessor of sufficient capital can hire radio time to present his case to the public. He can also place full-page advertisements in the nation's newspapers or, if he is more shrewd, he may get his point of view represented on the editorial pages, or even on page one under the guise of being "news" rather than "opinion." He can hire attorneys for the best of legal advice, consultants of all sorts, and lobbyists to work directly upon the legislators. If he is so inclined, he may (and sometimes does) even hire thugs and hoodlums to use physical force on those persons who oppose his plans or interests! In a society dominated by pecuniary values, the possessor of wealth (whether individual person or organized group) holds strong advantages not shared by the so-called "common man."

2. *The Employment of Propaganda.* The operations of pressure groups are generally far more subtle, however, than the open employment of force or financial pressure. Long ago, it became general knowledge that pressure tends to be most effective when it is hidden from view, so that individuals and groups do not realize they are being pressured but *believe* themselves to be acting in their own best interests. Thus the fine art of propaganda has become a principal tool in the pressure group's tool kit. To be successful the propagandist must, above all, conceal or distort his true motives.

The propagandist denies that he seeks to "indoctrinate" and insists that he wants to "educate" the public. This clever choice of words is one technique used by the propagandist to sway public opinion. Unless one is sufficiently critical to examine the legitimacy of the use of the terms *indoctrinate* and *educate,* it becomes logically very difficult not to accept the propagandist's conclusions. This technique has often been used to oppose liberal education in the nation's schools and colleges. The opponents of liberal education declare that the choice is between "indoctrinating" people with communism and socialism or "educating" them to the virtues of capitalism and free enterprise. The possibility of a comparative study of the merits and demerits of various economic and political systems is not even considered.

If the student is to guard against manipulation by pressure groups, he must examine some of the other techniques used by them for propaganda purposes. Four such techniques are: (*a*) to convince the public that it has the same interests as the pressure group; (*b*) to soft-pedal its true identity and promote acceptance as something else; (*c*) to use emotional rather than rational arguments; and (*d*) to employ diversionary tactics to divert attention away from the real issues.

a. Most pressure groups *presume* to speak not only for themselves but for the public at large. Thus in wage and price disputes both labor unions and manufacturers' associations claim to represent the public interests against the "narrow, selfish interests" of the other. The U. S. Chamber of Commerce has skillfully "sold" slogans to the effect that "a community prospers when its business prospers" and "that which helps business also helps the community." It is true, of course, that there is a correlation between general prosperity and the prosperity of business interests. But equally true is the labor contention that "business prospers when labor prospers." Each group attempts to use the general correlation between the prosperity levels of different segments of the population to demonstrate that anything which helps "its side" automatically aids everyone else at the same time. Thus, from one point of view, a price rise enables the businessman to make a profit which will be reinvested in the business, providing work for others who may in turn purchase more goods. From the other viewpoint, a wage increase enables laborers to buy more goods which means more profit for businessmen to be reinvested to produce more jobs and higher wages, and so on.

Both of these arguments obscure the fact that, in the short run at least, the interests of labor and business are by no means synonymous. The one benefits from higher wages, or higher prices, much more immediately and directly than does the other. Modern society is sufficiently complex so that no pressure group can adequately represent the interests of the entire population. But if the pressure group can *maintain the illusion* that it is fighting for the interests of all, it has won a real advantage in the struggle for power.

b. Since the arguments of pressure groups tend to be somewhat discounted as the nature and motives of the organization become known, many pressure groups have profited by taking titles which are either ambiguous or which have little to do with the real purposes of the organization. Until very recently, however, the propaganda advantage accruing from this situation has not been so much the result of purposive action on the part of pressure groups as it has of ignorance and apathy on the part of the general public. Most people make little or no effort to establish the identity and interests of an organization before evaluating its published statements. Consequently, pressure groups can hardly be blamed for taking full advantage of the situation. Probably only some of the more recently formed pressure groups have consciously selected their titles to conceal their true identity.

To illustrate the difficulty of accurately assessing the nature of a group from its title, consider a few which appear frequently in our newspapers. The *American Federation of Labor* is a respectable labor organization, whereas the *World Federation of Trade Unions* is a tool of Russian policy-makers. The *Chamber of Commerce of the United States* is not an official government agency but is a pressure group for business interests. The *Freedom Forum* also is supported by an impressive array of industrial and business interests and serves those interests well in the public forums which it conducts. The *Civil Rights Congress* is listed by the Attorney General as a subversive organization. The *Small Business Economic Foundation, Inc.*, follows closely the line of the *National Association of Manufacturers*. The student will notice that practically all of these organizations load their titles with words which carry a definitely favorable emotional connotation. This leads us directly into the next point.

c. Pressure groups generally attempt to discourage any critical thought on issues where they have an interest. Their goal is not to promote analysis of the problem but to induce others to accept the solution which yields maximum benefit to themselves. One way in which they accomplish this end is by attaching positive word symbols to their own cause and negative ones to that of the opposition. The use of such terms as *freedom, American, rights, crusade,* and *liberty* in its official title serves among other things to encourage outsiders to identify themselves emotionally with the organization and its causes.

Recently it has become fashionable among some groups to insist that we must have "a return to basic principles." Whether the complaint is directed toward the growth of labor unions, evidences of influence peddling in government, the regulation of prices, or participation in the United Nations, it is cried that we must have a return to "basic principles." One is soon forced to the conclusion that the term *principles* apparently refers to any situation or condition deemed desirable by the pressure group.

Terms such as *socialism, collectivism, statism, communism,* and *bureaucracy,* which have acquired unfavorable connotations, are applied indiscriminately to almost any cause opposed by the pressure groups, whereas those espoused by these interests are identified in terms of *morality, integrity,* and *the American way.* It is perhaps significant that at the very moment when we are locked in struggle with world communism, that the term *communism* seems to be devoid of any *rational* or *clear* meaning for most of the population. The use of the term *communism* as an epithet applied to such diverse phenomena as federal aid to education, municipal light and power companies, the government of the Soviet Union, the United States postal system, and the economic and political theories of Karl Marx seriously interferes with our ability to develop any constructive program for dealing with the most potent threat to democracy in recent centuries.

d. A fourth tactic employed by pressure groups is to divert public attention from the important issues by seeking to center attention on other matters. This is the so-called "red-herring" technique.

In many instances organized labor has opposed the adoption of labor-saving machinery on the grounds that the resulting products would be inferior and that "craftsmanship" would be lost. Objective analysis might lead one to suspect that the unions were far more fearful of loss of jobs and income than of the possible lowered quality of consumer products—especially since mass-production techniques have been instrumental in creating the highest standard of living the world has ever known. But if attention could be concentrated on the possible loss of "craftsmanship," the unions would have a much stronger case. Similarly, in the current struggle over the desirability of a union shop in much of American industry, the opposition forces claim that the granting of this demand would deprive the American worker of his right "not to join" the union. Regardless of the intrinsic merit of the argument, is it reasonable to assume that management is primarily concerned with the rights of the workers? Again it is obvious that the enactment of a union shop would mean a more powerful union with which management would have to bargain. To admit this fact, however, is to open the possibility that the public would support the unions' desire for more power in relation to that of management. If management can make it appear that it is really concerned with the right of the worker himself, then who can disagree with management's conclusion that the union shop would be an evil thing?

The preceding four points are illustrative of the type and range of techniques employed by pressure groups to propagandize the public into accepting the pressure group's point of view. They are not intended as a comprehensive analysis of propaganda techniques [8] but only to stimulate the student to greater awareness of the general pattern, so that he may be on the alert for and able to cope with those who seek to prevent an objective analysis of social problems.

Vested Interests

Interests and Vested Interests. Each of the numerous organizations which have appeared on the American scene is, in a sense, an interest group. In some cases the interest is obvious and coextensive with the pur-

---

[8] For a refresher on general propaganda techniques, refer back to the discussion in Chapter 3, pp. 35-42.

pose of the organization. The Society for the Preservation and Encouragement of Barbershop Quartet Singing in America and the Anti-Nicotine League of America were formed for the purposes indicated by their respective titles and generally do not participate *as organizations* in more general economic and political issues. Other organizations such as the American Medical Association, the C.I.O., and the American Farm Bureau Federation operate in practically all situations where their collective interests might be threatened. They actively compete in the contest to sway public opinion, they attempt to influence legislators, they support certain economic policies, and they apply subtle and sometimes not-so-subtle pressures to achieve their ends.

A basic distinction for analytic purposes is that between *interest groups* and *vested interest groups*. An interest group is any number of people who share a common aim or goal. The group may be of any size from two persons, theoretically, up to whole nations or even larger. The interest may be fundamental and all-pervasive—for example, democracy or freedom—or it may be trivial and isolated—for example, in the preservation of the custom of wearing high-button shoes. The group may be highly organized with officers and funds or it may have no formal organization at all. A *vested* interest group is a special kind of interest group—one which receives some special advantage from the status quo.

The Nature of Vested Interests. The real significance of the vested-interest concept goes far deeper than might appear at first glance. This significance derives from the facts that the vested interest (1) owes its position to past definitions, (2) has the support of tradition, (3) generally has a firm basis for wielding power, and (4) operates to impede the process of social change.

1. Vested interests appear whenever a group derives special advantage from the status quo. When our Puritan forefathers settled the coasts of New England they restricted voting rights to property holding males who were also church members. Their voting status then led this group to manage the colonies largely in their own interests and to oppose any changes which would have weakened their position. *A vested interest had been created.* This original definition in the New World, while gradually being modified, has persisted right down to the present time when a substantial proportion of the Negro population, for example, is effectively disfranchised through the use of poll taxes, literacy tests, and other questionable devices. The basis for such obvious, and occasionally illegal, discrimination was laid down in definitions formulated more than two centuries ago.

To cite another example, there are at the present time in the United States various groups of psychiatrists and clinical psychologists feuding over the right of the latter to be licensed by the state to deal with problems of mental illness. From the time of Hippocrates the professional treatment of bodily pathologies has been limited to physicians. Physicians have had a vested interest in the treatment of disease. That vested interest in the treatment of bodily pathologies has been extended to include mental illness and, so far, the psychiatrists have been rather successful in frustrating the attempts of the psychologists to gain official recognition. If the issue were to be decided on the basis of the nature of mental illness and of the efficacy of current treatments therefor, the psychiatric position might be considerably weakened. But vested interests have the advantage of favorable *past* definitions.

2. Ideas of right and wrong, justice and injustice, morality and immorality, are parts of culture which come to us out of the past. Thus the foundations for our standards of judgment lie in the very definitions, discussed above, which create vested interests. Not only do these definitions create vested interests but they lend the support of custom and tradition to the maintenance of the advantages thus established. During the first century of this country's existence, for example, there were not even serious questions concerning whether women should have the right to vote. "Woman's place is in the home," and for women to seek the vote was considered ridiculous, presumptuous, unladylike, and even immoral. Only after a long and sometimes bitter struggle with the tradition-supported male vested interests were women granted full suffrage.

The tradition that supports the right of vested interests to maintain their advantage operates, of course, in other than the abstract. Customs and traditions are likely to be embedded in the law, so that an attack upon the vested interests is likely to run afoul of the law itself. Agitators are likely to be jailed in accordance with laws that give support to and are supported by the vested interests. Opinion, too, of the legislators who make the laws and of the jurists who interpret the laws, tends to favor the vested interests against those who would challenge them. Negroes in the United States have continuously faced this very situation. In most any altercation between whites and Negroes the law technically and operationally favors the whites. Negroes are jailed and punished on the flimsiest of pretexts, whereas whites are often excused even for direct physical assaults on Negro persons. The advantages established by tradition are maintained by present institutions and opinion.

3. The struggle of emerging interest groups against vested interests is rendered more difficult by the fact that power tends to be concentrated in the hands of the vested interests. On the American scene, holding the financial advantage enables one in essence to purchase support for and allegiance to his cause. The possessor of wealth can influence newspaper presentation of the issue both by purchasing advertisement space and by withholding advertisements unless the paper's editorial policy is a "satisfactory" one. Such coercive measures are not usually necessary, however, since the newspapers are for the most part controlled by one set of vested

interests who would logically be in sympathy with another set of vested interests. The theoretically equal access which "both sides" of an issue have to radio and television facilities is likewise of little meaning when only one side has the necessary means to purchase their use. Concentrated propaganda campaigns involving the use of the mass-communication agencies, the hiring of public halls and speakers, the most expert of legal advice, and preferential treatment under the law are all potent weapons in the hands of the vested interests.

Perhaps almost as important as the above is the fact that the vested interests are in a better position to mobilize and use effectively the resources they possess. Being long established, they usually have already formed some sort of organization to further their common goals. They are apt to have formed a "consciousness of kind" that makes it easier for them to join forces when they are threatened from the outside. Conversely, the emerging interest groups are likely to suffer from a lack of "we" feeling and from the absence of any formal machinery through which to express their ambitions. The consumer movement in the United States is a good example. Though in isolated instances consumer groups have organized concerted campaigns to force down prices, the absence of long-standing common interests among them has frustrated all major attempts at organization.

4. Vested interests are identified with the forces of conservatism and reaction in the community and seldom with those of liberalism and change. Having attained a position of special advantage, the vested interest seeks to retain that advantage by discouraging any innovation which might remove it. Among the favorite phrases are pleadings for a "return to the good old days" or, more accurately, to the days before the vested interest was seriously challenged. In this way, the tendency for memory to be selective and for past conditions to take on a golden glow which they never really had is exploited for purely selfish reasons.

It is in the realm of technology that the undesirable social effects of this factor may be most easily seen. Time and again vested interests have prevented or delayed the adoption of inventions which were decided improvements over anything then in existence. The self-starter, six- and eight-cylinder motors, the "V" engine, four-wheel brakes, low-pressure tires, and automatic transmissions are only a few of the improvements which were eventually accepted after long periods of delay by the automobile manufacturers.[9] The telephone and telegraph companies have been guilty of the same sort of obstructionism in the field of communications. Davis, Bredemeier, and Levy report that in 1937 the Federal Communications Commission charged the Bell Telephone System with

[9] For a fuller development of this general thesis, see Kingsley Davis, Harry C. Bredemeier, and Marion J. Levy, Jr., *Modern American Society* (New York, Rinehart and Company, 1949), pp. 145-149.

suppressing 3400 patents in order to protect itself against competition.[10] Similar examples could be cited from other areas where vested interests have a secure hold.

Interest Groups and Social Change. In the process of social change, interest groups and vested interest groups continually oppose one another. The former tend to be the forces of action, the latter of reaction. Objectively, many advantages are possessed by the vested interests. They are solid, respectable people who are only seeking to protect what by law and custom is theirs. They have power and organization and generally the weight of public opinion behind them. Yet the fact that vested interests find it necessary to marshal and employ their resources with ever increasing skill indicates that the advantages are not all on their side.

On the side of the emerging interests is a potential advantage that may eventually prove greater than the combined advantages of the vested interests. That potential advantage stems from latent dissatisfaction with things as they are and from widespread aspiration toward "a better world." It is the power which is latent in numbers. Vested interests by nature are likely to be a relatively small fraction of the total population. They can retain their hold only so long as the usually quiescent majority does not become fully aroused to its contrary interests. When and if the emerging interest groups can bring about that arousal, the vested interests are forced to settle for the best terms they can get.

Business: A Primary Vested Interest

In order to understand the role played by business—especially big business—in the current struggle of interest groups, it is necessary to know something of the historical developments that gave rise to the present situation. Very briefly, it was the emergence during the eighteenth century of a set of principles or definitions concerning (1) the relations of employers to employees, and (2) the right of individuals to acquire, hold, and use property, which paved the way for business to become a major vested interest.

1. *Free Contract.* At the time when these definitions were formulated, industry was still in the handicraft stage and large-scale corporate organization was far in the future. The individual worker and the small employer were the principals in the economic scene, and the emerging definitions pertained to the relation between these two. With production organized on a small, relatively nonspecialized basis, employers and workers had approximately equal bargaining power so that neither could unduly exploit the other. The employer was essential to the workers and his

[10] *Ibid.,* p. 148.

workers were essential to the employer. Each had to bargain with the other. This situation in which buyers and sellers of labor bargained with one another came to be embodied in the "principle" and the "right" of "free contract." The right of workers to benefit themselves by seeking out the most remunerative of employments and those which offered the greatest prospects for advancement, and the right of employers to hire at the lowest wages necessary to keep their businesses functioning, became integral parts of that philosophy of economics and government known as "laissez faire." Each person was a free agent with the right to enter into any contract as he saw fit. So long as the power wielded by employers and employees was approximately equal, "free contract" did indeed prevail.

2. *Private Property.* Just as owners and workers were free to make the best bargains they could, each claimed the right to hold and to use the fruits of his labors in his own best interest. The acquisition of property was both an end in itself and also the means to the acquisition of more property. Thus, the concept of "private property" developed along with that of "free contract." Each worker, by diligent effort and thrift, might advance himself eventually to the status of owner and employer. Then he, by paying wages, would enable others to climb the same ladder. The only restriction placed upon the use of property was that it should not be utilized so as to infringe upon the property rights of others. As the doctrine of laissez faire became firmly entrenched in the political and economic life of western European nations, property rights gradually became inviolable and, because property was a means to the acquisition of more property, its permanent possession and free use provided the cornerstone for the growth of modern industry and business.

Under the twin principles of free contract and private property, business quickly took on the character of a vested interest seeking to maintain intact the principles which gave it life. Then signs of disorganization began to appear.

SOCIAL DISORGANIZATION

Growth and Concentration

Even before the turn of the present century the concentration of business and industrial power had led to the passage of antitrust laws. The Sherman Antitrust Law in 1890 and the Clayton Act which followed in 1914 have been the chief weapons of government in its attempt to prevent and to break down the growth of business monopoly. That they did not succeed, however, in preventing the spread of semimonopolistic conditions throughout much of the American economy is readily indicated by the facts.

TABLE 4-1. Concentration in American Industry

Industry	Per Cent of 1947 Output Accounted for by First Four Companies
Primary aluminum	100
Electric lamps	92
Locomotives and parts	91
Cigarettes	90
Flat glass	88
Steam engines and turbines	88
Typewriters	79
Soap and glycerine	79
Phonograph records	79
Corn products	77
Sewing machines	77
Tires and inner tubes	77

U. S. Department of Commerce, Business Report, December, 1949.

Some indication of the amount of industrial concentration is provided by information compiled by the Temporary National Economic Committee before World War II. In the field of transportation and public utilities, less than one-twentieth of the total number of corporations owned 93 per cent of the corporate assets. In manufacturing, less than 2 per cent of the corporations owned 66 per cent of the industry's assets. Even in the construction industry and in agriculture, both of which are notoriously competitive, the few multimillion dollar corporations owned over one-fourth of the total corporate assets. These are not complete monopolies in the true sense, but neither do they permit free competition. Many industries today are dominated by one or a few corporate giants, surrounded in some cases by a number of smaller concerns. The domination of the "big three" in the automobile industry, of a few big steel producers, oil companies, and the like, is fairly typical of the "bigness" of modern industry.

One of the commercial fields in which consolidation has been occurring most rapidly is that of newspaper publication. The number of independent newspapers is growing smaller and smaller and the relatively few papers left are becoming larger and more standardized. One writer estimates that, so far as ownership is concerned, there are approximately one thousand fewer owners now than there were twenty years ago.[11] Over thirty-two hundred newspapers have disappeared from the market, and a single company controls more than three thousand of the remaining ones. Only about one town in eleven in the United States still has competing daily newspapers. Most existing papers depend on one of three major news services for all but local news and buy most of their columns from one of the large syndicates. Obviously, bigness extends into the com-

[11] For the source of these statistics and a fuller treatment of the problem, see Morris Ernst, *The First Freedom* (New York, The Macmillan Company, 1946).

munications field as well as into the more commonly recognized near-monopolies in manufacturing, transportation, and distribution.

Separation of Ownership and Control

An important accompaniment of industrial growth and concentration is a tendency for the control of large corporations to become more and more concentrated in the hands of management officials who own only a small fraction of the corporation stock. Boards of directors and a few high company officials often wield relatively complete control over the company, sometimes to the disadvantage of the numerous, heterogeneous, geographically distant stockholders. The significance of this development derives from the fact that the wresting of control from the majority of owners has markedly altered the nature of private property. The purchaser of shares of stock acquires no right to use his property as he sees fit, but surrenders that right to company officers and directors in return for the privilege of receiving dividends. Although, theoretically, directors are elected by the stockholders, they often become a self-perpetuating clique—and the interests of management and stockholders are not completely identical.

Actual control of corporations is increasingly held by *holding companies,* which are separate corporations that buy up the small fraction of stock needed to control the boards of directors. The producing corporation is then forced to pay large shares of its profits to the holding company rather than to its majority stockholders. Occasionally, too, the holding company, because it controls several corporations, may find it advantageous to discourage production in one company to benefit the others. Corporation management bitterly opposes any outside regulation of corporations on the grounds that such regulation would be in violation of the rights of private property. They fail to recognize, or find it expedient to deny, that there has been any alteration in the *nature* of this property itself.

Awakening Opposition. There is little question that the course of events until approximately the last decade of the nineteenth century served to favor and strengthen the role of business as a vested interest. It may well be that the last quarter of that century saw the business interests at the zenith of their power. The great industrial and financial empires of the Vanderbilts, the Mellons, the Rockefellers, the DuPonts, and the Morgans are all associated with that period. Since that time the situation has been gradually but steadily shifting in favor of other groups within the society.

Among the first signs that the validity of the free-contract and private-property concepts was seriously being questioned was the passage of antitrust legislation by the federal government. The Sherman and Clayton acts in effect served notice that other interests, operating through government, had arisen to challenge the favored position of the industrialists. Nor was this the only sign of forthcoming changes. At least since 1869, when the Knights of Labor was organized, there had been signs that working groups were actively seeking a redress in the balance of power with management. A short time later, in 1886, the American Federation of Labor appeared on the scene, to be joined by the rise of the Congress of Industrial Organizations after 1935. Beginning early in the 1930's, political policies traditionally sympathetic to business interests almost continuously lost ground to the "pro-common-man" policies of the New Deal.

The period since the end of World War II has seen the appearance of another movement of possibly great future significance. Small groups of consumers organized in numerous localities to protest and contest the inflationary trends in certain consumer prices. Moreover, the general phenomenon of consumer resistance to prices was more widespread than were the organized groups. Whether an effective consumer movement is about to develop in the United States is not at issue here. The important thing is that numerous and varied signs of opposition to the traditionally favored position of business are in evidence.

Recently a noted American economist has advanced the theory that whenever a vested interest arises there are set in motion forces which tend to foster the development of compensatory power in other segments of the population.[12] This *countervailing power* appearing in the United States is suggested by the above brief examples. Let us now examine more carefully the status of certain of these newly developed interest groups.

Countervailence:[13] Emergent Vested Interests

Big Government. The role of the federal government in the clash of interests and vested interests is a twofold one: (1) the government supports the efforts of emerging interest groups against the greater power of the established interests, and (2) the government itself has taken on the character of a vested interest.

1. Governmental efforts to limit the power of industry by means of antitrust legislation have already been mentioned. Perhaps here it is only necessary to remark that such efforts do not end with the passage of legislation but that the *prosecution* of combinations in restraint of trade is regularly carried forth by the Department of Justice.

In a more indirect, though not necessarily less effective, fashion, the government offers positive aid to groups attempting to cope with business power. Government support of the rising trade-union movement is a case in point. When the Sherman and Clayton acts, originally designed to

---

[12] John K. Galbraith, *American Capitalism, The Concept of Countervailing Power* (Boston, Houghton Mifflin Company, 1952).

[13] This term was coined but not systematically used by Galbraith, *ibid.*, p. 118.

apply to business, were held by judicial interpretation to apply to labor unions also, the Norris-LaGuardia anti-injunction law of 1932 protected the growing unions against this form of restraint. The Wagner National Labor Relations Act of 1935 was even more favorable to organized labor and is often credited, by spokesmen for the business world at least, with having given labor a position even more favored than that of industry. It is interesting to speculate as to whether the labor-restrictive Taft-Hartley Law now indicates that a new balance of power between business and labor has been achieved. In a similar fashion, the government has aided farm and consumer groups by giving a favored tax status to their co-operatives, thus aiding them to compete with business.

2. In addition to its role as a supporter of emerging interests, the number of activities involved in governing itself has increased tremendously in recent decades. This expansion has been accompanied by a tendency for government to become a self-perpetuating and self-aggrandizing

TABLE 4-2. Growth of the Federal Government

Year	Number of Civilian Employees in Federal Government
1929	596,000
1930	611,000
1934	719,000
1935	820,000
1939	969,000
1940	1,078,000
1944	3,337,000
1945	3,569,000
1949	2,101,000
1950	2,081,000
1952	2,612,000

U. S. Bureau of the Census, *Statistical Abstract of the United States:* 1953 (Washington), p. 379.

agency. It is extremely difficult, even when conscientiously attempted, to eliminate any kind of government service once it has been established. Big government has become another vested interest and business and government are engaged in preventing one another from exercising dictatorial control over the lives of the American people.

Big Labor. The past two decades especially have seen organized labor, with the aid of government, join the ranks of the big powers among the vested interests. The number of union members rose from over 3½ million in 1935 to 8½ million in 1940, and to 14 million in 1944. There are now approximately 16 million trade-union members in the United States. The two giants of the labor world, the American Federation of Labor and the Congress of Industrial Organizations, currently plan to merge their forces and to embark on a major drive to gain millions of new members.

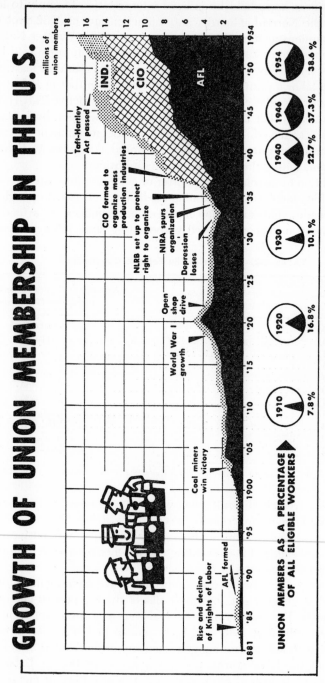

GROWTH OF UNION MEMBERSHIP IN THE U.S.

From "A Visual History of the United States," by Harold U. Faulkner & Graphics Institute; Abelard-Schuman.

FIG. 4-1

If the merger can be accomplished, organized labor may be in for another decade of rapid growth. The old stereotype of down-trodden labor hardly fits modern unionism.

Labor now claims the advantages secured to it under the National Labor Relations Act of 1935 as inherent rights while it bitterly opposes the subsequent Taft-Hartley Law as dictatorial, discriminatory, and unjust. Constantly striving to wrest a larger portion of the "profits pie" from business, organized labor is now obviously a vested interest of approximately co-ordinate standing with business and government. In at least some respects, it has ceased to be a disprivileged minority and has become a privileged group with a vested interest in the status quo.

Big Agriculture.[14] Agriculture is not "big" in the sense of having sixteen million farmers organized into unions as does labor. Nevertheless, over the past few decades agriculture has become a potent force, demanding its share of "the spoils" along with business and labor. Agriculture's efforts to gain vested interest status have taken two principal directions. First, co-operatives have appeared in the marketing of farm products and in the purchase of farm supplies and consumer goods. These co-operatives provide farmers with the savings to be derived from large-scale operation and give them some measure of control over the supply of farm products reaching the market at any given time. The tremendously large numbers of farmers involved and the difficulty of getting all to co-operate, however, have prevented the co-operatives from playing a major role in the development of countervailing power. It is in the second development that the major source of agriculture's bigness is to be found.

Though such measures were not new, the program of support for farm prices and the establishment of production quotas begun under the "New Deal" marked the first serious government effort to aid farmers to equalize the balance of power between themselves and industry. Beginning with the Agricultural Adjustment Act of 1933, the government has continuously kept "floors" under farm prices and has itself drained off excess quantities of various farm products. Many persons are of the opinion that this is a temporary situation which will disappear "when the time becomes right." Such reasoning neglects two important facts. First, the time was never conceived to be "right" during one of the most prosperous periods in American history. Second, and even more important, it is now one of the important functions of government to support the development and maintenance of "countervailing power" against the power of the established interests. Government has aided agriculture to become a vested interest and, with the aid of government, a vested interest it apparently will remain.

[14] The discussion in this and the following section draws heavily upon John K. Galbraith, *ibid.*

Big Distribution. Paradoxical though it may seem, certain developments within the business world itself have given rise to a new class of vested interests and have further limited the power of the original business and industry groups. Contrary to general belief, the interests of all large firms are by no means identical. Specifically, there has appeared in the American economy a class of very large retailers, for example, the grocery and department store chains, the large mail order houses, and the variety store chains, whose primary interest is to obtain goods as cheaply as possible from the manufacturers and then to sell them cheaply to the general public. The very size of these retailers gives them a great deal of power over the manufacturers from whom they buy. By threatening to take their business elsewhere or by proposing to set up their own sources of supply, they can generally force downward manufacturers' prices. That this situation has resulted in great savings to the consumer can be demonstrated by a simple stroll through any chain store supermarket. Curiously, the function of large retailers in limiting the power of manufacturers is not generally recognized, and there is much sentiment in Congress and among the general public for curtailing the buying power of such organizations. In any event, the chains are a powerful group with whom the other vested interests must reckon.

In the preceding sections we have seen how the privileged position allotted to business and industry following the Industrial Revolution has been gradually but surely encroached upon by other emergent vested interests. There is little question that business remains among the most powerful of these vested interests. The weight of tradition, the force of public sentiment, and the advantage of elaborate protective organization all help to preserve that supremacy. As government arose to challenge industry domination of the economy, however, one of its essential functions came to be to aid less powerful groups to buttress their positions against business power. At present, government itself, organized labor, big agriculture, and big distribution all rank alongside business as important vested interests. Each acts somewhat as a check upon the exercise of power by the others.

VALUE-CONFLICTS: THE ISSUE OF CONTROL

Obviously the passage of time is accompanied by more and more government regulation of the economy. This trend, however, is not unopposed nor necessarily enduring. Feelings run high and positions vary, but basically the issue appears to be bipartite: "Shall there be controls?", and if so, "in whose interests?"

Shall There Be Controls?

The issue is frequently stated as though it were a question of either continuing a set of thoroughly obnoxious controls or of completely freeing the economy from government interference. Stated in these terms, it implies that *all* government regulation is "bad" and that the proponents have nothing to lose by seeing all controls ended. Even casual reflection will show that this simply is not true.

Government regulation is not new. It is almost as old as the nation itself. The postal system, free public schools, tax-supported universities, and public-utility monopolies are just a few examples of areas where government participation is firmly entrenched and substantially to the advantage of the entire nation. More recently, the regulatory activities of such bodies as the Federal Communications Commission, the Food and Drug Administration, and the Interstate Commerce Commission have received general acceptance. In the field of social welfare, the government helps to finance unemployment compensation, the United States Employment Service, Aid to the Blind and to Dependent Children, Old Age Assistance, and Old Age and Survivor's Insurance. It is not even reasonable to suppose that opponents of government regulation oppose all of these and all other government aids.

The elimination of *all* government controls would destroy much of what has come to be known as the American way of life. The opposition to control is in reality opposition to *certain types* of control which are deemed inimical to someone's interests.

In Whose Interests?

Most of the opposition to government regulation of the economy is opposition to *certain types* of regulation *recently instituted* or *threatened* by the *federal* government. The main conflict is over *which* controls should be strengthened and which ones should be eliminated. The vested interests in business and industry favor one type of controls and the emerging vested interests in labor and agriculture, particularly, tend to favor another type of controls.

Neither side really wants a return to a laissez-faire economy. Business generally favors tariff regulations, fast tax write-offs on investments, subsidies to the maritime service, "mail" subsidies to airlines and railroads, and tax advantages for the holders of corporate stocks. Business is opposed to minimum wage laws, to the tax-free status of co-operatives, to anti-injunction laws, and to the subsidy maintenance of farm prices. Labor unions want government to force management to bargain with the unions and to enter the conflict as mediator or arbitrator whenever an impasse is reached. Labor opposes any limitation on its right to strike, the outlawing of secondary boycotts and jurisdictional disputes, and the right of management to fire union employees without good cause. Farm groups look to government to protect the farmer's purchasing power by maintaining parity price levels, by buying up crop surpluses, and by limiting the importation of farm commodities from other countries. The basic issue is not whether to have controls, but which side should benefit from them.

PERSONAL DEVIATION

As in all areas of conflict, deviant persons help to complicate the major issues. Deviant personalities who contribute to the clashes of economic interest groups are of at least two sorts: *extremists* who will brook no compromise, and *neurotics* whose involvements are primarily matters of emotional need.

The Extremists

Even though their prejudices may clearly favor one or another of the conflicting groups, most persons recognize and accept the fact that neither business nor labor nor any of the other groups is likely to gain complete control of the nation's economy. Not all persons are so convinced, however.

To some persons, nothing short of complete domination of all opposing factions is acceptable. The labor union fanatic points to the "exploitation of the masses" and urges labor "to fulfil its destiny." Other fanatics insist that only government regulation can prevent dictatorial control by both business and labor. Business die-hards point to revered traditions and to inevitable decadence if these traditions are sacrificed. Their allegiances vary, but each has a single purpose in mind—to gain an exclusive vested interest for his faction.

Such extremists people the "rear guards" or, perhaps, the "advance guards," depending upon which group they favor and upon the future course of events. In general, they harass the more moderate majorities who seek to work out reasonable compromises among the various interests. Many of these extremists, while motivated by genuine conviction, are also victims of personal difficulties that influence their behavior.

The Neurotics

The person whose convictions are greatly complicated by his own neurotic needs is even more troublesome than other extremists. The extremist whose conviction is primarily a matter of background, training, and group loyalty may, on related issues, be quite reasonable and, in the face of continued contrary evidence, may even be induced to modify his position somewhat. The extremist whose basic motivations derive from hate, fear, or anxiety, however, can seldom be reasonable on any important point. New evidence, instead of inducing change, tends to force him to ever more extreme measures for the defense of his position. He seeks not to understand issues but to incite; he attacks, uses emotional labels, and imputes motives. He plays no constructive role in the solution of problems but is generally to be found helping to intensify feelings and further to confuse the issues.

SUMMARY

Pressure groups, which operate in the field of practical power politics, have invaded almost every aspect of American life. Among the propaganda techniques employed by such groups to influence public and governmental opinion are (1) to convince the public that its interests are identical with those of the pressure group, (2) to soft-pedal its true identity and promote acceptance as something else, (3) to use emotional rather than rational arguments, and (4) to employ diversionary tactics to steer attention away from the important issues. Pressure groups are generally the power instruments of interest or vested interest groups. Vested interests (1) owe their favored position to past definitions, (2) have the support of tradition, (3) have a firm basis for wielding power, and (4) hinder the process of social change.

Big business traditionally has been the most powerful of the vested interests in the United States. Only within the past few decades has its favored status been seriously challenged. The rise of the giant corporation, however, grossly altered the nature of the "free contract" and "private property" definitions on which that vested interest was based, and business is losing some of its power to other groups. At least four other major groups have attained vested-interest status: the federal government, organized labor, big agriculture, and big distribution. In the present situation these five giants act to checkmate one another in the wielding of power. Considerable disagreement and conflict exists over what role government should play in the struggles among powerful interest groups. The problem is further complicated by extremists, some of whose motivations are complicated by their own personal inadequacies.

SUGGESTED READINGS

BLAISDELL, Donald C., *Government Under Pressure,* Public Affairs Pamphlet No. 67 (New York, Public Affairs Committee, Inc., 1946). Describes pressure-group operations resulting from the concentration of economic power in business and industry. A brief and lucid treatment.

DAVIS, Kingsley, BREDEMEIER, Harry C., and LEVY, Marion J., Jr., *Modern American Society* (New York, Rinehart and Company, 1949). An excellent book of readings in the area of social problems. See, especially, Part III, "The Economic Framework." Excellent discussion of impediments to technological change.

GALBRAITH, John K., *American Capitalism, The Concept of Countervailing Power* (Boston, Houghton Mifflin Company, 1952). A nontechnical discussion of the development of countervailing power in various segments of the U. S. economy. A novel formulation by a noted economist.

LYNCH, David, *The Concentration of Economic Power* (New York, Columbia University Press, 1946). Comprehensive account of concentration in the U. S. economy during the pre-World War II period. Based upon hearings before the Temporary National Economic Committee.

MILLS, C. Wright, and SCHNEIDER, Helen, *The New Men of Power: America's Labor Leaders* (New York, Harcourt, Brace & Company, Inc., 1948). Penetrating analysis of the personalities and philosophies of crucial figures in the vanguard of the American labor movement.

VEBLEN, Thorstein B., *The Vested Interests* (New York, Viking Press, Inc., 1933). An integrated series of lectures detailing the developing discrepancy between the definitions underlying the business management of industry and the conditions engendered by the material conditions under which modern industry operates.

AUDIO-VISUAL AIDS

America's Biggest Business (United States Rubber Co., Advertising Department, 1230 Sixth Ave., New York), 18 minutes, sound, black and white. An overview of the farming industry showing reasons for its comeback after the depression years. Tells of the importance of education, particularly extension, in helping to bring this about. Shows the farm as a market for rubber products.

Battle of Wall Street (Workers Education Bureau, A.F.L., 1525 H Street, N.W., Washington), 20 minutes, sound, black and white. Produced by the Seafarers International Union, Atlantic and Gulf District. The story of the 32-day strike of the employees of the New York Stock and Curb Exchanges. Emphasizes the role of the militant Seafarers Union which swelled the picket lines and organized food and literature dispersals. Documents press coverage and police action.

Capitalism (Coronet Films, Coronet Bldg., Chicago), 10 minutes, sound, black and white. Introduces such important aspects of the capitalistic system as private property, profit, competition, freedom of contract, and free enterprise. The students on a high-school radio forum then present conflicting opinions as each tells what capitalism means to him.

Pressure Groups (Encyclopaedia Britannica Films, Inc., 1150 Wilmette Ave., Wilmette, Ill.), 20 minutes, sound, black and white. Explains what pressure groups are and reveals that, when democratically used, they are a necessary instrument for decision-making in a democracy. Illustrates methods used by a representative democratic pressure group to bring about legislation for a desirable civic project. Contrasts these methods with the underhanded and behind-the-scenes manipulation employed by a group attempting to prevent the passage of a bill.

QUESTIONS AND PROJECTS

1. Define the terms *pressure group, interest group,* and *vested interest.*

2. Name and illustrate at least three techniques commonly used by pressure groups to propagandize the general public.

3. Interpret the statement that "vested interests tend to admire the past."

4. How were the doctrines of "free contract" and "private property" instrumental in creating a vested interest of business and industry?

5. Discuss two important changes in the economic system which served to encourage opposition to complete business freedom.

6. What is meant by the concept of "countervailing power"? What group or organization in the United States has played the most active role in the development of countervailing power?

7. Discuss the proposition that "government control is not new, and it is not likely to disappear."

8. How does the possession of capital by pressure groups make their efforts more successful?

9. Discuss the proposition that organized labor has become a vested interest.

10. What role or roles do extremists play in the struggle of interest groups to acquire countervailing power?

11. Select from your local newspaper an issue upon which there is considerable public debate and gather the arguments which each side is using to support its position. Subject these arguments to critical analysis in terms of what you have learned about propaganda and the distortion of facts. What techniques are being used by each side in the struggle? Try to arrive at an objective picture of the issue and test the accuracy of each side's position against that objective view.

12. Interview some man of your acquaintance who is in business for himself concerning his attitudes about private property. Note the particular kind of private property he talks about, whether it be land, buildings, merchandise, or corporate stock. Would his arguments apply equally well to all kinds of private property? Is he aware that there are important differences among the various kinds of property?

Part II

MAJOR AMERICAN SOCIAL PROBLEMS

The sequence of chapters in Part II is unavoidably arbitrary. Few will dispute, however, that each of the problems treated is a bona fide contemporary American social problem. Some of these are more traditionally recognized as problems—crime, race relations, and certain aspects of marriage. Others have become problems of somewhat general concern much more recently —civil liberties, the mass media, and problems of health. The chapters have been arranged so that the problems judged to be most clearly recognized as problems by the student, such as crime, would be studied first, leaving for later treatment some of the newer and less obvious problems.

CHAPTER 5

Crime in American Society

In the United States, criminals force us to spend each year more than four and two-thirds as much on them as we spend on all forms of education, both public and private.[1]

New York police arrested 55-year old Mrs. Beatrice Kam for possession of narcotics, and then jailed her son, Herbert, 33, despite her protests. "Herbert," said his mother, "is a good son. He never brought me anything but the pure stuff."[2]

Department of Agriculture inspectors have arrested and obtained convictions of eleven resturant owners since January 1 for serving butter returned from tables and mixed with oleomargarine on buttered toast.... Apparently the practice of scraping unused butter from plates and mixing it with oleo for this purpose is prevalent. It is illegal, since it constitutes coloring the oleo.[3]

Gamblers in 29 northern Illinois counties [gambling is illegal in Illinois] paid federal taxes on bets amounting to $14,213,320 for the year ending Nov. 1.[4]

In Toledo, onetime Conscientious Objector Charles Cline, 30, who had served two years in a Michigan federal prison for refusing to shoulder a gun, was given one to three years in Ohio Penitentiary for carrying a concealed weapon.[5]

Whistling under water is against the law in the state of Vermont. An Arkansas law provides that school teachers who bob their hair will not get a raise. A Montgomery, Alabama, ordinance forbids sitting on garbage cans. In Iowa a kiss lasting more than five minutes is against the law.[6]

A salesman was arrested in Medicine Lodge, Kansas, for burglarizing business places, although he sold them burglar insurance in order to quiet his own scruples of conscience.[7]

[1] J. Edgar Hoover, *New York Times*, January 4, 1953, p. 29.
[2] *Time* (November 5, 1951), p. 26.
[3] Associated Press, March 2, 1950.
[4] *Chicago Sun-Times*, December 11, 1952, p. 9.
[5] *Time* (March 17, 1952), p. 12.
[6] From "It's the Law," *American Magazine* (April, 1954), p. 72; (October, 1954) p. 133; (December, 1954), p. 126; (January, 1955), p. 119.
[7] *New York Times*, November 23, 1952, p. 54.

The public seems to be concerned about prison riots only when riots occur—and then wonders why riots occur.[8]

Text accompanying a cartoon—"Before you read this note from teacher, Pop, will you tell me again about the time you put limburger cheese in the school's hot air register?"

AT first reading, this series of items may seem flippant and trivial. Yet each is significant, for each touches upon a different aspect of the crime problem. The first indicates the cost of catching and caring for those criminals we succeed in catching. The second reveals something of the value-system of the professional criminal; the third illustrates how imperfectly the law reflects the actual social danger or injury of certain "criminal" acts; the fourth shows how openly certain laws are violated; the fifth shows how it is often the *conditions* of the act, not the act itself, which determine whether one is a criminal or a hero; the sixth calls attention to the many obsolete and foolish laws that clutter our lawbooks; the seventh tells one form of the fairly common practice of "playing both ends against the middle"; the eighth reminds us that part of the problem lies in the popular indifference to the problem; the last illustrates one of the many ways in which our culture encourages delinquent behavior.

There is perhaps no social problem which has been studied longer or more intensively than the crime problem. Although we have learned much, our knowledge is far from complete. To the questions, What causes crime? and What will cure crime?, nobody has an entirely satisfactory answer. There is no certainty that a fully satisfactory answer will ever be found. Meanwhile, our knowledge is steadily increasing, and each increase brings a fully scientific program of crime prevention and treatment closer to attainment.

NATURE OF THE CRIME PROBLEM

Definition: What Is "Crime"?

Whenever something impresses us as being simply awful, we say, "Isn't it a crime!" To call any shocking or socially injurious happening a "crime" reveals the popular rather than the scientific use of the term. In technical usage, *a crime is any violation of the law.* Since there are thousands of laws, one has an interesting variety of ways to become a criminal. Some of these laws define quite harmless acts as crimes. There are so many of these foolish and obsolete laws that everyone unconsciously violates them by the dozen, and it has been estimated that the average urban citizen violates enough of these every day to imprison him for five years and "fine" him nearly $3000.[9]

---

[8] W. A. Buchanan, warden of Eddyville, Kentucky, prison, in *New York Times,* October 12, 1952, p. 35.

[9] See L. M. Hussey, "Twenty-four Hours of a Law Breaker," *Harper's,* 160 (March, 1930), pp. 436-439.

Meanwhile, many acts which are highly injurious to society are perfectly legal. If one is quite careful how he does it, it is entirely legal to defraud widows and orphans of their savings, to sell useless and harmful medicines to people who will soon die unless they find competent medical treatment, to destroy people's self-confidence and mental efficiency by frightening them with a host of imaginary or unlikely ailments, to reduce the American standard of living by encouraging premature obsolescence through the promotion of endless style changes—these and many other activities operate within the law, taking advantage of people's ignorance, gullibility, and defenselessness. To kill a person by selling him a useless nostrum when he needs medical treatment is entirely legal, if done carefully, but to sell him this useless junk for a nickel less than the official "fair-trade" price is a crime (in 45 states; in the other three, it is legal).

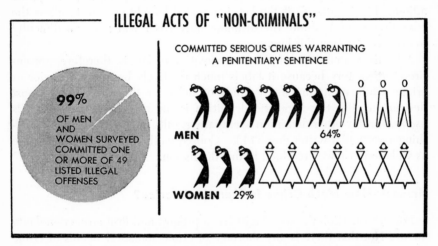

ILLEGAL ACTS OF "NON-CRIMINALS"

99% OF MEN AND WOMEN SURVEYED COMMITTED ONE OR MORE OF 49 LISTED ILLEGAL OFFENSES

COMMITTED SERIOUS CRIMES WARRANTING A PENITENTIARY SENTENCE

MEN 64%

WOMEN 29%

FIG. 5-1. (Based on a study reported in *Probation* [April, 1947])

Although it is the intent of the lawmakers (most of the time) to insure justice and protect society from injury, they do not always succeed. Aside from the fact that some lawmakers may be ignorant or venal, there is the fact, first, that *there is no common agreement upon whether many acts are socially injurious.* Are gambling, prostitution, and drug addiction social menaces or matters of private morality which the law should not attempt to regulate? Are holding companies, high-pressure advertising, "closed shops," or jurisdictional strikes socially destructive or socially beneficial? Wherever there are conflicting value-judgments, each with many passionate defenders, law is relatively ineffective. Law is effective and enforceable only when it reflects the moral consensus of the society. As the supporters of prohibition learned to their sorrow, law cannot create a consensus where none exists.

Even when there is general agreement that a particular act is socially injurious, it is not always practical to try to prevent it *by law*. It is widely recognized that overeating kills many times more people than all forms of crime combined, yet as long as people cherish their constitutional right to chew their way into their coffins, a law against overeating would be impractical. Furthermore, there are certain technical difficulties in law-making, in that any law worded broadly enough to forbid the injurious act often unintentionally forbids other harmless acts or invites other abuses. For example, there is general agreement that misleading advertising or the sale of useless "medicines" is socially injurious. But how could a workable law fully control these practices? Any procedure for preventing all dishonest or misleading advertising would be impractical; if the law is worded tightly enough to prevent all misleading statements, it would be unsafe for even an honest advertiser to say anything emphatic lest it be adjudged "misleading"; if the law is phrased loosely enough to allow the advertiser some latitude, the dishonest advertiser will have no difficulty in operating within this law.

A legalistic definition of crime as violation of law is, therefore, not entirely satisfactory because it labels much relatively harmless behavior as crime, while excluding many kinds of behavior that are socially most destructive. But this legalistic definition is the only definition which is *usable,* for any other definition eventually results in labeling as crime anything a particular writer doesn't like. Consequently, the definition of crime as violation of law is retained in this discussion.

Amount: How Much Crime Is There in America?

For this question the sociologist has a prompt and firm answer—*nobody knows!* Not that there is any shortage of crime statistics! Reams of crime statistics are collected by the Federal Bureau of Investigation and published semiannually in *Uniform Crime Reports,* listing arrests and convictions under 27 headings ranging from "homicide" to "suspicion," and classifying crimes by type of crime, urban-rural rates, by region, by size of city, by age, and by sex. This source reports that 2,160,000 serious crimes were reported in 1953, or about one every 15 seconds. All reported crimes increased 6 per cent over 1952, with robberies increasing by 8.5 per cent, while murders decreased by 1.2 per cent. While the population increased about 5 per cent between 1950 and 1954, crimes reported increased by 20 per cent during the same period. The amount of our annual crime bill is estimated by the FBI Director J. Edgar Hoover at about $20 billion, ten times as much as our annual donation to churches, and about $500 for each family in the United States.[10] Yet statistics such as these cannot

[10] *Time* (February 15, 1954), p. 21.

give an accurate measure of the amount of crime and only a very rough estimate of crime trends. There are several reasons for this. First, *much crime is never reported* and never appears in the crime statistics. The most successful crime is that which is never detected at all—the murder that looks like accidental or natural death, the fire that looks accidental, the shoplifting by customers and pilfering by employees that is never noticed, or the frauds whose victims never realize that they have been defrauded. In other cases, although the victim realizes a crime has been committed, he is *unwilling to prosecute*. Many sex criminals escape because the victims shrink from the notoriety of a prosecution. Many embezzlements are covered up and the dishonest employee quietly discharged because the firm wishes to avoid unfavorable publicity. Although it is widely believed that store employees steal far more than shoplifters, the dishonest employee is rarely prosecuted.[11] Victims of robbery, theft, or embezzlement often lose interest in prosecution once their money is returned. Hotels do not prosecute their highly "respectable" guests who steal the hotel linen, silver, and anything else small enough to carry, although the practice of quietly billing them for the loot seems to be spreading.[12] Victims of confidence games rarely report the crime, since they are usually swindled while engaged in an effort to turn a shady dollar for themselves. Graft, bribery, extortion, blackmail, and "protection" payments are rarely reported to the police, since secrecy is a basic feature of all these. Much petty crime is not reported because the victims doubt that the police will find the culprit. In some areas, especially rural areas, many known crimes are not reported or officially recorded.[13] It is impossible to know how much crime is unreported, but all authorities agree that it is tremendous, probably far greater in dollar cost than the crimes reported to the police.

In the second place, *much reported crime remains "unsolved."* Sometimes the police are unable to find the culprit; sometimes they are disinterested. Table 5-1 shows that for 226 cities over 25,000 population, only about one-fourth of the crimes reported to the police were "cleared" by the arrest of a suspect, and this is in the larger cities where police are presumably better organized and more efficient than in small towns and rural areas.

Finally, *not all arrests result in convictions*. As Table 5-1 shows, 226 cities convicted an average of 70 per cent of those brought to trial, with wide variations among different cities. The number of arrests made in a particular city is no accurate measure of its amount of crime. A low

[11] Gene Boyo, "Case of the Vanishing Profit—Chances Are It's an Inside Job," *New York Times,* July 25, 1954, p. 1.

[12] *Life,* "Souvenir Stealers" (November 4, 1946), pp. 2 ff.

[13] T. C. Esselstyn, "The Social Role of a County Sheriff," *Journal of Criminal Law and Criminology,* 44 (July-August, 1953), pp. 177-184; also Mabel A. Elliott, *Crime in Modern Society* (New York, Harper and Brothers, 1952), pp. 61, 80, 135, 146, 147.

arrest rate may indicate either a small amount of crime or an inactive police force. A high arrest rate may indicate a police force which makes arrests on slight pretext and is making a great show of combating a "crime wave." In one such "battle" against the underworld, the New York police arrested 652 persons, of whom 152 pleaded guilty to "vagrancy" (having no job or means of support). Of the 500 who pleaded innocent, only three were convicted of anything.[14] Wholesale arrests like this may make the local arrest rate meaningless as a measure of crime.

TABLE 5-1. Not All Criminals Are Caught and Convicted

Offenses known to the police	464,664
Offenses "cleared" by arrest	123,119
Suspects charged (held for prosecution)	87,809
Suspects found guilty	
of offense as charged	52,406
of a lesser offense	8,947
Total found guilty	61,353

Major crimes reported to police, arrests, and disposition of arrest, 226 cities over 25,000, January-June, 1952. *Uniform Crime Reports*, Semi-Annual Bulletin, 1952, p. 57.

For these reasons it is impossible to determine the exact amount of crime actually committed by tabulating crimes reported, arrests, or convictions. All authorities agree that criminal behavior is far more common than most people care to admit. One recent study claims that of 6000 cases of delinquent behavior admitted by a representative group of youths, only 1.5 per cent of these acts were followed by arrest or juvenile court hearing.[15] The same study reveals that of a representative sample of 1698 adults, 99 per cent admitted having committed one or more adult offenses, felonies carrying prison sentences of one year or more. The men in the sample admitted an average of 18 crimes, ranging from a low of 8.2 for ministers to 20.2 for laborers, while the more law-abiding women admitted an average of only 11 penal offenses! These and many similar studies proved beyond all doubt that no existing crime statistics are reliable as measures of the amount of crime committed in America.

Type: What Kinds of Crime Predominate?

Again, no one can be certain. It is conventional to classify crimes into *felonies* (major crimes carrying imprisonment for longer than one year) and *misdemeanors* (minor crimes with a maximum penalty of less than a year's imprisonment in a local jail or workhouse). They are also divided into *crimes against persons* and *crimes against property,* and under these headings are classified the specific crimes—burglary, murder, rape, lar-

[14] Irwin Ross, "You're Under Arrest," *Coronet*, 31 (November, 1951), pp. 5 ff.

[15] James S. Wallerstein and Clement J. Wyle, "Our Law-Abiding Law-Breakers," reprint from *Probation*, April, 1947 (New York, National Probation Association).

ceny, and so on—with enumeration of each. These statistics are notoriously unreliable. As already shown, some types of crime are more likely to be reported than others. An arrest on a particular charge is no proof that a crime has been committed by that person. Nor are convictions a reliable measure of the relative frequency of different types of crime. Occasionally a suspect agrees to plead guilty to a lesser crime in a "deal" to avoid prosecution for a more serious crime upon which the prosecutor lacks complete evidence. Consequently, many rapes appear in the statistics as convictions for "disorderly conduct," many "armed robberies" as "carrying concealed weapons," many "murders" as "manslaughter," and much "petty larceny" as "vagrancy," and conviction for a particular crime is sometimes a better indication of ease of conviction than of frequency of commission.

Trends: Is Crime Increasing?

Although some criminologists suspect so, it is difficult to be certain. It is clear that many "crime waves" are newspaper nonsense, as there is no evidence in statistics or elsewhere to suggest that the actual crime rate changes rapidly or violently. But even more gradual changes are difficult to determine, since there is no satisfactory measure of the amount of crime at any time. Changes in crimes reported may reflect either a changing frequency of criminal acts or changed attitudes toward reporting them.[16] The arrest rate is a better indication of police behavior than of criminal behavior. For example, more efficient law enforcement would produce more arrests and convictions and would thereby appear to increase the crime rate. The annual statistics regularly show increases in some types of crime and decreases in others. As a final confusion, there is the fact that each new law tends to increase the crime rate by defining another act as criminal. Auto theft, black marketing, and bootlegging were crimes great-grandfather was *unable* to commit! Many of the opportunities for "white-collar crime" have developed only within recent decades. All things considered, it is likely that the amount of crime has been increasing for at least several decades, although the exact degree of this increase cannot be measured. It is by no means certain, however, that this apparent increase means that people are growing more lawless, deceitful, or untrustworthy than they used to be. In fact, there is some evidence that present standards of private and public behavior are higher than they used to be,[17] and that our rising crime rate may be an indication of a stricter public conscience rather than of more flagrant misconduct.

[16] See Daniel Bell, "What Crime Wave?" *Fortune,* 51 (January, 1955), pp. 96 ff.
[17] See Estes Kefauver, "Past and Present Standards of Public Ethics in America: Are We Improving?" *The Annals,* 280 (March, 1952), pp. 1-8.

Regional, Seasonal, Racial, and Class Variations

None of these is very important. There are *slight regional variations,* especially in type of crime; for example, crimes against persons are slightly higher in the South and crimes against property slightly higher in the North, but regional differences are quite small. Cities show higher crime rates than rural areas, but it is probable that rural crime is less fully reported. The city also attracts those intending to commit crimes, as it provides more opportunities for crime and provides greater anonymity for those seeking an unconventional mode of life. But there is no evidence that country-reared persons are conspicuously less criminal than their city-reared compatriots.

There are *slight seasonal variations* in type of crime, with more rapes and assaults in the summer months, and more thefts and larcenies in the colder months, but these variations are only moderate.

Racial and national variations in crime rates are substantial but misleading. Both Negroes and American Indians show very high arrest and conviction rates. This is partly due to prejudice and injustice, for it has been conclusively shown that these minorities often are more severely treated by police and courts.[18] It is likely that much of the remaining Negro-white differential is actually a class variation, since most Negroes are in the less-favored social and economic classes in which the reported and prosecuted crimes are the highest. Shaw found that while juvenile delinquency was high in the slums and low in the prosperous suburbs, Negro and white rates *within* the slum area were approximately the same.[19] There is no evidence, therefore, that Negro crime rates differ very greatly from those of whites in the same area and social class.

Class variations, as indicated by statistics, are spectacular! Arrests and convictions are conspicuously rare in the upper classes and frequent in the lower classes. The Gluecks found that of 1000 juvenile delinquents, about three-fourths were from families below the "level of comfort" (defined as having resources to survive four months of unemployment without going on relief).[20] In Chicago, Shaw and McKay found a correlation of $+.89$ between boy delinquency and proportion of families on relief in each square mile area.[21]

[18] See Guy B. Johnson, "The Negro and Crime," *The Annals,* 217 (September, 1941), pp. 93-104; Thorsten Sellin, "The Negro Criminal, A Statistical Note," *The Annals,* 140 (November, 1928), pp. 52-64; Albert Deutsch, "No Glamor," *PM,* July 27, 1952, p. 20; William M. Kephart, "The Negro Offender," *American Journal of Sociology,* 60 (July, 1950), pp. 46-50.

[19] Clifford R. Shaw and others, *Delinquency Areas* (Chicago, University of Chicago Press, 1929).

[20] Sheldon Glueck and Eleanor T. Glueck, *1000 Juvenile Delinquents* (Cambridge, Harvard University Press, 1934).

[21] Clifford Shaw and Henry D. McKay, *Juvenile Delinquency and Urban Areas* (Chicago, University of Chicago Press, 1943).

But to criminologists, these and similar studies of adult crime prove only that conventional crime statistics are unreliable as measures of the criminality of the different classes. There is no accurate measure, but there is scattered evidence which casts doubt upon the belief that the lower classes are the more criminal. For example, it is the expensive hotels catering to the "best" people which have the heaviest losses from thieving guests—six times as great as the hotels catering to the ordinary trade.[22] One plush hotel placed 300 expensive down comforters in its rooms, and exactly one month later the last one disappeared. This is genuine crime, but rarely reported as such. Most criminologists suspect that the lower classes are no more criminal than the middle and upper classes, but are simply less successful in evading punishment.[23]

The upper-class person has a better chance of evading punishment for a number of reasons. (1) He has enough education and sophistication to know something of his legal rights and how to secure them. He is less easily bluffed into a confession or persuaded into pleading guilty. (2) He can generally afford a good lawyer who can make a skillful defense. (3) If he lacks resources, he generally has friends or relatives who can provide for his legal defense. (4) He can conduct himself with the disarming poise and dignity of a good citizen and a gentleman, and avoid the guilty confusion which makes one resemble the "criminal type." (5) He is the social superior of the police officers, the jury, and most of the court personnel. He represents a class which they have been conditioned to treat with deference and respect, and whose "story" their class culture has predisposed them to accept. (6) His education, his occupation, and his social life have all cultivated verbal skills that enable him to speak convincingly in maintaining his innocence or in rationalizing his error. (7) He is often able to offer restitution or bribery to the victims to dissuade them from prosecuting. (8) He may be able to offer bribes of money, position, or power to law-enforcement officials or jurors. (9) He may have many powerful connections of friendship, kinship, or business affiliation with the judge, the prosecutor, or others in a position to influence the prosecution. (10) He can frequently point to a record of community service and occupational success—as a good citizen, as a humane employer, as a Red Cross Drive chairman, as a generous physician—which helps destroy the image of him as a "criminal." (11) He can frequently secure highly respected and prominent citizens to witness to his past reputation and character. (12) There is considerable feeling that public humiliation is a great penalty to an upper-class person, making further punishment less necessary than for a lower-class person. (13) For all of these reasons, the judge is more likely to suspend sentence, use probation

[22] *Life, op. cit.*
[23] See Edwin H. Sutherland, *White Collar Crime* (New York, The Dryden Press, 1949), Ch. 1.

rather than imprisonment, or to impose a very light punishment in case the accused is found guilty. (14) For all these reasons, the upper-class convict is likely to be paroled at the earliest possible date, whereas less fortunate prisoners may serve the full sentence.

The upper classes commit a different kind of crime. It is likely that the greatest single advantage held by the upper-class criminal is the fact that much of his crime is of the sort which has recently come to be known as *white-collar crime.* This is not merely crime committed by white-collar persons; white-collar crime is crime committed by business and professional people *in the course of their occupation.*[24] If a physician shoots his wife, forges a check, or burns his house for the insurance, this is conventional crime; if he commits an illegal abortion, falsifies a prescription for a drug addict, or "pads" a bill, this is white-collar crime. A businessman who systematically short-weights his product, misbrands it, embezzles the firm's funds, manipulates a phony bankruptcy, or falsifies his financial statement is engaging in white-collar crime. When upper-class people engage in crime, it is more likely to be of this sort, rather than the conventional armed robberies, assaults, auto thefts, and the like.

There is no way of knowing the extent of white-collar crime, but criminologists agree that it is tremendous, "probably several times as great as the cost of all the crimes which are customarily regarded as the 'crime problem',"[25] and producing "infinitely more damage to the community."[26] An officer in one chain store embezzled $600,000 as against $100,000 lost by the same store in over five hundred burglaries and robberies.[27] Lie detector tests of all employees of several Chicago banks showed that 20 per cent of them had stolen bank property, and similar tests of a sample of store employees showed that 75 per cent had stolen money or merchandise from the store.[28] In one legal action, 30 of Chicago's 67 hog dealers were suspended for concealing actual profits by "willfully falsifying" annual reports as required by the Packers and Stockyards Act.[29] A certain chain store systematically short-weighted and overcharged its customers for many years, netting as much as 3.4 per cent profit on its entire capital investment through this policy. In one year, 456 of its stores showed "stock gains" of more than 2 per cent, meaning that its customers were cheated enough to make up all the stores' losses from spoilage, breakage, and pilferage, and net two cents on each dollar in addition.[30] Hundred-thousand-dollar robberies are ex-

[24] *Ibid.,* p. 9.
[25] *Ibid.,* p. 12.
[26] Morris Ploscoe, "Crime in a Competitive Society," *The Annals,* 217 (September, 1941), pp. 105-111.
[27] Sutherland, *op. cit.*
[28] F. P. McEvoy, "The Lie Detector Goes into Business," *Reader's Digest,* 38 (February, 1941), p. 69.
[29] *Chicago Sun-Times,* September 11, 1948.
[30] *Consumer Reports,* February, 1950, p. 84.

tremely rare, but hundred-thousand-dollar swindles, embezzlements, and stock frauds have become rather commonplace, and hundred-million-dollar frauds not unknown in American financial history. The Senate Banking and Currency Committee estimated that fraudulent profits of over $500 million were realized by builders who secured federal loans far in excess of the cost of building projects.[31] During a single week, one newspaper reported a "million dollar swindle," a $600,000 dollar embezzlement, and an $81,500 extortion.[32] Sutherland tabulated convictions for violation of federal laws (restraint of trade, misrepresentation in advertising, patent infringement, unfair labor practices, illegal rebates, and other violations of business laws) by 70 of America's largest and most famous corporations during the past half-century. He found two corporations which a federal court or commission had found guilty 50 times during the fifty-year period—one major violation a year. During the 1940-1948 period, the 70 corporations amassed a total of 340 convictions.[33] White-collar crime is not confined to clerks and stenographers!

Incomplete reporting and limited publicity discourages a full public awareness of the extent of white-collar crime. For example, if each of the *known* cases of bank embezzlement was given national publicity, they would be announced at the rate of nearly two cases per day; but wide publicity is discouraged in the belief that it would undermine confidence in our banking institutions.

Attitudes toward white-collar crime. Public indignation at conventional crime contrasts sharply with public tolerance of white-collar crime. To most people, many forms of white-collar crime are not viewed as being "real crime." They are not defined as genuine crime either by the public or by the perpetrators. The business executive who is convicted of violating the antitrust laws generally assumes not the guilty manner of a criminal caught in the act, but the righteous indignation of a victim of government tyranny. Most of his business associates reassure him in his martyrdom. The newspaper editors and radio commentators—those of them who raise their voices at all—usually raise them not in condemnation of the criminal for violating the law, but in condemnation of the government for enforcing it. This merely illustrates the fact that many forms of white-collar crime are not generally considered to be real crime, but instead are viewed as merely technical errors, or perhaps even as courageous opposition to government meddling. There are substantial groups who are strenuously opposed to much of our regulatory law—antitrust laws, labor-relations legislation, wage-hour laws, securities and exchange laws, and others regulating business conduct. Lacking any strong body of supporting public opinion, the government finds it

[31] *New York Times,* July 4, 1954, p. 1.
[32] *Chicago Sun-Times,* January 26, 1953, p. 3; January 31, 1953, pp. 3, 7.
[33] Sutherland, *op. cit.,* Ch. II.

politically difficult to enforce them very enthusiastically. It is also argued that there are so many confusing and contradictory regulations that a businessman can scarcely avoid breaking some of them—an argument for which there is considerable justification. This argument is rarely used, however, to excuse the violations of lower-class offenders jailed for vagrancy, nonpayment of alimony, or some other offense which, in many cases, the offender may have no desire to commit, but be unable to avoid.[34]

This lack of any strong condemnation of many forms of white-collar crime, either by the public or by one's business associates, helps to account for the popularity of white-collar offenses. This attitude that white-collar crime is not real crime is further expressed in the mode of its treatment. Violators are usually dealt with not in the ordinary criminal courts, but by special quasi-judicial commissions and agencies—the Federal Trade Commission, the National Labor Relations Board, the Securities and Exchange Commission, and other agencies. These agencies are empowered to determine facts, make settlements, and recommend criminal prosecution in federal courts when they think it advisable. They rarely do the latter. Usually the guilty violator is permitted to sign a consent decree (a promise not to break the law any more) and allowed to go free. Sometimes he is required to give some of the money back. In cases of especially flagrant violation, or where the accused maintains his innocence, the case may enter a federal court, where the accused is aided by all the advantages of status and position mentioned earlier in this chapter. If found guilty, the penalties are in sharp contrast to those given conventional criminals. Insofar as this writer can determine, no violator has ever gone to prison for violating the antitrust laws, the labor-relations laws, or most other regulatory laws. Fines are usually nominal and are usually assessed to the corporation rather than to the officers personally, meaning that if the officers break the law, the stockholders pay the fine. It has been suggested that the antitrust laws be enforced by dissolving any corporation which repeatedly violates them, or punishing any corporate officer involved in repeated violations by prohibiting him from holding any corporate office thereafter. Such proposals have found little support among businessmen, the press, or the public. This lack of severe penalties for white-collar violators of regulatory law is often explained by the doctrine that the object of these quasi-judicial agencies is not to punish the offenders, but to gain compliance with the law. This point—that law enforcement should seek to gain compliance rather than to inflict punishment—sounds reasonable and humane. Curiously enough,

---

[34] In most states, one commits the crime of vagrancy by being without a job, money, or means of support. In most states, one can be jailed for failure to pay alimony as ordered by the court, irrespective of one's ability or inability to make the payments as ordered.

however, it seems to be reserved for white-collar offenders and is less often applied to ordinary criminals.

The purpose of this discussion, however, is not to debate the ethical justification or the practical utility of this differential treatment. These facts are cited to show that the assumption that crime is largely a lower-class phenomenon is entirely unjustified. Although different classes specialize in different types of crime, the evidence does not warrant the conclusion that one class is more criminal than another. Differential social definitions and modes of treatment, although perhaps justifiable, serve to conceal the criminal behavior of one class while dramatizing that of another, leading to a highly distorted impression of the relative criminality of the different social classes in America.

In summary, then, there are few significant variations in probable actual crime rates of different regions, seasons, races, or classes in America. Most variations are due largely to statistical illusions and imperfections. There is one point at which such comparisons have been useful—in showing that American Indians, second-generation immigrants, and urban slums all have very high crime rates (even after allowing for statistical inaccuracies), the relationship between crime and social disorganization is suggested. Beyond this, any genuine variations which remain are quite small and of little significance in analyzing the causes or treatment of crime. For it is of little value to know that one group commits 10 per cent more crime than another; what is important is to know why either commits crime at all!

SOME POPULAR FALLACIES ABOUT CRIME

1. The Fallacy of the "Criminal Class"

We hear frequent references to the "criminal class," the "criminal type," or the "typical criminal." There is no such person! There is perhaps no other group in society whose members differ so greatly in motive, in background, and in conduct as the "criminal class." The confirmed drunkard, the professional racketeer, the confidence man, and the abortionist physician have remarkably little in common. It is absurd to speak of the "typical criminal," for he does not exist.

2. The Romantic Stereotypes of "the Criminal"

Around such highly dramatic but little-understood behavior as crime, it is inevitable that a number of highly romantic stereotypes should develop. One is the stereotype of the "mad killer" who kills without reason or remorse. Such psychotic killers are rare, but their high publicity value encourages an exaggerated notion of their numbers. Another is the

"Robin Hood" stereotype who robs the rich to feed the poor, a type whose popularity in fiction is matched by his rarity in real life. Another is the "tough softie," a Damon Runyon-style character whose menacing exterior conceals a heart of gold that melts at the mew of a kitten or the quaver of somebody's dear old mother. Opposed to this is the "insensitive clod" stereotype, a passionless, unfeeling creature who cares not what anyone thinks of him and has abandoned all hope of status or respectability. This stereotype rests upon complete ignorance of the manner wherein status and recognition are actually secured by professional criminals. Then there is the "gay desperado," a soldier of fortune whose life of crime is an adventuresome flirtation with death in search of fortune. There is the "secret society" stereotype of the underworld as a vast brotherhood united by eternal oaths of loyalty, practicing a chivalrous code of "honor among thieves," and united in eternal warfare against the forces of law and order. Finally, there is the "master brain" stereotype of the king of the underworld, a commander-in-chief over a vast criminal network which he rules with iron hand.

All of these florid conceptions are largely untrue, some entirely untrue. All are romantic oversimplifications of highly complex phenomena. None is consistent with the known facts about the actual organization and operation of crime, and none contributes anything to an understanding of the behavior of criminals.

3. The Fallacy That Criminals Are "Abnormal"

Many people believe that criminals are the physical, mental, or psychological inferiors of the general population. Many early studies seemed to support this conclusion, but these early studies suffered from two serious defects. First, they were based upon convict samples, and the prison population represents the failures of the criminal profession—the clumsy beginners, the stupid bunglers, the impulsive and careless, and so on. Presumably the more intelligent and skillful criminals are more successful in staying out of prison. Although studies of prison samples have some value, they cannot be carelessly generalized for criminals as a whole. To study a sample of businessmen who go bankrupt would provide useful knowledge about business failures, but would tell nothing reliable about businessmen as a whole. Any studies of prison inmates must be interpreted with equal caution. In the second place, many early studies did not compare their convict samples with a control group of persons from the general population; the scholar often compared his survey findings with what he merely *assumed* to be true of the general population. Consequently, the theory of the inferiority of the prison population rested upon an inflated notion of the characteristics of the general population.

Inasmuch as there is no way to define, locate, and measure those criminals who have not been convicted, it is impossible to determine accurately their qualities. Most criminologists are now of the opinion, however, that criminals, taken as a group and including those not in prison, probably form a relatively representative cross section of the general population physically, mentally, and psychologically.[35]

4. The Fallacy of the "Born Criminal"

It is a common habit of mankind to attribute to instinct any behavior for which he has no other explanation. Lacking any satisfactory explanation for criminal and other perverse behavior, further perplexity could be neatly avoided by assuming that some instinct was responsible. This assumption was buttressed by the observation that criminal behavior often "ran" in certain families and was absent in others. It might also be observed, however, that membership in the Catholic Church, preference for large breakfasts, or the use of correct grammar also run in certain families without being considered instinctive.

No reputable American criminologist today accepts the notion of a "criminal instinct," for they are agreed that *criminal behavior is learned,* a conclusion most biologists share.[36] An instinct is an inborn, relatively inflexible and specific behavior pattern, rigidly uniting a specific stimulus with a specific response. But a given pattern may be a crime in one period or one society and a noble benefaction in another. The criminal act could scarcely be an inborn pattern, for nature has no way of knowing which acts will be criminal and hence cannot know which acts to implant in human heredity. Furthermore, a given act may be criminal in some circumstances and legal in others. Under some circumstances we hang the man who kills another; in other circumstances, we hang medals on him. It is obviously impossible to implant in heredity only those acts which will, when committed, be defined as criminal, and the notion of a criminal instinct becomes fantastic nonsense.

It remains currently fashionable to maintain that although crime may not be actually instinctive or inherited, "criminal tendencies" may still be inherited. This is merely a diluted version of the original proposition. If nature cannot know what acts to implant, how can she know what "tendencies" to implant? Furthermore, exactly what is a "criminal tendency"? It cannot be an inclination toward a particular act, since the criminality of an act is a constantly changing matter of social definition. It cannot be a general resistance to social expectation since, as will be shown later, actual criminals are as hungry for status and social recogni-

---

[35] Cf. Harry Elmer Barnes and Negley K. Teeters, *New Horizons in Criminology* (New York, Prentice-Hall, Inc., 1951), pp. 247-250.

[36] Cf. M. F. Ashley-Montagu, "The Biologist Looks at Crime," *The Annals,* 217 (September, 1941), pp. 46-57.

tion as other people. In fact, the term *criminal tendency* illustrates the "naming fallacy" wherein a suitable name serves as a substitute for knowledge. Unable to find any firm evidence of an hereditary basis for criminal behavior, but feeling that there ought to be one, hereditarians use the term *criminal tendency* to conceal their lack of any exact knowledge upon the matter. In other words, if you can't prove it, just call it a "tendency!" Meanwhile, no one has yet defined a "criminal tendency" or proved that one exists, and the term remains scientific nonsense.

5. The Poverty and Broken-Homes Fallacies

Many people firmly believe that much crime is caused by poverty and most delinquency by broken homes. Although it is true that most of those convicted of conventional crimes are in the low-income class, this does not prove that poverty is a *cause* of crime, since there are many facts about the distribution of conventional crime which poverty cannot explain. For example, an equal number of boys and girls suffer poverty and broken homes, yet boy delinquents outnumber girl delinquents by four or five to one. Many poverty-stricken groups in the slum, such as the Chinese, have very low crime and delinquency rates despite their poverty. Certain immigrant groups with historically low crime rates have developed high crime rates in America, even though they are more prosperous than before.[37] Fluctuations in crime rates show little or no association with variations in the level of national prosperity.[38] Poverty, by itself, is a negligible factor in crime.

The "broken-homes" cliché is almost religiously believed by many people. Numerous studies have been made and have disagreed widely in finding anywhere from 20 to 60 per cent of delinquents coming from broken homes.[39] These figures cannot be interpreted without knowing what proportion of all children live in broken homes, and this figure is not accurately known. Earlier studies underestimated the proportion of children living in broken homes, and therefore made it appear that the broken homes were more common to delinquents than to the general child population by a ratio of several to one. Later studies, using more scientific methods of determining how many children are exposed to the influence of broken homes, have found only slight associations, with Shaw and McKay's study showing a ratio of only 1.18 to 1, which they consider insignificant.[40] It appears that broken homes are *not* contributing much

[37] See Pauline V. Young, *The Pilgrims of Russian-Town* (Chicago, University of Chicago Press, 1932).

[38] Thorsten Sellin, *Research Memorandum on Crime in the Depression* (New York, Social Science Research Council, 1937).

[39] See Barnes and Teeters, *op. cit.*, pp. 210-213.

[40] Clifford R. Shaw and Henry D. McKay, "Social Factors in Juvenile Delinquency," National Commission on Law Observance and Enforcement, *Report on the Causes of Crime*, No. 13, Vol. II, pp. 261-284.

more than their share of delinquents, and recent research has shifted from study of the physically broken home to study of the psychologically disrupted home, a factor of far greater importance.

6. The Fallacy That Violent, Dramatic Crime Constitutes the "Crime Problem"

From reading newspaper headlines, one would infer that the crime problem is largely concerned with such crimes as murder, armed robbery, rape, and other sex crimes, for these are the ones which crowd the front pages. For every woman killed by a "sex fiend," a dozen are slaughtered by their husbands; but the sex crimes attract more interest and arouse far greater anxiety. For every person murdered in calculated detective-story fashion, dozens are killed by drunken and reckless drivers (negligent homicide, if it can be proved). For every dollar taken in armed robbery, hundreds or thousands are taken quietly by gamblers, racketeers, and white-collar criminals. The corruption of police and government officials by organized and white-collar crime wreaks an injury to public life and public morals beside which the depredations of pickpockets, shoplifters, bank robbers, and homosexuals seem hardly worth mention. Yet these crimes rate the headlines. It would be only a slight exaggeration to say that the genuine social destructiveness and financial cost of a form of crime varies *inversely* with the publicity it receives and the public concern it arouses.

A REALISTIC CLASSIFICATION OF CRIMINALS

As already indicated, a classification of criminals according to type of crime is of little value. It tells nothing of the criminal's motives and contains no suggestions for effective treatment. A useful classification should give some insight into the purposes of the criminal and be of some practical aid in analyzing different methods of treatment. For this, criminals should be classified not according to type of crime, but according to personality orientation of the criminal.[41]

1. "Legalistic" Criminals

a. Some persons become *criminals through ignorance*. Feeble-minded persons unable to understand the nature of their actions may, in certain instances, be dangerous, but they are problems of custody, not of

[41] The classification that follows is one which has not yet been commonly used by sociologists, excepting perhaps the last three terms—situational, habitual, and professional. Although the classification which follows is an unconventional one, the present writers consider it a useful one.

punishment or treatment. Anyone convicted for an act done in genuine ignorance of its illegality is a genuine "criminal," even though he had no criminal intent and obviously presents no difficult problem of treatment. Some laws are so unclear that it is difficult to know whether a specific act is legal or illegal. Businessmen often complain that there are so many confusing and overlapping regulatory laws that they cannot be certain what is legal. Sometimes the only way to tell whether a particular act is covered by the law is to commit it and invite the government to try to get a conviction. If it succeeds, the act was illegal! There are hundreds of such "test cases" every year, many resulting in convictions. These convicts are not criminals in the usual sense, nor do they require any conventional "treatment."

b. Other legalistic criminals include the *victims of unjust law enforcement.* In any kind of court system, an entirely innocent person of good reputation will occasionally be convicted, either through a freak of mistaken identity or circumstantial evidence, or perhaps through a frame-up. Although such cases are relatively rare, scarcely a month passes without one or more convicts being cleared when another person confesses.[42] In other cases the police and prosecutor may "hang" a crime on an innocent suspect whose bad reputation and limited resources make it difficult for him to defend himself. A past record of misdemeanors—drunkenness, tavern brawls, nonpayment of bills, and so on—prejudices the police, prosecutors, and jurors to reject one's protestations of innocence. Negroes, Mexicans, and other racial or national minorities are usually handicapped by prejudice, poverty, and ignorance when they are suspected. Quite a few are convicted on incredibly flimsy evidence, or are easily frightened into signing false confessions. One Negro was recently convicted of "assault by leering" at a white woman from a distance of 60 feet![43] While this particular conviction was reversed by a higher court, not a year passes without several cases of similar "justice" appearing in the liberal press (The Nation, New Republic, and so on). Such cases rarely receive wide publicity in the conventional press.

c. Still another group of legalistic criminals are those whose *alleged crime is merely the pretext for action* against someone with unpopular social or political ideas. In a few instances, of which the Sacco-Vanzetti case is a celebrated example,[44] political radicals are convicted of a conventional crime on very flimsy evidence by a court whose lack of judicial objectivity results in nothing less than a legal lynching. Labor organizers have been arrested for "loitering" while waiting for a street car; while

[42] See Erle Stanley Gardner, *The Court of Last Resort* (New York, William Sloane Associates, Inc., 1952), for popularized accounts of such cases.

[43] *New York Times,* November 13, 1952, p. 22; January 29, 1953, p. 29; *Chicago Sun-Times,* February 26, 1953, p. 31.

[44] See pages 488-489 of this textbook.

talking to one another, they have been arrested for "obstructing the sidewalk"; while handing out handbills they have been arrested for "littering the sidewalk." A currently fashionable way to punish suspected subversives is to place them before a Congressional committee for extensive questioning and then prosecute them for perjury if they make a false statement in their defense. In such cases, although one may be guilty of the specific offense as charged, he is being prosecuted not primarily because of what he did, but because of who he is or what he believes in.

All of these legalistic criminals have little in common with conventional criminals. Granted some of them may be very poor citizens, they generally lack criminal intent, lack criminal orientation, and need no criminal treatment. If convicted and punished, they are likely to become far worse citizens than before.

2. "Moralistic" Criminals

These are violators of laws forbidding certain vices that inflict direct injury mainly upon one's self, if upon anyone. The moral views of a powerful segment of the community, possibly a hundred years earlier, have written into law many regulations of matters involving private morality as well as public protection. These include laws forbidding gambling, prostitution, illegal use of liquor or narcotics, homosexuality, adultery, fornication, and perhaps certain other sex offenses. All of these laws are of debatable effectiveness. The attempt to suppress gambling and prostitution, despite a great market for these services among "law-abiding" citizens, tends to result in widespread violation of the law and in corruption and demoralization of law enforcement agencies through protection payments and political pressures from "respectable" citizens. Some of the laws are obviously absurd, since if they were enforced, virtually the entire adult population would be imprisoned. Laws forbidding adultery are violated by perhaps half the male population,[45] and those forbidding fornication by perhaps nine-tenths of the male population.[46] These laws are usually enforced only when the police want to convict somebody of something, or when an offended third party wishes to make trouble. For all practical purposes, adultery and fornication are crimes only when somebody wants to make an issue of it. Kinsey has shown that if existing sex laws were strictly enforced, 95 per cent of the male population could be imprisoned, while not less than 60 per cent of the male college graduates could be imprisoned for certain illegal techniques of love-making in which they engage with their own wives.[47] Such laws

[45] Alfred C. Kinsey, Wardell B. Pomeroy, and Clyde E. Martin, *Sexual Behavior in the Human Male* (Philadelphia, W. B. Saunders Company, 1948), pp. 249, 585.
[46] *Ibid.*, p. 552.
[47] *Ibid.*, pp. 392, 576.

which make criminals of nearly the entire adult population are pointless.

Although many of those engaged in the illegal sale of narcotics are professional criminals, it is useless to class the drug addict as a criminal. The main direct effect of narcotics is to quiet him, and if he commits a crime, it is usually in an effort to insure his supply of drugs. He plays no part in organized crime, for a drug addict is untrustworthy. There is good reason to control the sale of narcotics, but many criminologists agree that to make the use of drugs by an addict a crime serves only to aggravate a difficult problem. The addict is a problem in medicine and psychiatry, not in criminology.

The moralistic criminals are, as a group, a relatively harmless lot. Although much of their behavior is highly offensive to others, they have little in common with professional criminals. Neither their motives nor their life organization is basically criminal. Their successful treatment should be viewed primarily as a problem in public morality rather than in criminology.

3. "Psychopathic" Criminals

In this class fall all those who are unable to control their behavior in a legally acceptable way because of a major emotional maladjustment. This includes not only the legally insane but all others with more or less permanent complexes, phobias, manias, and other instabilities or disturbances which result in criminal acts. In some cases, the behavior is of a wildly erratic sort which may result in any one of a wide variety of types of crime. In other cases, one suffers an uncontrollable compulsion to commit a particular act which he does not particularly want to do, and may receive no enjoyment from doing, yet must do to find relief. The *kleptomaniac* is a compulsive thief, often specializing in a single kind of merchandise for which he has no use, whose stealing has some symbolic meaning. In one case, a lonely, unattractive girl accumulated a trunkful of costume jewelry, as the act of stealing jewelry became a substitute for gaiety and companionship. In another, a timid, ineffectual housewife found a temporary sense of power and accomplishment in the act of stealing. The kleptomaniac should not be confused with the ordinary shoplifter who steals for use or sale, nor should the arsonist who burns his barn to collect the insurance be confused with the *pyromaniac* who cannot resist setting fires. The pyromaniac gains nothing from the fire except a sense of power, excitement, or revenge upon society and the temporary release from a driving compulsion he is powerless to understand or subdue. The sexual psychopath is not merely one caught in a sex act that offends the moral or esthetic sensibilities of the community; he is one who commits an illegal act under uncontrollable compulsion, not because it brings enjoyment, but because it brings relief. These range from window-peeping and lingerie-stealing to knifings and murderous assaults. The sexual psychopath finds sexual excitement and sexual relief through these acts rather than through normal sex activities.

All these "psychopathic" criminals have little in common with professional criminals. They seek not profit, status, or recognition, but release from uncontrollable impulse. Punishments are futile, for their acts are nonrationally motivated. Imprisonment gives them no aid and eventually releases them uncured. To view them as criminals is both ineffectual and medieval. Many of the sexual psychopaths are not curable and must be kept in permanent custody in an appropriate institution if society is to be protected. A few are susceptible to psychiatric treatment, after which they can be safely released.

4. "Institutional" Criminals

Institutional crime refers to certain criminal acts regularly committed, usually in the course of one's occupational behavior, yet so widely practiced and rationalized that these acts are not defined as crime by those committing them, or perhaps even by the community. These are not professional criminals, for crime is not a career but is only incidental to a legitimate career.

The slot machines in American Legion halls and private clubs, and the bingo parties and raffles which certain churches sponsor are examples of institutional crime. They are actual crimes as defined by law but are not viewed as such by those promoting them, by the law-enforcement officials, or by most of the general public. Instead, they are standard, customary practices of these groups and are likely to be testily defended with the argument that "the law is foolish," or that "the law isn't intended for this," with the added comment that it isn't polite to mention the matter.

A different example is found in the systematic, deliberate fraud practiced on some tenant farmers or sharecroppers in certain areas, at least until recently. The landowner advances seed and "keep" (living necessities) to the sharecropper during the year, markets his crop, subtracts his share and the accumulated advances, and gives the sharecropper the remainder, if any. In certain areas it appears to be a common practice for the landowner to "juggle" the accounts so that there is little or nothing left for the sharecropper. Although the sharecropper may suspect he is being cheated, he is prevented by ignorance, fear, status, and perhaps race from demanding an honest audit of the books. The landowners justify the practice by claiming that in the poor years they are still "stuck" for the sharecropper's advances and often lose money themselves; consequently, they must cheat the sharecroppers in the good years to recoup their losses in the poor years. They further charge that the sharecroppers regularly steal whatever they can from their landlords, mostly tools and food, to

which the sharecroppers reply that they are merely reclaiming their due.[48]
Here is a pattern of reciprocal stealing which is so highly systematized
and so neatly incorporated into the local social structure that it may be
termed institutionalized.

Longshoremen on the New York waterfront engage in systematic pilfering as a means of supplementing their irregular earnings. This practice is
encouraged both by their actual need and by their awareness of the huge
"take" of the waterfront mobsters.

"If five per cent of everything moving in and out is systematically siphoned off
by the mob, why shouldn't I take a few steaks home for the wife and kids?" a
longshoreman figures. "Taking what you need for your own table is never considered pilferage," it was explained to me rather solemnly. Shortly before
Thanksgiving a longshoreman who could double for Jackie Gleason noticed
barrels of turkeys being unloaded from a truck. He was not working that day
but he simply got in line and waited for a barrel to be lowered onto his back.
Everybody in his tenement got a free turkey. Another longshoreman . . . in a
whole year . . . made less than $1500, and he had kids to feed. "We couldn't 've
made out if I hadn't scrounged the groceries on the dock," he said.[49]

Income-tax frauds are widespread among occupational groups such as
physicians, dentists, waitresses, cab drivers, and others who receive income in the form of fees. It is easy to "forget" to report part of this income,
and in some groups, it appears to be only the exceptional person who files
a completely honest return. Few storekeepers report as personal income
all the merchandise they take home for family use, as is required by income-tax law. A growing business practice is the loading of the business
expense account with the private expenditures of the officers. If the
owner's dinner party or week end at Sun Valley can be listed as a business
expense, much of its cost can be shifted onto the taxpayer. It is said that
some businessmen never eat a meal, light a cigar, see a show, or take a
trip except on the expense account.[50] The persons engaged in systematically evading the tax collector do not define it as "real" crime, but as a

---

[48] Allison Davis and Burleigh Gardner, in *Deep South* (Chicago, University of Chicago Press, 1941), quote one white planter as saying, "The only way a man can
make money from farming is by stealing it from the Negroes, or by living close. [Some
live close, saving every penny] . . . and then there are lots that steal from the Negroes.
Some of them will take everything a Negro has, down to his last chicken and hog"
(p. 351). Davis and Gardner also report a conversation in which a white planter asks
a colored landlord why colored tenants so often stole from their landlords, and is
told that the white man "has beat him, and kicked him and shot him, and hurt him,
and lynched him, and cheated him, and stolen from him for so long that the Negro
feels that anything he can steal or cheat the white man out of is no more'n what's
been done to him." To this, the white planter replies, "You know, I believe you're
right about that" (p. 396).

[49] Budd Schulberg, "Joe Docks, Forgotten Man of the Waterfront," *New York
Times Magazine*, December 28, 1952, pp. 3 ff. See also "Last of the Business Rackets,"
Fortune, 43 (June, 1951), pp. 89 ff.

[50] Richard A. Girard, "They Escape Income Taxes—But You Can't," *American
Magazine*, CLVI (December, 1952), pp. 15 ff.

game of wits with the government. It therefore fits the definition of institutional crime—criminal acts which are widespread and generally tolerated by an occupational group and not treated as real crime either by them or by most of the community.

In the American Southwest, most large growers employ Mexican labor, partly contract labor brought in by agreement with the Mexican government, and partly "wet-back" labor consisting of Mexicans who illegally cross the river bed at night.[51] Some growers prefer the wet-backs, as they are not protected by contract and can be hired more cheaply and can sometimes be cheated out of even their meager earnings.[52] It is no secret that some growers connive at violation of the immigration laws and strongly oppose their rigid enforcement. The Immigration Service has accommodated these growers by staging "roundup" raids near the end of the work season, "so they haven't interfered seriously with the farm labor force."[53]

Dozens of other examples of institutional crime could be documented. Violation of the highway weight laws by commercial truckers is a widespread practice, and some haulers consider it more profitable to pay the fines than to stay within the legal weight limits.[54] Violation of fire, sanitary, and other building regulations is a standard practice of many owners of slum property. In Chicago, a recent survey showed one owner who had accumulated a total of 418 violations, but since half of all violation suits were dropped and fines averaged only $10 each in the other half, it was more profitable to continue to violate the law than to repair the property.[55] These institutional criminals have little in common with conventional criminals, or even with each other, for the tax evader, the longshoreman, and the wet-back employer differ greatly from one another. "Treatment" would not be a conventional effort to reform criminals, since neither they nor the public consider them as criminals. Institutional crime is not a problem in conventional criminology, but a problem in social organization, in jurisprudence, or in public morality.

5. "Situational" Criminals

Every prison contains a number of persons who, under pressure of overpowering circumstances, have committed a criminal act entirely out of harmony with their basic life organization. A melodramatic illustration

[51] New York Times, January 18, 1953, p. 6; January 17, 1954, p. 62; January 24, 1954, p. 10.
[52] New York Times, May 10, 1953, pp. 1 ff.
[53] Farm Journal (September, 1952), p. 34.
[54] New York Times, March 21, 1954, p. 21. See Time (December 20, 1954), p. 61, for a report of Illinois' unsuccessful effort to bar from its highways a trucking company with 157 overweight violations. Time concludes, "Most of them [the truckers] count fines as simply another routine cost of doing business."
[55] Chicago Sun-Times, May 28, 1953, p. 16; June 9, 1954, p. 28.

is that of the clerk or cashier who embezzles to pay for his wife's operation. A high proportion of murders are committed by husbands, wives, or in-laws who are caught in an intolerable domestic conflict from which they see no escape and which they eventually "solve" with a shotgun or meat-axe. Many a normally law-abiding businessman, faced with ruin through adverse circumstances, will consider a profitable fire or a fraudulent bankruptcy. The debts from a single gambling spree may involve one so deeply that he tries a little larceny as a way out. Many a long-honest employee becomes dishonest when he acquires an expensive girl friend. Occasionally a thoroughly respectable citizen commits a serious crime while intoxicated. In rare cases a timid, mousy employee, taunted once too often, flares into towering anger and parts his tormentor's hair with a sledge hammer. Such situational criminals as these form a moderate share of our prisoners, because they rarely escape detection and prosecution. Courts are inclined to be lenient if one's prior life was exemplary, but when the offender's past life has been somewhat unsavory, he may find the judge inclined to treat him severely as an "example."

No social purpose is served by *punishing* most of these situational criminals. Inasmuch as their basic life organization is not criminal, they are in no need of the treatment or reformation needed by conventional criminals. They are no more likely to commit another crime, in most cases, than are their neighbors. Imprisonment serves only to satisfy the community's sense of "justice" and usually to embitter and brutalize the offender.

6. "Habitual" Criminals

There are some whom circumstances overpower very easily—persons who repeatedly yield to temptation. Such persons repeatedly get into financial crises from which a little larceny is needed to extract them. Or they are easily provoked to violence. Or, while they may not deliberately seek opportunities for thievery, when one arises they readily seize it. They do not view themselves as criminals and defend each lapse with a succession of excuses. Repeatedly criminal, they have not adopted crime as a career and organized their lives around it. Therefore, they are habitual rather than professional criminals.

Unlike the situational criminals who are frequently sober and industrious, the habitual criminals contain a high proportion of shiftless "ne'er-do-wells." Those who lack vocational skills and industrious working habits and lead the irregular life of a marginal worker may be more likely to engage in many forms of petty mischief. Many habitual (not professional) criminals have a long record of petty offenses—disorderly conduct, drunkenness, moving traffic violations, nonpayment of bills, vagrancy, nonsupport, perhaps minor sex offenses, arrests "on suspicion," and the like.

Lacking a dependable source of income, lacking any long-term life goals, and having little of the conventional sort of status or respectability to sacrifice, the border line between criminal and noncriminal behavior becomes chronically faint and easily breached.

This group probably provides the major share of our prison inmates. Lacking the training, skills, and "connections" necessary to pursue crime successfully, they are easily apprehended and convicted. They play no important role in organized crime and receive scant profit from their efforts. For these, it is true that "crime does not pay." Crime "pays" only those who pursue it systematically and intelligently.

7. "Professional" Criminals

These are the career criminals. Although there are important differences between "con" men and hijackers, all professional criminals have many common characteristics. They all define themselves as criminals and consciously organize their lives around a criminal career. They prize professional competence, are contemptuous of amateurs, and value their standing among their fellow professionals. They crave status and respectability and secure it through demonstrated skill in criminal behavior. Flashy clothes, jewelry, and expensive cars are prized as symbols of status, even as in polite society. To go to prison is humiliating because it is inconvenient, because it is a confession of professional failure, because one's skills and "connections" get rusty, and because possible partners lose faith in one who gets caught too often. To have to sell the pawn ticket to one's "hock piece" (a large diamond which can be pawned when sudden cash is needed) is a humiliating symbol of professional decline.

The professional criminal is, of all criminals, the least likely to get caught. His crimes are not impulsive, but planned as carefully and often as skillfully as a military campaign. Professional criminals are loath to undertake any criminal activity unless the "fix is in"—unless protection has been arranged by making a deal with law-enforcement officials. The professional criminal plans so as to receive a minimum punishment if caught; thus he never kills or resorts to violence unless actually necessary. The professional "second-story man" (house robber) never carries a gun; he would be a fool to use it, and it increases his "rap" if he is caught with it. If the professional is caught, an expert "mouthpiece" (lawyer) obstructs the wheels of justice with a skillful delaying action, further aided by frequent bribery and occasional intimidation of witnesses or jurors. If convicted, the professional becomes a model prisoner and is usually paroled in the shortest possible time, with his "connections" sometimes applying fiscal grease to the wheels of the parole machinery. It is easy to see why professionals comprise a relatively small part of the prison population.

The mental outlook of the professional criminal is somewhat like that of a professional soldier. He kills without passion, but only when there is something to be gained by it. He takes calculated risks, carefully weighed against the objective to be gained. He has a set of firm beliefs that justify his career. The professional criminal believes that "only saps work" and that "everybody has a racket." He attributes his choice of career to his superior perception, not to any lack of moral sensitivity. He may use the "I'm a victim of society" or the "My parents abused me and the street was my home" arguments in a shrewd bid for sympathy if it will help him escape punishment, but he does not really pity himself for being a criminal—only for being caught.[56]

Some romantic notions of criminal chivalry are quite inaccurate. Professional crime is a business, not a fraternal order. No chivalrous code of honor binds the professional criminal. He generally keeps his word because it is professionally and personally unwise to break promises; yet the double-cross is well known. Sharing a common contempt for the police, the professional will ordinarily give them no assistance and will occasionally "cover up" for a stranger whom he recognizes as a fellow professional, but not to the extent of endangering himself. He sometimes disposes of competitors by betraying them to the police; when caught by the police himself, he occasionally will "sing," betraying his partners in exchange for a promise of leniency.

ORGANIZED CRIME

Professional crime varies in degree of organization. Some kinds, such as picking pockets, armed robbery, or confidence games (swindles) do not lend themselves to large-scale organization, and are ordinarily handled singly or by groups of two or three. In others, such as gambling, prostitution, and narcotics peddling, large-scale organization has certain advantages.

Successfully organized crime operates smoothly and quietly, rarely rating headlines, whereas unorganized and nonprofessional crime fills the front pages and gives the public an incorrect notion of its relative importance. But all authorities agree that the cost of organized crime greatly exceeds that of unorganized crime and that organized crime is largely responsible for the corruption of public officials.

A number of journalistic descriptions have fairly accurately pictured the structure and functioning of organized crime,[57] and these populariza-

[56] See Chic Conwell, *The Professional Thief*, annotated and interpreted by Edwin H. Sutherland (Chicago, University of Chicago Press, 1937).

[57] Courtney Riley Cooper, *Here's to Crime* (Boston, Little, Brown & Company, 1937); Martin Mooney, *Crime Incorporated* (New York, McGraw-Hill Book Company, Inc., 1935).

tions are generally supported by more scientific sociological investigations.[58] The investigations of the "Kefauver Committee" focused national attention upon organized crime and brought wider public recognition of the tie-up between crime, business, and government, but the Kefauver investigations added nothing new to our knowledge of organized crime beyond certain up-to-date details.[59] The general pattern of organized crime was well known to sociologists, journalists, and public officials long before Senator Kefauver helped to popularize this knowledge.

Connivance of Law-Enforcement Agencies

The term *organized crime* is not applied to small roving bands of robbers, pickpockets, shoplifters, confidence men, and the like. Organized crime is crime conducted by rather large, organized groups of criminals, with a more or less clearly defined territory in which to operate, and maintaining constant connections with law-enforcement officials. The most elaborately organized crime is found in gambling, prostitution, and narcotics, with bootlegging recently growing in importance.[60] In each of these instances, there is a large market among "respectable" people who have no interest in seeing the law enforced. This large and highly profitable market, combined with considerable public opposition to law enforcement, guarantees the development of organized crime and provides a ready-made rationalization for the law-enforcement officials who must co-operate. For *without exception, organized crime cannot long exist without the connivance of law-enforcement officials.* When a "book" or a house of prostitution opens, police almost invariably know about it within a matter of hours or days. For it is a patrolman's duty to know what goes on in his district, and even a sudden increase in the number of cars parked before a building or in the number of people entering it calls for an investigation. Therefore it is safe to conclude that wherever gambling or prostitution continue for long, it is always by courtesy of our public officials.

This does not mean that *all* the public officials are corrupt; in fact, it would be too costly to "pay off" all of them. Only a few strategically placed officials need to be "reached" in order to provide effective protection. A few judges, one or two assistant district attorneys, and a few police captains are enough to guarantee that the business can operate with only occasional minor annoyance. There are many subtle ways to avoid effective prosecution while going through all the motions of deter-

---

[58] William Foote Whyte, *Street Corner Society* (Chicago, University of Chicago Press, 1943).

[59] See Estes Kefauver, *Crime in America* (Garden City, Doubleday & Company, Inc., 1951).

[60] *New York Times,* December 7, 1952, p. 78; III, pp. 1, 7.

mined law enforcement, and there are many points at which one corrupt public official can neutralize the integrity of a dozen honest companions and frustrate honest law enforcement. The "honest cop" soon learns who is under protection and discovers the futility (and the danger) of attempting to molest them. So the honest cop concentrates on catching traffic violators, pickpockets, and other small fry and closes his eyes to that which he cannot do anything about. It is, therefore, quite possible to have a "wide-open" town even though most of the police are honest.[61]

The "connections" of organized crime reach very high. Mayors of great cities and district attorneys by the dozen have been revealed to have very amiable relations with the "mob." Even federal judges and state supreme court judges sometimes owe their appointments to the mobsters. A famous telephone conversation in which Thomas A. Aurelio thanked gangster Frank Costello for arranging his nomination as Justice of the Supreme Court of the State of New York is only the best authenticated of many such cases.[62]

Role of Respectable People in Organized Crime

Is it possible to suppress organized gambling and prostitution when there are so many customers for these services? There is no clear answer to this question. It is difficult to suppress organized gambling while permitting private organizations to raise funds through gambling operations, yet former Governor Stevenson of Illinois has described the opposition of many "good citizens" when he instructed his state police to remove the slot machines from veterans' posts and private clubs.[63] This widespread toleration of gambling, coupled with the powerful connection of "the syndicate," makes it extremely difficult to suppress gambling even when officials determine to do so. Whether such laws should be repealed or enforced is a moot question. Most attempts at enforcement are only temporarily successful, and the existence of these laws forbidding what many people want and will pay for leads directly to the corruption of law-enforcement officials. Yet, Nevada's experience with legalized gambling is anything but encouraging, and the question remains debatable.[64]

Organized theft and burglary could not exist without dishonest businessmen who sell the stolen merchandise through normal trade channels.

[61] See Albert Deutsch, "The Plight of the Honest Cop," *Collier's*, 132 (September 18, 1953), pp. 23 ff; 133 (May 28, 1954), pp. 29 ff; 134 (July 23, 1954), pp. 33 ff.

[62] *New York Times*, September 1, 1943, pp. 1, 31.

[63] Adlai E. Stevenson, "Who Runs the Gambling Machines?" *Atlantic Monthly*, 189 (February, 1952), pp. 35-38.

[64] Virgil Peterson, "Gambling—Should It Be Legalized?" *Journal of Criminal Law and Criminology*, 40 (September-October, 1949), pp. 259-329; Joseph F. McDonald, "Gambling in Nevada," *The Annals*, 269 (May, 1950), pp. 30-34; Estes Kefauver, *op. cit.*, Ch. 16, "Nevada: A Case Against Legalized Gambling"; Albert Deutsch, "The Sorry State of Nevada," *Collier's*, 135 (March 18, 1955), pp. 74 ff.

As in the days of piracy when pirate loot (mostly merchandise) was marketed through dishonest merchants under the benevolent eye of conniving government officials, organized crime is not profitable without the co-operation of other supposedly honest persons.[65]

National or Regional Organization

Although gambling and prostitution form the backbone of organized crime, other forms include narcotics, hijacking, bootlegging, gold and diamond smuggling, labor racketeering, "protection" rackets, and possibly others. Each gang ordinarily confines itself to a single line, while the "big shots" may have their fingers in several rackets. Territories are worked out through a combination of negotiation and intimidation and enforced by occasional beatings or killings, with possible outbreaks of gang war-fare when boundaries are in dispute. An informal network of contacts provides a means of communication, serves to identify new arrivals, and is used in arranging deals and co-operative arrangements among different gangs. This structure of organized crime does not, as sometimes alleged, parallel that of a business monopoly, with a nation-wide network of branch offices, regional managers, and a national board of directors; it is instead a loose network of relatively autonomous local or regional organizations whose leaders know one another and are willing to co-operate when mutually advantageous, and are equally ready to "muscle in" on one another whenever they feel strong enough. But the picture of a "general staff" of criminal overlords jointly planning and directing the organized crime of the nation is more fiction than fact.

SUGGESTED READINGS

Since Chapters 5 and 6 constitute a unit, the summary, bibliographies, and study questions for both chapters will be found together beginning on p. 141.

[65] See Cyrus H. Karraker, *Piracy Was a Business* (West Rindge, N. H., Richard R. Smith, Inc., 1953); Patrick Pringle, *Jolly Roger: The Story of the Great Age of Piracy* (New York, W. W. Norton & Company, Inc., 1953).

CHAPTER 6

Crime: Causes and Treatment

THE PROBLEM OF CAUSES

WHAT causes crime? This is a question many would ask at the beginning of the discussion. But the classification of crime shows that much criminal behavior is properly a problem in jurisprudence, or public morality, or in education and social organization rather than a problem in criminology. It is only the habitual and professional criminals whose behavior need be explained in terms of crime causation, for they are the only ones whose motivation is criminal.

The search for causes is not new. Throughout most of human history, criminal behavior, along with most other out-of-the-ordinary phenomena, was explained by theological assumptions of evil spirits, devils, and demon possession. The scientific search for causes begins with Lombroso's bodily measurements, from which he developed the theory of the "born criminal," biologically different from normal people. Although Lombroso's approach was scientific, his method was defective; and no reputable American criminologist today accepts any of the biological theories of crime causation.

The search for causes among environmental factors seemed more promising. Shaw found that certain slum areas maintained extremely high delinquency rates quite consistently over many years; even though a succession of racial or ethnic minorities might have occupied an area, the delinquency rates remained constant regardless of the group living in it.[1] Obviously, crime was not a product of the kind of people in the area but a product of the physicial and social life of the area. Other studies showed some association between juvenile delinquency and broken homes, parental neglect, school failure, parental alcoholism, and other social circumstances. But these studies did not indicate *causes,* for in each instance the associations were too low. For example, while broken homes apparently contribute somewhat more than their share of delinquents, ap-

[1] Clifford R. Shaw and others, *Delinquency Areas* (Chicago, University of Chicago Press, 1929).

proximately half the delinquents come from nonbroken homes, and most of the children living in broken homes are not delinquent! A *cause* must be more dependable than this! Furthermore, in some cases, such as delinquency and school failure, it is difficult to determine which is cause and which is effect. Rather than listing environmental factors as causes, it is more correct to list them as "risk factors," since they increase the risk of coming into contact with and learning criminal behavior. For criminal behavior is *behavior*, and like all other social behavior, *criminal behavior must be learned*. This discovery has led to the formulation of a *differential-association theory of crime*.

a. The *differential-association* theory states that *most criminal behavior is learned through contact with criminal patterns which are present, are acceptable, and are rewarded in one's physical and social environment.* As Sutherland states it,[2]

The hypothesis of differential association is that criminal behavior is learned in association with those who define such behavior favorably and in isolation from those who define it unfavorably, and that a person in an appropriate situation engages in such criminal behavior if, and only if, the weight of the favorable definitions exceeds the weight of the unfavorable definitions.

In a "delinquency area," where perhaps one-fourth or more of the youths are officially delinquent each year, and many of the rest are delinquent without being caught, it is no exaggeration to say that *delinquency is normal*. Although not every youth is delinquent, most of them are delinquent some of the time, some of them are delinquent most of the time, and delinquent behavior is an integral part of the area culture. Since such areas are also high in adult crime, an easy and natural graduation for the juvenile is provided.

Yet not all children living in a delinquency area become delinquent, and not all juvenile delinquents become adult criminals. Although criminal patterns are an integral feature of the area culture, even the delinquency area is not totally isolated from noncriminal patterns and anticriminal definitions. In many cases a stable family life, strongly integrated around the conventionally-approved values, may insulate the child against the criminal patterns in the area. In some instances the influence of the church or school may acquaint the child with ambitions or values that oppose these criminal patterns. A child may adopt as model some teacher, church worker, social worker, or other person whose image encourages a noncriminal orientation for the child. Life in a deteriorated area of crowded, substandard housing and dubious business enterprises increases the chances for contact with counteracting influences. Lack of affection or understanding in the home often leads the child to reject the values

[2] Edwin H. Sutherland, *White Collar Crime* (New York, The Dryden Press, 1949), p. 234.

and definitions of parents and to accept the moral definitions of the street life to which he turns. In ways such as these, an unsatisfactory home life, unsolved emotional problems, or the influences of a deteriorated neighborhood all function to increase the risk of delinquency and eventual adult crime by tending to increase contact with criminal patterns and their supporting values, while reducing contact with noncriminal patterns and anticriminal values.

This holds true not only for the slum delinquent but for the middle-class delinquent as well. Since middle-class and upper-class delinquents do not live in deteriorated neighborhoods, delinquent behavior is much less a normal part of their cultural world. In a certain sense, delinquency is normal for the slum child and abnormal for the middle-class child. The middle-class child has less contact with delinquent patterns and more contact with anticriminal evaluations than has the slum child. Yet the middle-class child is not isolated from contact with criminal behavior, for he reads about it, sees it portrayed in movies and on television, and observes a certain amount of unreported crime in his social world. As long as there is no serious rupture of his emotional life, his close and frequent association with anticriminal definitions is likely to keep him from criminal behavior. But if his emotional life is seriously disturbed—by parental conflicts, by social difficulties with his age group, or by other unsolved emotional conflicts—he frequently becomes immune to the anticriminal evaluations and becomes delinquent.

This differential-association theory is equally applicable to white-collar crime. The discovery that a great many of one's associates are chiseling on their income tax, and that they view it as "smart" rather than shameful, is a powerful temptation to follow suit. An acquaintance of the author, a small businessman, was recently told by the auditor who inspected his books that he was claiming less for "business entertainment" than most comparable firms, and the auditor suggested that the tax officials would not question a somewhat larger deduction; thereafter he loaded much of his personal entertaining on the business expense account, thereby avoiding income taxes on the cost of this entertainment. Anyone operating a business observes this practice so frequently among his associates, and so rarely hears it strongly condemned, that he may easily slip into the practice himself. The manner in which contact with white-collar crime tends to lead to its adoption is seen in the following brief case history, only one of many such cases.[3]

A man who had been a school teacher and had never been officially involved in any delinquencies secured a position as agent of a book-publishing company and was assigned to public school work. He soon learned that the publishing company bribed the members of the textbook committee in order to secure adoptions of their books. With considerable shame he began to use this

[3] *Ibid.*, pp. 238-239.

method of bribery because he felt it was necessary in order to make a good record. Partly because he disliked this procedure but principally because this work kept him away from home much of the time, he decided he would become a lawyer. He moved to a large city, registered in a law school, and secured a daytime job as a claim agent for a casualty insurance company. About two years later he was convicted of embezzling the funds of the insurance company. A portion of his autobiography describes the process by which he got into this difficulty: "Almost immediately after I got into this business I learned two things: first, the agents who got ahead with the company were the ones who made settlements at low figures and without taking cases into court; second, the settlements were generally made by collusion with the lawyers and doctors for the claimants. Most of the lawyers for the claimants were ambulance-chasers and were willing to make settlements because they got their fees without any work. The claim agent for the insurance company got a secret kick-back out of the settlement. When I learned this was the way to get ahead in the casualty insurance business, I went in for it in a big way. Accidentally I left some papers loose in my office, from which it was discovered that I was 'knocking down' on the settlements. The insurance company accused me of taking money which belonged to them, but actually I was taking money which belonged to the claimants."

Although the differential-association theory may not provide a complete explanation for all criminal behavior, it is probably as satisfactory an explanation as we have. And yet it should be noted that differential association is not the *cause* of crime, but describes a process whereby criminal behavior is transmitted. The basic causes of crime are unknown and probably unknowable, perhaps because they are inseparable from the same drives and motives that impel all other behavior. A search for understanding of the conditions under which criminal behavior appears and spreads has proven to be far more useful.

APPROACHES TO THE CRIME PROBLEM

The Personal-Deviation Approach

This approach views a social problem as an outgrowth of certain individuals who, for one reason or another, fail to absorb and internalize the conventional attitudes, habits, goals, and values. The criminal is viewed as a deviant person who has failed to form the normal value-judgments, ambitions, and habits, but instead has developed socially disapproved ones.

Such an approach is not too applicable to slum delinquents, since delinquency is a normal part of their cultural system. It would be inapplicable to legalistic, institutional, situational, and at least part of the moralistic criminals, for in none of these cases have the persons rejected the conventional value-system. They have in some way become criminals despite the conventionality of their value-system and life organization.

But some of the moralistic criminals (those engaged in sex "perversions," for example) are deviant personalities, as are many of the habitual and professional criminals. In these cases, the individual has rejected major portions of the conventional value-system and consciously identifies himself as different from other people in this respect.

The reasons for criminal deviation are probably similar to the reasons for any other form of personal deviation. *Any factor in inheritance, environment, or social experience can become either a factor in a conventional or in a deviant personality organization.* Lack of maternal affection drives one child to the streets, another to books, still another to the church. A number of biographical studies have shown how the influences of a deteriorated neighborhood interact with an unsatisfactory home life in producing many juvenile delinquents who graduate into adult criminals.[4] Yet even a "desirable" characteristic may be defined and interpreted in social experience in such a way as to contribute to a deviant personality orientation, as seen in this case: [5]

School was always easy for me. By just sitting and listening to what happened I could always learn enough to pass the examinations pretty well. I never bought a textbook and never studied one single lesson throughout high school. My grades were never high but I never failed a course and my grades averaged more than satisfactory. . . . I also learned quite young that if one is smart he can outwit the ordinary suckers who are really pretty dull. Only dopes work for a living. I've never really done a day's work in my life and I don't intend to. I have always found it possible to work out some kind of a racket and you can always be sure to find some sucker who will do the work for half the gain. I live on the other half. . . . I am now 40 years old and in this scrape which will probably land me in jail. I just over-stepped a little—didn't cover up too well. My lawyer tells me I won't get over four years and I may be out in two and a half for good behavior. You can bet that my behavior will be ___ ___ good. And the guys who sent me up will be working for me yet.

This deviant of extremely high native intelligence, whose parents and teachers never required him to do any real work, developed a pattern of "getting by" without work. His home life failed to cultivate conventional ambitions and values, but did provide him with poise, vocabulary, and refinement which were helpful to him in his criminal career. As this case shows, high intelligence, a pleasing personality, and a "good" home background can be incorporated into either a deviant or a conventional personality organization.

No one knows exactly how large a proportion of criminals are emotionally maladjusted. It is clear that a good many of the prison inmates show

[4] See Clifford R. Shaw, *The Jack-roller; A Delinquent Boy's Own Story* (Chicago, University of Chicago Press, 1930); Clifford R. Shaw and M. E. Moore, *Natural History of a Delinquent Career* (Chicago, University of Chicago Press, 1931); Clifford R. Shaw, H. D. McKay, and J. F. McDonald, *Brothers in Crime* (Chicago, University of Chicago Press, 1938).

[5] Quoted from John F. Cuber, *Sociology*, 3rd ed. (New York, Appleton-Century-Crofts, Inc., 1955), pp. 227-228.

evidences of some emotional maladjustment, ranging from mild neurotic symptoms through many forms of psychoses. Those who are chronically insecure, who harbor intense resentments, who are erratic and unstable, or who have some other emotional difficulty, are likely to have difficulty in conforming to social expectations.

The study of criminal deviation is, then, only a phase of the larger study of personality development in general. In any society, a number of persons develop badly adjusted personalities or fail to internalize the conventional values and are therefore deviant; some but not all of these come from "bad" environments. Among the possible behavior outlets for deviant persons are a number which are termed criminal. The specific study of criminal careers in terms of personality deviation helps to understand much, if not all, crime. Intelligent treatment is impossible without this understanding.

The Value-Conflict Approach

This approach analyzes the problem in terms of the conflicting values of our society. Values differ both on the questions of what acts are crimes and what should be done about them. In moralistic and institutional crime, the value-conflict is obvious. These are widespread crimes because the value-judgments of certain groups have been written into law, forbidding acts which the value-judgments of many other groups fully tolerate. Gambling and prostitution become problems purely because of such value-conflicts. If disapproval of these activities were unanimous, there would be no question of what to do about them, and suppression would not be too difficult. Or if these activities were unanimously accepted, there would be no problem, since no critical judgments would define them as situations needing correction. But wherever there is a substantial number of people whose values define acceptably a form of behavior forbidden by law, widespread violation of the law and persistent corruption of law-enforcement officials are inevitable.

There is another manner in which value-conflicts function as a "cause" of crime. This is through the corrosion of personal morality by the value-conflicts inherent within the culture. At home, church, and school the child learns a set of moral values—truth, honesty, loyalty, and so on, and a set of copy-book maxims—"honesty is the best policy," "crime does not pay," "truth wins out in the end," and the like. Eventually he discovers that these are only half true. He comes to realize that a considerable amount of business or professional success is based upon a subtle betrayal of trust.[6] He learns that a salesperson's job is to sell not necessarily what the customer needs, but what the store has to sell. He realizes that most

[6] See Donald B. Cressey, *Other People's Money: A Study in the Social Psychology of Criminal Violation of Financial Trust* (Glencoe, Ill., The Free Press, 1953).

advertising is somewhat exaggerated and that some of it is completely untruthful. He learns about grafting politicians, about physicians who split fees and collect "kick-backs" from pharmacists and opticians, about bribery of purchasing agents, about falsification of financial statements, about the many legal and semilegal ways of avoiding tax obligations, about the padded repair bills collected by over half the garages and repair houses, according to one set of surveys.[7] If he works in a cleaning shop he learns how many customers will misrepresent the value of a lost or damaged garment. If he is an insurance adjuster he learns how many claimants view each accident as a fresh opportunity to defraud the insurance company. He generally comes to accept those forms of "sharp practice" that are current in his occupation, along with the rationalizations which justify them, and he is constantly reminded of the many other forms of exploitation and fraud going on around him. Meanwhile, it is theorized, his moral sensitivity is blunted and his lofty moral principles are relegated to a remote island of life, available for ritualistic repetition when needed, but carefully insulated from any controlling influence upon economic practice. Some criminologists consider this process to be a primary explanation of the prevalence of crime in modern society.[8]

This indictment is, however, in some respects an exaggeration. Although in practically every business or profession there are certain dubious or dishonest practices that are very common, it is probably true that the dishonest acts are vastly outnumbered by the honest acts, and false statements outnumbered by truthful ones. After some experience with the business world, one learns to expect scrupulous honesty in some activities and dishonesty in others. For example, it is likely that most people do not expect complete truth in advertising and are calmly prepared to discount what they read. Meanwhile they do expect a businessman to be honest in weighing hamburg or making change, and in these respects businessmen are probably more honest than their customers. In securing a proper perspective, one must not assume that most business activity is dishonest or fraudulent, for this would be highly unjustified. But it is true that there is enough of misrepresentation, of exploitation of ignorance and gullibility, and of deliberate fraud in the business world to make the maintenance of a strict moral conscience more difficult.

Many people were shocked to learn in 1951 that a number of college athletes had been bribed by gamblers to manipulate the winning or losing margin so that the gamblers could not lose in predicting the "spread."

---

[7] R. W. Riis, "The Repair Man Will Gyp You If You Don't Watch Out," *Reader's Digest,* 39 (July, 1941), pp. 1-6; "The Radio Repair Man Will Gyp You If You Don't Watch Out," *Reader's Digest,* 39 (August, 1941), pp. 6-10; "The Watch Repair Man Will Gyp You If You Don't Watch Out," *Reader's Digest,* 39 (September, 1941), pp. 10-12; Discussion of series, *Reader's Digest,* 39 (October, 1941), pp. 144-148.

[8] Harry Elmer Barnes and Negley K. Teeters, *New Horizons in Criminology* (New York, Prentice-Hall, Inc., 1951), p. 22.

Yet these students had long been "secretly" selling their services to their colleges while both connived to maintain an illusion of amateur status. The facts of the long and sordid story of deception and subterfuge wherein many great colleges and universities have paid their athletes is no secret to any newspaper reader. Some of these athletes entered college on forged high-school credentials; some colleges were widely accused of maintaining their star athletes' eligibility through gifts of grades never earned, while at least one college corrected past oversights by doctoring grades already recorded in the registrar's office. Is it really so surprising that students who have already sold themselves to a college in an atmosphere heavy with deception should see nothing very wrong in selling themselves again? When the line between crime and "being practical" becomes so indistinct, it is not surprising that this line should frequently be breached.

The role of cultural values in producing crime, however, goes beyond the tendency for shady practices to beget criminal ones or for white-collar crime to encourage shirt-sleeve crime. It also involves the basic ethos of our culture. There are good reasons to suspect that *the basic values of our competition-success seeking culture must inevitably produce a high crime rate.* No other culture in the world has so persistently trained people to want so many things that most of them have no remote possibility of ever getting. No other culture has so strongly conditioned them to view themselves as failures unless they attain status and living standards that are utterly unattainable to most of them. That many of the people in this bitter struggle for status and respectability should overstep the line of legality should surprise nobody, especially when that line of legality is so confused.

It is quite possible that there is no prospect of a low crime rate in a society which pays greater attention to the possession of status and wealth than to the means used in gaining them. It is unlikely that America can achieve a greatly lowered crime rate without major changes in American values. In place of the present Cadillac-and-country-club measure of success, it might be necessary to measure status and respectability in terms of some values more readily attainable by all who put forth a reasonable effort. For only when the rewards of status and respectability represent genuinely attainable probabilities to all those who are willing to strive for them—only then will the resort to shady short-cuts be discouraged.

There is little prospect of any such sweeping change in American cultural values. The entire American value-system would need to be overhauled and most of the present incentives of our economic system reinterpreted. Even to blueprint these value-changes, together with the other institutional changes they would produce, would be a task few sociologists would care to attempt. Furthermore, values do not change because some sociologist suggests it; values emerge from the social life of a people and change only as it changes. Therefore to call for a revolution in American values is unrealistic; realism consists simply in recognizing that part of the cost of our present competition-success value-system will be paid in the form of crime rates which remain high.

The Social-Disorganization Approach

This approach studies the crime problem as a product of social change. A stable, well-integrated society has very little crime. Those habits and practices that are necessary and useful will have become institutionalized and thoroughly supported by the moral values of the culture. In time, an objectionable practice will be dealt with in a stable culture, either by a gradual change of values so as to accept it, or by suppressing it through the compelling system of social control found in a stable society.

Social change disorganizes the existing network of arrangements and values of a society. Many old norms become inapplicable and numerous conflicts of value appear. Children are taught a series of expectations which do not fit the realities they eventually find. Traditional standards seem remote and meaningless, and traditional behavior controls lose power. Change produces new groupings with special interests to promote and new situations and pressures to reconcile. Such rapid and sweeping change as Western civilization has experienced means that before adjustment to one set of changes is completed, still more changes rush upon it.

A social-disorganization analysis of crime emphasizes how change from a rural agricultural society to an urban industrial society has revolutionized our values and disorganized our traditional social-control machinery. The hard-work-and-thrift value orientation of a peasant people has been replaced with the get-it-and-spend-it materialism of today. The informal controls of neighborhood and community are largely sterile in our anonymous urban civilization. Parental supervision of children and adolescents suffers from modern transportation, commercialized recreation, the smallness of homes and apartments, employment of mothers, and the daily scattering of the family for work and play. Modern employment schedules, with work at all hours of day or night, disrupt the traditional family routines and subject millions of families to temptations unknown to our grandparents. In numerous subtle ways the conditions of modern life tend to break down traditional controls and to increase temptations; for example, the mere fact that one passes jewelry stores and auto salesrooms instead of brooks and fence rows on the way to work probably serves to increase wants and temptations. For the first time in history, a society is expending great energies, through advertising and salesmanship, in the deliberate encouragement of people to want more than they can possibly get. Although advertising and salesmanship doubtless are necessary parts of our economic system, this mass promotion of unlimited wants is a development whose impact is only beginning to become apparent. Many of the traditional values, such as thrift, simplicity of life, and pride in craftsmanship, become increasingly remote as the urge for "conspicuous consumption" is nursed into full bloom.

Social change produces many new situations and practices for which the traditional mores have no clear-cut guide. Although the existing mores clearly condemn murder or rape and clearly support private property and marriage, they provide no positive definitions concerning the propriety of labor unions, selling watered stock, or the set-back requirements for a skyscraper. In order to regulate such technical matters, thousands of laws have been passed without any strongly supporting mores attached. There are too many such technical matters, they have developed too rapidly, and are too complicated for any coherent set of moral definitions to have crystallized and preceded the passing of the law. Such laws which are not buttressed by a strong supporting morality are difficult to enforce; neither the violator, the enforcement officials, nor the public view these violations very seriously, but are likely to dismiss them lightly as minor administrative errors instead of criminal acts. Severe punishments for such technical violations probably would be unwise, yet it remains likely that widespread violation and lax enforcement of certain laws tends to break down the habit of obedience to law in general.

Social change also produces new interest groupings of people and alters the complexion of old ones. New occupations appear, new industries arise, new recreational groups develop, and new pressure groups of all sorts are constantly being organized. A constant battle rages for position and power, in which the law is often violated. Again, the existing morality often provides no clear-cut guides. Is the wire-tapper, who secretly (and illegally) records telephone conversations for the use of police, politicians, business competitors, suspicious husbands, or sometimes blackmailers, a menace or a benefactor? Should corporations or labor unions be permitted to make contributions to political campaign funds? Should the "closed shop" and "industry-wide bargaining" be viewed as labor rights or labor abuses? The rise of new interest groups always produces considerable new legislation and considerable confusion.

Another disorganizing feature of American life is found in its ethnic heterogeneity—in the variety of racial and national backgrounds represented among the American people. Settled by a mixture of peoples, America has never possessed an integrated cultural tradition. Immigration during the past century brought a heavy infusion of Slavic and Latin elements into the predominantly Anglo-Saxon culture, resulting in increased cultural conflict and confusion. Many of our value-conflicts stem from the clash of cultural backgrounds—for example, Catholic-Protestant disagreement over gambling, or over relations of church and state. In this clash of cultural backgrounds, each cultural tradition loses some of its power to control the behavior of individuals. The high crime rates of second-generation immigrants reflect the assimilation problems which they confront. With parental authority undermined by the clash of cultures, the immigrant's child readily absorbs the delinquent patterns of the slum areas in which most immigrants live. With the virtual disappearance of immigration, this problem rapidly fades, but the lack of a single coherent cultural tradition will continue to create moral confusion for generations.

Of all the approaches to the crime problem, sociologists have made most use of the social-disorganization approach. It provides a very plausible explanation for much criminal behavior. The high crime rates of disorganized groups, such as second-generation immigrants or the American Indians, and the increase of crime in war-devastated countries, clearly show how social disorganization is accompanied by a high crime rate. Yet no one approach gives a complete picture. The social-disorganization approach indicates the conditions under which crime may be expected to increase or decrease; the value-conflict approach reveals how people may rationalize and justify their criminal behavior; the individual-deviation approach helps understand why some become more criminal than others.

SOME POPULAR PROPOSALS FOR TREATMENT

1. Severe Punishment

Each "crime wave" produces a backwash of clamor for more severe punishment. A string of murders arouses a cry for the death penalty among people who do not realize that the homicide rate in states having the death penalty is approximately three times as high as in states without it.[9] This clamor for punishment is understandable, if not scientific. There are *three conventional reasons for punishment—revenge, reformation, and deterrence.* Although punishment for revenge may have been abandoned in theory, the popular thirst for revenge is brutally apparent whenever a highly revolting crime captures public attention. It is entirely respectable, however, to believe in punishment for reformation or deterrence, and meanwhile vent one's hostilities very effectively. Consequently, many people see the crime problem as simply a matter of imposing more severe punishments.

The facts about the frequency with which criminals revert to crime after being punished are revealing, if not exactly encouraging. Glueck quotes a number of studies showing that from half to three-fourths of the convicts in penal institutions have a record of at least one earlier conviction,[10]

[9] Karl F. Schuessler, "The Deterrent Influence of the Death Penalty," *The Annals,* 284 (November, 1952), pp. 54-62.

[10] Sheldon Glueck, *Crime and Justice* (Boston, Little, Brown & Company, 1936), pp. 207-209.

and that from two-thirds to four-fifths of them became officially delinquent again within five years after release.[11] Since these records are an incomplete measure of later criminality, it is reasonable to estimate that somewhere between three-fourths and nine-tenths of all criminals commit further crimes after they have been punished and presumably "reformed." And there is no evidence that states with more severe penalties have lower crime rates or recidivism rates than states with lighter penalties.

The "practical" people who continue to advocate punishment seem unaware that their proposal has had several thousand years of trial without conspicuous success. Among our oldest written documents are the Code of Hammurabi, the Book of Leviticus, and the laws of the Pharaohs, each providing exact and severe penalties for a long series of offenses. The severity of ancient and medieval punishments is beyond the comprehension of most students today. A long list of offenses were normally punished by amputation of ears, noses, hands, genitals, tearing off scalps, tearing out tongues, by branding, and by other mutilations. Severe and often fatal floggings were commonly used for relatively trivial offenses. One decree of William the Conqueror stated:[12]

We decree that no one shall be killed or hung for any misdeeds, but rather that his eyes shall be plucked out and his feet, hands, and testicles cut off, so that whatever part of his body remains will be a living sign to all of his crime and iniquity.

No historical movie begins to depict the brutality of medieval punishments, for it would sicken the patrons. These cruel punishments were finally abandoned by civilized societies and replaced with imprisonment when it became apparent to eighteenth- and nineteenth-century critics that they were ineffective.[13] One of the arguments against mutilation was that the sight of mutilated convicts had become so commonplace that it was no longer deterrent. One of the arguments leading to the abolition

[11] Sheldon and Eleanor Glueck found that 80 per cent of 510 men released between 1911 and 1922 were unreformed five years later. (*Five Hundred Criminal Careers* [New York, Alfred A. Knopf, Inc., 1930].) After ten years, 68 per cent were still unreformed. (*Later Criminal Careers* [New York, The Commonwealth Fund, 1937].) Of 1000 juvenile delinquents, 88 per cent were delinquent after five years; after fifteen years, 37 per cent were nondelinquent, 30 per cent were serious delinquents, and 33 per cent were minor delinquents. (*Juvenile Delinquents Grown Up* [New York, The Commonwealth Fund, 1940].) Of 500 delinquent women, 76 per cent were again delinquent during a five-year period. (*Five Hundred Delinquent Women* [New York, Alfred A. Knopf, Inc., 1934].) All these studies were made upon convicts released from the Massachusetts penal system, probably a much better-than-average system. Numerous recidivism studies are summarized in George B. Vold, "Does the Prison Reform?" *The Annals*, 293 (May, 1954), pp. 42-50, with the conclusion that from 60 to 80 per cent of the offenders receive further convictions.

[12] Barnes and Teeters, *op. cit.*, p. 344.

[13] Cf. Dr. Benjamin Rush, *An Inquiry into the Effects of Public Punishments upon Criminals and upon Society* (Philadelphia, 1787). Quoted in Barnes and Teeters, *op. cit.*, p. 346.

of public hangings was the claim that, at the very moment when the trap was being sprung, and the observers presumably being deterred from crime by the awesome spectacle—at this moment of fascinated concentration, the pickpockets and thieves were the busiest. It almost seemed as though public hangings produced more crime than they prevented.

It becomes more clear why punishment is relatively ineffective if the different kinds of criminals are again considered. Since "legalistic" criminals have no criminal intent, deterrence is impossible and reformation unnecessary. Severe punishment of "moralistic" criminals (excepting certain sex offenders) is impractical, for our society will not tolerate strict enforcement of these widely violated laws. Punishment of "psychopathic" criminals is repugnant to all who realize that the psychopath is emotionally incapable of directing his behavior and that punishment will neither reform nor deter him. The "institutional" criminals form another group which society will not allow to be severely punished; furthermore, since this "criminal" and his associates agree in justifying his behavior, punishment will not make him penitent, but only bitter. The "situational" criminals need no reformation, since their life organization is not criminal and their crimes are committed only under desperate circumstances wherein it is unlikely that any threats of punishment would deter them. The "habitual" criminals are generally ineffectual, unstable personalities, repeatedly surrendering to impulse or getting into "desperate" jams; they are unlikely to be deterred by some remote punishment, nor will punishment transform them into well-integrated or responsible personalities. The "professional" criminal discounts the likelihood of punishment. There is no evidence in the life histories of professional criminals to indicate that they gave much thought to the possibility of punishment during their apprenticeship; nor do the life histories of law-abiding folk show that they ever seriously considered a criminal career and recoiled from it through fear of punishment. Neither is there any convincing evidence that many professionals have actually been reformed through punishment, although it may be that some are reformed in spite of it. It would seem that an examination of the values, motivations, and life organization of each type of criminal reveals none for which punishment is likely to prove either deterrent or reformatory.

This misplaced faith in punishment may rest upon the unrealistic assumption that people consciously *decide* whether to be criminal—that they consider a criminal career or a criminal act, rationally balance its dangers against its rewards, and arrive at a decision based upon such pleasure-pain calculations. It supposedly follows that if the pain element is increased by severe punishments, people will turn from crime to righteousness. A little reflection reveals the absurdity of this notion. How many of the readers of this textbook can recall when they seriously considered a criminal career, not as a vague daydream but as a concrete possibility? How many weighed this possibility and, after balancing all the considerations, "decided" against it? For most law-abiding citizens this decision is not a conscious, rational choice, thoughtfully made at some crucial moment; it is an unconsciously-developed way of life, a set of values, and a group of expectations, all emerging from the thousands of events and incidents forming their social experience. Nor is it any more likely that the professional criminal ever makes such a conscious choice. For him, too, the "decision" is a gradual, imperceptible crystallization of habits and values which emerge from the totality of his social experience. For him, the question of *whether* to commit crimes has never arisen; the only question is one of *how* to commit them most profitably. Just as most people "decide" whether to be Catholic or Protestant without having to think it over at all, so do most people decide whether to be criminal or noncriminal. Since a rational choice between criminal and noncriminal careers is rare, deterrence is unnecessary for the law-abiding and ineffective upon the criminal.

For all these reasons, criminologists and penologists agree in doubting the effectiveness of punishment either as a deterrent or as a means of reformation. One distinguished criminologist even draws the startling conclusion that punishment leaves a man seven times more likely to commit further crime than those convicts treated in some other manner.[14] This conclusion is supported by the informal testimony of many criminals, of which the following, related by a famous warden, is typical.[15]

Before Morris Wasser's execution, when I told him the governor had refused him a last-minute respite, he said bitterly: "All right, Warden. It doesn't make much difference what I say now about this here system of burning a guy, but I want to set you straight on something."

"What's that?" I asked.

"Well, this electrocution business is the bunk. It don't do no good, I tell you, and I know, because I never thought of the chair when I plugged that old guy. And I'd probably do it again if he had me on the wrong end of a rod."

"You mean," I said, "that you don't feel you've done wrong in taking another man's life?"

"No, Warden, it ain't that," he said impatiently. "I mean that you just don't think of the hot seat when you plug a guy. Somethin' inside you just makes you kill, 'cause you know if you don't shut him up it's curtains for you."

"I see. Then you never even thought of what would happen to you at the time."

"Hell, no! And lots of other guys in here, Harry and Brick and Luke, all says the same thing. I tell you the hot seat will never stop a guy from pullin' a trigger." That was Wasser's theory, and I've heard it echoed many times since.

14 Thorsten Sellin, quoted in Barnes and Teeters, *op. cit.*, p. 74.
15 Lewis E. Lawes, *Meet the Murderer* (New York, Harper and Brothers, 1940), pp. 178-179.

2. Better Law Enforcement

The popular faith in punishment is coupled with an equally blind faith in law enforcement as a means of reducing crime. The *immediate* effect of better law enforcement, however, would be to increase crime *rates,* since many unreported crimes and unidentified criminals would be added to the crime statistics. The long-run effects are more difficult to measure.

It is possible that the popular faith in law enforcement is not entirely misplaced. It is a fact that organized crime cannot long survive determined law enforcement. It is probable that the relative immunity enjoyed by many professional criminals helps encourage youths to follow suit. The wholesale violation of many rarely-enforced laws may tend to undermine respect for law in general. It is quite likely, therefore, that more effective law enforcement would eventually reduce the amount of crime committed while perhaps increasing the number of criminals apprehended and under treatment. A *certainty* of punishment would probably be a more effective deterrent than severity of possible punishment. If prompt punishment were absolutely certain, there might be few crimes except those of accident, compulsion, or passion.

The unreality of this proposal lies in the difficulty of securing better enforcement. There are many laws which the public is unwilling to repeal, yet unwilling to enforce. The public calls for honest officials, but gives them little support.[16] The public desires a competent police force, but is unwilling to bear the financial cost of one. Our localistic bias prevents us from organizing the competing and overlapping police agencies of an area into an effectively integrated unit. We are concerned about police corruption, but not concerned enough to provide a form of city government that makes a politically-independent police force more easily attainable. Although better law enforcement might prove effective, there is little prospect of any sudden changes. Meanwhile, gradual improvement in police organization and efficiency is discernible.

3. Education

The plea to "build schools instead of jails" is doubtless a fine idea, but a doubtful cure for the crime problem. *More* education of the conventional sort will not reduce crime, for there is no conclusive evidence that poorly-educated people are more criminal than high-school or college graduates, even though the highly-educated are less frequently caught. It is possible, however, that the *kind* of schools we have may affect delinquency and crime. It is plausible to argue that a school with an indifferent staff, a dull and unchallenging curriculum, and a slender program of activities offers no help to an unadjusted child and may drive him to truancy and

[16] See Anonymous, "Are You *Sure* You Want an Honest Mayor?" *Collier's,* 132 (October 30, 1953), pp. 64 ff.

the influences of street life. There can be no doubt that a fully adequate school has many opportunities to aid in the development of well-adjusted personalities and in the guidance of poorly-adjusted ones. Since the school has regular supervision of nearly all children, it is the institution through which guidance and counseling can most easily be arranged. The effectiveness of such services in reducing delinquency and the degree of success with which schools are employing them are not known. Concrete evidence of the effectiveness of superior schools in controlling delinquency is lacking, except in a few isolated instances. Meanwhile, the overcrowding and understaffing of our public schools at present is less than encouraging. The proportion of students taught in substandard schools by substandard teachers remains high, so the possible contributions of the school will for some years remain largely unrealized.

4. Religion

Many assert that our crime rates rise because we have "forgotten God," and that only a "return to faith" will lower them. Just wherein we have "forgotten God" is not clear, since church membership, participation, and financial support appear to be at record levels.

Few would doubt that if all Americans were good Christians (or good Jews, or good humanists) all of the time, there would be little crime. It is equally clear that no church has succeeded in getting all of its members to act like good Christians all of the time. In fact, it is by no means clear that church members are much more law-abiding than nonmembers.

There is a remarkable lack of carefully-controlled comparisons of the behavior of members and nonmembers. The famous Hartshorne-May studies of the honesty of children found no significant behavior differences between children who attended Sunday School and those who did not.[17] Although this study is neither recent nor conclusive, it does raise questions about the effectiveness of traditional religious education as a behavior control.

Religious education as a means of crime control is limited in at least two ways: first, the church is unable to reach half of each generation of children at all and has only fleeting contact with many of the remaining half; second, there is no clear evidence that the church has effective techniques of preventing delinquency among those it does reach. While it is known that church-connected children are less likely to be recorded as delinquent, this does not prove that their actual delinquency is less than that of other children of the same social class. Neither does it

[17] Hugh Hartshorne and Mark A. Way, Studies in Deceit (New York, The Macmillan Company, 1930). They conclude, "Attendance at Sunday School or membership in at least two organizations which aim to teach honesty does not seem to change behavior in this regard, and in some instances there is evidence that it makes children less rather than more honest." p. 15,

separate cause from effect—it does not indicate whether the "good" children are good because they go to church, or whether they go to church because they are good children. In other words, lower crime rates among church people may be true because the church *attracts* the conventional and orderly folk rather than because it *produces* them. In the absence of more detailed and carefully-controlled research, nothing conclusive is known about the relation of church membership and criminal behavior.

The suggestion that religious education be promoted by, or in co-operation with, the public schools is attracting considerable interest, and is often presented as a means of delinquency control. There is an almost total lack of evidence to support this belief, and few if any criminologists are convinced that such a program would have an appreciable effect upon delinquency.

SOME PROFESSIONAL PROPOSALS FOR TREATMENT

1. *Legal Reforms*

Criminologists, penologists, and leaders in the legal profession are in considerable agreement upon a number of suggestions, including the following:

a. Revision of the Criminal Law. Present laws make crimes of many trivial and harmless acts, and most people agree that the legal code should be cleared of a considerable clutter of outmoded legislation. Laws that treat alcoholics and drug addicts as conventional criminals are outmoded. Some progress has been made in treating drug addicts as medical and psychiatric problems, but alcoholics are still ordinarily given a futile succession of jail sentences. All experts agree that special provision should be made for all psychopathic offenders—pyromaniacs, kleptomaniacs, sex deviants, and others. Only a few states have such laws, and even these often fail to follow the special procedures provided for such offenders.

b. Revision of the Jury System. It is widely felt that whatever justice we enjoy is secured not because of the jury system but in spite of it. It is argued that the method of selecting and excusing jurors now operates to eliminate most of those who are well educated, who have important business, or who impress the lawyers as uncomfortably intelligent and critical, leaving the average jury composed mostly of average or below-average persons, semiliterates, and loafers. This jury views an elaborate stage show, with carefully-rehearsed witnesses and with every possible appeal to the vanities, prejudices, and gullibilities of the jury serving as substitutes for a rational weighing of evidence.[18] To correct this travesty

[18] See Barnes and Teeters, *op. cit.*, Ch. XIV, "The Jury Trial"; J. Warren Madden, "Is Justice Blind?" *The Annals*, 280 (November, 1952), pp. 60-66.

is suggested either (1) the replacement of the jury by one or more judges who weigh evidence and render decision, or (2) a revised method of jury selection to insure a higher proportion of educated and intelligent members. Either method would probably be an improvement, for although juries probably convict few who are innocent, there is little doubt that they free many who are guilty.

c. *The Indeterminate Sentence.* Since no judge can possibly know how long it will take to reform a convict, the *limited indeterminate sentence* (such as one-to-five years, or three-to-ten years) is now practically universal in America. This permits a prisoner to be freed after serving the minimum term, or to be held for the full term if prison and parole officials think advisable. But even under the limited indeterminate sentence the prisoner must serve the minimum term whether he needs it or not, and he must be freed at the end of the term whether reformed or not. Penologists believe that for every prisoner who is ever worthy of release, there is a certain moment in his development when he is ready to be released; to release him before this moment, or retain him after it is reached, is to invite failure. So there is considerable support for a *fully indeterminate* sentence, under which a convict is committed for no specified period, to be released whenever prison and parole officials consider him ready for release. Since such a program could easily be abused, it would require a professionally trained prison staff and an incorruptible, politically-independent parole board for its successful operation.

2. Penal Reforms

There is no such thing as a really *good* prison. To remove a man from all stabilizing contacts with family, friends, job, and community and isolate him among a choice selection of our poorest citizens, in an environment to which he can adjust only by forgetting most of the habits necessary to normal adjustment on the outside—to do all this and then hope that the convict will somehow purge himself of bitterness, adopt a conventional value-system, and be prepared to resume family life and useful citizenship upon his release is to expect a miracle. One can scarcely learn conventional behavior patterns by being isolated from them. The facts are that prison tends to brutalize convicts. Their vocational skills deteriorate, their family life is interrupted, and all the routine habits of living and taking care of one's self become inoperative. Instead the inmate receives a graduate course in criminal skills and attitudes, often develops homosexual practices or other sexual deviations, and ordinarily learns nothing that will be useful in a noncriminal career.[19]

[19] See Victor Nelson, *Prison Days and Nights* (Boston, Little, Brown & Company, 1932); also Norman Hayner and Ellis Ash, "The Prison as a Community," *American Sociological Review,* 5 (August, 1950), pp. 577-583.

Upon release, he must forget prison habits and resume the forgotten ones necessary to making a living and operating a family, and meanwhile overcome the stigma of an "ex-convict." [20] The disorganization of prison life is indicated by English studies showing that mental disease rates of prisoners are positively correlated with length of time in prison.[21] The demoralization of prison life is further suggested by the fact that much recidivism takes the form of petty crime instead of major crime.[22] It seems that long imprisonment unfits one to be either a good citizen or a good criminal. All prisons are bad, and their futility is widely recognized. The public continues to support them because it can think of nothing else to do with its criminals. That locking them up is no solution, however, is clear when we remember that in an average of less than two years each will be released,[23] usually worse than when he entered, while even those sentenced to "life imprisonment" are released after an average of ten years.[24]

All prisons are bad; some are incomparably worse than others. Wretched food, filthy quarters, indifferent medical care, brutal and sadistic guards, lack of any educational or training program, and a demoralizing system of convict "self-government" by the more vicious of the convicts—all these conditions are still common in many American prisons, although considerable improvement has occurred. To most people, "prison reform" means correcting these things—providing good food, decent medical care, humane guards, clean quarters, and an educational program. Adequate financing and enlightened administrators can easily accomplish these things, yet many prisons still lack them, and there is scarcely a prison in the country which is not so overcrowded as to place any serious attempts at reformation under a severe handicap.

But there are certain basic features that make prison life demoralizing no matter how good the food or humane the treatment. The sex starvation, monotonous routine, isolation from conventional behavior patterns, lack of opportunity for self-direction, and stigmatizing of the convict as "criminal"—all these are unchangeable features of prison life. For the vast majority of inmates, prison brings a demoralization which the most enlightened warden cannot possibly change.

Since prisons do not reform, it would seem logical to abolish them, at least for those whom there is any hope of reforming. It would seem sensible to use conventional prisons only for those whom there is little hope of reforming, imprisoning them permanently for the protection of

[20] See Frank O'Leary, "The Twilight World of the Ex-Convict," *Reporter*, 10 (June 8, 1954), pp. 38-40.

[21] Stephen Hobhouse and A. F. Brockway, *English Prisons Today* (New York, Longmans, Green & Company, 1922).

[22] Sheldon Glueck and Eleanor T. Glueck, *Later Criminal Careers*, pp. 121, 350.

[23] Elliott, *op. cit.*, p. 730.

[24] Alfred M. Harries, "How Long Is a Life Sentence for Murder?" *Proceedings*, American Prison Association (1939), pp. 513-524.

society. Since prisons are more likely to corrupt and demoralize than to reform, it would seem to follow that *no one who is expected to reform should remain in prison for any great length of time.* If not prison, then what? There are at least two practical alternatives: probation, and various sorts of minimum security institutions with generous parole.

Under *probation,* the convict's sentence is suspended provided he stays out of trouble for a specified period of time, during which the probation officer checks upon his activities. The probation officer supposedly functions as a guide and counselor, helping the convict to work out a more successful life organization. This task requires a person who combines professional social casework training with certain qualities of personality that relatively few people possess. Inasmuch as many communities pay their probation officers less than they pay their janitors and truck drivers, it is not surprising that the probation officer is sometimes a political hack, a semiliterate ignoramus, or a well-meaning but incompetent busybody. In other instances a well-trained probation officer is given such a heavy case load that he can do little more than keep an address file of his probationers. Since it costs several thousands of dollars to convict each criminal and costs (in 1949) some $3.12 a day to keep him in a federal prison and only about 18 cents a day for probation supervision,[25] our niggardly probation programs are revealed as penny-wise-pound-foolish. Probation is generally sucessful in from 70 to 80 per cent of the cases,[26] and there is perhaps no place where there are better prospects for eventual savings than through a professionally-adequate probation program. This would involve paying probation officers something more than factory workers, and setting case loads which make genuine individual casework possible.

Minimum security institutions are those in which walls and locks are partly replaced by the cultivation of intelligent self-direction by the convict. Prison farms and work camps are the most familiar examples, but any institution that places emphasis upon self-direction and personal responsibility instead of locks and iron bars is a minimum security institution. Whereas a conventional (maximum security) prison concentrates upon keeping the prisoners from escaping, the minimum security institution must emphasize rehabilitation, for the inmates will walk away if they see no reason for remaining. Minimum security institutions do have gates and fences, but anyone who wants to break out has little difficulty in doing so.

Since minimum security institutions are not pervaded with the preven-

<hr />

[25] Richard A. Chappell, "The Federal Probation System Today," *Federal Probation,* 14 (June, 1950), pp. 30-40.
[26] According to a United Nations survey of probation in Britain, Denmark, Norway, Sweden, the Netherlands, and the United States. (*New York Times,* August 29, 1954, p. 19.)

tion-of-escape atmosphere, it is simpler to arrange brief furloughs or temporary releases for visiting one's family, thereby keeping contact with family and community and helping prevent the loss of routine life habits. Many variations of part-time custody are possible in a minimum security institution, although such plans are not yet widely used. Most of the inherent defects of a conventional prison can either be eliminated or greatly reduced in the minimum security institution.

There are other suggestions for improving penal treatment. The *classification program* aims to separate the hardened professionals from those for whom there are prospects of reform. Although the suggestion for classification and segregation of hardened offenders is at least a hundred years old, the perennial overcrowding and understaffing of most penal institutions means that the classification program is often little more than a pious hope. The *educational program* is nonexistent in some institutions and chronically neglected in many of the remainder. Realistic vocational education is expensive, so prison workshops are operated mainly to supply the needs of the prison, not to train the prisoners. Academic education is cheaper but is not highly appreciated by most convicts. The *local jail*, often a filthy, vermin-ridden dungeon, and nearly always a human wastebasket filled with all kinds and degrees of offenders—thieves, murderers, sex deviants, and bums, mixed with traffic violators, drunks, and wide-eyed first offenders and suspects awaiting trial—is widely regarded as a source of criminal contagion.[27] Suggestions for dealing with the jail nuisance [28] are as obvious as is our general failure to do anything about it.

3. Guidance and Counseling Programs

Since many adult criminals were more or less delinquent as children, the suggestion for a comprehensive guidance and counseling program is a logical one, with the school probably the most convenient place to locate it. There is some scientific evidence concerning the effectiveness of such programs in reducing delinquency,[29] and an impressive array of educational, criminological, and psychiatric opinion supports them.

If a child is harassed by fears, anxieties, and insecurities, professional

---

[27] See Joseph F. Fishman, *Crucibles of Crime* (New York, Cosmopolis Press, 1923); Austin H. McCormick, "Children in Our Jails," *The Annals,* 261 (January, 1949), pp. 150-157.

[28] *Proceedings,* American Prison Association (1937), p. 320; Roy Casey, "Catchall Jails," *The Annals,* 293 (May, 1954), pp. 28-34.

[29] One study (Elise Martens and Helen Ross, *The Adjustment of Behavior Problems of School Children* [Washington, U. S. Office of Education, 1932]) reports a 20 per cent reduction in misbehavior of problem children who were treated and no reduction in those not treated. Healy and Bronner (*Treatment and What Happened Afterward* [Boston, Judge Baker Foundation Center], p. 42) reported favorable results in 70 per cent of the delinquents receiving psychiatric interviews.

counseling may relieve him. If his well-meaning parents lack understanding, a counseling program may show them how to handle their children more wisely. If a child is lonely and rejected, counseling may help teach him how to gain acceptance among his group. If he has sex anxieties, counseling may provide needed orientation and assurance. Because unsolved problems of these sorts frequently appear in the life histories of criminals, professional treatment of them may help reduce criminal behavior.

A guidance and counseling program is less effective wherever delinquency is a normal aspect of the local culture, as in the high-delinquency slum. Delinquency in a slum child does *not* denote maladjustment; delinquent behavior is a normal adjustment pattern in his social world. The counseling program rests upon the assumption that delinquency stems from compensatory strivings of the frustrated, maladjusted child, groping for some means of release or satisfaction. This assumption correctly applies to many middle-class delinquents, but not to those in whose social world delinquency is normal. Nor can the counseling program be expected to prevent much institutional or white-collar crime, or any other form of crime indulged in by normal, well-adjusted people. It is only where crime is a compensatory response of frustrated people that the counseling services are likely to be effective. "Problem" children in school, incipient sex deviants, drug addicts, chronic alcoholics, and certain other emotionally disturbed offenders represent the most promising opportunities for guidance and counseling, from various sources ranging from the classroom teacher to the psychiatrist.

Many school systems have a guidance and counseling program of some sort, often using the services of psychiatrists, psychologists, social caseworkers, and other specialists working with the classroom teacher. Children with problems can be located and aided in developing a well-adjusted personality before they have become psychotic or seriously delinquent. Almost without exception these programs are understaffed and overworked, and can treat only a few of those who might benefit from treatment, while still fewer counseling services are readily available to adults. This is especially true in the case of sex deviants. Although sixteen states had sexual-psychopath laws by 1952, most of them make no provision for treatment and neglect preventative work.[30] In scarcely any jurisdictions is there any systematic provision for psychiatric examination and treatment of sex deviants *before* they have committed serious sex crimes, and surprisingly few jurisdictions even make systematic provision for treatment after serious sex crimes have occurred. While counseling programs of various sorts offer our best prospects for the prevention of certain sorts of crime, the almost universal lack of legal authorization,

[30] Manfred Guttmacher and Henry Weihofen, "Sex Offenders," *Journal of Criminal Law, Criminology, and Police Science*, 43 (July-August, 1952), pp. 153-175.

funds, and staff for an adequate program means that this opportunity is largely wasted. Until such time as our society is willing to finance an adequate counseling program, these crimes will continue unabated, and news items like the following will appear with monotonous regularity.[31]

The grand jury voted six true bills against Theodore Schermerhorn, 25, confessed "walking doll" molester of little girls. . . . Meanwhile, the *Sun-Times* learned that careful court surveillance, plus psychiatric treatments, was recommended for Schermerhorn as long ago as May 29, 1947 . . . [when he] was examined by the Psychiatric Institute of the Municipal Court . . . [at which time] psychiatrists learned, that, when he was 14 years old, Schermerhorn had been caught molesting a young girl. . . . Dr. Theodore Dulin of the institute staff made the recommendation for surveillance and treatment at that time [1947]. Dr. Edward Kelleher, director of the institute, said there was no record that the man had ever received the treatment and attention called for. "This happens to us repeatedly," said Dr. Kelleher. "Too often we are forced into the position of saying, 'We told you so'."

4. Social Group Work

Boy Scouts, Girl Scouts, Y.M.C.A., Y.W.C.A., summer camps and playgrounds, and other organized activities are widely supported as means of delinquency prevention. It is not known to what extent these activities actually prevent delinquency or merely attract the nondelinquent. Nevertheless, these activities are widely supported by both laymen and specialists.

Aside from their other possible values, social-group activities under the leadership of a skilled leader offer strategic opportunities for aiding in personality development and, indirectly, in crime prevention. Such activities provide the leader with many opportunities to locate children with problems and to help them develop ways of meeting them. The leader can gently draw the shy, inadequate child into more active group participation; he can help the rejected child find better ways of seeking group acceptance; he can manipulate the group in such a way that the bully and the "prima donna" are trapped and disciplined by the group, and thus taught the necessity for consideration and self-control; he can guide the normal energies and exploratory interests of young people into acceptable and constructive activities. To the extent that the group leader is able to do these things, he helps develop well-adjusted personality.

To do this, however, requires not merely an athletic director or a well-intentioned adult, but a skilled social worker who has both the personal qualities and the professional training for his task. Lack of properly qualified social-group workers seriously limits the effectiveness of present group-work activities. Meanwhile, even though the effectiveness of group

[31] *Chicago Sun-Times,* January 14, 1953, p. 3.

work as a crime preventative is undetermined, there are plausible reasons for believing that it may be helpful, and it continues to receive the support of most sociologists as a constructive measure.[32]

5. Area Rehabilitation

It is difficult to reform individuals when they live in a community whose basic characteristics produce crime. This recognition has led to attempts to change the area culture so that it will be easier for its members to behave acceptably. Area rehabilitation may be of two kinds.

a. *Physical Rehabilitation.* The effort to change area culture may focus upon the physical aspects of the area, especially housing. Although housing is not the sole "cause" of delinquency, every study yet made shows a striking association between substandard housing and delinquency rates. There is also considerable evidence that when slum people are moved into adequate housing, delinquency rates decline significantly. One study cites a delinquency rate seven times as high in the adjacent slum area as that among the residents of a slum-clearance housing project.[33] Another shows delinquency rates in a slum-clearance housing project to be less than half those of the entire city.[34] Another shows delinquency rates for a group of 317 slum families dropping almost one-half after moving into a project.[35] One very carefully controlled study showed delinquency to be 21 per cent lower in a project than in adjacent comparable slum areas.[36] These and similar studies show quite clearly that slum clearance is accompanied by a substantial reduction in delinquency rates. Whether slum clearance can best be accomplished through public or private housing is a separate question, and one upon which there is bitter disagreement. But there can be little doubt that slum clearance, by whatever means, reduces delinquency.

b. *Social Reorganization.* A different approach aims to unite the people of the area in a joint effort to reduce delinquency and improve area life. The Back of the Yards Neighborhood Council in the stockyards area of Chicago represents a successful attempt to promote neighborhood welfare through uniting its existing groups and agencies. The Roman Catholic Church (in an area 90 per cent Catholic) and the labor unions are the main forces, joined by the local Chamber of Commerce, veterans'

[32] See National Conference on Prevention and Control of Juvenile Delinquency, *Report on Case Work–Group Work* (Washington, Government Printing Office, 1947).

[33] Cincinnati Metropolitan Housing Authority, *Tenth Annual Report,* December, 1943.

[34] Philadelphia Housing Authority, *Homes for War Workers and Families of Low Income* (July, 1941-June, 1943).

[35] Naomi Barer, "Delinquency Before, After Admission to New Haven Housing Development," *Journal of Housing,* 3 (January, 1946), p. 27.

[36] Newark Housing Authority, *Public Housing in Newark* (November, 1944).

organizations, athletic groups, and fraternal groups. The Council is made up of persons living in the area, not of outsiders; and the program is developed by them, not imposed upon them by outside agencies. Expert personnel are used as advisors, and the members of the area have developed greatly in leadership ability and in their understanding of the area's problems.

One of the eight committees works with delinquency prevention at the common-sense level. If a boy needs a job, they help him find one. Recreation centers have been established, numerous littered vacant lots have been turned into small parks and playgrounds, and young people have been invited to organize and join with older people in seeking to meet common problems. The Council has not made the mistake of promoting amateur psychiatry or amateur counseling, but it has unified an area in a successful approach to its problems on a common-sense level.[37]

The Chicago Area Project operates in a somewhat similar manner, concentrating primarily upon delinquency prevention. One writer summarizes as follows: [38]

The Chicago Area Project is founded on the idea that the roots of delinquency are to be found in the deteriorated area and that social workers (or psychiatrists and psychologists) cannot prevent delinquency. They can help in lending professional advice, but the motivation and the effort to improve a community must come largely from the people themselves. Those who live in the community set the community standards and these cannot be imposed from without. Hence the Area Project has enlisted the support of local leadership, who are organized into neighborhood committees for an orderly attack on problems. The local leaders include professional people (usually neighborhood boys who return to practice medicine, dentistry, or law in their old community), clergy, teachers, truck drivers, butchers, grocers, druggists, factory workers, and housewives.

The Area Project provides trained personnel, usually a sociologist who is interested in helping the local residents provide their children with a decent and attractive place in which to live. By and large the committee is composed of citizens whose children are growing up in the community.

Local institutions, the church and the school, parks, and health and welfare agencies are enlisted in the co-operative project, in which the social workers advise but do not direct. They are merely members of the committee. Where practicable, local trained persons are recruited for dealing with delinquents, whether as probation, parole, or truant officers.

Many activities are sponsored by the neighborhood committees of the project.

[37] See Saul D. Alinsky, "Community Analysis and Organization," *American Journal of Sociology*, 46 (May, 1941), pp. 797-808.

[38] Mabel A. Elliott, *Crime in Modern Society* (New York, Harper and Brothers, 1952), pp. 788-789. See also, Saul D. Alinsky, "Community Analysis and Organization," *American Journal of Sociology*, 46 (May, 1941), pp. 797-808; Clifford R. Shaw, *Annual Report, The Chicago Area Project, 1949-1950* (mimeographed); Chicago Area Project, *Change the Street* (Chicago, 1951); Clifford R. Shaw, Solomon Kolbein, and Richard T. McClaughry, *Bright Shadows in Bronzetown* (Chicago, University of Chicago Press, 1949).

Some are purely recreational, in the shape of community centers, camps, sports tournaments, etc. But the committees have also tried to build up the community in other ways, by promoting housing projects, community forums, adult education classes, etc. A major activity has been the rehabilitation program for delinquents or adults who are returned to the community from courts, correctional institutions, or prison. Here there is an attempt to help the child (or adult) readjust by reintegrating him into the life of the community and helping him help himself. The Chicago Area Project maintains that constructive leadership of the residents can do more to prevent delinquency than any diagnostic skills of psychiatrists or social workers. . . .

The Chicago Area Project is now organized in 10 different high-delinquency areas with 28 separate projects. . . . [In one of these projects] volunteer committees were organized, some 11 neighborhood centers and clubs were established, recreational programs were initiated, funds were recruited from public and private sources. The project itself was an experiment in democracy.

What the Chicago Area Project is doing is converting the values of a delinquency-ridden community to concepts of social responsibility and an acceptance of standards of conduct which are approved by the middle class.

These area-rehabilitation programs represent a highly practical approach to certain aspects of the crime problem. Although no approach or combination of approaches is likely to eliminate criminal behavior, delinquency rates in the areas concerned appear to be substantially lower than would normally be expected. In high-delinquency areas, such area-rehabilitation programs are probably the most effective approaches yet developed.

SUMMARY

Crime is a problem whose exact extent is not known. It probably exists in much the same degree in nearly all areas, races, and classes in the United States, although it is mainly the lower-class violators who are caught and convicted and the prevalence of "white-collar crime" has only recently become recognized. Popular thinking about crime is confused by a number of fallacies, including the notions that there is a "criminal type," a wide variety of romantic stereotypes of the criminal, the view of the criminal as necessarily abnormal, the notion of the "born criminal," the idea that poverty and broken homes cause most crime, and the assumption that the dramatic crimes are the serious ones.

A classification of criminals in terms of their motivation reveals several types—legalistic, moralistic, psychopathic, institutional, situational, habitual, and professional. As these differ greatly in motivation, each poses a different problem of treatment. The "causes" of crime seem to be mainly environmental. Sutherland's *differential-association* theory holds that one acts largely according to his contacts with favorable or unfavorable social definitions of criminal actions.

The *personal-deviation approach* sees the criminal as a deviant person who has failed to develop the conventional codes of behavior or as a maladjusted person who is unable or unwilling to follow them. The *value-conflict approach* notes that many common actions are defined as crimes because of the conflicting values of different groups, and that the numerous value-conflicts in our poorly-integrated society are inimical to effective social control. The *social-disorganization approach* shows how social change has produced these value-conflicts, and has undermined the traditional morality and control system of an earlier society.

Popular proposals for crime reduction are of dubious practical value. Punishment has proved ineffectual in both deterrence and reform. Better law enforcement might reduce crime, if it could be secured. Neither education nor religion, of the conventional sort, is likely to reach and reorient many of those who actually commit crimes.

Professional proposals include: (1) legal reform, with revision of laws, jury system, and system of sentencing; (2) penal reform, recognizing that all imprisonment is inherently injurious, and using probation, parole, and minimum security institutions for all those who are believed reformable; (3) guidance and counseling programs, especially at the school level; (4) social-group work, mainly with children and youth, and (5) area rehabilitation in deteriorated areas where criminal behavior is a normal part of the area culture. At present, crime appears to be increasing, and may continue to increase unless all of these professional proposals are vigorously employed.

SUGGESTED READINGS

ELLIOTT, Mabel A., *Crime in Modern Society* (New York, Harper and Brothers, 1952). A comprehensive, readable textbook in criminology.

GLUECK, Sheldon, and GLUECK, Eleanor T., *Unraveling Juvenile Delinquency* (Cambridge, Harvard University Press, 1951). A study of juvenile delinquents, and especially of the kinds of family experience which encourage the development of antisocial attitudes.

KEFAUVER, Estes, *Crime in America* (Garden City, Doubleday & Company, Inc., 1951). A popular summary of the findings of the famous Senate investigations into organized crime.

KEVE, Paul W., *Prison, Probation, or Parole? A Probation Officer Reports* (Minneapolis, University of Minnesota Press, 1954). The warmly human accounts of some 30 cases which the writer handled as a probation officer.

PETERSON, Virgil W., *Crime Commissions in the United States* (Chicago, Chicago Crime Commission, 1945). A report of action by various state and local crime commissions to reduce crime.

"Prisons in Transformation," *The Annals*, 293 (May, 1954). A number of articles on prisons, their operation, effects, costs, and alternatives.

SHAW, Clifford R., *The Jack-roller; A Delinquent Boy's Own Story* (Chicago, University of Chicago Press, 1930); or (with M. E. Moore), *Natural History of a Delinquent Career* (Chicago, University of Chicago Press, 1931); or (with H. P. McKay and J. F. McDonald), *Brothers in Crime* (Chicago, University of Chicago Press, 1938). Intensely interesting biographical accounts of delinquents, showing the interaction of social factors in producing delinquent behavior.

SHAW, Clifford R., KOLBEIN, Solomon, and McCLAUGHRY, Richard T., *Bright Shadows in Bronzetown* (Chicago Southside Community Committee, University of Chicago Press, 1949). A report of area improvement in a Negro district in Chicago.

SUTHERLAND, Edwin H., *White Collar Crime* (New York, The Dryden Press, 1949). A well-documented analysis of a type of crime whose importance has only recently been recognized.

THRASHER, Frederick H., *The Gang* (Chicago, University of Chicago Press, 1927). A classic study of adolescent boys' gangs in Chicago.

WHYTE, William Foote, *Street Corner Society* (Chicago, University of Chicago Press, 1943). An absorbing analysis of an urban slum, showing the integration of criminal and noncriminal activities in an area where organized crime is an accepted part of the area culture.

AUDIO-VISUAL AIDS

Boy in Court (National Probation and Parole Association, 1790 Broadway, New York), 12 minutes, sound, black and white. Shows in detail the operation of a juvenile court when a boy is brought before it.

Children of the City (British Information Services, 30 Rockefeller Plaza, New York), 30 minutes, sound, black and white. Shows working of British juvenile courts through handling of three youths in trouble.

Children on Trial (British Information Services, 30 Rockefeller Plaza, New York), 1 hour, sound, black and white. Describes juvenile delinquency and British efforts through story of three resentful and un-co-operative delinquents who eventually respond to treatment.

Prison with a Future (McGraw-Hill Book Company, Inc., Text-Film Department, 330 West 42nd, New York), 18 minutes, sound, black and white. Shows how the Reformatory for Women at Marysville, Ohio, seeks to rehabilitate its inmates.

Probation Officer (British Information Services, 30 Rockefeller Plaza, New York), 32 minutes, sound, black and white. Tells how a girl, treated unsympathetically at home, gets into difficulty and is helped by probation.

Why Did He Do It? (Columbia University, Center for Mass Communications), six 15-minute, 16-inch, 33⅓ rpm transcriptions. Impressive documentaries giving life stories of six delinquents and criminals.

QUESTIONS AND PROJECTS

1. What is a "crime"? Why is it difficult to find a fully satisfactory definition of crime?

2. Why is it difficult to determine the amount of crime or the direction of crime trends? If informed of a "crime wave," what information would be needed to tell whether the report were sound?

3. What comment would you make at hearing a reference to "the criminal class"?

4. What reason is there to doubt that crime statistics accurately indicate the "criminality" of the different social classes?

5. What is the main distinction between the professional and other types of criminals?

6. Is the "moralistic" criminal, as classified in this chapter, a product of conflicting social values or of personal moral weakness?

7. Why should substandard housing or disorganized family life be classed as "risk factors" rather than as "causes" of crime?

8. How does the differential-association theory of crime causation explain the occasional crimes by persons of "good" family and respectable associations?

9. Could all three of the approaches be used to explain the criminal behavior of the same individual? Illustrate.

10. What theories lie behind the "practical" proposal to curb crime through severe punishment? Could punishment "work" even if the theories are unsound?

11. What reasoning lies behind the limited indeterminate sentence? Does this reasoning also support the fully indeterminate sentence?

12. What may be gained through area rehabilitation which cannot be accomplished through guidance and counseling programs? Would this make guidance and counseling programs unnecessary?

CHAPTER 7

Marriage and the Family: Transitional Problems

The extensive mobility in this country has finally torn people so far from their roots that we now have probably the largest number of marriages that history has ever known of couples who have no visible reason for ever getting on together, who share no common background whatsoever, who have no common friends, no common past, not even a dog they can both remember....

For the first time we have a generation of young people who have witnessed, not necessarily in their own homes, a great deal of divorce, who are beginning to think of divorce as something that is done.... There is a large proportion to whom it still does not apply, but on the radio, in films, in the magazines, and in our urban secular communities, the idea that marriage is terminable... permeates every quarrel.... We now have set up the family, therefore, as a terminable situation.[1]

THIS short quotation goes straight to the heart of what is happening to the American family. Some people, professionals as well as laymen, conclude that the family itself is "breaking down." A less extreme, and probably more typical, reaction is that the family is an institution in trouble; that catastrophic social changes have rocked it to its very foundations. Typical symbols of present confusion are wives who "insist on wearing the pants," husbands "still tied to their mothers' apron strings," and children who use the home as a kind of human "filling station," coming home only to "gas up" on food and sleep in preparation for the next day's risky adventures far from the control of responsible adults.

MARITAL UNHAPPINESS

Practically everyone disapproves of divorce. The legislators who provide for them, the attorneys who file for them, the judges who grant them, and the men and women who get them, all are convinced that divorce is "bad." Yet the divorce rate rises steadily. In the year 1900 there was only one divorce for every thirteen marriages in the United States. By 1930 one out

[1] Margaret Mead, "What Is Happening to the American Family?" *Journal of Social Casework,* 28 (November, 1947), p. 325.

of every six marriages was ending in divorce, and by 1950 the ratio was almost one in four. The long depression of the 1930's cut down the number of divorces temporarily and the postwar 1940's brought a sizable upsurge, but after each of these major fluctuations, the long-time trend toward more divorce reasserted itself. Barring a major reversal, we may predict that over one-fourth of all future marriages will eventually end in divorce.

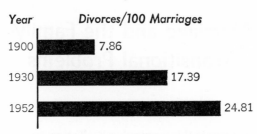

FIG. 7-1. The Increase in Divorce. (Computed from U. S. Bureau of the Census, Statistical Abstract of the United States: 1954 [Washington], p. 59; and The World Almanac, 1954 [New York], p. 310)

Startling as these divorce figures are, they do not tell the whole story. They simply indicate the number of marriages which are completely dissolved in the eyes of the law. Many families break down without benefit of law. Especially among lower income groups (in 1950, nearly 12 per cent of U. S. families earned less than $1000) husbands often simply leave their families and never return. By its very nature, there are no accurate statistics on the number of such desertions. Unless the deserted family turns to a social agency for help or police are enlisted to find the missing spouse, there is likely to be no official record of the desertion having occurred. Certainly the deserting husband will not call the matter to anyone's attention! It is variously estimated that there are about one-fourth as many desertions as divorces in the United States. At present this means approximately 100,000 cases of desertion annually.[2]

This kind of desertion should not be confused with another kind of *fictitious* desertion that is often a prelude to divorce. In states where divorces are granted for desertion or gross neglect, many couples agree to live apart for the prescribed period in order to have legal grounds for divorce. There are reported instances of "deserted" persons living "across the hall" or "down the street" from their spouses. That many cases of so-called desertion do not involve actual physical disappearance of the husband is indicated by the findings of a recent study that "... husbands and wives were still living in the same household in about one-third of Philadelphia desertion and nonsupport cases."[3] The same

[2] Ray E. Baber, *Marriage and the Family* (New York, McGraw-Hill Book Company, Inc., 1953), pp. 493-494.

[3] William N. Kephart and Thomas P. Monahan, "Desertion and Divorce in Philadelphia," *American Sociological Review,* 17 (December, 1952), p. 719.

study also reports that over the past thirty years, the number of new desertion and nonsupport cases in the Philadelphia courts has been almost double the number of divorces granted during that period.[4] There is unquestionably a great deal of overlap between bona fide and fictitious desertion and between desertion and divorce cases, but many cases of desertion never reach the divorce courts.

Together desertion and divorce account for the breakdown of approximately a half million American marriages each year. To get an accurate picture of the number of marriages actually broken each year, however, there would have to be added an undetermined number of marriages where the spouses agree to separate without any intention of either going back together again or ever securing a divorce. One insurance company estimated, in 1947, that two million spouses were separated from one another without having been divorced.[5] Middle-class and professional people often resort to such separation in order to avoid the scandal of divorce. Also, some religions prohibit divorce but do permit separation when the marital situation becomes intolerable. Approximately half our states provide for formal *legal separation* under the supervision of the courts. Such legal separation may be instituted at the request of the married couple or upon the order of the court. The couple are still married to one another, but they are forbidden to live together and the husband must contribute a specified amount for the support of the wife and children. Neither in such separations nor in desertion has the marriage actually been dissolved, but families are certainly broken when their members no longer live together.

No one knows just how many married couples are unhappy and dissatisfied. Studies of the matter have generally shown the vast majority to be fairly well satisfied and only 20 or 25 per cent to be definitely unhappy.[6] Yet if some 25 per cent eventually seek divorce, logic and common sense suggest that the number who are unhappy must be far greater. One possibility is that, when reporting to investigators, people overestimate their happiness and underestimate the seriousness of their problems. If people thus fool themselves, however, they must also fool their friends, for estimates of the happiness of a marriage by the couples' friends tend to correlate highly with the couples' own ratings. Another distinct possibility is that the degree of happiness and satisfaction in marriage is not a constant. Most everyone expects to be happy in marriage and most people do achieve some happiness. But as marriage continues, new adjustment problems keep cropping up. After a couple have ironed out their initial differences and worked out a *modus operandi* along come children,

[4] *Ibid.*

[5] Harriet F. Pilpel and Theodora Zavin, *Your Marriage and the Law* (New York, Rinehart and Company, 1952), p. 300.

[6] Ernest W. Burgess and Leonard S. Cottrell, *Predicting Success or Failure in Marriage* (New York, Prentice-Hall, Inc., 1939), p. 32.

aged and infirm parents, and with the demands created by these, recognition of insufficient income. Unfortunately, American culture does not have any one set of rules on how to discipline one's children or how to give them the proper religious background, on how to deal with aged and dependent parents, or just what to do when the wife decides that she ought to go to work. In more theoretical terms, the traditional roles which men, women, parents, and children play in this society have been changing. In trying to adapt to these changing roles, families inevitably encounter some frustration and, often, more or less prolonged conflict.

CHANGED ROLES

Man's traditional right to "wear the pants in the family" shows signs of being replaced by a "His-Hers" arrangement such as that found on guest towels and pillow slips. The uncertainty as to who-should-play-what-role is possibly greatest in the husband-wife relationship, but similar problems plague other family members from teen-agers to grandparents.

Women's Roles

Woman's place today is in the office and factory as well as in the home. Nor is it just single women, for by 1949 over half of all employed women were married. Not that single women are less employed, for the number of single women in industry has increased steadily. But the number of married women working has increased even faster. Working *before* marriage has been modified to include working *after* marriage and working *instead of* marriage.

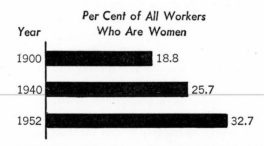

FIG. 7-2. The Increase in Women Workers. (Women's Bureau, *Handbook of Facts on Women Workers*, Bulletin 242, 1952, p. 1)

The revolution in women's roles goes far beyond the mere facts of women working, however. Women no longer have to fit into the wife and mother role, but face a bewildering number of alternatives. The most basic choice of all permits women to marry or to avoid marriage if they prefer. Financial independence of males is possible for most women, and at least that broad group of women whom we generally label as middle class are consciously prepared in high school and college to earn a living after graduation. Given this possibility, some women deliberately choose not to marry. Many others never actually choose to remain single, but because of their financial independence are able to reject specific suitors until largely by default they have drifted into spinsterhood.

Within marriage many different roles are possible. The ever-present concern of young people to know whether it is possible to combine marriage and a career attests to the wife as an economic *partner* in marriage. It is probable again that most of the wives who work are not career women in the conventional sense. Most young women now work during the early years of marriage but drift into a fairly conventional housewife pattern following the birth of their children. Some of these women go back to work, part or full time, after their children are in school or after they have grown up and left home. Gradually rising life expectancies mean more years of active life beyond the childbearing period and more and more middle-aged women suddenly find themselves with too little useful work to do.

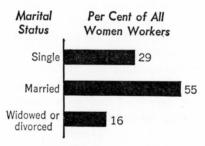

FIG. 7-3. Marital Status of Employed Women. (Women's Bureau, *Handbook of Facts on Women Workers*, Bulletin 242, 1952, p. 17)

From the very beginning, the working wife faces a dilemma. Employers are reluctant to hire her for occupations with a future because of the probability that she will soon be having children and the time and money spent training her will be wasted. Consequently, even professionally trained young women are forced to settle for positions as stenographers, clerks, sales persons, and similar "fill-in" jobs. After a few years of this work and from six to twenty or more years spent rearing their children, very few women can quickly pick up and use their earlier professional training. After all the effort in high school and college, women with grown families find themselves a drag on the labor market and prepared for only the most menial of jobs.

Whether she works or not, the modern wife is apt to find that she faces multiple expectations in marriage for which she is only partly prepared. Moreover, many of her roles are flatly contradictory. She is taught that she must be a good wife but that she has equal rights with her husband, that she should bear children but that she should keep her figure, that she should like to sew and wash dishes but be capable of entering a profession, that she should be a home-body but also a clever hostess, that she should be modest and unassuming but able to keep her husband's interest, that she should be frugal and thrifty but dressed in excellent taste. How are such contradictions to be reconciled and what role or roles can married women play? How well adapted will the clever, glamorous college girl be to scrubbing floors and changing diapers? For that matter, how well adapted is she to play *any one role* in life? She is likely to have some desire, or compulsion, to follow in her mother's footsteps. Also she will likely have acquired notions that her mother's role is "old fashioned," or degrading, or just plain boring. She probably will want to "make something of herself" but also to have children, to stand on a par with her husband but to expect "chivalrous" courtesies from him. She will probably be ambivalent no matter what role she plays!

The conflicts in women's roles also create problems for men. When his wife shows little disposition to make herself available for the "pipe-and-slippers" routine, the husband must make adjustments also. He too may be torn between the intellectualized belief that men and women should be social equals and nostalgic longing for the deference which "mother showed to father." The husband is perhaps more likely to feel comfortable in the traditional male-dominant role than is his wife in the female-subordinate role, but again ambivalence is probable. His wife's independence is a sign of disrespect and her acquiescence makes him feel guilty. Not only has the husband's role been challenged but he must suffer with the confusion in women's roles.

Changed Notions of Morality

Modern America can scarcely be said to have *a* moral code. Rather, it has at least several such codes flatly contradicting one another at numerous points. The most widespread and best known is the Judeo-Christian code requiring chastity before and faithfulness in marriage, but punishing females much more heavily for any transgressions. We frequently act and talk as though this code were the only one and apply it alike to all groups in the society.[7] Discussions of morality generally hinge upon how widely the Judeo-Christian code is adhered to and whether violations of it are on the increase.

In the present century, with the advent of two world wars and the "roar-

[7] Actually sex patterns and moral standards vary widely from one society to another and among different social and educational levels in American society. Cf. George Murdock, *Social Structure* (New York, The Macmillan Company, 1949), pp. 260-322, and Alfred C. Kinsey and associates, *Sexual Behavior in the Human Male* (Philadelphia, W. B. Saunders Company, 1948), pp. 327-393.

ing twenties" in between, discussions of sex became fashionable and it became common knowledge that violations of the code are much more widespread than had formerly been admitted. People quickly jumped to the conclusion that violations were increasing rapidly and consequently that the moral code was breaking down. Not until the middle 1940's was this conclusion seriously challenged.

When analyzing changed sex patterns it is a mistake to consider men and women together. Men, contrary to expectations, are not having more premarital experience than they had in decades past. A comparison of the total amount of premarital experience for older and younger men, shows them to be almost identical. Because of their greater freedom men have generally been much more active than women. For women there has been a definite increase in premarital sex experience. Whereas only about 40 per cent of women who were born before 1900 had sexual intercourse before marriage, 60 per cent of those born between 1900-1909 had done so,[8] and it is confidently predicted that by the time all of the women born after 1920 are married the figure will also have climbed to approximately 60 per cent.

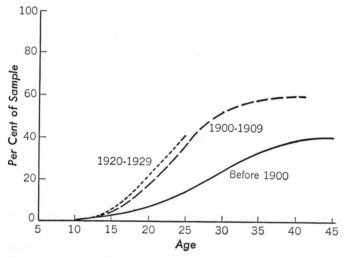

FIG. 7-4. **Premarital Sex Relationships in Three Groups of Females, According to Decade of Birth. (After A. C. Kinsey and associates, *Sexual Behavior in the Human Female* [Philadelphia, W. B. Saunders Co., 1953], p. 299, by permission)**

What conclusions can be drawn from this comparison? First, the increase in premarital experience even among women has not been large, and considerable experimentation occurred in past generations. Predictions that premarital sex relationships are becoming universal are not

[8] Alfred C. Kinsey and associates, *Sexual Behavior in the Human Female* (Philadelphia, W. B. Saunders Company, 1953), pp. 298-299.

borne out. How can we account for such widespread misbelief? Undoubtedly, one factor is our greater freedom to talk about sex. For the first time boys and girls discuss sex freely and demand to have some academic preparation for sex adjustment before they marry. Until recently, such efforts were unheard of. Consequently, older people who grew up under rigid taboos upon any mention of sex equate the breakdown of taboos in this one area with the breakdown of moral standards in general. It does not occur to them that open consideration of sex matters might be coupled with a pattern of reserving full sexual involvement for marriage. Furthermore, older persons constitute a kind of vested interest in the relations between succeeding generations. Tendencies to "forget" what their own early experiences were like, coupled with enough remembrance to make them fear for their children's safety, and the habitual resistance to change itself, encourage oldsters to take a dim view of their offsprings' behavior. Some of the adult reaction is a direct effort to control the behavior of specific youngsters against dangers with which the adults themselves are familiar.

Second, the failure to find any increase in premarital sex relationships for boys together with the increase for girls suggests that there may be less relative promiscuity now than formerly. Sexual experiences seemingly are now more confined to couples from similar social groups who are potential marriage partners. These couples reject the notion that their relationships should be asexual up to the point of marriage and drastically changed immediately thereafter. Their standards of morality include the gradual progression of intimacy as part of the total relationship.

Problems of Older Persons

Middle and old age are often periods of tragedy. Suddenly there is nothing to do. Aged men and women sit and rock on porches or wander about the neighborhood waiting out their lives. The problems of age often begin before the period of physical disability, however. Two events are crucial in initiating them: the marriage of children, and retirement.

"No mother ever delivered a child at adolescence with less pain than at the hour of birth." [9] The sudden exodus of grown children from the home is often a distinct shock. Mothers, especially, find that suddenly they have little or nothing to do during the many hours each day that they formerly spent in looking after their children's needs. Superficially one might say, "What an opportunity for leisure," "What a chance for Mother to do the things she has always wanted to do." Fine, except that twenty or more years of caring for her offspring likely have destroyed the desire for many of the things she once wanted and, more important, she is left to do them

[9] John Levy and Ruth Munroe, *The Happy Family* (New York, Alfred A. Knopf, Inc., 1938), p. 9.

alone! Her children, who are her chief affectional outlet, are building new ties for themselves—which means weakened ties to the parents. She is largely "left out" of the lives she formerly shared.

Nor is her own marriage prepared to fill the void. Often during the child-rearing period, fathers become more engrossed in earning a living and mothers become more engrossed in their children. Though the affectional ties between them may continue strong, large parts of their daily lives are built apart from one another. When the children leave, the father to assuage his own frustration may become even more involved in his work and even less available to his wife. She is left even more alone. Without existing habits to fall back upon many women tend toward one of two extremes: a pattern of idleness, self-pity, and despair; or a frantic cycle of activity in almost any group that will take them and serve as partial outlet for their unmet needs.

At retirement, frequently "the shoe switches to the other foot." The husband and father faces the most serious problems of adjustment. Enforced retirement "at age 65" or at any other age will be unwelcome to many men who are physically able to continue working. Moreover, even those who look forward to retirement often find it a disappointing experience. The status of adult males is very largely their status as "breadwinners." Take away the job and you take away the status. For a man to think, "I am retired," is often equivalent to, "I am no longer useful." He tends to an orientation of "I was . . ." and finds in that orientation no place for the present. His wife can at least cook and clean house and baby-sit for the grandchildren, but what is there to do for a retired grandfather? The few alternatives most available, such as caring for lawn and garden and household repair, often require more strength and agility than he can muster. There aren't even any "men's clubs" for him to join. Retirement often turns still capable men into helpless, useless creatures in a remarkably short period of time.

LEGAL PROBLEMS

The tangle of legal hazards facing married couples today might well discourage marriage altogether were the forces of love not so imperious! Some of the common practices of at least 90 per cent of all married persons are illegal, and a majority of couples face possible criminal prosecution for behavior that they regard as right and proper, but concerning which the law takes a different view.[10]

[10] Harriet F. Pilpel and Theodora Zavin, *op. cit.*, p. 213.

Family Planning

American families are small. The modal number of children per family is two. There is no reason to believe, however, that couples are less capable of reproduction than they have ever been. Today people plan their families, or at least try to. Certainly families are successfully *limiting* the number of children they have. Such limitation has been made possible by modern techniques of contraception. Perhaps nowhere is contraception more widely condemned or more widely practiced than in the United States.

Between 80 and 90 per cent of American women believe that birth-control knowledge should be made available to them. Devices for the prevention of conception are sold in an estimated 300,000 retail outlets.[11] The Planned Parenthood Federation of America has over 700 centers scattered throughout the United States. The American Medical Association promotes medical school instruction on various factors affecting fertility; the American Federation of Women's Clubs, the Federal Council of Churches, and countless other groups have endorsed the principle of family planning. Yet powerful groups forbid contraceptive practice and many aspects of it are illegal.

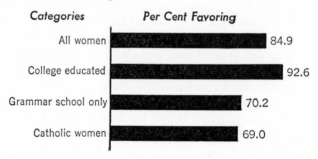

FIG. 7-5. American Women Believe That Birth Control Knowledge Should Be Available to Married Couples. (Redrawn by special permission of the editors from the August, 1943, issue of *Fortune*, pp. 24, 30)

In 1873 a man named Anthony Comstock was influential in getting Congress to pass a law prohibiting the transportation or sale of obscene literature and, though it apparently was not the intent of Congress to do so, articles for the prevention of conception were included in the ban. Later about half the states passed similar laws which came to be known as "little Comstock laws." Massachusetts and Connecticut both have particularly stringent anticontraceptive legislation. The Massachusetts law forbids a physician to provide contraceptive information even though a pregnancy would mean the certain death of his patient. The Connecticut law that forbids only the "use" of contraception is enforced chiefly by

[11] *Fortune Magazine*, 17 (February, 1938), p. 85.

prosecuting doctors and nurses as "accessories to the crime." Despite wholesale violation, all but one of the original laws still remain on the statute books. Attempts on the part of legislators to repeal them have amounted to political suicide. Most of the "teeth" of the federal law have been removed by Supreme Court decisions rendering physicians and druggists relatively safe from prosecution. Ironically, several of the states which have little Comstock laws have since established state-supported "planned parenthood" clinics, often providing free-of-charge information and devices whose sale is illegal.

The practical effect of existing legislation has been to make contraceptive information available to upper income groups who can afford the services of private physicians but to deny it to the lower income groups who may feel the greatest need. It also increases the use of the least reliable devices which generally do not require medical prescription and decreases the use of the more reliable methods that do require such prescription. Despite the discrepancies between law and practice, it seems unlikely that any of the laws will be repealed. Any future changes are likely to come about through court decisions which modify application of the laws while permitting them to remain unchanged on the law books.

Migratory Marriage and Divorce

The fact that some states have more lenient laws than others encourages people to "migrate" temporarily to secure the advantages of marrying and divorcing under the easier laws. Some states require that there be a waiting period between the time of application for a marriage license and the marriage itself. That this requirement serves to discourage hasty, ill-considered marriages is demonstrated by the experience of California where in the first full year following the institution of a three-day waiting period there were ten thousand fewer marriages.[12] The states also vary in requirements certifying freedom from venereal disease and in the minimum ages at which people may legally marry.

Desire to escape the stricter requirements of some states has led to the development of many "Gretna Greens" or marriage-market towns especially along state borders. License bureaus may remain open twenty-four hours a day to catch the "night trade," and the securing of a blood test, marriage license, and the marriage ceremony itself can all be completed in a few hours. Mercenary ministers and justices of the peace co-operate by providing quick ceremonies with none of the "frills" attached. During the 1920's and 1930's towns such as Elkton, Maryland, and Crown Point, Indiana, were noted marriage-market towns. At the present time certain towns along the northern and eastern borders of Indiana are pro-

[12] Ray E. Baber, *op. cit.*, p. 62.

viding "quick service" for residents of Ohio and Michigan. Though Indiana does not have a formal waiting period, the necessity for securing a blood test and sending it through the United States mails to the laboratory is supposed to serve the same purpose. Some "enterprising" cities, however, permit the couple to carry the blood sample to the post office, have it postmarked, carry it to the laboratory, back to the post office for another postmark, and then to the license bureau and on with the ceremony. One county with a population of approximately 17,000 records, according to one estimate, approximately 6500 marriages per year.[13] This situation in the Midwest is duplicated in many other areas.

In relation to migratory divorce an even more obvious situation exists. The length of residence required before a divorce can be secured varies from six weeks in Nevada and Idaho to five years in Massachusetts for persons who were not married in that state. New York provides only a single legal ground for divorce, whereas other states provide a dozen or more grounds. Actually only about 6 per cent of United States divorces are migratory,[14] but this amounts to approximately 24,000 migratory divorces each year. According to precedent, such divorces are valid even though they obviously violate the intent of the laws of the states in which the persons actually live.

Recently in cases where residence was obviously established for divorce purposes the courts have shown some tendency to declare the divorces invalid. Whether such divorces stand now seems to depend on whether anyone decides to contest them. Many persons remarry after securing migratory divorces. At present such persons cannot be sure if they are legally single, or married, or even if they are bigamists. Such confusion will exist until the courts take a firm stand one way or the other.

Divorce Law

All states in the United States now grant divorces. The number of *legal grounds* upon which divorce may be secured ranges from one to more than a dozen. The legal grounds for divorce are generally not, however, the actual *reasons* or *causes* for divorce. The grounds for divorce are the reasons the courts will accept, so whatever the actual reasons, people pretend to seek divorce for "adultery" or "desertion" or some other reason recognized by the law. Actually most people seek divorce because they are no longer willing or able to live together. Generally they are agreed, if reluctantly, that the divorce should take place. Yet if it should come to the official attention of the court that both partners want a divorce they cannot legally get one.

American law is such that in any litigation there must be two parties,

[13] *Indianapolis Star Magazine,* June 1, 1952, pp. 4-7.
[14] Ray E. Baber, *op. cit.,* p. 473.

the plaintiff (or accuser) and the defendant (or accused). One of the parties must have committed some act contrary to the law; there must be a *guilty party*. Though generally no such violation has occurred, the fiction must be maintained that there has. Consequently, one spouse must agree to be charged with some offense that is a legal ground for divorce in that state. For the spouses to make any such agreement is known technically as collusion, and evidence of it requires the judge to throw the case out of court. In sum, the law which requires that there be a guilty party and that there be no agreement between husband and wife concerning the divorce means that if the law were adhered to, very few divorces would be granted. In actual practice the law is winked at, and judges, lawyers, and clients conspire to prevent the law from interfering with the divorce procedure. It is estimated that collusion is involved in at least 75 per cent of American divorces.[15]

There are at least two other interesting "legal fictions" in current divorce practice. The first of these is the "noncontestant petition," whereby collusion is made less obvious. By not appearing in court to defend himself, the accused spouse is held to be guilty by default. His absence is supposedly an admission of guilt. This is a popular technique because it does not require any lengthy airing of the charges in court. The second legal fiction is the "counter-petition," wherein the spouse who is the defendant in a divorce case files another suit and himself brings suit for divorce. The court then maintains the fiction that these are separate cases and grants the divorce to the partner with the better case.

There is some awareness of this ridiculous situation and isolated efforts are being made to deal with it. Two jurisdictions, New Mexico and Alaska, now grant divorce for "incompatibility," which is a rather radical departure from traditional American practice. It is the first recognition that two normal, essentially law-abiding people might have reason for divorce. As yet, no state grants divorce for "mutual consent" as do Sweden and Norway. Although accepting nonjudgmental grounds such as incompatibility and mutual consent as recognized grounds for divorce would not eliminate the problem, it would reduce the inconsistency between legal practice and current values.

FAMILY DISORGANIZATION

The Old Rules

The American family that adapted to colonial and frontier life was a strong and stable organization. It was a rural family oriented toward agriculture. Families were large, for children were highly valued, not much additional expense, and they were a chief source of labor. The husband

---

[15] See the figures cited in Pilpel and Zavin, *op. cit.*, p. 299.

and father was the undisputed head of the household. The biblical admonition that "husbands should be the head of their wives" was interpreted quite literally and children were supposed to be "seen, not heard." Divorce was rare. Marriages were contracted to meet the necessity for earning a living and rearing a family. A lack of compatibility between the spouses was no reason for destroying an otherwise good marriage. The family grew most of its own food, made its own clothing, furniture, and other household goods, and often built its own house. It was a large, patriarchal, stable group which performed numerous functions for its members.

It was not difficult either for men or women to decide "what they would do in life." By and large, they did what their parents had done. Boys learned to farm and to carpenter and to assume their place as caretakers and disciplinarians for women and children. Girls learned to do all the things required of a farmer's wife, to expect marriage, and to bear large families. For neither were there any real alternatives. Farming is a family business. Men could not run their farms without the help of wives and children, and for women the only alternative to marriage was to live in the home of a relative with a status somewhere between that of a hired servant and that of a child who needs special attention. Family unity also had its positive side. Men, women, and children shared the same basic values in addition to the many tasks required to make a living. Each performed services for the other and each was rewarded in turn. Parents provided apprenticeships for their children and gradually turned over property and responsibility to them. As their vigor declined, the parents withdrew to part-time work without fear of economic deprivation or social isolation. The clearly defined roles for family members fitted together smoothly and provided security for all.

The Transition

The Industrial Revolution had profound effects on the family. It removed farming as the principal occupation, it brought the growth of cities, and it was accompanied by the development of a much more secular outlook on life.

As we have seen, prior to the Industrial Revolution farming was the chief occupation, and what little industry was carried on was organized under the "cottage" system. Small producers fabricated goods in their own homes with the aid of family members and one or two hired workers. On the farm and off, the family was an economic unit with production activities helping to build up and maintain its solidarity. The appearance of the factory changed all this. No longer was work carried on in the home and no longer did all of the family members participate. The husband or father was likely to be employed at some distance from his home and to be effectively removed from contact with other family members throughout most of the waking hours. Both the satisfactions and the frustrations encountered on the job came to have less and less meaning for the remaining family members who were similarly intent on going their separate ways.

The appearance of factories required large numbers of laborers to be congregated near by. Stores and other retail businesses sprang up to cater to the needs of the factory workers, and already the modern city was in the process of development. Land close to the factories became expensive and living space scarce. Families crowded into smaller quarters and spent less time in the home. Children became economic and social liabilities, expensive to raise and troublesome in the city environment. They went out of the home to the school and church and to centers of commercialized recreation.

It was not only the material aspects of life which changed, however. Customs and traditions which formerly had been accepted as eternal God-given verities became the objects of rational scrutiny. Just because it had "always been done that way" was no reason for continuing it, if a better way could be found. People began to look for new and better ways of regulating their personal lives as well as for producing goods. Marriage assumed the character of a humanly sanctioned relationship from which the sanction could be withdrawn by divorce or separation. The requirements and expectations which formerly held families together began to give way to a new pattern.

The New Rules

A complete and accurate list of the new rules governing family behavior is not possible, for the transition is not yet complete. Though the large patriarchal family has largely given way, vestiges of it remain and the character of its successor is not fully established. From past changes and present trends, at least the following seem definite.

The primary goal of marriage (and the family) is happiness—with the emphasis on the personal happiness of each family member. The family is subordinate to its members' needs and is modified or dissolved when individual needs are not met. Permanence of a marriage is no longer a wholly satisfactory criterion of success, and family responsibility does not require a large number of children. Parents consider their own happiness as well as that of their children and plan the size of their families to provide the maximum benefits for all concerned. More stress is placed on the quality of child care than on the number of children. Parents strive to achieve wholesome, well-adjusted personalities in their children as well as to feed, clothe, and educate them.

No longer are husbands the undisputed masters, and neither men nor women know beforehand what to expect in marriage. Though women largely have gained equality with men, the nature of that equality remains vague and undefined. To some it is equality based upon the traditional division of labor between the sexes, the husband being breadwinner and the wife homemaker. To others it means that beyond bearing children the division of labor should be worked out according to the temperaments and needs of the two spouses. To still others it means something intermediate between these two extremes. Above all, it means confusion and dissatisfaction, because there is no one role for which persons are trained and in which they can feel comfortable. Perhaps a satisfactory set of new roles will appear, but more likely not. Rigid, unvarying roles for men and women may be incompatible with our highly individualistic, technologically advanced culture. Rather than develop any one set of satisfactory roles, we appear to be moving toward the acceptance of various role patterns. Flexibility of attitude toward roles for men and women with several possible alternatives for each may be about as much uniformity as can be achieved in the equalitarian family group.

Parents, though they may continue to aid their children, are forced to let go of their offspring at marriage. The marriage of children demands again the equivalent of the prechildbearing relationship between the mother and father—and the problems of adjustment are often more difficult at age 50 than they were at age 20. Parents are expected to be emotionally self-sufficient and to prepare for financial independence during their old age. Modern homes are small and efficient. They assume the presence of only one set of parents and children. About the only entrée into the child-rearing family for grandparents is in the role of baby-sitters and occasional visitors. The independence of the young family requires also the independence of the grandparents.

Many groups bitterly oppose some or all of these changes in the family. Even where the changes are not actively opposed, people are disoriented by them. They are torn between loyalty to the values of old and acceptance of new, supposedly better ways. The conflict rages between groups and within persons.

VALUE-CONFLICTS

Permanence versus Adjustment

History is replete with accounts of unsatisfactory marriages. Biblical heroes, European monarchs, and American presidents have succeeded or failed because of or in spite of the sharp tongues of their wives. Noble women of all countries have assumed increased stature in comparison to the incompetence and debauchery of their husbands. Outsiders have, for centuries, admired and pitied these (un)fortunate men and women. Only recently, and mostly in America, has anyone had the temerity to try to do anything about it. And rarely have efforts at change met such concerted opposition.

Self-sacrifice has never been the least highly regarded of virtues, and permanence of the family somehow is supposed to compensate for any sacrifices made by its members. The basic assumptions underlying this position are at least two: (1) family life itself is "sacred" and not to be trifled with; and (2) protection of the family against dissolution is necessary for the well-being of all its members. Husbands and wives who remain together, even if unhappy, reputedly are building "character" in themselves and will be "better men and women" for the tribulations they have undergone. Children similarly need their parents. Even though the home be strife-ridden, its continuance is presumed to be better than having the parents separate. For persons who hold these beliefs, the only solution to family problems is to seek a return to the stable family of the past. Generally they advocate stricter divorce laws or the permission of no divorce at all, a clearly defined set of obligations for husbands, wives, and children to follow, and punishment for those who disobey.

These "permanence" values are opposed by the emerging "happiness" or "adjustment" goals in family life. Many people now deny that benefits inevitably or automatically result from preserving marriages intact. On the contrary, they claim that continuance of conflict-ridden marriages may be harmful both to parents and children and that such marriages had best be dissolved so that other more satisfactory relationships may be formed. Presumably, unhappy parents are in no position to provide the necessary affection and security for their children. Moreover, the emotional trauma resulting from the unhappy parental relationship may be greater than that involved in divorce. In support of this position, it is true that most divorced persons remarry and that second marriages are often happy ones.[16] Very few of these persons actually favor divorce. They merely regard it as less undesirable than the existence of unhappy marriages.

State and Regional Conflicts

Depending on one's point of view, United States domestic-relations law is characterized either by "charming individuality" or by a "reprehensible lack of uniformity" among the several states.[17] The laws in no two states are identical, and efforts to establish uniformity have failed miserably. Each jurisdiction asserts its right to legislate in terms of the

[16] Andrew G. Truxal and Francis E. Merrill, *The Family in American Culture* (New York, Prentice-Hall, Inc., 1947), pp. 701-702.

[17] Ray E. Baber, *op. cit.*, p. 450.

mores of its own area. Conflicts among the states focus at two separate points: (1) What is a good law?; and (2) Do some states have the right to subvert the laws of other states?

Arbitrarily, states might be divided into two groups according to where they stand on the permanence versus adjustment issue raised in the preceding section. In general, where permanence values prevail the laws support them. The age at which persons may legally marry is low in order to discourage premarital sex relationships and to encourage marriage. Divorce is difficult to secure, children born out of wedlock are stigmatized as illegitimate, and a general philosophy of punishing "wrongdoing" is incorporated into the law. In other states where adjustment values are making headway, the reverse situation exists. There is a tendency toward raising the legal ages for marriage to prevent the immature and unprepared from marrying, numerous grounds are provided and divorce procedure is relatively simple, and the underlying concept stresses the ultimate welfare of the persons involved rather than the need to punish them for their difficulties.

It is unlikely that there will be any agreement on these issues in the near future. Meanwhile, many persons cross the border to escape their own states' laws, and the laws of some states if not designed "to attract trade" actually do serve that purpose. Should states be permitted to pass laws that in effect sabotage the laws of other states? The controversy, rather than being ended, is becoming sharper. The final right of each state to legislate for its own population is not likely to be questioned. Where far-reaching changes may be expected is in the administration of the laws. Individual states are coming under increasing pressure to provide legal services only for persons who can demonstrate that they are bona fide residents of that state.

PERSONAL DEVIATION

The United States is both a much married and a much divorced nation. A larger proportion of the adult population is married today than ever before, but one out of every eight persons is in a second or subsequent marriage.[18] High marriage and divorce rates in the United States are not new, nor do they show any real signs of declining. Apparently they are a fundamental part of modern American culture. Yet the vast majority of people maintain that the situation is "abnormal" and should be remedied as soon as possible. Only a small group who are convinced that the instability is here to stay have the temerity to suggest that it is man's ideas and expectations of marriage which must change rather than the nature of marriage itself. They are deviants who believe that the individualistic,

[18] Harold T. Christensen, *Marriage Analysis* (New York, The Ronald Press Company, 1950), p. 441.

materialistic values of modern society require that institutions, the family included, be flexible enough to fit themselves to individual needs. It is yet near heresy to proclaim that divorce may serve socially useful purposes, that some marriages may cause or aggravate personality problems for the spouses, and that divorcées and remarried people should not automatically be suspected of having special personal difficulties. The few persons who take this extreme position may themselves lead quite conventional family lives, but they are deviant in the attitudes they take toward family problems. They are important because their ideas are so directly contrary to prevailing family traditions. If these deviants are correct in the assertion that a universal permanent monogamy is incompatible with modern conditions, they may prove to be the vanguard in a movement to reorient most of our thinking on the family.

Ordinarily, deviant behavior is considered to be the unusual—or atypical—behavior deriving from motivation which differs in kind or in force from that experienced by most people. But this is not always true. For example, sex relationships before marriage are regarded as deviant behavior in the United States. Yet more than half of all boys and a sizable proportion of girls eventually have such relationships.[19] Premarital relationships are then, the majority pattern! The forces that give rise to them are deeply rooted in biology and culture. The deviancy in this case is from a verbal norm, not a behavorial one. Premarital sex relationships are still so strongly disapproved that most young people are forced to attempt to rationalize for themselves behavior that they condemn in anyone else.

It would not be correct to assume, however, that premarital relationships result inevitably from biological and cultural forces without individual personalities playing an important role. Especially among boys, the need to prove they can "carry it off" and thereby assure themselves and others of their adequate masculinity is an important factor. Boys who feel inferior to and hostile toward girls frequently use sex conquests as a means of "getting even" with the girls to whom they feel inferior. Both boys and girls unwittingly use sex relationships as weapons against parents and others in authority. In addition to indicating complete defiance of authority, if these relationships are discovered they cause parents great anguish or concern. Girls, too, who do not receive sufficient feelings of security and being loved in their families sometimes resort to sex relationships for the temporary feelings of being loved and desired that these relationships provide. In all the cases mentioned here, premarital sex relationships are furthered by failure of the individual to establish satisfying interpersonal relations with other people.

Divorced persons are generally regarded as deviant, and frequently with

[19] Alfred C. Kinsey and associates, *Sexual Behavior in the Human Male,* p. 550, and *Sexual Behavior in the Human Female,* pp. 330-331.

good reason. Certainly not all divorces, however, involve maladjusted persons. Differences in social background or temperament of the spouses may be so extreme as to thwart adjustment and indicate divorce, even though each of the spouses might be quite successfully married to some other person. Such divorced persons cannot realistically be considered to be personality deviants. The really deviant divorcés are those who would not likely make good marriage partners no matter whom they married. They are the persons whose needs for security, affection, approval, to dominate or be dominated are too great a burden for almost any marriage partner to bear. After failing with one partner, they often seek out a second and a third and destroy each of these relationships by their insatiable demands. In a minority of cases the neurotic need appears to be for the notoriety of marrying and divorcing itself. Such people go through a series of marriages, attracting a great deal of attention to themselves on the way.

To some extent divorce itself *creates* deviancy. Even though it may be anticipated for months or years, the experience of divorce is frequently traumatic. Habit patterns and personal relationships of long duration are suddenly uprooted. The person must finally face up to having failed in marriage and having been rejected by the marriage partner. Extreme bitterness and despair often follow. To assuage the hurt and to cope with the frustrations of suddenly being unmarried again, the individual often enters a more or less promiscuous series of sex relationships. Gradually as he reorients himself, these symptoms of deviancy are replaced by a more conventional pattern. Some persons, of course, never completely recover from the divorce experience, and it may be expected to remain at least temporarily disorganizing in the foreseeable future.

SUMMARY

The family is a victim of change. Compared to the stable family of the past, much seems wrong with the family of today. Marital unhappiness is one of the most widespread symptoms of trouble. Approximately one out of four marriages ends in divorce, perhaps one hundred thousand more are effectively broken each year by desertion, and still other couples separate even though they remain legally married.

Much of the dissatisfaction with marriage and family life stems from far-reaching changes in the accepted roles for various family members. Women's roles have changed most drastically. Women may now work and/or marry and/or bear children and/or choose any one of several other roles. Whatever the role she selects, it is likely to cause adjustment problems for both her and her husband. Adolescents and young adults are questioning openly the validity of a moral code which has in the past been observed in the breach as well as in actual practice. Mothers and fathers today live long past the usual child-rearing period often without sufficient interests and opportunities to round out their lives.

The unrealism of family law creates another range of problems. Some form of birth-control practice is practically universal and, more often than not, illegal. Though each state makes its own marriage and divorce law, evasion is generally a simple matter. One has only to cross the state border. Divorce is widespread, but the nature of our divorce law forces most applicants to become liars and perjurers as well as serving further to embitter the already embattled spouses. Few of these laws are likely to be changed except, perhaps, through judicial interpretation.

Changes resulting from the Industrial Revolution and the shift to urban living underlie modern family problems. A new, equalitarian, happiness-centered family is emerging. Powerful groups oppose the transition. Particularly they oppose the assumption that marriages should be dissolved if happiness and personal satisfaction are not forthcoming. Very few persons can completely accept present family instability as being an integral part of modern family life. Personality problems both create and are created by the new patterns. Immature and neurotic people swell the ranks of those involved in premarital sex relationships and divorce.

SUGGESTED READINGS

CHRISTENSEN, Harold T., *Marriage Analysis* (New York, The Ronald Press Company, 1950). A basic sociological textbook on marriage and the family. Takes a positive approach to the amelioration of present family problems.

CUBER, John F., *Marriage Counseling Practice* (New York, Appleton-Century-Crofts, Inc., 1948). The first systematic treatise on the new field of marriage counseling. Treats both the theory of marriage counseling and the professional status and problems of the field.

HILL, Reuben, and others, *Families Under Stress* (New York, Harper and Brothers, 1950). Interprets family reactions to the crises of separation and reunion during World War II.

KINSEY, Alfred M., POMEROY, Wardell B., and MARTIN, Clyde E., *Sexual Behavior in the Human Male* (Philadelphia, W. B. Saunders Company, 1948). The most exhaustive study of the sexual behavior of American males. The data are analyzed in terms of relevant social variables.

KINSEY, Alfred M., and associates, *Sexual Behavior in the Human Female* (Philadelphia, W. B. Saunders Company, 1953). Companion volume to the earlier volume on sexual behavior among American males. Weighted toward the better educated segments of the population.

MEAD, Margaret, *Male and Female* (New York, William Morrow and Company, 1952). Synthesis of twenty-five years of study, by an anthropologist, of problems of masculine and feminine roles in various cultures including modern American society.

PILPEL, Harriet F., and ZAVIN, Theodora, *Your Marriage and the Law* (New York, Rinehart and Company, 1952). An excellent nontechnical treatment of the legal problems surrounding marriage in the United States. Interprets the law and points the way toward a more rational legal philosophy.

AUDIO-VISUAL AIDS

Date of Birth (Seminar Films, Inc., 347 Madison Ave., New York), 16 minutes, sound, color. Produced by the National Film Board of Canada for the Department of Labor of the Government of Canada. Presents the actual record of employees in the over-45 age group, indicating that there is less absenteeism, a lower turnover rate and an equal standard of production among older workers.

Jealousy (McGraw-Hill Book Company, Inc., Text-Film Department, 330 W. 42nd, New York), 16 minutes, sound, black and white. A young wife learns that her jealous misunderstanding of her husband is really an expression of her dissatisfaction with her role as homemaker and her tendency to distort events in her own imagination.

Life with Grandpa (McGraw-Hill Book Company, Inc., Text-Film Department, 330 W. 42nd, New York), 17 minutes, sound, black and white. Produced by March of Time. Discusses the problems of old age including degenerative diseases and economic insecurity. Various remedies are suggested to these and other problems including the feelings of loneliness and uselessness that so often come with old age.

Marriage and Divorce (McGraw-Hill Book Company, Inc., Text-Film Department, 330 W. 42nd, New York), 15 minutes, sound, black and white. Produced by March of Time. Surveys the problems of broken homes and the increasing divorce rate by examining the effects of mechanization on present-day family relations. The opinions of several experts as to what should be done are included.

A Planned Parenthood Story (Mayo-Video, 113 W. 57th, New York), 18 minutes, sound, black and white. Produced for the Planned Parenthood Federation of America, Inc. Deals with a young couple who lost two babies in rapid succession because the wife had not regained her strength after the birth of their third living child. They learn of the service of "Planned Parenthood" and are able to space the arrival of their next baby. During the clinic scenes, the action shows how other services of "Planned Parenthood" are carried on.

Social-Sex Attitudes in Adolescence (McGraw-Hill Book Company, Inc., Text-Film Department, 330 W. 42nd, New York), 22 minutes, sound, black and white. Shows how teen-agers meet, and are helped to meet, the problems in becoming aware of and adjusted to the opposite sex. Takes a boy and girl through their entire adolescent experiences, culminating with their marriage.

QUESTIONS AND PROJECTS

1. The divorce rate, alone, is an inadequate measure of the rate of family breakdown. Explain.

2. Indicate how changed roles for young adults, for husbands and wives, and for older persons have contributed to disorganization in the American family.

3. How does variation in marriage and divorce law among the separate states encourage violation of the laws? What dangers are inherent in these procedures for the persons involved?

4. Why is it true that if the partners to a marriage agree that they wish to be divorced, technically they cannot get a divorce?

5. What are "legal fictions" in the area of domestic-relations law? Discuss at least two such fictions.

6. How are changes deriving from the Industrial Revolution basic to most of today's family problems?

7. Debate, with some other student in the class, the desirability of "permanence" values in marriage as opposed to "adjustment" values.

8. Evaluate the statement that "there are many otherwise normal people among the ranks of the divorced."

9. Define the terms *divorce, desertion,* and *legal separation.*

10. Relate the clichéd expression, "The younger generation is going to the dogs," to the fact that we have not one but several moral standards in modern society.

11. Investigate your community to see what resources it provides for the welfare of older persons. Evaluate the programs of church groups, fraternal societies, and community agencies. How much are these agencies doing to provide meaningful goals and interpersonal relationships? What is the prevailing attitude within the community's families upon the place of grandparents within them? What can be done to provide more satisfactory arrangements for both the older and younger generations?

12. Interview the judge in your county who is responsible for administration of the divorce laws. What does he think are their major strengths and weaknesses? What changes does he recommend in existing laws? Do you agree with him on what changes are needed? Why?

CHAPTER 8

Religious Problems and Conflicts

AT no time in American history has the institutional status of the church in America been more secure than it appears to be today. When we became a nation, only one American in fifteen was a church member.[1] Today, three out of five are members, and church membership during the past quarter-century has been growing twice as fast as the general population.[2] Church contributions are at an all-time high and have been rising faster than the cost of living in recent years.[3] Organized opposition to religion is weaker than it has been in generations. Not a single widely-known professional atheist or agnostic carries the mantle of the Robert Ingersolls and Tom Paines of earlier generations, and popular interest in atheism appears to have faded. The leadership of the American labor movement, once sharply anticlerical, is now composed of leaders who are either devoutly religious or discreetly silent. No American president today dares, like Lincoln, to remain unaffiliated with any church, and one president within recent decades was hastily baptized and enrolled after his nomination.

Despite such evidence of institutional stability, however, religion remains an area of conflict and discontent. Religious bodies expend much of their energy in rivalries with one another, while a host of unheeded Jeremiahs call for repentance. After a long period of comparative religious toleration, it seems possible that America is drifting into a period of intensified religious strife. What is the nature of these conflict areas? Why have they developed?

RELIGIOUS PROBLEM AREAS IN AMERICAN LIFE

Alleged Lack of Religious Faith

Despite the record level of church membership, there is a continuous chorus of lament over the "lack of faith," the "godlessness," and the "falling away from the faith" of the American people. Church membership

[1] William W. Sweet, "The Protestant Churches," *The Annals*, 256 (March, 1948), p. 50.

[2] National Council of Churches, *Trends of Church Membership of the Larger Protestant Bodies* (New York, National Council of Churches, 1952).

[3] *Christian Century*, 70 (January 21, 1952), p. 94.

alone is not a satisfactory measure of functional religious faith, and something beyond mere membership is insistently demanded. Statements that "the world crisis is basically a *moral* crisis," that "the only hope for our nation is in a rebirth of religious faith," and that "the only way to solve national and world problems is to seek God's way" pour from the pulpit and the lecture platform. All such views agree in holding that some sort of religious inadequacy is basic to (or even the sole cause of) our national and international problems. It follows that no solution is possible unless it involves these religious elements. In its more naively uncritical form, this viewpoint proposes personal religion as a substitute for political or sociological approaches. In its more sophisticated form, this viewpoint insists that economic and political reforms must spring from religious motivations and be guided by profound religious convictions if they are to be fully effective.

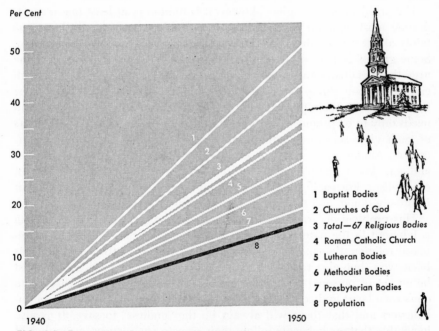

Per Cent

1 Baptist Bodies
2 Churches of God
3 Total—67 Religious Bodies
4 Roman Catholic Church
5 Lutheran Bodies
6 Methodist Bodies
7 Presbyterian Bodies
8 Population

FIG. 8-1. Percentage Increase in Membership of Religious Bodies and in Population, 1940-1950. (From J. Frederic Dewhurst and associates, *America's Needs and Resources: A New Survey* [New York, Twentieth Century Fund, 1955], p. 422)

Such anxieties about our faith are nothing new. Every period in recent history has heard denunciations of godlessness and exhortations to repentance. At one time in the early nineteenth century it was seriously charged that only three students at Yale University professed to believe in God. Although it is impossible to determine just how godly our ancestors were, it is clear that certain of them were deeply disturbed about the godlessness of the rest of them.

It is difficult to determine whether religious faith and devotion are actually declining. There is some scientific evidence that people no longer accept certain traditional religious beliefs (belief in a personal God, a Heaven as a physical place of reward and Hell as a physical place of torment, and so on) as widely as formerly.[4] But is this a *lack* of faith or a *change* in faith? Not all agree.

If it is uncertain whether religious faith is declining, why is the alleged lack of religious faith a social problem? Simply because a number of people *view it* as one. When a considerable number of people think a condition poses a problem, express concern over it, and discuss ways of meeting it, then it *is* a social problem. In this instance it may be a problem to only a minority of people, but to them it may be the most serious of all problems—may even be the only problem they recognize.

The problem of "irreligion," however, is unique in at least one respect. Among most of those who consider it a problem, each has little uncertainty about the solution. But there are *disagreements* about the solution. Some groups call for a great "revival" similar to those of the past; some urge the socializing and modernizing of the program of the church, with emphasis upon group activities and attention to current social issues; some feel that their present church program is entirely adequate and needs only to be promoted with greater zeal and enthusiasm. The holders of each view seem to be thoroughly convinced that their approach is correct. Among many religious groups there is a relative lack of interest and an almost complete lack of research into alternative methods of evangelism. For each group the solution lies in continuing to do what it is already doing, and no "search for the answer" is necessary.

This problem of "irreligion" may never be "solved," since the problem is inherent in the nature of Christianity. The Christian religion is a universal religion, demanding that its members not rest until every soul has been won, but also teaches that one's acceptance of Christianity must be an act of personal faith, voluntarily and willingly taken according to one's own heart and conscience. It is inevitable that some will remain unbelievers and that there will always be the "godless" to save. It is also inevitable that, as believers follow their private consciences, a number of religious sects arise, some of whom view the others as corrupters of the faith. Even if *all* persons were devout followers of some Christian church, there would be many who considered the others still "unsaved," and the problem of "godlessness" and "lack of a saving faith" would remain.

This problem, however, is one with which social scientists, *as scientists,* are not deeply concerned. Most of the groups who are the most concerned

[4] James H. Leuba, "Modern Man and Religious Faith," *Survey Graphic,* 28 (April, 1939), pp. 277-279.

with this problem have neither sought nor accepted the services of social scientists in analyzing the problem or evaluating their techniques of meeting it. Furthermore, since the problem consists of states of faith whose concrete effects upon persons or society cannot be objectively determined, social scientists have been somewhat disinclined to study it. This problem will probably remain a long-time concern of certain groups of people, while most of the rest remain untroubled by it.

The Fundamentalism-Modernism Battle

The first quarter of the twentieth century saw a theological battle which still continues as a sort of guerrilla warfare. Unlike many social controversies, this was not deeply rooted in changing technology, human migration, or economic interest clashes; its causes were found in the clash of increasing scientific knowledge with intrenched religious belief. Such a clash is not new, for intellectual history since Galileo is littered with the remnants of cherished beliefs which scientific discoveries have demolished.

The last half of the nineteenth century, however, saw a rapid accumulation of scientific fact and theory which impinged upon traditional theology with devastating effect. From natural science came facts and theories about the age of the earth and the evolution of life which conflicted sharply with the biblical account of creation as it was generally interpreted at that time. From psychology and the infant field of sociology began to come insights into human motivation and behavior that cast doubt upon the traditional religious interpretation of "good" and "bad" behavior as results of an individual's voluntary "free-will" choices between good and evil. From anthropology there came some fairly complete and sympathetic pictures of primitive life which caused some people to wonder whether it was entirely civilized to consign all the unsaved heathen to eternal damnation. A developing school of "higher criticism" arose which began to study the cultural background of the biblical writings, with a suspicion that bits of mythology and tribal folklore may have crept into the Bible.

Most church leaders were appalled at these heresies and rallied to defend the faith. The battle lines were drawn between those who wished to accommodate their biblical interpretations and church doctrines to the discoveries of science, and those who denounced as "false science" all claims and theories which conflicted with traditional religious doctrines. These rival camps came to be known as "modernists" and "fundamentalists." The *fundamentalists* generally agreed: that all parts of the Bible are divinely inspired and unalterably true; that man was created by God in his present form without intermediate stages; that Christ was born of a virgin and was a Divine Being who died on the cross to atone for our sins; that only those who accept and profess these (and other) beliefs can enter Heaven, a physical place of eternal reward, whereas all others must go to Hell, a physical place of eternal torment. With only minor changes, these views are retained by fundamentalist groups today. The *modernists* (or "liberals" as they often prefer to term themselves) generally believed that the Bible contained the word of God along with bits of literature and folklore, and that not all parts of the Bible were true in a literal sense; that earth and man developed through a long evolutionary process; that Christ may have been a mortal man, of natural conception and birth; that Christ's crucifixion was a symbolic rather than a literal atonement for our sins; that the acceptance and professing of religious belief is less important than the living of a Christian life; that little is positively known about Heaven and Hell, and that the idea of eternal punishment for unbelief is untenable; that religious beliefs should be revised whenever they conflict with the studied conclusions of science.

These opposing positions gradually crystallized during the closing decades of the nineteenth century, and the battle reached its peak during the first quarter of this century. Within each major Protestant denomination, the issue was debated at their periodic conferences, in their colleges and theological seminaries, and sometimes in their local congregations. Modernists were accused of being atheists, agnostics, agents of the Devil, and other assorted kinds of villains. Fundamentalists were accused of being narrow-minded bigots and ignorant reactionaries. In several states, fundamentalists secured the passing of laws forbidding the teaching of evolutionary theories in the public schools. These led to the 1925 "monkey trial" in Tennessee, where a teacher, John Scopes, was tried for the teaching of evolution. Few trials in American history have excited such intense national interest. William Jennings Bryan and Clarence Darrow, possibly the most famous lawyers of their day, met in what became less a trial of Scopes than a trial of the law itself. The fundamentalists won the battle but lost the war. Scopes was convicted and later freed on a technicality, but Darrow succeeded in picturing the law as undemocratic and its supporters as ignorant bigots. The attempt to prevent by law the teaching of evolutionary theories quickly collapsed, and acceptance of evolutionary ideas soon became practically universal among scientists and others fully familiar with the evidence.

The modernists also won the war within most of the major Protestant denominations. They captured the leadership of most denominations, but not without a struggle which left the churches deeply divided. In several instances, groups of dissatisfied fundamentalists withdrew and organized separate denominations. Many ministers and laymen drifted away to join denominations which had remained fundamentalist or to join one of the new fundamentalist denominations which appeared. The battle within each denomination has subsided, leaving a considerable realignment of religious bodies in America.

During the later days of this battle, a new theological movement, *neo-orthodoxy,* was already gaining momentum. Led by such men as Barth, Tillich, and Niebuhr, neo-orthodoxy arose largely as a reaction against the easy optimism which was swept away in the disillusionment of two world wars and the depressions and tyrannies which followed them. Neo-orthodoxy agrees with the fundamentalists that man is self-centered and tyrannical and in need of divine salvation, that sin is real, and that social progress must come through God's grace. Neo-orthodoxy agrees with the liberals that the Bible should be criticized like any other human document, that traditional religious beliefs should be revised as scientific knowledge requires, and that the good society can be attained in this world and need not be postponed until the next. Neo-orthodoxy represents a partial rapprochement between fundamentalism and liberalism. It appears to be the dominant theological movement at present and may have helped reduce the sharpness of theological controversy.

If this is largely a past battle, wherein is it a present social problem? Guerrilla warfare continues both between denominations and *within* denominations. The American Council of Christian Churches, comprising fifteen national fundamentalist denominations, is sharply critical of the more liberal National Council of Churches of Christ in the United States, which includes twenty-five Protestant and five Eastern Orthodox bodies with over 35,000,000 members. Relations between the two councils are far from cordial.[5] The fundamentalist churches maintain a continuous drumfire of attack upon the liberal or modernist churches as traitors to the faith. The more extreme fundamentalists believe that the liberal churches are not only mistaken but are positively pernicious, since people may fail to find salvation because of its false teachings. Some even consider the modernist a greater menace to true religion than the atheist or agnostic. The liberal churches tend to ignore these charges, having apparently concluded that further argument is pointless.

For this determined fundamentalist minority, the task of recapturing the faith from the modernists and propagating this faith remains the *only* important social problem. If this could be done, and all people won to the true faith, they believe that all ordinary social problems would be easily solved, not through social reforms, but as a natural by-product of religious faith. This leads the fundamentalist to reject both the attempt to reform society through legislation and the "social gospel."

The Social-Gospel Controversy

The roots of Christianity extend far back into the history of an agricultural people living in small groups within which all relations were primary group relations. Most of the Bible is written in the language

[5] Cf. *Time* (December 28, 1953), p. 33.

of the primary-group association of person with person. Little is said about impersonal group relations of the sort rare in a primitive agricultural society but so important in an urban industrial society. A half century or more ago it became increasingly apparent that many men who were moral and generous in their relations with other individuals were thoroughly ruthless and nonmoral in dealing with impersonal groups. A number of churchmen concluded that the teachings of the Bible and the church must be reinterpreted in the language of impersonal, secondary group relations in order to fit the needs of the present society. This would mean that, in addition to such personal sins as murder, theft, greed, or lust, the church must also *define* and condemn such "social sins" as economic exploitation, racial injustice, and fraudulent business practice.[6]

Another root of the social gospel is found in the insights of social science. Nineteenth-century folklore held that each person consciously and freely chooses whether he will be good or evil, Christian or pagan, lazy or ambitious, honest or deceitful. Poor people were poor because they were lazy, and the evil man was evil because he wished to be evil. Social scientists began to cast doubt upon these assumptions, showing how a man may be lazy and unmotivated because he has experienced only poverty and lack of ambition in his environment, and how the "choice" between good and evil is usually a more or less mechanical response to the balance of environmental influences surrounding him.

Whereas the traditional approach was to seek converts and assume that a better society would incidentally follow,[7] the social gospel seeks to improve the institutions and practices of society directly, in the belief that they are obstacles to Christian life. In 1910, the social gospel included support of labor's right to organize and bargain collectively, and opposition to the twelve-hour day and the seven-day week. Today the social gospel calls, for example, for slum clearance and equal rights for Negroes and other minorities. The exact content of the social gospel changes along with changing social needs and issues.

The social gospel has been hotly attacked ever since its appearance. The fundamentalists charged that reforming the society was no proper business of the church, and was a betrayal of the church's real purpose of saving souls. Vested interests sought to forestall clerical criticism by urging that the church confine itself to "spiritual" matters and stay out of "politics." Still others feared that the church would be torn with dissen-

---

[6] For statements of the "social gospel," see Henry F. May, *Protestant Churches and Industrial America* (New York, Harper and Brothers, 1949); Walter G. Muelder, *Religion and Economic Responsibility* (New York, Charles Scribner's Sons, 1953). For a Catholic view, see John F. Cronin, *Catholic Social Action* (Milwaukee, The Bruce Publishing Company, 1948).

[7] Some groups, however, are uninterested in a better society, believing that the society is unalterably bad and that the church should concentrate upon the rescue of individuals from sin through personal salvation.

sion if it became involved in social controversies. The social-gospel debate accompanied the fundamentalist-modernist battle, with much the same participants and outcome. The leadership of the liberal churches accepts the social gospel, whereas the fundamentalist bodies generally reject it. The National Council of Churches tends to promote the social gospel while the much smaller American Council of Christian Churches strongly opposes the social gospel and lends tacit support to the economic status quo. These positions having crystallized, there is not much debate today about the social gospel within any denomination.

It is uncertain just how effectively the liberal churches are applying the social-gospel approach. Many official resolutions about social issues produce little activity in the local congregations. In recent years church organizations promoting the social gospel have been subjected to increasingly sharp charges of "communism," and their effectiveness may have been curtailed.[8] Possibly the most effective promoter of the social gospel in America today is the Catholic Church, which has combined a fundamentalist theology (differing somewhat from Protestant fundamentalism) with a social gospel.[9] Catholic participation in the Back of the Yards Council in Chicago and the Rural Life Association are examples of Catholic applications of the social gospel, although Catholics usually use the term *social action*. Their purposes are both ameliorative and evangelistic; through identifying the church with the economic needs and social problems of Negroes, workers, and other *groups*, the Catholic Church hopes both to improve social conditions and to develop a rapport with these groups which will lead to individual conversions.

Among those who accept the social gospel, the question of how to apply it is not an easy one. If the church uncritically supports the status quo, it invites the charge that it is an instrument of exploitation. If it promotes extensive reforms, beyond those for which its membership is prepared, it ceases to lead anyone. If it develops detailed programs of social action, it tears itself apart in controversy over them. It cannot make a frontal attack upon vested interests, for it depends upon them for support. Most important of all, both the clergy and the membership are products of our culture. For all these reasons, the social-action program of the church consists mainly of repeated reminders of unsolved problems and a quiet insistence that the Christian conscience should not rest while they remain untreated.

The Released-Time Controversy

The American Constitution provides for separation of church and state and forbids the state to use any public funds for the support of religious

[8] Cf. *Time* (October 12, 1953), p. 70.
[9] See Cronin, *op. cit.*

bodies or sectarian religious education. In a country of multiple religious bodies, each wishing that *its* beliefs be taught, the public school can avoid giving offense only by refraining entirely from the teaching of sectarian religious doctrines.

In recent years there has arisen a determined and well-organized effort to induce the public school to co-operate in the teaching of religion.[10] Under one plan, classes in religion were held in the school during school hours with attendance voluntary. The classes were taught by local ministers of the various faiths, serving without pay. Although this involved no compulsion and no direct expenditure of public funds, the use of school facilities and time involved an indirect use of public funds, and this plan was ruled unconstitutional by the Supreme Court.

This adverse ruling encouraged another plan whereby those children who wish may be released during school hours to receive religious instruction off the school premises. This appears to be constitutionally acceptable, but has still provoked violent debate. Supporters are convinced that the presumed benefits of such religious training far outweigh any possible inconveniences or objections. Opposition comes partly from those who doubt that such religious training is as effective as claimed and partly from those who maintain that the school should not be expected to assemble classes for the church. Opposition also comes from school personnel who object to the disruption of the school's schedule. To release part of the children while retaining the rest creates a dilemma for the school. If, for those children who do not elect to take the religious training, the school arranges an interesting activity, then it draws children away from the religious program; if the school does not plan an interesting activity for those remaining, then a discipline problem develops.

In some communities this has become a bitter issue. Dispute becomes intense; neighbors attack one another's character and impugn one another's motives. In an earlier period when the church functioned as a community center, no such problem arose. But in recent decades the school has increasingly become a center of community life and has absorbed a growing share of the children's time. It is perhaps not surprising that some in the church should move to reclaim a portion of that time which they feel the school has usurped. At present only a minority of communities have responded. Whether the released-time program will become general is doubtful.[11]

[10] See American Council on Education, Committee on Religion and Education, *The Function of the Public Schools in Dealing With Religion* (Washington, American Council on Education, 1952); R. H. Martin, *Our Public Schools: Christian or Secular* (Pittsburgh, National Reform Association, 1952); Clyde L. Hay, *The Blind Spot in Public Education* (New York, The Macmillan Company, 1950).

[11] See V. T. Thayer, *The Attack on the Secular School* (Boston, The Beacon Press, 1951), Ch. IX, "Religion in the Secular School: Religious Instruction on Released Time."

The Rising Tide of Catholic-Protestant Hostility

Of all religious controversies in America, the one most likely to disrupt orderly social life is the apparent increase in antagonism between Protestants and Catholics. Relations between Catholics and Protestants in America have never been entirely cordial. Since the Catholic Church was mainly composed of working-class immigrants, a variety of nationalistic and class prejudices were intermingled with religious prejudices on the part of each group. Organized anti-Catholicism appeared at times, as in the Know-Nothings of the 1830's, 1840's and 1850's and the Ku Klux Klan of the 1920's. These were short-lived and localized protests and attracted little following among Protestants of education and responsibility. In recent years, however, there is evidence of increasing tenseness and anxiety among both Catholic and Protestant leaders.[12]

1. Catholic Evangelism

Throughout most of its history in the United States, the Catholic Church was fully occupied in caring for an immigrant membership. Many of the priests were foreign-born and trained and would have found little response among non-Catholics. With the ending of mass immigration and the gradual assimilation of the immigrants, the Catholic Church has now become aggressively evangelistic and has announced its intention to win America for the Church.

This increase in Catholic evangelistic activity has been paced by a mounting Protestant anxiety lest their efforts prove successful. There is no evidence of great Catholic gains in church-membership statistics, which, if accurate, show the Catholic Church to be scarcely holding its own in proportionate membership.[13] But church-membership statistics are notoriously unreliable, as not all churches define a "member" in the same way, nor are all churches equally prompt to prune duplications and inactive members from the roll. And the mere fact of aggressively evangelistic efforts by the Catholic Church, together with a number of highly publicized conversions (for example, Henry Ford II, Clare Booth Luce) still arouses anxiety among Protestant leaders. For they consider that more than merely religious doctrines are involved. As the editor of a leading Protestant journal sees it: "Rome is a cultural competitor of Protestantism

[12] John F. Kane, "Protestant-Catholic Tensions," *American Sociological Review,* 16 (October, 1951), pp. 663-672.

[13] For the quarter-century, 1926-1950, the National Council of Churches of Christ reports that the larger Protestant bodies (over 1,000,000 members) made membership gains of 59.7 per cent, compared with Catholic membership gains of 53.9 per cent. (*Christian Century,* 69 [March 26, 1952], p. 357. A prominent Protestant interdenominational journal, *Christian Herald,* estimates over 4 million Catholic conversions to Protestantism within the past decade—very possibly an exaggerated estimate. (*Time* [April 5, 1954], p. 65.)

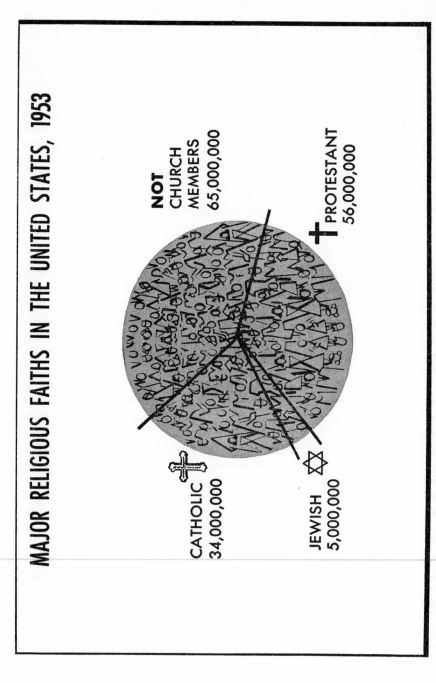

FIG. 8-2. Membership in Major Religious Faiths, 1953. (Data from the *Yearbook of American Churches*)

wherever the two coexist in the same society. The differences between them are radical and irreconcilable. The ascendancy of one spells one kind of America. The ascendancy of the other spells another kind." [14]

It is futile to point out that America's tradition of religious liberty grants Catholics the same right to seek converts that Protestants enjoy. The fact is that Protestants have long assumed that this would remain a Protestant country and are now disturbed to discover that their assumption is being challenged. A great many Protestants feel that the Catholic Church in America has never really accepted the principles of religious liberty and of separation of church and state. They fear that Catholic ascendancy in America would mean persecution of Protestants, church domination of the state, religious censorship of the movies, radio, and press, and suppression of free inquiry and expression in many areas of life. They cite the reported existence of some of these conditions in present Catholic countries in evidence.[15] To these charges, American Catholics reply that the practices of the Catholic Church always reflect the cultural setting in which it functions, that American fears of loss of liberties through Catholic action are completely unwarranted, and that a strong Catholic Church in America strengthens American freedom.[16] Yet Protestant fears continue, leading to charge and countercharge, hostility and resentment.

2. Differing Mores: Divorce, Birth Control, Gambling

In an earlier period when divorce was rare and strongly condemned by all church folk and birth control was virtually unknown, there was no reason for Catholics and Protestants to disagree. But among the social changes of the past half-century, divorce has become commonplace and birth control a widespread practice, each with a measure of carefully-qualified approval from most Protestant churches. The Catholic Church does not recognize divorce for any reason whatever and condemns all chemical or mechanical devices for the prevention of conception. Catholics have sought to impose these views upon the entire society through

[14] C. C. Morrison, "The Protestant Task," *Christian Century,* 63 (May 15, 1946), p. 619.

[15] See the editorials, "What Is the Truth About Columbia?" *Christian Century,* 69 (October 1, 1952), pp. 1116-1117; "More 'Americanism'?" *Christian Century,* 69 (July 25, 1952), pp. 741-743; "Protestant Freedom and Italian Law," *Christian Century,* 69 (October 1, 1952), p. 1117; also *New York Times,* February 14, 1954, p. 6; *Time* (February 8, 1954), p. 36. See also Paul Blanshard, *American Freedom and Catholic Power* (Boston, The Beacon Press, 1953).

[16] Cf. George H. Dunne, *Religion and American Democracy: A Reply to Paul Blanshard's American Freedom and Catholic Power* (New York, America Press, 1949); James M. O'Neill, *Catholicism and American Freedom* (New York, Harper and Brothers, 1952).

law and in some states have been partly successful.[17] Most Protestants have no objection to Catholics applying these views to themselves, but bitterly resent the attempt to impose them on non-Catholics by law. Catholics contend that these practices are forbidden by the "natural law of God," and that this law is binding upon all people, whether Catholic or not. The basic issue, therefore, is not whether divorce or birth control are socially desirable or harmful, but whether they are contrary to the "natural law of God," and this question cannot be *scientifically* proven or disproven. No real settlement or satisfactory compromise is possible unless one side surrenders its beliefs. Meanwhile, this situation produces a great deal of mutual resentment.

The fact that many individual Protestants like to gamble does not alter the fact that the Protestant churches are practically unanimous in condemning all gambling as immoral and socially injurious. The Catholic Church believes that certain games of chance, such as bingo or lotteries and raffles, are harmless when conducted by religious or benevolent organizations.[18] In a number of states, the question of legalizing "charity bingo" and certain other games of chance has provoked bitter political controversy.[19] This issue generally arrays Catholics and Protestants in opposition, issuing critical and self-righteous remarks about each other. Since differences in mores can rarely be resolved by discussion and compromise, extreme bitterness is sometimes provoked by this issue.

3. Parochial School Aid

The Catholic Church educates a growing proportion of its children in Catholic schools, controlled and entirely financed by the church. In 1938, the nonpublic schools, mainly Catholic, enrolled one-tenth of the nation's pupils; by 1953, this had risen to one-eighth and is expected to reach one-seventh by 1960.[20] At a time when most students quit school early, when equipment was limited and teachers needed little training, the costs of a private-school system were not too burdensome. As the school term lengthened, as students prolonged their education, and as standards of equipment and teacher training were raised, the burden of supporting

[17] E.g., Connecticut law forbids the use of contraceptives, or the giving of contraceptive information. Repeated attempts to pass a law permitting Connecticut physicians to prescribe contraceptive devices for married women where their health was concerned "have failed because of strong Roman Catholic opposition." (*New York Times,* April 19, 1953, p. 52.)

[18] Cf. Ansley C. Moore, "The Case Against Gambling," *Christian Century,* 69 (February 20, 1952), pp. 218-219; Thomas N. Numson, S.J., "Gambling, A Catholic View," *Christian Century,* 69 (April 9, 1952), p. 437.

[19] Cf. *New York Times,* August 24, 1954, p. 15; September 2, 1954, p. 23; September 3, 1954, p. 1; September 4, 1954, p. 6; September 10, 1954, p. 1, 17; September 15, 1954, p. 35; September 8, 1954, p. 27; September 17, 1954, p. 12, 29; September 23, 1954, p. 1; January 9, 1955, p. 1.

[20] *New York Times,* April 12, 1953, IV, p. 11.

parochial schools mounted. Catholics are now seeking public funds for the partial support of these schools. They state that their taxes help support public schools, that they are being "doubly taxed," and that the parochial schools relieve the taxpayer of much expense. They ask for tax assistance of various forms; that school taxes be refunded to Catholics, that their schools share in state or federal aid payments, that their children be transported in public-school buses, or that certain other expenses be assumed by the state.

Relations between public-school leaders and Catholic educators are, on the whole, amiable and co-operative.[21] But there are questions of value which cordiality does not erase. Since state aid to parochial schools would presumably aid Catholic evangelism, those who fear the spread of Catholicism are opposed to all such proposals. Opposition also comes from those who fear the destruction of the public-school system through its atomization into the series of church-controlled school systems which they predict would follow. They consider the public-school system an essential unifying agency in a democracy and fear that multiple school systems would foster divisiveness and lack of mutual understanding.[22]

4. Censorship

When the Catholic Church in America was busy with its immigrant membership, it paid little attention to the newsstands. Today the Catholic Church keeps a watchful eye on the newsstand and the movie screen. The Legion of Decency urges that all Catholics boycott such movies as, in its opinion, are obscene or critical of the church. Since movie-makers seek to avoid offending any group, this often results in deleting from the movie script any material that may offend the Catholic Church. In certain localities, Catholics have provided strong backing for censorship ordinances or boards that seek to remove "obscene" material from the newsstands. In one celebrated case, Catholic leaders succeeded in banning from public-school libraries a periodical which published articles critical of the Catholic Church.[23] Since all of these moves involve censorship of the reading material and movie fare of non-Catholics as well as Catholics, opposition and hostility develops. Opposition also comes from those who object to censorship by any private group because of a belief that all

[21] Cf. New York Times, April 12, 1953, IV, p. 11.

[22] See V. T. Thayer, The Attack Upon the American Secular School (Boston, The Beacon Press, 1951), or James B. Conant, "Education, Engine of Democracy," Saturday Review, 35 (May 3, 1952), pp. 11-14 for a vigorous statement of this thesis; see criticism by Archbishop Richard J. Cushing, "The Case for Religious Schools," Saturday Review, 35 (May 3, 1952), pp. 14 ff; see an intermediate view by Allan V. Helly, "A Call for Diversity," Saturday Review, 35 (May 2, 1952), pp. 15 ff.

[23] Cf. New York Times, June 24, 1948, p. 1. For numerous citations covering this two-year controversy, see New York Times Index, 1948, p. 918; 1949, p. 615; 1950, p. 678.

censorship is oppressive or self-defeating, and this resentment falls heavily upon Catholics.

For all of these reasons, it appears to many observers that relations between the Catholic and non-Catholic segments of our society are growing more tense than they have been in the recent past. Since present social trends promise to aggravate rather than to eliminate these sources of hostility, it seems that these antagonisms may become still more bitter as time passes. While no blood bath is even remotely probable, a lengthy period of tenseness and distrustful hostility seems likely. Many nonreligious issues will become complicated by religious antagonisms. Political campaigns will continue to have religious overtones, with the religion of the candidate taking precedence over other qualifications for many voters. Such programs as "federal aid to education" will be complicated by disagreements over public aid to parochial schools. Periodic outbursts will betray inner tensions, like the violent Protestant protest at President Truman's appointment of a personal ambassador to the Vatican [24] or the Catholic criticism of former Harvard President James B. Conant for his endorsement of the principle of the public school.[25] Neither incident was highly important in itself, but each assumes importance as a symbol of an accumulation of anxieties and frustrations.

ANALYSES OF RELIGIOUS SOCIAL PROBLEMS

Social-Disorganization Analysis

Although America has never been free from religious conflicts, most of them have developed as a result of some change in the religious status quo. Either an invasion by a new religious group or the rise of a dissenting local group threatened the security of existing religious institutions. Insecurity breeds anxiety and distrust of the character and motives of one's rivals.

The religious problems here presented are not exceptions. The religious heterogeneity of America gives many opportunities for conflict, while the American tradition of religious liberty and tolerance has been relatively effective in minimizing these conflicts. With so many religious faiths, many claiming absolute and exclusive truth, it is remarkable that conflict has been so limited. But the rise of an aggressive Catholic evangelism in a traditionally Protestant country will place a heavier strain upon the American tradition of tolerance than it has borne for many generations. In some Latin American countries, where Protestants appear to be gain-

[24] See "An Ambassador at the Vatican," *Christian Century*, 68 (November 7, 1951), pp. 1272-1275.

[25] *New York Times*, April 16, 1952, p. 29; June 9, 1952, p. 17; August 22, 1952, p. 22.

ing strength,[26] Catholic anxieties are revealed in scattered acts of violence and suppression directed at aggressively evangelistic Protestants.[27] Should the Catholic Church make substantial membership gains in the United States, increased anti-Catholicism would probably develop.

The march of science has been perhaps the most disorganizing single factor, primarily responsible for the fundamentalist-modernist battle and the social-gospel controversy. It is unlikely, however, that the discoveries of natural and social science will be as disorganizing in the future as in the past. The liberal church has already adapted a theology which can readily accommodate itself to any further discoveries that are likely to appear. The fundamentalist churches have quite effectively insulated themselves from the impact of science upon theology and will confine their membership to those who accept such a divorcement.

Urbanization, industrialization, and secularization have had an impact upon the church which it has not yet fully recognized. The Protestant Church is still a largely rural institution insecurely transplanted into an urban environment. The oft-lamented "loss of influence" of the church, to the extent that it is a genuine loss, may be a result of the church's relative isolation from many of the real problems of people in an urbanized, specialized, impersonal, secondary-group society. The Catholic Church, with its membership mainly among urban workers, has been more prompt to recognize this than most Protestant churches. Both Catholic and Protestant churches have elaborated their programs of activities in an attempt to cater to the diversified interests of people today. But whereas the Protestant churches still appear to consider the individual mentality to be the proper unit for evangelistic effort, the Catholics also direct their

[26] According to *Gentes*, missionary organ of the Jesuits, Protestant membership in Latin American countries has increased 500 per cent in the last 25 years. (Reported in *Christian Century*, 69 [April 23, 1952], p. 484.)

[27] See footnote 15. See also "Colombian Mob Stones Presbyterian Church," *Christian Century*, 69 (April 9, 1952), p. 422; "Priest Leads Children in Stoning Church," *Christian Century*, 69 (April 23, 1952), p. 483; "Causes of Violence," *Commonweal*, 56 (August 22, 1952), p. 476.

It appears that in Catholic countries, Protestant churches are not likely to be disturbed unless they engage in active, public efforts to gain members, thereby threatening to disorganize the status quo. One Catholic writer, describing certain Protestant bodies which have long existed in Spain without molestation, states that they "have loyally co-operated. They abstain from proselytizing and open propaganda. Unfortunately certain smaller sects use political means and large funds of foreign origin for their propaganda by which they seek to undermine Church and State." (Archduchess Adelaide of Austria, "Cardinal Segura and The Protestant World," *Catholic World*, 175 [July, 1952], pp. 266-272.)

In a predominantly Catholic country, the propaganda of a small Protestant minority, largely inspired and financed by foreigners, arouses a reaction somewhat similar to that aroused in many Americans by communist propaganda. In each case, it appears to be an attack upon both God and country. It is also possible that, in at least some cases, Protestant missionaries may have been unnecessarily provocative and insulting in a (conscious or unconscious) desire to invite persecution. A little persecution may be highly beneficial to an obscure sect struggling for recognition.

appeal to "collectivities"—the Negroes, the workers, ethnic groups—in what represents a rational adaptation to the structure of modern society.

The Value-Conflict Approach

In a number of respects, value-disagreements enter into religious conflicts. The clash between the sacred and the secular values which our scientific progress and our economic materialism have encouraged lies at the root of the "problem" of godlessness—certain people are more secular-minded than other people think they should be. A "secular-minded" person is one who is inclined to be preoccupied with worldly goals and interests and to seek explanations in terms of physical cause-and-effect sequences instead of in terms of divine influence. Both fundamentalists and liberals consider secularism a threat to religion, possibly an even greater threat to religion than communism or atheism.

That secularism and materialism are enemies of religious faith cannot be denied, but it is not clear even to churchmen how they are to be overcome. Our scientific and mechanical civilization encourages secularism, as people are conditioned to look for physical rather than supernatural causes for events of all sorts. Most daily "problems" consist of the malfunctioning of some human contrivance—the car breaks down, traffic jams up downtown, a government policy works out badly, and so on. When faced with such problems, we call a mechanic, engage some traffic engineers, or revise government policies. We do not pray about these, for both the causes and the cures are well within human understanding and control. The urban factory worker, operating a machine which he can feel, control, and perhaps repair, is less likely to feel a constant sense of dependence upon supernatural forces than the primitive hunter or the farmer. Knowledge—sometimes superficial knowledge—often leads to secularism, a point which some faiths have recognized by attempting to discourage the spread of knowledge.

Materialism—a preoccupation with worldly possessions and interests—competes with religion for man's time and money, but how is materialism to be curbed? Our economic system rests squarely upon the deliberate cultivation of materialism, and there is no immediate prospect that this will change. Our status system is largely sparked by material symbols. The core of our system of incentives lies in an appeal to man's carefully stimulated thirst for possessions and conspicuous consumption. Materialism is too deeply rooted in our culture to be easily replaced, and the clash of materialistic with religious values is not likely to diminish.

Other value-clashes, real or imaginary, are central to the tension between Catholic and non-Catholic. Many non-Catholics do not believe that the Catholic Church in America has really accepted the principle of religious liberty and separation of church and state. These values are not highly developed in most Catholic countries, and occasional Catholic pronouncements have encouraged Protestant fears that a Catholic America would bring religious persecution, domination of the state by the church, and widespread suppression of scientific and academic freedom.[28] Repeated avowals of devotion to democracy by American Catholics fail to allay these fears.

Any sociologists would readily predict that a Catholic America would differ greatly from Catholic Ireland, Spain, Italy, or Peru even as these countries differ from one another. The American cultural heritage will continue to shape American values and practices, regardless of which religious group gains ascendancy. It is also true that the profound differences between the Catholic and Protestant churches would significantly affect our culture, should one supersede the other. No sociologists can predict exactly what these effects would be, or to what degree these Protestant fears may or may not be justified. But the *existence* of these Protestant fears is an objective fact, and there appears to be little prospect for more congenial relations between Catholics and Protestants as long as such fears survive.

The Personal-Deviation Approach

To what extent are deviant persons involved in religious problems? To a great degree, in the opinion of most observers. Every minister has suffered with the parishioner who, with great professions of religious devotion and divine guidance, proceeds to wreck his church by stirring up all sorts of trouble. Such persons are not usually hypocrites; they are simply neurotics who happen to be religious. For a neurotic who belongs to the church is still a neurotic. He still imagines slights and insults; he defines all disagreement as personal opposition; he insists on having his own way, impugns the religious sincerity of any who block him, and finally leaves to disrupt another congregation.

The number of people who are seriously mentally ill is vastly exceeded by those who are in a state of neurotic adjustment. These persons are oriented to reality, but their reactions to reality are considerably distorted by their unconscious fears, hostilities, insecurities, and unsatisfied longings. Such people are likely to be oversensitive, overcritical, jealous, aggressive, uncompromising, and very intense in their opinions and dislikes. Frequently they are prodigious workers, but their labor is often wasted because others find them so hard to work with for long. Religious activity is one of the many possible outlets for such people. Religion has certain advantages as an outlet, for the members of a religious body are required to welcome the newcomer, to refrain from too sharp criticism, and to refrain from ejecting even the troublesome member. Furthermore, the

[28] Cf. Blanshard, *op. cit.*, pp. 112, 114-115, 121.

neurotic may find through religion an effective rationalization for his motives. Where else can one sanctify his selfish and petty impulses and raise them above examination by attributing them to the will of God? The Protestant tradition of the "priesthood of the individual believer" [29] means that each person's prayerful conclusion as to the will of God must receive respectful recognition from others. Most ministers need no study of psychology to arrive at the suspicion that sometimes a member's "divine commands" arise not from the voice of God, but from the depths of his own unconscious compulsions and yearnings. Usually these people are intensely earnest and deeply hurt at the suggestion that their inner motives are other than purely spiritual.

Every church is plagued with some of these maladjusted troublemakers. The Catholic Church, with its authoritarian structure, can control them with a minimum of confusion. Casual observation suggests that they are most numerous not among the major Protestant denominations, but among the marginal Protestant sects and fundamentalist bodies. These groups are somewhat unconventional and therefore may attract the deviant person. They are bitterly and vocally critical of the major denominations, and provide the neurotic with an approved outlet for his hostilities. Being relatively small congregations, they offer many opportunities for leadership. Aggressively evangelistic, they offer an approved opportunity to lose one's self in purposeful activity. There would appear to be much more to attract and hold the interest of the deviant or the neurotic in these groups than in the sedate downtown churches. It is *not* suggested that most of the members of these bodies are neurotics, but merely that those persons who are neurotic may tend to gravitate to them.

Neurotic behavior appears to play an important part in religious conflicts, as in most conflicts of any sort. In most such controversies, the extremists on both sides appear to be neurotic persons who are more interested in making issues than in resolving them and taking greater pleasure in scoring points than in settling them. The most bitter anti-Catholicism among Protestants is found not among the leaders of the major liberal denominations, but among the most narrowly fundamentalist sects, who merely include Catholics in their violent condemnations of all who disagree with them. And the Catholic Church has recently felt it necessary to suspend an intolerant priest who has attracted a following of "scowling fanatics." [30] It is clear that much neurotic behavior is expressed through religious activity and that much of the bitterness of many religious controversies stems from the compulsions and emotional mal-

---

[29] All Protestant churches teach that the believer may approach God directly, without any intermediary priests or officials, and that God may reveal his will directly to the believer. A member of a Protestant church is taught that the layman may, on occasion, administer sacraments, perform other offices, and some Protestant bodies (e.g., Jehovah's Witnesses) operate largely or entirely without a professional clergy.

[30] *Time* (May 2, 1949), p. 67; (October 13, 1952), p. 78.

adjustments of the more violent participants. Even if all doctrinal disputes, power struggles, and value-conflicts among religious groups were resolved, it is likely that the emotional compulsions of the neurotic minority would still provoke a measure of religious controversy.

CONCLUSION

Religious problems may be unique among social problems in several respects. For perhaps no other problem are so many people confident that they have "the answer." Since each group already has "the answer," no search for an answer is necessary. As each group's "answer" often consists of converting all the others, it is clear to the sociologist that these "answers" provide no solution in the foreseeable future. Meanwhile, there is little point in suggesting new answers to groups who are complacently satisfied with their present ones. There are other groups, of course, to whom the problem is not this simple, and who are actively seeking ways and means of resolving religious differences.

With few if any other problems is there so great an opportunity to use *tolerance as a solution*. To "tolerate" crime, ill health, or waste of natural resources would be no solution, for the social effects of these conditions would remain unaffected but still be defined as undesirable by our values. But intolerance is itself the cause of much of our religious tension, and "a decent respect for the opinions of mankind," which includes a respect for the "wrong" opinions we cannot accept, would relieve much needless conflict. If all persons, however firm in their own religious convictions, sought a tolerant understanding of the views of others, it would be far easier to confine "the problem" to those issues which actually require an agreement.

Although no genuine "solution" for religious problems is in immediate prospect, considerable progress has been made in certain areas. The fact that many different faiths exist in the United States with practically no violence is a substantial achievement. The ecumenical movement, seeking to unite similar churches into common denominations, has brought several mergers and may bring still more. Co-operation between denominations in areas where they can work together is being promoted at the national level by the National Council of Churches, and at the regional and local levels by appropriate church councils and ministerial associations. Although in certain areas, religious tensions appear to be growing, there are others in which discord and rivalry are being replaced by amity and co-operation. The sharpness of religious conflicts in the future will be highly affected by the strength of the American traditions of religious tolerance and democratic regard for the rights and beliefs of others, and there is reason to believe that these may become stronger than ever before.

SUGGESTED READINGS

BERNARD, Jessie, *American Community Behavior* (New York, The Dryden Press, 1949), "Religious Competition," pp. 242-257. A section dealing with competition between religious groups in the United States.

CRONIN, John F., *Catholic Social Action* (Milwaukee, The Bruce Publishing Company, 1948). A description of Catholic activities in dealing with social problems and social reform.

JOHNSON, F. Ernest, ed., *American Education and Religion: The Problem of Religion in the Schools* (New York, Harper and Brothers, 1952). A presentation of the issues by a number of educational and religious leaders.

MAY, Henry F., *Protestant Churches and Industrial America* (New York, Harper and Brothers, 1949). A history of the rise of the "social gospel" in the United States during the nineteenth century.

MAYER, F. E., *The Religious Bodies of America* (St. Louis, Concordia Publishing House, 1954). A reference book describing the history, doctrines, and practices of the churches of America and of the various interdenominational councils; statistical data from 1954 Census of Religious Bodies.

MUELDER, Walter G., *Religion and Economic Responsibility* (New York, Charles Scribner's Sons, 1953). A statement of the "social gospel" attempting to interpret Christian principles in terms of the structure and problems of modern society.

STUBER, Stanley I., *Primer on Roman Catholicism for Protestants* (New York, Association Press, 1953). An appraisal of the basic differences between the Roman Catholic Church and Protestantism, written not to convert but to inform, and probably as objective and nonpolemical as any book available in this field.

YINGER, J. Milton, *Religion in the Struggle for Power* (Durham, Duke University Press, 1946). An empirical study of religion as a factor in human behavior.

QUESTIONS AND PROJECTS

1. How can an intangible like "lack of religious faith" be a social problem?
2. Is it possible to resolve religious disagreements scientifically?
3. What conflicts of value enter into Catholic-Protestant tensions?
4. Why has the assimilation of the Catholic immigrant group in the United States failed to produce a disappearance of tension between Catholics and Protestants?
5. Jews receive no mention in this chapter, but receive considerable attention in the chapter on race. Why, since the Jews are not a race, are they discussed in that chapter rather than this one?
6. In what sense is the "social gospel" a product of social change?
7. Read Marshall Wingfield, "One Preacher in Politics," *Christian Century,* 69 (September 24, 1952), pp. 1094-1096. Do you think these activities proper for a Christian minister?
8. The article by David S. Burgess, "Place: A Georgia Town. Time: 1952," *Christian Century,* 69 (August 27, 1952), pp. 971-973, raises a number of questions about the role of the church in capital-labor controversies. Should it remain aloof? Should it defend the interests of its larger contributors? Should it encourage the unionization of workers? Is there any way for the church to avoid "taking sides" in economic conflict?

CHAPTER 9

Population Problems: Nation and Globe

Every *day* the increase almost equals the total of all the people living in Muncie and New Castle, Indiana.

Every *week* it almost equals those in Indianapolis and South Bend. Every month it exceeds the population of the state of Mississippi.

In a *year* it adds up to the population of three cities the size of New York, or of a nation equal to Mexico.

If this expansion continues at its present rate the world will be three times as crowded with people in 100 years. . . . [1] If the population expands only to a "medium" degree . . . here are some samples of how much extra food would have to be produced [in the U. S.] . . . by 1975.

About 5,500,000,000 pounds of beef, veal, pork, lamb and mutton. This is equal to the entire 1950 pig crop of two important meat-producing states, Nebraska and Iowa, or to the entire beef output in 1950 of the big cattle states of Texas, Oklahoma, and Minnesota, or to the entire 1950 lamb crop of Nevada, Utah, Wyoming, and Montana.

About 30,000,000,000 pounds of milk. This is an amount equal to the entire production of New York, Wisconsin, and Michigan.

About 15,000,000,000 more eggs—equal to all the eggs produced now in California, Kansas, Pennsylvania, Missouri, and Illinois. [2]

THIS book focuses on American social problems. Most of its chapters present data for the United States alone. One can discuss crime, traffic control, and the divorce rate without considering capital punishment in England, the flow of traffic in Ceylon, or divorce in Uruguay. The American aspects of such problems can be treated relatively apart from the status of the same problems in other parts of the world. But not always can this be done. In a few instances the *American problem* is inseparable from the *world problem*. The two are so interrelated that the American problem must be considered in the perspective of the larger world problem. Such is the case with population problems and also with war, which will be treated in a later chapter.

---

[1] Associated Press news release appearing in the *Indianapolis Star*, February 24, 1952. Italics not in original.

[2] Associated Press news release appearing in the *Indianapolis Star*, March 16, 1952. Data from *The 5th Plate*, U. S. Department of Agriculture, Production and Marketing Administration, December, 1951, p. 12.

THE PROBLEMS

Population problems may be summed up in three words: size, distribution, quality.

Size

The world's population has been characterized by irregular but continuous growth ever since the appearance of man on earth. Moreover, as time passes the average rate of growth increases. The world's people are multiplying faster now than ever before.

Demographers estimate that man has been on earth for a hundred thousand years or so. During the first ninety-eight thousand (more or less) years, or up to the time of Christ, the population increased to between 200 million and 300 million people. In the next 1650 years the population doubled to approximately 550 million, a rate of growth almost sixty times that which existed before. In the last three hundred years the population of the world has quadrupled again—to 2,400,000,000. According to the United Nations the next thirty years may see another 50 per cent increase, to 3,600,000,000.[3] Though it is impossible accurately to predict the size of the population fifty or a hundred years from now, the estimates vary only in the *rate* of increase predicted. Population growth in the past has been accompanied by both high birth rates and high death rates. Both rates remain high in most of the world today. Since a drop in the death rate generally precedes a lowering of the birth rate, large population increases seem inevitable in the near future.

Distribution

The almost two and a half billion people who populate the earth are not distributed equally over its surface. Nor are all nations or continents equally capable of supporting large populations. Differing ratios of population to resources and techniques of food production mean that population pressures are quite severe in some areas and practically nonexistent in others. In general, population pressures are greatest in Asia and the Near East and least in the United States, Canada, Australia, and in parts of Europe.

Asia contained in 1950 approximately 60 per cent of the world's population, Europe had 17 per cent, North America 9 per cent, Africa 8 per cent, and Australia less than 1 per cent. India, with a total land area of 1,353,364 square miles, has nearly 358 million people. Japan with only

[3] United Nations, Department of Public Information, Press and Publications Bureau, Press Release SOC/1341, 18 April 1952.

152,357 square miles has 83 million, the Soviet Union has 193 million people in a 8,400,000 square mile area, England has 44 million people in 58,343 square miles, and the United States has approximately 151 million people in 3,022,387 square miles.[4]

Within the United States, New York State has a density of 309 persons per square mile, Rhode Island has 748 people per square mile, Nevada has 1.5, and Wyoming has 3 people per square mile. In New York City the density is almost 25,565 persons per square land mile while in some parts of rural Montana the population density is less than 1 person per square mile.[5]

Bound up with these differences are problems of war and peace, famine and plenty, disease and health. Tens of millions of people have migrated from China, India, Japan, and Korea without materially reducing the size of their populations. The shrill cry for *lebensraum* (space for living) threatens the world with future disasters.

Quality

Ever since Darwin, the notions of "struggle for survival" and "survival of the fittest" have emphasized the idea of inequality within both animal and human species. Theoretically the fittest do survive, and the inevitable result of natural competition within the species should be to produce a constantly improving biological stock. A major difficulty with the theory, however, is that among human beings competition is not the simple biologic process that it is among lower species. Human competition is complicated by the existence of *culture*. Rarely do human beings meet in mortal combat. And when they do, the meeting is not likely to be a chance occurrence. Each combatant is likely to be a chosen representative of his group, specially armed and trained for the purpose. Each is equipped with weapons designed to minimize physical advantage. Wars are fought and won through technological superiority rather than through the quality of the germ plasm. High mortality rates among infants and children generally are considered bad, and efforts are made to save the weak as well as the strong. Within human groups, *social* selection is as important as *biological* selection.

It is widely feared that human interference with the operation of biological selection means a lowering of population quality. If the inferior and incompetent are protected against extinction, will they not go on to perpetuate their kind? May they not gradually lower the quality of the entire population and, perhaps, eventually bring about its destruction? Such fears have given rise to "eugenics," a movement to improve

[4] All population figures taken or computed from *United Nations Demographic Yearbook*, 1951, pp. 91-103.

[5] All figures taken or computed from *The World Almanac*, 1953, pp. 208 and *passim*.

population quality. The eugenics movement is based upon two principles: (1) discourage reproduction of the hereditarily unfit; and (2) encourage reproduction of the "better" biological stocks.

POPULATION GROWTH

The rapid rate of world population growth has already been noted. The figures themselves are staggering. But what do they mean? If the world already holds more than 2¼ billion people, is it not capable of holding twice as many, or even more? If there are limits that may not be surpassed, what are they? And how do they operate? A partial and classic answer to some of these questions was provided nearly a hundred and fifty years ago by Thomas R. Malthus in his famous *An Essay on the Principle of Population.*[6]

Malthus' Theory

According to Malthus, population tends to grow faster than the food supply can be increased. Population tends to increase in geometric fashion (1, 2, 4, 8, 16) while the food supply increases only arithmetically (1, 2, 3, 4, 5). Consequently, at any given time the size of a population is limited by the amount of available food. So long as they can be fed, additional children will live. Most of the population exists at a minimum subsistence level, barely staying alive and ready to be wiped out by a variety of possible calamities.

Malthus went on to define the nature of the calamities that result when population size presses too closely upon the food supply. These he called *positive* and *preventive checks.* The term *positive checks* refers to those means of population limitation which operate through the taking of human life. Chief among them are war, disease, and famine. Up until the time of Malthus these had been the principal forces holding down the rate of population growth. They result from the blind operation of societal forces, relatively independent of human control. The *preventive checks* reduce population size not through the taking of lives but through the preventing of additional births. They depend primarily upon the exercise of human will power. To Malthus this meant chiefly that people should delay the time of marriage. The longer they waited and the older they were at marriage, the fewer children would result. He did not, as is often assumed, advocate birth control in marriage. Modern contraception had not come into existence at that time and even if it had it is not likely that Malthus, who was a minister, would have regarded it as desirable. He placed great emphasis on the exercise of "moral restraint" through delay in the time of marriage.

[6] *First Essay on Population,* 1798 (New York, The Macmillan Company, 1926).

Malthus' theory was the first comprehensive one to see great danger to standards of living, to political freedom, and even to human survival in too rapid population growth. Drawing his illustrative material from the experience of the United States, which was growing rapidly through immigration and natural increase, Malthus postulated that under ideal conditions populations would double in size about every twenty-five years. In the absence of "moral restraint" this could mean only increased dependence on the undesirable positive checks—war, disease, and starvation.

Is Malthus' theory applicable today? Instead of there being a real shortage of food, the United States government is holding millions of pounds of surplus butter, farmers are operating under production quotas designed to limit the size of crops, and millions of bushels of grain are being "dumped" into foreign countries. At least in the United States, population does not seem to be pressing very hard upon the means of subsistence. Important changes have occurred since Malthus' time which must be taken into consideration in evaluating his theories.

England at the beginning of the nineteenth century was still very much an agricultural nation and was beset by a series of ever lengthening economic recessions. It was in this atmosphere that Malthus wrote. Poverty was widespread and was being rendered more acute by population increases. Malthus did not live to see the tremendous changes which were wrought by industrialization. The Industrial Revolution in Europe and the United States transformed agricultural nations into manufacturing ones, and food production increased at an almost unbelievable rate. Unparalleled growth and expansion followed. Population increased rapidly but the food supply increased even faster. Especially in the United States, Malthus' theory seems to have been invalidated by the course of social change. But before asserting that such is necessarily the case, let us examine more closely the current picture in the world at large and then in the United States.

The World Picture

Over one-half of the world's population is concentrated in Asia. China, India, Japan, Java, the Philippines—all have exceedingly large populations and all are threatened by inadequate food supplies. The Industrial Revolution has not been a world-wide revolution, since many of these areas have been relatively untouched by it. Undoubtedly industrialization could relieve the situation somewhat. But whether even full-scale industrialization could accomplish what it has in the United States is open to serious question. The United States is blessed with a large, fertile land area and relatively low population density. The world at large is much more crowded. According to one estimate, it takes a minimum of 2½ acres of arable land to provide a minimum adequate diet for each person. There are now less than 2 acres per person available.[7]

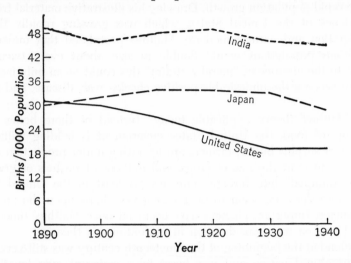

FIG. 9-1. Crude Birth Rates in Japan, India, and the United States. (Data from Warren S. Thompson, *Plenty of People* [New York, The Ronald Press Company, 1948], p. 34; and Kingsley Davis, *The Population of India and Pakistan* [Princeton, Princeton University Press, 1951], p. 69, by permission)

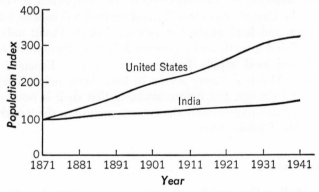

FIG. 9-2. Relative Population Growth in India and the United States, 1871-1941. Population expressed as an index: 1870-71 = 100. (Adapted from Kingsley Davis, *The Population of India and Pakistan* [Princeton, Princeton University Press, 1951], p. 27, by permission)

Especially in Asia, populations are characterized by exceedingly high birth rates and are held in check only by extremely high death rates. Malthus' positive checks seem to be in full operation. Poverty, malnutri-

[7] Fairfield Osborn, "Crowded Off the Earth," *Atlantic Monthly*, 181 (March, 1948), p. 18.

tion, and even starvation are widespread. Contrary to widely held opinion, not all Asian populations are increasing rapidly. Near saturation points were reached decades ago and increases have been limited to the additional persons who could be supported by the slight technological advances that have occurred. Unfortunately, accurate data for most of these countries are lacking. Adequate censuses are unknown and only estimates are available. The most reliable information comes from India where the population has been under intensive study for a number of years. Since 1870 the rate of population growth in India has been only about one-fifth that of the United States. Yet the birth rate in India has been nearly twice as high. In Asia, generally, the "positive checks" continue to operate with undiminished fury.

U. S. Population Growth

American population experience up to the present has been that of rapid and almost continuous growth. From approximately 4 million people in 1790 the United States had grown to 151 million in 1950, and the total has now passed the 160 million mark. This represents an increase of 3900 per cent in 160 years. For analytic purposes, United States population growth may be considered in three separate stages: before 1900; 1900-1940; and from 1940 onward.

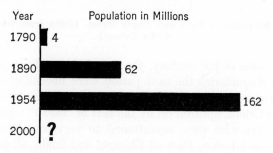

FIG. 9-3. United States Population Growth, 1790-1954. (Data from the U. S. Bureau of the Census)

Before 1900. Superficially, population growth would appear to be due to high or increasing birth rates. Equally important, however, are the size of the death rate and the amount of migration. These latter factors have been of great importance in the United States. Until very recently, the trend in American birth rates was steadily downward. Past gross reproduction rates [8] are shown in Figure 9-4. But American death rates have been dropping even faster. Between 1880 and 1950 the death rate dropped by 60 per cent while the birth rate decreased only 43.4 per cent.

[8] The number of births per 1000 population.

The decreasing death rate means a larger population *in spite of* a declining birth rate.

Some forty millions of the United States population were gained through immigration, coming primarily from Europe. During most of the nineteenth century the United States government looked with favor upon immigration and did little to discourage it. Land was to be had almost for the taking and immigration was a means of developing and strengthening the country. Most of the immigrants were coming from the countries of northwestern Europe such as England, Ireland, and Germany. Similar in cultural background to those who were already here, the immigrants adjusted easily and were rather quickly accepted by the "Americans."

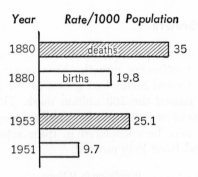

FIG. 9-4. The Decrease in Birth and Death Rates. (Data from the U. S. Bureau of the Census)

Before the turn of the century, the population policies and problems that were to characterize the next period were becoming evident. Birth rates were dropping rapidly, and the government began to curb immigration from the Orient. Spurred on by the fear of "unfair" competition from Chinese laborers who were accustomed to very low living standards, first the Chinese laborers, then all Chinese, and finally all Japanese were excluded.

1900-1940. Though the population continued to grow during the early decades of the twentieth century, the increment added each decade was smaller than the one before. Reproduction dropped below replacement requirements and by the 1920's immigration virtually ceased. The prolonged depression of the 1930's depressed birth rates even further, and from 1931-1935 for the first time the number of persons emigrating *from* the United States exceeded the number migrating *to* the United States.[9] The steady decline in birth rates led demographers to predict that soon the population would stop growing. That very thing had already hap-

[9] U. S. Bureau of the Census, *Statistical Abstract of the United States: 1952* (Washington), p. 95.

pened in Europe, particularly in France and Scandinavia. Eventually, they predicted, the population would even start to decline. At first it was believed that a stable population size would be reached by 1970 or 1975. But then World War II loomed on the horizon, the nation began to come out of the depression, and things began to happen to the birth rate.

From 1940. Fluctuations in the birth rate from 1938 to 1945 can be ascribed almost wholly to the war. Birth rates rose at first and then dropped as more and more men left their homes and the country. Beginning in 1946 the number of births increased rapidly, reaching an all-time high of 3,786,000 in 1947. The figures for the years 1948-1950 were only

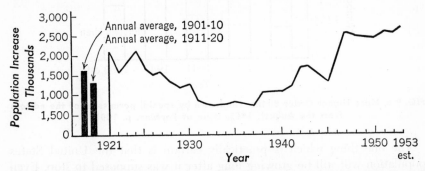

FIG. 9-5. Net Population Increase, 1921-1953. (Redrawn by special permission of the editors from the August, 1953, issue of *Fortune*, p. 100)

slightly lower. Demographers generally "stuck to their guns," maintaining that no real reverse had occurred. We were simply experiencing, they said, the effects of the backlog of marriages which had built up during the depression of the 1930's and the war of the early 1940's. They pointed out that most of the births were of first or second children—the result of the formation of new families rather than an indication that families were getting larger. The birth rate would drop soon, and drastically. It did not. In 1951 the number of births totaled approximately 3,900,000, a new high. Since then the annual number of births has passed 4,000,000.[10] The marriage rate reached its peak in 1946 and has declined gradually since that time. Not as many new families are being formed and yet the number of births continues to climb. People are having more children! The number of first births has declined somewhat since 1947; second, third, and fourth births are becoming more numerous. In 1953 it was estimated that there would be born: [11]

```
1,300,000 first    children (47 per cent increase over 1940)
1,170,000 second      "    (91  "    "     "      "      "  )
  620,000 third       "    (86  "    "     "      "      "  )
  310,000 fourth      "    (61  "    "     "      "      "  )
```

[10] *Fortune,* 48 (August, 1953), p. 103.
[11] *Ibid.*

Percentage-wise, even the increase in fourth-order births is higher than that for first-order births. What has happened to the predictions of a continuing decline in birth rates and eventually a stable population?

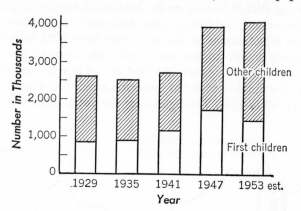

FIG. 9-6. More Higher Order Births. (Redrawn by special permission of the editors from the August, 1953, issue of *Fortune*, p. 100)

The one thing which is practically certain is that the United States population will still be growing long after it was supposed to stop. Even if birth rates should immediately resume their long-time downward trend, the present crop of youngsters would ensure continued growth till about the end of the century, And, at present, there is no sign that birth rates will drop again. Demographers, with the traditional caution of scientists, have adopted a "wait-and-see" attitude. They are revising their predictions and examining the bases for the present "bumper crop" of babies to see how long it may be expected to continue.

The question is whether or not we are witnessing a real reversal of the long-time trend. Heretofore, modern contraception has permitted, and the emphasis on material goods and rising standards of living has encouraged, small families. The pattern was supported by rationalizations that "small families permit each child to be better cared for and to receive more of the *advantages*." The advantages in large part were construed to be material advantages, such as new refrigerators, bicycles, and college educations. Perhaps, if the apparent reverse is real, the satisfaction value of having additional children is rising relative to that of automatic dishwashers and longer-wheel base automobiles. At least some people feel that families, especially large families, are becoming increasingly important to their members. If true, the new rationalizations may be that "the give-and-take of living in a large family is worth more than any material goods."

It should be remembered, however, that the last ten years have been a period of almost unparalleled economic prosperity. Additional children have not for the most part required families to "take in their belts." It has been possible to have additional children *and* luxuries. The real test may come when and if living standards drop. Continued large families in the face of some financial hardship might well mean that a new cycle of growth is under way, and that perhaps the validity of some of Malthus' original formulations needs to be re-examined.

DISTRIBUTION: THE PROBLEM OF IMMIGRATION

For more than two hundred years the United States immigration policy was officially an "open-door" policy. The inscription on the base of the Statue of Liberty, presented to the United States by France, indicates how this policy was received abroad:

> Give me your tired, your poor,
> Your huddled masses yearning to breathe free,
> The wretched refuse of your teeming shore,
> Send these, the homeless, tempest tossed, to me:
> I lift my lamp beside the golden door.

The United States was a haven of refuge for the surplus population of Europe and, to a very slight extent, for that of Asia. She became known as the "melting pot" where diverse peoples and cultures were fused into a new entity of great vigor and promise. Culturally and politically, the new nation remained tied to northwestern Europe. English-speaking people outnumbered other immigrants and established their prejudices in the new land. The first restrictions which barred the poverty-stricken, the insane, the disabled, and criminals from entering the country included also the first of a series of bans against Orientals, who were conceived as threats to the "native" population. Until after World War I, no further restrictions were imposed.

The stage for the drastically altered policies which followed World War I was set by the changed character of immigration during the last of the nineteenth and the first of the twentieth century. During this period, immigration from northwestern Europe had virtually ceased and increasing numbers came from the south and east—from Italy, Greece, and the Balkans. There were language barriers to be overcome, ethnic communities multiplied in the cities, and whereas the original migrants had been predominantly Protestant, the newcomers were more often Catholic. The antagonism and resentment first directed against Asiatics were extended to the south Europeans. The situation came "to a head" following 1918. There was much clamor "to keep America for Americans" and to protect American jobs by halting the flood of immigration. Laws passed in 1921 and 1924 laid down the basic policy which is with us yet today.

The concept of "national origins" underlies the legislation. Nations are allotted immigration quotas on the basis of the proportion of the United States population already made up of persons from those nations. The 1921 law stated that immigration from any country in any one year should be limited to 3 per cent of the persons of that nationality who were residents of the United States in 1910. The law of 1924 was even more drastic in that the proportion was reduced to 2 per cent and the base year was moved back to 1890. The practical consequence of this immigration policy has been virtually to cut off immigration to the United States.

Since the northern Europeans were the first to migrate to the United States, the national-origins system gives them very large quotas. People from central and southern Europe who had begun to migrate in large numbers only from about 1870 have very small quotas. Moreover, unused portions of one country's quota cannot be used by other countries, and unused portions cannot be carried over into the following year. Large parts of the quotas for England and other northern European countries remain unused while southern Europeans who seek admittance are refused. There seems to be little question but what prejudices against the Italians, Poles, Greeks, and others were both instrumental in the formation of this policy and were furthered by it. The "land of the free" is freer to northern than to southern and eastern Europeans!

Though the national-origins theory was established in the 1920's, it should not be interpreted as being solely a product of the past. In 1952, the question of immigration policy came up before the Congress again. The law that was passed, popularly known as the McCarran immigration law, did little to remove existing inequities, but simply consolidated and simplified the provisions of earlier laws.

QUALITY: THE DIFFERENTIAL BIRTH RATE; AN AGING POPULATION

The Differential Birth Rate

Up to now we have discussed population in terms of the total society. All elements in the population do not reproduce and increase uniformly, however. The societal birth rate is an average which derives from the higher birth rates of some groups and the lower rates of others. The higher-birth-rate groups account for a larger proportion of succeeding generations than do the lower-birth-rate groups. To paraphrase a Beatitude, "The high-birth-rate groups ... shall inherit the earth." The fact of such differential birth rates has long caused speculation on what they might mean. Any characteristics found disproportionately among the high-birth-rate groups would appear disproportionately in future generations. If these characteristics are desirable, the quality of the population should be improved; if they are undesirable, quality would be lowered. Upon these premises the eugenics movement exists, attempting to encourage reproduction of the hereditarily fit and to discourage reproduction of the hereditarily inferior.

Within the United States two instances of birth-rate differentials have received considerable attention. Rural birth rates are higher than urban ones, and birth rates vary inversely with socioeconomic status. Rarely is it contended that the rural population is either markedly superior to, or inferior to, the urban. The rural-urban differential is generally agreed to be of primarily social significance. Therefore, it will be treated in the chapter on urban and rural problems rather than here. Birth-rate differences according to socioeconomic status, on the other hand, are frequently conceived to have social *and* biological significance! These must be treated in the present section.

TABLE 9-1. Immigration Quotas to the United States

Great Britain	65,361
Germany	25,814
Greece	308
India	100
China	100

Based on Immigration and Nationality Act of 1952.

It is widely known that the economically dispriviled segments of the population tend to have large families, whereas white-collar, business, and professional groups are more likely to be childless or to limit the number of children to one or two. The inference is generally not that the lower economic groups are biologically more capable of having children but that the upper economic groups marry later and make more successful use of birth control. Generally, the higher the income, the more respected the occupation; and the higher the educational level, the lower the birth rate. That portion of the population which is college educated has never had enough children even to replace itself while groups with little or no formal education overreproduce themselves.

What does this mean for population quality? The arguments advanced stress biological factors or social factors, or both.

Biological Factors. Francis Galton, the English biologist, was among the first to recognize and systematically explore the possible consequences of birth-rate differentials. His conclusions have since been taken over in more or less modified form by large numbers of scholars and lay persons. Galton assumed that the biological struggle for survival and "natural selection" result in persons with greater innate ability or superior genetic endowment rising to the top of the social ladder while the less talented remain on the lower rungs. Hence, the upper classes of society are by and large the superior biological stocks. The fact that these groups do not adequately reproduce themselves means that the quality of the population is reduced accordingly. The human race, thus, might be breeding itself into mediocrity and, perhaps, eventually out of existence.

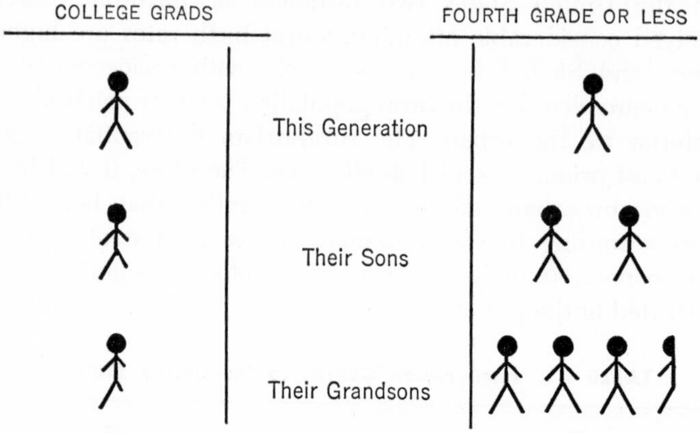

FIG. 9-7. The Uneducated Have Most of the Children. (Especially prepared by the Population Reference Bureau, Washington)

To many persons these conclusions have come to represent unquestioned fact and, though it would be error to assert that the eugenicists have uncritically accepted them, many eugenic proposals do in fact rest upon them. That which is commonly called "negative" eugenics calls for the sterilization of certain classes of people *believed* to have defective heredity. Since 1907 over two-thirds of the states have passed laws permitting or requiring the sterilization of certain groups. Most commonly, the laws call for sterilization of the feeble-minded, but some laws include the psychotic, the epileptic, certain criminal classifications, and certain types of hereditary malformation. The goal, of course, is to prevent the multiplication of hereditarily inferior types. However desirable the goal, the laws fall far short of achieving it.

The fatal weakness in this approach is in its original assumptions; namely that feeble-mindedness, psychosis, epilepsy, and criminality are *completely hereditary* and that they can be eliminated or even markedly reduced through sterilization procedures. The difficulties are twofold. First, the role of hereditary factors in causing these difficulties has been greatly overestimated. Probably not more than half of all feeble-mindedness is strictly hereditary, the other half being the product of very adverse environmental conditions, birth injuries, disease, and still other factors.[12] Adverse social conditions, as well as genetic factors, can produce feeble-

---

[12] For a balanced, readable account of the role of heredity in mental deficiency and mental illness, see Amram Scheinfeld, *The New You and Heredity* (Philadelphia, J. B. Lippincott Company, 1950).

mindedness in generation after generation, with whole families being affected. Similarly, only a part of all epileptic cases are hereditary and even fewer cases of mental illness are entirely genetic in origin. With regard to criminality, hereditary factors now are regarded as negligible. It is the consensus of social scientists that wholesale sterilization of such groups would result in sterilizing large numbers of people who are not organically defective but it would do little to reduce the number of defectives in the next generation.

The second difficulty derives from the fact that most defective organisms are produced not by defectives but by the so-called "normal" population. At least some of the genes which cause conditions such as organic feeble-mindedness are carried recessively, so that they may be present even when there are no observable signs in the individual. They may remain "hidden" for several generations, only to unexpectedly appear again. According to a reliable estimate, there are ten times as many normal persons as morons carrying a simple recessive "black" gene for mental deficiency. Most of the carriers of recessive harmful genes cannot be identified. But if they could, and sterilization were recommended, *"Almost every one of us would have to be sterilized!"* [13]

Social Factors. Galton and his followers generally failed to recognize the role of *social selection* in determining the placement of individuals within the socioeconomic structure. They assumed, but could not demonstrate, that it is superior innate ability which accounts for the movement of people upward in the class system. It is probable, however, that such nongenetic factors as motivation, shrewdness, and ruthlessness play a role in determining "who gets to the top." Moreover, the class system itself exerts a major selective influence. A given class status, once attained, becomes somewhat hereditary. The upper classes may contain many persons of decidedly inferior ability who are able to stay there simply because of the competitive advantages which upper-class status provides them. Similarly there is believed to be a vast reservoir of potential ability among lower socioeconomic groups which is not tapped because of unfavorable social environment. On these assumptions, a somewhat more realistic eugenics program has been developing.

Poverty-stricken adults beset by malnutrition and illness and living in ignorance, whether or not there is any organic inferiority, are not the societal groups best fitted to bear and raise the young. The upper economic groups, however, with their higher standards of housing, nutrition, medical care, education, and awareness of personal and social responsibility have traditionally had few children. Beyond the question of biologic capacities, large numbers of children have had "the cards stacked against them" *socially*. Consequently, eugenicists advocate larger families among

[13] *Ibid.*, p. 549. Italics in original.

the upper economic groups and lower birth rates among the economically disprivileged. The expansion of "planned parenthood" facilities, including adequate and inexpensive birth-control information, is basic to the latter. Legal implications of such a program are discussed in the chapter on the family, pp. 154-155. Efforts to raise the birth rates of middle- and upper-income groups have been less widespread. Reports by occasional public and private agencies have stressed the low reproduction rates among college graduates and have urged that these rates be raised. By and large, however, not much has been done. Yet family size among these same middle- and upper-income groups seems to be on the increase. A disproportionate part of the "baby boom" since World War II has been concentrated in the great middle-income group. Other recent statistics indicate that college graduates may be having enough children to replace themselves for the first time in recent history.[14] To further this trend seems to be the chief eugenic possibility. Little is known about and even less control can be exerted over the biological quality of the population. Within existing biological limits, however, considerable use might be made of the superior cultural advantages possessed by upper-income groups.

An Aging Population

Ordinarily we think of "population" as including persons of all ages and seldom stop to think that some populations may be "younger" or "older" than other populations. Expanding populations with high birth rates tend to be "young" because of the large proportion of infants and children in them. Stable or decreasing populations tend to be "older" because of their low birth rates and smaller numbers of children. Traditionally the United States has had a young population, and more recently there has been a rapidly increasing proportion of older persons.

During its early history the average age of the United States population was kept down by high birth, death, and immigration rates. That high death rates would keep ages down is obvious; the effect of high birth rates has already been mentioned. As for immigration, it is primarily people in the very young adult ages who migrate. Married immigrants also tend to have high birth rates. But birth and death rates have dropped steadily, at least since 1790, and immigration from Europe has virtually ceased. In 1800 the median age was 16 years, in 1920 it was approximately 25 years, and in 1945 it was almost 30 years. The average life expectancy increased from 49.2 years in 1900 to 67.5 years in 1950. In 1900 there were only three million people in the United States who

[14] The College Project, Population Reference Bureau, Milton, Massachusetts, News Release, June 11, 1952.

were over 65 years of age. The number had increased to 12 million in 1950 and will reach 22 million by 1980. This great increase in the number of aged persons will have extensive repercussions for the population at large.

Before discussing the effects of an aging population, however, the post-World-War-II birth rate again needs to be brought into the picture. Up to 1940 the increased proportion of older persons was accompanied by steadily decreasing proportions of younger persons. The "baby boom" has again raised markedly the numbers of children up to 10 years of age. The net changes since 1940, by age groups, are shown in Figure 9-8.

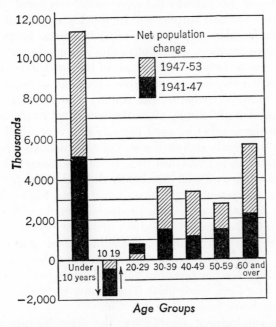

FIG. 9-8. Net Population Change by Age Groups, 1941-1953. (Redrawn by special permission of the editors from the August, 1953, issue of *Fortune*, p. 100)

If the birth rate remains high, then the *proportion* of older persons will not increase as rapidly as the *number* of older persons. If the birth rate should begin to drop again, then both the proportion *and* number of older persons will increase rapidly. The additional number of older persons to be expected is not subject to question. What we do not yet know is how many young people there will be to balance the older ones.

In any event, the presence of a large number of older people poses a variety of problems. In many industries, age 65 is the compulsory retirement age. Persons beyond this age are largely a dependent population—dependent for even the barest living upon their children and other younger adults. As the proportion of older dependent persons becomes larger, the burden of support will fall more heavily upon each younger adult. Here the birth rate is most important. If the birth rate remains high, the proportion of young adults will rise considerably beginning about 1960 and will remain relatively high. If it falls, the burden will be great. With rare foresight, the federal government anticipated this situation during the 1930's and instituted the Social Security program to help care for the increasing numbers of aged. Widely misunderstood, this program has been subjected to continuous criticism as "needless taxation." Up to the present, social security taxes *have* built up a considerable surplus (on paper, for actually the government has spent the money for other purposes) *but* that surplus will be quickly exhausted and a deficit built up as the number of persons over 65 increases. Labor unions, and to a lesser extent business, are emphasizing retirement and annuity programs as one way to help meet the needs of the aged. The next twenty or thirty years will likely see considerable expansion of such efforts. It is questionable, however, whether the country can afford to continue its arbitrary retirement philosophy no matter how great its old-age-assistance efforts. When the number of aged persons was very small, their retirement did not materially reduce the size of the effective labor force. But when the number of persons over 65 years of age exceeds 10 per cent of the total population, as it well may before the end of the present century, their enforced retirement might mean lower standards of living for the entire nation. Certainly per-capita production would suffer. Many persons of 65 years and beyond are still capable of performing their jobs efficiently and many physically undemanding tasks now performed by younger men might well become the province of older persons. In managerial and executive positions the value of increased maturity and experience has long been recognized. These same traits should be at least useful in many lesser jobs.

Beyond its employment significance, the changing age structure of the population will have other consequences for the economy. The bright young man of today who desires a rosy financial future should not overlook the expanding market for hearing-aids, bifocals, wheel chairs, canes, crutches, and other products in demand among older persons. Clothing manufacturers will need to devote more attention to the conservative styles and colors and, if the birth rate remains high, the market for children's apparel will continue to expand. Contractors will likely find increased demand for one-floor plan bungalows with no stairs to climb and, perhaps, for near "child-proof" houses with four bedrooms or so. Pediatrics and geriatrics (care of the aged) may be the "coming" medical specialties. Attorneys specializing in probate matters (wills and estates) will be in demand. From a "young adult" culture we may be entering a "youth *and* age" culture with ramifications yet undreamed of.

SOCIAL DISORGANIZATION

Population problems differ from most other social problems in the closeness of the tie to biological factors. Many writers have recognized this relationship by referring to population problems as "bio-social." In the present section we need to elaborate upon this interrelation and examine the association between population growth and social organization.

Throughout human prehistory and during most of the historic period populations were small. Food production techniques were crude and large population aggregates were not possible. Both history and natural science indicate that populations rather continually pressed upon the *available* resources and the available resources were definitely limited. Both technology and population developed gradually, probably through a large number of minor crises. Though Malthus did not write until the beginning of the nineteenth century, the principles he expounded probably had been operating throughout the millennia—population growth up to the maximum permitted by the state of the arts and then relative stability until some new technological advance permitted growth to be resumed. Not only did growth continue, but the *rate* of growth continued to accelerate. Small population groups were replaced first by civilizations, great in achievement but still comparatively small in numbers, and eventually by nation-states great in achievement *and* numbers. The stage of the nation-states had been achieved largely by the dawn of the industrial and agricultural revolutions—the greatest stimuli of all to rapid population growth. Until the beginning of the present era, growth meant gradual movement into yet virtually uninhabited areas and the opening up of small segments of vast untapped resources. Since the agricultural and industrial revolutions, however, the vast majority of the earth's habitable areas have become thickly populated and the earth itself has been rapidly relieved of its mineral and soil resources. Population size has been moving closer and closer to the theoretical maximum attainable. Previously unlimited resources have become limited through depletion. The seeming endless prosperity created by machine methods is being threatened by the familiar specter of *too many people!*

Modern technology not only has permitted population figures to push up into the billions but it has possibly provided the first large-scale interference with the quality of population. The limitation of the number of offspring through scientific birth-control is disproportionately the prerogative of the middle and upper classes. Whether or not it has any ultimate biological significance, the socio-cultural advantages possessed by the upper classes are not being used to fullest advantage. Modern medicine permits the survival and reproduction of *constitutionally* inferior persons whether or not they are *genetically* inferior. We may only speculate concerning whether there is also genetic inferiority, for hundreds of years will be required for any results of this process to become evident. Human beings cannot be quickly bred through several generations in the laboratory as is done with the fruit fly.

The most immediate threat to the existing social organization lies in *differential population pressure*. The pressure of numbers on available resources is relatively low in nations such as the United States and Canada and extremely high in many other nations. Population pressure, coupled with the existence of all-out war as a cultural technique, poses a serious threat to civilization itself. Satisfactory means of redistributing population do not exist. Migration barriers have become increasingly rigid. The countries experiencing the least population pressure are, by and large, the most successful ones in limiting population growth. The most crowded nations are prevented from using birth control effectively by a combination of ignorance and the incompatibility of contraceptive practice with other elements of the culture. Even surplus goods from wealthy nations are prevented from moving to needy countries by problems of currency exchange, trade barriers, and aggressive nationalism. The past few centuries have witnessed unparalleled technological advance and the crowding of the earth with people, but the population policies of today show no significant advances over those which existed four hundred years ago.

VALUE-CONFLICTS

Population values clash at many different levels. For discussion purposes we might distinguish those conflicts that rage among nations from those which are more nearly domestic matters.

International Conflicts

Many people in the United States are prone to assert that "if other nations just were not so backward, we wouldn't have to worry about populations getting too large." The implication is that science has now provided the means for population limitation and sensible persons (or nations) would not hesitate to use them. People who make such statements generally are not aware, of course, of their ethnocentric implications; namely, that our system of values should seem equally reasonable to persons reared in a different value-context. American values typically ascribe great worth to life itself and to high living standards, subordinating most other values to these goals. In some other nations, India is perhaps the best example, human life and welfare must yield to more sacred values. India's economic capacity is greatly reduced by having to support large numbers of sacred cattle and monkeys. The fact that Americans would say, "slaughter these animals," is of little help when "these animals" are valued higher than the people who would do the slaughtering. The unrealism of arbitrarily attempting to impose our values in such situations may become more evident when we realize that a somewhat similar situation exists *within* the United States. Though most Americans favor the limiting of family size to preserve at least minimum adequate living standards, the religious values of some groups define any attempts at limitation to be one of the gravest of sins. The "logical" conclusions of the majority make little difference if the behavior they advocate is *wrong* or *sinful*. Nor are there any more ready solutions when the conflict is between nations where even a clear majority belief does not exist.

There is an additional factor making it difficult to reach agreement at the international level—the power that is latent in numbers. So long as there is a struggle for supremacy among nations, numbers will be a factor in that struggle. Numbers and technological superiority are crucial. With them wars are won and without them wars are lost. When some nations such as the United States have definite technological superiority, less advanced nations are forced to rely upon the *size* of their armies. Programs for population limitation have little meaning when survival itself may depend on size.

Domestic Conflicts

Homogeneity versus Melting Pot. "To preserve the national character!" —"To maintain our homogeneity!"—"To exclude the inferior, the subversive, the unwanted!"—"Discrimination!"—"Racism!"—"Fascism!"—"Ignorance of the facts!" These are some of the most frequent battle-cries.

The issue is immigration, its extent and its character. The battle is being fought in local communities, in the press, on radio and television, and in Congress.

Proponents of the national-origins theory urge that the United States is no longer a developing country in need of population but a mature nation whose distinctive character has made it the leader among nations. They urge further that the existing composition of the population be maintained; that fairness to the people of the United States and to future citizens requires protection against our being overwhelmed by "foreign" elements. They maintain also that "the realities" of international struggle must be recognized and that the United States must exclude all persons who might possibly subscribe to subversive ideologies. As indicated earlier in this chapter, it is the national-origins theory which is currently supported by law.

Opponents of the national-origins theory do not regard the battle as lost, however. They declare that the present policy is un-American, auto-cratic, and unrealistic. Democracy in the United States, they insist, is built upon the recognition of differences and the faith that out of the free mingling of diverse peoples and philosophies a vigorous nation can be maintained. They see in the doctrine of national origins the implicit as-sumption that southern Europeans and Asiatics are "less desirable," and compare this reasoning to the former Nazi German notion of "Aryan superiority." They assert that the leading national exponent of representa-tive democracy is behaving shamefully like the fascist nations it fought to suppress. Just what the provisions of acceptable immigration legisla-tion would be have not been spelled out in detail. So far, the struggle has been limited to the fight against national origins. But the arguments used indicate a desire to allot immigration quotas on the basis of need and desire to immigrate, with far larger quotas going to non-English speaking nations and the elimination of categorical restrictions against Asiatics. Feelings run high on both sides of the issue and it will likely be reopened in future sessions of Congress.

Freedom versus Responsibility. Does everyone have the right to repro-duce? Or *should* everyone have the right to bear children? Is the *freedom* to bear children tied to the *responsibility* to bear normal healthy children who are not likely to become wards of the state? Should such freedom and responsibility be contingent on one another? One set of values as-sumes that reproduction is a basic human right not to be abridged, no matter what the eugenic implications. According to this view, one might encourage some groups to have children and discourage others, but the decision is ultimately a personal one. Often this reasoning is buttressed by our admittedly limited knowledge of human genetics. Though in some cases the quality of potential offspring may be predicted, in many cases it cannot. Especially when sterilization is recommended as a technique for preventing the reproduction of the unfit, the holders of these values see grossly unwarranted interference with one of the most basic of human rights. The situation is even further complicated by the necessity for providing adequate safeguards. Even should one grant the eugenic de-sirability of *selective* sterilization, how could its unintentional or, perhaps, calculated misuse be prevented? The possible benefits they say could never be worth the inherent risks in such a program.

Opposing factions, on the other hand, claim that the right to reproduce may be withheld when the exercise of that right would knowingly be detrimental to the group at large. They see, even in our limited knowledge of genetics, the possibility of greatly reducing the financial and social burden of caring for large numbers of mental and physical incompetents. Frequently they point to selective sterilization surrounded by "adequate" safeguards as the most humane and only rational approach to the prob-lem. About half the states, today, have sterilization laws and the *principle* of sterilization has been upheld by the Supreme Court. The actual number of sterilizations performed, however, has been quite low, and more than a third of the total have been performed in one state—California.[15] The California program is both looked to for leadership and a chief target in the maneuverings and conflicts of other states.

Pension Battles. The name Townsend recalls to many adults the largest scale pension struggle in the United States to date. The Townsend Plan to provide adequate pensions for aged persons, which enjoyed great vogue in the 1930's, is only one example, however, of similar campaigns large and small over the entire country. Increased numbers of older persons, often in dire financial straits, are politically a potentially powerful group. Shrewd politicians, recognizing this fact, have advocated everything from minimum subsistence plans to pensions providing $200 a month for every person over 65 years of age. The large pensions supposedly would stimulate purchasing power and general prosperity to the point where the states would be able to afford to pay the pensions. Such proposals are less common today than they were twenty years ago, probably because of the advent of Social Security and the high economic levels that have prevailed. Retirement plans in industry are also becoming increasingly common. Relatively few older persons can live adequately on the benefits available today, however, and future years may see pension proposals again take on increased importance.

PERSONAL DEVIATION

The Genetically Inferior

One of the most difficult problems facing biological and social scientists is to define the role played by hereditary and environmental factors in the production of defective, deficient, and deviant organisms. The problem is the more difficult because in many instances it is not heredity *or* environment but heredity *and* environment which bring the undesirable condition into being. Frequently a hereditary potential or "tendency" will not come out unless the environmental conditions are adverse, and adverse environmental conditions will not bring the condition about unless there is some hereditary tendency present. To be hereditary or genetic, the condition must definitely be tied to the operation of one or more genes. The genetic composition is determined at the moment of conception and normally cannot be changed by anything that happens during the lifetime of the individual. The presence of unfavorable genes is not always sufficient to produce a deviant organism, however. Geneticists estimate that practically all persons carry some unfavorable genes. Because it generally takes two or more such unfavorable genes, the deviancy does not

[15] Scheinfeld, *op. cit.*, p. 544.

appear unless unfavorable genes from the father "match up" with similar genes from the mother. Thus the deviancy may appear several generations apart, in seemingly unpredictable fashion, and still be hereditary. In other instances, the condition may repeat itself in successive generations. Certain recurrent physical abnormalities as, for example, the presence of additional or fewer than the usual number of fingers and toes is known to be hereditary. Blindness, gross physical deformities, deafness, and mental deficiency are *often* hereditary. It is further believed that some family lines carry greater than ordinary susceptibility toward certain diseases such as tuberculosis and schizophrenia. The difficulty as we move down this list is that environmental factors come to play larger and larger roles. Between those conditions which are purely hereditary and those which are purely social lie an intermediate group of "constitutional" deviancies.

The Constitutionally Inferior

Not all conditions that are present at birth are hereditary. Some of these "congenital" conditions are produced by the intra-uterine environment and some are contracted during the birth process. In hemolytic disease, for instance, the genetic combination of an Rh-negative mother and an Rh-positive fetus permit development of the disease *when and if* there is sufficient transmission of antigens and antibodies between mother and child. Hereditary factors alone will not produce the condition and yet, when found, it is present at birth. Syphilis is a good example of a disease frequently believed by the uninformed to be hereditary. Syphilis cannot be inherited but it may be transmitted to the child during birth by a syphilitic mother. Birth injuries, particularly to the head and to the central nervous system, occasionally produce defective and deficient persons for whom little can be done. Such conditions are congenital and organic, yet they are not hereditary. In still other cases there may be no abnormality present at birth but there is a proneness toward diabetes, tuberculosis, epilepsy, or yet other conditions. The genetic structure may be such that the individual is constitutionally weak in one or more regards, not having inherited any specific diseases but being especially susceptible to them.

The Socially Inferior

Research tends to ascribe continually increased importance to social-environmental factors in the production of deviants. Conditions which formerly were thought to be purely or principally hereditary in origin are found instead to be socially transmitted. It is now recognized that merely because a given condition tends to run in certain families is not sufficient reason to label it as biological. Many of the ills associated with lower population quality can be reduced through the bettering of environmental conditions alone. Slum conditions, poverty, malnutrition, and filth are capable of producing as much havoc in the *physical* functioning of human beings as are genetic factors. Among the diseases, tuberculosis is an excellent illustration. In the year 1900 tuberculosis resulted in more deaths in the United States than any other disease. Now, thanks largely to improved sanitary conditions, the TB death rate is only about one-sixth what it was then. To illustrate further: Negroes are widely *believed to be* more susceptible to tuberculosis than are whites. True, Negro death rates from TB are generally far higher than white TB death rates. *But* Negroes generally live under economic and social conditions far inferior to those of the whites. Examination of the situation in the city of Milwaukee in 1940 revealed that: [16]

The Tuberculosis mortality rate among Negroes living in a slum area was fifteen times as high as for Whites of the city. But a generation before (in 1915), the rate among Whites, mostly foreign-born, who lived in the same depressed environment *had been almost exactly the same as it now was among the Negroes who succeeded them there.* And among descendants of those same Whites, now living elsewhere and under much better conditions than their forebears, *the tuberculosis mortality rate had dropped to one-fifteenth*—to the same rate current for other Whites in the city.

Not all diseases result so directly from environmental conditions as does tuberculosis, of course, but much of the deviancy in any population is less closely tied to physical factors than is true in the case of physical disease. Adverse environmental conditions play an even larger part in the development of mental and emotional malfunctioning. Fuller discussion of these factors will be reserved for the chapter on personal pathologies.

SUMMARY

Population problems are chiefly those associated with size, distribution, and quality.

The tremendous size of modern populations is a relatively recent development. The world's population has more than quadrupled in the past 300 years. Throughout history, however, operation of the Malthusian principle, that population size tends to press upon the available means of subsistence, has been evident. Most of the world today has too many people in proportion to the available resources. The United States and part of Europe have escaped the struggle, temporarily at least, through

[16] From *The New You and Heredity,* by Amram Scheinfeld, Copyright, 1939, 1950, by Amram Scheinfeld, published by J. B. Lippincott Company, p. 172. Italics in original.

the tremendous production advances which followed the industrial and agricultural revolutions.

The United States has shown a continuous pattern of growth ever since its founding. Though both birth and death rates have dropped steadily, immigration sustained the pattern of growth until approximately 1920. The period beginning about 1940 saw a reversal in the birth rate and a trend toward larger families. How long this trend will continue is not yet certain.

Since 1921 the United States has followed a policy of drastic limitation of the volume of immigration according to the theory of national origins. This policy, in effect, discriminates against southern Europeans and Asiatics and has virtually cut off immigration to this country.

The quality of the United States population has been affected by the tendency for lower economic groups to have the highest birth rates, and by the gradual aging of the population. Although the lower economic groups may not be biologically inferior, the upper economic groups probably are best fitted to care for large families. The problems created by the aging of the population will depend greatly on whether the birth rate remains high. In any event, the production of goods and services will have to take cognizance of the changing age structure.

Rapidly growing populations pose a threat to the entire social organization. Mineral and soil resources formerly believed inexhaustible have become limited and are being used up at a rapid rate. Differences in population pressure among nations support international antagonisms and are one stimulus toward war. The various nations do not agree upon what are desirable population policies and how these may be achieved. Within the United States a bitter conflict rages over immigration policy, some eugenicists favor sterilization of people believed to be hereditarily unfit, and pensions, large and small, are sought for the aged.

Among the deviant persons in any population there may be distinguished the genetically or hereditarily inferior, the congenitally or constitutionally inferior, and the socially inferior. The socially inferior are probably the largest of these three groups and offer the quickest and surest route to improvement of population quality.

SUGGESTED READINGS

DAVIS, Kingsley, *The Population of India and Pakistan* (Princeton, N. J., Princeton University Press, 1951). The most thorough analysis, to date, of the population of India and Pakistan. For the serious student.

HANSEN, Marcus L., *The Immigrant in American History* (Cambridge, Harvard University Press, 1940). A readable account of the role played by European immigrants in American history.

OSBORN, Fairfield, *Our Plundered Planet* (Boston, Little, Brown & Company, 1948). Neo-Malthusian treatise, highlighting wastage of the world's resources and predicting dire consequences for the world's population.

Osborn, Frederick, *Preface to Eugenics* (New York, Harper and Brothers, 1940). An able introduction to the eugenics field by a leading United States authority.

Smith, T. Lynn, *Population Analysis* (New York, McGraw-Hill Book Company, Inc., New York, 1948). An excellent up-to-date treatment of United States population problems.

Thompson, Warren S., *Plenty of People* (New York, The Ronald Press Company, 1948). Discussion of population growth and population problems in various areas of the world. Intended for the lay reader.

Whelpton, P. K., and others, *Forecasts of the Population of the United States: 1945-1975* (Washington, Government Printing Office, 1947). Predictions of U. S. population growth according to varying fertility and mortality assumptions. Includes predictions of the age structure of the population and various problems resulting therefrom.

AUDIO-VISUAL AIDS

Food for Asia (British Information Services, 30 Rockefeller Plaza, New York), 10 minutes, sound, black and white. Produced for the British Foreign Office. Shows that in a war-stricken world the Far East is the greatest sufferer from lack of food. Tremendous efforts are being made to increase the acreage for growing rice and to step up production so that by trade the people may get the food they so desperately need.

Heredity and Environment (Coronet Films, Coronet Bldg., Chicago), 10 minutes, sound, black and white. Visual examples are shown of heredity and environment at work. An overview is given of cultural inheritances, genetics, environmental influences, and their interrelationships.

Immigration (Encyclopaedia Britannica Films, Inc., 1150 Wilmette Ave., Wilmette, Ill.), 11 minutes, sound, black and white. Photographs and animated maps show how the United States became populated, and why Europeans left the Old World for the New. Scenes of families leaving their homes for this country tell the human side of the story.

QUESTIONS AND PROJECTS

1. Why can we not consider American population problems in isolation from world population problems?

2. Describe the Malthusian theory of population growth. What are the "positive" and the "preventive" checks? How applicable are Malthus' theories today? in the United States? in Asia?

3. Explain how the tremendous growth of the United States population was accompanied by a steadily falling birth rate.

4. Why is it not possible to state definitely that a real reversal in birth rate trends has occurred since 1940?

5. What is "the differential birth rate"? Evaluate the belief that the differential birth rate is leading to a lowering of the quality of the United States population.

6. What kinds of problems are likely to be augmented due to the increasing proportion of oldsters in the population?

7. Evaluate the usefulness of the argument that, "India would have no excess population problem if only the Indians would kill off all the sacred cows and monkeys."

8. In what ways is the "national-origins" theory consistent with American traditions? In what ways is it contrary to basic American values?

9. Write a short paper on the topic, "Resolved: the unrestricted freedom to reproduce *is not* a universal human right." Now write a second paper on the topic, "Resolved: the unrestricted freedom to reproduce *is* a universal human right."

10. Distinguish among the genetically inferior, the constitutionally inferior, and the socially inferior. Which type or types of inferiority offer most promise for elimination?

11. Read Fairfield Osborn's *Our Plundered Planet*. Now relate the point of view of this book to Malthus' original theory of population growth. Why is this book described as neo-Malthusian? Evaluate the validity of its arguments.

12. Check the number of births for your county for the years 1930-1934 and for 1950-1954. What is the proportion of increase? To what factors do you ascribe the increase? What effects are the increased numbers of births having upon the community? What are community institutions, schools and hospitals, doing to adjust to the higher birth rate?

CHAPTER 10

Educational Problems and Conflicts

I was completely unprepared for the afternoon of August 14, 1952. I was quietly sitting in the audience of the board of education as an observer, when the anti-UNESCO group [opposing school study of the United Nations Educational, Scientific, and Cultural Organization and its work] launched into a series of scurrilous, demonstrably untrue attacks.

I looked around me at the wild cheering accorded each speaker. The room was packed. There must be one articulate supporter here, I thought, just for the record. In almost intuitive foreboding, I had requested a place on the agenda but had specified that I might not care to use it. Suddenly I found myself standing up to claim it.

As I, by then a notorious supporter of UNESCO, walked to the front of the room, I shuddered. The air was thick with hate. Snickers and sneers followed my progress. I had a blurred picture of the angry, flushed faces. My legs trembled as I braced myself against the speaker's stand. I was shaken at being so surrounded by hate, but I was furious, too. I shouted with all my strength above the din of the boos and jeers. Accompanying my words was the insistent rapping of the chairman's gavel, trying to silence the crowd.

This must be a nightmare, I thought. These are my fellow citizens. This is my beloved country. I couldn't believe my eyes and ears. What awful thing was I doing, what dreadful betrayal, to become an object of loathing, the target of glares and catcalls?

I had been allotted two minutes to speak, but I did not need a watch. At exactly two minutes I was stopped by shouts: "Her time's up . . . Get her off the stand!" For a moment I stood there, helpless and humiliated. Then, trembling, I walked through their ranks back to my seat. The meeting ended. Reporters came up to ask for the names I had read aloud: the noise had made it impossible for them to hear me accurately. Two members of the school administration, walking up the aisles to the exit, reached over the heads of the now standing crowds to shake my hand.

But I knew that I was surrounded by hostile glances and I heard venomous remarks about my character and patriotism. Two elderly women, tight-lipped and flushed, edged in on me exclaiming loudly, "You don't belong in this country! Why don't you get out?"

I got out—out of the auditorium to the parking lot as fast as I could. I was sufficiently afraid of physical reprisal to ask a friendly male teacher to stand by my car until I started the motor. The meeting had lasted so long it was dark, and I still could feel the waves of hate.

As I drove homeward, the once familiar Hollywood freeway appeared strange and ominous. Never in my life had I felt hate from strangers, people I'd never seen before, who knew nothing about me except that I believed in the teaching of world understanding.[1]

THESE paragraphs are taken from the harrowing story of an ordinary housewife who found herself swept into a local school battle of the sort which occasionally appears. The story reveals most of the elements of a community row over its schools—opposing views about the curriculum, conflicting values which the school is asked to protect, differing willingness to pay school costs, and the collapse of democratic processes as rational, orderly discussion of differences is crowded out by hostility, name-calling, and intimidation.

What crisis has arisen to excite such violent passions? Although American schools have always aroused public concern and debate, rarely has the debate become so bitter and ill-mannered. Not only are the educator's journals expressing alarm [2] but a number of books and general magazines have expressed concern.[3] What is the background of change and value from which this educational crisis arises?

PROBLEM AREAS IN AMERICAN EDUCATION

1. Costs: Education Is Expensive

In 1952 the people of the United States spent about $7 billion on their public schools. This is an amount equal to about $270 for each school child, and does not include the parent's expense of keeping the child in school, nor does it include the cost of private and parochial schools, nor of colleges and universities. Education, obviously, is a big and costly business.

Just how good is the education provided at such cost? The education editor of the *New York Times* reports: "Nearly 4,000,000 children are receiving an impaired schooling because of double sessions, lack of teachers, poor buildings, and inadequate financial support of the school program." [4]

a. Schools Are Obsolete and Overcrowded. A survey in 1950 showed that one in five schools needed to be remodeled or demolished, at a cost

---

[1] Dorothy Frank, "I Was Called Subversive," *Collier's*, 131 (March 28, 1953), pp. 68 ff.

[2] Cf. Agnes E. Meyer, "Freedom of the Mind," *American Association of School Administrators Official Report; 1953* (Washington, 1953), pp. 85-102; reprinted *N.E.A. News,* 7 (February 27, 1953); condensed in *National Education Association Journal,* 42 (April, 1953), pp. 207-210; L. Morey, "On Academic Freedom," *School and Society,* 79 (March 6, 1954), p. 761.

[3] E.g., H. Gordon Hullfish, ed., *Educational Freedom in an Age of Anxiety,* 12th Yearbook of the John Dewey Society (New York, Harper and Brothers, 1953), Ernest O. Melby and Morton Puner, *Freedom and Public Education* (New York, Frederick A. Praeger, 1953); Symposium, "Let's Attack the Problems ... Not the Schools," *Ladies' Home Journal,* 71 (October, 1954), pp. 54-57 ff.

[4] *New York Times,* February 28, 1954, IV, p. 9.

estimated in 1950 at nearly $15 billion.[5] In 1953 the nation was short 345,000 classrooms, and one in five pupils attended school in a building which did not meet minimum fire safety requirements.[6] In the single state of Michigan, to have adequately housed all public school pupils in 1952 would have required additional space equal to a building 43 feet wide and 85 *miles long*—stretching from Lansing to Detroit.[7]

At no time in our recent history has our school system been fully "adequate." Schools are always overcrowded, because a community will rarely build a new building until serious overcrowding has already developed. With a growing population, a new building is often already overcrowded by the time it is completed. Overcrowding and understaffing of schools are no new problems. What *is* new, however, is record governmental expenditures and the coincidence of a sharp rise in school enrollment at a time when taxes are at a level already considered intolerable.

School enrollments remained about the same during the 1930's and declined during the war years, partly because of the low birth rate of the depression 1930's and partly because of drop-outs for war jobs or enlistment during the 1940's. Few new school buildings were built either during the depression when money was scarce or during the war when materials were scarce. The birth rate, however, increased considerably during the war and still more greatly after the war. School enrollments began to zoom after the close of the war. During the first half of this century, public-school enrollments increased by 10 million pupils, but are expected to grow by another 10 to 15 millions in the *single decade* of 1950-1960!

A much smaller increase following World War I produced a great wave of school building. The situation now differs, however, in that taxes now claim over one-fourth of our national income, far more than after World War I. Taxes at such a level during peacetime are contrary to the traditions and expectations of our people, and they are borne with strong protests and widespread evasion. Candidates who are elected to office on a promise to "try to" cut taxes find that the voters wish to retain most of the governmental services and handouts, and that no great tax reductions are politically possible; meanwhile, the voters fret with a confused sense of helpless frustration. In this frame of mind, the voter may be asked to approve a bond issue and an increased school tax for a new building, and he may express his irritation at taxes in general by voting a thunderous "No!" For most citizens, the school budgets provide almost their only opportunity to vote *directly* against higher taxes. Even many

[5] Citizens Federal Committee on Education, Federal Security Agency, *Citizens, Look at Our Schoolhouses* (Washington, Government Printing Office, 1951), pp. 6, 10.
[6] *Michigan Education Journal*, 31 (October, 1953), p. 132-A.
[7] *Michigan Education Journal*, 31 (October, 1953), p. 81-A.

who claim to "believe in" schools appear to be so resentful of high taxes in general that they seize the first opportunity to register a protest, even at the expense of their own children's future.

There are few examples of a problem which can more easily be established and measured than the classroom shortage. Present classroom needs can be measured and future needs for a decade or so estimated with a high degree of accuracy. It can easily be shown that the present rather active rate of school construction will barely keep up with the growing school population, and that little real progress is now being made in relieving the shortage—that nearly as many children as before are still attending classes in antiquated school buildings, basements, warehouses, and other substandard buildings. The cost is simply more than our society is willing to pay.

b. The Teacher Shortage Becomes Steadily Greater. For much the same reasons, a national shortage of teachers grows steadily worse. The present (1954) shortage is estimated at from 120,000 to 150,000 teachers and is expected to double by 1960. The nation's schools need about 100,000 new teachers a year but are now getting only about 60,000 from all teacher-training institutions.[8] At present, the number of new teachers prepared by teacher-training institutions is declining (from 115,000 in 1950 to 91,000 in 1953),[9] while the number of teachers on "emergency" or substandard certificates is growing (from 70,000 in 1952 to 72,000 in 1953).[10]

Why does such a shortage exist? The work is not unpleasant; one who is temperamentally fitted for teaching finds it to be a stimulating and emotionally rewarding task! The work is socially useful, the profession commands a certain respect,[11] and the vacations are the envy of other occupational groups! But the income of teachers does not compare very favorably with that of other occupations which demand far less training, native ability, and self-discipline. The average teaching salary of $3605 paid to public school teachers in 1951-1952 is only slightly above the $67.04 a week (equivalent to $3352 for a 50-week year) received by the average factory worker in January, 1952. Although differences in working year, regularity of employment, and other factors make an exact comparison impossible, it is clear that teachers receive meager financial reward for the extended training, the exemplary character, the pervasive insight, and the unwavering sense of responsibility they are expected to display.

[8] While 91,000 graduates were qualified for certification in 1953, only about 65 per cent of these entered teaching. (See *Journal of Teacher Education,* 5 [March, 1954], pp. 20-21.)

[9] *New York Times,* September 12, 1954, IV, p. 11.

[10] *New York Times,* February 28, 1954, IV, p. 9.

[11] Cf. Frederick W. Terrien, "Who Thinks What About Educators?" *American Journal of Sociology,* 59 (September, 1953), pp 150-158.

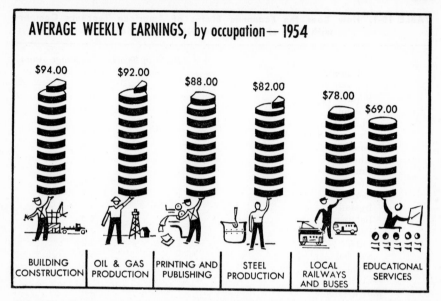

AVERAGE WEEKLY EARNINGS, by occupation— 1954

$94.00 — BUILDING CONSTRUCTION
$92.00 — OIL & GAS PRODUCTION
$88.00 — PRINTING AND PUBLISHING
$82.00 — STEEL PRODUCTION
$78.00 — LOCAL RAILWAYS AND BUSES
$69.00 — EDUCATIONAL SERVICES

FIG. 10-1. (Based on data from U. S. Department of Labor and National Education Association)

Other factors also help explain the teacher shortage. Teachers are overloaded; over 90 per cent of the nation's classes are over the ideal limit of 25 members, and a third are over 35 members.[12] Excessively large classes not only make teaching more tiring; they also prevent good teaching and oppress the teacher with a sense of futility. The burden of "extracurricular" responsibilities grows heavier as more and more tasks are piled onto the school. Some of the 75,000 teachers who leave teaching for other jobs each year complain about lack of administrative support and co-operation, and some even complain that the vigilante activities of self-styled "patriots" have made it unsafe to teach realistically in certain areas.[13]

The greatest shortage appears to be in the sciences and the industrial arts, perhaps because teachers in these fields can so easily make more money by leaving teaching. Since it is these fields which are most closely connected with technological progress and national defense, this shortage has sobering implications.

The results of the teacher shortage are not hard to recognize. Over-crowded classrooms and neglect of individual needs of pupils may be the most obvious consequences. But in other, less spectacular ways, the

[12] Cf. "Class Size Is Out of Hand," *N.E.A. Journal*, 42 (December, 1953), pp. 555-556.

[13] See "Why I Quit Teaching" as told to Victor Boesen, *Reporter*, 11 (July 6, 1954), pp. 18-20.

TABLE 10-1. How Does the Economic Status of American Teachers Compare with That of Teachers in Other Countries?

Country	Ratio of Teachers' Average Annual Salaries to Per Capita Income
Syria	10.2
Colombia	9.6
Philippines	8.5
Union of South Africa	6.8
Israel	5.8
Chile	5.6
France	5.1
Austria	5.0
Germany	4.7
Ireland	4.7
Belgium	4.5
Peru	3.9
India	3.6
Sweden	3.6
Cuba	3.5
Ceylon	3.4
Switzerland	3.3
Yugoslavia	3.3
Denmark	3.2
Italy	3.1
Netherlands	3.0
Norway	2.7
Scotland	2.7
England	2.5
New Zealand	2.0
UNITED STATES	1.9
Canada	1.8
Iran	1.7
Australia	1.6

Yearbook of Education, 1953 (Yonkers, N. Y., World Book Company, 1953), p. 106.

quality of teaching is impaired. Many schools, especially those in the poorer states and in the lower-paying towns and rural areas, must accept teachers with little college training and with *no professional training* whatever. While some of these persons may become good teachers anyway, many are not really *teachers* but are merely collective babysitters! Many failures continue to teach because there is no better candidate to replace them. As with any profession, some beginners prove to be temperamentally or emotionally unqualified. Some are too erratic or unstable to teach; some cannot "keep discipline"; some can do no more than merely "keep discipline"; some have no understanding of children; some do not like children; some are simply dull and ineffectual. But in today's teaching market, especially in the lower-paying systems, a teacher will be retained as long as she can keep the classroom from explosion and the parents from revolt. The normal process of weeding out the incompetents has virtually ceased. It is very rare today for a teacher to be "let out" for any reason other than immorality, "subversion," or utter failure to keep discipline.

There is little likelihood that the teacher shortage will disappear in the near future. It is doubtful that teaching salaries will be increased enough to attract a greater number of suitable persons into the teaching profession. Some communities show little interest in raising salaries or improving teaching conditions as long as they can staff the schools with baby-sitters. Teachers themselves show little interest in organizing themselves into the aggressive kind of teachers' organization which might succeed in improving their financial status. In fact, our school enrollment is growing so rapidly that the question becomes not, How soon will the teacher shortage be relieved? but, How much worse will it get before it gets better?

c. *Federal Aid to Education: Threat or Promise?* It is a common practice in America for states and localities to clamor for "federal aid" whenever they want something they are unwilling to pay for themselves. The proposal for federal aid to education, however, arises in part from a different motive—the desire to equalize the educational opportunities of our nation's children. For, to a far greater degree than most people realize, "success" for America's youth begins with picking the right state to be born and educated in. The average Mississippi child in 1946 attended school in a building worth $101 per pupil, was taught by a teacher who received $856 a year, while $45 covered the entire public expense of his year's education. The child in New York State attended school in a building worth $659 per pupil, with a teacher paid $2946 per year, and had $209 of public funds spent on his year's education.[14]

Although the amount of money spent is not an *exact* measure of the quality of education, there is some relation between educational expenditures and educational achievements. Of 1000 Mississippi children who completed the fifth grade, only 204 continued to the twelfth grade, whereas in New York, 565 out of 1000 entered the twelfth grade. In New York State, 13 of each 1000 draft registrants were classed by the armed services as "educationally deficient"; in Mississippi, ten times as many (132 per 1000) were so classed, and the war had to wait while the Army educated them. Of those rejected as unfit for military service, 2.8 per cent of New York's rejections and 29.2 per cent of Mississippi's rejections were for educational deficiencies. In nine states, over one-third of all young men called for military service during the Korean war failed to pass the armed forces (educational) qualification test. In one state, 58 per cent failed the test.[15]

[14] These and following data on federal aid are from *The Facts on Federal Aid to Education* (Washington, National Education Association, 1948).
[15] Cf. *New York Times*, February 27, 1954, p. 27.

Does this situation exist because Mississippi is *unable,* or *unwilling* to give its children a first-class education? Mississippi's educational expenditures in 1945-1946 from state and local tax funds equaled 1.80 per cent of the total income of the people of the state, as against 1.72 per cent for New York. Since Mississippi is spending a larger share of its income for schools than New York, it is clear that Mississippi is not unwilling, but is unable to provide equally good schools. Mississippi, along with a number of other states, cannot afford first-class schools because it has *more children to educate and less wealth with which to pay the costs.* Of each 1000 people in Mississippi, 281 are of school age, as compared with only 170 in New York State; meanwhile the per capita income (1946) in Mississippi is $575, against New York's $1651. New York, therefore, has nearly five times as much income per school-age child as Mississippi. A number of the less prosperous states are in very much the same predicament as Mississippi. Less complete data for recent years have altered these figures without altering the contrasts. By 1950-1951, Mississippi was spending $85 per pupil, compared with New York's $324—still a one-to-four ratio. And New York by 1952 had $17,340 of personal income to each school-age child, as compared with Mississippi's $3539—still a one-to-five ratio.[16]

The "vicious circle" of educational inequality now becomes apparent. The low per capita income of these states is both cause and effect of inferior schools. The low incomes make it a practical impossibility for these states to provide schools equal to those of more prosperous states, even though some of the states with the poorest schools are spending a *larger proportion* of their income on education than many states having the highest per pupil expenditures. The inferior schooling, in turn, helps to keep the income of the region low by failing to help children to increase their earning power. Thus, the circle of low productivity and inferior education is completed—and perpetuated.

These educational deficiencies affect the national interest in time of war, both by reducing the productivity of our economy and by reducing the efficiency of our armed forces. In peacetime the national interest is also involved, since the "graduates" of substandard schools do not stay home. Those states with the lowest school expenditures are also the states with the highest birth rates. It is these states which provide a great many of the migrants to the industrial towns and cities of the North and West. These migrants are, then, coming from the areas where the schools are least able to prepare them to migrate, to enter the urban labor market advantageously, and to become useful citizens of their new communities. In these and other ways the people of New York and Illinois share the

[16] N.E.A. Research Division, "Educational Differences Among the States," *N.E.A. Research Bulletin,* 32 (March, 1954), pp. 1-21; condensed in *Education Digest,* 20 (September, 1954), pp. 14-18.

results of poor schools in Mississippi and Alabama, whether they wish it or not.

The proportion of unskilled workers in our economy has been declining for some decades. Under the recent impact of automation (self-operating and self-controlling machinery), our need for unskilled workers is falling more rapidly than ever before. No longer will large numbers of functionally illiterate workers from educationally impoverished areas be of much use in the kind of economy which we are developing.

It is for these reasons that the National Education Association favors a program of federal grants to the states, to bring the educational expenditures of the poorer states closer to the national average. This proposal has been considered and defeated in several sessions of Congress. Opposition comes from several sources, including: (1) those who are more interested in reducing federal expenditures than they are in improving education; (2) those who fear that federal aid would eventually result in undesirable degrees or forms of federal control of education; (3) those who consider federal aid "socialistic" or "communistic"; (4) Catholic groups which withhold support unless parochial schools share in federal grants.

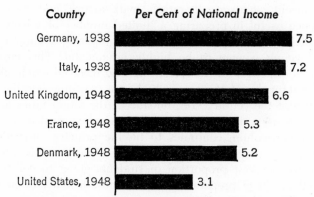

FIG. 10-2. Can We Afford to Improve Our Schools? Proportion of national income devoted to education in selected countries for the last year for which comparable figures are available. (Data from Lawrence Beal, "Democratic Education," *Michigan Education Journal*, 30 (April, 1952), p. 462)

The various problems connected with the cost of education cannot be solved in a way that satisfies everybody, for not all have the same values. How important *is* education, after all? In 1900, our annual educational expenditure equaled one-half the annual budget of our federal government; in 1953, they equaled only one-sixth of the federal budget. How much *should* we sacrifice to improve education—or perhaps, to keep it from deteriorating any more than it has? When one compares the share of our national income spent for education with that of other less prosperous nations (Figure 10-2), one begins to suspect that Americans may love learning with all their hearts but with somewhat less than all their pocketbooks.

2. The Curriculum: What Should American Schools Teach?

Neither educators nor laymen are agreed upon what the school should be and do. One survey of pressures upon school superintendents reports that 59 per cent were under community pressure to concentrate upon the three R's, and 64 per cent reported pressure to offer a greater variety of courses, with some obviously under pressure to do both. Some 39 per cent reported protests against addition of new school services such as guidance and health programs, while 63 per cent had demands for such services. Twenty-nine per cent were pressed to introduce new teaching methods, while 43 per cent faced protests against such innovations. Forty per cent faced demands for less emphasis on athletics; 58 per cent reported pressure for more emphasis on athletics.[17]

At least three different kinds of curricula are in use in American schools. *The classical curriculum* is the traditional one, emphasizing foreign and ancient languages, literature, mathematics, and pure science. This was once useful in preparing a limited number of selected young men for college and the professions and in preparing a limited number of selected young women to be highly ornamental. This curriculum, although quite practical for the select few who received much education, was less useful for the great masses who began crowding into high school after the turn of the century. Yet, outside of the larger cities and more progressive towns, a basically classical curriculum, called a "college-preparatory" curriculum, continues to be the primary curriculum emphasis in a great many of the high schools. Ironically, it is often those towns with the smallest proportion of students going to college which emphasize the college preparatory course most heavily, often because they have nothing else to offer.

The vocational curriculum abandons such "ornamental" material in favor of preparing the student for a "job." To many students, the vocational curriculum has brought a chance to learn something which appeared useful to them, in place of studies which had little meaning in terms of their interests and values. Many students have had their interests stimulated, their school adjustment transformed, and their adult earning power developed as a result. But often there is little relation between the vocational training offered and the job opportunities available in the locality. In many an agricultural village, more boys study auto mechanics than study agriculture. Many high schools crank out a

[17] Neal Gross, *The Pressures and Dilemmas of the School Superintendent,* summarized in *New York Times,* May 2, 1954, IV, p. 9.

dozen "secretaries" or "bookkeepers" each year in villages where only one secretary or bookkeeper is hired each decade. Much allegedly "vocational" training is offered not because that particular training is needed by the students, but because many students will not accept the college-preparatory curriculum. Students of limited ability or of lower-class origin who have little interest in a college-preparatory course are herded into "vocational" courses in order to keep them occupied until they may legally drop out of school.[18] For these students the vocational curriculum is just an educational waiting-room rather than an avenue to employment.

The life-adjustment curriculum describes a third curricular approach. Consisting of a wide variety of courses and combinations, this is the approach most widely supported (and less widely employed) by educators. Emphasis is placed on the personality development of the student and the social usefulness of what he learns. Many traditional course titles may remain, but course content is vastly changed. Although much traditional subject matter is learned, much of it is learned through projects and group activities rather than through traditional recitation and drill. Personality characteristics such as initiative and self-confidence, and social skills such as ability to participate in a discussion, organize a work project, or conduct a parliamentary meeting, are considered to be at least as important as the ability to parse a sentence or prove the binomial theorem. This is an eclectic approach, drawing from many sources and seeking to functionalize all learning areas and levels.[19]

Critics of the life-adjustment curriculum charge that pupils are not required to work but are permitted to loaf and bluff, that basic factual learnings and intellectual skills are neglected, and that much school time is wasted in noneducative activities and frivolities.[20] Some very sweeping indictments of present school practices have been issued, based largely upon the technique of generalizing on single cases.[21] (For example, a

[18] Cf. A. B. Hollingshead, Elmtown's Youth (New York, John Wiley & Sons, Inc., 1949), Ch. 8.

[19] For a concise statement of the life-adjustment curriculum, see National Association of Secondary School Principals, Planning for American Youth: An Educational Program for Youth of Secondary-School Age (Washington, National Education Association, 1944). This pamphlet is a condensation of a larger treatment by the Educational Policies Commission, Education for All American Youth (Washington, National Education Association, 1944).

[20] Cf. Arthur E. Bestor, "Life Adjustment Education: A Critique," American Association of University Professors Bulletin, 38 (Autumn, 1952), pp. 413-441; Arthur E. Bestor, Educational Wastelands: The Retreat from Learning in Our Public Schools (Champaign, University of Illinois Press, 1953); Albert Lynd, Quackery in the Public Schools (Boston, Little, Brown & Company, 1953); Paul Woodring, Let's Talk Sense About Our Schools (New York, McGraw-Hill Book Company, Inc., 1953).

[21] See Howard Whitman, "The Struggle for Our Children's Minds," Collier's, 133 (February 5, 1954), pp. 23-28; 133 (March 19, 1954), pp. 34-36 ff; 133 (May 14, 1954), pp. 32-36; 134 (August 6, 1954), pp. 58-61; Howard Whitman, "Report Cards: EGFU, SNUX, or ABC," Collier's, 134 (September 17, 1954), pp. 58-60 ff. This critic, although he apparently wishes to be fair and objective, does not always

charge that "schools waste students' time" is "proved" by describing a single school where the students spend several days making a stage set.) Charges that pupils are not learning basic subject matter as well as formerly are easily disproved by dozens of surveys of comparative learning achievements, all showing that the present generation of children know as many or more basic facts than their parents did at the same grade level.[22]

There is little doubt, however, that *in some instances* charges of wasted time, aimlessness, and sloppy standards are justified. Like most new developments, life-adjustment education has sometimes carried a practical approach to an impractical extreme.[23] As in every field, there are some teachers and administrators who "go off the deep end" with each innovation. And it probably requires far more judgment and teaching skill to develop "an integrated unit of meaningful activities" than to conduct a spelling drill. In some instances, the language of life-adjustment education has been invoked to excuse aimlessness and inefficiency.

The progressive-education movement formed the main guide for the changes taking place in the curriculum during much of the second quarter of this century. Finding its original inspiration in John Dewey, progressive education sought to replace mechanical drill and memorization of unrelated facts with purposeful integrated learning. It sought to make education a process of pupil growth *through learning activities which appear interesting and worth while to the pupil now*, rather than making education a process of storing away information for use in some remote future. Thus motivated, it was believed that pupils would not only learn subject matter more quickly but would also develop a set of study methods, social skills, attitudes, and other personality outcomes vastly superior to those developed by the traditional school.

The basic viewpoints of progressive education have been widely accepted (and somewhat less widely applied) in American education. The progressive-education movement, as an organized movement, has recently languished for lack of spirited opposition *among educators*. The Progressive Education Association has disbanded as its major principles, shorn

---

understand what educators are trying to do. For example, he fails to realize that in grading children according to their *efforts* instead of their achievement, the school is not seeking to eliminate competition but to *equalize* competition so that all children will be encouraged to work harder.

[22] See A. Conrad Posz, "We Just Want the Facts, Sir," *Michigan Education Journal,* 31 (March, 1954), pp. 316-318, for a summary of numerous such studies; see also Louis E. Raths and Phillip Rathman, "Then and Now; Some Research Findings on the Effectiveness of Teaching the Three R's," *National Education Association Journal,* 41 (April, 1952), p. 214.

[23] For a development of this viewpoint, see Paul B. Horton and Rachel Y. Horton, "False Dichotomies and Educational Perspective," *Michigan Education Journal,* 29 (September, 1951), pp. 5-8; condensed in *Education Digest,* 17 (November, 1951), pp. 19-21.

of their more extreme enthusiasms, have ceased to be controversial *among educators.* Most educators and teachers feel that they have incorporated the enduring contribution of progressive education into their thinking and that the label has become meaningless. *Laymen,* however, often invoke the term *progressive education* in making their criticisms of whatever they dislike about the school system. Progressive education often gets the blame for everything that goes wrong in the school, whether it is actually a part of the philosophy of progressive education or not.

The athletic program is another highly controversial aspect of the curriculum of the school. Should the athletic program of the high school or college be primarily an activity program, urging *all* students to develop a number of athletic interests and skills? Or should it emphasize the production of winning teams and sporting events in which a highly trained few perform while the student body and townspeople watch, identify, and cheer? Recent exposés have made common knowledge of the commercialization of athletics, especially by many of the larger colleges and universities. It is no secret that academic standards are sometimes corrupted, student athletes exploited, coaches reduced to nervous wrecks, and college finances jeopardized so that the students and others may enjoy a spectacle.[24] It is no secret that many, possibly most, big-time football teams are composed of professional players, secretly paid through devious subterfuges which enable them to maintain the pretense of amateur status. Both the athletes and the rest of the student body receive a liberal education in the art of "getting around" the laws and regulations one pretends to honor—a point which has provoked caustic comment about the campus as a center of moral and spiritual growth and about football as a builder of character.

Although the subsidization problem affects mainly the larger universities, the small college and the high school face the question of whether to sacrifice the general athletic program in a bid for a winning team. Seldom is there money and staff enough to do both. And, more important, emphasis on the big and the winning team means that both students and faculty come to feel that this is important, while ordinary participation is less important. The promotions and the testimonial banquets go to those who coach winning teams, not to those instructors who instill in masses of students a fondness for archery or handball. The wealthy alumni, who are often said to control college athletics, are unlikely to excuse a coach's failure to have a winning team by his success in encouraging intramural sports.

An occasional high-school principal or college president attempts to

[24] Cf. Virginius Dabney, "The Ivy-Covered Fraud," *Reporter* (November 27, 1951), pp. 38-40; "Excerpts from Judge Streit's Comments on College Basketball Fixing Scandal," *New York Times,* November 20, 1951, pp. 1, 26; Jeff Cravath and Melvin Durslag, "The Hypocrisy of College Football," *Collier's,* 132 (October 30, 1953), pp. 30-33.

shift emphasis from competitive athletics. He may not last very long.[25] Many educators severely criticize the emphasis upon winning games and would like to encourage general student participation in athletic activities,[26] but they cannot easily challenge the status quo. Alumni are powerful, and alumni good will is necessary. Private colleges would die without the contributions of loyal alumni, and public institutions need loyal alumni to lobby for them in the legislature. High-school coaches seldom forget that the townspeople are more interested in seeing spectacular games than in knowing how many students have learned how to swim. Manufacturers of sporting goods remember that a football team will wear out a highly gratifying number of suits, balls, and footwear in an active season. The students themselves, who have never been offered any real choice in the matter, appear to be well satisfied with the status quo. So the educator who is dissatisfied (and not all are) finds it expedient to invoke the folklore of sportsmanship to sanctify the athletic status quo and direct his attention to matters he can more easily control.

3. The Parochial-versus-Public School Controversy

A growing proportion of American school children attend nonpublic schools, rising from one-tenth in 1938 to one-eighth in 1953, and expected to reach one-seventh by 1960.[27] Although most of these schools are Catholic, some other bodies including the Missouri and Wisconsin Synods of the Lutheran Church, the Christian Reformed Church, and the Seventh Day Adventist Church also maintain parochial schools.[28]

Both Catholic and Protestant critics of the secular public school agree in making these accusations:

a. That the public school in seeking to be neutral in religion actually becomes godless, training children to view religion as unimportant. According to Harry Emerson Fosdick, a noted Protestant clergyman, "Public schools that rigorously exclude religion are not neutral; the dice are loaded against religion." [29]

b. That religious training is essential for the development of moral character, and that the school which fails to teach religion undermines

[25] Cf. "Normalcy in Denver," *Time* (March 23, 1953), p. 54.

[26] Cf. Educational Policies Commission, *School Athletics: Problems and Policies* (Washington, National Education Association, 1954).

[27] *New York Times,* April 12, 1953, IV, p. 11.

[28] Some of these schools may not be strictly "parochial" in that they are administered by boards of laymen rather than by the church officials directly; for simplicity in this discussion, they will all be referred to as parochial schools.

[29] Harry Emerson Fosdick, "Shall American School Children Be Religiously Illiterate?" *School and Society,* 66 (November, 1947), pp. 401-406; same, *Reader's Digest,* 54 (February, 1949), pp. 97-100. See also R. H. Martin, *Our Public Schools— Christian or Secular?* (Pittsburgh, National Reform Association, 1952), Ch. VI, "Secular Public Education Not Neutral but Against Religion."

public morality.[30] Some of these critics hold the "godless" public school largely responsible for crime, juvenile delinquency, and most other misconduct.[31]

There are many who would answer these criticisms through the teaching of religion in the public schools. The Committee on Religion and Education of the American Council on Education proposes that the public schools include the "objective" study of religion and encourage the acceptance of "a minimum body of religious doctrines" while not teaching any sectarian beliefs.[32] The International Council of Religious Education and many local organizations (such as the Division of Christian Education of the Protestant Council of the City of New York) have sought public-school co-operation in released-time religious education programs, in which children are released for a period each week to receive religious instruction in the faith of their choice. A survey in 1949 indicated that about one-fourth of the public-school systems were following some sort of religious education program, with two-thirds of these being of the released-time variety.[33] Only 14 per cent of the students in these schools were taking advantage of this religious instruction, however, and interest in such programs appears to be waning.

To the supporters of parochial education, the defects of the public school cannot be corrected by any incidental religious offerings, for they consider the public school to be basically and inescapably pernicious. Catholic and Protestant supporters generally agree, in addition to the earlier criticisms, that (1) it is God's will that the school should be directed by the church,[34] and that (2) the entire educational process should be permeated with religious interpretations and overtones. One noted Protestant clergyman explains,

I do not mean that [children] need instruction in all the various subjects taught plus a little instruction in the Bible. . . . What is necessary is that every subject shall be taught in the light of the Scriptures. When history is taught the child must be instructed to see the unfolding of the eternal counsel of God, and must learn to see the age-old struggle between God in Christ on the one hand and

[30] R. H. Martin, op. cit., Ch. VII, "Shall Moral Training in our Public Schools Be With or Without Religion?"; also, "Report of the Committee on Religion and Education of the American Council on Education," American Council of Education Studies: Reports of Committees and Conferences, Vol. XI, No. 26 (April, 1947).

[31] R. H. Martin, op. cit., pp. 36-38; W. S. Fleming, God in Our Public Schools (Pittsburgh, National Reform Association, 1942).

[32] Report of the Committee on Religion and Education of the American Council on Education, op. cit.

[33] N.E.A. Research Division, "Status of Religious Education in the Public Schools," National Education Association Journal, 38 (November, 1949), pp. 610-611.

[34] The Catholic view is that "education belongs pre-eminently to the Church, by reason of a double title in the supernatural order, conferred exclusively upon her by God Himself; superior therefore to any other title in the Natural Order." (Encyclical of Pius XI, Christian Education of Youth, 1929.) Through somewhat different reasoning, Protestant supporters arrive at much the same conclusion.

Satan on the other. Geography and other related subjects should be taught from the point of view that the earth is the Lord's. Every subject must be taught from the God-centered point of view.[35]

This clergyman concludes by agreeing with Bishop John F. Noll's characterization of the public-school system as "Public Enemy Number One."[36]

To all these charges, the defenders of the public school system make spirited replies that:

a. The public-school system is a democratizing agency. In a country of multiple religious faiths, either the school must be neutral or there must be as many school systems as there are religious faiths. The latter would be both expensive and socially divisive. As former Harvard President James B. Conant states, "A dual system [of schools] serves and helps to maintain group cleavages,"[37] whereas a public school system, embracing all faiths and minorities, tends to reduce prejudices and create unity. The public school is perhaps our greatest unifying institution.

b. There is no proof that the public schools are inferior to parochial schools. The "proof" of the superiority of the parochial school consists of unsubstantiated assertions by supporters who keep telling one another how superior it is. Although parochial-school advocates state that "Christian" schools are necessary to combat delinquency, they present no objective evidence that their pupils are less delinquent or more honest and trustworthy than comparable groups of public-school children. Such a comparison would, in fact, be very difficult to control, since many variables of social class, ethnic group, and school administration would be involved. It is significant, however, that the assertions of the parochial schools' superiority in moral and ethical training are almost entirely unsupported by factual evidence.

These disagreements over the respective merits of parochial and public schools do not necessarily lead to conflict, except in the area of school finance. Here, bitter controversy has arisen over (1) the Catholic request for tax funds for parochial schools, and (2) occasional parochial opposition to tax increases for public schools.[38]

Public Funds for Private Schools? This has become a spirited issue. The Lutheran and Seventh Day Adventist Churches seek no public funds for their schools, insisting upon a very rigid "separation of church and state." The Christian Reformed Church has made no official demands for pub-

[35] Rev. William Kok, "When Foundations Are Destroyed: Education," Radio address on Christian Reformed Church's "Back to God Hour," September 29, 1946.

[36] *Ibid.*

[37] Quoted in *Time* (April 21, 1952), p. 82.

[38] For two different points of view, see Cletus Healy, S.J., "Catholics and Public Schools," *The Catholic World,* 169 (September, 1949), pp. 451-455; and John K. Norton, "Church, State, and Education," *National Education Association Journal,* 38 (January, 1949), pp. 21-24.

lic funds, although some semiofficial leaders believe it should do so.[39] The Catholic Church, however, actively seeks public funds for the support of parochial schools. Catholics maintain that a democratic society should support the right of the parent to educate his child at public expense in a school of his choice. They argue that they are subjected to "double taxation" by paying school taxes for schools they do not use, in addition to supporting a private school system. They point out that the parochial-school system greatly reduces the costs of public education and ask that the community reimburse them for a part of the expense they have absorbed.

For these reasons, Catholics seek whatever form of public aid they believe they may be able to get. At present, they are pressing their request for the same auxiliary services (bus transportation, health services, free textbooks, and so on) which public-school pupils receive, and asking that they share in state-aid or federal-aid payments along with public schools. It is widely believed that a proposed Federal Aid to Education program would have been adopted by the 82nd Congress had its supporters not been divided upon whether to permit states to include parochial schools in distributing federal grants. Catholics opposed any bill which forbade aid to parochial schools,[40] and many Protestants opposed any bill which would permit such aid. Objections to public funds for parochial schools come from various sources: from taxpayers who object to the added taxation, from Protestants who fear that such aid would increase the power and membership of the Catholic Church, from educators and others who are dedicated to the public-school system and oppose tax encouragement to a competing system. Critics also fear that tax support for Catholic schools might lead to the growth of a series of parochial-school systems, one for each denomination, resulting in an inefficient atomization of the school system and the virtual destruction of the public school. No mutually satisfactory "solution" of the question of parochial-school aid is possible, since an apparently irreconcilable conflict of values is basic to the controversy.

In communities where many belong to churches supporting parochial schools, it may become difficult to maintain the public-school system. New public schools can be built and operating funds increased only by bonding and taxing the community. Already burdened with the heavy costs of maintaining a private-school system, the parochial-school sup-

[39] See remarks of Prof. Henry Van Zyl, of Calvin College, speaking before Michigan Christian School Alliance, quoted in *Christian Science Monitor*, April 9, 1948.

[40] Cardinal Spellman stated that "The Catholic school is an American school, equal in right with the public school because our theory of democratic government protects the inalienable right of the human person to freedom of religion and freedom of education. We must oppose any bill that fails to guarantee at least non-religious textbooks, bus rides, and health services for all the children." Quoted in *The Nation's Schools*, 44 (September, 1949), p. 27.

porters often take a dim view of increasing their taxes to improve a school system which they do not use and in which they may not believe. They are not cynically indifferent to the welfare of the community, but they are not easy to convince that increased taxes for public schools are justifiable. Often their own private-school system is badly overcrowded and lacking in buildings and equipment; it is understandable that they should be unenthusiastic about taxing themselves more heavily to improve the public-school system when the needs of their own schools may, in fact, appear still more urgent.

However understandable these reactions may be, they nonetheless form a serious obstacle to adequate public-school financing in some communities. In some communities, feelings have become most bitter, and vindictive and futile reprisals inflicted. In others, parochial and public school leaders have co-operated cordially in promoting bond drives. Here, again, a basic conflict of values may make any complete "solution" impossible, but a spirit of mutual understanding and compromise often makes these value differences more tolerable.

4. Academic Freedom: How Much Freedom Do We Want?

Socrates was neither the first nor the last teacher to suffer because he persisted in teaching ideas that other people disliked. For, in most times and places, the teacher has been commanded to be not a searcher for truth but a propagandist for the approved values. During only a few brief moments in history have teachers been permitted to encourage students to search for truth, regardless of where the search might lead. These islands of rationality represent, in part, the achievement of those for whom truth itself comprises a worthy value, and who believe that truth is best protected from corruption by maintaining an atmosphere of freedom of speech and inquiry. Jefferson, founder of the first state university in America, the University of Virginia, expressed this faith in writing, "This institution will be based on the illimitable freedom of the human mind. For here we are not afraid to follow truth wherever it may lead, nor to tolerate error, so long as reason is left free to combat it." [41]

But truth is costly. It often demolishes cherished beliefs and hallowed traditions. It often undermines comfortable vested interests and threatens a profitable sinecure. The scientific truth about the composition of Jewish and gentile blood would have undermined Hitler's political propaganda, so scientists dared not publish this truth. The true biographies of the persons who are Russian heroes and villains at any particular moment would not always fit the roles in which they are cast, so Russian biography must be rewritten as persons rise or fall in official favor. The truth about the

[41] Jefferson to William C. Jarvis, September 28, 1820 in *The Writings of Thomas Jefferson* (Library Edition, Washington, 1903), Vol. XV, p. 278.

relative nutritional qualities of butter and oleomargarine was most unpopular with those who wished to protect the market for butter, and some professors who published objective nutritional studies soon faced demands for their dismissal. For every truth, there are usually a number of people whom it will distress and who may wish to suppress it.

Still more dangerous to the search for truth, however, may be those who lack Jefferson's faith in the ability of truth to defend itself, but feel it necessary to protect truth by suppressing error. To suppress error requires that books and magazines be censored, that movies and television shows be censored, that textbooks and teaching materials be inspected and approved, and that teaching be purged of all who harbor unconventional thoughts. It is a determined effort to do just this which has provoked what many educators are calling the greatest academic-freedom battle of American history.[42]

What Is Academic Freedom? By "academic freedom" is meant *the freedom to seek and impart knowledge without any limitations except those inherent in the search for knowledge.*[43] If one really searches for knowledge, he must accept facts honestly, he must consider *all* the relevant facts, he must welcome honest debate and be willing to revise his conclusions in the light of new-found facts. These limitations are inherent in the search for knowledge. Other limitations—that one must not shock students with material for which they are too immature, that one must operate within the standards of good taste and personal discretion, that one must not propagandize for pet ideas but must present objectively all sides of controversial issues—these limitations inhere within the task of *imparting* knowledge. Academic freedom does *not* include the right to do or say whatever one wishes. Academic freedom includes the right to reach

---

[42] See Robert M. MacIver, "The Freedom to Search for Knowledge," *New York Times,* April 12, 1953, VI, p. 12; see also Louis Joughin, "The Current Questionings of Teachers: Notes for a Social Pathology," *Social Problems,* 1 (October, 1953), pp. 61-65.

[43] The American Association of University Professors defines academic freedom as:
(*a*) ... full freedom in research and in the publications of the results, subject to the adequate performance of his other duties....
(*b*) ... freedom in the classroom in discussing his subject, but he should be careful not to introduce into his teaching controversial matter which has no relation to his subject....
(*c*) The college or university teacher is a citizen, a member of a learned profession, and an officer of an educational institution. When he speaks as a citizen, he should be free from institutional censorship or discipline, but his special position in the community imposes special obligations. As a man of learning and an educational officer, he should remember that the public may judge his profession and his institution by his utterances. Hence he should at all times be accurate, should exercise appropriate restraint, should show respect for the opinions of others, and should make every effort to indicate that he is not an institutional spokesman. (From "1940 Statement of Principles," as printed in *American Association of University Professors Bulletin,* 39 [Spring, 1953], pp. 122-123.) See also pamphlet, *Academic Freedom and Academic Responsibility* (New York, American Civil Liberties Union, 1953).

conclusions through scholarly investigation, but does not include the right to *act* in accord with these conclusions if such action is against the law. Academic freedom is not license.

Academic freedom does imply the freedom to seek and impart knowledge *without any external authority* telling teachers what they may or may not teach. Academic freedom grants neither the church, nor the state, nor any private organization the right to tell teachers what facts or ideas they may not teach. The state may properly require that certain *subjects* be taught but may not decree *how* they must be taught, or which ideas must be taught. For example, the state may legitimately require the teaching of American history; but for the state, or a newspaper, or a "patriotic" society to insist that teachers depict the United States as a saint and Great Britain as a villain would be an invasion of academic freedom.

There have been many such invasions in our history.[44] Every great crisis in American thought—the Revolution, the sedition controversy between Federalists and Republicans, the slavery question, the evolution debate, the temperance issue, the surge of nationalism following World War I—each provoked determined efforts to control the ideas taught in schools and colleges. Earlier periods allowed far less academic freedom than is enjoyed today, for it was generally assumed that teachers should reflect the conventionally-approved opinions of the period. The slavery question, for example, resulted in wholesale firings of teachers, college professors, and ministers in both North and South, together with the burning of some newspaper publishing offices. For more than a half century following the Civil War, two sets of history books were published—Northern and Southern—for neither the Grand Army of the Republic nor the Daughters of the Confederacy would allow an objective history textbook to be used.

The Present Invasions of Academic Freedom. At no time in American history has academic freedom aroused such a controversy as rages today. While earlier periods tolerated little academic freedom, a great many Americans today expect and treasure the academic freedom which many other Americans seek to curtail. There has been widespread popular acceptance of the idea that schools should study controversial issues, should "present both sides," and encourage students to "think things through." Recently, however, many groups who claim to intend no attack on academic freedom are nevertheless doing a number of things that tend to make academic freedom impossible to exercise. A series of Congressional investigations have located scarcely any *present* communists among teachers, but, according to the American Association of University Profes-

---

[44] See Howard K. Beale, *A History of Freedom of Teaching in American Schools* (New York, Charles Scribner's Sons, 1941); also, Howard K. Beale, "Teacher as Rebel," *The Nation*, 176 (May 16, 1953), pp. 412-414.

sors, have made teachers hesitant to join anything, sponsor anything, sign anything, or speak on anything at all unconventional or unorthodox.[45] A rash of loyalty oaths, some of them worded so vaguely that they might apply to practically anything, cause the more independent teachers to wonder what may become the test of "loyalty" tomorrow. According to a *New York Times* survey,[46]

A concerted campaign is underway over the country to censor school and college textbooks, reading materials, and other visual aids. Voluntary groups are being formed in nearly every state to screen books for "subversive" or un-American statements. . . . Librarians are intimidated by outside pressures in their choice of books and other materials. Unwilling to risk a public controversy, they meekly accept the requests of the self-appointed censorship groups. Several textbooks and other materials have already been removed from school or college libraries and are effectively on "the blacklist."

The Los Angeles *Mirror* polled 250 social science teachers and discovered that over half (53 per cent) of the teachers felt less free to discuss "all phases of social studies, history, geography, political science, and international relations" than they did five years earlier. Even more (55½ per cent) stated that teachers avoid "controversial subjects" for fear of losing their jobs. Over two-thirds were "cautious" about the books and magazines they read, one-fifth (21½ per cent) felt it hazardous to discuss the Bill of Rights, one-sixth (17 per cent) were afraid of "being spied upon" by loyalty investigators, and over half (54½ per cent) felt that students "are being deprived educationally as a result of the uproar about controversial subjects." [47]

The main line of attack is the charge that the schools and colleges are "tainted with communism and subversion." Beginning in 1952, the study of the United Nations and use of pamphlets of the United Nations Scientific, Educational and Cultural Organization (UNESCO) began to figure prominently as "evidence" of un-Americanism.[48] At the national level, the attack is encouraged by the general public anxiety cultivated by a continuing series of "revelations" by Congressional investigations of communism. Although these "revelations" consist in considerable part of gossip, rumor, and unsubstantiated accusation, and add up to nothing more than a few dozen specific cases of allegedly subversive teachers, these periodic driblets of accusation help to arouse public apprehension. Similar mixtures of fact and guesswork are given national circulation in newspapers and magazines, and are highlighted by certain writers and radio news commentators who love to dwell on this theme. The tellers of these

[45] "Professors Assail College Inquiries," *New York Times*, March 29, 1953, p. 20.
[46] Benjamin Fine, "Textbook Censors Alarm Educators," *New York Times*, May 25, 1952, I, p. 1.
[47] *Time* (April 5, 1954), p. 46.
[48] See Dorothy Frank, *op. cit.*; also Mark A. Hennessey, "Saving Los Angeles from the U. N.," *Reporter*, 7 (November 11, 1952), pp. 28-31.

tales quote one another's unproved accusations and rumors back and forth until, through sheer repetition, many people come to accept them as facts. Although such articles or broadcasts usually carry a sentence stating that the vast majority of teachers are loyal, the remainder of the text piles rumor upon fact and supposition upon rumor until the reader or listener quite forgets the one-sentence affirmation of the loyalty of most teachers and instead visualizes a school system simply crawling with subversion.

At the local level the attack ranges from minor unreported incidents to pitched battles attracting national attention. An example of the former is found in the experience of a student of the writer's who, in his practice-teaching, encouraged students to discover and list the characteristics of communism and democracy in parallel columns; he soon heard from an officer of a local veterans' organization who inquired whether he was teaching about communism and democracy "from the objective or from the patriotic point of view." National publicity has attended the pitched battles fought in Pasadena, Denver, Englewood, Los Angeles, Battle Creek, and some other cities,[49] while some other cities such as Chicago averted a battle by a prompt and quiet surrender.[50]

The Technique of Attack. That these attacks have shown remarkable similarity in pattern may be due in part to the guidance of Allen A. Zoll, who proudly accepts credit for assisting in them, and whose pamphlets attacking "progressive education," the United Nations, and "Communist infiltration" of the schools have figured prominently in all or nearly all of the recent school battles.[51] The attack is sometimes, but not always, preceded by some school problem that provokes local controversy—a costly building program, a revision of school-district boundaries, a dispute over the merits of a superintendent, or some other issue. The attack may open with a series of letters to the editor, charging the schools with wastefulness, inefficiency, lack of discipline, and especially with promoting "one-

---

[49] Cf. Morris Mitchell, "Fever Spots in American Education," *The Nation*, 173 (October 27, 1951, pp. 344-347; Carey McWilliams, "The Enemy in Pasadena," *Christian Century*, 68 (January 3, 1951), pp. 10-15.

[50] Cf. "School Civics Revised: Take Emphasis Off U.N.," *Chicago Sun-Times*, September 17, 1952, p. 44.

[51] Allen A. Zoll, executive vice-president of the National Council for American Education (not to be confused with the National Education Association) publishes the *Educational Guardian*, in which he wages his crusade. His pamphlets include "They Want Your Child" (charging that "ninety per cent of the texts and teaching in our schools today are in considerable measure subversive . . ."), "Progressive Education Increases Delinquency," "Must American Youth Be Taught That Communism and Socialism Are Superior to Americanism?", "Should Americans Be Against World Government?" For critical appraisals of Zoll, a long-time agitator for various pro-Nazi and undemocratic causes, and his activities, see Robert A. Skaife, "They Sow Distrust," *The Nation's Schools*, 47 (January, 1951), pp. 27-30; Robert A. Skaife, "They Oppose Progress," *The Nation's Schools*, 47 (February, 1951), pp. 31-33; Robert A. Bingham, "Public-School Enemy No. 1?" *Reporter*, 5 (October, 1951), pp. 27-30.

worldism," "socialism," and "communism," and with undermining patriotism and Americanism. The letters have the appearance of spontaneity and give the impression of widespread dissatisfaction, but usually turn out to be the work of a tiny but vocal minority. One or more newspapers give publicity and some measure of support to these charges. Without some newspaper support, it is extremely difficult for an attack to attract enough interest to gain momentum. With publicity, the attackers begin to gain supporters—neurotics seeking an outlet for their hostilities, who generally join the side making the most lurid charges; people who think they see in the school situation a chance to "do something" about communism; persons with a grudge against the school system; disgruntled school employees who see a chance to settle old scores (and who are extremely useful to the attackers); and a good many average citizens who have been conditioned to believe that communists are lurking everywhere, so are ready to believe that the local schools are infested with them. A series of protest meetings are held in which the charges are repeated and quoted back and forth until they become accepted as fact, and where the lurid pamphlets of Zoll and others are conveniently available. Skillful management of such a meeting enables a small minority to create the appearance of a vast ground swell of popular discontent. Public meetings are held in which the attackers and defenders of the school "discuss" the issue. The attackers nearly always win these meetings through two simple techniques: (1) they fill the air with so many charges that the defenders cannot possibly answer more than a fraction of them; (2) they shout, hoot, and heckle the defenders so that they have no chance to speak effectively. Even so highly respected a businessman as Paul Hoffman (former president of Studebaker Corporation, later head of Ford Foundation) found his voice drowned by the raucous clamor of Los Angeles attackers who had no interest in anything the schools' defenders might say.[52]

Once such an attack gets under way, it is very difficult to stop. To date, the attackers appear to have won many more battles than they have lost. Still more disquieting to educators is the fear that even when the attackers lose a battle, they still win the war, by having increased the distrust and suspicion under which the school must operate. Each renewal of the attack may find more people beginning to suspect that "so much smoke must mean there is some fire." Educators and friends of the school, however, have become alerted and are organizing for more effective defense. A number of books and articles have recently appeared to instruct school people in defensive strategy.[53] This strategy emphasizes:

[52] Dorothy Frank, op. cit.
[53] See John H. Haefner, "The Battle of the Books," *National Education Association Journal*, 42 (April, 1953), p. 227-228; H. Gordon Hullfish, op. cit.; Ernest O. Melby and Morton Puner, op. cit. (described by publisher as "A Combat Manual").

(1) interpretation of the school to the community so that citizens understand what the school is actually doing and why; (2) periodic surveys of local attitudes toward the school, both to locate areas of grievance and to provide a basis for dismissing foolish charges as the work of a tiny minority. The co-operation of the local newspapers in not playing up or supporting irresponsible charges is invaluable, but cannot always be secured.

The public-school battles have attracted the greatest interest, but the colleges have by no means escaped somewhat similar attacks. The attack leading to the discharge of Dr. Mundel from Fairmont College,[54] the attack upon the *Basic Economics* text at Phoenix College,[55] the nation-wide attack upon the Gemmill and Blodgett *Economics* textbook several years ago, and many other incidents all have much in common with the attacks upon the public school.

The Consequences: Who "Loses" When Academic Freedom Is Curtailed? That the schools and colleges have suffered is widely agreed, not only by educators but by many others. The United Automobile Workers adopted in March, 1953, a resolution declaring that teachers and administrators "have been hounded by McCarthy, Velde, Zoll, and others whose objective is to reduce the level of public expenditure for education and to frighten the schools into the service of reaction." [56] The *Inland News*, official publication of the Inland Steel Company (and hardly a radical publication), editorializes:[57]

> We have permitted political opportunists and hysterical anticommunists to single out our schools and colleges and question their right to teach freely and without direction from the state. ... The inevitable outcome has been to make teachers afraid of teaching conflicting theories of government and freedom to their students. ... High school students of today are not going to be able to weigh the merit of "isms" if parents and teachers alike fail to explain the values of democratic rights.

A *New York Times* survey of 72 colleges in 1951 reported "a reluctance to speak out on controversial issues in and out of class," "neglect of humanitarian causes because they may be suspect in the minds of politically unsophisticated officials," and "shying away from association with the words, 'liberal,' 'peace,' and 'freedom.' " [58]

Statements of concern from such responsible sources as these make it clear that *academic freedom is not merely a convenience for the teacher*

[54] See William Manchester, "An Enemy of the People?" *The Nation,* 175 (August 9, 1952), pp. 111-112.

[55] See Joseph Stocker, "The Corporal and the Textbook," *The Progressive,* 16 (March, 1952), pp. 24-25.

[56] Quoted in *National Education Association Journal,* 42 (May, 1953), p. 259.

[57] Quoted in editorial, *Chicago Sun-Times,* May 31, 1952.

[58] Cf. "New York Times Survey Shows Liberalism Declining Under Current Political Tensions and Pressures," *New York Times,* May 10, p. 1; May 11, pp. 26, 29.

but a necessity for a free society. When academic freedom is impaired, the main casualties are *not* the teachers, most of whom form a quite conservative group who can easily accommodate themselves to the prevailing orthodoxies.[59] The real casualty is *independent, critical thinking.* The dominant note in nearly all discussions of academic freedom in educational journals is concern over "the growing paralysis of thought in the nation's classrooms. The play-safe attitude in teaching, induced largely by the activities of fanatical vigilantes, has been one of the main concerns of national educational organizations." [60]

The Real Issue. The issue is not whether communism should be taught, or whether communists should teach. Every major educational organization in America has agreed that an actual communist, having abandoned the objective search for truth by submitting to the discipline of an absolute faith, is unfit to teach. No responsible person familiar with the facts believes that any significant number of genuine communists remain among American school and college teachers, and in this most critics agree. Any communist can remain a teacher in the present atmosphere only by refraining from all communistic propagandizing. The real issue is not communism, since it is no present ideological threat and has no influential defenders in American education. The real issue in the academic-freedom controversy is between (1) those who believe that truth can protect itself and those who believe that truth must be helped out by suppressing the expression of error; and between (2) those who want an objective treatment of social issues and those who want special treatment for their ideas. There are some people who label as "communism," "social-ism," or "subversion" almost any ideas which disagree sharply with their own. In attacking "subversion," these people are really insisting that none but their own ideas should be taught. Their ideas seem so unmistakably right to them that they do not realize the bigotry of their position. Like an Illinois congressman who was surprised when people criticized his statement that a proposed antisubversive bill's "purpose was not to prohibit exploration of ideas but to prevent people from reaching the wrong conclusions," [61] they are puzzled and hurt when critics suggest that they have no understanding of democratic freedom. But their benign intentions make them nonetheless the enemies of academic freedom. And whether, in the decades which follow, academic freedom will regain the ground it has lost, or lose still more greatly, is a question few social scientists would care to answer.

[59] See William H. Kilpatrick, ed., *The Teacher and Society* (New York, D. Appleton-Century Company, Inc., 1937), Ch. VIII, "Social Attitudes and Information of American Teachers."

[60] Malvina Lindsay, "Intimidating Teachers," reprinted from *Washington Post* (D.C.) in *National Education Association Journal,* 41 (October, 1952), p. 411.

[61] Quoted in *Civil Liberties* (monthly publication of American Civil Liberties Union), September, 1953, p. 3.

5. ... And Still Other Educational Problems ...

There are many other educational problems that might be explored, although there is space to mention only one or two. *The financial plight of the private colleges* in a period of rising costs has attracted widespread concern.[62] To meet this crisis, the private colleges within a region often band together for co-operative fund-raising, with a strong appeal for contributions from corporations. A number of business leaders have responded, saying that American business should support the private colleges which educate so many business executives and which serve as insurance against the possibility of a politically-dominated government monopoly of higher education. Business concerns donated over $60 million to private American colleges in 1954, plus additional funds for equipment and research.[63] This increasing dependence of private colleges upon corporate contributors gives rise to still another problem: Will this dependence result in subtle pressures to teach only those points of view most agreeable to business interests? The generous provision of free pamphlets, films, and other materials by business concerns, trade associations (and, to a lesser extent, labor organizations) also raises the question of how schools and colleges shall use such free materials without becoming propagandists for the donors.[64]

In a society in which agriculture becomes steadily more highly specialized and is highly dependent upon migrant, seasonal labor, *the education of the children of migrant laborers* becomes a growing problem. Yet the federal government spends more to protect migratory birds than it spends to educate migratory children. This is a problem to which a chapter could easily be devoted.[65] *The problem of social class and education*—of the manner in which social class affects pupil motivation, classroom behavior, and school organization and administration—is worthy of attention.[66]

The question of *who should go to college* is claiming growing interest. The National Manpower Council finds that there is a serious national shortage of nearly every kind of highly educated man power; yet only half the students who are mentally capable of going to college ever enter, and only one out of 25 who are capable to earning a doctoral degree ever

[62] Benjamin Fine, "Grave Fund Crisis Confronts Colleges," *New York Times,* June 1, 1952, p. 1.

[63] "Business and the Colleges," *Time* (January 18, 1954), p. 82.

[64] See J. Austin Burkhard, "Big Business and the Schools," *The Nation,* 173 (November 10, 1951), p. 401.

[65] Cf. Morris McClure, "Make Room for the Migrants," *Michigan Education Journal,* 30 (April, 1953), pp. 428-431; also Lester Velie, "The Americans Nobody Wants," *Collier's,* 125 (April 1, 1950), pp. 13 ff.

[66] Cf. A. B. Hollingshead, *Elmtown's Youth* (New York, John Wiley & Sons, Inc., 1949), Chs. 6, 8, 13. Also Lloyd A. Cook and Elaine F. Cook, *Sociological Foundations of Education* (New York, McGraw-Hill Book Company, Inc., 1950), Ch. 11.

complete one.[67] It would be easily possible to persuade many more of our young people to go to college and graduate school, but to do so would cost money and might also involve some changes in the class system. Either of these would arouse bitter value-controversies.

APPROACHES TO THE PROBLEMS OF EDUCATION

1. The Social-Disorganization Approach

Change and disorganization are involved in some way in each educational problem. The recent rise in the birth rate has swelled the child population at a time when a long depression and a major war had curtailed the building of schools. Add to this the fact that the costs of recent war and the present defense program have kept taxes at record peacetime levels, and the origin of the classroom shortage is clear.

The existence of a continuing teacher shortage is a clear symptom of social disorganization. A well-organized society includes means of attracting sufficient workers to do the work believed necessary. In a free society, a continuing and disproportionate shortage of workers in a particular occupation means that the society is failing to reward them well enough to attract the right number and type of workers.[68] Although our society rewards teachers fairly well in terms of status, working conditions, and vacation time, its persistent exclusion of teachers from sharing in the general rise of living standards has helped to drive college students away from teaching careers. While the *real income* per employed person in our country was rising by more than one-third between 1939 and 1954, the real income of public-school teachers has shown no substantial increase, that of teachers in state colleges and universities has fallen by about 7 per cent, and the real income of teachers in private colleges and universities has fallen by nearly 30 per cent.[69] For a society to prize education so highly yet support it so poorly—to be so emphatic about *wanting* teachers, yet so unwilling to pay enough to get them—this is prime evidence of social disorganization.

The curriculum controversies can be very neatly analyzed in terms of social disorganization. A changing society imposes upon its schools a set of changing responsibilities. A curriculum that very successfully prepares a small and selected class for college entrance and professional careers may work very poorly in preparing *all* classes of people for effective citi-

[67] National Manpower Council, *A Policy for Scientific and Professional Manpower* (New York, Columbia University Press, 1953). Summarized in *New York Times*, May 24, 1953, IV, p. 10.

[68] Provided there is no artificial restriction of supply, such as in medicine or in some of the skilled trades, which restrict entrance in order to protect their economic status.

[69] *New York Times*, March 15, 1955, IV, p. 2.

zenship. Our changing patterns of work, of play, of family life, of mass communication, of political behavior—all require constant revisions of the curriculum if the school is to be an active guide to effective social living and not merely a museum of ancient lore and ornamental refinements. But none can be entirely certain just what sort of adaptations a changing society requires, and this makes the curriculum an area of constant debate, experimentation, and compromise.

The academic-freedom battle, although it is a continuous one, has been intensified by recent changes. The rising tension with Russia and a growing recognition of the totalitarian nature of communism have strengthened the hand of those who have never really believed in academic freedom, and increased the number of those who feel that academic freedom may have become a weakness we must correct. Many have accused the schools and colleges of encouraging the liberalism of the New Deal-Fair Deal era, and consider the present more conservative period as a fine time to comb "socialistic thinking" out of the textbooks and classrooms. The net result of *any* group's effort to delete all but their pattern of thinking from the school inevitably becomes a grave assault upon academic freedom.

The parochial-public school controversy has fed upon a number of social changes: the growing maturity of the Catholic Church in America which, having completed the assimilation of its immigrant membership, has now become aggressively evangelistic; the rising level of school costs and the growing difficulty of meeting parochial-school costs through private contributions; the high level of postwar taxation that makes parochial-school supporters especially reluctant to support school tax increases; the rise of the federal-aid-to-education issue which presents the highly explosive question of whether parochial schools should share in such aid— all these changes have helped to intensify the clash of values that lies at the base of this controversy.

While a social-disorganization analysis does not fully explain all current educational problems, neither can they be understood without reference to the changing social setting in which they grow.

2. The Value-Conflict Approach

A conflict of values is basic to every one of these educational problems. From the question How much is education worth? to the question Who is worth educating?, it is clear that people disagree partly because they do not want the same outcomes. In school tax balloting, parents of school-age children generally vote about two to one for school improvements, whereas elderly people and owners of rental properties often vote about two to one for low taxes instead of school improvements. Although nearly all people desire "good schools," they are not equally intense in their desire for good schools or in their willingness to sacrifice for them.

The factual case for federal aid to education is overwhelming. It is clear beyond debate that (1) there is no practical possibility that certain states will be able to provide "first-class" education to all their children at any time within the near future through their own resources; (2) these educational deficiencies help to retard the economic and cultural development of these areas and inflict economic and military burdens upon the entire nation. *But a number of value-choices are involved.* Federal aid means more taxes to be paid by somebody, striking at the nerve center of many a person's value-system. Federal aid would tax the more prosperous states for the direct benefit of the poorer states. Although circumstances may force us to be our brothers' keepers, few of us seem to enjoy the privilege. Federal aid would enlarge the function and possibly the control of the federal government, and the values of many are furiously opposed to this. Federal aid is further complicated by the value-conflicts inherent in the parochial-public school controversy. Among the seldom discussed issues are the changes in social structure that federal aid would promote. Better schools for southern Negroes and "poor-whites" would make them less docile as workers and would accelerate the decline of the plantation and tenancy systems of agriculture. Better education probably would encourage farm mechanization and industrialization and encourage the organization of co-operatives and labor unions. Since federal aid would almost certainly have some sort of nondiscrimination provision, it would be a powerful lever for equalizing educational and occupational opportunities for Negroes. Better education would accelerate the trend toward Negro voting and might also weaken the one-party system in the South. In short, better education would tend to alter the social structure and power system of the South in many respects. There are those in both South and North who do not enjoy the prospect of such changes.

The academic-freedom controversy is, above all else, a conflict of values. Some prize the *unrestricted search* for knowledge and object to any authoritarian labeling of truth and error; some desire an authority in which to find confidence and security and want all "wrong" and "right" ideas officially labeled, for they dislike confusion, uncertainty, and debate. Some desire change and "progress," secured through constant examination and debate; some prefer stability of thought and social structure and seek to insure it through an educational indoctrination of the young. Some prize the average citizen's ability to study data, analyze competing propagandas, and arrive at valid conclusions; some doubt that the average citizen can develop any such ability and prefer that he be trained to believe and obey his leaders. And the child of average ability who has been trained to think independently, ask questions, and join with his neighbors in forming an action organization when he is dissatisfied—some would consider him an educational achievement; others would view him as a social menace. The academic-freedom controversy is, therefore, more than a debate over whether indoctrination or critical analysis is the better way to preserve social order; *it is also a debate over what kind of a social order is to be preserved*—a society of loyal, united, obedient, intolerant believers, or a society of inquiring, discussing, quarreling, relatively tolerant searchers for truth.

The most inescapable fact about each educational problem is the existence of such irreconcilable value-conflicts. The value-conflicts of the society become the problems of the school, since the members of the society cannot agree upon what the school should be and do. Not only differences upon *means,* but differences upon *ends* are involved. People who disagree about the kind of society they want must also disagree upon how children should be trained to live in society. As long as such value-conflicts persist—and they will persist at least as long as our society continues to change—educational controversies are inevitable.

3. The Personal-Deviation Approach

Educational problems are ones in which deviant persons are incidental rather than major factors. If there were no value-conflicts involved, deviant persons would be unable to transmute their private grudges into social issues. Since there *are* important value-conflicts, plus many misinformed people, it is possible for deviant persons to play a major role in mobilizing people for school battles. People who have closely observed local school battles have been impressed by the large number of hostile, aggressive, resentful, hate-filled persons who appear at the mass meetings.[70] Many persons who throughout an adult lifetime have shown no particular interest in the school suddenly become bitter participants in a school battle. It would appear that these are maladjusted people who have displaced their inner emotional conflicts upon the school or upon some group of school people. Of course, the success of an attack requires that many ordinary, well-adjusted citizens be induced to join, but the contagious intensity of the neurotic core helps to build such a mass following.

Not all who criticize the school, of course, are neurotics. Some are cynical opportunists, planning to cut school costs or to capture the school as an instrument of their propaganda. Some are honest critics, calling attention to the genuine failures and dubious aspects of the school's operation. And not all the neurotics are found among the attackers. Educators and teachers have their share of eccentric and maladjusted personalities, apparently in about the same proportion as other professions.[71] Although the neurotic person appears more likely to join the free-

70 Dorothy Frank, *op. cit.;* Carey MacWilliams, *op. cit.*

71 Cf. Lloyd A. Cook and Elaine Forsyth Cook, A *Sociological Approach to Education* (New York, McGraw-Hill Book Company, Inc., 1950), p. 435; Lloyd A. Cook, *Community Backgrounds of Education* (New York, McGraw-Hill Book Company, Inc., 1938), p. 355.

swinging attackers, he may also turn up among the defenders. The cause of academic freedom has suffered greatly from neurotic, exhibitionistic, and communistic teachers who have invoked "academic freedom" to evade legitimate criticism. Although a genuine communist is prevented by his doctrine from accepting the responsibilities of academic freedom as a teacher, when he is discharged he almost unfailingly raises the cry that academic freedom has been despoiled. In each instance, it is important to determine whether a real interference with academic freedom has occurred, or whether there are entirely proper reasons for the teacher's dismissal.[72]

In each educational problem, then, deviant persons play a similar role. They do not *cause* educational problems, but can *greatly aggravate* them. The basic causes of educational problems are found in the value-conflicts of a changing (disorganized) society. Since there are value-conflicts that produce tension and misunderstanding, a small band of neurotics can capitalize on this to organize an attack. Many local school battles, text-book controversies, and dismissal quarrels *would* not occur if they were not promoted by aggressive neurotics, and they *could* not occur if basic value-conflicts had not provided the background of controversy. In this way, deviant persons may function as precipitating factors in educational controversies.

PROSPECTS FOR THE FUTURE

Since educational problems are rooted in the value-conflicts that a changing society inevitably produces, no complete or final solutions are possible. Whether the immediate future brings a relaxation or aggravation of tensions depends partly upon developments in other fields. If no major war develops, it is likely that the classroom shortage will be considerably relieved after a decade or so. A major depression would quickly end the teacher shortage, however unpleasantly. A relaxation of international tension and reduction of military expenses would make it easier to pay the salaries necessary to help alleviate the teacher shortage. If most teachers were to join an aggressive union—which appears unlikely—they perhaps could raise salary levels and increase the teacher supply. If a genuinely peaceful accord with the Soviet Union were to develop, the anxieties which lead to a fear of academic freedom would greatly subside. The

[72] The Committee of Academic Freedom and Tenure of the American Association of University Professors investigates complaints to determine whether academic freedom has actually been infringed, although it has no powers beyond those of publicity and persuasion. Each issue of the AAUP *Bulletin* publishes a list of "censured administrations" where "unsatisfactory conditions of academic freedom and tenure have been found to prevail," a list currently numbering five colleges and universities. State education associations and the N.E.A. also seek to offer public-school teachers some protection against arbitrary discharge.

parochial-school controversy will be greatly affected by the general course of Catholic-Protestant relations. Such external developments as these will have great effects upon educational problems.

Even if final solutions for educational problems were possible, further social change would soon produce new problems. All major educational problems—curriculum, teaching methods, finances, academic freedom—are *permanent problems* in that social changes will continue to excite debate and call for readjustment. The prospect is for a continuing process of *accommodation* through which the conflicting wishes and pressures of a democratic society can be compromised. Wherever ultimate solutions are unavailable, accommodation provides democracy's alternative to chaos, and nowhere is this more true than in education. This is a far from gloomy prospect, since most of us consider the argumentative and wordy compromises of democracy far preferable to the orderly discipline of monolithic authority.

SUGGESTED READINGS

American Library Association and American Book Publishers Council, *The Freedom to Read,* American Association of University Professors Bulletin, 39 (Summer, 1953), pp. 209-214. An eloquent statement of the thesis that book publishing and circulation should be free from censorship, labeling, or other restraints on freedom to read.

Association for Supervision and Curriculum Development, *Forces Affecting American Education* (Washington, National Education Association, 1953), Ch. 3, "Groups Affecting Education," by Robert A. Skaife. A survey of national pressure groups interested in the school, and several brief-case histories of local school controversies.

Cook, Lloyd Allen, and Cook, Elaine Forsyth, *A Sociological Approach to Education* (New York, McGraw-Hill Book Company, Inc., 1950), Ch. 8, "Unity-Disunity, Change, and Planning," describes the social changes in a rural hamlet and their significance for education. Ch. 11, "Social Class in the School," considers the effect of social class differences on school behavior and learning, and shows how the school functions to perpetuate rather than eliminate class differences.

Hullfish, H. Gordon, *Keeping Our Schools Free,* Public Affairs Pamphlet No. 199, September, 1953 (New York, Public Affairs Committee, 1953). A concise pamphlet clearly stating a number of possible threats to the freedom of the schools.

Hunter, Evan, *Blackboard Jungle* (New York, Simon & Schuster, Inc., 1954); condensed in *Ladies' Home Journal,* 71 (October, 1954), pp. 60 ff. A highly readable and disturbing novel which portrays many of the problems and difficulties of the school in an underprivileged neighborhood. Written with knowledge and insight by a former teacher in such a teaching situation.

Nordskog, John Eric, McDonagh, Edward C., and Vincent, Melvin J., *Analyzing Social Problems* (New York, The Dryden Press, 1950), Ch. 9, "Analyzing Educational Problems." A collection of readings on various aspects of educational problems and issues.

Scott, C. Winfield, and Hill, Clyde M., *Public Education Under Criticism* (New York, Prentice-Hall, Inc., 1954). A collection of many short articles dealing with criticisms of the public-school system; stimulating and readable.

AUDIO-VISUAL AIDS

Children Must Learn (New York University Film Library), 15 minutes, sound, black and white. Depicts a poverty-stricken rural family and the inadequate one-room school which cannot meet the needs of life in the area.

Design of American Public Education (McGraw-Hill Book Company, Inc., Text-Film Department, 330 West 42nd, New York), 16 minutes, sound, black and white. The structure of American education, as it might be under a centrally controlled system, and as it actually is in a democratic society.

Freedom to Learn (National Education Association, Washington), 27 minutes, sound, black and white. A charge of teaching communism in the classroom, hurled at a high-school teacher, raises the issue of freedom to learn. Asks whether the freedom to study and evaluate can be controlled or restricted and still be freedom.

Sixth Chair (National School Service Institute, Chicago), 18 minutes, sound, black and white. Presents such problems as school construction and modernization, class size, teacher shortages, and public complacency toward education.

Who Will Teach Your Child? (McGraw-Hill Book Company, Inc., Text-Film Department, 330 West 42nd, New York), 24 minutes, sound, black and white. Raises the questions of how to attract, train, and retrain superior teachers.

QUESTIONS AND PROJECTS

1. Why is the "cost" of education a problem during a period of unprecedented national prosperity?

2. What are the causes of the teacher shortage? How does the shortage illustrate the disorganization approach? The value-conflict approach?

3. Why has federal aid to education been proposed? Why has there been opposition? Are the disputes mainly over facts or over values?

4. Nearly everyone seems to "believe in" athletics in the school, so what is the argument about?

5. How would one "prove" whether a private-school education is generally superior to a public-school education, or vice versa? What variables would have to be controlled in making any comparisons?

6. What is academic freedom? Whom is it supposed to benefit? Is academic freedom threatened? By whom?

7. What responsibilities does academic freedom place upon the teacher? Upon the school administrator? Upon the citizen?

8. Is the "freedom" of the schools endangered only by those who do not "believe in" education?

9. How would you distinguish between "constructive" and "destructive" criticism of the schools? Do you think educators and administrators have generally received criticism less fair-mindedly, or more fair-mindedly, than have other professional groups (such as lawyers, physicians, or businessmen)?

10. Should schools and colleges accept free pamphlets, films, and other free teaching materials from corporations and trade associations, labor organizations, or other sources which may have an "ax to grind"?

11. Read Robert Maynard Hutchins' essay, "What Price Freedom?" (in Nordskog, *Analyzing Social Problems*, pp. 438-441; also in American Association of University Professors Bulletin, 35 [Summer, 1949], pp. 211-215). If the viewpoints in this statement are accepted, what present tendencies and practices in America would need revision?

CHAPTER II

Social Class and Class Struggle

Tom Brown, the ordinary boy, is ten years old and in the fifth grade. His father owns and runs a grocery store in Hometown. The family lives in a large well-kept house in the "better" part of town. Tom's mother is proud of her home but she recognizes that their part of town is inferior to the Hillcrest region where the Peabodys and families like the Peabodys reside. . . .

The Peabodys are "one of the town's old families," and their kind are often referred to in Hometown as "our Four Hundred," or by those hostile and often envious as "small-town aristocrats." Tom's mother and father, while respected as pillars of society, are never spoken of in such terms.

Neither Tom's nor Kenneth's [Peabody] father knows or has heard of the Jones family. Tom's father knows of Joe Sienkowitz's big brother, who was a great football player, and he says, "That Sienkowitz boy's football career goes to show how everybody who wants to, and who tries, can go places in this country." Kenneth's father thinks too many people now go to high school. His interest in football is confined to the annual game between Yale and Princeton.[1]

"ALL men are equal" is a favorite cliché of many Americans. But what does it mean? And is it true? If we add the phrase ". . . in the sight of God," it indicates belief that *to the Almighty* one human soul is as important as any other. Such propositions, which are a matter of faith, cannot be proved or disproved scientifically. If we limit the question to whether all men are equal *here on earth,* a much more definite answer is possible. It is really rather ridiculous to assert that all men are equal without qualifying that phrase very markedly. They are certainly not equal in height, intelligence, in the ability to drive a car, or in ability generally. Neither are they equal in the benefits they receive from society. Some men drive Cadillacs, more men drive Chevrolets, and many have no automobiles at all. Houses range from twenty-room mansions to converted chicken coops. Debutantes have "coming out" parties, and slum youth quit school to help support their families. Cities maintain welfare departments, and civic organizations distribute baskets at Christmas.

[1] W. Lloyd Warner, Robert J. Havighurst, and Martin B. Loeb, *Who Shall Be Educated?* (New York, Harper and Brothers, 1944), pp. 2-3, by permission.

CLASSES AND DEMOCRACY

The American Ideology

In their enthusiasm for democracy, many people are convinced that there are "no important" social distinctions in the United States. A moment's sober reflection will show that this is not true. The United States from the beginning had social inequality, and indeed our free-enterprise system assumes that extraordinary initiative and ingenuity should be rewarded by the acquisition of wealth, power, and prestige. The "American dream" does not include an undifferentiated mass society but rather holds out to each person the prospect of climbing the class ladder. American history is replete with stories of the "poor boy who made good," of the "office boy who became president of the firm," and of the open road from "log cabin to White House." The United States is founded not on the idea of a classless society, but upon the notions of an "open" class system. The opportunity to change class position in accord with one's ability is the essence of such a system.

The kind of equality so much admired in this country is *equality of opportunity*. Men are supposed to be *equal at birth*, if not at any time thereafter. Given the same initial advantages, one person should have as much chance to succeed as any other. It is allowed that some persons may be more favored biologically than others, but aside from the uncontrollable aspects of heredity, success is regarded largely as a matter of ambition, hard work, and, perhaps, a little "luck." Prestige, wealth, and power are the rewards for diligent application of one's talents and are equally available to all who strive for them.

The course of American history has been such as to give real meaning to this philosophy of free movement from one social class to another. Two factors have been instrumental in supporting the pattern of extensive interclass mobility. These are (1) the expansion of the economy, and (2) the differential birth rate.

1. *Expansion of the Economy.* One of the striking features of American life has been the stimulus provided by the Western frontier and our rapidly growing population. The frontier served at least two functions. It acted as a kind of safety-valve, draining off excess population and goods from the East and it constantly added to the material wealth and natural resources of the nation. Ever expanding markets gave tremendous impetus to production. In a mere century and a half the United States moved from a group of semi-autonomous colonies to the world's most highly industrialized nation. Expansion created new jobs by the thousands. New businesses grew up and a whole new class of entrepreneurs was created. It was relatively easy for a man to go into business for himself and eventually to become the head of a large business organization. This

is, perhaps, the kind of *vertical mobility* most highly valued in the United States.

Not all upward movement was of this type, however. In fact, much of the mobility occurred within the ranks of workers who were not, themselves, owners of businesses. Large-scale corporate organization with its intricate specialization and complex problems of financing and management brought into being a great new "middle class," midway between the "laborers" and the "bosses." This army of white-collar workers, technicians, scientists, and managers was recruited mainly from the ranks of the lower economic groups. The more rapidly the economy developed the more new positions were created. Either by striking out on their own or by rising through the occupational hierarchy, the sons of working-class families could outstrip their fathers and raise their standards of living.

2. *The Differential Birth Rate.* Throughout most of Western European culture, upper-class groups are known for their low birth rates. Their failure to have enough children to replace themselves again results in some interclass mobility. The groups at the top of the class structure are always in the process of slowly dying out and being replaced by "new blood" from the lower classes. In most cases it is not a matter of individuals rising from the lowest to the highest class in a single generation but is felt instead in a gentle upward pressure upon whole segments of the population. Advances up the ladder are generally made a rung or two at a time, rapidly enough to keep alive the American's faith that at least his son, if not himself, can achieve a higher class status.

The Nature of the Problem

One might well ask at this point, What, then, is the problem with regard to social class? If an expanding economy and the differential birth rate assure continued mobility, and if the American people are confident that the system is fair and equitable, is there "... a situation believed to be undesirable by a large number of people ..."? To answer these questions, certain other facts must be noted. One set of facts is concerned with the question, Are conditions *today* the same as they were during the early part of our national history?, and the other with, Does the class system itself prevent the existence of any real *equality of opportunity?*

Have Conditions Changed? The basic role played by economic expansion in maintaining the pattern of upward mobility has led many persons to speculate on the possible effects of the disappearance of the Western frontier. There is at least a strong possibility that the rate of expansion had passed its peak by the early part of the present century, and that the American economy is losing some of its dynamic character. In terms of the class structure, such a slowdown would be apt to increase the rigidity of present class lines and to discourage large-scale upward mobility.

Middle- and upper-class groups would be forced to consolidate their positions and lower-class persons would find it more difficult to escape their present lot. Since *mobility rather than the absence of social classes* has been the key to the American system, this turn of events would be cause for re-examination of the whole system in terms of its significance for the continuance of our democratic pattern.

Classes and Equality of Opportunity. Increasingly, thoughtful people are questioning whether there is not a basic incompatibility between the ideal of equal opportunity and the existence of social classes. It is just possible that protecting persons from any *legal disabilities,* as does the Constitution, is not the same thing as guaranteeing them an equal chance to get ahead in the world! On purely logical grounds, it appears that the possession of some power, wealth, and prestige makes it easier to acquire more of these. The cliché expression, "It takes money to make money," is tacit recognition of this fact. Though education and technical training are available to everyone, it probably is easier to take advantage of these opportunities if one's parents can afford to support a family member who is not making any contribution to the family income. There is also a far more positive kind of advantage that is likely to accrue to the children of upper-class families. Becoming a member of the middle or upper classes requires that one acquire the attitudes, values, manners, and social graces characteristic of those groups. Some children, because they are reared in upper-class surroundings, will acquire these traits rather automatically. Mobility for lower-class persons requires the unlearning of behaviors learned in childhood and the substitution of other patterns for them. In the individual case, having lower-class parents may take much of the meaning out of equality of opportunity!

Thus, there are at least two points of view concerning the operation of social class in the United States. One group stresses relatively free mobility and opportunities for advancement; the other faction points to increasing rigidity of class lines and the advantages possessed by the upper classes. With these two viewpoints in mind, let us examine the available data before attempting to draw any conclusions. First of all, just what is the class structure in the United States? Is it open and fluid or are there elements of rigidity? Do people identify with class groups? What is the objective evidence concerning class placement? How much mobility is there? Is mobility becoming more or less frequent? Do some groups have "most of the advantages"? Are there any trends which can be discerned? These are the questions we shall try to answer.

THE AMERICAN CLASS STRUCTURE

The United States is a large and diversified country. With large rural and urban populations and regional differences from north to south to west it is unlikely that there can be presented a single class picture which accurately describes each segment of the total society. Class interaction is very much influenced by the degree of specialization within the economic structure and by the kind of history the community has. There can be presented, however, certain broad outlines which are sufficiently typical that with appropriate modification they can be applied to the local situation. The student of the American scene must recognize that there are both "class" and what have been called "caste" aspects to be considered.

Caste Aspects

One of the most glaring inconsistencies between the "American dream" and the real situation is to be found in what have been called "caste aspects" of the American system. A caste system differs from a class system in that once born into a given caste there is no possibility of rising above or falling below that caste. Placement is hereditary and mobility is nonexistent. Pre-modern India is frequently offered as a good example of a caste system. The rigid distinctions and the great social distance between castes from the "brahmin" down to the "untouchables" are fairly well known.

Ordinarily one would not consider caste to be relevant to the American class structure, but the challenge has been made that certain aspects of the system do *approximate* a caste system. Specifically it is charged that the 10 per cent of our population who happen to be Negro are impressed into a caste apart from the rest of the class structure and out of which they cannot rise. In most sections of the country, strong taboos forbid any kind of intimate contact suggesting equality between Negroes and whites. White persons are taught that Negroes are inferior and are to be "kept in their place." Especially in the South, any white man no matter how poor, ill educated, and incompetent, considers himself above the most eminent Negro business and professional men. A rigid barrier separates the highest ranking Negroes from the lowest ranking whites. This means that the vast majority of Negroes are denied certain opportunities available to whites. Negroes, even if they acquire professional training, wealth, and prestige within the Negro group, are forced to recognize the superior position of lower-class whites.

Defenders of the "open-class" theory in the United States point out that Negro-white relations are really not caste relationships and they point to such persons as Dr. Ralph Bunche, highest ranking American in the United Nations, as evidence that Negroes can overcome the handicaps of their race. There are separate classes in Negro society and there is possibility of mobility within the Negro group. Moreover, the caste aspects of Negro-white relations are probably more marked in the South than in other areas of the country. Even there the caste-like suppression of Negroes is breaking down somewhat as it becomes more difficult for the American people to reconcile "discrimination" with "democracy." Eventually there may be no special class distinctions between the white and Negro groups. Some groups such as the National Association for the Advancement of Colored People are working to bring this about. Other groups, predominantly white, see the gains made by Negroes in recent years as dangerous trends leading to the breakdown of segregation, to intermarriage, and eventually to the deterioration of the population. It appears that the special restrictions on the freedom and upward mobility of Negro persons are tending, in the long run, to break down. Nevertheless, it is evident that the vast majority of Negroes are a disprivileged group in the struggle for status. The success achieved by a mere handful of Negroes serves only to accent the plight of the many.

Class Aspects

The emphasis on equal opportunity and upward mobility has discouraged the development of any real *class consciousness* on the part of the American people. The prospect of better things, at least for one's children, encouraged people to identify themselves with the prosperous and powerful elements in the community rather than with the so-called common man. Conscious recognition of class has generally been confined to vague differentiations between the "business class" and the "working class," or to casual references to upper, middle, and lower classes. It is not surprising, then, that the class distinctions made by ordinary people in ordinary speech do not mirror very closely the actual status differentials which exist within the population. Consequently, one may look at the class system either in terms of the *identifications* made by individual persons or in terms of *objective differences* which exist among them.

Self-Identifications. Most Americans identify themselves with the middle class. *Fortune* magazine some years ago conducted a survey in which people were asked to identify the class to which they belonged. Seventy per cent of the respondents called themselves middle class, 7 per cent claimed upper-class status, and 22 per cent identified themselves with the lower class. This pictures the population as a remarkably homogeneous one in terms of social class, with seven out of every ten persons belonging to the middle class, two to the lower class, and one to the upper class. Even casual observation would indicate that the actual class system is quite different and that wealth, power, and prestige are distributed among the population in a different fashion.

HOW AMERICANS CLASSIFY THEMSELVES

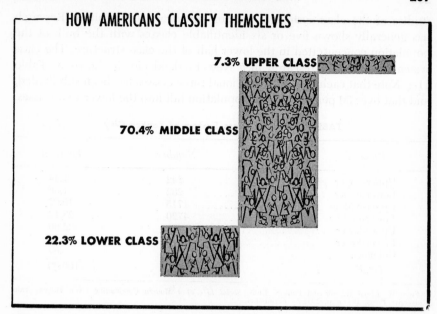

7.3% UPPER CLASS

70.4% MIDDLE CLASS

22.3% LOWER CLASS

FIG. 11-1. The United States Says It Is Middle Class. (Data from the February, 1940, *Fortune* Survey of Public Opinion, by special permission of the editors)

Rather than accept these identifications at face value, it would seem prudent to ask *why* people overwhelmingly conceive of themselves as middle class. The explanation probably is to be found in the peculiar American attitude toward class. The prevalent belief that one's present status is temporary encourages lower-class persons to identify with the middle class toward which they aspire. School teachers and some other low-paid white-collar workers, for example, who income-wise might well be lower class, are prone to identify themselves with middle-class business and professional interests. Upper-class persons, too, find it advantageous to support these beliefs and are reluctant to admit, at least to others, that they hold positions of special benefit. Thus, in spite of wide differences in income, wealth, and prestige, most people act *as if* they were middle class. Now let us compare these self-identifications with some other indices of class placement.

Objective Placement. Fifty per cent of United States families and individuals in 1950 received less than $3000 total money income,[2] some 16 million people belonged to labor unions, and up to one-third of the nation was said to be ill-housed. Offhand, these do not sound like characteristics of the great middle class. Moreover, the class identifications discussed above are not consistent with the results of many comprehensive

[2] U. S. Bureau of the Census, *Statistical Abstract of the United States: 1952* (Washington, Government Printing Office), p. 264.

studies of the class system in various American communities. Research has generally shown five or six identifiable classes with the bulk of the population concentrated in the lower half of the class structure. The class system revealed by research in a New England city is shown in Table 11-1. Note that each of the conventional three classes has been subdivided, and that over 50 per cent of the population fall into the lower two classes.

TABLE 11-1. The Class System of Yankee City

Class	Number	Per Cent
Upper-upper	242	1.44
Lower-upper	262	1.56
Upper-middle	1715	10.22
Lower-middle	4720	28.12
Upper-lower	5471	32.60
Lower-lower	4234	25.22
Unknown	141	.84
Total	16,785	100.00

From W. Lloyd Warner and Paul S. Lunt, *Social Life of a Modern Community* (New Haven, Yale University Press, 1941), p. 203, by permission.

Slightly under 40 per cent are middle class and some 3 per cent belong to the upper classes. A number of criteria including family background and the patterns of association within the community were used in identifying these classes, but it is interesting to see how this alignment parallels that provided by the distribution of money income among the population. The comparison is made in Table 11-2. One-fourth of the population in 1950 had less than $1500 money income and 60 per cent had incomes of less than $3500. The income picture and the Yankee City data show the major part of the population to be concentrated in the lower half of the socioeconomic structure, with the proportions getting steadily smaller as one moves toward the upper-class and upper-income brackets. *By their own assertion,* most people are middle class. *But according to other evidence,* much of this "middle class" is concentrated in the bottom half of the income and prestige structure.

People in the United States, then, apparently believe or want to believe that status differences are at a minimum and that most people are middle class. Objective studies, however, show status differentials to be greater than believed and a class structure with a broad base which narrows to an almost needle-like top. The popular conception of a great middle class ignores the fact that there is an even larger lower class among whom incomes and living standards are very low. The opportunities provided by the American technology and whatever equality of opportunity prevails have not been enough to eliminate problems of gross inequality in the class system. We still have a large lower class which is potentially capable of challenging the prerogatives of the middle- and upper-class groups. To date, the development of any real class consciousness among the lower class seems to have been forestalled by the widespread hope of climbing into the middle class. Whether this situation continues indefinitely may well depend upon the reality of the hope of upward mobility.

TABLE 11-2. Money Income and Social Class

Total Money Income, 1950	Per Cent		Yankee City Classes
Under $500			
$ 500-999			
1000-1499 . . . . .25.4%	25.22%	. . . .	Lower-lower
1500-1999			
2000-2499			
2500-2999			
3000-3499 . . . . .35.4	32.60	. . . .	Upper-lower
3500-3999			
4000-4499			
4500-4999			
5000-5499			
5500-5999 . . . . .27.3	28.12	. . . .	Lower-middle
6000-6999			
7000-7999			
8000-8999			
9000-9999 . . . . 9.1	10.22	. . . .	Upper-middle
			Lower-upper
$10,000 and over 2.7	3.0	. . . .	Upper-upper

Income data from U. S. Bureau of the Census, *Statistical Abstract of the United States: 1952* (Washington, Government Printing Office), p. 264.

MOBILITY AND THE CLASS STRUCTURE

Being able to move freely from one class to another has been an important part of the American class picture. The expanding economy and the differential birth rate, at least formerly, made widespread upward mobility possible. But now we need to know, Do people have equal chances to acquire upper class status? and, Is mobility decreasing?

Equal Chances?

The American ethos proclaims that all children regardless of origin, whether from upper- or lower-class families, shall have equal opportunities to prove themselves and to make good. To that end we have a free public-school system and the competitive filling of openings in business and industry. But does, in fact, this system guarantee equality of opportunity? Let us examine the available data in the areas of *education* and *occupation*.

Education. Since education has been one of the chief routes to upward mobility, equal opportunity depends upon the school system remaining equally open to children from all social classes. *Legally*, of course, all children are guaranteed a public-school education. College attendance is not quite so free in that some fees must be paid, books and supplies purchased, and living costs met, even at the tax-supported state universities. Especially in recent years, however, more and more scholarships have been made available to help needy and deserving persons to finance their educations. All these provisions are meant to be a bulwark protecting and maintaining the avenue to improved social position.

TABLE 11-3. Number of College Graduates, 1870-1950

Year of Graduation	Number of Graduates
1870	9,371
1880	10,353
1890	14,306
1900	25,324
1910	34,178
1920	48,622
1930	122,484
1940	186,500
1950	432,058

U. S. Bureau of the Census, *Statistical Abstract of the United States: 1952* (Washington, Government Printing Office), p. 121.

Education, and especially higher education, is more widely received today than ever before. The number of persons attending college and doing postgraduate work has grown by leaps and bounds. Unfortunately, national information is not available to indicate how these persons attending college are distributed in the class structure. Probably it can be assumed that college enrollments represent largely middle- and upper-class backgrounds. Especially with the aid of the "G.I. Bill," however, more lower-class persons may be attending both private and state universities. At least some of the evidence points to ever widening use of the educational system, but contrary evidence also exists.

TABLE 11-4. College Attendance of High School Graduates in Old City

Class	Per Cent of Each Class Attending College
Upper	72
Upper-middle	69
Middle	58
Lower-middle	16
Lower	0

Adapted from W. Lloyd Warner, Robert J. Havighurst, and Martin B. Loeb, *Who Shall Be Educated?* (New York, Harper and Brothers, 1944), p. 59, by permission.

Much of our information indicates that the educational system itself operates as a selective mechanism tending to discourage the continuance of lower-class children and encouraging those from the middle- and upper-class groups. In one study of an anonymous Southern city identified as "Old City," Warner, Havighurst, and Loeb found (Table 11-4) that 72 per cent of the high-school graduates from the upper class, 16 per cent from the lower middle class, and none from the lower class attended college. These figures do not speak well for a "democratic" educational system. Table 11-5 portrays the situation discovered in one Pennsylvania school system. Some 910 students with I.Q.'s of 110 or above were classified by economic status into two groups. *Though the two groups were of equal ability,* the "below-average" economic group showed a higher proportion of drop-outs at every grade level, and a much larger percentage of the "above-average" economic group eventually attended college. How can we explain this situation?

TABLE 11-5. Effect of Economic Status on Educational Achievement of Students With I.Q.'s of 110 or Above

Educational Advance	Socioeconomic Status Above Average	Socioeconomic Status Below Average
Dropped school at eighth grade or below	.7	7.9
Completed ninth, tenth, or eleventh grade but did not graduate from high school	6.2	20.2
Graduated from high school but did not attend college	36.3	59.0
Attended college	56.8	12.9

Adapted from W. Lloyd Warner, Robert J. Havighurst, and Martin B. Loeb, *Who Shall Be Educated?* (New York, Harper and Brothers, 1944), p. 52, by permission.

Apparently, the theoretical opportunity to complete one's education is in certain ways abridged for many lower-class children. Some of the relevant factors are to be found in the way of life of the lower class and some of them are to be found in the school system. Much of the lower class has not been thoroughly indoctrinated with the ideals of success and mobility that characterize middle-class groups. Instead, large families and low, uncertain incomes combine to create a resignation and apathy which tend to perpetuate the lower-class pattern. Boys and girls are encouraged to quit school, as soon as they can legally do so, to help support their families. Moreover, because they can see little use for education in their way of life the children often *want* to quit school. Defenders of the traditional American system use this fact of many lower-class children not wanting to go to school to indicate that lower-class children really are not discriminated against. The opposite viewpoint maintains that the desire for education must be learned and that many *lower-class children never really have a chance to want to go to school!*

TABLE 11-6. Social Class Distribution of Teachers

Class	Hometown Per Cent	Yankee City Per Cent	Old City Per Cent
Upper-upper	0	2	2.5
Lower-upper	0	1	2.5
Upper-middle	26	76	72.5
Lower-middle	72	21	20.0
Upper-lower	2	0	2.5
Lower-lower	0	0	0.0
	100	100	100.0

From W. Lloyd Warner, Robert J. Havighurst, and Martin B. Loeb, *Who Shall Be Educated?* (New York, Harper and Brothers, 1944), p. 101, by permission.

Within the school system, too, there are pressures which operate against lower-class and for middle-class children. Not without foundation, it has been said that the school itself is a middle-class institution. School boards and school teachers are both drawn primarily from the middle class. Middle-class teachers, even without realizing it, are prone to reward middle-class children for their clean faces, tidy clothes, nice manners, and interest in pleasing their elders. To lower-class children, who have not learned these middle-class "virtues" and who see in school work only a compulsory and not very pleasant task, the lack of understanding and discouragement encountered reinforces a latent hostility toward schools and teachers. Taken together, these pressures that operate in the home and in the school deprive lower-class children of much of their "opportunity."

TABLE 11-7. Occupations of the Sons of Unskilled Workers

Occupations of Sons of Unskilled Workers	Per Cent
Unskilled workers	41.7
Semiskilled workers	16.5
Skilled workers	13.7
Clerks	13.7
Proprietors	10.3
Professionals	4.1

Data from P. E. Davidson and H. D. Anderson, *Occupational Mobility in an American Community* (Stanford, Calif., Stanford University Press), 1937.

Occupation. Occupational mobility probably is as good a single index as we have of the amount of class mobility in the United States. Davidson and Anderson, in analyzing the data from a California sample, report that over 40 per cent of the sons of a group of unskilled workers became unskilled workers themselves. Sixteen per cent became semiskilled, and 27 per cent became skilled workers or clerks. Ten per cent of the sons became proprietors and 4 per cent entered the professions.[3] Thus, slightly over half of the sons remained in lower-class occupations, some 27 per cent moved into middle-class occupations, and 14 per cent into occupations which might be either middle or upper class. Judging from these data, lower-class boys have a better than average chance to remain lower class. On the other hand, a substantial number of them will move up to the middle class and a few may even attain upper-class status.

Is Mobility Decreasing?

The "American dream" assumes relatively free interclass mobility and, as we have seen, some mobility does take place. However, since lower-class youth most frequently seem to remain at the same class level as their parents, it is important to ask whether it is becoming more difficult to move upward in the class system. Many authorities believe that the rate of upward movement is slowing down. Of the two chief sources of upward mobility, the differential birth rate and the expansion of the economy, it is in the latter that opportunities may be becoming stabilized or even decreasing. Warner reflects this point of view when he says, "Such economic mobility as now exists in our society is made possible largely by the fact that people in the upper classes do not have enough children to replace themselves." [4]

Empiric data on trends in the amount of mobility have not been wholly conclusive. Taussig and Joslyn attempted to discover possible trends by collecting data on the occupations of fathers of present leading businessmen and then separating the businessmen into older and younger age groups. If mobility is decreasing, the fathers of the younger men should have higher ranking occupations than the fathers of the older men. Part of their data are presented in Table 11-8. The data are not as clear as one might desire but one trend stands out. A considerably larger proportion of the younger men had fathers who were major executives. The only other large difference, for farmers' sons, is complicated somewhat by the fact that the proportion of farmers in the population has been declining steadily. What little evidence there is, seems to point toward a somewhat decreased amount of mobility, and this evidence is supported by the beliefs of a considerable number of well-informed experts.

As it stands, we have neither the completely "open" class system claimed by some groups nor the down-trodden proletariat postulated by some others. The United States has a large middle class based on income and material possessions, an even larger lower class with depressed

---

[3] Percy E. Davidson and H. Dewey Anderson, *Occupational Mobility in an American Community* (Stanford, Calif., Stanford University Press, 1937).

[4] W. Lloyd Warner, Robert J. Havighurst, and Martin B. Loeb, *Who Shall Be Educated?* (New York, Harper and Brothers, 1944), p. 153.

standards of living, and a relatively small upper class founded on current or former wealth and family lineage. Again, the actual lines drawn will vary with the local community, but the basic pattern is never very far removed. *Mobility from one class to another is still a fairly frequent occurrence, but the surest way to attain upper-class status is to be born of upper-class parents.* From "office boy to president" is greatly admired, but from "president's son to president" is surer.

TABLE 11-8. Father's Occupation of Business Leaders Classified According to Present Ages

Occupation of Father	Present Ages of Business Leaders		
	Age 35-39	Age 50-54	Age 65-69
Laborer—unskilled or semiskilled	2.6	1.6	2.2
Laborer—skilled	7.4	8.7	8.4
Farmer	7.5	12.9	17.0
Clerk or salesman	5.7	6.0	3.7
Minor executive	8.0	6.3	4.9
Owner small business	18.2	20.6	22.4
Major executive	23.5	17.9	12.4
Owner large business	14.4	13.5	16.0
Professional	12.7	12.5	13.0
Totals	100.0	100.0	100.0

Adapted from F. W. Taussig and C. S. Joslyn, *American Business Leaders* (New York, The Macmillan Company, 1932), p. 103, by permission.

SOCIAL DISORGANIZATION

Many people deplore open discussion of class differences and class consciousness. Such talk implies that there is something wrong and that somehow the system is at fault. Sociologically, it means that social change has created new conditions to which people have not yet adequately adjusted. Many of the old familiar definitions are being challenged or denied altogether; many of the new ones seem strange, incongruous, and radical. These are the familiar symptoms of social disorganization. Some of the old rules have broken down; new ones are beginning to emerge. Which are the old rules that no longer function effectively? What groups are dissatisfied? And what solutions are proposed?

The Old Rules Challenged

Most people apparently still believe there is a substantial amount of upward mobility in the United States. Growing numbers, however, are coming to the belief that class status tends to persist; that mobility is possible but that remaining in the same social class is more probable. Perhaps for the first time many people are beginning to act and think not only as participants in the American way of life but also as members of a given social class. Such class consciousness encourages awareness of *conflicts of interests among the classes.* Manual and white-collar workers find it more difficult to identify themselves with the business and professional interests. They become more prone to oppose the economic and social advantages of middle- and upper-class groups. Labor unions, for example, have grown tremendously and have found support among such white-collar groups as school teachers and clerical workers. The recent political affinity of Negroes, farmers, and white-collar workers for New Deal and Fair Deal national administrations also suggests a developing class alignment at variance with the traditional American pattern. Articulate groups at all social levels vigorously deny both the basis for and the existence of such trends. But the argument continues and grows louder. From widespread denial of even the existence of classes, the focus is shifting to more class consciousness and the prospect of possible class conflict.

The Dissatisfied Groups

Much of the stimulus to increased class consciousness has come directly or indirectly from the intelligentsia. Scholars and academicians have long debated among themselves the extent to which society is organized along class lines and the benefits and injustices that derive therefrom. Nonetheless, not until recently has this concern spread to the general population. The new public awareness is tied to political and economic conditions that have brought it to the fore.

One of the effects of the great depression of the 1930's was to shatter some of the American's naive faith in the inevitability of progress. Long hard years of unemployment and breadlines rendered people susceptible to new and radical social philosophies. It remained for the government to do what private enterprise could not—to pull us out of the depression. The idea of government responsibility for the welfare of the masses gained favor and grew in popularity. Two radical economic philosophies—socialism and communism—received eager attention from the adventurous, the liberals, and the disgruntled. Both of these philosophies stress the conflict of interests between the "masses" and the "bourgeoisie." Subsequent events in the form of elaborate government regulation of the economy in World War II and the "cold war" were heartily applauded by some groups and bitterly opposed by others.

Probably the most vociferous and articulate of the dissatisfied groups are the "liberals." Class-wise, the liberals are a heterogeneous lot. For the most part they appear to be drawn from the better educated segments of the society, although they include persons from all economic levels except perhaps the very lowest. A principal requirement for "liberal" status seems to be the ability to conceptualize *class* and to sympathize with the lower classes. As a group, the liberals are not effectively organized. Being drawn from such varied backgrounds, they have little in common other than their liberality.

Intellectuals, and particularly social scientists, are often thought to be in the vanguard of the liberal movement. In one sense they are and in another sense they are not. Its social scientists are among any society's most persistent critics. Their social science training frees them from the narrow perspective which people generally have of their own society, conflicts among the society's basic values become apparent, and the social scientist is apt to lend his authority to reconciling them. However, just as he cannot share the conservative's naive acceptance of the status quo, the social scientist generally cannot accept the liberal's naive faith in alleged panaceas. Consequently, conservatives tend to regard him as dangerous and radical while liberals eventually find him stodgy and conservative. As in the matter of class, social scientists through their teaching and research have done much to arouse awareness, but only in rare instances have they been actively involved in liberal movements.

Just as liberals are the vocal chords of the opposition, the lower classes are its muscles. The liberals are likely to be heard, but as a group they wield relatively little power. The lower classes on the other hand are handicapped by their inability to conceptualize the problem. Theirs is more of a latent than an actual awareness. They are prone to see the problem in terms of their individual inability to get ahead rather than as a collective problem requiring collective action. Potentially, they have the power inherent in large numbers, and should they become aroused to a "class" interest, fundamental changes would likely follow. Largely leaderless and only partly aroused, the lower classes are at present not a major threat to the existing order. But some persons in both groups envision the time when the liberals and the lower classes will "get together."

Proposed Solutions

Among the dissatisfied groups, only a minority segment of the intellectuals seem unwilling to accept the inevitability of a rigidly stratified society. Those academicians who want to preserve the benefits of the original system ask, How can we ensure that people will be given advantages in accord with their abilities rather than because they belong to certain class groups? The obvious but not easily achieved answer is to make education and technical training available on the basis of I.Q. scores or some other measures of ability. "Availability" would have to mean much more than just a free public-school system, however. To *guarantee* equal opportunity, lower-class children of superior ability would have to be given a type of education which might seem meaningless both to them and their families—education based on middle-class rather than lower-class values.

Whether such goals could be achieved within the structure of existing social institutions is doubtful. Many children would soon be destined for social levels either above or below that of their parents and families would be disrupted. Probably few persons really imagine that such wholesale changes will be effected. An important step toward more equality of opportunity could be taken, however, simply by reducing the middle-class bias of the existing educational system. Teachers would need to become familiar with lower-class culture patterns and to become aware of their own tendencies to discriminate in favor of middle-class children. They would have to learn to interpret the goals and values of an education in terms which lower-class children can understand and appreciate. Some progressive school administrators are already aware of this situation and are attempting to put the above recommendations into practice. Only the barest beginning has been made, however.

Both the lower class and most of the liberals tend to orient their solutions toward improving the position of the lower class *as a class*. The emphasis is on securing new benefits for the class rather than aiding people to escape the class. Many workers have come to accept labor unions as a major weapon in this struggle and their goals are largely identified with those of the unions—higher wages, shorter hours, improved working conditions, unemployment insurance, retirement plans, and paid vacations. The liberal emphasis, on the other hand, attacks much more directly the prerogatives of the upper classes. The liberals favor such measures as excess-profits taxes and higher tax rates on larger incomes to reduce the inequalities in wealth and living standards. They see a need to end the "exploitation of the masses" by restricting the privileges of the "elite." Because their attack is a direct and frontal one, the liberals are most bitterly opposed by the upper classes. The lower class demands for higher wages and better living conditions seem relatively nonthreatening by comparison. One effect of the presence of an articulate liberal group may be to aid lower-class efforts by making them seem to be the lesser of two evils.

PERSONAL DEVIATION

Class conflicts cannot be explained solely in terms of economic interests. Though there is an observable alignment along income lines, certain groups seem to act in a fashion contrary to their own best interests. It is easy to see why the lower classes might want to challenge the existing order, but it is not so easy to see why many prosperous middle- and upper-class persons should be involved. Most of the liberals stand to lose, financially as well as prestigially, if the reforms they propose are adopted. Moreover, they are frequently scorned and regarded as traitors by their own class. Some few liberal persons have gone far beyond rejecting upper-class values in favor of lower-class ones, and have flirted openly with communist and socialist movements. Knowledge of this fact brings condemnation not only by the upper classes but by the majority of people at all social levels. People do not reject the approval of class or society without paying heavy penalties. How can we explain the actions of these deviants in the class structure?

To state that liberals are disloyal to the traditional and customary values tells only part of the story. The rest of it is that the liberals *are loyal to a different set of values!* For our purpose we may divide liberals into two groups: (1) those who are loyal to socially *approved* values; and (2) those who are loyal to socially *disapproved* values.

1. The existence of liberals in society is provided for by the culture itself. American culture is not a uniform and homogeneous mass. Rather, it is a composite of many different subcultures which differ considerably among themselves. What agreement exists among them is agreement that stems from diversity and heterogeneity as well as from similarity. One subculture exists among academicians and intellectuals, part of whose function is to direct the society to more adequate realization of its basic values. Discerning some inconsistency between our basic democratic values and the operation of the class system, many academicians feel duty-bound to press for change even at the expense of their own personal welfare. They place the values involved in belonging to a democratic society, and in the ethical obligations of their profession, above personal economic advancement. Though they reject the values of their class, they act in terms of a *different* set of *socially approved values.*

A like situation exists for other deviants such as those who sympathize with or are active in organized labor. In attempting to live up to our democratic ideals, some middle- and upper-class people have allied themselves with the lower classes. Instead of accepting and defending their own privileged statuses these persons have chosen to side with the less fortunate. Just why people should act in such an unexpected fashion has never been adequately explained. Certainly it is true that in all complex cultures some people reject the standards of the many for other minority values which they consider to be more worthy. Their past experiences have encouraged them to identify with a subculture rather than with the larger culture. Another interesting hypothesis is that upper-class persons sometimes join the liberals as compensation for not being readily accepted by their own group.[5] It may be that failure to achieve recognition commensurate with one's position in society is a powerful stimulus to seek recognition from other groups.

Though many groups violently disapprove of these liberal positions, the loyalty and integrity of the persons concerned generally are not ques-

[5] Seymour Lipset and Reinhard Bendix, "Social Status and Social Structure: a Re-examination of Data and Interpretations: II," *The British Journal of Sociology,* II, No. 3 (September, 1951), p. 243.

tioned. Such liberals often are regarded as foolish, misguided, and stupid, but seldom as vicious or unprincipled.

2. "Liberals" who are loyal to certain other values do not share the tolerance accorded the above groups. Loyalty to the values of socialist and communist movements, for example, is generally disapproved. These economic and political ideologies involve much more than just theories of social class. They question the very foundations upon which our society is built. This brand of liberality is seen not only as disloyalty to a given segment of society but to the society as a whole, and some persons feel justified in taking action against the individuals involved.

The sociological explanation in this case is not very different from that above. Socialist and communist ideologies, even though bitterly condemned, have become part of American culture. Communism seems very far from acceptance by the total society, but socialism today is not much more vigorously opposed than were labor unions fifty years ago. The same factors of participation in subcultures and lack of adequate recognition can explain why some people become involved in some socialist and communist movements. In the foreseeable future, such deviant liberals can expect only rather harsh suppression. Whether eventually such ideologies will guide the alteration of the class system cannot now be determined.

VALUE-CONFLICTS

The Original Values

The American economy traditionally has been a free economy—free from unwarranted interference by government or other outside agencies. This free economy unquestionably has produced the greatest volume of goods and the highest standard of living the world has ever known. It is not necessary to assert that the free economy *caused* the high production, for it is apparent that other factors—abundant resources, a vast land area, and a vigorous young population—were also involved. But neither can we be sure that a different economic system would have used these factors so effectively. The simple historical fact is that *American prosperity has been associated with a free economy.*

The American free economy, as stated earlier, was built not upon equality but on a *relative* equality of opportunity. The system has always embraced—in fact even assumed—wide differences in incomes and living standards. According to our traditional values, there is nothing morally wrong with low standards of living. Humble beginnings and the chance to rise above one's origins have been considered to be compatible with our other values of "democracy" and "freedom." What has been regarded as morally suspect is remaining in a lower-class position when one has the opportunity to escape it. According to this traditional view, the responsibility for one's status lies with the individual! The responsibility of society ends with the maintenance of a free economy, so that the individual may rise *if* he is capable of rising. Within this framework, a sizable lower class becomes natural and even inevitable. Each man should profit according to his own merit and the class structure should accurately reflect individual differences in ability.

This free economy, along with its supporting theory of class placement according to individual ability, has to many Americans become almost synonymous with freedom itself. "Freedom" has meant the freedom to rise above the masses and become wealthy. Supposedly every man has an inherent right to become as prosperous as he possibly can. Whether these inherent rights are God-given or man-made, justice presumably depends upon their being maintained. Traditionally the point of view of society as a whole, the maintenance of "freedom" to rise in the class structure and to amass wealth is perhaps becoming the limited value position of the conservative middle and upper classes. Increasingly, another set of values is rising to challenge it.

The Ideology of Minimum Standards

Increased awareness of the tendency for lower-class status to be self-perpetuating has encouraged people to question the whole set of assumptions on which the class structure is built. It is now widely recognized that income and class status are not distributed simply on the basis of ability alone. People have begun to ask such questions as, Is it just ability or is it also somewhat less desirable characteristics such as ruthlessness and greed which permit people to get ahead? Should some people be permitted to earn as much as half a million dollars per year while one-fifth of the population earn less than $1000 per year? Is any man worth five or six hundred times as much as any other man? Should "freedom" include the freedom to live in poverty—to be underfed, ill-housed, ill-clothed, and without adequate medical care? Can democracy exist side by side with filth and squalor?

Few serious people contend that the answer lies in the elimination of all class differences. Relatively few people see the issue in the extreme form of "freedom" versus "equality," but many people feel that the harsher effects of the class system need to be lessened through raising the living standards of the lowest classes. This position is sometimes referred to as "the ideology of minimum standards." The growing numbers of people who hold these values advocate such measures as minimum-wage laws, guaranteed annual wages, publicly financed health insurance, vacations with pay, retirement programs, and the like. The student will recognize that these are among the "hottest" issues on the American scene. These are measures which conservatives, in an effort to forestall their acceptance, label as socialistic or communistic and which liberals ardently support. Theoretically, such gains might come, over the years, out of increased production alone without taking anything directly away from the upper classes. Practically, the conflict of values is too deep for this solution to be really satisfactory to either side. Middle- and upper-class conservatives bitterly oppose any measures which would put a "floor" under living standards. Raising the "floor" for the lower classes would mean, directly or indirectly, lowering the "ceiling" on the upper classes. Especially the liberal and probably the lower-class groups would applaud this philosophy. They favor limiting the freedom of the wealthy to become more wealthy in order to help the poor to become less poor! The fundamental nature of the conflict underlying these two positions cannot be overemphasized. For at least twenty years now, the whole issue of "social welfare" measures to aid the lower classes has occupied a central place in American politics. Elections are being fought, won, and lost over it. To date, the United States has been less disposed to accept the "minimum-standards" ideology than have been many European nations. Conservatives maintain that any further steps in this direction will result in considerable loss of "freedom" for all; liberals argue that freedom and dire poverty cannot exist together. In any event, resolution of this conflict will have to be part of any solution to existing problems of social class. For now, one may safely predict that many future elections will raise the same issue.

SUMMARY

American democracy is built not upon the notion of a classless society but upon an "open" class system: "All persons should have equal opportunity to get ahead, so that the more capable individuals will be those who achieve upper-class status." The low birth rates of upper-class groups and the expanding nature of the American economy have favored considerable upward movement in the class structure.

There is considerable evidence, nevertheless, to suggest that there is a basic incompatability between the existence of *social classes* and *equal opportunity*. In the American scene, for example, the one-tenth of the population which happens to be Negro is forced into an almost "caste-like" position beneath the white group. Although most whites tend to identify themselves with the middle class, objective studies reveal the existence of an even larger lower class. Identification with the middle class is apparently based upon the hope of being able to rise into that group. Again, objective studies show that while mobility is possible it is less probable for lower-class than for middle-class persons.

There is a growing body of opinion that class status tends to be permanent and that it is becoming more difficult to rise into a higher class. Some liberals, intellectuals, and members of the lower class have begun to challenge the justice of the original system and are agitating for change. They advocate either opening wider the channels for mobility or improving the lot of the lower classes as a whole. The role of the liberals, who are the most active opponents of the existing system, is explained as resulting from loyalty to the values of a subculture within the over-all American culture. The actions of these opposing groups reflect a basic conflict of values—the freedom of the individual to become wealthy or to live in abject poverty against the right of all people to at least a minimum adequate standard of living.

SUGGESTED READINGS

CENTERS, Richard, *The Psychology of Social Classes* (Princeton, N. J., Princeton University Press, 1949). Penetrating analysis of social class structure in the United States. Stresses class consciousness as a variable in social stratification.

CUBER, John F., and KENKEL, William E., *Social Stratification in the United States* (New York, Appleton-Century-Crofts, Inc., 1954). The first systematic textbook in the field of social stratification. A good introduction to both theoretical analysis and empiric research.

DAVIS, Allison, GARDNER, Burleigh, and GARDNER, Mary, *Deep South* (Chicago, University of Chicago Press, 1947). A comprehensive study of class patterns in a city in the deep South. Includes both the white and Negro populations.

MILLS, C. Wright, *White Collar* (New York, Oxford University Press, 1953). An extensive treatment of the "white-collar" portion of the American middle classes. Relates the rise of the white-collar classes both to historical trends and to economic forces.

WARNER, W. Lloyd, HAVIGHURST, Robert J., and LOEB, Martin B., *Who Shall Be Educated?* (New York, Harper and Brothers, 1944). Impressive analysis of social class influences on the operation of the American educational system.

WARNER, W. Lloyd, and LUNT, Paul S., *The Social Life of a Modern Community* (New Haven, Yale University Press, 1941). A comprehensive picture of the social class structure of a New England city. Includes several chapters on the techniques used to determine a community's class pattern.

AUDIO-VISUAL AIDS

Again Pioneers (Broadcasting and Film Commision, 220 Fifth Ave., New York), 1 hour, 10 minutes, sound, black and white. Produced by the Protestant Film Commission. Shows the efforts of leading citizens in an average American town to rid the community of a group of migrants settled in shacks on the outskirts of town which they feel threaten health and welfare. A home missions field worker helps the citizens to see the needs of these, their neighbors, and to see something of the total task of the church in relation to the underprivileged of the nation.

One Tenth of Our Nation (International Film Bureau, Suite 308-316, 57 E. Jackson Blvd., Chicago), 26 minutes, sound, black and white. A picture of the education of Negro children in the rural South, from one-room shacks to high schools and colleges.

Two Views of Socialism (Coronet Films, Coronet Bldg., Chicago), 15 minutes, sound, black and white. Specially designed to stimulate an intelligent discussion on the difference between socialism and capitalism. The basic charges leveled by socialists against capitalist society are made and answered.

You and Your Attitudes (Association Films, Inc., 347 Madison Ave., New York), 10 minutes, sound, black and white. The Barrett family gathers around the dinner table to discuss social attitudes—money and allowances, foreign groups, the new girl on the block, and the prejudices which create unintelligent attitudes. The film does not attempt to solve the questions raised concerning social attitudes. Appropriate for high school and beginning college groups.

QUESTIONS AND PROJECTS

1. How accurate is the unqualified statement, "all men are equal"? What kind of equality is highly valued in the United States?

2. Define the concept "open-class system." What two factors have been important in maintaining a relatively open class system in America?

3. Differentiate between the concepts "class" and "caste." Where are there caste-like elements in the United States stratification pattern?

4. With what social class group do most Americans identify themselves? How do you explain this identification?

5. How do the results of community studies and the distribution of money income compare with the self-identifications referred to in the previous question?

6. How does class status influence one's chances to acquire higher education? professional status?

7. What role do "liberals" typically play in relation to social class problems? Evaluate the statement that "social scientists are frequently among the most active of the liberals."

8. Explain the "ideology of minimum standards."

9. List as many pro's and con's as you can for each of the value-positions involved in the issue "freedom versus minimum standards."

10. Interview two young men in or just graduated from college and two middle-aged men who have college degrees, concerning what life goals a young man should select for himself. Relate their responses to the theory that upward social mobility is diminishing. Are the young men more security and less adventure minded, or do their responses contradict this point of view? Are the middle-aged men aware of the new philosophy or do they continue to interpret the situation in terms of unlimited opportunities for self-improvement?

11. Map out roughly the main lines of class division in your home community. Are there a few fairly well defined classes or does there seem to be a continuous range of variation? How large is your community? How does this factor of community size influence the precision with which class lines can be drawn?

CHAPTER 12

The Race Problem in America: I

The woman with the pink velvet poppies wreathed round the assisted gold of her hair traversed the crowded room at an interesting gait combining a skip with a sidle and clutched the lean arm of her host. . . .

"Listen," she said. "I want to meet Walter Williams. Honestly, I'm just simply crazy about that man . . . Oh, when he sings! When he sings those spirituals! Well, I said to Burton, 'It's a good thing for you Walter Williams is colored,' I said, 'or you'd have lots of reason to be jealous.' I'd really love to meet him. I'd like to tell him I've heard him sing. Will you be an angel and introduce me to him?"

"Why, certainly," said her host. "I thought you'd met him. The party's for him. Where is he, anyway?"

"He's over there by the bookcase," she said. "Let's wait till those people get through talking to him. Well, I think you're simply marvelous, giving this perfectly marvelous party for him, and having him meet all these white people, and all. Isn't he terribly grateful?" . . .

"Now, me, . . . I haven't the slightest feeling about colored people. Why, I'm just crazy about some of them. They're just like children—just as easygoing, and always singing and laughing and everything. Aren't they the happiest things you ever saw in your life? Honestly, it makes me laugh just to hear them. Oh, I like them, I really do. Well, now, listen, I have this colored laundress, I've had her for years, and I'm devoted to her. She's a real character. And I want to tell you, I think of her as my friend. That's the way I think of her. As I say to Burton, 'Well, for heaven's sakes, we're all human beings!' Aren't we?" . . .

They reached the tall young Negro standing by the bookcase. The host performed introductions; the Negro bowed.

"How do you do?" he said. "Isn't it a nice party?"

The woman with the pink velvet poppies extended her hand at the length of her arm and held it so, in fine determination, for all the world to see, until the Negro took it, shook it, and gave it back to her.

"Oh, how do you do, Mr. Williams," she said. "Well, how do you do. I've just been saying I've enjoyed your singing so awfully much. I've been to your concerts, and we have you on the phonograph and everything. Oh, I just enjoy it."

She spoke with great distinctness, moving her lips meticulously, as if in parlance with the deaf.

"I'm so glad," he said.

"I'm just simply crazy about that 'Water Boy' thing you sing," she said.

"Honestly, I can't get it out of my head. I have my husband nearly crazy, the way I go around humming it all the time. Oh, he looks just as black as the ace of —er. Well, tell me, where on earth do you ever get all those songs of yours? How do you ever get hold of them?"

"Why," he said. "There are so many different—"

"I should think you'd love singing them," she said. "It must be more fun. All those darling old spirituals—oh, I just love them! Well, what are you doing now? Are you still keeping up your singing? Why don't you have another concert sometime?"

"I'm having one the sixteenth of this month," he said.

"Well, I'll be there," she said. "I'll be there, if I possibly can. You can count on me. Goodness, here comes a whole raft of people to talk to you. You're just a regular guest of honor! Oh, who's that girl in white? I've seen her someplace."

"That's Katherine Burke," said her host.

"Good heavens," she said, "is that Katherine Burke? Why, she looks entirely different off the stage. I thought she was much better-looking. I had no idea she was so terribly dark. Why, she looks almost like— Oh, I think she's a wonderful actress! Don't you think she's a wonderful actress, Mr. Williams? Oh, I think she's marvelous. Don't you?"

"Yes, I do," he said.

"Oh, I do too," she said. "Just wonderful. Well, goodness, we must give someone else a chance to talk to the guest of honor. Now, don't forget, Mr. Williams, I'm going to be at that concert if I possibly can. I'll be there applauding like everything. And if I can't come, I'm going to tell everybody I know to go, anyway. Don't you forget!"

"I won't," he said. "Thank you so much."

The host took her arm and piloted her firmly into the next room.[1]

THIS incident, notable for the subtlety of the prejudice it reveals, suggests but a few of the many facets of the American race problem. Of all social problems, there is perhaps none more serious, and certainly none more unnecessary, than the race problem. If the first terrestrial expedition to Mars should find that the Martians (if any) have a social structure stacked into layers according to length of proboscis or coloration of antennae, we should think this very odd. And if the Martians, because of slight variations of coloration of thorax, worried themselves into neuroses, drifted into rioting, lynching, and warfare, and excluded many of their members from doing useful and valuable work, we would think this incredibly wasteful and inefficient (and conclusive evidence of Martian inferiority an unfitness to rule themselves!). Would the conclusions of a Martian visitor to our globe be greatly different?

How could such a situation have developed, to become a genuine and serious problem in America? What is the nature and extent of the race problem? How does it affect all the groups involved? What are the current trends in treatment? Will they prove effective?

[1] Dorothy Parker, "Arrangement in Black and White," Viking Portable Library: The Portable Dorothy Parker (New York, The Viking Press, 1952), pp. 41-47.

THE SCIENTIFIC FACTS ABOUT RACE

The facts about race are no longer a mystery to social scientists. They are well established by scientific research and are easily summarized. Most social scientists believe that, *in biological inheritance, all races are alike in everything that really makes any difference.* There are differences in coloration and slight differences in facial features and bodily proportion but, according to all evidence available, these have no effect upon learning or behavior. With the exception of several tiny, isolated, inbred tribes of primitives, all racial groups seem to show the same distribution of every kind of ability. All races learn in the same way and at the same average speed under the same circumstances. All important race differences in personality, behavior, and achievement are purely a result of environmental factors. Such differences (for example, ignorance and shiftlessness among Negroes) are cited by the majority group to justify its discrimination which, in turn, perpetuates those very differences. Thus the "vicious circle" is completed, and an *illusion* of innate race differences is preserved.

These are the conclusions of science. Vast numbers of people are unaware of them and of the evidence upon which they rest, and many other people are unable to accept them. For those who wish to study them, the scientific facts about race differences are easily available.[2] This chapter will not attempt any further review of these facts, but will assume that the student has some awareness of them.

Cost of the Problem

1. *The financial cost* of the race problem will surprise most people, who are unaware of the many ways in which they pay for the luxury of enjoying their alleged race superiority. Although there is no fully satisfactory way of measuring the direct and indirect cost of the race problem, there are a number of ways of suggesting that the total cost is enormous.

Race riots with their destruction of life and property give most dramatic evidence of the cost of the race problem. The 1919 Chicago riot killed 38 persons, injured 537, destroyed the homes of nearly a thousand, and caused over $250,000 destruction.[3] "The newspapers in 1942 and 1943 reported more Negro casualties from racial friction in the United States

[2] See Ruth Benedict and Gene Weltfish, *The Races of Mankind,* Public Affairs Pamphlet No. 85 (New York, Public Affairs Committee, 1943), for a brief, popularized treatment of race differences and race prejudice. See Otto Klineberg, *Race Differences* (New York, Harper and Brothers, 1935), for a comprehensive analysis of scientific research about race differences.

[3] Chicago Commission on Race Relations, *The Negro in Chicago: A Study of Race Relations and a Race Riot* (Chicago, University of Chicago Press, 1922), p. 1.

than [Negro] casualties in the World War for the same period." [4] Disorders in Chicago, where whites sought to keep Negroes out of a public housing project in 1953-1954 caused over $200,000 property damages, and total costs (for police protection, etc.) of over $2,000,000.[5]

But these losses are as pennies compared to the cost of economic inefficiency which the race problem produces. Since scientists are in general agreement that whites and Negroes have *equal native abilities,* it follows that *all important differences in group behavior are due to prejudice, discrimination, and lack of opportunity and encouragement.* This means that if Negroes work less energetically, receive less income, have more illness, spend more time on relief, commit more crimes and spend more time in jail than whites, all such differences are part of the cost of discrimination. The indirect economic loss from these 15,000,000 people, so many of whom are ignorant, poor, and unmotivated, reaches an impressive total. Oveta Culp Hobby, the Secretary of Health, Education and Welfare in the Eisenhower administration, places the annual cost of racial discrimination in the United States at from 15 to 30 *billion* dollars, about four to seven times as much as it cost to run the nation's schools in 1949-1950. She comments, "Individuals who suffer discrimination cannot be full partners in an economy of plenty. They cannot afford to purchase their share of the goods we produce nor pay their potential share of the taxes for the common good." [6]

Lack of education, lack of motivation, and denial of employment work together to keep the Negro's productivity low and his income small. Median income of all persons over 14 years old who received income in 1949 shows this distribution:

Male total	$2699
Male non-white	1456
Female total	1089
Female non-white	640

The Negro worker received, in 1949, barely half as large an income (52 per cent) as did the "average" American worker. Why is this true? He is educationally handicapped by having an average of 6.4 years of schooling, compared with 9.3 years for whites (persons over 14 years of age, 1950 census). He is often barred from the jobs where he could make his greatest contribution. Although 24,000 Negro veterans worked as carpenters in the armed forces, they were barred from the trade as civilians during a period of acute shortage of skilled labor.[7] Although teaching is the principal Negro profession, Negroes have only about half the repre-

---

[4] A. Clayton Powell, *Riots and Ruins* (New York, Richard R. Smith, 1945), p. 17.
[5] Cf. "Racial Problems Trouble Chicago," *New York Times,* July 25, 1954, p. 50.
[6] *New York Times,* March 3, 1954, p. 25.
[7] Elmo Roper, in R. M. MacIver, *Discrimination and National Welfare,* Institute for Religious and Social Studies (New York, Harper and Brothers, 1949), pp. 21-22.

sentation in the teaching profession that they have in the general population. Failure to use Negro talent, and failure to provide opportunities and rewards that stimulate his efforts and ambitions have helped keep the Negro unmotivated and unproductive.

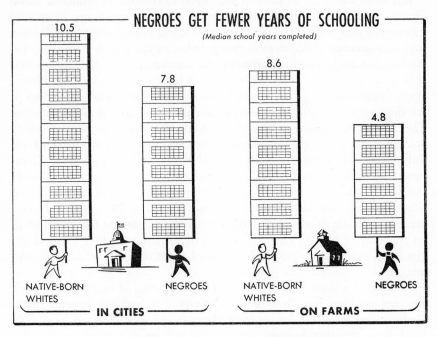

FIG. 12-1. (Data from the U. S. Bureau of the Census)

2. *The political costs* cannot be measured in dollars, but must be measured by the degree to which unsolved race problems disrupt democratic processes and impair national unity. Although Negro voters are rapidly increasing, millions of Negroes are still prevented from voting through such devices as the poll tax, by white primaries, by various "tests" of voting fitness which local officials permit few Negroes to pass, and sometimes by threats and even violence. In no part of the country can Negroes be confident that they will receive the equal protection of the law, and frequency of charges of police brutality toward Negroes are "proof that improper conduct by police is still widespread." [8] The Negro's constitutional right to a fair trial is often violated, and Negroes are not infrequently convicted on evidence on which no white person would even be tried. One Negro was convicted of "assault" for having "leered" at a white girl from an admitted distance of 50 feet.[9] Virginia executed seven

[8] President's Committee on Civil Rights, *To Secure These Rights* (Washington, Government Printing Office, 1947), p. 25.
[9] *Time* (November 24, 1952), p. 22.

Negroes in 1951, bringing to 45 its total of Negroes executed for a crime (rape) for which no white man has ever been executed in Virginia.[10] One recent celebrated case comes not from the South but from New Jersey, where six Negroes were condemned to death on exceedingly flimsy evidence in a flagrantly unjust trial, and did not gain their freedom until several years and many thousands of dollars later.[11] Although such cases are unusual, the monotonous regularity of their appearance shows that Negroes are still far from receiving equal treatment from courts and enforcement officers. In *no* respect—the right to vote, to hold office, to buy and own property, to travel about the country, to be justly arrested and fairly tried when suspected of crime, and even to be buried when dead— do Negroes fully enjoy the promises of the Fourteenth Amendment, reading in part: "No State shall make or enforce any law which shall abridge the privileges or immunities of citizens of the United States, nor shall any State deprive any person of life, liberty or property without due process of law, nor deny to any person within its jurisdiction the equal protection of the laws...."

It is ironical that the political inequities imposed upon Negroes should often prove even more costly to the whites themselves than to the Negroes. The poll tax, a device to prevent Negroes from voting, actually disfranchised an *even greater* number of whites in some Southern states. In allowing the maintenance of white supremacy to dominate its political life for nearly a century, the South curtailed its national political influence and largely destroyed its power to resist three-quarters of a century of commercial exploitation by the North. Her preoccupation with white supremacy prevented serious discussion of other issues. Candidates for public office who sought to present a constructive program for dealing with the real problems of the South were likely to be defeated by candidates who posed as saviors from a terrifying nightmare of Negro revolt. Beneficiaries of the political and economic status quo found the white-

---

[10] Henry Lee Moon, "The Martinsville Rape Case," *New Leader,* xxxiv (February 12, 1951), p. 18.

[11] In this case of the "Trenton Six," the only evidence consisted of "confessions" secured by long interrogation and use of drugs upon the suspects. The New Jersey Supreme Court reversed the verdict and ordered a new trial, at which four were acquitted and two convicted, four years after the original arrest. One of these two died while further appeal was pending, and the other finally pleading "no defense," was sentenced and paroled after serving six months. It is likely that all were entirely innocent. For numerous citations covering this lengthy case, see *New York Times Index* (heading, Murders; New Jersey; Horner, W.), 1948, p. 688; 1949, p. 665; 1950, p. 729; 1951, p. 704; 1952, p. 719; 1953, p. 696. See also Claire Neikind, "The Case of the Trenton Six," *Reporter,* 4 (May 1, 1951), pp. 31-34; (May 29, 1951), pp. 33-38.

A significant sidelight is the fact that the communist-front Civil Rights Congress successfully exploited this miscarriage of justice to raise an estimated $300,000 defense fund, most of which was diverted to other party uses. The eventual release was secured mainly through the efforts of the NAACP and the American Civil Liberties Union.

supremacy issue an easy device for diverting attention from possible reforms, and thus political interest was largely diverted from the discussion
of economic issues to the ritualistic exorcism of racial bogeymen.

The political costs of prejudice are not confined to the South. By keeping its Negroes poor and half-educated, the North has kept them prime
subjects for political "bossism." The seat of a boss's power rests in a
group of voters so poor, so ill-informed, and so neglected that a few small
favors will buy their support. Negro politics is often corrupt politics, for
wherever there is poverty, ignorance, and limited opportunity, political
corruption appears. Both the North and the South have, as one critic
observed, "sold their political birthright for a mess of racial pottage."

3. *The psychic costs* of the race problem are less tangible but no less
real. For Negroes the race problem means a variety of anxieties, fears,
and frustrations which the remainder of this book could not fully describe.[12] These differ among regions and individuals, ranging from the
fear of violence to the fear of embarrassment, from anxiety over finding a
job to anxiety lest a remark be misunderstood—the list is endless. The
Negro's dilemma is that *no matter what he does, he irritates some white
folks.* If he is docile and easygoing, that only proves his inferiority; if he
seeks a nice house and good car, he is an "uppity nigger"; if he doesn't, he
is "content to live in filth." He gets along best with whites by appearing
to be stupid, unambitious and contented, but this pattern conflicts with the
competition-success ideology of our culture. Thus the Negro, particularly
the better-educated Negro, is constantly frustrated by the contradictory
pressures imposed upon him. The more successful Negroes often find that
increasing frustration is the reward of their efforts, for success fails to
bring the Negro the full rewards of status, acceptance, and freedom to
spend his money where and as he wishes—the rewards success brings
to white folks.

Whites, too, harbor fears, anxieties, and above all, a bad conscience.
Whites are fearful of Negro violence, especially in the South, where a
long succession of bloody slave revolts disprove the myth that Negroes
were ever very contented. Many whites fear Negro invasions of their jobs,
their schools and neighborhoods, even their resorts and clubs. Many
whites fear sexual aggression by Negro men against white women, a fear
which may spring from the white's own guilt feelings.[13] Lillian Smith has

[12] See Richard Wright, *Black Boy* (New York, Harper and Brothers, 1945); Allison
Davis and John Dollard, *Children of Bondage: The Personality Development of Negro
Youth in the Urban South* (Washington, American Council on Education, 1940).

[13] Simpson and Yinger say, "Most of the sex contacts between Negroes and whites
are initiated by white men; most of the violence is used by whites against the
Negroes; yet there is an emotionally vivid belief in the violent and sexually aggressive
nature of the Negro. This belief is needed, not only to rid many white people of a
sense of guilt for having violated their own standards, but to help them resist the impulses toward violation. The Negro, a designated inferior group, symbolizes the repressed impulses one must not admit are still motivating him." George E. Simpson

suggested that white men have impoverished their own sexual life with white women through their sexual affairs with Negro women. She suggests that the white man's morbid preoccupation with Negro sexual aggression (and the tendency for every racial discussion to arrive at the "would-you-want-your-daughter-to-marry-a-Negro" rhetorical question) may be only a displacement of the white man's own guilt feelings and his sternly repressed fear that white woman may also find Negro men attractive.[14]

In a hundred lesser ways the race problem afflicts the white man's peace of mind and makes him uncomfortable. He does not really want to give up the many discriminations and subtle forms of exploitation from which he thinks he benefits, and yet he is not always comfortable with them. As Myrdal has pointed out, a moral conflict rages within him, for "even a poor and uneducated white person in some isolated and backward rural region in the Deep South, who is violently prejudiced against the Negro and intent upon depriving him of civic rights and human independence, has also a whole compartment of his valuation sphere housing the entire American creed of liberty, equality, justice, and fair opportunity for everybody." [15] The white who believes both in democracy and in white supremacy, and reconciles the contradiction with a set of artful rationalizations, is sometimes bedeviled by an uneasy awareness that they *are* rationalizations. Whites cannot enjoy the luxury of professing democracy and practicing discrimination without paying a price, either in guilt feelings or in double-talk which they can only half believe.

4. *International costs.* When the Nazis invaded Russia, many of the people welcomed them as liberators. If they had treated the Russian people as human beings, Russia might have been defeated, and Hitler might have become master of all Europe. Instead, guided by the "master-race" theories of Hitler, the Nazis' contemptuous brutality united the Russian people and helped insure German defeat.[16] It is well known that Nazi persecution of Jewish scientists largely explains why we, and not they, first developed the atomic bomb. There are times when a people's notions about "race" can be their destruction or their salvation.

In this sense, the future of America rests in the hands of foreigners, for it is doubtful that we can remain free and democratic if the rest of the world embraces communist totalitarianism. With roughly a third of the

---

and J. Milton Yinger, *Racial and Cultural Minorities* (New York, Harper and Brothers, 1953), p. 80.

[14] Cf. Lillian Smith, *Killers of the Dream* (New York, W. W. Norton & Company, Inc., 1949).

[15] Gunnar Myrdal, *An American Dilemma* (New York, Harper and Brothers, 1944), p. xliv.

[16] Cf. J. A. Lukacs, "Story Behind Hitler's Biggest Blunder," *New York Times Magazine,* June 17, 1951, pp. 10-11 ff.

world's people under communist rule, perhaps a fifth of the world's people democratic, and the remainder undecided, the eventual outcome depends largely upon whom this undecided half of the world's people choose to follow. Since *most of the undecided half of the world's peoples are colored*, they are much more interested in our treatment of our Negroes than they are in statistics about our plentiful telephones and bathtubs. For example, when Ethiopian Princess Sybel Desta visited Chicago, she "immediately" asked about racial disorders at Trumbull Park housing development and even knew the name of the Negro whom whites were seeking to expel.[17] As our recent ambassador to India reports: [18]

"Do you know the Number One obstacle to Asian friendship for America?" a Pakistani business man once asked me. He provided the answer which I had heard over and over again, from Lebanon to Japan. "It's racial discrimination against your colored citizens. If you want to win our respect and to encourage democracy in our part of the world, you must make dramatic progress in the next few years in establishing full equality for American Negroes. Not only will we Asians admire you for what you accomplish, but your own success will give us new faith that the reforms which are so urgently needed in Asia can be achieved through democratic means."

No American returning from Asia can doubt that the status of the American Negro is the key to our country's relationship with the awakening nations of Asia and Africa.

It may shock Americans to realize that much of the world considers us insincere, cynical hypocrites whenever we talk of democracy. They ask, "How can you really mean what you say when you treat your Negroes as you do?" In many such ways our international influence is impaired. Our delegates to the United Nations are repeatedly put on the defensive. We must overlook many acts of Russian injustice to minorities because we, too, are to some degree vulnerable to a similar charge. Thus, many opportunities to discredit communism must be sacrificed, while our denial of equality to Negroes has provided communist propagandists with a most effective theme.

Many have predicted that the final outcome of the world contest between communism and democracy will be determined not on battlefields but in the minds of men. If the colored peoples of the world come to feel that their best chance for a better life lies in following communism, neither American talk nor American guns will long delay the outcome. We cannot garrison the whole world. Only if the people of the world feel that democracy offers a practical solution of their problems of poverty, insecur-

[17] *Chicago Sun-Times,* July 7, 1954, p. 44.
[18] Chester Bowles, "The Negro—Progress and Challenge," *New York Times Magazine,* February 7, 1954, p. 7.

ity, and injustice will they follow America's lead. This is why they watch American treatment of Negroes with such avid interest.

In all these ways and in still others, the race problem is costly to whites and Negroes, to North and South. A Southern sociologist writes, in words also applicable to the North: [19]

The South pays dearly for the economic bondage and the political impotence of its black folk. For, in one way or another—in inefficiency, in waste, in poor health, in low moral standards, in excessive rates of dependency and delinquency—the Negro has levied a tax on the South just as surely as if the states themselves had levied it.

SOME FACTS ABOUT RACE DISCRIMINATION

From before he is born until after he is dead the Negro knows discrimination in countless forms. In many parts of the country, he has his choice of being born at home or in a second-class hospital. North or South, he attends schools that are often inferior to those of white children. Whatever test is used—expenditures per pupil, salary of teachers, pupils per teacher, adequacy of school plant and equipment, length of school term— Negroes in many states are at some disadvantage and in some states are at a great disadvantage. Some colleges will not admit him at all; others he can enter only by hurdling a quota. Upon graduation, the Negro finds most of the jobs open to him are the jobs nobody else wants. Although he earns lower wages, he generally pays a much higher rent than whites pay for comparable housing, because of the very limited supply of housing available to Negroes.[20]

If he is highly successful, he cannot buy a home in the better parts of

[19] Guy B. Johnson, "Does the South Owe the Negro a New Deal?" *Social Forces*, 13 (October, 1934), pp. 100-103.

[20] In a news story headed "Edgewater Beach Units Cheaper Than Ratty Flats Where 10 Burned to Death," the *Chicago Sun* (October 17, 1947, p. 5) reported, "Today, October 17, 1947, a two-room apartment at the plushy Edgewater Beach Apartments, 5555 Sheridan Road, rents for $69 to $74.50 a month. You have a view of Lake Michigan from the $74.50 apartments. Today, October 17, 1947, Mrs. Ernestine Lyles and her family of six pay $78 a month for two rooms at 934 W. Ohio St. This is the unburnt section of the rat-infested tenement where 10 persons were killed in a fire on midnight, October 9. Here from Mrs. Lyles' front window you have a view of garage doors and the back porches of another tenement up the street. Mrs. Lyles and her family share with other tenants a community kitchen in the rear and, down the hall, a community toilet. . . .

All the tenants at the Ohio Street building are Negroes. In 1945, before the flats were carved up into small box-like units and before the steam boiler was installed, the flats rented to white tenants for $11 to $13 a month.

One tenant who managed to escape the fire told a reporter the other day: 'If you think these rents are high, you should see what some of the other colored people in the neighborhood are paying. Their places aren't even furnished. There's nothing we can do about it. There just isn't any other place we can move to'."

town without facing the certainty of discourtesy and humiliation and the possibility of violence. In no city can he patronize first-class hotels, restaurants, and theaters and be confident of the respectful service which whites receive. If he takes a vacation trip, his itinerary is limited to those resorts and lodges—rarely first-class—which accept Negroes, and all sight-seeing is attuned to the urgent need to reach a town which allows Negroes to stay overnight. In some places, when he dies he is buried in a separate cemetery.[21]

In hundreds of ways Negroes and other "racial"[22] minorities endure discrimination based not upon their qualities as individuals but upon their status as Negroes, Jews, Indians, and so on. Most of this discrimination rests on the theory of segregation—"separate but equal" facilities. In practice, most segregated facilities are neither fully separate nor fully equal. *Completely* separate facilities—schools, churches, stores, hotels, theaters, buses, waiting rooms, and so on—are impractical because of the cost of duplicate accommodations. In many places there are not enough Negroes to support separate Negro accommodations, especially first-class ones. Strict separation of races is often inconvenient for whites, so segregation is constantly being breached and compromised by whites for their own convenience (for example, the Negro servant traveling with a white family and sharing their accommodations). Nor are the facilities fully equal. It would be unrealistic to expect that whites who insisted upon separation from their "inferiors" would always be concerned about equality of accommodations. In practice, Negro housing, schools, and other segregated facilities have often consisted largely of hand-me-downs, left-overs, and makeshifts.

Patterns of segregation and discrimination differ for different minorities and are very rapidly changing. Most Southern states have been sharply reducing the gap between Negro and white schooling, as seen in Table 12-1. In 1950, over a thousand Negroes were attending colleges and universities, mostly Southern, to which no Negroes were being admitted ten years earlier. Any current description of discriminatory practices will

[21] Even his pet dog is unacceptable for burial in one of the plush pet cemeteries which accept pets from only white, gentile owners. Apparently, one can't be too careful!

[22] Jews are generally considered as a race, although, being biologically a highly mixed group, they are not a genuine racial group. Neither are they a religious group, as many Jews have left the Jewish faith; nor are they a cultural group, since many "emancipated" Jews have abandoned traditional Jewish rites and behavior, and are fully assimilated. Jews, then, are a group defined by cultural myth—Jews are a group composed of whomever is generally considered as and treated as Jewish. (See Arthur Miller's novel, *Focus* [New York, Reynal and Hitchcock, 1945], for the story of a gentile who was forced to become a "Jew" when he started wearing glasses which so altered his appearance that people decided he was Jewish.) Since Jews are generally thought of as a race, anti-Semitism is race prejudice, even though Jews are not actually a race.

need rapid revision to keep pace with present changes, especially as the recent Supreme Court decision on school segregation is implemented.

TABLE 12-1. Expenditures for Negro and White Education in States Having Segregated School Systems, 1949-1950 *

State	Annual Expenditures Per Pupil in Average Daily Attendance		Annual Expenditure for Instruction Per Classroom Unit	
	White	Negro	White	Negro
Alabama	$130.09	$ 92.69	$2214	$1901
Arkansas	123.60	73.03	1900	1416
Florida	196.42	136.71	3056	2643
Georgia	145.15	79.73	2081	1680
Maryland	217.41	198.76	3600	3575
Mississippi	122.93	32.55	1884	760
North Carolina	148.21	122.90	2675	2721
South Carolina	154.62	79.82	2149	1515
District of Columbia	289.68	220.75	3963	3863
Average of eight states & District of Columbia	169.79	115.20	2613	2230
Negro expenditure as per cent of white expenditure		61		85
Average per pupil expenditure of ten states, 1935-36 †	49.30	17.04		
Negro expenditure as per cent of white expenditure, 1935-36		36		

* Data unavailable for some states with segregated school systems. Data from Federal Security Agency, Office of Education, *Biennial Survey of Education, 1948-50* (Washington, Government Printing Office, 1952), Ch. 2, p. 105.
† *Statistics of the Education of Negroes*, 1933-34 and 1935-36, U. S. Office of Education Bulletin No. 13 (1938), p. 15.

SOME FACTS ABOUT RACE PREJUDICE

Prejudice is not the same as discrimination. Prejudice refers to one's *judgments* of others, whereas discrimination refers to one's *actions* toward others. A prejudice is, literally, a *pre-judgment*, a judgment arrived at before having really examined any evidence upon the case or person involved. *A racial prejudice is any judgment of a person based upon knowledge of his race rather than upon knowledge of his individual qualities.* Both the teacher who expects the Negro boy to be dull in algebra and the teacher who expects him to be gifted in music are showing their race prejudices, for both impute qualities to him because he is a Negro instead of discovering his qualities by observing him as a person. A prejudice is a stereotyped image, favorable or unfavorable, which one "sees" in place of the actual individual.

1. *Prejudices Are Learned.* No one is born with prejudices. Small children show no race prejudices until they begin to observe them in their elders.[23]

2. *Prejudices Are Largely Unconscious.* Several studies have offered informants a check-list including many prejudiced statements and have asked them to indicate how highly "prejudiced" they considered themselves to be. In general, those who accepted the largest number of prejudiced statements rated themselves as "unprejudiced," whereas those who checked the fewest prejudiced statements classed themselves as somewhat prejudiced. Apparently those who have the most prejudices are unaware of them—to them, their prejudices are "facts"—while those with the fewest prejudices are acutely aware of and feel somewhat guilty about the few which they hold. This unconscious quality of prejudice makes it possible for many kindly, humanitarian people to remain unconcerned with race problems, for if one considers it a "fact" that Negroes are naturally dirty and shiftless, then an announcement that many Negroes are living in squalor suggests to him not a problem to be treated but simply another illustration of the Negro's nature.

3. *Prejudice Is Learned Through Contact with Prejudice, Not Contact with Other Groups.* It is firmly established that there is very little relationship between the amount of contact one has had with a particular group and his attitudes toward that group. Although in certain cases, the *kind of contact* has an important bearing upon attitudes, it is safe to say that, in general, race attitudes are based far more on contact with the *attitudes* of others around us than upon contact with the other race or group. Studies have shown no important differences between the race attitudes of children in towns where no Negroes or Jews live and children in towns having Negro and Jewish residents. Radke found that children who had *no* personal experience with Negroes and Jews had strong and definite prejudices against them.[24] A *Fortune* survey found that resentment of Catholic and Jewish economic and political power was greatest in areas where such "power" was the weakest, and that "Jews evoke the greatest hostility in the areas where there are very few of them."[25] Hartley dramatically showed the irrelevance of personal contact in a study in which three *imaginary* groups—the Danireans, the Wallonians, and the Pireneans—were included in a list of races and nationalities.[26] Informants made much the same responses to these nonexistent groups that they did to other actual groups, with coefficients of correlation rang-

[23] Bruno Lasker, *Race Attitudes in Children* (New York, Henry Holt & Company, Inc., 1929), pp. 4-6, 39.

[24] Ronald Lippitt and M. Radke, "New Trends in the Investigation of Prejudice," *The Annals*, 244 (March, 1946), pp. 167-176.

[25] "The Fortune Survey," *Fortune*, 36 (October 1947), pp. 5 ff.

[26] Eugene Hartley, *Problems in Prejudice* (New York, The King's Crown Press, 1946), p. 26.

ing from .78 to .85. People who disliked Negroes and Jews also disliked the fictitious Danireans and Wallonians, and vice versa. From such data it is clear that prejudices are learned mainly through contact with prejudiced people rather than through contact with the group toward whom prejudice is felt. The prejudiced person may defend his views with a string of unpleasant anecdotes, but it is likely that his vivid memory of these experiences is *a result of his prejudice, rather than its cause.* For those experiences which dominate our recollections are those which our attitudes define as significant.

4. *Prejudice Is Unrelated to Reality.* Since prejudice is learned mainly through contact with prejudice rather than through contact with the people concerned, prejudice need bear no relationship whatever to the real characteristics of the group concerned. Once a prejudice has become absorbed, one can readily "see" in another person whatever his prejudice tells him must be there to see. Like attitudes, prejudices are subject to a *circular reinforcement.* This enables one to interpret *any* evidence in such a way as to confirm the prejudice. A classic illustration is General J. L. DeWitt's remark on the "need" for interning Japanese-Americans during the war: "The very fact that no sabotage has taken place to date is a disturbing and confirming indication that such action will be taken." [27] Only a tremendous ability to rationalize one's prejudice can explain a responsible official's interpreting a *lack* of sabotage as "evidence" of *disloyal* intent!

Circular reinforcement enables one to "find" in Negroes or Jews whatever traits his prejudice prompts him to look for, and having thus found them, his prejudice is reinforced. To one who thinks Negroes stupid, a dull-acting Negro confirms his prejudice. An intelligent Negro, however, is an "exception" who also confirms the prejudice, for, if *he* is an "exception," then *all the rest must be stupid.* Thus, even the "exception" proves the rule and confirms the prejudice, and the prejudice becomes totally divorced from the reality it supposedly describes. Perhaps this is why many people remain in undisturbed possession of a set of prejudices which are not even consistent with one another. One study found that most of those who claimed that Jews were too "pushy," trying to force themselves upon gentiles, were the same informants who reported that Jews were too "clannish," refusing to mix with other people.[28] Jews are said to be invariably rich and grasping, and to be a bunch of communists and radicals intent on confiscating all wealth; Negroes are "contented and easygoing" and "getting out of hand"; Negro athletes are second-raters who "blow up in a pinch," but who are so good that they "are taking over

[27] United States Army Western Defense Command and Fourth Army, *Japanese In the United States, Final Report: Japanese Evacuation from the West Coast* (Washington, Government Printing Office, 1943), p. 34.

[28] D. J. Levinson and R. N. Sanford, "A Scale for the Measurement of Anti-Semitism," *Journal of Psychology,* 17 (April, 1944), pp. 339-370.

athletics"; Jews are instantly recognizable by their "Jewish" features, yet have successfully concealed themselves in industry, finance, the professions, and everywhere else. Such absurdities of contradiction remind one of the well-known comedian who specializes in contradiction (for example, "A tall short little fellow stood running down the street . . ."). Only by remembering that prejudices are unrelated to reality can one understand how a person can hold prejudices that contradict one another so flatly.

5. *Prejudice Exists Because It Is Satisfying.* People hold prejudices because they enjoy them. Some may feel a bit guilty about them, but people enjoy a great many things which bring feelings of guilt. Prejudice can bring many emotional satisfactions—a feeling of superiority, an excuse for failure, an outlet for aggression and hostility—and can be a very useful weapon in power struggles between groups. Some of the emotional values of prejudice are implied in the following section.

THEORIES OF THE CAUSES OF PREJUDICE[29]

The causes of prejudice are hard to evaluate, for there appear to be several causes, often operating in combination with one another.

1. *Economic Theories*

a. The *economic-competition* theory notes that when groups compete, hostilities and prejudices often arise. If the competing groups differ in race or religion, the prejudice takes the form of race or religious prejudice. The more highly identifiable the two groups are (or are imagined to be), the more easily such prejudice can be focused on the differences which identify them—race, religion, or nationality. Thus, prejudice against the Irish, once intense, largely disappeared as the Irish immigrants became assimilated, whereas prejudice against the easily recognized Japanese remains.

There is considerable evidence to support this theory. Both in Hawaii and on the West Coast, little prejudice against Japanese developed until the Japanese immigrants began to enter types of work which competed with white occupations. Medieval anti-Semitism in Europe increased greatly when banking and finance, previously left to the Jews, grew profitable enough to be attractive to gentiles. Yet, although one can cite many instances of prejudice following competition, it is unlikely that competition is the sole factor in prejudice. The intensity of prejudice is not exactly proportionate to the strength of competition or the strength of the competing minority. Furthermore, as Mydral points out, the economic ambi-

[29] As outlined in Brewton Berry, *Race Relations* (New York, Houghton Mifflin Company, 1951), pp. 104-116.

tions of the Negro meet much less white verbal opposition than the Negro's social and political aspirations.[30]

b. The *economic-exploitation* theory notes that prejudice is very helpful in maintaining economic privilege. It is much easier to keep Negro wages low if Negroes are believed inferior. As Margaret Halsey wrote in her "Memorandum to Junior Hostesses" serving in a nondiscriminatory servicemen's canteen during the war: [31]

> The real reason back of the refusal of some of you to mingle with Negroes at the canteen isn't nearly so romantic and dramatic as you think it is. The real reason has nothing to do with rape, seduction, or risings in the night. The real reason can be summed up in two extremely unromantic little words: cheap labor. As long as you treat Negroes as subhumans, you don't have to pay them so much. When you refuse to dance with Negro servicemen at the canteen, you are neither protecting your honor nor making sure that white Southerners won't have their homes burned down around their ears. All you are doing is making it possible for employers all over the country to get Negroes to work for them for less money than those employers would have to pay you.

There is considerable evidence to support this exploitation theory. Modern race theories first appeared when European nations established colonial empires and needed a theory to sanction their exploitation of the native peoples. Prejudice against the Japanese-Americans appears to be, at least in part, a result of agitation by vested interests.[32] The use of "white supremacy" as a political issue in the South long served to keep Negroes and poor whites in hate and fear of each other, and prevented them from discovering their common interest in modifying an economic status quo that impoverished them both. The conversation at many a bridge luncheon shows that middle-class housewives are quite aware of the relationship between "equality of opportunity" and the wage rate for Negro cleaning women. There is ample evidence that prejudice has often been used, both consciously and unconsciously, as a "mask for privilege," but since prejudice also exists between groups where there is no exploitation, there must be other causes as well.

2. Symbolic Theories

A great many theories, some of them fantastic, claim that prejudice arises because we see in another group certain traits which become symbols of what we hate, fear, or envy. Therefore, we hate Negroes because their (supposedly) uninhibited sex life symbolizes a freedom we envy; or we see in their lazy, easygoing life a symbol of a wish that our ambi-

[30] Gunnar Myrdal, *op. cit.,* pp. 60 ff.

[31] Margaret Halsey, *Color Blind* (New York, Simon & Schuster, Inc., 1946), pp. 56-57.

[32] See Carey McWilliams, *Japanese-Americans: Symbol of Racial Intolerance* (Boston, Little, Brown & Company, 1944).

tions force us to renounce. The symbolic theories have most often been applied to anti-Semitism. The Jew is seen as a symbol of urbanism and of the impersonality and sophistication which rustic folk envy and distrust. Other theories see the Jew as a symbol of internationalism, of capitalism, of communism, or of "nonconformity," and accordingly the Jews are hated by the nationalists, the communists, the capitalists, and the worshippers of conformity.[33] Such symbolic theories, although difficult to prove or to disprove, find some acceptance among students of prejudice.

3. Psychological Theories

a. The Scapegoat Theory. Nearly two thousand years ago the Emperor Tertullian wrote, "If the Tiber rose to the walls of the city, if the heavens did not send rain, if an earthquake occurred, if famine threatened, if pestilence raged, the cry resounded, 'Throw the Christians to the lions'." After the Christians became the majority, Jews took their place as scapegoats. During the great plague of the fourteenth century, some 350 Jewish communities were exterminated within a two-year period on the charge that they had poisoned, or might poison, the water supply and spread the plague.[34]

People have always sought to blame something or someone else for their troubles. The ancient Hebrews each year loaded their sins onto a goat and chased him into the wilderness; [35] this goat, allowed to escape, came to be known as a "scapegoat," and the term came to be applied to anyone forced to bear blame for others' misfortunes. Most minority groups have, at some time or other, served as convenient scapegoats. According to one analysis,[36] a suitable scapegoat should be: (1) easily recognizable, either physically or through some trait of dress or behavior; (2) too weak to fight back; (3) available near at hand; (4) already unpopular; (5) a symbol of something that is hated and despised.

The scapegoat theory helps to explain German anti-Semitism under Hitler, as the Jews were blamed for the loss of World War I and for the postwar difficulties. Hitler actively cultivated the scapegoating tendency, for without the Jews to fill the role of devil, the Nazi movement might have failed.[37] Scapegoating is evident in American anti-Semitism

[33] See Arnold Rose and Caroline Rose, *America Divided* (New York, Alfred A. Knopf, Inc., 1948), pp. 285-292.

[34] Isaque Graebner and S. H. Britt, eds., *Jews in a Gentile World* (New York, The Macmillan Company, 1942), p. 95.

[35] Leviticus, 16:5-26.

[36] Gordon W. Allport, *ABC's of Scapegoating* (New York, Anti-Defamation League of B'nai B'rith, 1948), pp. 42-43.

[37] When asked whether the Jew should be destroyed, Hitler replied, "No . . . we should then have to invent him. It is essential to have a tangible enemy, not merely an abstract one." (Herman Rauschning, *Hitler Speaks* [New York, G. P. Putnam's Sons, 1940], p. 234.) When a member of a Japanese mission studying the Nazi movement

also, as the great depression, the war, the wartime shortages and rationing inconveniences, and the postwar inflation were successively blamed on the Jews by certain groups of people. Prejudices against Negroes are less easily explained by scapegoating, since Negroes are hardly powerful enough to have created our troubles.

b. *The Frustration-Aggression Theory.* There is some experimental evidence showing that aggressive impulses arise when one is frustrated.[38] All persons, children and adults, are often unable to do the things they wish to do, and their frustration produces aggressive impulses which can find a socially approved outlet through race prejudices and hatreds. The abuse and mistreatment of a minority serves to drain off these irrational, latent hostilities which the frustrations of social living produce. Thus the "poor white," prevented by custom and by the power system from any attack upon the landlord or the industrialist, vents his hostilities upon the Negro. The businessman, struggling to survive in a competitive system but enjoined from hating his competitor and fellow-Rotarian, hates the Jew instead. The incompetent, unsuccessful person would be particularly tempted to find in racial prejudice a compensation for his own failures.

This theory is not easy to prove or disprove. There is some evidence that unsuccessful people show greater than average amounts of prejudice. One study finds that veterans who were downwardly mobile expressed more aggressive attitudes than those who were moving into better jobs and improved social status.[39] The same study reports that those who believed they had received a "bad break" in the army were the more anti-Semitic. The spectacular growth of organized anti-Semitism during the New Deal era, mainly among groups bitterly opposed to New Deal policies, suggests that many who were frustrated by "that man in the White House" may have found an outlet for their anger in anti-Semitic hostilities.[40]

The theory, however, overlooks the fact that aggression is only one of the several possible consequences of frustration (including identification, conversion, repression, retreat into fantasy, and others), and that aggressions need not be directed at a minority group. Nor does the theory explain why one group rather than another becomes an object of abuse.

c. *The Social-Neurosis Theories.* There are several versions of the theory which views race prejudice as *a symptom of a maladjusted, neu-*

---

in 1932 was asked what he thought of the movement, he replied, "It is magnificent. I wish we could have something like it in Japan, only we can't, because we haven't got any Jews." (Fritz August Voigt, *Unto Caesar* [New York, G. P. Putnam's Sons, 1938], p. 301).

[38] John Dollard and others, *Frustration and Aggression* (New Haven, Yale University Press, 1939), especially pp. 151-156.

[39] Bruno Bettelheim and Morris Janowitz, *Dynamics of Prejudice, A Psychological and Sociological Study of Veterans* (New York, Harper and Brothers, 1950), p. 59.

[40] Donald S. Strong, *Organized Anti-Semitism in the United States* (American Council on Public Affairs, 1941), records five anti-Semitic organizations founded between 1915-1932, nine in 1933, and 105 between 1934-1939.

rotic personality. According to this theory, people who are insecure, troubled, and discontented find refuge in prejudice. As Ben Hecht says, "Prejudice is our method of transferring our own sickness to others. It is our ruse for disliking others rather than ourselves. . . . Prejudice is a raft onto which the shipwrecked mind clambers and paddles to safety." [41]

The high proportion of maladjusted persons among race agitators and fanatics has often been noted.[42] Of the eleven student leaders of a school strike against a move to integrate Negro students into local schools, all but one or two were reported to be frustrated and unhappy.[43]

These boys who initiated the Barstow strike and who chose the anti-Negro goal were ones whose lives both at home and in school had been largely unhappy and difficult. . . . They were unhappy in their relations with other boys and girls as well as with teachers and principals. This spurred them to try to build more satisfactory pictures in their own minds of what their own status was. . . . They were driven to become attention-seekers, "zoot-suiters," extremists in behavior, speech, and appearance.

Several studies seem to show some rather striking differences between the personalities of prejudiced and unprejudiced persons. Hartley, after testing several groups of college students, reports that: [44]

The *relatively tolerant personality* in this type of collegiate sample is likely to exhibit some combination of the following characteristics: a strong desire for personality autonomy associated with a lack of need for dominance, a strong need for friendliness, along with a personal seclusiveness, fear of competition, a tendency to placate others along with a lack of general conformity to the mores. He is likely to be fairly serious, to be interested in current events, to have ideas about bettering society, to be a member of a political group and to have great need for personal achievement in the vocational area. He is likely to be an accepting personality, disliking violence, able to appreciate the contributions of others, conscious of feeling that people tend to be more or less alike and adopting a nurturant rather than dominant attitude toward those younger than he. He is conscious of conflicts concerning loyalties and duties, and thinks very seriously about moral questions. His interests center about what are commonly called social studies, reading, and journalism. Although personally seclusive, he has a great need to be socially useful.

The *relatively intolerant personality* might be expected to combine in varying degrees the following characteristics: unwillingness to accept responsibility, acceptance of conventional mores, a rejection of "serious" groups, rejection of political interests and desire for groups formed for purely social purposes,

[41] Ben Hecht, *A Guide for the Bedeviled* (New York, Charles Scribner's Sons, 1944), p. 31.

[42] See John Roy Carlson, *Under Cover* (New York, E. P. Dutton & Co., Inc., 1943); *The Plotters* (New York, E. P. Dutton & Co., Inc., 1946); Leo Lowenthal and Norbert Gutterman, *Prophets of Deceit* (New York, Harper and Brothers, 1949); Elton Mayo, "Routine Interaction and the Problem of Collaboration," *American Sociological Review,* 4 (June, 1939), pp. 335-340.

[43] James H. Tipton, *Community in Crisis* (New York, Bureau of Publications, Teachers College, Columbia University, 1953), pp. 68-69.

[44] Eugene Hartley, *Problems in Prejudice* (New York, The King's Crown Press, 1946), pp. 62-63.

absorption with pleasure activities, a conscious conflict between play and work, emotionality rather than rationality, extreme egocentrism, interest in physical activity, the body, health. He is likely to dislike agitators, radicals, pessimists. He is relatively uncreative, apparently unable to deal with anxieties except by fleeing from them. Often his physical activity has in it a compulsive component; it may be that his compulsion to be on the move, that is, constantly occupied with sports, motoring, traveling, etc., serves for him the same function that study and activities with social significance serve in the case of the individual with high tolerance.

This picture of the intolerant personality is quite similar to Frenkel-Brunswik and Sanford's findings that: [45]

... those with high scores on prejudice tests exhibit, among other tendencies, rigidity of outlook (inaccessibility to new experience), intolerance of ambiguity (they want to know *the* answers), pseudoscientific or antiscientific attitudes (more superstition, reliance on accidents as explanations, attribution of behavior to heredity), suggestibility and gullibility, and autistic thinking in goal behavior (unrealistic views of what will achieve the desired goals). Those low in prejudice, on the other hand, show more flexibility of judgment, greater tolerance of ambiguity, a more scientific-naturalistic explanation of events, greater autonomy and self-reliance, and realistic thinking about goal behavior.

From a number of such studies, Adorno constructs a picture of the basically prejudiced type of personality with these tendencies: [46]

a. Conventionalism. Rigid adherence to conventional, middle-class values.
b. Authoritarian submission. Submissive, uncritical attitude towards idealized moral authorities of the in-group.
c. Authoritarian aggression. Tendency to be on the outlook for, and to condemn, reject, and punish people who violate conventional values.
d. Anti-intraception. Opposition to the subjective, the imaginative, the tender-minded.
e. Superstition and stereotypy. The belief in mystical determinants of the individual's fate; the disposition to think in rigid categories.
f. Power and "toughness." Preoccupation with the dominance-submission, strong-weak, leader-follower dimension; identification with power figures; overemphasis upon the conventionalized attributes of the ego; exaggerated assertion of strength and toughness.
g. Destructiveness and cynicism. Generalized hostility, vilification of the human.
h. Projectivity. The disposition to believe that wild and dangerous things go on in the world; the projection outwards of unconscious emotional impulses.
i. Sex. Exaggerated concern with sexual "goings-on." These variables were thought of as going together to form a single syndrome, a more or less enduring structure in the person that renders him receptive to antidemocratic propaganda.

[45] Else Frenkel-Brunswik and R. Nevitt Sanford, "Some Personality Factors in Anti-Semitism," *Journal of Psychology*, 20 (October, 1945), pp. 271-291; summarized in Simpson and Yinger, *op. cit.*, p. 89.
[46] T. W. Adorno and others, *The Authoritarian Personality* (New York, Harper and Brothers, 1950), p. 228.

These studies, then, generally agree in finding the prejudiced personality to be highly active, preoccupied with strength and toughness, non-studious, self-centered, domineering, immature, somewhat puritanical, critical of others, ethnocentric, superficial in interests and cliché-bound in thinking, whereas the unprejudiced personality is seen as more studious and serious, co-operative rather than domineering, tolerant of others, benevolent and humanitarian, and relatively free of stereotypes and rigid categories in his thinking. These conclusions, however, are based upon rather small samples, not fully representative of the entire population; therefore, they cannot be accepted as definitely established or final.

It seems probable that both tolerance and extreme prejudice generally are functions of the *total* personality rather than of isolated experience. It is doubtful, however, if this can explain all prejudices. It is known that the prejudiced person generally shows similar prejudices against many groups, irrespective of his knowledge of or contact with them, but there are many exceptions—prejudiced persons who are tolerant towards certain groups and tolerant persons who are prejudiced about certain groups. It is also true that many widespread prejudices are simply learned as supposed "facts" (for example, "Jews have an instinct for making money," "Negroes are naturally easygoing"). Such "facts" may have no particular impact upon the personality, merely being filed away as part of one's store of information. It is probable that the social-neurosis theory may be applicable only to the extremes of the prejudice continuum, with the central group of mildly or moderately prejudiced persons explained by some other theory. It is clear beyond all question, however, that *we find the explanation of prejudice in the personality and experience of the person holding the prejudice, not in the character of the group against whom the prejudice is directed.* The utter irrelevance of the true characteristics of the victims of prejudice has been demonstrated again and again! The precise manner in which and degree to which prejudice and tolerance identify different kinds of basic personalities can be learned only through much further research.

These are the principal theories of the origin of race prejudices, although there are several others of lesser import.[47] These principal theories are more than idle speculation; each is supported by a respectable body of research. None explains *all* prejudice, for prejudices are of many kinds and degrees and may have as many origins. Each helps to understand certain kinds of prejudice. Taken together, they provide a good deal of insight, and place the problem of controlling prejudice somewhere between a science and an art.

[47] Cf. Brewton Berry, *op. cit.*, pp. 113-116.

SOME COMMON MYTHS, EVASIONS, AND RATIONALIZATIONS

A favorite way of dealing with one's guilt feelings is to change one's vices into virtues through the art of rationalization. As Myrdal insistently repeats, the conflict between the ideals of Christianity and democracy and the realities of racial discrimination produce in white folks an uneasy guilt that becomes a powerful force for change in race relations.[48] This same guilt feeling also gives birth to an elaborate folklore of myth, evasion, and rationalization that permits people to view themselves as unprejudiced without sacrificing any of their treasured prejudices. Included are such comforting beliefs as the following.

1. "It's Their Own Fault"

Minorities are variously accused of being lazy and shiftless, aggressive and overambitious, clannish and seclusive, pushy and intrusive, artful and deceitful, simple and trusting, miserly and grasping, extravagant and wasteful, and so on. The inconsistency of such characterizations seldom occurs to those who hold them. The fantastic inaccuracy of many such characterizations has been demonstrated repeatedly by cases such as this: [49]

. . . in Fresno County, California, where a colony of first- and second-generation Armenians has settled . . . LaPiere found that the reasons given by non-Armenians for their antipathy revealed three distinct stereotypes: (1) They are dishonest, deceitful liars. The manager of the Merchant's Association said, "I can safely say, after many years of work that the Armenians are, as a race, the worst we have to deal with." (2) They are parasitic; they do not contribute their fair share to community life and welfare. (3) They have a low moral code; they are "always getting into trouble with the law." LaPiere attempted to determine the truth of these accusations, and he could find no support for them. Far from being dishonest, the records of the Merchant's Association revealed that the credit standing of the Armenians was "remarkable." A study of admissions to the County Hospital and of the requests at the Welfare Bureau proved that the Armenians' demands for charity were very small, considering their ratio in the general population. As for their being a lawless group, LaPiere's analysis of the police records revealed that Armenians were involved in only 1.5 per cent of the cases, although they make up 6 per cent of the population.

In some cases, however, the unflattering characterizations have a measure of truth. There is no doubt that, as compared with whites, a greater

[48] Gunnar Myrdal, op. cit., pp. xli-lv.
[49] Brewton Berry, op. cit., pp. 119-120; summarizing study by R. T. LaPiere, "Type-Rationalizations of Group Antipathy," Social Forces. 15 (December, 1936), pp. 232-237.

proportion of Negroes are uneducated, unskilled, and unrefined. This fact may be interpreted either as a challenge to do something about it, or as an excuse for doing nothing about it. To the prejudiced person, the ignorance and poverty of Negroes serves as an excuse for preserving those conditions which keep Negroes ignorant and poor. And the stereotype of the greedy, grasping Jew becomes a basis for slights and insults that encourage Jews to become grasping and exploitative, just as a child who is repeatedly called a "bad boy" eventually becomes one. The ironic significance of the unflattering minority stereotypes is not merely that they are often untrue, but that these stereotypes tend to become true by creating the conditions which make the stereotype come true. If there were no other forces at work counteracting it, the stereotype of the lazy, shiftless, sexually-promiscuous Negro might already have converted all Negroes into just such persons. Any characterization of a group is not merely an inert description; it is functionally active! To describe a group as "lazy" or as "ambitious" not only affects that group's view of itself; it also affects the treatment and opportunities the group receives.

This is why the description of the supposed characteristics of any group might be termed the "self-correcting description," for, in the absence of other counteracting forces, *any group tends to become whatever it is commonly said to be.* The greatest error of those who justify discrimination by pointing out the offensive habits of a minority is in their utter failure to realize that their own prejudices and accusations are among the causes of the traits they dislike.

2. "They Like It That Way"

Many white people confidently assert that "they know the Negro" and insist that they know exactly what pleases and displeases him. Having seen that part of the Negro's personality which the Negro wished to show them, many whites feel that they understand Negroes better than Negroes understand themselves. Such whites would be much chagrined to know how deliberately and contemptuously the Negro has exploited the vanity of whites by assuming whatever pattern of outward behavior is most useful in "handling" white folk. Negroes "know" white folk infinitely better than whites "know" Negroes.

The belief that Negroes like poverty and Jews prefer "their own" resorts can be supported by occasional anecdotes that make the belief sound reasonable. It is true that many Negroes show no active discontent with the poverty and squalor which have been their only experience. Some Jews prefer a segregated resort to the uncertainties and humiliations encountered elsewhere. But the belief that any American minority has been long contented with inequality is nonsense. The magnolia-scented, technicolored picture of the Old South peopled with considerate masters and contentedly grateful slaves is marred by the historical fact of a succession of bloody slave revolts,[50] the 100,000 Negroes who served with Union armies during the Civil War,[51] and the steady migration of Negroes away from the South. There is no record of adequate housing remaining vacant because Negroes preferred to sleep five to a bed. In a society which trumpets the virtues of opportunity and self-advancement, no group will long be satisfied with poverty or discrimination.

3. "Discrimination Really Benefits the Minority"

It protects them from disastrous competition with the dominant group, so the argument runs, and is an evidence of the dominant group's unselfishness and altruism. Segregation in particular is defended as an arrangement supposedly beneficial to Negroes; the "separate but equal" schools, churches, public services and occupations protect them from direct competition with whites and help them gratify a supposedly irresistible desire to be with "their own" people. The historical fact that segregation was invented to protect the *whites* from competition is conveniently obscured by a rationalization which permits members of the dominant group to continue their discriminatory practices without interrupting their pious professions of kindness and sympathy.

4. "Whites Have Troubles, Too"

This is a device for avoiding the issue by changing the subject. Many people, confronted with the facts about Negro poverty, housing, or job discrimination, reply that there are lots of miserable white folks too, implying that if some whites are poor, Negroes should not complain. It is true, of course, that (a much smaller proportion of) whites share the poverty and squalor which a great many Negroes suffer, and for reasons often beyond their control. But the proportions of white and Negro poverty, for example, are far apart because of the added handicap of race discrimination which Negroes endure. The "whites-have-trouble-too" argument shifts attention away from race discrimination as a *cause* of poverty and instead centers attention upon poverty itself; then it is another short jump to a discussion of the general worthlessness of the poor, and the original issue is now neatly buried.

Of these and other rationalizations there is no end. It is often futile to attack them or to cite the facts which disprove them. If one's rationalizations are destroyed, he invents newer and better ones. For rationaliza-

[50] Cf. Melville J. Herskovits, *The Myth of the Negro Past* (New York, Harper and Brothers, 1941), pp. 91 ff.

[51] Monroe N. Work, ed., *Negro Year Book*, 1931-32 (Tuskegee Institute, Alabama, Negro Year Book Publishing Co., 1931), pp. 327-334; also, Benjamin Quarles, *The Negro in the Civil War* (Boston, Little, Brown & Company, 1953).

tions are not believed because they are demonstrably true, but because they protect and sanctify those beliefs and prejudices one is unwilling to change. But with the gradual popularization of natural and social science, it grows steadily more difficult to find convincing rationalizations, and annoying doubts persist in arising. As Myrdal repeats, this is the white man's dilemma—that he only half believes his own rationalizations. His shrill professions of innate white superiority sound less and less like a confident statement of a self-evident fact, and more and more like a whistling in the dark.

MINORITY "ADJUSTMENTS" TO PREJUDICE AND DISCRIMINATION

Of all popular nonsense about race, perhaps none exceeds the nonsense of attributing racial behavior to instinct rather than to experience. People note what they see, or think they see, in a particular race or group and attribute it to their "racial nature." They fail to realize that all group behavior is a product of group experience, and all racial behavior is a product of the conditions under which that race has lived. In a noted rabbi's remark that "I have been a Jew for a thousand years," we see that many generations of experience—of working, of struggling, of interaction with other groups, and of traditions and legends told and retold—enter into the making of the so-called "racial nature" of a group.

A minority which endures discrimination and inequality in a society that professes democracy and equality of opportunity is doubly affected by this experience. The *fact* of discrimination and inequality promotes certain behavior outcomes in the minority, while the cultural *ideal* of democracy and equality of opportunity promote quite different outcomes. Consequently, there is no single "racial personality" for any minority in America, but a variety of personality outcomes, all of which represent minority "adjustments" to the conditions under which they live.

1. Acceptance

The stereotype of the contented, easygoing Negro is not entirely untrue. A considerable number of Negroes, especially in the South, accept wholeheartedly the doctrine of innate Negro inferiority and view white domination as entirely proper. These are probably the most successfully "adjusted" Negroes of all, since they escape most of the frustrations and resentments which bedevil other Negroes. These Negroes also gain the approval of those whites who describe as a "good nigger" the Negro who is obedient, docile, and deferential. This white stereotype also defines the "good nigger" as hard-working but unambitious. Such Negroes are rare, for few people will work hard and well unless driven by an ambition. In attempting to limit Negro ambition to those simple and childish goals which in no way jeopardized white status or income, whites have also deprived Negroes of their main reason for working, and have guaranteed that many Negroes would be "lazy." But if Negroes will not work hard unless motivated by ambition, many whites would prefer that the Negro be lazy, for, while the lazy Negro is an irritation, the ambitious Negro is a threat. Many whites may be unaware of making such a choice, but the effects of their choice remain. *For the Negro, laziness is a normal, intelligent, and functionally useful adjustment to his lack of opportunity.*

2. Accommodation

There is an apparently growing number of Negroes who resent white domination but will make expedient compromises with it in order to advance themselves. Fearful of attacking the white man's prejudices, they seek to manipulate these prejudices to their own advantage. This involves the studied use of flattery, cajolery, and humble petition. It involves observing the racial etiquette and making no challenge to the racial status quo. It entails acting the way whites expect Negroes to act, and requires the use of many subterfuges to avoid disturbing any of the white man's illusions about Negroes. By preserving an outward appearance of acceptance of white domination, many Negroes have achieved a tolerable existence and even some advancement.

The accommodation pattern often includes *avoidance,* an effort by the minority to minimize contacts with the majority. The "clannishness" of a minority is an avoidance technique. The medieval ghetto originated as a voluntary clustering of Jews for common protection and escape from insult; only later did it become compulsory. Many Negroes travel by automobile to avoid segregated public transportation, and middle- or upper-class Negroes often shop by telephone and pay bills by check in order to avoid contacts with disrespectful whites.[52]

3. Aggression

Not all who resent discrimination are able to accommodate themselves successfully. Some find outlet for their frustrations in some form of aggression against someone—the majority, another minority, or even against each other. The many forms of aggression range from revolts, riots, and street fights to such subtle provocations as loud talk or the intentional withholding of deference. Johnson has described numerous subtle ways

[52] See C. S. Johnson, *Patterns of Negro Segregation* (New York, Harper and Brothers, 1943), pp. 267-293, for a description of the many subtle ways in which Negroes minimize contacts with whites.

in which Negroes vent hostility upon whites—"talking back," quitting jobs without notice, spreading gossip, paying exaggerated courtesies, committing acts of petty sabotage, and so on.[53] In the North, Negro boasts and hints of white girl friends are an effective aggressive device; in the South, this would probably be too dangerous.

Certain numbers of the minority develop what has been called the *oppression psychosis,* an oversensitivity to discrimination that leads them to imagine discrimination even where it is absent. Some Negro students who receive low grades because of poor work are quick to accuse the teacher of injustice. A prominent Negro explains the oppression psychosis in saying: [54]

... when I was a barefoot boy in Franklin County, Virginia, sometimes I stubbed my toe in the spring and it would not heal until the fall. It seemed that everything in nature, including the leaves, wind and grass, conspired to hit that toe. The children, dogs, flies, and cats always deliberately selected that toe to brush against or to trample upon. My suffering, I admit, was more psychological than physiological, for I was always expecting somebody or something to pick on that sensitive toe.

The Negro has been stubbed and snubbed so constantly by prejudice, that he not only reacts to the slightest rebuff in word or act, but he often reacts when there has been no intended action.

One with the oppression psychosis blames all disappointments and failures upon discrimination and is likely to be highly aggressive in venting his hostilities. Such persons irritate and alienate the majority group and embarrass the minority whose complaints they exaggerate and caricature.

4. Organized Protest

Whereas aggression is merely a way to vent one's hostile feelings, organized protest is a calculated campaign to change things. Organized protest often uses aggressive devices, but as part of a carefully organized plan. Organized protest goes beyond the humble petitions of a Booker T. Washington to include an insistent demand that the promises of the Constitution be fulfilled. The National Association for the Advancement of Colored People (NAACP) is perhaps the most effective organization in the country militantly fighting for Negro rights. It vigorously demands enforcement of existing laws and enactment of additional laws to end lynching, insure equal police protection, and reduce occupational, educational, and social discriminations against Negroes. While it has had limited success in securing new legislation, it has successfully pressed many legal actions resulting in court rulings which have weakened and reduced many kinds of discrimination.

[53] *Ibid.,* pp. 294-315.
[54] A. Clayton Powell, *op. cit.,* p. 28.

In organized protest, the minorities have their most effective weapon. For lack of effectively organized protest (among other reasons) the Negroes made no important "gains" during World War I. In World War II, however, well-organized plans for a "March on Washington" to dramatize failure to employ Negroes in defense industry—an incident which would be highly embarrassing to a nation fighting a war against fascism—resulted in President Roosevelt's establishment of the Fair Employment Practices Committee. Organized protest can be quite effective when it can appeal to a set of democratic professions such as ours. The membership of protest organizations such as the NAACP indicates that increasing numbers of Negroes are rejecting both placid acceptance and quiet accommodation in favor of organized protest as their reaction to life in America.[55]

SUGGESTED READINGS

Since Chapters 12 and 13 constitute a single unit of study, the bibliography and study questions for Chapter 12 are included at the end of Chapter 13, beginning on page 325.

[55] This partial list of minority reactions, largely taken from Brewton Berry, *op. cit.*, pp. 414-443, is not the only such listing. Davie finds seven Negro responses: acceptance, resentment, avoidance, over-compensation, race pride, hostility and aggression, and protest. (M. R. Davie, *Negroes in American Society* [New York, McGraw-Hill Book Company, Inc., 1949], pp. 434-455.) Johnson sees four Negro reactions: acceptance, avoidance, direct hostility and aggression, and indirect or deflected hostility. (C. S. Johnson, *Patterns of Negro Segregation, op. cit.*, pp. 244-315.)

CHAPTER 13

The Race Problem in America: II

APPROACHES TO THE RACE PROBLEM

1. The Social-Disorganization Approach

RACE problems can be viewed as products of social disorganization. Some factor—migration, population growth, technological change—disturbs an existing equilibrium between races, or between groups who are imagined to be races. In America, migration brought into successive contact whites and Indians, whites and Negroes, Protestants of northern and western European extraction and Catholics of southern and eastern European extraction, gentiles and Jews, and several other combinations. Each developed into a "problem." The status of the Negro aroused some debate and soul-searching from the very beginning, but not until the Civil War period did it become a major social concern. Although it is widely believed that the war was fought to free the slaves, the historical fact is that Lincoln freed the slaves in order to win the war by disrupting the South's labor force. Negroes received freedom as a bit of war strategy from a government which had no clear idea of what Negroes were to be and do after they were free. Following the war, the North ruled and more or less looted the South, ruling with the help of the Negroes whom they gave the vote and placed in political office. After a decade, the North abandoned the Negroes to the tender mercies of an embittered South as part of a deal which secured the presidency for Hayes. The South promptly disfranchised the Negro, removed him from political offices, and set about returning him to servitude. An elaborate etiquette developed to regulate all contacts between whites and Negroes [1] (for example, Negroes were never addressed as "Mr."; white and Negro children might play together only while small; Negroes never sat down in the presence of adult whites, and so on). This etiquette sought to permit close and intimate contacts

---

[1] See Charles S. Johnson, *Growing Up in the Black Belt* (Washington, American Council on Education, 1941), pp. 277-280; also Bertram Doyle, *The Etiquette of Race Relations in the South* (Chicago, University of Chicago Press, 1937).

but to prevent any suggestion of equality; therefore Negro servants might live on the same block or in the same house with whites, prepare their food and even nurse white babies at their own breasts, yet could not eat with whites or wear hats in their presence.

Before the war many of the skilled workmen were Negro slaves,[2] and Negroes worked in nearly all occupations except the professions. After the war, a popular classification of all jobs as either "white man's work" or "nigger's work" developed, and each postwar census showed a decline in the proportion of skilled workers among Negroes. Within a generation, Negroes were largely excluded from all but the most menial jobs.

In this way a new equilibrium developed to replace the prewar slave-oriented society of the South. Although there were many local variations and minor uncertainties, this new equilibrium did tell each person, white or Negro, where he stood and what he might do. This equilibrium persisted without great change for over half a century. Meanwhile, Negroes made some gains in education and in ownership of farms and businesses, but made few gains and suffered some net losses in their bid for political and occupational equality. But the northward migration of Negroes, the accumulating findings of natural and social science, and the development of industrial unionism after 1933 all eventually undermined this post-Civil War equilibrium. During the 1930's the C.I.O. organized many industrial unions, which include all the workers in a particular *industry* rather than those in a given *trade* or skill (as in the A.F.L. trade unions). The industrial union cannot exclude Negroes without weakening itself, nor can it allow race animosities to disrupt union affairs. Although discrimination against Negroes has been the rule in trade unions, enlightened self-interest led most industrial unions to admit Negroes, and the national office of the C.I.O. and some locals have waged an energetic campaign to reduce race prejudice and discrimination.[3]

The outbreak of World War II found the traditional race patterns beginning to weaken, and greatly accelerated their decay. The war produced a serious labor shortage together with an emphasis upon the values of democracy and equality. Negroes and sympathetic whites took full advantage of this unique opportunity to press for minority rights. They succeeded in gaining Negro access to many job areas formerly reserved for whites and made successful attacks in the courts upon many forms of discrimination in higher education and public services. Negroes are now working in hundreds of thousands of jobs formerly closed to Negroes,

[2] There were many abolitionists, both North and South, who argued that slavery penalized the great mass of whites by largely excluding them from the skilled trades, as the slaveowner found it cheaper to train a slave as a carpenter or blacksmith than to hire white tradesmen.

[3] H. R. Northrup, *Organized Labor and the Negro* (New York, Harper and Brothers, 1944); Robert Weaver, *Negro Labor* (New York, Harcourt, Brace & Company, Inc., 1946).

attending dozens of colleges and universities which formerly excluded them, and are even being elected to some local elective offices in the South. The effects of such changes will be further to disorganize and destroy the traditional pattern of race relations in all of the country. No new equilibrium is yet in sight, and it appears quite possible that relatively complete political and economic equality for Negroes may not be far distant.

The old equilibrium owed much of its stability to the fact that the status of the Negro was fully consistent with the beliefs of the period. Since nearly all people, including even the Negroes, believed that Negroes were innately different from and inferior to whites, it seemed perfectly sensible to treat them as inferiors. The "all men are created equal" dictum did not apply to Negroes, since they were not really "men" anyway. Theories of a biblical Hamitic curse, of incompleted or separate evolutions, of geographic determinism, and of intelligence test evidences were successively employed to justify treatment of Negroes as inferiors. As long as such notions were believed—and most people did believe them—there was no inconsistency in professing democratic ideals while practicing discrimination.

But as natural and social science destroyed the intellectual respectability of such beliefs, the inconsistencies between democratic ideals and racial practice became increasingly apparent. A society which professes democracy and equality of opportunity yet practices race discrimination is to this degree disorganized. This disorganization gives whites a bad conscience and drives Negroes into frustrated confusion.

It is unlikely that such inconsistency will be tolerated indefinitely in a technologically-advanced society such as ours. Only when a group is consistently trained to expect and desire the treatment it receives can that group be content. It is unlikely that any intermediate equilibrium—granting Negroes certain privileges while withholding others—will be satisfactory either to whites or to Negroes. A stable equilibrium can be secured only by bringing current practice into harmony with current beliefs, and this means either (1) admitting Negroes into full democratic citizenship, or (2) suppressing the ideas of freedom and equality of opportunity which make Negroes discontented. If whites desire an enduring racial peace with a clear conscience, they must surrender either the practice of discrimination or the ideal of democracy. They cannot enjoy both.

2. The Value-Conflict Approach

As repeatedly implied in this chapter, the race problem is basically a moral problem—a choice of values. The existence of race discrimination is a problem only to him whose values define race discrimination as abhorrent. Although practically everyone agrees that there is a race problem, some define the problem as the task of eliminating prejudice and discrimination, while others define the problem as one of putting the Negroes back in "their place." What some hail as "progress" in race relations, others view with alarm and dismay. If all, or even most, Americans could agree upon what kind of a solution of the race problem they wished, such a solution might not be long in coming. We have enough knowledge to "solve" the problem if we could gain consensus upon objectives. But there can be no agreement between those who want Negroes to be ambitious citizens and those who wish them to be servile inferiors.

Even among sympathetic whites, there are difficult value-choices to make. Should we seek the prevention of race conflict, the reduction of discrimination, or the reduction of prejudice? In at least the short run, these objectives may conflict. A consistently enforced segregation may reduce conflict for the present, but (aside from being uneconomic) it multiplies discrimination and perpetuates prejudice. Techniques of reducing discrimination may produce at least a temporary increase in conflict and prejudice. While, over the long run, it is likely that conflict, prejudice, and discrimination may move together, some short-run sacrifices may be necessary.

3. The Personal-Deviation Approach

Race problems are not *caused* by deviant individuals, but deviant persons can greatly *aggravate* them. Each minority has its maladjusted neurotics who, in one way or another, increase their brothers' burdens. The aforementioned "oppression psychotic," with his chip hopefully perched on his shoulder, is an embarrassment to his fellows as he constantly confirms the worst suspicions of the enemies of his race. Another minority response which plays into the hands of the enemy is the self-hatred response. The anti-Semitic Jew or anti-Negro Negro is a maladjusted person who seeks to escape the stigma of inferiority by agreeing with and repeating the criticisms commonly directed against his group.[4]

Among the dominant group the maladjusted person is more likely to be highly prejudiced than is the well-adjusted person. Furthermore, the frustrated neurotic may be far more likely to express his prejudices in violent action than the well-adjusted person with the same prejudices. Observers of organized anti-Semitic movements (most of which are also anti-Negro) have been impressed by the numerous tight-lipped, sadistic fanatics and the almost complete absence of relaxed, genial folk among the followers.[5]

This deviant person is a noisy nuisance, making serious race problems

---

[4] Cf. George E. Simpson and J. Milton Yinger, *Racial and Cultural Minorities* (Harper and Brothers, 1953), pp. 192-195, 304-307.

[5] Cf. John Ray Carlson, *Under Cover* (New York, E. P. Dutton & Co., Inc., 1943); *The Plotters* (New York, E. P. Dutton & Co., Inc., 1946).

even more explosive, yet he is not the primary cause of them. Without a background of widespread prejudice, the racial fanatic could not be effective. So both the sadistic street rioter and the well-mannered teller of the racial joke play a role in perpetuating the race problem.

The totally unprejudiced person is also a deviant, in that he has not absorbed the normal prejudices and racial stereotypes of his fellows. Racial equality may even become a "cause" to which he is fanatically dedicated. The more fanatical equalitarians often have a personality structure very similar in some respects to that of the fanatically prejudiced person. In this as in most other problems, the extremists at both ends of the continuum are likely to be deviant, even neurotic, persons.

TECHNIQUES FOR REDUCING PREJUDICE

1. *Education*

To many people, education is *the* answer. But it is naive to expect either church or school to educate people toward beliefs and values very different from those already held by the community. Both church and school are dependent upon the community for financial support and are staffed and directed by persons who share most of the views and prejudices of the community. Angry denunciations as "communist," "radical," "atheist," "subversive," or "un-American" await the school superintendent or minister whose concern over race problems goes much beyond the conventional platitudes. Certain church bodies, and especially the National Council of Churches, have been quite active in issuing liberal racial pronouncements and supporting minority rights. Although these pronouncements may have helped promote a national atmosphere more favorable to minority rights, not much of this interest in race problems has filtered down to the local congregational level. Several studies, while inconclusive, suggest that prejudiced persons tend to be more often conventionally religious, although the least prejudiced persons often showed a strong, though unorthodox, religious interest.[6] There is certainly no basis for assuming that conventional or traditional religion reduces prejudice. The church remains a stronghold of discrimination, lagging far behind labor unions and professional organizations in this respect.[7] At no other moment during the week are white and Negro as rigidly segregated as when engaged in the worship of the God of all Mankind.

While the church reaches only part of the population, the school reaches virtually everyone, and at impressionable ages. But this strategic location is largely nullified by both the prejudices of the school staff and the toleration of the community. Teachers and administrators appear to

[6] G. E. Simpson and J. Milton Yinger, *op. cit.*, pp. 94-95.
[7] See Dwight W. Culver, *Negro Segregation in the Methodist Church* (New Haven, Yale University Press, 1954).

be somewhat less prejudiced than the rest of the community, and in a few places have succeeded in introducing realistic programs of "intercultural" education.[8] But even these programs have a habit of dying a quiet death after the novelty wears off or their promoter moves on to a new position.

Race relations conferences, interracial meetings, and "brotherhood" assemblies have little educational effect because they consist mainly of racial liberals busily talking to one another. Such conferences may maintain morale among race liberals and may provide exceedingly valuable instruction in techniques of effective action, but can play no real role in the direct reduction of prejudice as long as the prejudiced people will not attend them.

2. Exhortation and Propaganda

This is a double-edged weapon. Exhortation at the level of platitudes and generalities, like the posters, radio plugs and sermons, saying "All men are brothers," "Prejudice is un-American," and the like, are ineffective. The prejudiced person applies them to other people, since he is unaware of his own prejudice. His own prejudices are so fully rationalized as to be immune to such slogans. In fact, such exhortation may have a negative effect, since it allows the prejudiced person to feel self-righteous, while it gives the liberal the illusion that he is "doing something" about race problems, and thus serves as a substitute for more effective action.

More specific propaganda also has its dangers. Publicizing the achievement of minority members (especially Jews) may arouse jealousy rather than respect. Publicizing recent Negro gains may inspire jealousy and insecurity among whites, while describing Negro poverty and handicap may confirm prejudices instead of arousing sympathy. Attempts to "answer" false rumors and racial accusations may spread the falsehood even more widely. Propaganda must be used very skillfully or it will defeat its own purposes.

Propaganda is even more seriously limited by the facts that (1) it fails to reach the right audience, since many prejudiced persons read and watch little beyond comics and sports events; and (2) the prejudiced person reinterprets propaganda in such a way that his prejudice remains undisturbed or even strengthened.[9] All in all, it is doubtful that propa-

[8] See Clarence A. Chatto and others, *The Story of the Springfield Plan* (New York, Barnes & Noble, Inc., 1945); Theodore Brameld, *Minority Problems in the Public Schools* (New York, Harper and Brothers, 1946); Lloyd Allen Cook and Elaine Cook, *Intergroup Education* (New York, McGraw-Hill Book Company, Inc., 1954).

[9] For experimental evidence of this, see Patricia Kendall and Katherine Wolf, in Paul Lazarsfeld and Frank Stanton, eds., *Communications Research, 1948-49* (New York, Harper and Brothers, 1949), p. 158. For evidence of the "boomerang" effect,

ganda can have very much effect in reducing the general level of prejudice.

3. Personal and Group Therapy

Since, in at least some cases, intense prejudice seems to be a function of a maladjusted personality, it might be more effective to attack the maladjustment instead of the prejudice. If the personality disorder can be cured, then the violence of one's prejudice should fade and the prejudice be far more easily removed. This approach is probably sound, but there are serious difficulties in its use. Mass psychotherapy, even on a group basis, would be fantastically expensive. Many maladjusted persons sense no maladjustment ("It's *other* people who are queer!") and have no desire for treatment. Finally, the problem of how to produce stable, prejudice-free personalities in a prejudice-prone environment is not easy to answer.

But psychotherapy is not always necessary. Often a change in *situation*, reducing one's pressures and frustrations, will reduce one's maladjustment and lessen his active prejudice. The use of *guidance* techniques by teachers, employers, military officers and others in supervisory roles may indirectly reduce prejudices by steering pupils and adults into situations which are less frustrating.

4. Contact

Contact between peoples produces a variety of attitudes, depending upon the *kind of contact*. A mere "getting together" of whites and Negroes or Jews and gentiles does not automatically reduce prejudices; it may even increase them. The lack of a consistent relationship between amount of contact and amount of prejudice between two groups has already been mentioned in the preceding chapter.

Certain kinds of contact, however, produce spectacular changes in attitudes. In military service, in employment, in housing projects, the "integration" (mixing) of Negroes and whites has not fulfilled the dire predictions of "trouble," but has resulted in striking reductions in prejudice with surprisingly little "trouble." Deutsch and Collins studied two integrated housing projects in which Negroes and whites were scattered indiscriminately, and two segregated projects in which Negroes and whites occupied separated sections of the project. They found agreeable rela-

---

in which propaganda is interpreted in such a way as to strengthen the prejudice, see Eunice Cooper and Helen Dinerman, "Analysis of the Film, 'Don't Be a Sucker': A Study in Communication," *Public Opinion Quarterly*, 15 (Summer, 1951), pp. 243-264.

tions between whites and Negroes ten times more common and bad relations only one-fourth as frequent in the integrated projects.[10]

Lazarsfeld [11] reports on an interracial housing project in which:

Before they moved into the project only one out of every 25 whites thought that race relations would turn out well, while five times as many felt that there would be nothing but conflict between the people of the two races. After a few years, one out of every five whites said that race relations were better than they had thought they would be, while only about one-fourth as many [one out of twenty] thought they were worse than they had expected. But of the people who had anticipated really serious race conflicts, three out of every four were willing to say that their fears had been proved groundless. Moreover, people who had worked with Negroes were considerably more willing to live in the same community with them.

A survey of attitudes in private residential areas shows that those whites living closer to Negroes are more willing to approve the idea of mixed racial housing areas than those living at a greater distance.[12] Although the attempt to bring about mixed housing often produces temporary tensions, serious "trouble" usually develops only where police encourage it by sympathizing openly with the troublemakers.[13] Where police and

[10] Morton Deutsch and Mary Evans Collins, "Intergroup Relations in Interracial Housing," *Journal of Housing* (April, 1950), pp. 127-129 ff., reprinted in Arnold Rose, ed., *Race Prejudice and Discrimination* (New York, Alfred A. Knopf, Inc., 1951), p. 556. It should be noted that, of those persons who reported *any* relations with Negroes, "bad" relations formed 19 per cent of all relations in the segregated group, and only 5 per cent of all relations in the integrated group.

NATURE OF WHITE HOUSEWIVES' RELATIONS WITH
NEGRO PEOPLE IN THE PROJECT

Kind of Relations Reported	Integrated		Segregated	
	Koaltown	Sacktown	Bakersville	Frankville
Friendly relations	60%	69%	6%	4%
Accommodative relations	24	14	5	1
Mixed relations	7	11	2	3
No relations	5	0	87	88
Bad relations	4	6	0	4
Total cases	102	90	100	101

[11] Quoted from President's Committee on Civil Rights, *To Secure These Rights* (Washington, Government Printing Office, 1947), p. 85.

[12] Arnold M. Rose, Frank J. Atelsek, and Lawrence R. McDonald, "Neighborhood Reactions to Isolated Negro Residents: An Alternative to Invasion and Succession," *American Sociological Review*, 18 (October, 1953), pp. 497-507.

[13] After extended disorders at Trumbull Park housing project in Chicago, the Chicago Congregational Christian Association, representing 87 Congregational Churches in the Chicago area, adopted unanimously a resolution denouncing groups fomenting racial disorder there "with apparent assurance that the law will not be enforced," and calling on Mayor Kennelly to "fulfill his duty in this regard by securing the appointment of an officer to be in charge of the police detail there who will enforce the law impartially." (*Chicago Sun-Times*, April 29, 1954, p. 30.)

prosecutors act promptly and firmly to enforce the law, "trouble" rarely develops. After the mixed housing is established, both prejudice and conflict decline.

The armed services experienced "endless trouble" with segregated units and found that integrated units produced less race friction and a more efficient use of manpower.[14] Owing partly to pressure from the civilian government, and partly to military necessity in the Korean conflict,[15] the armed services rather reluctantly proceeded to integrate Negro troops into white units and fill ratings and training programs irrespective of race. Integration is now virtually completed, and, to quote General Mark Clark, "Integration of Negro troops in white units on a percentage basis proved an unqualified success—against the predictions of many military men, including myself."[16] The Defense Department reports that integration has been carried out "more rapidly than had been considered possible," that "there have been no untoward incidents," and that integration has produced "a marked increase in over-all combat effectiveness," along with "economies in manpower, materiel, and money...."[17]

The policy of complete integration was pursued only after experimentation and testing had established its practicality. After some experimental integrated units had been established, 1710 white enlisted men were asked, "Some Army divisions have companies which include Negro and white platoons. How would you feel about it if your outfit was set up something like that?"[18] Two-thirds of the white men in the mixed com-

---

Another organization, the Independent Voters of Illinois, made similar charges. (*Chicago Sun-Times,* June 4, 1954, p. 12.)

[14] See President's Committee on Equality of Treatment and Opportunity in the Armed Services, *Freedom to Serve* (Washington, Government Printing Office, 1950).

[15] See Lee Nichols, *Breakthrough on the Color Front* (New York, Random House, Inc., 1954).

[16] *Collier's,* 133 (February 5, 1954), p. 881.

[17] "Services Abolish All-Negro Units," *New York Times,* October 31, 1954, p. 23, quoting Defense Department publication by James C. Evans, *A Progress Report on Integration in the Armed Services.*

[18] Information and Education Division, United States War Department, "Opinions About Negro Infantry Platoons in White Companies of Seven Divisions," reprinted in Theodore M. Newcomb and Eugene L. Hartley, eds., *Readings in Social Psychology* (New York, Henry Holt & Company, Inc., 1947), pp. 542-546.

Groups polled on Negro and white platoons serving in same company	Percentage of white enlisted men answering: "Would dislike it very much."
Cross section of field force units which do not have colored platoons in white companies (1450 cases)	62
Men in same division, but not in same regiment as colored troops (112 cases)	24
Men in same regiment, but not in same company as colored troops (68 cases)	20
Men in company with a Negro platoon (80 cases)	7

panies reported that they had been opposed to the idea beforehand and had expected it to fail; yet nearly all of these men agreed that it had succeeded despite their fears. When white company-grade officers and platoon sergeants involved in the experiment were asked, "Has your feeling changed since having served in the same unit with colored soldiers?," over three-fourths replied that their feelings had become more favorable.[19] When asked, "How well did the colored soldiers in this company perform in combat?", 84 per cent of the white officers and 81 per cent of the white non-coms replied, "Very well" (the most favorable answer on a four-point scale) to this question.[20] While all these percentages are based on too small samples to be highly accurate, they leave no doubt that integration produced a dramatic reduction in prejudice.

A number of other surveys support the conclusion that certain kinds of contact reduce prejudice. A study of the prejudices of 400 merchant seamen with varying amounts of shipboard experience with Negroes shows that: [21]

... whether a man had been born in the North or the South was not important in determining whether he was prejudiced against Negroes. The extent of his education and the jobs he held before he went to sea were not important. What was important was whether the men were members of unions with tolerant policies toward Negroes; how many trips to sea a man had made; how many times he had been under enemy fire; and how many times he had been to sea with Negroes. Here again what determined whether a white man was prejudiced against Negroes was the kind and amount of experience he had with them. Where there was contact with Negroes on an equal footing in a situation of mutual dependence and common effort, prejudice declined.

Simpson and Yinger summarize our present knowledge of the effects of contact on prejudice in these four propositions: [22]

1. Incidental, involuntary, tension-laden contact is likely to increase prejudice.
2. Pleasant, equal-status contact that makes it unnecessary for the individuals to cross barriers of class, occupational, and educational differences ... is likely to reduce prejudice.
3. Stereotype-breaking contacts that show minority-group members in roles not usually associated with them reduce prejudice ...

[19] *Ibid.*

Response to question, "Has your feeling changed since having served in the same unit with colored soldiers?"	White Officers (per cent)	White Non-coms (per cent)
"No, my feeling is the same."	16	21
"Yes, have become more favorable."	77	77
"No answer."	7	2

[20] *Ibid.*

[21] President's Committee on Civil Rights, *op. cit.*, p. 85.

[22] George E. Simpson and J. Milton Yinger, *Racial and Cultural Minorities* (New York, Harper and Brothers, 1953), p. 675.

4. Contacts that bring people of minority and majority groups together in functionally important activities reduce prejudice . . . When white soldiers find Negroes fighting side by side with them, they are more likely to see them as fellow soldiers, less likely to see them as "Negroes." When white seamen shipped with Negroes, their prejudice declined, even though mixed crews were compulsory union policy, not freely chosen situations.

CURRENT TRENDS IN RACE RELATIONS IN AMERICA

1. Decline of Regional Variations in Race Attitudes

Regional variations of all sorts—rural-urban, agrarian-industrial, East-West and North-South—are rapidly fading. Mass communication, migration of peoples, and decentralization of industry are fast dissolving the quaint provincialism of region, hamlet and mesa. Georgia Negro and Georgia white not only work at the same bench and belong to the same union in Detroit; they are doing so in growing numbers in Georgia as well. The noble pose of moral superiority which Northerners are wont to strike is today losing whatever validity it may have possessed. The barriers to Negroes voting in the South are rapidly crumbling, and this inevitably means better schools, more hospitals, and better jobs. The improvements now taking place in the South in Negro education at all levels and Negro success in gaining better jobs and more nearly equal pay have been remarkable. Although regional differences may never entirely disappear, they are diminishing at an impressive rate.

2. Application of Scientific Knowledge to Race Problems

Earlier periods had no alternative but to wallow in their own ignorance and guesswork. Our knowledge is not complete (is it ever?), but we already have enough knowledge to separate the blind alleys from the practical approaches. We now know that most racial fears are groundless, that prejudice is unnecessary, and that amity is attainable. We know how to isolate racial clashes and prevent race riots,[23] and we know the conditions necessary for racial peace. If all, or even most, of us really wished to attain it, we could do so quite quickly. We know in which areas to press for early action, and in which to remain silent. Myrdal points out that whites do not oppose all kinds of racial "equality" with equal fervor. His "rank order of discrimination" suggests that whites will oppose, in declining order of intensity, the following "equalities": [24]

[23] See Alfred McClung Lee, *Race Riots Aren't Necessary*, Public Affairs Pamphlet No. 107 (New York, Public Affairs Committee, 1945).
[24] Gunnar Myrdal, *The American Dilemma* (New York, Harper and Brothers, 1944), pp. 60-61.

1. Sexual equality—intermarriage and Negro sex relations with white women.
2. Social equality—dancing, eating, hand-shaking, bathing, and so on.
3. Civic equality—common use of schools, churches, conveyances, and other public services.
4. Political equality—voting and holding office.
5. Legal equality—use of police, law courts, and governmental services.
6. Economic equality—jobs, credit, property ownership, relief and welfare services.

Myrdal concludes that whites will most willingly grant the last of these, and most bitterly fight to preserve the first. Negroes have an almost identical rank order, but in reverse. This means that *what Negroes most want, whites are most willing to give*—equal jobs and equal pay—while that which whites are least willing to surrender—sexual segregation—is a thing in which Negroes have little interest anyway. Knowing what to seek and what to bypass is of great importance in race relations.

McWilliams counts over 500 local, state, and national organizations working to reduce prejudice and discrimination—many of them working very skillfully—and over half of them organized since 1943.[25] Both in demolishing the rationale of white supremacy and in indicating effective techniques of reducing prejudice and discrimination, scientific knowledge is playing a crucial role.

3. Shift from Laissez-Faire to Action

Even as recently as fifteen or twenty years ago, it was widely believed that any attempt to "do anything" about race would only "make things worse." Even social scientists who privately desired action were paralyzed by the prejudiced person's threat of "trouble" (usually a threat that someone else would make trouble).[26] Thus the prejudiced would blackmail the unprejudiced into inaction, while proceeding to fix the status of minorities according to their own prejudice. Thus the tolerance of the unprejudiced was neutralized and largely wasted as they were reduced to talking to one another and expressing hopes for the future.

Today this is changed. Social scientists have become increasingly aware of the ineffectiveness of talk unless supported by action and have learned how action—legislation, political pressure, and organized publicity—can be effectively used. Today people who desire a reduction in discrimination are busily promoting legislation and planning local campaigns to break down discrimination in local employment; in restaurants, barber shops, and other public services. Action has replaced hopeful waiting as the program of race liberals.

[25] Carey McWilliams, *Brothers Under the Skin* (Boston, Little, Brown & Company, 1951), p. 17.
[26] See Gunnar Myrdal, *op. cit.*, pp. 19, 580 fn, 831.

4. Shift from Attack Upon Prejudice to Attack Upon Segregation

Social scientists long accepted the popular assumption that segregation was necessary to prevent race conflict in a prejudice-ridden society. Only after prejudice had declined, it was believed, could segregation be relaxed and equality be achieved; meanwhile the races might enjoy "separate but equal" facilities and opportunities. People interested in minority rights were urged to tolerate and work within segregation—to seek to reduce prejudice first, after which discrimination and segregation would disappear.

One of the significant discoveries of the past two decades is the discovery that attempts to reduce prejudice while retaining segregation and discrimination are ineffective. For segregation prevents the sorts of contacts that reduce prejudice and channels the races into the kinds of contact that create and reinforce prejudice. To seek to reduce prejudice by exhortation and propaganda is largely futile when segregation is so busily creating it. Segregation even fails in its primary objective of preventing conflict, at least in a society whose democratic values make segregation frustrating to Negroes and embarrassing to whites. The President's Committee on Civil Rights sums up the matter: [27]

The separate but equal doctrine stands convicted on three grounds. It contravenes the equalitarian spirit of the American heritage. It has failed to operate, for history shows that inequality of service has been the omnipresent consequence of separation. It has institutionalized segregation and kept groups apart despite indisputable evidence that normal contacts among these groups tend to promote social harmony.

Sociologists generally support these views in statements such as this: [28]

It has been pointed out again and again that segregation produces ignorance and superstition, and that it perpetuates the status of minority groups and makes it impossible for them to participate fully in the main stream of American life. Instead of producing social order, it produces chaos. In the Detroit race riot, Negroes and whites who lived close together as neighbors, those who were fellow students at Wayne University, and those who worked side by side in the Detroit war plants, showed no disposition to fight. Disturbances occurred in segregated residential areas and segregated plants.

Today in North and South efforts to change race relations focus directly on the effort to reduce segregation. Both through legal means discussed in later pages, and through organized pressure of various sorts, segregation is under attack. At the local, state, and national levels, voluntary organizations—NAACP, National Urban League, American Civil Liberties Union, Anti-Defamation League of B'nai B'rith, and many local "Human

[27] Op. cit., p. 87.

[28] A. M. Lee and N. D. Humphrey, Race Riot (New York, The Dryden Press, 1943), p. 17.

Relations Councils" and other organizations—are highly active. In addition to supporting civil rights legislation, such groups publicize local instances of discrimination; they use persuasion and pressure upon business concerns to accept minority members as employees and as patrons; they put unions and professional organizations "on the spot" and urge them to abandon discriminatory practices. Especially in local public services—hotel and restaurant, commercialized recreation, and so on—local groups have sometimes been able to reassure proprietors that their businesses will not suffer if they cease to discriminate.

With the fear of attacking segregation removed by recent knowledge, the attack is being vigorously pressed wherever segregation is found. And segregation and discrimination are crumbling with a speed which few if any social scientists, two decades ago, would have predicted.

5. Shift from Education and Conciliation to Legal and Administrative Action

In the days of Booker T. Washington, conciliation was probably the only approach open to the Negro. To *demand* anything from whites would only infuriate them; but to *petition* whites—to appeal to their sympathy, generosity, and vanity—was sometimes effective in getting schools, hospitals, and other benefits which would not seriously disturb the status quo. But today a better educated and more restive Negro group faces a less self-satisfied white group which has been repeating the slogans of democracy so fervently it almost believes them. Today minority leaders, aided by many members of the dominant group, are making a determined legal attack upon every form of segregation. Although Negroes are the main beneficiaries of this movement, Jews, American Indians, Americans of Mexican or Oriental ancestry, and other minorities share in the accomplishments. The legal approach involves: (a) enforcing existing laws; (b) seeking court interpretations which extend the coverage of existing laws; and (c) passing additional laws.

a. *Enforcing Existing Laws.* Many rights legally guaranteed to Negroes (and other minorities) are in fact unavailable. Rights to vote, to use of public facilities, and to equal protection of the law have often been denied. Violence and threats of violence often deterred Negroes from claiming their legal privileges. Negroes seeking service in hotels and restaurants were often met by a bland refusal of proprietors to obey the law, or else by evasion, inattention, and humiliation. Law-enforcement officials were likely to "stall" when legal action was sought. Such situations are now changing. The NAACP, the Civil Liberties Union, and other organizations often prod local law-enforcement officials into action when necessary. The proprietor who refuses service to Negroes, in a state whose laws forbid such discrimination, now knows that a lawsuit is a real possibility. Hundreds of legal actions have been pressed for the sole purpose of demonstrating that noncompliance with the law will not be accepted without complaint. While not yet entirely successful, the effort to gain enforcement of existing laws has produced a great many changes.

b. *Extending Interpretations of Existing Laws and Constitutional Provisions.* Civil rights organizations, mainly the NAACP, have pressed many court cases seeking legal ruling that a particular discriminatory practice is contrary to law, usually the Fourteenth Amendment. Every recent year has brought one or more Supreme Court rulings which extended the legal rights of Negroes. One decision held that "Jim Crow" segregation on interstate trains and buses was unconstitutional, another had the effect of requiring Negro admission to tax-supported university graduate and professional schools of most Southern states, another ruled that restrictive racial covenants (preventing resale of real estate to Negroes or other "undesirables") are unenforceable, and so on. This approach has been quite successful and has greatly weakened segregation in housing, education, and certain public facilities.

In the most important decision affecting Negroes in decades, the Supreme Court in 1954 declared segregation in public schools to be unconstitutional. In a unanimous decision written by Chief Justice Warren, the Court declared that, even though physical facilities and other "tangible" factors might be equal in segregated Negro schools,[29]

> To separate them [Negroes] from others of similar age and qualifications solely because of their race generates a feeling of inferiority as to their status in the community that may affect their hearts and minds in a way unlikely ever to be undone. . . .
> A sense of inferiority affects the motivation of a child to learn. Segregation . . . has a tendency to retard the educational and mental development of Negro children and to deprive them of some of the benefits they would receive from a racially integrated school system. . . .
> We conclude that in the field of public education the doctrine of "separate but equal" has no place. Separate educational facilities are inherently unequal.

The Court did not order the *immediate* end of school segregation, but invited the states to send representatives to later hearings (not yet held as this is written) to consider ways and means of implementing the decision. When schools opened in the fall of 1954, desegregation was either accomplished or under way in most of the border states and in the District of Columbia. Twelve Deep South states took no action immediately, pending completion of the Supreme Court's hearings. In four states, Georgia, South Carolina, Mississippi, and Louisiana, political leaders announced their determination to maintain segregation by whatever "legal" means necessary, and three of these have set up legal machinery for turning over the public schools to private operators. In

[29] *New York Times,* May 18, 1954, p. 15.

several states, groups have been formed to exert economic pressure and intimidation upon Negroes and whites who favor school integration.[30]

Schools enrolling many tens of thousands of children were quietly integrated in the fall of 1954, with only a handful of "incidents." It appears likely that desegregation will proceed quite rapidly and with little "trouble" in the border areas where Negro school enrollment is relatively small. In the "Deep South" areas where Negro enrollment is heavier, where patterns of segregation are more rigidly enforced, and where the financial cost of expanding school facilities to accommodate the Negroes on an integrated basis is a major obstacle, strenuous opposition to integration may be expected.[31] It is too early to predict the eventual pattern which may emerge in these areas, although it seems doubtful that the "Deep South" can permanently avoid the national trend toward racial integration.

c. *New Laws Against Discrimination.* After a half-century of comparative inactivity, the past decade has brought a flood of proposals for new legal curbs on discrimination. In a single year (1949) no less than 149 bills opposing discrimination were introduced into state legislatures.[32] These proposals are of many sorts—anti-defamation laws, anti-segregation laws, and laws defining and affirming the rights and privileges of minorities.[33] The most important have been proposals for a "fair employment practices" law which would forbid employment discrimination on a basis of race, color, religion, or national origin.

Fair Employment Practices Legislation

Although efforts to extend employment opportunities of minorities are not new, agitation for fair employment practices legislation is a postwar development getting its initial impetus from the wartime Fair Employment Practices Committee. After much pressure and the threat of an embarrassing Negro "march on Washington," [34] President Roosevelt

[30] "Integration Finds Varied Reception: 'Old South' Resists Strongly But Progress in Border States Is Impressive," *New York Times* (October 3, 1954), pp. 1, 74; also "South Marking Time Now on School Segregation," *New York Times,* March 27, 1955, IV, p. 12.

[31] For a scholarly analysis of the problems involved in the attempt to desegregate Southern schools, see Harry S. Ashmore, *The Negro and The Schools* (Chapel Hill, University of North Carolina Press, 1954); see also Cabell Phillips, "What Happens When Segregation Ends," *New York Times Magazine,* May 30, 1954, pp. 7 ff., for a case history of local desegregation; also, Robin M. Williams and Margaret W. Ryan eds., *Schools in Transition: Community Experiences in Desegregation* (Chapel Hill, University of North Carolina Press, 1954).

[32] American Council on Race Relations, supplement to *Report,* Vol. IV, No. 8 (August, 1949).

[33] See John H. Burma, "Race Relations and Antidiscriminatory Legislation," *American Journal of Sociology,* 55 (March, 1951), pp. 416-423.

[34] Louis Ruchames, *Race, Jobs and Politics; The Story of FEPC* (New York, Columbia University Press, 1953), pp. 17-21.

established, in 1941, a Fair Employment Practices Committee (FEPC) [35] by executive order 8802 under his war powers as president. All federal departments and agencies "concerned with vocational and training programs for defense production" were ordered to administer these programs without discrimination, and all defense contracts were to include a "provision obligating the contractor not to discriminate against any worker because of race, creed, color, or national origin." After some confusion and further extension of authority,[36] the FEPC operated throughout the war. The committee was empowered to receive complaints, conduct investigations, hold hearings, issue subpoenas, issue findings of fact, and make recommendations. It could impose no legal penalties or fines but could threaten an employer with loss of man-power priorities or a striker with loss of draft deferment. It could recommend cancellation of a defense contract, but never did so lest the war effort suffer.[37] Despite these limited powers, the committee was successful in helping promote a great enlargement of Negro employment opportunities. "Between July, 1943 and December, 1944, the committee docketed a total of 5,803 complaints of discrimination which, at first glance, seemed to be valid. Of these, about 64 per cent were dismissed soon after docketing because of lack of merit, insufficient evidence, and other causes. The remaining 36 per cent were satisfactorily adjusted." [38] The proportion of Negroes among workers in war production nearly trebled, and the proportion of Negroes in the more highly skilled jobs showed striking increases.[39] In 1938, 90 per cent of Negro government employees in Washington were doing custodial work; this fell to 40 per cent, meaning that 60 per cent were in other (often better) jobs. Dozens of industries which had employed no Negroes, or who limited them to unskilled jobs, began hiring Negroes for many sorts and grades of service. During four years of FEPC, the Negroes made more progress towards occupational equality than they had made in the preceding half-century. The wartime labor shortage, the wartime emphasis upon democratic values, and the FEPC were all necessary for this accomplishment; but without FEPC, little change would have been likely. The violent and bitter attacks upon FEPC [40] appeared only after its success became apparent.

Following the end of FEPC in 1945, a revival of discriminatory practices began,[41] and stimulated proposals for permanent legislation.

[35] The abbreviations FEP, FEPC, and FEPA have become widely used to refer to "fair employment practices," "fair employment practices committee" and "fair employment practices act."

[36] Executive Order 9343 (1943).

[37] See Louis Ruchames, *op. cit.*, Ch. IX, "The Committee in Structure and Function."

[38] *Ibid.*, p. 159.

[39] *Ibid.*, p. 159-163.

[40] *Ibid.*, Chs. V, VI.

[41] *Ibid.*, pp. 134-136.

Although both Republican and Democratic parties supported fair employment practices legislation in their campaign platforms of 1944 and 1948, and numerous bills have been presented in the federal Congress, none has ever even come to a vote. There is more than a suspicion that certain members of both parties have been more interested in FEPC as campaign bait than as a legislative objective.[42]

Eleven states and twenty-eight cities had by 1953 enacted some sort of fair employment practices legislation. Eight states have laws with commissions empowered to enforce them.[43] One (Colorado) has a law applying only to public agencies, and two (Indiana and Wisconsin) have commissions with conciliatory powers only. The city ordinances vary widely in scope and provision for enforcement.

Unless FEP legislation includes provision for enforcement, including legal penalties and procedures for court action, the laws are relatively ineffective. All successful FEPC action relies heavily upon publicity and persuasion,[44] but these are likely to be effective only when backed by the implied threat of real penalties. Such penalties need rarely be used, if it is known that they *can* be used. Up to 1952, state FEPC's had investigated over 5000 complaints, but had ordered only five public hearings to enforce compliance, and resorted to court action only four times.[45] Purely voluntary and conciliatory programs are ineffective, as the Cleveland experience illustrates. After a thirteen-month trial of a voluntary program which the Cleveland Chamber of Commerce planned, directed, staffed, and financed at a cost of over $30,000, the Chamber of Commerce agreed that it was a failure and joined in support of a compulsory FEP ordinance.[46]

Business management strongly opposed FEP legislation when first proposed. Like all other groups, businessmen include a share of prejudiced persons busily rationalizing their prejudices. And the businessman's traditional dislike of "government interference" and his fear that FEP laws would provoke "trouble" and disrupt production led him to prefer to drop the entire matter. These fears have proven to be largely groundless. The expected "trouble" did not materialize, and there is little business opposition and considerable business support for FEP legislation in those places where it has been tried. A survey of employers reported in 1950 by *Business Week* revealed that "employers agree that FEPC laws haven't caused near the fuss that opponents predicted.... Personal friction hasn't been at all serious ... even those who opposed an FEPC aren't actively

---

[42] *Ibid.*, Ch. XIII.

[43] New York, New Jersey, Massachusetts, Connecticut, New Mexico, Oregon, Rhode Island, and Washington.

[44] Louis Ruchames, *op. cit.*, pp. 143 ff., 154, 183.

[45] John A. Davis, "Negro Employment: A Progress Report," *Fortune,* 46 (July, 1952), pp. 102 ff.

[46] *Ibid.*

hostile now." [47] Employers find that FEP laws "get management off the hook" and help them in dealing with those who threaten "trouble." [48]

Organized labor support has varied. In general the industrial unions (C.I.O.) do not practice discrimination and have supported FEP legislation. The trade or craft unions (A.F.L. unions, railway unions) often practiced discrimination, and unions have been the respondents (offenders) in 10 per cent of the complaints made to the New York Commission.[49] Many of these trade unions have shown little enthusiasm for FEPA. Numerous chuch groups, racial conciliation groups, and assorted liberal groups have strongly supported FEPA. Public opinion appears to be generally favorable, with one survey showing that even in the South, the supposed citadel of discrimination, 48 per cent of the workers favor FEPA.[50]

The Legal Approach to Discrimination

How successfully can prejudice and discrimination be reduced by law? The cliché, "you can't prevent prejudice by passing a law," is true, but the *expression* of prejudice can be controlled by law. No law can force Catholics and Protestants to like each other, but laws do prohibit them from burning each other's churches; and by discouraging the violence upon which hatred feeds, the law indirectly encourages Catholic and Protestant to like each other better. Wherever law can reduce the *expression* of prejudice, the prejudice itself tends to decline.

A law is enforceable in a free society only when backed by a preponderant public opinion. In civil rights legislation, the problem is one of determining what measures will receive enough support to be enforceable. A proposal such as FEPA might find the people of an area divided roughly into five groups:

a. Strong supporters, who will contribute time and money to pass a law, and actively press for its enforcement.
b. Passive supporters, with definite approval but limited interest; will not become active unless prodded and organized by others.
c. The indifferent, with little interest and no definite convictions; likely to follow course of least resistance and side with the majority.
d. Passive opponents, with definite disapproval but limited interest; will not become active unless prodded and organized by others.
e. Strong opponents, who will contribute time and money to defeat a proposed law, and will actively seek to prevent its enforcement.

[47] "Does State FEPC Hamper You?" *Business Week*, No. 1069 (February 5, 1950), pp. 114-117.
[48] John A. Davis, *op. cit.*
[49] "FEPC: New York Version," *Fortune*, 42 (September, 1950), pp. 50 ff.
[50] Conducted by McGraw-Hill Research Department, reported in "What the Worker Thinks," *Factory*, CVII (November, 1949), p. 105.

The possibility of passing and enforcing a law depends upon the relative size, and the power and influence, of groups *a* and *b* compared to groups *d* and *e*. Law can check the intolerant only when the actively intolerant form a relatively small minority. But in the absence of law, *this intolerant minority can nullify the good will of the majority* by insisting that all social policy be fitted to their prejudice. A bigoted 5 per cent, by loudly refusing to work beside Negroes, can neutralize the good will of the remaining 95 per cent. If one-tenth of the hotel guests object to Jews, they are permitted to outvote the 90 per cent who do not object. The absence of law allows an intolerant minority to coerce the majority into acceding to their prejudices, and forces the liberal into the role of the busybody who "stirs up trouble."

The passing of an antidiscrimination law, if accompanied by publicity, machinery for enforcement, and a determined effort at enforcement, alters this picture dramatically. *It reverses the "trouble-maker" role;* the intolerant person now becomes the "trouble-maker" when he darkly hints of "trouble" or demands that the employer or restaurateur evade the law. *The burden of action is shifted;* it is now up to the bigot to "start something," and experience has shown that in most cases the dire predictions of the bigots peter out into futile grumbling. *The pattern of conformity behavior is changed;* nondiscrimination becomes the approved status quo, and all those who follow the course of least resistance now find that nondiscrimination is the least bother. While it is often possible to evade the law through various subterfuges, this may become such a nuisance that compliance with the law is the lesser inconvenience. For all these reasons, a carefully-drawn law with machinery for enforcement *changes the balance of power* between tolerant and intolerant groups. In the outline above, if groups *a* and *b* are larger than, or even as large (influential) as, groups *d* and *e*, it should not be difficult to enforce the law under consideration. Groups *a* and *b* will actively support the law; group *c*, the indifferent, will "go along with" the law because that has become the course of least resistance. These three groups now comprise the majority, whereas *d* and *e* are the deserted minority. Group *d*, the passive opponents, will grumble, but are unlikely to take obstructive action in the face of a determined effort to enforce the law. "Trouble" is likely to develop only when law-enforcement officials betray a disinterest in energetic enforcement. Group *e*, the strong opponents, find themselves a small and lonely minority, hesitant to "start anything" without support.

Where a proposed antidiscrimination law finds those who are actively opposed to be more numerous or influential than those who support it, that law is obviously unenforceable and probably will not even be enacted. We have generally been quite conservative in passing such laws, for we have usually overestimated the opposition to their enforcement. Recent efforts at enforcing such laws have produced remarkably little of the "trouble" hopefully predicted by the intolerant and uneasily feared by the tolerant.

The Administrative Attack Upon Discrimination

In a "folk society," people behave according to the attitudes and values they have absorbed through primary-group association. In the modern "mass society," however, much of one's behavior consists of playing a designated role as a member of some secondary group. Behavior in secondary-group relationships is impersonal and segmental, dictated less by personal attitudes and feelings than by the formal obligations of one's role. Thus, the teacher, salesman, and porter regularly display behavior which is contrary to their private feelings, because such behavior is part of their job—is demanded as part of the role they fill. In the mass society, deliberately organized collectivities—labor unions, professional organizations, administrative officials of business organizations and governmental departments, and others—define the behavior expected of personnel in specific situations.

This helps explain many inconsistencies in racial attitudes and behavior. The teacher is, as a teacher, expected to treat Negro and white pupils alike, but as a homeowner is likely to support other homeowners in seeking to "protect" the neighborhood against Negro invasion. Studies have shown little or no statistical correlation between acceptance of Negroes as fellow-workers and acceptance of Negroes as neighbors.[51] Many other inconsistencies may be due to the fact that people increasingly act in specific situations in terms of their respective roles as workers, homeowners, merchants, and so on.

Such an analysis suggests that a person's race attitudes and prejudices may be less important than his role obligations in controlling his behavior. Instead of trying to change his over-all race attitudes and prejudices, it may be more effective to ignore these and simply redefine his expected behavior in specific situations. The National Maritime Union has been successful in a policy which bluntly tells its members, in effect, "Feel as you wish, but if you refuse to ship out with Negroes, you don't ship out."[52] Police in several cities have been highly successful in preventing racial incidents from blossoming into violence[53]

... after a program of training of the police, which stressed their role and responsibility in the maintenance of law and order without reference to their personal feelings and beliefs.... The training of the police was not designed

[51] Joseph D. Lohman and Dietrich C. Reitzes, "Note on Race Relations in Mass Society," *American Journal of Sociology*, 58 (November, 1952), pp. 240-246.

[52] Cf. *New York Times*, May 27, 1946. "The Stand of the U.M.N. on Discrimination" is stated in the union's publication, *Equality for All*.

[53] Joseph D. Lohman and Dietrich C. Reitzes, *op. cit.*

to effect changes in their personal attitudes and prejudices but solely to redefine and set forth their role as professional law-enforcement agents in the
implementing of public policy.

It is uncertain just how far it is possible to alter racial behavior by
ignoring race attitudes and redefining roles. Presumably, there are limits
to the degree to which collective or administrative redefinition of roles
can be expected to overpower traditional habits and attitudes. To date,
however, the combination of legal and administrative redefinitions has
been highly effective in altering racial behavior, and continued use of
these techniques may be expected. Since there is evidence that each
change in racial behavior has an eventual effect upon race attitudes,
thereby reducing the potential resistance to further changes in racial
behavior, it is conceivable that this technique may eventually "solve"
the race problem in the United States.

PROSPECTS FOR THE NEAR FUTURE

In a highly dynamic society, race relations cannot possibly stand still.
For a half century or more, educational opportunities for Negroes were
steadily being extended while occupational opportunities were being contracted. This paradox put explosive pressure behind the Negro demand
for greater equality of treatment. The growing insistence of Negro demands, the destruction of the popular theories supporting discrimination,
the wartime labor shortage, the wartime emphasis on democratic values,
and the election of a pair of highly sympathetic presidents (Roosevelt and Truman) all combined to create a period of the most rapid
Negro advance in our history. In a little more than a decade, the gap between white and Negro educational expenditure was reduced by one-
half,[54] and the median income of Negro workers rose from 40 per cent
up to 52 per cent of the median income for white workers.[55] This is far
from equality, but it also is a very rapid improvement in Negro status.

How long the present equalitarian wave will continue is uncertain. A
business depression with serious unemployment would almost certainly
reverse the present trend towards more and better jobs for Negroes. Only
those who feel relatively secure themselves are likely to feel generous
toward minorities. Tension and warfare between America and fascist
countries, noted for their persecution of minorities, stimulated America
to emphasize the democratic values of political freedom and equality,
but tension with communist countries seems to be having an opposite
effect. In communist countries, persecution on a basis of *race* has virtually

[54] See Table 12-1.
[55] U. S. Department of Labor, *Negroes in the U.S.* (Washington, Government
Printing Office, 1952). Income figures for 1939 and 1950.

ceased,[56] and communist propagandists talk greatly about racial equality and justice. This means that tension with communist countries—since we emphasize our *differences* from them—does not particularly encourage our movement towards racial equality. It may even retard it, since those who are actively supporting racial equality then come under attack as "pro-communist." [57] In these respects, the next decade looks far less favorable for racial "advance" than the last two decades.

But there are other forces more favorable to minority rights. The popularization of the scientific facts about race and race prejudice continues to demolish the popular rationale behind race prejudice, which year by year grows more tattered and disreputable. The momentum of the drive for racial opportunity will not abruptly subside. Negroes and their friends have a taste of victory and are gaining the income and status from which to press effectively for further improvements. The probability that no national administration will permit a severe depression to develop is a measure of protection of present Negro gains. The industrialization of the South, and the industrial unions which follow, are possibly the most important single factor promoting Negro advance in the South. The economic development and rising prosperity of the South give her greater means with which to finance better schools and public services for Negroes. Most important of all, recent experience has shown that it is not necessary to purchase racial peace at the price of supine inaction, for we now know that there are areas where segregation and discrimination can be attacked directly, and that such an attack will result in reducing prejudice and conflict.

For all these reasons, it is likely that the present trend towards racial equality will continue for at least another decade or more. The segregated past is irretrievably gone, and the present generation is learning to live in an increasingly nonsegregated society. As a distinguished Southern newspaper editor writes, "Segregation is on its way out, and he who tries to tell the people otherwise does them a great disservice. The problem of the future is how to learn to live with the change." [58] Although these changes are deeply disturbing to many persons, and sporadic minor conflicts will appear, the trend of race conflict turns downward as segregation and

---

[56] It should be needless to add that many other forms of persecution abound in communist lands, and that freedom, as we know it, does not exist under communism. The "racial justice" of a communist state is based not on principles of human dignity and spiritual equality, but upon political expediency. To a communist movement seeking the loyalty of the world's discontented masses, racial persecution would not "pay." It is quite possible, however, that at some future moment, racism might become useful to a communist regime. In fact, it appears that anti-Semitism was being considered in Russia just before Stalin's death.

[57] Every major organization seeking to advance minority rights in America has been accused of "communism" by one or more of the Congressional committees which claim to be "exposing communism."

[58] Ralph McGill, editor of the *Atlanta Constitution*, quoted in *Time* (December 4, 1953), p. 51.

discrimination are reduced. Although these developments are primarily concerned with whites and Negroes, the problems involving the other minorities—Jews, American Indians, Americans of Oriental or Mexican ancestry, and still others—differ only in detail, and the developments are likely to be much the same.

Whether viewed on a local or a world scene, the race problem is both America's Achilles heel and her opportunity. Which we choose to make it is a choice between values, with moral confusion, economic waste, and international debility the price we must pay for protecting our prejudices. As Myrdal sums it up: [59]

If America in actual practice could show the world a progressive trend by which the Negro became finally integrated into modern democracy, all mankind would be given faith again—it would have reason to believe that peace, progress, and order are feasible. And America would have a spiritual power many times stronger than all her financial and military resources—the power of the trust and support of all good people on earth. *America is free to choose whether the Negro shall remain her liability or become her opportunity.*

SUGGESTED READINGS

ALLPORT, Gordon W., *ABC's of Scapegoating* (New York, Anti-Defamation League of B'nai B'rith, 1948). A concise pamphlet describing the scapegoat theory of race prejudice.

BENEDICT, Ruth, and WELTFISH, Gene, *The Races of Mankind*, Public Affairs Pamphlet No. 85 (New York, Public Affairs Committee, 1943). Probably the finest brief summary of the scientific facts about race available, interestingly written in nontechnical language.

BERRY, Brewton, *Race Relations* (Boston, Houghton Mifflin Company, 1951). A highly stimulating and readable textbook in race relations.

DAVIS, Allison, and DOLLARD, John, *Children of Bondage* (Washington, American Council on Education, 1940). Uses the case-analysis method to reveal the differing effects of racial experience upon Negro children in the South.

FRAZIER, E. Franklin, *The Negro in the United States* (New York, The Macmillan Company, 1949). A history of Negroes in the United States, and of their progress and frustrations in American society.

HALSEY, Margaret, *Color Blind* (New York, Simon & Schuster, Inc., 1946). An entertaining, popular account of a nonsegregated service mens' club operated successfully by the author during the war.

PUBLIC AFFAIRS COMMITTEE, *Segregation and the Schools*, Pamphlet No. 209 (New York, Public Affairs Committee, 1954). A summary of Harry S. Ashmore's *The Negro and the Schools;* describes the special problems of education in the South, and their bearing upon the imminent integration of its schools.

RUCHAMES, Louis, *Race, Jobs, and Politics* (New York, Columbia University Press, 1953). A history and evaluation of fair employment legislation in the United States.

SIMPSON, George E., and YINGER, J. Milton, *Racial and Cultural Minorities* (New York, Harper and Brothers, 1953). An encyclopedic textbook in race relations; useful as a secondary source on almost any racial topic.

[59] *Op. cit.*, pp. 1021-1022.

U. S. Department of Labor, *Negroes in the United States* (Washington, Government Printing Office, 1952). A booklet giving much statistical data about the employment and economic status of American Negroes.

AUDIO-VISUAL AIDS

Americans All (McGraw-Hill Book Company, Inc., Text-Film Department, 330 West 42nd St., New York), 16 minutes, sound, black and white. A March of Time film, surveying racial and religious tensions in the United States, and of programs for reducing them, especially through intercultural education.

Brotherhood for Survival (National Conference of Christians and Jews, 381 Fourth Ave., New York), 11 minutes, sound, black and white. Describes the program of the National Conference of Christians and Jews for promoting understanding.

Brotherhood of Man (Brandon Films, Inc., 200 West 57th, New York), 10 minutes, sound, color. An animated film, humorously showing that dissimilarities between peoples result from environmental influences. Based on the pamphlet, "Races of Mankind," by Ruth Benedict and Gene Weltfish.

Picture in Your Mind (McGraw-Hill Book Company, Inc., Text-Film Department, 330 West 42nd, New York), 16 minutes, sound, color. A highly effective film depicting the tribal roots of prejudice and the manner in which distorted images of other groups arise.

Prejudice (Broadcasting and Film Commission, 220 Fifth Ave., New York) 60 minutes, sound, black and white. A man who imagines himself to be unprejudiced comes to realize his prejudice when prejudice is directed at his own family, and he learns that bigotry threatens everyone.

That All Men Are Created Equal (United Auto Workers—A.F.L., Milwaukee), 15 minutes, sound, color. A cartoon film based on the pamphlet, "Turnover Talks for Fair Practices," which labor groups have used for some years in fighting discrimination against minority groups.

The Challenge (McGraw-Hill Book Company, Inc., Text-Film Department, 330 West 42nd, New York), 30 minutes, sound, black and white. Based on findings of the President's Commission on Civil Rights, revealing many kinds of discrimination in the United States.

The High Wall (McGraw-Hill Book Company, Inc., Text-Film Department, 330 West 42nd, New York), 32 minutes, sound, black and white. A case study showing how a young bigot became "infected" and how his home life encouraged the development of prejudice.

QUESTIONS AND PROJECTS

1. What are the scientific facts about race differences?

2. Define the "race problem" according to each of two or three different sets of values.

3. Who bears the "costs" of the race problem? In what ways?

4. What is race prejudice? Is lack of race prejudice closely correlated with intelligence, knowledge about other races, or contact with other races?

5. Why do prejudiced people usually deny that they are prejudiced?

6. What are the theories of the causes of prejudice? Is any one adequate?

7. What is the function of myths and evasions in protecting prejudice?

8. Is it possible for the minority member to remain unaffected by prejudice and discrimination? What are some common minority reactions?

9. What effect does discrimination against a minority group have upon members of the majority group?

10. How have race problems grown out of the disorganization of earlier social arrangements? Is a new equilibrium in process of development?

11. How did World War II affect race relations in the United States?

12. In what way is every race "problem" the product of a value-conflict?

13. What value-judgments are implied in Fair Employment Practices Legislation? In the doctrine of "separate but equal" facilities?

14. Is the prejudiced or the unprejudiced person the "social deviant"?

15. Why do extremist social movements so often include violent race prejudices in their ideology?

16. To what extent will prejudice be reduced by spreading the scientific facts about races and race differences?

17. What difficulties are met in the effort to reduce prejudice by propaganda?

18. Under what conditions will increased social contact between races lead to a reduction of prejudice?

19. Why were racial liberals so long fearful of taking any action in seeking to change race relations? How and why has this attitude changed within recent years?

20. Is segregation a "successful" way of dealing with race relations? What are its results? What value-judgments are involved in answering this question?

21. Which do social scientists think more effective: to reduce discrimination by first reducing prejudice, or to reduce prejudice by first reducing discrimination? Why?

22. Is passing laws an effective means of changing race relations?

23. Do race relations in the United States automatically "get better" as time passes?

CHAPTER 14

Problems of Urban and Rural Communities

... From samples of Los Angeles air (collected on both smoggy and clear days), the experimenters filtered out the chemicals. They painted the resulting gook on the backs of black mice. In little more than a year, 29% of the surviving mice developed malignant tumors.[1]

The sky over Chicago turned an eerie shade of yellow-brown one afternoon last week, and a menacing twilight fell over the Loop—powdery topsoil, blown in from the Great Plains, was drifting once more in the upper atmosphere. It was a fearful reminder that the flatlands of the midcontinent, which had a green and healing decade of rain in the 1940's, are dry again. This spring dust storms such as have not been seen since the 'black blizzards' of the 1930's are blowing in the Southwest, in western Kansas, in areas of Nebraska, Missouri, Wyoming, and Colorado. ... The wreckage of field is only one aspect of the drought. Almost everywhere in the drought area and in many peripheral regions the water table has dropped alarmingly. Thousands of wells have run dry. In Missouri as in many a nearby state water is being hauled in trucks, tank cars and barrels from more fortunate spots. The drought has even affected cities. Some residents of Oklahoma City are drilling wells in their yards as insurance against shortage, and many houses in St. Louis and Kansas City are settling and cracking in the ash-dry earth.[2]

... at the last count, only a fraction of 1% of the available office space was unoccupied. But people who remember Frank Lloyd Wright's prophecy that cities will die and grass grow in the streets are worried about the new office buildings choking the midtown area. Grass may never grow in the streets, but it may some day grow on the roofs of the cars caught in the daily 5 o'clock traffic jam.[3]

BOTH city and country are vast—and heterogeneous. The city means theaters and taxis, squalid slums, teeming traffic, graft and corruption, housing developments, areas of "homeless men," penthouse apartments, juvenile gang wars, quiet streets, "smog" and "smaze," and much more. The country includes the sharecropper's windowless shack, prosperous dairy farms, one and one-half acre plots, the "dust bowl," outhouses, and ruined crops from rain and drought. Neither city nor country has a

[1] Reprinted from *Time;* copyright Time Inc. 1954.
[2] Reprinted from *Time;* copyright Time Inc. 1954.
[3] Reprinted from *Time;* copyright Time Inc. 1953.

monopoly on poverty, debauchery, or disaster. To understand the problems of one requires knowledge of the other. One aspect of the problem is relatively new—the tremendous growth of cities. We shall start with that.

THE GROWTH OF CITIES

It is not the city as such that is new, for ancient history revolves around such cities as Rome, Athens, Jerusalem, and Constantinople. That which *is* relatively new concerns (1) the large size of many modern cities, (2) the large number of modern cities, and (3) the growing proportion of the total population which now lives in cities.

Large Size

The cities of ancient and medieval times were not at all large by modern standards. London in the year 1400 had only about 35,000 inhabitants and was the largest city in Europe. Modern cities by contrast are behemoths. If we consider only that portion of the city population living within the corporate limits, the United States has five urban centers each with more than a million people. New York, Chicago, Detroit, Los Angeles, and Philadelphia together contain more than 17 million people. To define as urban, however, only the population living inside the corporation limits is sociologically unrealistic. A large proportion of the people who are functionally a part of large cities actually live outside the city limits. New York City contains approximately 8 million people, but greater New York contains over 12 million people. In 1950, for the first time, the United States Census reported "urbanized areas" in order to include as urban all of the people who effectively are a part of urban life. There are *twelve* urbanized areas in the United States *each with over a million population.* According to preliminary counts of the 1950 census, they are: [4]

New York-Northeastern New Jersey	12,222,963
Chicago	4,902,801
Los Angeles	3,970,595
Philadelphia	2,913,516
Detroit	2,644,476
Boston	2,218,893
San Francisco-Oakland	1,997,303
Pittsburgh	1,525,966
St. Louis	1,394,051
Cleveland	1,372,274
Washington, D. C.	1,281,572
Baltimore	1,151,050

[4] "The Urban Population of the United States, 1950 Census of Population: Preliminary Counts" in Paul K. Hatt and Albert J. Reiss, Jr., eds., *Reader in Urban Sociology* (Glencoe, Ill., The Free Press, 1951), p. 62. Statistics in this and the following two sections draw heavily upon this very excellent summary.

The Number of Cities

Unfortunately, there is a tendency among many people to equate urban life with that which exists in New York or Chicago. There are 4270 urban places in the United States. Most of these are incorporated places of 2500 or more population, but also included are some smaller incorporated places and some unincorporated areas, around cities, that are definitely urban in character. The United States is not organized primarily around any one city, any five cities, or any hundred cities. Certain industries and certain products may be identified with a particular urban center, for example, automobiles in Detroit and garment-making in Philadelphia and New York, but there are at least several hundred cities serving as primary sources for employment, commerce and trade, public utility services, newspaper publication, and many other goods and services that are an essential part of modern life. Just as the early part of the present century saw unparalleled growth and centralization in the largest cities, more recent decades have witnessed increases in the numbers of smaller cities. The present 4270 urban places represents a gain of 806 over 1940 and a gain of 1105 over 1930.

Population in Cities

In 1790 only 5 per cent of the United States population was urban. New York has less than 60,000 people. By 1950, 64 per cent of the population was defined as urban. The urban portion of the population ranged from

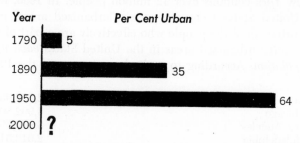

FIG. 14-1. The United States Becomes an Urban Nation. (Data from Historical Statistics of the United States, 1789-1945, p. 25; and U. S. Bureau of the Census, Statistical Abstract of the United States: 1954 [Washington, Government Printing Office], p. 27)

less than half in the South to almost four-fifths in the Northeast. Five separate states had more than four out of every five inhabitants living in urban areas, and thirty states had half or more of their population living in urban areas.[5] One-fourth of the total United States population resides in the twelve urbanized areas of a million or more population listed in the

[5] *Ibid.* p. 59.

preceding section, and over half of the total population lives in standard metropolitan areas.[6] Thus the United States has become a very much urbanized nation. Large central cities and extensive metropolitan areas are a fundamental part of modern life. The development of such urban centers has been accompanied by the appearance of a whole series of problems to which we now turn.

THE PROBLEMS OF CITIES

The census usually defines urban places in terms of whether or not incorporation has occurred and in terms of the absolute numbers of people involved. For some purposes this kind of definition is adequate; for others, it is not. Even the census is moving toward a *social* definition of city, toward a definition which recognizes the peculiar qualities of urban life as well as the number of people included. The classic sociological definition of city is, "... a city may be defined as a relatively large, dense, and permanent settlement of socially heterogeneous individuals."[7] Many of the special problems of cities result from large numbers of very unlike persons living very close together.

Heterogeneity and Anonymity

Birth rates vary markedly from one part of the city to another but for the city as a whole they are quite low. City people do not have enough children even to replace themselves, let alone enough to account for the continuous growth characteristic of many cities. Most sizable cities, consequently, include large numbers of persons who were not born there—people who have come from the most varied of backgrounds and with widely divergent expectations of urban life. Moreover, these migrants move into certain areas of the city with sufficient regularity that the city takes on a *pattern* defined by the types of people and the types of living that characterize each area. The pattern will vary in detail from one city to another according to the type of economic base, special features of topography, the age of the city, and still other factors. If these limitations are kept in mind, however, it is possible to specify some of the dominant features of each area as one moves outward from the center of the city. The major areas indicated by Roman numerals in Figure 14-2 are somewhat self-explanatory. The central business district generally has little or no permanent residency, with some permanent residence beginning in Zone II amid the manufacturing and wholesale businesses frequenting

---

[6] Standard metropolitan areas contain at least one, and sometimes more than one, city of at least 50,000 population plus an adjacent county or counties meeting specified criteria of urban character. *Ibid.*, pp. 63-67.

[7] Louis Wirth, "Urbanism as a Way of Life," *American Journal of Sociology*, 44 (July, 1938), p. 8.

that area. Moving outward from Zone II, dingy rooming houses, flats, and apartments are gradually replaced by better single houses with larger yards and relatively more absence of business establishments. As one approaches the periphery, large open spaces, farms, new housing developments, and even heavy industry may appear to disrupt and distort the pattern. Often, too, features most characteristic of Zones II and III may extend outward in a narrow belt well into Zone IV and even Zone V.

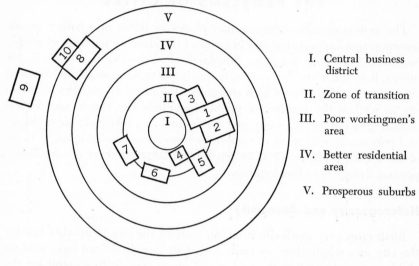

I.   Central business district

II. Zone of transition

III. Poor workingmen's area

IV. Better residential area

V.   Prosperous suburbs

1. Negro area
2. Italian, Greek, and other ethnic areas
3. Slums, tenements
4. Homeless men area
5. Red-light district
6. "Bohemian" colonies
7. Rooming house area
8. New housing development
9. Large industry
10. Shopping center

FIG. 14-2. Social and Spatial Plan of the Modern City

Superimposed upon this general pattern are likely to appear all and more of the features designated by Arabic numerals in Figure 14-2. Generally it is the areas closest to the center of the city that are most heterogeneous, most anonymous, and where "social controls" are least effective. Family and neighborhood ties found in the suburbs are often weak and even lacking. Landlords "don't ask questions," and frequent moving discourages the establishment of close friendships. The high ratio of men to women, and the lack of adequate finances in both sexes, discourages the normal drift into marriage and respectability, and increases the proportion of temporary illicit unions. Thus the curious paradox that the most densely populated areas of the city are often the loneliest. Deviant persons of all sorts drift into the area because of the protection which its anonymity affords. The still fairly conventional persons obliquely witness the deviancy all around them and gradually become more vulnerable themselves. Heterogeneity and anonymity not only draw deviants, they produce deviants.

Not only is there extreme heterogeneity within the central areas of the city, but there are wide differences between areas. Communication between areas is even less adequate than that which exists within the central zone. Most suburb-dwellers know little and care less about the problems of the slum-dwellers, and vice versa. Common values and goals shared by all the population are conspicuous by their absence. The population of a city is an aggregation or a conglomeration; rarely is it an *organization*. The importance of the absence of ties among the various areas of the city will become evident in a later section.

Blighted Areas

Certain areas of the modern city may be likened to malignant growths on a living organism. They develop through the same processes which give life to the city as a whole, but they are largely parasitic, continuously growing, and draining more and more of the city's life blood. These are the blighted areas—the areas undergoing, or having undergone, degeneration. Crime, poverty, delinquency, prostitution, gambling, drug addiction, mental illness, tuberculosis, infant and maternal mortality, all are concentrated here. Rat-infested slums, filthy streets, crumbling buildings long since declared firetraps and frequently condemned, pawnshops, second-hand clothing stores, taverns, and "greasy spoons"—these are the physical habitat. Such blighted areas literally "prey" upon the rest of the city. The run-down buildings of the area pay relatively little in the way of taxes, though landlords often charge extremely high rents and reap fantastic profits. The cost of providing police and fire protection, borne by the city at large, may be two or three times as high as in other areas. The proportion of gainfully employed is painfully low, and "relief" payments of all sorts flood into the area. Children play in the streets; there is no other place. Graduation from grade school is frequently followed by "matriculation" at reform school. Then it is an easy step to prison, all at the rate of $600 per prisoner per year, paid by taxpayers. Health needs are met, if at all, by public-health departments and by "free" clinics which are exorbitantly expensive to run. Slum clearance and "low-cost" public housing is still an additional form of subsidy. The modern slum embodies all that is un-American. "The promised land?"—a cruel joke! "Faith in the future?"—resignation and despair! "Responsibility for self and family?"—at the mercy of economic conditions and charitable agencies! "A benefit of democracy?"—ready-made propaganda for the totalitarian world!

Congestion

Death by strangulation! Both literally and figuratively, the metropolis bodes to be choked out of existence.

Depletion and Contamination. As it expanded upward, the city became a densely packed conglomeration of industry upon industry, apartment upon apartment, store upon store, and people upon people. Little thought was given to the adequacy of two previously unlimited and essential commodities—air and water. For many decades no limitations became apparent. More recently both air and water have sometimes been in short supply. The potential shortage of water appeared first.

Cities over much of the nation have been faced by two uncomfortable facts: tremendously increased needs for water, and a dropping water table. Modern industry uses water in prodigiously increasing quantities. The location of many modern plants depends as much upon the availability of an adequate water supply as upon the nearness to raw materials and labor. And many cities no longer have water to spare. Even a slight drought lowers many reservoirs dangerously. The summer pastime of sprinkling one's lawn has occasionally become a matter for legal regulation, and toward evening the water pressure may lower noticeably. Nor is it just a matter of inadequate storage facilities. Wells must be drilled deeper and deeper and communities struggle bitterly for their fair share of river and lake water. Parts of the West and South have already found their programs to encourage growth and industrialization frustrated by inadequate water resources. The rest of the country is not far behind.

Obviously, there is no shortage of air in the absolute sense. But cities are increasingly producing a shortage of uncontaminated, "breathable" air. As much as twenty years ago it was fashionable to point out that the lungs of urban adults tended toward a dirty black, whereas those of rural adults remained a healthy pink. The soot, dust, and grime of city life showed up here even if they did not materially shorten the life span. Twenty years ago it was largely a matter of amusement. Today, however, it has become quite serious. The most serious incident to date was the great London "smog" of 1952 that directly and indirectly caused the deaths of 4,000 people. But the United States doesn't have fogs comparable to those of England. True. But just as this is being written a new term, *smaze,* has come into our vocabulary. A pall of smoke, dirt, pulverized asphalt and rubber, "fly ash" and haze, hanging for several days over New York City, resulted in thousands of cases of respiratory irritation, created a need for greatly increased medical attention, and kept people indoors to protect their health. Los Angeles is now as famous for its "smog" as for its sunshine, and from out on the highway a murky cloud up ahead is often one of the first signs of entrance into a city. In scattered instances, the clouds over industrial cities have been directly, though temporarily, lethal. Investigating commissions have been appointed to reduce the possibility of such occurrences in the future. Yet they promise to increase both in severity and number in the years to come. Cities are, literally, showing signs of strangulation.

Traffic Congestion. The spread of cities outward has encouraged strangulation of another sort. The development of the automobile and other rapid transportation encouraged people to live at some distance from the city's center where substantial proportions of them work, shop, and do business. Early in the morning they pour through highways and streets into the city's center, there merge with the heavy flow of commercial traffic which keeps business and industry operating, and in the evening fight their way back out again. Until recently, the system worked fairly well. The same streets which once accommodated horse and wagon now handled automobile traffic, and great superhighways were constructed to move traffic quickly from one city to another. But the city has proved the bottleneck. Central city streets fronted by ten-story buildings cannot easily be widened and it is no longer merely a joke that pedestrians move more rapidly than automobiles.

One problem is that of "parking." Practically all cities face a shortage of convenient parking space and in large cities the thousands of cars milling around and jockeying for parking places greatly increase the over-all congestion. The problem is complicated by two factors: first, land values are so high in the city's center that the woefully inefficient, traditional parking garage frequently cannot pay its way financially; and second, the motorist demands parking space convenient to his destination. One estimate states that if he has to walk over a thousand feet, the average motorist would rather park in a restricted area and take a chance of getting a ticket.[8] Many city-planning specialists believe that part of the answer to the problem is a yet-to-be-invented satisfactory automatic parking garage. The increased efficiency of an automatic system that would take automobiles off the street and disgorge them again at the rate of several per minute would make it a paying proposition. Varying numbers of strategically placed "parketerias" would largely solve the parking problem.

Unfortunately, the parking problem cannot really be solved apart from the larger traffic problem. Even if automobiles could be quickly taken off and put back on the streets again, the roadway system could not handle the volume of traffic. Within minutes the super-efficient parking garage would grind to a halt because of the traffic jam in the street before it. Some means of rapidly shuttling tremendous numbers of cars out of the central city is essential. Limited access, express roadways seem to be the

[8] William Zeckendorf, "Parking in the Sky," *Atlantic Monthly,* 191 (June, 1953), p. 34.

only answer. But the doing is not so simple. Many expensive buildings would have to be condemned and torn down, the cost of the roadway system alone would be tremendous, and opposition would be forthcoming from myriads of vested interests who derive some profit from present conditions. We can only conclude that any large-scale solution to these problems is many years in the future. Some cities will move faster than others, and here and there a specific parking or roadway system will be held out as a "shining example," but parking and traffic will remain a major urban headache.

That extreme concentration of facilities and population around a single urban center is not an unmixed blessing is indicated by the course of events of roughly the past twenty years. Up to 1930, growth was most rapid in the largest of cities. But the 1930 census indicated the start of a new trend—suburbanization. Some of the population was literally forced outward by the density farther in, but there also appeared a positive ideology in favor of suburban living. The desire to escape soot, grime, noise, and traffic, to have yards, gardens, and a healthy place to raise children, helped create a new urban pattern. Since 1930 the rate of growth of medium-sized cities has generally outstripped that of the great population centers, and the growth of the largest cities has been concentrated in outlying areas. Moreover, service facilities, shopping centers and the like, and even industry, have followed the population outward. Many suburban centers today are almost as self-sufficient and as heterogeneous as the central city. Some of them are incorporated separately, some are within the central city limits, some fall within two or more political subdivisions, and most of them keep spreading outward into what politically is rural territory. This transformation and expansion aggravates some existing problems and helps create some new ones.

Political and Economic Problems

It is unrealistic in many ways to define the city as that which exists within the corporation limits. Yet, *legally* the city is just that—that which lies within the corporate boundaries. In actual practice, large open spaces may lie within the city limits and the urban population extend for many miles beyond them. The power of the city to legislate and to regulate is determined by the location of the corporation limits, not by the location of the population.

Governing Problems. American cities have rarely been known for good government. On the contrary they have been fountainheads of graft, corruption, and inefficiency. To be a city official has more than occasionally been a forerunner to public disgrace and even to imprisonment. Names such as Hague and Kelly symbolize the city bosses and the intricate sub-rosa structures they represent. The internal corruption characteristic of so many cities is further complicated by inability to enforce the law outside the city limits. Where suburbs are incorporated separately or two central cities exist side by side, there are two or more sets of laws and law-enforcement agencies in a single urban area. "Businesses" and practices such as gambling, liquor sales, and prostitution, vigorously prosecuted in one area, simply move "across the line" and operate virtually un-molested. Even when there is no conflict of policy among the separate municipalities, rarely is there sufficient co-operation among them to make effective law enforcement feasible. Communities quarrel over "who is to blame," and the illicit activity goes on and on.

Efficient city government depends upon both a responsible administration and the relative absence of conflicting jurisdictions. The most satisfactory solution to date to the problem of general administration seems to be the "city-manager" plan where management of the city and its affairs is taken out of politics and vested in the hands of an "expert" who is expected to run the city much in accord with the practices involved in running large businesses. The chief limitation of this plan is that since he may be "fired" as well as "hired," the city manager is sometimes dominated by the very groups whom he is supposed to replace. Even at its best, however, the plan offers no solution to the relationships among several adjacent city corporations.

Financing Problems. City taxes have generally shown large increases over the past fifteen years. Real-estate taxes have risen, city income taxes adopted, city automobile taxes appeared, school taxes increased, personal property levies raised, and so on. Life has become increasingly expensive for urban residents, and yet many cities are in dire financial straits. The suburban trend is a major factor in this situation.

Urban facilities such as banks, businesses, theaters, and streets serve the neighboring suburban and rural populations as well as that of the central city. Large proportions of the noncity population work in the city, drawing sustenance from it, helping deteriorate its streets, contributing to its traffic and police problems, benefiting from its administrative machinery, but paying it no taxes. Even the groups who do not *work* in the city generally use it for shopping and recreation. Many persons are suburb-dwellers precisely *because* it gives them all the urban advantages without the disadvantages and the *expense*. As the proportion of suburb-dwellers increases, the proportion of nonpaying users increases. No wonder many suburbs can afford well-kept streets, new schools, and garbage collection twice a week. On the other hand, the population of some central cities, and consequently the tax base, has actually declined while the financial burden has been getting heavier. In many areas considerable strife has developed as central cities seek to regain financial solvency and as suburbs resist being drawn into the "city's" problems.

There are probably two major ways in which cities seek to spread more equitably the costs of providing city services. (1) One way is to *annex* the suburban areas which are socially but not politically or legally a part of the city. Such annexation is frequently frustrated, however, by prior incorporation of the suburb, by resistance to incorporation on the part of the surburban residents, by reluctance of the central city to take on an even larger burden of support for the suburb, and by still other factors. (2) The second means, which is more frequently used, is to alter the scheme of taxation so as to more nearly *tax "city use"* than "city residence." Traditionally, cities have relied heavily upon real-estate taxes borne by those who own property within the city. More recently the trend is toward city income taxes and sales taxes. The income tax is generally collected upon all income earned in the city regardless of where the person may live. The sales tax, of course, is collected upon purchases made.

RURAL PROBLEMS

For many people the illusion persists that while the city is a polyglot mixture of variant social and personal types, the rural environment is homogeneous. The facts do not support this belief. The rural environment includes cattle ranches in Texas, turkey farms in Ohio, mining camps in Colorado, logging operations in Washington, oil fields in Oklahoma, shanty-towns scattered in all sections, migratory labor, trailer habitués, and so on.

The relative size of the rural population has been declining (though not the absolute size) from 95 per cent of the total population in 1790 to 43 per cent in 1940 and to 36 per cent in 1950. The census divides the rural population into two broad categories—*farm* and *nonfarm*. Nearly three-fifths of the rural population is engaged in occupations other than farming. Much of this nonfarm population lives in villages and towns of various sizes and adjacent to the cities we have just discussed. Much of it is partly rural and partly urban in its way of life, its attitudes, practices, and beliefs. Evidence that the nonfarm group is really intermediate between the urban and farm groups is provided by examination of birth rates in the three areas: from 1944 to 1949 the net reproduction rate in urban areas was 119, in rural nonfarm areas it was 163, and in farm areas it was 181. Some of what we have to say in the following sections is oriented directly toward the rural farm population, but most of it applies to large segments of the nonfarm population as well. Whenever possible, the context will indicate just where the problems apply.

Dependence on Nature

Urban residents with their central heating, air conditioning, street-cleaning departments, and indoor occupations are prone to be unaware of how direct a role climate and weather play in the life and livelihood of the rural population. But rural residents are fully aware of it. A successful growing season makes it possible to obtain some luxuries as well as the necessities—providing of course that the season is not so successful that the market is glutted by overproduction. If the farm population prospers, then associated nonfarm businesses—stores, hatcheries, storage elevators, feed and seed suppliers—prosper also. If the farmer suffers, then his suppliers suffer. One might contend that the city resident suffers also—and he does—but much less directly. The urban resident may suffer from the scarcity and high price of beef, but he can still get pork or lamb or even meat substitutes. Urban business may decline in proportion to the loss of buying power among part of its customers, but to the farmer a single year's drought may destroy most of the benefits of from one to several years' labor and financial investment. The farmer is more directly subject to climatic and weather conditions over which he has no control and against which he has little recourse. Too much rain at planting time and too much or too little thereafter, a single violent hail storm, excessive winds, a late or an early frost, an invasion of insects, an outbreak of contagious animal disease—all are enemies of the farmer. One bad year may mean considerable tightening of the belt, two in a row may mean debt for the next ten years, three in a row—ruin. His standard of living is higher, but the conditions of the farmer's livelihood are almost as precarious today as they were a thousand years ago.

Low Living Standards

The price paid for rural residence can be measured in many ways, for almost any index of material living standards shows up the inferior position of country people. If cash income is used as a criterion, the median income of farm families in 1950 was only $1970, whereas in urban areas the average was $3673. In 1950, 98.8 per cent of urban residences had electricity, but only 77.7 per cent of rural-farm homes had it. Mechanical refrigeration is found in 86.1 per cent of urban homes, but in only 62.7 per cent of rural ones. And whether the criteria used are bathtubs or inside bathrooms, telephones, radios, television sets, central heating, or any number of others, the results are the same.

Many people reply to such comparisons by saying in effect, "Ah, but look at the advantages of rural living. It's a healthier place in which to live and rear children." The intangibles of living are, of course, hard to measure. Moreover, all would not agree as to what is desirable in a "way of life." There is considerable evidence, however, that the nostalgia which many people feel for rural living is a matter of stereotype and of prior conditioning as much as of rational choice.

In the matter of health facilities, there is approximately one doctor for every 650 people in urban areas but only one doctor for every 1700 persons in rural areas.[9] There are over 28,000 physicians in greater New York City, and there are hundreds of square miles of rural territory without even one doctor. In the matter of personality adjustment, Mangus presents some carefully qualified evidence from one county that "The proportion of children of superior personality adjustment was found to be highest among farm and village children and lowest among city children." [10] He goes on to say, however, that "The proportion of children

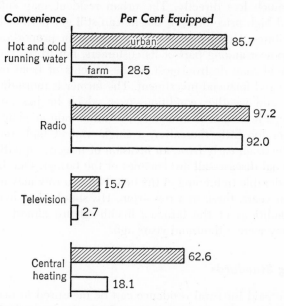

FIG. 14-3. Disadvantages in Farm Living. (Data from U. S. Bureau of the Census, Statistical Abstract of the United States: 1954 [Washington, Government Printing Office], pp. 798-799)

classified as very poorly adjusted was not significantly different among farm, village and city children." [11] Some additional evidence derived from draft rejection rates during World War II when farm youth had the highest rejection rate for physical, mental, or educational defects of any occupational group.[12] It can only be concluded that the evidence is very fragmentary and subject to varied interpretation. Most important of all, many important comparisons have never been made.

[9] David E. Lindstrom, *American Rural Life* (New York, The Ronald Press Company, 1948), p. 315.
[10] A. R. Mangus, "Personality Adjustment of Rural and Urban Children," *American Sociological Review,* 13 (October, 1948), p. 575.
[11] *Ibid.*
[12] Lindstrom, *op. cit.,* p. 309.

Unfavorable Age Structure

One of the most pervasive of rural problems is born of the customary pattern of migration from rural to urban areas. As pointed out above, rural birth rates, particularly farm birth rates, are well above replacement requirements whereas urban centers fall short of reproducing themselves by approximately 25 per cent. Moreover, productivity per man hour on the farm is steadily increasing, requiring consistently fewer farmers to feed the same urban population. As a consequence of these two factors, there is a steady stream of migration from rural to urban areas. The migrants are predominantly young adults. Children ordinarily cannot migrate alone, but once they are of age or have completed school, many of them trek into the cities to find employment.

The problem is not migration, per se, but the fact that it is heavily concentrated among the young adult age groups. The high rural birth rates mean a relatively *large dependent population* which must be fed, clothed, housed, and educated. The burden of supporting this large number of children falls upon the productive adults whose ranks are seriously depleted via urban migration. Not only are the rural areas poorer to begin with but they bear a large part of the cost of raising future urban adults. Each young man or woman who migrates represents a lost investment to the country and a financial gain to the city. Thus rural areas inadvertently subsidize city life.

RURAL AND URBAN DISORGANIZATION

Rural Disorganization

Throughout its history the United States has been becoming more and more urbanized. The proportion of persons living in rural areas and engaged in farming has been steadily dropping. Until recently, however, most rural areas actually have been gaining population, but not gaining as fast as the urban areas. The United States population, as a whole, has been growing so rapidly that rural areas could gain millions of people in a decade and still decline in proportion to the urban increases. So long as the rural-urban difference was purely a matter of *relative growth,* there was little general rural disorganization. Evidence of disorganization appeared as the rate of rural growth declined and as at least some areas actually began to lose population.

To select any one date as the point where depopulation became disruptive of the rural social organization would be to artificially break into a long-term process. Nevertheless, it seems clear that the period of the 1930's both aggravated and served as a further causal factor in the rural decline. The great depression of the early 1930's actually reversed the usual flow of migration and sent many city persons scurrying back to the farm where at least they could grow some food to eat. But at the same time the depression dealt a serious body blow to the prestige and security of farming as an occupation. Foreclosures were frequent and tenancy increased rapidly. When economic conditions finally bettered, the appeal of immediate high wages in the city often seemed more attractive than years of struggle to build up a farm again, perhaps to have it all destroyed in the next crisis. The 1930's also saw several years of the most severe drought, especially in the Middle West. The term *dust bowl* came into existence to indicate large areas of several states which as farm lands were virtually destroyed by the combined forces of sun and wind. The mass migrations to California and elsewhere were part of the first large-scale decreases in local rural populations. Then the increased mechanization of farming in most areas during the 1940's and 1950's has favored the combination of farms into larger holdings and further stimulated rural depopulation. In some areas the population has nearly or completely ceased to grow. In others, the population is declining.

But why disorganization? Community institutions by and large must be supported by the local population. Schools and churches, the Granges, police and fire protection, medical and legal services, mills, elevators, feed stores, groceries, clothing stores, and all the rest must be paid for. In a growing community this is relatively easy for, in a sense, the population can mortgage its future inhabitants. Services of all sorts are attracted to the community because of the "promise" of the future. But when growth stops, the burden shifts. Each existing family unit must bear a larger share of the costs. The mortgage for a contemplated new church, or even the minister's salary, becomes a much more serious problem. When the population actually begins to decline, the maintenance of *existing* services becomes difficult. Churches may have to double up and share a single minister's salary. Physicians drift away in search of patients, and the local elevator "merges" with one 30 miles away. The decline renders the community a less attractive place in which to live and further stimulates the decline. Thus the relation between depopulation and disorganization. As farming becomes even more efficient and requires fewer people, rural institutions will become still more difficult to maintain.

Urban Disorganization

Urban disorganization stems more frequently from growth than from depopulation; and from shifts in population and institutions *within* the city, rather than to or from the city. Disorganization appears (1) in the physical conditions of life, and (2) in city government and administration.

1. The stultifying effects of the outpouring of wastes and dirt into the atmosphere and the paralyzing chaos of traffic congestion have been dis-

cussed above. In this section we must trace another aspect of urban breakdown. Just outside the city's central business district there generally lies an area of the utmost dilapidation. Much of the blighted area is concentrated here; human misery is its watchword. It has the misfortune to be cast between the high land values of the business district and the lower values of residential districts, and between the land use of a former day, and, hopefully, that of the future. It has been largely deserted by its wealthy former residents and has been eagerly seized upon by businesses which cannot afford the high rent district. Landlords hope that the highrent district will expand outward and that, consequently, their properties will multiply in value. It is a short-run venture that has a distressing way of seeming to become permanent. In the meantime, the smellier, dirtier, noisier businesses move in, knowing full well that the area will go to ruin, in anticipation of one day selling the land at a fantastic profit. When, and *if,* that day arrives, the existing buildings will have to be torn down anyway to make room for more modern structures. So why bother to maintain them? Besides, taxes will be lowered as the buildings deteriorate and, since it is primarily the location which tenants are paying for, rents will not suffer.

Not all of this area is converted to business use. People also live in it. The processes are the same. The smells and dirt accumulate. Disgusts, resentments, and antisocial tendencies are fostered. There, too, are tenements, warehouses, and all the symptoms of blight discussed earlier in this chapter. The processes involved are as normal as those that create the new suburbs. The old patterns of land use have broken down and the new ones not yet appeared, unless, of course, the present patterns become permanent. When the new patterns do appear, the blighted areas will move a little farther out.

2. Fifty years ago, in *Shame of the Cities,* Lincoln Steffens described the graft, corruption, and maladministration typical of large United States cities. So it is not new. Showing the sagacity which made him famous, Steffens drew upon the Old Testament and said in effect, "The cause of sin was not Adam nor Eve, *but the apple!*" Had he been more social scientist than journalist, he might have gone on to explain. The factors that keep men honest, including among others, the unavailability of anything worthy of stealing, the high probability of being caught, and the searching eyes and souls of moralistic primary groups, are frequently absent in the city's governing circles. "Gang-busters" to the contrary, this kind of corruption often does pay—and handsomely. And, Steffens concluded, so long as it pays it will exist.

Techniques for assuring conformity to group expectations have not kept pace with the growth of city government. Officials are able to avoid the careful scrutiny of their constituents and are supported in their malfeasance by others, legitimate and not, who stand to profit thereby. By and large, no effective techniques exist to combat this situation. Occasional "exposés" redistribute the grafting opportunities but most of the graft goes on. The city-manager system shows some promise but suffers seriously from the generalized lack of public awareness and support.

CONFLICTS OF VALUES

Price Supports

Since the early 1930's the United States government has been committed to a program of "price supports" for farm products. The details of the program and the method of its administration have varied, and both have been rather continually embroiled in conflict. Basically the goal has been to keep farm prices at or near "parity." Parity, in effect, is a measure of the relationship between farm prices and the prices of goods and services which farmers must purchase. To maintain farm prices at parity means to raise them when the prices of other commodities go up and to lower them when other prices fall. Most farmers and their supporters have been enthusiastically behind the idea, at least, of price supports. Many other groups have been bitterly opposed, attacking the program as "favoritism" and frequently, "socialism." To place "floors" under farm prices, they argue, is to give unfair protection to one segment of the economy, to nullify the operation of supply and demand, and to encourage overproduction. These groups generally call for the elimination of all price supports and a return to a completely "free" economy.

The advocates of price supports reply that the above arguments involve gross distortions of fact, that farm production and industrial production are not comparable, that industry does not operate in a "free" economy, and that industrialists are seeking only to preserve their own special advantages. First of all, they point out, industrial production is frequently concentrated in the hands of relatively few producers who arbitrarily restrict output in order to maintain or to raise prices. Farmers, on the other hand, number in the millions and no few farmers control even a small fraction of the market. The farmer must produce and sell in a market over which he has no control. Farm produce cannot be held from the market indefinitely until prices rise. Without price supports, individual farmers face ruin with each small adjustment in the market. Furthermore, they claim, industry has long enjoyed the same kind of protection through the existence of tariff barriers, and more recently in the form of fast, tax-write-offs and rapid depreciation allowances on plant and machinery. The "free" economy advocated by business interests, they assert, is one in which industry would be free to profit and farmers would be free to go bankrupt!

Objectively, the issue seems to be not whether any kind of market protection exists, but how much and what kind of protection is desirable and whether the government has the right or the obligation to protect those who cannot protect themselves.

Education

The distorted age structures and usual patterns of migration from country to city already have been described. Rural areas have both larger numbers of dependent young children and less cash income with which to educate these children. And large numbers of them will migrate to the city as soon as their education is completed. Which area should bear the costs of this education?

As indicated in the chapter on education problems, education traditionally has been the responsibility of the local community. The different states vary widely, however, in their financial ability to provide adequate educational facilities, and federal aid to education has been proposed as a technique for reapportioning the costs of educating the nation's children. A similar problem and conflict of financial interests exists between the rural and urban communities within each state. Urban communities resist taxation to help support schools in the "backward" rural areas and point with pride to the fine job they are doing of educating their own children. Rural communities, on the other hand, are likely to point to their higher *per capita* expenditures for education and to remind the cities that many rural children are future urban residents. Rural communities are prone to turn to the state government and even to the federal government for aid.

The basic issue questions the whole theory of education being primarily a matter of local concern. That doctrine was founded in an era of isolation and self-sufficiency which for the most part has disappeared. The present era is becoming one of mobility and interdependence. The conflict rages around whether the traditional values are appropriate to the new conditions or must give way to new definitions.

PERSONAL DEVIATION

Rural

"Deviation" can be meaningfully discussed only in terms of the standards of norms of *some* group. Any given kind of deviancy—thievery, bohemianism, homosexuality, or what have you—becomes meaningful only as the group gives it approval or disapproval. Such deviation from group norms must be distinguished from cultural variability, or the variation in norms themselves from one group to another.

Considerable cultural variability is to be found in both rural and urban areas. Amish settlements, Ozark mountaineers, and snake-worshiping religious cults are all a part of rural culture—and all play a role in the creation of certain social problems. The Amish refusal to bear arms in time of war, their insistence that formal education cease with the completion of the eighth grade, and the rebellious adolescents with secretly acquired "jalopies" pose police problems at the very least. Mountain-cultivated patterns of distilling "moonshine," and the exacting of personal vengeance for actual or alleged wrongs; religious frenzies accompanied by floggings, self-mutilation, and even death; these make headlines in urban newspapers, reflect urgent preoccupations of the people involved, and forecast the clash of cultures. These all represent variability in group norms and the contribution of such variability to problem situations. They tell us little about deviation within each of these groups and the role of *personal* deviation in rural and urban problems.

One of the most striking characteristics of rural culture is its tendency to suppress deviation *within* the group. Rural communities are generally small, at least in terms of the number of people involved, ties to the land make it a highly permanent and stable population, and relations between families are informal and personal rather than formal and impersonal. The group typically is quite homogeneous in religious and economic background, in attitudes, feelings, and beliefs, and in definitions of "right and wrong." Constant pressure is brought to bear upon the individual to make him conform to the expectations of the group. Conform he must, for there is nowhere to go and no one to whom to turn to escape the pressure. Rebellion is impractical, for it is quickly discovered and easily punished. Complete conformity to group expectations cannot be secured, of course, but no group sanctions can be expected to support the deviant behavior and every effort is made to minimize its effect on the community as a whole.

Statistics on such matters generally show deviant behaviors—crime, for example—to be relatively infrequent in rural areas. There are fewer recorded arrests, fewer trials, fewer jail sentences, and fewer admissions to mental hospitals. The burglaries and larcenies *are* fewer in number precisely because of the closer regulation of individual behavior. But the means of handling violations that do occur make them seem even less frequent than they actually are. A teen-ager apprehended in a minor violation is likely to be turned over to his parents for "correction" rather than to be "booked" and to appear before a judge. The community is law-enforcement officer, judge, and penal agency all rolled into one—and an effective one at that. Whether mental illness is less frequent in rural areas is open to serious question. There *is* more likely to be an extra room for the "not-quite-right" relative, and the distance involved prevents him from "bothering" neighbors and other people. Besides, rural families are supposed to take care of their members. The whole of rural culture is oriented toward the discouragement of deviant personal behavior and, then, toward the elimination of its disruptive effects.

Urban

Variability among group norms is at least as common in urban as in rural areas—probably more so. Large urban centers are the characteristic locations of many ethnic and racial groups. The "Little Sicilies," the "Greek towns," the "Ghettos," the Harlems—all signify diverse cultural patterns. "Americanization" battles between the first, second, and third generations of immigrant families, the encroachment of one group upon another's territory, restrictive covenants, and the like, are all parts of typical intergroup conflict.

But more importantly, perhaps, the city is also a haven for *personal* deviation. It provides protection for many persons whose common denominator is the rejection of group norms and the determination not to be bound by them.

The anonymity and impersonality of the city are the keys to its nature as a haven for deviancy. Urban residents are perhaps no more tolerant of deviancy *within their own groups* than are rural residents. But in the city, one's face-to-face primary group association is limited to a very small proportion of the total population. There is no one set of mores or other agreed upon definitions, and each small group is unconcerned with the other's activities unless directly and seriously threatened by them. In a small rural area any deviant behavior is likely to bring censure, for "most everyone knows" and "most everyone cares." In the metropolis, on the other hand, it is not too difficult a matter to find other persons who share one's problems and to congregate with them in areas unmolested save by curiosity-ridden tourists and the minions of the law. Most large cities will embrace within them the local counterparts of the "Bowery" and "Greenwich Village." Though these terms identify actual places in New York City, they have come to identify patterns of deviant behavior which extend far beyond their geographical limits.

The Bowery (or "Skid-row," or the "Area of Homeless Men," or "Hobohemia") houses illiterates and Ph.D.'s, the always-poor and the formerly-rich, generally middle-aged and older men with one thing in common: failure! Each has been unable or unwilling to continue to meet the requirements of his personal life or his stratum in society. An intolerable marriage, public disgrace, too much responsibility, sexual deviation, drug addiction, and alcoholism are all among the factors frequently found in their backgrounds. Each has found his way into an environment of flophouses and sheltered doorways, of soup kitchens and missions, of cheap wine and liquor, and of anonymity. No one will ask where he is from, or what he has done, or why.

"Bohemianism" has come to mean, among other things, economic and political radicalism, "free love" and tolerance of sex deviation, and "patronage of the arts." Young unmarried men and women, students and clerks, aspiring musicians, writers, and artists dwell in the shabbiness of nondescript rooming-houses where landlords have learned not to inquire about the informal sleeping arrangements of many of their tenants. These practically nameless young people make a fetish out of being "emancipated," but at the same time are precariously dependent upon being able to conform to bohemian mores. For weeks or months or years they dwell in a world apart. Theirs is a way of life wholly foreign and almost unbelievable to most outsiders.

Homeless men die and are buried, bohemians marry and raise children, but the patterns continue on. Replacements are always headed toward each of the city's characteristic areas. The city provides the areas of refuge and torment.

A GLANCE INTO THE FUTURE

Inexorable time already has drastically altered the relation between city and country. The very terms *city* and *country* are no longer adequate to connote housing conditions, standard of living, occupation, political attitudes, or recreational patterns. Farmers now include trips to the grocery among their "chores" and many city people have large gardens. The rural residents who can be identified on the street by their dusty and dilapidated automobiles, by the uncomfortable Sunday-dress appearance of their clothes, and by their twangy or drawling speech, are a small minority. The labels *rube* and *city slicker* are fast losing what little meaning they have left. One can drive for miles along many highways and never be quite sure whether he is in the city or the country, and it would take this entire page to describe all the types of settlements that the census now defines as urban.

High-speed transportation and transmissible electric power have done much to urbanize the entire nation. Together they reduced the need for cities to be concentrated around a single center and stimulated suburbanization. They made it possible for urban residents to move outward and for rural people to have daily contacts inside the city. The rate of growth of the largest cities has slowed appreciably while satellite cities around the central one are growing at a furious rate. Urbanized areas are expanding, and the number of farmers required to feed a given urban population steadily declines. There is every reason to believe that these trends will continue—at least in the near future.

The central city will probably be one of the big problems of the next few decades. As its buildings and streets deteriorate, the unwillingness to pour large amounts of capital into reconstruction fosters slum conditions. The suburban movement narrows the tax base but increases the tax load, which somehow must be redistributed. Soot and grime will become greater enemies, and vehicle traffic may have to be banned from the city's center.

Traffic problems in general threaten to grow worse before they get better. Much of the nation's street and highway system is in need of improvement or replacement, and even the most adequately planned thoroughfares are overcrowded almost from the time of completion. Again, large capital outlays will be required. How these improvements are to be financed already is a matter of bitter conflict among trucking interests, railroads, city, state, and federal governments, plus "John Q.," automobile driver. The carnage of life and property from accidents is hardly recognized as yet, but probably will come to the fore relatively soon.

A multiplicity of overlapping political and economic units can be expected. Many small communities, incorporated and unincorporated, rural and urban in varying degree, and with varying degrees of dependence upon larger communities, are coming to be the rule. As people dwell in one area, perhaps work in a second, and seek recreation in still a third, residence-based communities become more difficult to maintain. Police, financial, and administrative problems are not coextensive with community boundaries. Action taken by one administrative or police body directly affects neighboring ones and interferes with the efficiency of both. Adequate representations of interested parties becomes almost impossible.

These are but some of the "undesirable conditions" now being created and of which we are gradually becoming "aware," but for the solution of which no wholly satisfactory techniques have yet been invented.

SUGGESTED READINGS

GEE, Wilson, *The Social Economics of Agriculture* (New York, The Macmillan Company, 1954). A mine of information on rural life and rural problems. Designed for textbook use in courses in rural sociology and agricultural economics.

GIST, Noel P., and HALPERT, L. A., *Urban Society* (New York, Thomas Y. Crowell Company, 1948). A leading textbook in urban sociology.

HATT, Paul K., and REISS, Albert J., Jr., eds., *Reader in Urban Sociology* (Glencoe, Ill., The Free Press, 1951). Comprehensive and sophisticated readings in urban sociology. For the serious student.

LINDSTROM, David E., *American Rural Life* (New York, The Ronald Press Company, 1948). A basic textbook in rural sociology.

PARK, Robert E., BURGESS, Ernest W., and McKENZIE, R. D., *The City* (Chicago, University of Chicago Press, 1925). A pioneer treatise on the city by three pioneers in the study of urban problems.

WIRTH, Louis, "Urbanism as a Way of Life," *American Journal of Sociology*, 44 (July, 1938), pp. 1-24. A classic statement of the nature of urbanism and a definition of the field of study of urban sociology.

ZECKENDORF, William, "Parking in the Sky," *Atlantic Monthly*, 191 (June, 1953), pp. 34-35. An imaginative attack on a growing problem, by one of America's leading real-estate magnates.

AUDIO-VISUAL AIDS

America's Disinherited (Brandon Films, Inc., 200 W. 57th, New York), 33 minutes, sound, black and white. Produced for the Southern Tenant Farmers Union. Aims to portray the plight of the Negro and white share-croppers in the South and their efforts to organize for more equitable conditions. Shows the Delta co-operative farm as one of the possible remedial measures.

Farm and City (United World Films, Inc., Government Films Department, 1445 Park Ave., New York), 8 minutes, sound, black and white. Classroom version of a longer film produced by the U. S. Department of Agriculture in 1939. Shows the relation of farm to city and that the economic status of one affects the other.

A Place to Live (Brandon Films, Inc., 200 W. 57th, New York), 18 minutes, sound. A schoolboy leaves his classes and walks home through city streets and back alleys infested with rats. There in a "band box house," three rooms, one above the other, his mother awaits. Scenes follow of their squalid way of living and we learn of their hopes for a better place to live. No over-all solution is offered but several suggestions are made.

Water for the City (University of California, Extension Division, Visual Department, 2272 Union St., Berkeley), 30 minutes, sound, color. Shows how watershed areas act in receiving and storing water and in releasing it for future use; the interaction between the water cycle and the various parts of the watershed. Intended to acquaint the city-dweller with the importance of California's watersheds in providing water for use in the city.

QUESTIONS AND PROJECTS

1. What proportion of the United States population is now defined as urban?

2. Explain the need for a *social* definition of "city."

3. Describe the blighted area of a large city. What is the social significance of such blighted areas?

4. Discuss several ways in which congestion has become a major urban problem.

5. Explain the seeming paradox of more pressing financial problems in cities even though city tax rates have been rising steadily.

6. Is rural life synonymous with farming as an occupation? Why or why not? Illustrate your answer.

7. Comment upon the alleged superiority of the rural way of life.

8. How does the age structure of the rural population augment the problems of rural living?

9. Depopulation contributes to rural disorganization in some areas of the country. Explain.

10. Evaluate the statement that "there is less personal deviation in rural than in urban areas."

11. Take a field trip to the slum area of a modern city and visit one or more

of the social agencies there. Inquire of the persons in charge concerning the nature of the problems they encounter. How are the agencies financed? What portion of the costs are paid by the people who receive the agency services?

12. See if you can locate the rural counterpart of the slum, mentioned above, in your area. In what ways are living conditions better in the rural area? In what ways are they worse? What agencies exist to provide aid for poverty-stricken rural inhabitants?

CHAPTER 15

Mass Communication in Modern Society

Now the whole earth had one language and few words. And as men migrated in the east, they found a plain in the land of Shinar and settled there.... Then they said, "Come, let us build ourselves a city, and a tower with its top in the heavens, and let us make a name for ourselves, lest we be scattered abroad upon the face of the whole earth."

And the Lord came down to see the city and the tower, which the sons of men had built. And the Lord said, "Behold, they are one people, and they have all one language, and this is only the beginning of what they will do; and nothing that they propose to do will now be impossible for them. Come, let us go down, and there confuse their language, that they may not understand one another's speech."

So the Lord scattered them abroad from there over the face of all the earth, and they left off building the city. Therefore its name was called Babel, because there the Lord confused the language of all the earth; and from there the Lord scattered them abroad over the face of the earth.[1]

Germany had surrendered; Japan had been left to fight alone, and the American forces had moved in their relentless stepping-stone advance all the way to Okinawa. Out of the Potsdam Conference held in defeated Germany there came on July 26 the Potsdam Declaration, signed by the United States, Britain, and China, a demand that Japan surrender or be crushed.

The Allied world waited for Japan's answer. Two days later ... the word flashed that Premier Kantaro Suzuki and his cabinet had decided to "ignore" the Potsdam Declaration.

The rest is familiar history. Within three weeks the Japanese turned about and accepted the Potsdam terms. But in those three weeks two events took place which were to have a profound effect on the history of the world. Atomic bombs were dropped on Hiroshima and Nagasaki—giving birth to the atomic age—and Russia declared war on Japan and sent her troops sweeping south and east into Manchuria and Sakhalin—thus vastly strengthening her position in the Far East.

Japan in fact had been on the verge of collapse, [and] her leaders had been negotiating desperately for many weeks with the then neutral Russians in an effort to surrender. . . .

The almost unbelievable fact seems to be this: the Japanese cabinet decided to accept the Allied ultimatum, but by a mistake the Prime Minister made an announcement that was taken to mean the opposite! . . . The Premier told the

[1] Genesis, 11:1-9.

Japanese newspapermen that his cabinet was holding an attitude of *mokusatsu,* a word that is difficult to translate directly into English. He meant that the cabinet was withholding comment on the ultimatum, that a decision was not yet to be announced. But the Domei News Agency, in translating Suzuki's statement into English for shortwave broadcast to the West, put the wrong meaning on *mokusatsu* and mistranslated it as "ignore." The Allied Powers— waiting for Japan's answer to Potsdam— were informed that the Suzuki cabinet was "ignoring" the surrender ultimatum. On the basis of this apparent rejection, the final effort to crush Japan was launched and the surrender came nearly three weeks later, *after* the atomic bombs had been dropped and Russia had entered the war.[2]

WITHOUT a common language, the builders of the tower of Babel could not proceed. Because of the imperfect translation of a word, the war with Japan may have been prolonged and the world balance of power altered. Without communication, human social life becomes impossible. It is by the nature and quality of our communication processes that the character of our social life is molded.

THE COMMUNICATIONS REVOLUTION

In their effects upon the daily lives of the people, the processes of communication have probably changed more in the last fifty years than in the preceding five thousand. At the turn of the century, radio and television were unknown, the motion picture was a laboratory curiosity, and telephone and telegraph were largely confined to business use. Books rarely reached below the upper-middle class, while the "muck-raking era" was beginning to produce the mass magazine. Newspapers, though many in number, were limited in scope and had just begun to reach a sizable fraction of the population. It is difficult for today's college student, who has been immersed in the mass media of communication throughout his entire recollection, to visualize the atmosphere of local isolation, provincialism, and homemade recreation of his grandparent's childhood.

1. *The Press.* From the publication of the first daily newspaper in 1783, the number of daily English-language newspapers in America rose to a peak of 2600 in 1909 and has settled to a present figure of 1785. Daily circulation totals about 55 million,[3] more than one for each household in the United States. Once a medium devoted to news and opinion, the modern newspaper is primarily a medium for advertising and entertainment. Advertising occupies much of the space and supplies two-thirds of the income. Although the modern newspaper prints more news, and more accurately than in earlier periods, newspaper circulation campaigns

[2] W. J. Coughlin, "The Great Mokusatsu Mistake," *Harper's,* 206 (March, 1953), pp. 31-40.

[3] Most statistics on mass media in this chapter are given in round numbers; such statistics are not entirely reliable; the data are constantly changing, and different sources compile and classify data differently, so that figures are not always comparable.

stress "features"—syndicated columns, comics, sports sections, style shows, lovelorn columns, and the like—more than news coverage, and many news stories are selected for oddity or "human interest" rather than for social significance. Opinion, once scattered through the news stories, is now (theoretically) limited to the editorial page and to the signed columns of the commentators.

About 8000 periodicals are now published, ranging from mass magazines like the *Reader's Digest* (American circulation 10,275,000) and *Life* (5,475,000) to many tiny, obscure journals. In 1954, there were 36 magazines with circulation over one million copies per issue. Book publishers currently print over 12,000 new titles each year, while an unknown number of booklets, pamphlets, tracts, leaflets, and handbills appear in constant succession.

The complexity of the press is revealed in its tremendous variety of publications. Newspapers include not only the mass-circulation daily and Sunday press but some 10,000 weekly and semiweekly papers, while included in the totals are the foreign language press, the labor press, the Negro press, and several other varieties. Different magazines are aimed at every level of age, occupation, class and region, and every variety of religious, political, intellectual, and recreational interest. Hundreds of trade journals cater to the special interests of each industry or trade association. A relatively new type of publication, the *house organ*, has mushroomed into an estimated ten or twelve thousand titles. Often a single corporation publishes many different journals, one or more each for its salesmen, customers, managers, stockholders, foreign employees, domestic employees, teen-age daughters of domestic employees, and so on. DuPont alone publishes 75. Usually distributed free (at a cost of over $100 million a year), the main purpose of the house organ is to promote prestige and good will and to mold attitudes. With a combined circulation far greater—possibly twice as great—than that of all daily newspapers, the house organ has quietly developed into a potent medium for the shaping of social and political thinking.[4] This paragraph only hints at the great diversity of the American press, which, after all, reflects the complexity of the society it serves.

2. *The Motion Picture*, born about the turn of the century, reached its peak of popularity and profit during World War II and has declined somewhat since the spread of television. Despite this decline, the "average" American over six and under senility goes to the movies about once every two weeks, where he is exposed to probably the most effective of all media in shaping the attitudes and conditional responses of the subjects.[5]

[4] "How to Play the House Organ," *Fortune*, 46 (October, 1952), pp. 144 ff. The official 1952 circulations figures of 70,000,000 are far too low, since a *Fortune*-estimated 5,000 nonreporting publications are not included.

[5] Several studies have established that motion pictures can produce striking changes in attitudes and beliefs. See Solomon P. Rosenberg "Change of Socio-economic Atti-

The motion-picture medium also includes: (1) the *newsreel,* with its abbreviated but intensely dramatic capsules of information and commentary; (2) the *educational* film whose use in schools, colleges, and adult education groups is steadily expanding; (3) the *promotional* film, loaned out by vested interests—corporations, trade associations, labor organizations—and containing a mixture of education and propaganda.

3. *Radio Broadcasting,* in a third of a century, has developed from a novel toy into an industry with 2600 standard broadcast stations, over 600 FM stations, over a 100,000 special-purpose radio stations (aeronautical, marine, public safety, industrial, experimental, disaster communications), and over 100,000 amateur stations and operators. No other communications medium reaches as many people as does radio, which enters about 97 per cent of all homes (with nearly two sets per home) and is found in two-thirds of the automobiles. Although the advent of television brought some decline in radio listening and broadcast income, the number of stations and receiving sets in use continues to rise, and it seems assured that television will supplement and not replace radio.

4. *Television* has grown even more rapidly. At the end of 1954, there were 33,000,000 sets in use, 415 stations on the air, 197 under construction, and 219 license applications pending. Television is still growing so rapidly that any statistics will be out of date before they can be published. In areas where stations have been broadcasting for five years or more, nearly 90 per cent of the homes are equipped. Before long, nearly all the homes in the nation will have television.

The communications *revolution,* however, consists not so much in the statistical growth of the media as in the ways in which they have altered the lives and feelings of the people. One measure of this is in the way they spend their leisure time. One study gives these national averages for men, women, and children in the United States: [6]

Hours Weekly

Radio listening	25
Movie attendance	1
Newspaper reading	3½
Magazine reading	1¾
Attendance at classroom— average during a lifetime	4
Legitimate theatre and concerts	negligible

tudes under Radical Motion Picture Propaganda," *Archives of Psychology* No. 166 (Columbia University Press, 1934); L. L. Thurstone, "Influence of Movies on Children's Attitudes," *Journal of Social Psychology,* 2 (August, 1931), pp. 291-305; Herbert Blumer, "Molding Mass Behavior Through Motion Pictures," *Publications of the American Sociological Society,* 29 (1934), pp. 115-117. See also the twelve volumes of the Payne Fund studies. So conclusive were these earlier studies that little recent research in this area has been pursued.

[6] Quoted in Carroll V. Newsom, ed., *A Television Policy for Education* (Washington, American Council on Education, 1952), p. 58.

This study is imperfect in that it neglects age differences and the effects of television, but it does reveal that the average American spends many times the hours in mass communication than he has spent in the classroom. Even school children spend "at least as much time with the mass media of communication as they spend in school." [7] After subtracting the hours spent in work, sleep, and personal and family chores, it would appear that the average American spends *most* of his remaining free time in mass communication—far more than in all other avocational activities combined! A century ago, the average person's free time was probably spent, in declining order, in (1) conversation, (2) games and participation sports, (3) spectator sports and organized or commercialized "entertainment," (4) mass communication. Today this order has been approximately reversed. Robert M. Hutchins has even suggested that conversation may become a lost art, as television may convert us into "a high order of plant life."

For many people the mass media appear to have created an imaginary world more vivid and "real" than the real one. Many children become so absorbed while reading comic magazines that they become utterly unaware of what goes on about them.[8] Many adults agonize over soap-opera tragedies as though they were genuine. So real do the comic-strip and soap-opera characters become that a "wedding" brings in truck loads of gifts for the imaginary couple, a "funeral" inspires a soggy mountain of tearful letters, and cartoonist Chester Gould is prodded (by uncomfortable Chicago law-enforcement officials) into explaining to his readers how Dick Tracy can drive a Cadillac and live in a $100,000 mansion on a policeman's salary.[9]

The mass media of communication have an effectiveness and dramatic impact unknown to our predecessors. Through mass media, one's eye and ear can roam the universe of time and space, and experience the re-creation of spectacle which far surpass even their originals in dramatic intensity. Few battles, seen in person from a single viewing point, are as dramatic as a battle in Cinemascope.[10] Seldom is the real-life hero as godlike or the villain so demoniac as the celluloid one! The famous Orson Welles "Invasion from Mars" broadcast sent millions of people into a

---

[7] National Council on Research in English, *Education and the Mass Media of Communication* (Chicago, National Council of Teachers of English, 1950), p. 27.

[8] Paul F. Lazarsfeld and Frank N. Stanton, *Communications and Research, 1948-1949* (New York, Harper and Brothers, 1949), p. 23.

[9] He "pinches his pennies." (*Time* [November 26, 1951], p. 57.)

[10] In an early attempt at film realism, D. W. Griffiths and a camera crew accompanied Pancho Villa, the Mexican bandit, on an actual military campaign. Unknown to Griffiths, Villa accommodatingly arranged to inject realism by having some 30 or 40 prisoners actually massacred in one battle scene. The resulting picture was so dull that it had to be padded out with studio shots before it could be released. "Real-life" is seldom dramatic in its entirety; only when carefully selected bits and pieces of "real-life" are skillfully arranged (via the "documentary") does "real-life" become dramatic and compelling to watch.

panic such as even the wartime reality of falling bombs and crashing buildings does not produce. [11] Of course, the fear of the theater patron shrinking into his cushion differs from the feelings of the soldier pinned down by enemy fire. The point is that the mass media which claim so much of our attention have a tremendous capacity either to inform or to inflame. Neither capacity has been fully exploited, perhaps the one because it is too unprofitable, and the other because it is too dangerous.

PROBLEMS OF THE MASS MEDIA

As each new medium appeared and grew, it raised both hopes and fears—hopes that it would checkmate tyranny and arm justice, that it would bring to the masses the benefits of learning and "culture," and unify a people; fears that it would became an instrument of tyranny, that it would adulterate learning, degrade "culture," and promote social unrest. Each medium has been an object of social concern and controversy almost from its inception. Among the topics of concern are the following.

1. THE PROBLEM OF "MONOPOLY"— OF CONCENTRATION OF CONTROL

The development of the mass media illustrates both the ideal of vigorous competition and the tendency towards noncompetitive practice which pervade our economic system. As in all forms of modern business and political organization, the pressing problem is, What degree of centralized organization and management is in the public interest?

a. The Press

The doctrine of the "freedom of the press," protected by the First Amendment, implies that books, magazines, and newspapers may be published and distributed by any who wish, without any official permission or censorship. This freedom to publish was considered the indispensable bulwark of democracy. Through the free press, tyranny would be challenged, corruption exposed, and a market place provided for the free competition of ideas, in which truth would finally prevail. This passionate faith in the eventual triumph of truth through the free competition of ideas lies behind Jefferson's statement that "Were it left to me to decide

[11] "Long before the broadcast had ended, people all over the United States were praying, crying, fleeing frantically to escape death from the Martians. Some ran to rescue loved ones. Others telephoned farewells or warnings, hurried to inform neighbors, sought information from newspapers or radio stations, summoned ambulances and police cars. At least six million people heard the broadcast. At least a million of them were frightened or disturbed." (Hadley Cantril. *The Invasion from Mars* [Princeton, N. J., Princeton University Press, 1940], p. 620.)

whether we should have a government without newspapers or news-papers without a government, I should not hesitate to prefer the latter."

This "free competition of ideas" is complete only when the publication of conflicting opinions is politically *and economically* possible. In the days of the hand-operated press, a paper could be established quite cheaply, and a large paper had little competitive advantage over its smaller competitor. Even more recently, E. W. Scripps stated that none of his papers cost over $30,000 to establish, and declared in 1911 that any two young men with brains, ambition, and a little money could found a successful newspaper.[12] Today, newspaper publishing is a big business. To establish a new competing newspaper in a small town is virtually a commercial impossibility; to establish one in a large city requires an investment of millions, with probable losses of millions more before it becomes self-supporting.[13]

Changing technology and the advantages of large-scale operation have steadily reduced the number of newspapers from the 1909 figure of 2600, serving a population of 90,000,000, to its present 1785, for a popu-lation of 165,000,000. By 1945, daily newspaper competition had disap-peared from all but 117 American cities; by 1954, this number had fallen to 74, while the remaining 1575 cities were either one-newspaper towns, or had two newspapers under a single management. By 1954, there were 21 states in which no city had competing daily papers. Last year, 22 dailies were merged or suspended, and one prominent publisher pre-dicts that soon no city under half a million will have more than a single paper.[14] Over much of America, local newspaper competition has disappeared!

The amount of effective newspaper competition is further reduced by absentee-ownership of many papers. Over one-fourth of our newspaper circulation is attained by a few newspaper chains. Except for purely local news, most of the news that reaches print passes through one of the three major newsgathering services—the Associated Press, a co-operative to which most papers belong; the United Press, affiliated with the Scripps-Howard chain; and the International News Service, affiliated with the Hearst chain. Most newspapers rely on syndicated features both for "entertainment"—comic strips, lovelorn columns, fashion features, and the like—and for their columns of news interpretation and opinion (Walter Lippmann, the Alsops, Roscoe Drummond, and others). Even

---

[12] Quoted in Frank Luther Mott, *American Journalism* (New York, The Macmillan Company, 1950), p. 548.

[13] The only new large-city dailies in the past twenty years have been financial rat-holes. Marshall Field's *Chicago Sun* lost millions until virtually liquidated in a merger with the *Times*. Norman Chandler's Los Angeles *Mirror* lost millions, and "... is still losing at the rate of an estimated $20,000 to $30,000 a week." (*Time* [June 21, 1954], p. 79.)

[14] *Time* (June 21, 1954), pp. 79, 80.

the editorials are sometimes "canned," supplied by the chain owner or some other nonlocal source.

In magazine publishing, although about 8000 periodicals are published by 2200 publishers, the top five publishers with ten magazines account for about one-fifth of the total circulation. The top ten of these 2200 publishers employ one-third of the total persons employed in the industry and supply nearly half the weight of second-class mail carried in the country. Although the magazine publishing field is fiercely competitive, the need for a large circulation makes it hazardous and expensive to launch a new general-interest magazine. In book publishing, although the top dozen publishing houses dominate the field, the relatively modest cost of having a book privately published makes it fairly easy to get one's ideas into print. But book distribution is another matter! Unless a new book is reviewed and discussed in the "book review" section of newspapers and magazines, it is usually doomed to remain unsold and unread; therefore the promotional "connections" of a major publishing house assume great importance.

The total picture of the press is one that is far from freely competitive in the traditional sense, yet is far from complete monopoly. The degree of concentration in the industry vests in a relatively small number of persons a great power to determine what shall reach the presses. If most of them should chance to think alike on some issue—and sometimes they do—other points of view may have difficulty getting into print where many people will see them.

b. Motion Pictures

Although the five largest production studios dominate the industry, the smaller studios and the independent producers are highly active, and movie-making is highly competitive. In film distribution, ownership of chains of first-run theaters by the major studios gave them a monopolistic advantage, until antitrust action forced them to dispose of their theater chains. Yet both the independent producers and the smaller theater-owners still complain of "monopolistic" practices. It is also charged that foreign films are discriminated against, and that the Breen Office (for movie self-censorship) sometimes discriminates against the independent producers in its rulings.[15]

c. Radio and Television

Since its infancy, radio has been subject to some governmental regulation, arising from the need for assigning frequencies in a spectrum that

[15] Ruth A. Inglis, *Freedom of the Movies* (Chicago, University of Chicago Press, 1947), p. 187.

has room for only a limited number of stations. Since the limitations upon the number of stations that can operate are technical rather than economic, broadcasting is not viewed as a strictly "free enterprise," but as a sort of public utility. The law creating the Federal Communications Commission (FCC) establishes the principle that the air waves belong to the public, that a station operator may own the studio equipment but does not own the frequency upon which he broadcasts, and that licenses to operate a station are to be granted only "in the public interest, convenience, or necessity." FCC rules allow one person or company to own no more than five television stations, six FM stations, or seven AM (standard broadcast) stations.

Concentration in broadcasting, therefore, rests not upon station ownership but in network affiliation and program sponsorship. Most of the 2600 standard broadcast stations belong to one of the four national or several regional networks. Most local stations give little time to locally-originated programs, especially during good listening hours, and most of the broadcast material consists of network shows.[16] Practically all network broadcasts are sponsored by advertisers. In a very literal sense, *the advertisers control radio* broadcasting, for the advertising agency not only supplies the "commercial" but supplies the entire show, with the station operator merely a supplier of radio time. White interviewed 40 radio executives of whom only two challenged the thesis that advertisers run radio broadcasting.[17] A few large advertisers, operating through a still smaller number of advertising agencies, supply the bulk of network income; a 1944 study showed that about one-fourth of the advertising income of each major network came from only four advertisers, and over one-third of the income from four agencies. In perhaps no other medium does so small a group have as great power to control what the people may see and hear.

The advent of FM radio and television has broadened the medium, but has not greatly affected the pattern of ownership and control. When FM radio developed, the FCC sought to establish policies that would attract "new blood" to broadcasting, but was defeated by industry opposition.[18] Aside from those granted to schools and colleges, about 90 per cent of the FM licenses are now held by operators of AM stations, who effectively discouraged outside competition by carrying their AM radio "commercials" and sponsored shows over their FM stations without added expense to the advertiser.[19] In television's earlier years, heavy financial

[16] Federal Communications Commission, *Public Service Responsibility of Broadcast Licensees* (Washington, Government Printing Office, 1946), p. 37.

[17] Llewellyn White, *The American Radio* (Chicago, University of Chicago Press, 1947), p. 94.

[18] Charles A. Siepman, *Radio's Second Chance* (Boston, Little, Brown & Company, 1947), pp. 244-251.

[19] *Ibid.*

losses were absorbed by the established radio industry. As television became profitable, the competitive advantages enjoyed by an established, experienced broadcaster enabled the existing radio station owners to retain control of most of the television stations.

d. Interlocking Concentration

When radio appeared, many predicted the death of the newspaper, but what followed was union, not conquest. Today nearly one-third of the radio and television stations are affiliated with newspapers under common ownership or control. In over one-third of the cities with only one radio station, that one is associated with the only newspaper, giving an absolute local monopoly of local news.

e. Significance of Concentration

Concern over concentration is nothing new. Jefferson complained of the great trading towns, that "though not one-twenty-fifth of the nation, they command three-fourths of its public papers." [20] In 1941, the FCC, finding 90 per cent of nighttime broadcast power in two network systems (NBC and CBS), forced NBC to dispose of one of its two networks. Nearly every serious study of ways of "improving" the mass media includes recommendations for reducing concentration. In a society wherein the mass media have replaced the town meeting and the cracker barrel, it is argued, "freedom of speech" has little meaning unless it includes the practical opportunity for each group to get its ideas into print and on the air. This freedom, many critics feel, is gravely weakened by the highly centralized managements of a motion-picture industry intent upon avoiding everything controversial, a radio industry seeking to offend nobody, and a press largely devoid of local competition. Critics also complain that centralized control imposes upon the media a dead level of mediocrity, squeezing out of the next-to-the-last drop of diversity, originality, and imagination. Most serious of all is the charge that an unhealthy degree of power is shared by too small a group. MacIver writes, "Of all such monopolies, the most immediately fatal to democracy is the monopoly of the media of opinion, or any approximation to it." [21]

No doubt centralization does pose a certain threat to freedom and to diversity, but the effects of centralization are not entirely pernicious. "Yellow journalism" was a product of the circulation wars of a half-century ago. Hearst's circulation battle with Pulitzer probably caused

[20] J. A. Pollard, *The Presidents and The Press* (New York, The Macmillan Company, 1947), p. 75.
[21] R. M. MacIver, *The Web of Government* (New York, The Macmillan Company, 1948), p. 221.

the Spanish-American War,[22] and his circulation battle with McCormick is widely agreed to have helped establish Chicago gangdom.[23] As one liberal journal comments editorially, "Too much competition can sometimes reduce all publishers to the lowest common denominator of sensationalism; whereas monopoly can sometimes encourage independence, letting a publisher feel that he can afford to put out a good paper." [24] From radio networks come not only many vacuous absurdities but also many artistic productions which no local studio could produce. Whether partial centralization of control of the mass media has done more "harm" than "good" remains debatable; meanwhile, any attempt to alter greatly the present pattern of control would probably be economically difficult and politically impossible. Large-scale activities are a necessity in modern society, and rather than try to destroy concentration, it may be more realistic, as Brady suggests, to develop forms of democratic participation in guiding them.[25]

2. THE PROBLEM OF BIAS AND RESPONSIBILITY

a. The Press—Free to Inform and to Misinform

The *New York Times* proclaims as its motto, "all the news that's fit to print," and is generally agreed to come very close to fulfilling its pledge. For certain other papers, a more descriptive motto might be, "all the news that fits the publisher's biases."

Bias is not easy to measure and is difficult to establish. Bias is practically universal among the human species, for all persons have their value-preferences, and the thinking of all or nearly all persons is colored by their values. It is almost inevitable, therefore, that the biases of those who control the mass media should affect their content. One would hardly expect the *C.I.O. News* to be fully objective in reporting labor-management affairs, the *Democratic Digest* to be impartial in reporting political affairs, or the *Lutheran Witness* and the *Catholic World* to agree in appraising the film, "Martin Luther." Although each is expected to refrain from falsehood or slander, it is expected that each will eloquently plead the cause which it was established to promote.

To a lesser degree, bias is charged against those media which are supposedly independent and neutral. Some papers, such as the *New York Times* and the *Christian Science Monitor,* are widely respected for maintaining a high degree of objectivity. Some others have a notorious record

[22] Mott, *op. cit.,* Ch. 31, "Yellow Journalism and the War with Spain."

[23] Ferdinand Lundberg, *Imperial Hearst* (New York, Equinox Cooperative Press, 1936), pp. 151-173.

[24] *Reporter,* 11 (August 17, 1954), p. 5.

[25] Robert A. Brady, "Monopoly and the First Freedom," *Hollywood Quarterly,* 2 (April, 1947), pp. 225-411.

of twisting the news to fit the views of the publishers. As a striking example, an article in *Harper's* magazine reproduces a news story from a well-known newspaper and lists 112 inaccuracies and unwarranted inferences found in this single news story, in the opinion of the article's writer.[26]

There is little doubt that the economic philosophy of newspaper editors and publishers, radio station owners, and movie producers is overwhelmingly conservative. Men of wealth and power are, understandably enough, defenders of the social system which allows them to hold that wealth and exercise that power. As veteran newspaperman Quincy Howe writes, "To criticize a newspaper because it supports the system under which it operates, or because it strives to please its advertisers and readers, is to criticize a bee because it stings or a dog because it barks. That is the nature of the beast."[27] A distinguished editor, Virginius Dabney of the Richmond *Times-Dispatch,* writes:[28]

Today newspapers are Big Business, and they are run in that tradition. The publisher, who often knows little about the editorial side of the operation, usually is one of the leading business men in the community, and his editorial page, under normal circumstances, strongly reflects that point of view. Sometimes he gives his editor a free hand but far oftener he does not. He looks upon the paper primarily as a "property" rather than as an instrument for public service. . . . (He) considers the important part of the paper to be the business management. . . . Of course, such a publisher sees that the editorials in his paper are "sound," which is to say that they conform to his own weird views of society. . . .

Every survey known to the authors reinforces the picture of the general conservative bias of the press. *Fortune* magazine a few years ago stated that "the United States press is prevailingly capitalistic and overwhelmingly conservative," and quoted Oswald Garrison Villard, a one-time Associated Press Director, as having "declared the (Associated Press) service constitutionally incapable of doing justice to the underprivileged."[29] Child-labor legislation, public housing, social-security legislation, securities-exchange regulation, the Wagner Labor Relations Act, wage-and-hour legislation were enacted despite opposition from the majority of the press. Newspaper publishers are employers, and news unfavorable to unions seems to get far more space than National Labor Relations Board findings of "unfair labor practices" against employers. Some papers have refused to sell advertising space to unions who felt that the editorials and

[26] Milton Mayer, "How to Read the *Chicago Tribune,*" *Harper's,* 198 (April, 1949), pp. 24-35.
[27] Quincy Howe, *The News and How to Understand It* (New York, Simon & Schuster, Inc., 1940), p. 39.
[28] Virginius Dabney, "What's Wrong with Newspaper Editorials?" *Saturday Review,* 28 (February 24, 1945), pp. 7-9.
[29] "Associated Press," *Fortune,* 15 (February, 1937), pp. 89 ff.

news columns were unfair, and the consumer testing organizations, *Consumers' Research* and *Consumer Reports,* have generally been unable to buy advertising space. Bias is also charged against consumer co-operatives, food and drug legislation, Federal Communications Commission orders, and Federal Trade Commission efforts to suppress fraudulent advertising. Even the comic strip may reflect a social philosophy, allegedly conservative in at least the case of "Little Orphan Annie." [30]

In the last several presidential elections, a steadily growing majority of the press has given editorial support to the Republican candidate, rising to about 80 per cent of the nation's newspaper circulation in 1952, with 10 per cent supporting the Democratic candidate and another 10 per cent uncommitted.[31] Leading Democratic spokesmen and friends have repeatedly complained about what they call the "one-party press," charging that not only are the papers editorially Republican, but also favor Republican candidates and policies in their news stories and pictures.[32]

Such charges are easy to hurl but difficult to evaluate. While in theory the news story is written "straight," there are many subtle ways in which bias can be expressed in the news story, yet is difficult to establish or measure.

1. *Space*—the favored cause or candidate may receive detailed reporting whereas the opponent gets little attention.

2. *Location*—favored candidates may be front-paged and headlined, and opponents buried in the inside pages.

3. *Selection*—the news story may quote the most moving and popular phrases of the favored candidate and spotlight the blunders of his opponent; or it may play up a trifling comment of a speaker and ignore his main theme.

4. *Headlines*—the headline may support and confirm a candidate's position, or may undermine it; the headline may focus attention on his main theme, or upon some irrelevance.

5. *Supporting quotations*—the favored candidate's quoted statements may be followed by supporting quotations from other respected persons, whereas his opponent's statements may be followed by opposing quotations from others, or by reminders of unpleasant events for which he is blamed.

6. *Audience reaction*—the audience may be described as highly enthusiastic, or as apathetic or hostile.

7. *Juxtaposition*—a news story or picture concerning a candidate may be placed next to a story or picture that will color the reader's reaction.

8. *General news selectivity*—the general news stories may play up news developments which are embarrassing to the party in power (e.g., unemploy-

---

[30] Donald Auster, "A Content Analysis of 'Little Orphan Annie'," *Social Problems,* 2 (July, 1954), pp. 21-32.

[31] Cf. Frank Luther Mott, *American Journalism* (New York, The Macmillan Company, 1950), p. 719; Nathan B. Blumberg, *One-Party Press?* (Lincoln, University of Nebraska Press, 1954), pp. 14-17.

[32] Cf. Blumberg, *op. cit.*, pp. 11-19; Robert Lasch, "Pride and Prejudice: The Fourth Estate," *Reporter,* 7 (November 25, 1952), pp. 9-11; M. R. Werner, "New York Newspapers—6 to 1 Against Stevenson," *Reporter,* 7 (November 25, 1952), pp. 13-16.

ment, taxes, debt, corruption, foreign troubles), or play up developments favorable to the party in power (e.g., tax cuts, prosperity, administration accomplishments).

9. *Picture selection*—may be folksy, appealing, heroic, or may be routine, nondescript, or even ludicrous.

It is difficult to see how a democracy could long survive a genuine "one-party press," and these charges of political favoritism in news handling are not to be taken lightly; neither are they to be accepted without conclusive evidence. At present, there is no comprehensive, reliable survey to warrant a conclusion. Following the 1952 presidential election, the national journalism fraternity, Sigma Delta Chi, called for such a survey, but encountered considerable opposition and the proposed survey was dropped.[33] *Editor and Publisher* also called for a survey, but the American Society of Newspaper Editors and the American Newspaper Publishers Association lent no support.[34]

Only one methodical, apparently objective study of newspaper performance in the 1952 campaign has been made, and it is too limited in scope to be fully conclusive. It covered a small sample of 35 newspapers, and concluded that slanting of the news columns was less widespread than critics have charged, with over half the papers in the sample meeting "the highest standards of fair news presentation."[35]

The mass-circulation magazines appear to show much the same patterns of bias as do the newspapers. The smaller journals, however, show a great variety of viewpoint, from the right-wing journals like *American Mercury* or *Freeman* to such liberal journals as *The Reporter, Nation, The Progressive,* or *New Republic.* Even communist journals are presently being published, although they may be suppressed before long. There is no important segment of American thought which is unable to get into magazine form. Comparative circulation figures, however, show that the liberals are talking mainly to one another, for these four liberal journals combined require nearly a full year to circulate as many copies as the more conservative *Saturday Evening Post* circulates each week. There is little evidence of bias on the part of book publishers as a whole. Certain publishers have their preferences, but, with a few possible exceptions, any manuscript likely to command a respectable sale is not difficult to market.

b. The Motion Picture—Image or Caricature of Life?

Whereas the press proudly proclaims itself a medium of public enlightenment, the motion-picture industry frankly announces that its primary pur-

[33] Cf. *New York Times,* December 21, 1952, p. 18; Nathan Blumberg, *op. cit.,* pp. 20-25.

[34] Cf. Blumberg, *op. cit.,* pp. 23-25; *Problems of Journalism: Proceedings of the American Society of Newspaper Editors, 1953,* pp. 184-185.

[35] Blumberg, *op. cit.,* p. 44.

pose is to sell entertainment at a profit, not to stimulate social criticism. As one movie executive remarked, "Messages are for Western Union; I sell entertainment." Movie-makers have avoided controversial plots and sought to delete anything that might give offense to anybody. But this technique has not avoided the problem of bias, for a variety of biases are claimed against the movie industry. They include the following.

1. *Race Bias.* The important, ambitious, successful people in the movie are almost invariably white Anglo-Saxons, with Negroes, Indians, and other minority members depicted in servile, stereotyped roles.

2. *Class Bias.* Most pictures deal mainly with persons in the upper income brackets and in executive or professional occupations, with the life of working-class people, when shown, often depicted unfavorably.

3. *Nationalistic Bias.* In pictures involving foreign locales or persons, the Americans are usually the heroes and the foreigners either villains or simpletons, whom any red-blooded American can easily dispatch by the score.

4. *Militaristic Bias.* It is charged that movies promote militarism by idealizing combat, glorifying force and belittling negotiation, and presenting military service in a colorful, glamorous, and adventuresome setting.

5. *Conservative Bias.* It is charged that movies promote conservatism in two ways: (*a*) by avoiding all controversial themes, especially anything which suggests social criticism or calls attention to social problems; (*b*) by presenting all problems as *personal* problems, caused purely by bad luck or bad people, not by defective social organization. An example is contained in a letter written to Samuel Goldwyn by Joseph Breen, production code administrator, regarding the 1937 picture, "Dead End," [36]

> We would like to recommend, in passing, that you be less emphatic, throughout, in showing the conditions of the poor in tenements and those of the rich in apartment houses. Specifically, we recommend you do not show, at any time, or at least that you do not emphasize, the presence of filth, or smelly garbage cans, or garbage floating in the river, into which the boys jump for a swim ... such scenes are likely to give offense.

A prominent movie executive suggests that today's producers are still more cautious, saying,[37]

> Hollywood has rarely ventured far into the field of films concerned with political or economic conditions. Nevertheless, one or two features of this type have appeared almost annually, providing a striking contrast to the mass of strictly escapist material that constitutes the industry's major contribution to American life. Even this small trickle has now dried up. One of the distributors

[36] Reprinted from *Freedom of the Movies* by Ruth A. Inglis by permission of The University of Chicago Press, p. 182.

[37] Arthur Mayer, "A Movie Exhibitor Looks at Censorship," *Reporter,* 10 (March 2, 1954), pp. 35-40.

of "Mr. Smith Goes to Washington" recently assured me that a remake of this fine picture, which showed some of our lawmakers in a less than favorable light, could not possibly be undertaken today. Even the mild legitimate comedy "Affairs of State" was passed up as potential dynamite by all the major picture companies.

Old movies as well as new stories are being shelved. After Harry Warner emerged from testifying before the House Un-American Activities Committee, he decided to issue instructions to take out of circulation, even by the educational film libraries, three great social documents that had made his company famous: "I Am a Fugitive from a Chain Gang," "The Story of Louis Pasteur," and "Emile Zola."

The student of social problems realizes that many personal difficulties are produced by social and cultural pressures, and that a realistic treatment requires social changes. But for the movies, with exceedingly rare exceptions, blame rests upon the people, not upon the system, and the problem is solved when the bad people are located and destroyed. In this way, the movies discourage social criticism and social reform and lend tacit approval to the status quo.

c. Radio and Television

Most of the comments made about movies also apply to the entertainment aspects of radio and television. The other aspects of radio and television—news broadcasting, discussion programs, political broadcasts, and the sale of time—involve some different problems. Since the air waves have room for only a limited number of stations—often only one to a locality—the FCC imposes upon radio a special obligation to be impartial. Time must be given or sold to all major political parties on the same terms, and a station is expected to provide balanced discussion of any controversial issues that are aired. Most station operators appear to have wholeheartedly accepted this obligation and make an honest effort to grant all points of view and equal opportunity to be heard. Radio probably comes closer to over-all objectivity than the press—at least, most people appear to think so. In a national survey inquiring of people how fair they thought newspapers and radio generally were in giving both sides of public questions, the following percentages replied that the media were generally fair: [38]

	Per Cent Saying Media Are "Fair"	
	1945 survey	1947 survey
Radio stations	81	79
Newspapers	39	55

There are, however, complaints that radio's impartiality is more apparent than real. The mere avoidance of controversy may, unintentionally,

[38] Paul F. Lazarsfeld and Patricia L. Kendall, *Radio Listening in America* (New York, Prentice-Hall, Inc., 1948), p. 54.

become a device for supporting the status quo. Lazarsfeld and Merton comment: [39]

Since our commercially sponsored mass media promote a largely unthinking allegiance to our social structure, they cannot be relied upon to work for changes, even minor changes, in that structure. It is possible to list some developments to the contrary, but upon close inspection they prove illusory. A community group, such as the PTA, may request the producer of a radio serial to inject the theme of tolerant race attitudes into the program. Should the producer feel that this theme is safe, that it will not antagonize any substantial part of his audience, he may agree, but at the first indication that it is a dangerous theme which may alienate potential customers, he will refuse, or will soon abandon the experiment. Social objectives are consistently surrendered by commercialized media when they clash with economic gains. Minor tokens of "progressive" views are of slight importance since they are included only by the grace of the sponsors and only on condition that they be sufficiently acceptable as not to alienate any appreciable part of the audience. Economic pressure makes for conformism by omission of sensitive issues.

More direct forms of bias are also claimed against radio. Until 1945, the code of the National Association of Broadcasters condemned sale of time to labor unions for any sort of program whatever, although the National Association of Manufacturers not only could buy time but on occasion received free radio time. Co-operatives were generally barred from the air until 1943.[40] Quincy Howe has remarked that sponsors prefer conservative news commentators, asserting that "... sponsors snap up the news programs with a conservative slant as they never snapped up the programs with a liberal slant." [41] *Variety*, a highly respected magazine of the entertainment world, appraised thirty radio news reporters and analysts, and reported a definite conservative unbalance, classifying 5 as reactionary or extreme reactionary, 7 as conservative, 6 as middle-of-the roaders, 7 as very cautious or midde-of-the-road liberals, 1 as an independent liberal, with 4 unclassified.[42] Several well-known radio newscasters have left the air protesting that they were pushed off because of their liberalism, whereas few conservative commentators have met such a fate.[43] Such charges of newscaster bias—difficult to evaluate—are aimed mainly at advertiser-sponsored newscasters. The news reporters sustained by the radio networks themselves enjoy a reputation for greater objectivity and balance.

[39] Paul F. Lazarsfeld and Robert K. Merton, "Mass Communication, Popular Taste, and Organized Social Action," in Lyman Bryson, ed., *Communication of Ideas* (New York, Harper and Brothers, 1948).

[40] White, *op. cit.*, p. 78.

[41] Quoted in Siepman, *op. cit.*, p. 89.

[42] *Variety* June 25, 1945.

[43] Siepman, *op. cit.*, pp. 91-92.

d. The General Problem of Bias

To summarize the data on bias is not easy. Charges are many, but evidence is scattered and conclusions must be tentative. It is clear that the degree of objectivity and responsibility of the mass media have greatly increased over earlier periods. With the possible exception of England, no other major country has a press as responsible and objective as ours. It also appears inescapable that a pronounced conservative bias pervades most of the mass media—which may be either a menace or a blessing, according to one's values. Although to some extent due to the pressure of advertisers,[44] who supply two-thirds of newspaper and magazine income and nearly all of the radio and television income, bias appears primarily as a consequence of the social and cultural values of those limited groups who own and control the media. As the famous editor William Allen White said, a few years ago, in words which also fit the owners of the other media,[45]

The publisher associates on terms of equality with the bankers, the merchant princes, the manufacturers, and the investment brokers. His friends unconsciously color his opinions. If he lives with them on any kind of social terms in the City Club or the Country Club or the Yacht Club or the Racquet Club, he must more or less merge his views into the common views of other capitalists. The publisher is not bought like a chattel. Indeed he often is able to buy those who are suspected of buying him. But he takes the color of his social environment.

He is pretty generally against organized labor. He is too often found opposing the government control of public utilities. He instinctively fears any regulation of the stock exchange. The right to strike seems to the rich publisher and his Chamber of Commerce friends to be sheer anarchy. It is inevitable that the managing editor and the editorial writers who want to hold their jobs take their professional views from their boss, the man who signs the payroll check.

Bias is not ended by denouncing or explaining it. It is unlikely that bias will be ended at all. Perhaps the most effective control lies in sensitizing students to the problem of bias, so that they will recognize that one cannot hope to be intelligently informed on any public issue by reading a single paper (with a few exceptions), or even a dozen papers reflecting the same viewpoint. Only by reading and comparing sources reflecting opposing biases is one likely to find the complete truth about any controversy.

[44] For example, *Editor and Publisher* (March 20, 1948), attributes the financial failure of Marshall Field's *Chicago Sun* partly to a boycott from some national advertisers who disliked Marshall Field's liberal editorial policies.

[45] William Allen White, in *Chicago Times*, June 2, 1939; quoted in George L. Bird and Frederic E. Merwin, *The Press and Society* (New York, Prentice-Hall, Inc., 1951), pp. 74-75.

3. THE PROBLEM OF CONTENT— "CULTURE" VERSUS COMMERCE

a. The Content of the Media

As each new means of mass communication developed, it was hailed as the key to cultural salvation—the ignorant could be enlightened and the uncouth refined. These bright—and perhaps unrealistic—visions have not materialized. Despite occasional exceptions, each medium is largely geared to bring entertainment to the public and profits to the owners. To those who demand mass improvement from the mass media, this is outrageous. Lee De Forest, whose inventions made modern radio possible, has attacked the radio broadcasting industry, saying,[46]

What have you gentlemen done with my child? He was conceived as a potent instrumentality for culture, fine music, the lifting of America's mass intelligence. You have debased this child, you have sent him out on the streets in rags of ragtime, tatters of jive and boogie-woogie, to collect money from all and sundry for hubba hubba and audio jitterbug. You have made of him a laughing stock to intelligence, surely a stench in the nostrils of the gods of the ionosphere. . . . Soap opera without end or sense floods each household daily. . . . Murder mysteries rule the waves by night and children are rendered psychopathic by your bedtime stories. This child of mine, now thirty years in age, has been resolutely kept to the average intelligence of thirteen years. Its national intelligence is maintained moronic, as though you and your sponsors believe the majority of listeners have only moron minds. . . .

Who has the right to say what the press shall print, movies show, and radio shall broadcast—the owners, the public, the government? The public overwhelmingly favors leaving primary control of the mass media right where it is—with the private owners.[47] But to the critics, this merely proves the truth of George Bernard Shaw's dictum that "if we do not get what we like, we shall grow to like what we get."

What *do* we get? Detailed up-to-date surveys of media content are not available. In general, newspapers give us news, comment and editorial opinion, and a variety of "features" that are entertaining and sometimes mildly informational. Books and magazines give us a great choice, with ample opportunity for everyone to gratify his tastes. Movies are almost entirely devoted to entertainment, either light frothy entertainment or rootless melodrama that carefully skirts all serious themes or challenging issues. The most recent detailed study of radio content (1946) shows that about three-fourths of all broadcast time was devoted to entertainment-type programs, about one-sixth to informational programs, and the remainder classed as "orientational." Classified differently, musical programs

---

[46] Quoted in "The Revolt Against Radio," *Fortune,* 35 (March, 1947), pp. 101 ff.
[47] Lazarsfeld and Kendall, *op. cit.,* pp. 89, 144.

occupied 41 per cent of broadcast time (8 per cent classical and semi-classical, the rest popular, dance, Western, hillbilly), 16 per cent to dramatic programs, 13 per cent to news and commentators, with the remainder divided among various types. Talks, farm programs, forums and panels, and homemaking programs combined to occupy 7 per cent— about as much as given to "soap opera." [48] Practically all commercial FM radio broadcasting duplicates the programs carried on affiliated AM stations, and television appears not to have greatly altered the pattern of program distribution, except that the purely musical show becomes a variety show when on television.

How well do people like what they get? Data on this are scattered. Movie attendance drops off rapidly as people mature, falling steadily from an average of about four movies per month at 19 to less than one per month for people over 60 years old.[49] How much of this drop is due to lagging interest and how much to increasing responsibilities is not known. A national sample of informants were asked whether they thought radio, schools, newspaper, churches, and local government were each doing "excellent," "good," "fair," or "poor" jobs; those replying either "excellent" or "good" totaled 76 per cent for churches, 70 per cent for radio, 63 per cent for newspapers, 59 per cent for schools, and 42 per cent for local government.[50] When asked to classify themselves into one of the three categories below, they divided themselves as follows: [51]

	Per Cent
A. I listen to the radio mostly for entertainment and very seldom listen to serious or educational programs	26
B. I like to listen to both serious and entertainment programs, and I'm satisfied with what I get now	52
C. I like to listen to both serious and entertainment programs, but I wish there were more serious programs	20
Don't know	2
	100

These figures show both that the majority is not actively dissatisfied, and that there is a sizable minority which is definitely dissatisfied. The 20 per cent who want more serious programs were not merely highbrow snobs, for they were evenly distributed over all educational strata.[52] A 1946 survey (before television) reports that during the daytime soap opera hours, approximately 77 per cent of the available radio listeners had the set turned off entirely[53]—certainly indicating disinterest, if not

[48] Kenneth Baker, "An Analysis of Radio's Broadcasting," in Lazarsfeld and Stanton, *op. cit.*, p. 58.

[49] Lazarsfeld and Kendall, *op. cit.*, p. 11.

[50] *Ibid.*, p. 115.

[51] *Ibid.*, p. 36.

[52] *Ibid.*, p. 38.

[53] Federal Communications Commission, *op. cit.*, p. 13.

discontent. The more highly educated people are the more highly critical of radio, listen less, and are far more interested in classical music and discussions of public issues,[54] of which radio gives comparatively little. Persons who were critical of any one of the media (radio, movies, newspapers) were from two to four times more likely to be critical of the others,[55] showing that a sizable minority is clearly dissatisfied with the mass media in general. Just what do they dislike?

b. The Criticisms of Media Content

Critics indict the mass media on three main counts: that much of the content is either (1) *trashy,* (2) *harmful,* or (3) so *limited in variety* that the public has little choice but to learn to like trash.

Trash—Where and Why? The charge of "trashiness" involves a value-judgment—by whose values is "trash" to be defined? This charge is rooted in the fact that most media content is scaled to mass tastes, to the dismay of those who view mass tastes as vulgar. Each of the media (excepting books and specialized magazines) seeks to attract as large an audience as possible for each issue, show, or broadcast. This means *scaling the content to the least common denominator of audience acceptability.* Since the average American adult has completed a fraction over nine years of schooling, the local newspaper can gain circulation by containing little that cannot be read and understood by a 15-year-old child. Since nearly everyone likes "human interest" stories whereas few will read a column about foreign trade, the serious but undramatic news must make room for lurid scandal and sentimental trivia. When Old Bob, the coon dog, got lost in a cave near Bedford, Indiana, he was on or near the front page of several papers for a full week—at a time when the war in Korea was in its most tense phase and the country involved in a hasty mobilization, price inflation, a political crisis, and a basic reorientation of foreign policy. In the search for excitement, newspapers tend to emphasize the bizarre, the exceptional, and the illicit, while sober but serious news developments get buried in the back pages. At times, newspaper treatment of crime may make impossible a fair trial of the accused, a situation that occasionally leads to judicial rebuke of the press.[56]

The least-common-denominator approach is most clearly revealed in movie and broadcast content. The crime-sex-adventure trio of themes accounts for most movie plots because movie-makers are under no illusions as to which kinds of pictures make money.[57] Despite occasional

---

[54] *Ibid.,* pp. 10, 83, 136.

[55] *Ibid.,* p. 140.

[56] E.g., see "Free Press and Fair Trial," *Time* (April 23, 1951), pp. 78-79; also Edwin H. Sutherland, *Principles of Criminology* (Philadelphia, J. B. Lippincott Company, 1947), pp. 187-189.

[57] It is revealing to note upon what assumptions some highly successful producers operate. Leonard Goldstein, described in *Time* as "Hollywood's top moneymaking

exceptions, serious drama and genuinely artistic films rarely make money, and no producer can afford to make many films like "The Treasure of Sierra Madre," widely acclaimed as an artistic triumph, but a box-office failure (no love interest!). Films involving social criticism and intellectual challenge are both commercially doubtful and politically dangerous. Dancing girls, horse operas, and "who-dun-its" are both safer and more profitable.

A similar situation is found in radio and television broadcasting. Most broadcast time during the best listening hours is sponsored by an advertiser who buys the time, and chooses and presents the entire program. Although an occasional sponsor disregards the least-common-denominator approach to sponsor a high-prestige program of more limited appeal (such as the Metropolitan Opera or the New York Philharmonic Orchestra), most sponsors try to attract the largest possible audience to hear the "commercial." This produces a great deal of entertainment and—except for news broadcasting—little else. The drama is mostly second- or third-rate, for serious drama requires an intelligent audience and, furthermore, serious drama is difficult to stage successfully in a 26-minute program with one or two breaks for commercials. Variety shows offer something for everybody and not much of anything for anybody. Quiz shows provide a brisk contest along with many tiny fragments of unrelated information. The forum or discussion show attracts a mass audience if it is a good fight, while a discussion which reaches agreement and conclusion is less exciting. The "confrontation" show offers the morbid a peek over the emotional transom of other people's lives. Although some educational and artistic values may occasionally emerge from this diet of entertainment, it is unrealistic to expect the sponsor to cater to minority tastes. Commercial sponsorship *must* scale the content to mass tastes if the sponsor is to sell his product and serve his stockholders. The blame—or credit, according to one's values—rests not with the sponsors for acting as sponsors should, but with the system wherein commercial sponsorship determines program content.

A further explanation for the allegedly poor quality of much movie, radio, and television drama lies in their fantastic appetite for story material. The movie studios, with a combined production of perhaps 500 hours showing time a year, have real difficulty finding enough suitable story material. Jerry Wald, production director at Columbia, is quoted as saying, "If you get six decent books in one year, it's a miracle. . . . We'd

---

producer," avoids sophisticated comedy and includes among his rules of operation: "avoid 'downbeat' (depressing) pictures—nobody ever bought tickets to watch inmates of a mental institution," and "adults are grown-up children, and should be entertained as such." (*Time* [April 28, 1952], p. 96.) Another producer, Hal Roach, Jr., who has been highly successful in making films for television, "accounts for his new success with the explanation that televiewers have even lower I.Q.'s than moviegoers." (*Time* [October 29, 1951], p. 48.)

make a hundred more pictures this year if we could find the stories." [58]
The radio and television studios, with the four major networks programming about 500 hours a *week,* have an even greater problem. The entire content of a quality magazine that appears once a month would not run a television studio for a single evening. All the Pulitzer Prize novels and plays ever written would not fill the broadcast schedules for more than a few days. A vaudeville routine, once usable for several seasons, is now gone in a few minutes. The insatiable appetite of modern media makes it inevitable that *as long as the emphasis is on newness and entertainment of the mass audience,* the average quality of output will be mediocre.

Media Content—Harmless or Vicious? The second criticism—*that much of the content is actively harmful—*is easy to hurl but difficult to test. The newspapers are accused of glamorizing crime and cultivating a preoccupation with sex through their lurid reporting. The movies, since their first appearance, have flickered in the baleful glare of those who distrusted their influence. Many studies, particularly the Payne Fund Studies, established that the movies had great influence on people, without clearly establishing whether that influence was "good" or "bad." As each new medium spreads, critical attention shifts to it, and at present television and comic books are the major culprits. By 1948, six of the ten highest-selling magazines were comic books, with their emphasis upon "sin, sex, and sadism." Present circulation approaches 100 million a month, with several readers per copy and is still rising. Child interest in comic books appears to reach its peak at age 8 or 9, declining slowly thereafter, but still outranking all other magazine reading at junior-high-school level and comprising about one-fourth of total magazine reading at senior-high-school level. Research findings on the effects of comics upon children vary widely. One group claims that comics fill genuine child needs for fantasy, adventure, and identification with heroes, and do no particular damage to children. Heisler compared excessive comic-book readers with non-readers, finding no significant differences in mental age, educational achievement, socioeconomic status, or social and personal adjustment. [59] Witty finds little difference in the amount or kinds of general reading by those who read comic books extensively and those who seldom read them. [60] After reviewing numerous studies, DeBoer concludes that "good books and magazines can compete successfully with comic magazines when children and youth have easy access to a great variety of reading materials." [61]

[58] *New York Times Magazine,* June 20, 1954, p. 43.
[59] Florence Heisler, "A Comparison of Comic Book and Non-Comic Book Readers of the Elementary School," *Journal of Educational Research,* 40 (February, 1947), pp. 458-461.
[60] National Conference on Research in English, *Education and the Mass Media of Communication* (Chicago, National Council of Teachers of English, 1950), p. 20.
[61] *Ibid.,* p. 22.

But other experts view comic books as highly injurious. Wolf and Fiske, after dividing comic book readers into "fans" and "moderate readers," find very few fans are normal children, while "a marked correlation is revealed between neuroticism and being a fan." They feel that comics not only attract neurotics, but actually *produce* neuroticism, saying,[62]

That the fan does indeed become a neurotic, i.e., that the habit and characteristics of comic reading gradually engulf his life and affect his entire behavior pattern, is empirically verifiable from the children's responses to interview questions. The fan is seen (1) to be interested only in the general aura of the story, as manifested by its triumphant conclusion; (2) to deliberately lift comic reading to a position superior to that of other activities, including eating; and (3) to extend to other activities the habits of thought characteristic of comic reading.

The well-known psychiatrist Dr. Frederic Wertham has been the most persistent and uncompromising critic of comic books, considering them highly injurious even to normal children, because of their continuous glorification of violence, crime, and sadism.[63] The consensus of recent research and opinion seems to be swinging to the belief that comic books are harmful, but there is no clear agreement upon a solution. Parent objections are generally evaded by the children,[64] industry self-regulation has thus far proven ineffective,[65] and any legal ban or censorship raises a number of other objections.

In the sale of violence, television is a brisk competitor. A recent monitoring survey covering the week of January 4-11, 1953, for New York City stations, showed an average of 9.2 acts and threats of violence per hour during "children's listening hours" (5 to 7 P.M. weekdays; sign-on to 7 P.M. week-ends).[66] Acts of violence were twice as high during children's listening hours as during other hours, and television violence in 1953 was up 10 per cent over 1952. During the early days of television, when broadcast time was cheap and the industry was seeking respectability, many highly-regarded children's programs were developed. As the industry became established and time becomes readily salable at good prices, children's programs waned; children's drama, for example, has dropped in New York from 30.4 per cent of total television time in 1951 to 6.7 per cent by 1953.[67] As with comic books, the effects of television violence upon children remain a matter of debate.

[62] Katherine M. Wolf and Marjorie Fiske, "The Children Talk About Comics," in Lazarsfeld and Stanton, *op. cit.*, p. 29.

[63] Frederic Wertham, "What Parents Don't Know About Comic Books," *Ladies' Home Journal*, 70 (November, 1953), pp. 50 ff; also, *Seduction of the Innocent* (New York, Rinehart and Company, 1954).

[64] Wolf and Fiske, *op. cit.*, pp. 37 ff.

[65] See "Reform of Comic Books Is Spurred by Hearings," *New York Times*, June 13, 1954, IV, p. 6.

[66] Diane Shipler, "Murder for Moppets," *The Progressive*, 18 (March, 1953), pp. 28-29.

[67] *Ibid.*

Limited Choice—The Triumph of Monotony. A third criticism is the charge that the media—mainly radio and television—fail to offer the public that wide range of choice which is supposed to be the particular virtue of free enterprise. Since each sponsor, with occasional exceptions, tries to attract the same mass audience, each tends to select much the same type of programs for a particular hour, with newscasts at mealtime, soap operas during daytime hours, and so on. This means that at many hours the listener has no choice whatever as to *type* of program. In the forenoon he may choose between several soap operas, all following much the same sudsy formula; during late evening hours, he may choose between rival disc jockeys; even during the "best," middle-evening hours, he is largely limited to a choice between comedy, variety, and mystery shows.

The "minority audience" is neglected most of the time. There are a number of minority audiences—groups each numbering far less than a majority of listeners—whose taste may run to classical music, to pure jazz music, to literary readings, to informative talks, to book reviews, to leisurely and complete dramatizations of the classics, and so on. For these listeners, radio and television offer relatively little—some jazz recordings intermixed with other popular music, a steadily shrinking offering of serious music, mostly semiclassical, and little else. For the lover of, say, chamber music or music of the baroque period, standard broadcast radio and television offer practically nothing.

In theory, radio stations are expected to offer something for everyone by carrying "sustaining" (nonsponsored) programs during some good listening hours, since sponsors obviously cannot afford to cater to minority tastes. In this way "program balance" is to be achieved.[68] In practice, much of the industry has failed to do this. Although the networks and some individual stations have developed some sustaining programs of high quality and high listener popularity, these programs have rarely been offered during good listening hours, have often been shifted around whenever a sponsor wanted the hour involved, or dropped unaccountably. Network sustaining programs are often not carried by local stations.[69] It would appear that the sustaining programs are used mainly to fill in any left-over time which no sponsor will buy at the moment.

Attempts to secure a more balanced offering encounter a fundamental obstacle—sustaining programs are not profitable. Promises of program bal-

---

[68] The FCC states, "The sustaining program is the balance-wheel by means of which the imbalance of a station's or network's program structure, which might otherwise result from commercial [sponsor's] decisions concerning program structure, might be redressed. . . . Stations have been asked on renewal, to set forth the average amount of time, or percentage of time, devoted to entertainment programs, agricultural programs, religious programs, educational programs, agricultural programs, fraternal programs, etc.; and the Commission has from time to time relied upon the data thus set forth in determining whether a station has maintained a well-balanced program structure." Federal Communications Commission, *op. cit.*, p. 13.

[69] See Federal Communications Commission, *op. cit.*, pp. 12-32.

ance and of local coverage made when applying to the FCC for a license are often disregarded after the license is secured.[70] The FCC remarks,[71]

The most immediately profitable way to run a station, may be to procure a network affiliation, plug into the network line in the morning, and broadcast network programs throughout the day—interrupting the network only to insert commercial spot announcements, and to substitute spot announcements and phonograph records for outstanding network programs.... Some stations are approaching perilously close to this extreme.

Efforts of the FCC to secure greater diversity and balance in programming have been generally ineffective, and have been sharply denounced by the industry and by much of the press as a government attack upon freedom of speech and free enterprise.[72] The development of FM radio raised hopes of increased experimentation and variety of offerings, but most commercial FM stations are jointly owned and operated with AM stations and broadcast the same programs. The industry opposed and defeated the FCC's proposed requirement that two or more hours of FM broadcast time each day should broadcast programs different from their standard AM broadcast schedule.[73] FM radio has increased the number of commercial outlets without changing the general character of the programs.

Dissatisfaction with the programs offered by commercial stations has led to several developments among the dissatisfied. Some of them have gazed longingly (and perhaps uncritically) at the noncommercial British Broadcasting Corporation with its emphasis on "highbrow" fare and its avowed intention to educate and elevate the public,[74] and at the Canadian broadcasting system, with its mixture of private and public enterprise. Serious listeners have turned to noncommercial stations wherever they are available. Serious music listeners in particular have turned to noncommercial FM radio and to phonograph records for classical music. Recent improvements in record-making and reproducing have produced a spectacular growth in the record industry, with an equally spectacular expansion in the repertory of music available on records. Thus, the minority audiences have largely abandoned commercial radio.

There are, of course, conspicuous exceptions to the general program pattern. Some stations come closer to "program balance" than others. Several commercial stations, such as WQXR and WFMT, located in the largest cities, have frankly catered to the minority audience with "high-

[70] *Ibid.*, pp. 3-9.
[71] *Ibid.*, p. 39.
[72] Cf. White, *op. cit.*, p. 84.
[73] Siepman, *op. cit.*, pp. 244-247.
[74] See William Clark, "The BBC, Britain's Favorite Monopoly," *Reporter*, 7 (December 9, 1952), pp. 27-30; Marga Mannes, "The Children's Hour," *Reporter*, 9 (October 27, 1953), p. 38; Andrew Roth, "British TV: Low-Budget Highbrow," *The Nation*, 176 (March 29, 1953), pp. 297-299.

brow" fare. New York City's publicly-owned WNYC, two or three listener sponsored and supported stations (WCFM, KPFA), and over one hundred stations operated by schools and colleges add considerable variety to the total radio programming available in certain areas.

No choice of content will please everybody. American radio and television aim to please the masses, but they alienate the intellectuals; British radio and television delight the intellectuals and perhaps bore the masses. It is clear that only a variety of sources, catering to the full range of interests, will come close to pleasing everybody—and this is not easy to arrange.

4. —AND STILL OTHER PROBLEMS...

Still other aspects of mass communication arouse concern and debate. The *problem of censorship* has excited continuous debate for over four centuries. To some, censorship appears as a *solution* for the defects of the mass media, whereas to others, censorship is part of the *cause* of those defects and a hindrance to be overcome. Government security classifications sometimes prevent disclosure of facts embarrassing to the party in power. Movie censorship makes it impossible to film some of the greatest works of literature, or to deal honestly with certain social issues. Various private groups have sought, by censorship, pressure, and intimidation, to prevent expression of any view of life and liberty which differs from their own. A widely circulated private black-list, coupled with the timidity of movie-makers and broadcast sponsors, has largely barred from employment in movies and broadcasting practically anybody whom practically anybody has ever called communist. The story of Robin Hood is branded as subversive by a member of a state textbook commission, and in a state library, John Bunyon's *Pilgrim's Progress*, Jules Verne's *20,000 Leagues Under the Sea*, and Hans Christian Andersen's fairy tales are reserved for "adults only." [75] These and many other incidents ranging from the serious to the absurd document the problem of the concern over censorship.

The general effects of mass communication upon modern man have become a fashionable new anxiety.[76] Some fear that modern man is being turned into a puppet, manipulated by words and slogans instead of wires. Advertisers are financing highly scientific sociological and psychological research to find out how people react to particular words, and why. There is some evidence that the sheer repetition of the product's name has more to do with the selling power of a radio commercial than the content of the commercial. In American political life, the cigar-smoking ward

[75] Cf. *New York Times*, November 14, 1953, p. 1; *Time* (February 15, 1954), p. 66.
[76] Cf. William H. Whyte, Jr., "Groupthink," *Fortune*, 45 (March, 1952), pp. 114 ff.

heeler gives way to the press agent and the publicity agency, and candidates are "merchandised" like laundry soap.[77] Are political campaigns becoming simply a contest to see who has the most money and the best publicity agents, or are the mass media merely revealing more candidly the strengths and weaknesses of our political system? In George Orwell's chilling novel, *1984,* he visualizes a society in which the mass media, monopolized and censored by a totalitarian party, strip the people of all privacy or independence and transform them into automatons conditioned mechanically to accept and enjoy their servitude. Is this the ultimate destiny of our inventiveness? Probably not; yet there are those who wonder.

APPROACHES TO COMMUNICATION PROBLEMS

1. *The Social-Disorganization Approach*

Without the technological revolution in communication, the social problems concerning communication would be few and simple. As long as books were few and expensive, and owned only by the wealthy, their rulers saw little need for censorship. When printing made books and handbills so cheap that they could be widely circulated among the common people who had less of a "stake" in the status quo, rulers began to fear books and demand censorship of printed matter. When newspaper publishing was small-scale, minority views could quite easily find expression; when the publisher must necessarily be a wealthy man, views of other groups reach a wide audience only by his grace. When the primary means of communication was face-to-face conversation, and the town meeting or country store the main forum, freedom of speech was secure if only the government kept hands off. Today the press, radio, and television become the main public forum, and effective freedom of speech—the chance for all groups to share in a discussion of all vital issues—is neither greater nor less than their owners decree. Under these conditions, *the protection of freedom of speech sometimes requires the intervention, rather than the abstention, of government.* Yet each governmental attempt actively to protect this freedom—an antitrust suit to keep a newspaper from throttling a competitor,[78] a senatorial proposal to reserve part of the radio frequencies for noncommercial stations,[79] or an FCC effort to require FM stations to broadcast some original material [80]—is denounced by the industry as an attack upon freedom. A widespread confusion as to what freedom of speech means and how it functions lies at the root of many current controversies.

[77] Cf. William Lee Miller, "Can Government Be Merchandised?" *Reporter,* 9 (October 27, 1953), pp. 11-16.
[78] Cf. "Unfair Competition," *Time* (June 9, 1952), pp. 64-67.
[79] White, *op. cit.,* pp. 155-156.
[80] Siepman, *op. cit.,* pp. 244-247.

This technological revolution is not ended. Television is still in its childhood, the facsimile newspaper is in prospect, and still other inventions are almost a certainty. And certain it is that each will bring new problems in the continuous process of adjusting the mass media to the needs of a changing society.

2. The Value-Conflict Approach

The value-conflicts of society produce the arguments over the mass media. Each group wishes to use the media to propagandize its own values, and often seeks to deny use of the media to its opponents. Liberals wish the media to give more discussion to social problems and social reforms; conservatives wish the media to support the status quo. "Highbrows" deplore the taste of the masses, while the masses snort at the "highbrows." The persistent concern over "obscenity" in literature is largely a representation of middle-class disapproval of lower-class tolerances. As long as values differ so widely, as they must in a changing, highly differentiated society, it is difficult to please everybody.

Perhaps the most fundamental value-clash concerns the basic question, What are the media for? Should the mass media be primarily (a) a profit-earning business enterprise, (b) a means of entertainment, or (c) an instrument of mass improvement? Although these objectives are not entirely incompatible, the choice of any one definitely limits the others. Owners generally favor the first, the masses prefer the second, while educators and "highbrows" usually choose the third. Behind most arguments and criticisms of the media lurk such basic value-judgments as these.

3. The Personal-Deviation Approach

This approach contributes relatively little to an understanding of communication problems. There are deviant persons who are somewhat of a nuisance—those who write "crank" letters to the editor, and who pester radio stations with complaints and demands—but they are no serious problem. At times a deviant person may secure leadership of a respectable local or national organization—a veterans organization, labor union, chamber of commerce, a D.A.R. chapter—and use the power of this position in an effort to intimidate the media into airing only his own neurotic viewpoints; but such persons cannot be effective for long unless they also express the character and viewpoint of the members of the organization. Occasionally a deviant person will secure control of a newspaper or radio station and seek to use it to promote his intemperate views. In radio, such behavior may soon get him into trouble with the FCC.[81] In the news-

[81] Cf. Charles A. Siepman, *Radio, Television, and Society* (New York, Oxford University Press, 1950), p. 234.

paper world, the neuroticism of the owner, or of a columnist, probably accounts for some of the most notorious abuses of press responsibility.

But even if all editors, writers, newscasters, and private citizens were perfectly adjusted personalities, communications problems would remain very much the same. Social change always disorganizes, and values differ even among well-adjusted persons. Deviant persons may complicate communications problems, but do not cause them.

SUGGESTIONS FOR IMPROVING THE MASS MEDIA

Although the owners and operators of the mass media have generally argued that they should be permitted to run their own affairs like any other business enterprise, some critics contend that the mass media owe a special obligation to the public, differing from the obligations of other business enterprises. For *the private citizen is forced by circumstance to support the mass media, whether or not he wishes.* Of each dollar he spends, a few cents go for advertising, which provides two-thirds of the income of magazines and newspapers and nearly all of the income of radio and television. As a taxpayer, he shoulders the expense of carrying newspapers and magazines through the mails at less than cost, giving the publisher an indirect subsidy which, for a very large publisher, runs into several million dollars a year. Each radio and television station is a partial monopoly; since the air waves are limited, the FCC in granting only a limited number of licenses also protects each station from having unlimited competition. As a result, the radio industry has enjoyed monopoly profits. In 1939, the net profit rate of the entire radio broadcasting industry averaged 125 per cent on their depreciated investment; in 1944, this had risen to 315 per cent.[82] By 1952 the profit rate for radio broadcasting had fallen to 41 per cent, but the profit rate for television had reached 66 per cent and was rapidly rising.[83] These profit rates, many times higher than those earned by competitive businesses, are possible only because the public grants to a limited number of operators the free use of the air waves. Meanwhile, the public's investment in receiving sets is about twenty-five times as great as the industry's investment in broadcasting stations, and the public spends nearly twice as much in operating these receivers as the industry spends in operating the broadcasting studios and transmitters.[84] Far from receiving the products of modern communication "free," the public pays the entire cost in one way or another, often in ways

[82] Federal Communications Commission, *op. cit.,* p. 50.
[83] Federal Communications Commission, *19th Annual Report* (Washington, Government Printing Office, 1954), pp. 115, 116.
[84] Federal Communications Commission, *Public Service Responsibility of Broadcast Licensees* (Washington, Government Printing Office, 1946), p. 54.

over which they have no individual control. In citing these facts, *it is not necessarily implied that this situation is "bad."* It may be (and probably is) in the public interest to subsidize the media in various ways, for the public's subsidies to the press, and the gift of the air waves which have earned such handsome profits for radio, have greatly aided in their development and expansion. Furthermore, they lay the basis for viewing communications as a *public utility,* answerable to the public for their standards of performance.

The owners and operators of the media have not welcomed this public interest and have usually denounced even highly responsible criticisms as attacks on press freedom and free enterprise.[85] But public criticism continues, and numerous and detailed proposals for the improvement of the media have been published,[86] many of which fall into a few main types of proposals.

1. Antimonopoly Action

Practically every set of proposals includes measures designed to preserve and increase competition or infuse "new blood" into the media. Specific proposals include vigorous application and prosecution of the antitrust laws, government encouragement to new ventures in communications, sponsorship of new ventures by philanthropic foundations, encouragement to noncommercial radio and television stations, control of radio program content by stations rather than advertisers, and many others.

To find the most widely acceptable balance between the efficiency of large-scale operation and the presumed benefits of competition is not easy. Any decision involves a value-judgment, and rearranges an array

[85] E.g., The Commission on Freedom of The Press, a highly responsible group of distinguished educators assembled by Robert M. Hutchins and financed by a $200,000 grant from Time, Inc., and a $15,000 grant from the Encyclopaedia Britannica, Inc., made its report and recommendations in 1947. A year later, Hutchins asked, "What did you, the newspaper editorial writers, do with it? Some of you read the commission's report incorrectly; some treated it unfairly; some used untruthful headlines; and some just plain lied about it." (Quoted in newsletter, *Between The Lines,* January 10, 1949, p. 1.) The commission's report on radio, prepared by Llewellyn White, states that "The monotonous references to 'free speech' and 'the American System' which greet each criticism of broadcasting, however temperate . . ." expose the broadcasting industry to both public ridicule and to the danger of eventual excessive governmental interference, because "the American people may react one day, when their support is really needed to defend genuine freedoms precisely as the shepherds of the fable reacted to the ultimate cry of 'Wolf! Wolf!'" (White, *op. cit.,* p. 84.)

[86] Commission on Freedom of the Press, *A Free and Responsible Press* (Chicago, University of Chicago Press, 1947), pp. 79-106; Federal Communications Commission, *Public Service Responsibility of Broadcast Licenses* (Washington, Government Printing Office, 1946), pp. 54-59; White, *The American Radio, op. cit.,* pp. 204-236; Inglis, *Freedom for The Movies, op. cit.,* pp. 172-204; Leon Svirsky, ed., *Your Newspaper* (New York, The Macmillan Company, 1947), pp. 188-194; Morris Ernst, *The First Freedom* (New York, The Macmillan Company, 1946), pp. 245-271.

of vested interests. At present, the trend towards concentration of control appears to be continuing. Whether it is either desirable or politically possible to reverse it is a moot question.

2. Censorship

Proposals and attempts at censorship and various forms of pressure and intimidation are too numerous to catalog. Wertham wants to prohibit the sale of comic books to children under 15,[87] and Mannes suggests that "the shot and the knockout" be prohibited on television shows for children.[88] Several private organizations are busily branding those textbooks which they consider unfit for student consumption. Several states and a number of cities have legal censorship boards who must approve any motion picture before public showing. In a number of cities, more or less official boards inspect the newsstands for obscene material. Sometimes the censorship efforts are directed at the author or producer rather than the content. Two states now have laws requiring that for each text in use, the publisher must supply anti-communist oaths from the authors and all others quoted therein. The American Legion claims credit for largely preventing showing of Charlie Chaplin's film "Limelight," not because of the film content, but because they disliked Chaplin's political beliefs and associations.[89] The Minute Women asked the banning of an edition of *Moby Dick* because it had been illustrated by Rockwell Kent,[90] a painter whom they considered subversive. Such examples could be added indefinitely. Dozens of state bills and hundreds of local ordinance proposals for censorship are offered each year and arouse bitter controversy. The American Library Association and the American Book Publishers Council are much alarmed, feeling that our basic "freedom to read" is in danger.[91]

Censorship has several fundamental limitations. (1) It is purely negative. Although it may eliminate "bad" content, it cannot produce "good" content. To censor obscenity does not produce noble drama; instead it is more likely to produce a studious playing at the fringes of the obscenity code. (2) There may be a "boomerang" effect. Nothing stimulates the sale of a book like being banned in Boston. A considerable number of third-rate books and shows have been rescued from commercial oblivion by the censors. To be fully effective, censorship must be imposed *before* publication or production. (3) To define unsuitable content is difficult. Sheer nudity is less provocative than gossamer covering. Obscenity codes

[87] Wertham, *op. cit.*
[88] Mannes, *op. cit.*
[89] See William Murray, "Limelight," *The Nation*, 175 (March 21, 1953), p. 247.
[90] See Martin Hale, "The Revolt Against Reason," *The Nation*, 178 (January 9, 1954), pp. 30-32.
[91] "The Freedom to Read," *Time* (July 6, 1953), pp. 62-64.

may produce a sophisticated sort of sexual innuendo which makes people even more sex-conscious than would occasional obscenity.[92] To define obscenity so as to prevent the cheap exploitation of sex without also preventing literary realism and artistic integrity seems to be impossible. To define subversion so as to prevent the deliberate undermining of the social system yet permit mature social criticism is still more impossible. In fact, many attempts to censor "subversion" are basically attempts to prevent the expression of any social criticism. (4) It is hard to place limits upon censorship. The power to censor indecency also includes the power to censor *ideas* personally offensive to the censors—and sooner or later, this usually happens. For these reasons, scholars and intellectuals seem generally to feel that censorship represents a treatment more dangerous than the disease. Unless the intellectual atmosphere of our society grows considerably more repressive and authoritarian—a distinct possibility—it seems unlikely that censorship will be greatly extended.

3. Development of Noncommercial Media

Although there are very few in America who oppose private ownership and commercial development of mass media, there are many who favor supplementing this system with some noncommercial facilities. It has been suggested that philanthropic foundations, educational institutions, labor organizations, co-operatives, farmer organizations, and other groups engage in the operation of mass media, thereby reducing concentration of control and increasing the variety of choices and biases. Support for noncommercial radio and television stations is particularly widespread.

The history of educational AM radio is not encouraging. Of over 200 licenses for educational stations granted since 1921, only 34 remained in operation in 1950. Some languished for lack of faculty interest; some died for lack of financial support; some were crowded out when commercial applicants wanted their frequencies.[93] Many commercial stations offered time to schools and colleges for educational broadcasts; often this time was not used, either because the schools lacked funds or interest, because good listening hours were not offered, or because the irregularity and uncertainty of the time offered prevented orderly programming and audience-building.

The appearance of FM radio and the perfection of tape recording opened new opportunities for educational radio, and by 1954 there were 123 educational FM stations in operation. Local broadcasts are supplemented by a wide variety of tape recordings interchanged through the National Association of Educational Broadcasters, which also distributes many tape recordings of British Broadcasting Corporation programs.

[92] Inglis, *op. cit.*, pp. 183-185.
[93] White, *op. cit.*, pp. 103-109.

The FCC has reserved 245 television channels for educational stations. About a dozen educational television stations were on the air by the end of 1954, with plans in various stages of completion for 130 more. Of the first 50 stations, 34 will be community stations, eight will be college stations and eight will be state-owned. Cost is a major obstacle, with an educational television station costing from $200,000 to $1,000,000 to build and from $100,000 to $200,000 a year to operate. Costs are being met largely through contributions from private citizens, foundations, commercial broadcasters, and in some cases, appropriations of public funds.[94] Programs include school programs for classroom viewing, after-school children's programs, adult education telecourses at college level sometimes carrying college credit, and general education and "cultural" programs. No educational television networks are planned, but programs of widespread interest will be kinescoped and distributed nationally on film through the Educational Television and Radio Center at Ann Arbor, Michigan.

It is too early to predict the fate of educational television. The statistics cited above will be "dated" soon after this book appears in print. And whether educational television can survive on voluntary contributions or must eventually depend upon appropriations of public funds is a vital question.

In radio and television, noncommercial outlets greatly increase the variety of total broadcast offerings in some localities without greatly impairing the commercial broadcast industry's freedom of action or opportunities for profit. In the movie industry, noncommercial films are largely limited to classroom educational films, or to the propaganda films of vested interest groups. In the press, the labor press offers a forum to a group which feels itself mistreated by the commercial press, while a small liberal press opposes the bias of the commercial press with a bias of its own, receives little advertising revenue, loses money steadily, and survives only through voluntary contributions of its supporters. All in all, the media gain much variety and diversity through the existence of some noncommercial and semicommercial facilities.

4. Self-Regulation

Each set of proposals includes a suggestion that the members of each industry develop and follow a set of standards for the self-regulation of the industry. Self-regulation, with its accompanying codes of performance, can be an effective means of regulating a medium, or it can be a smoke screen to confuse and disarm critics. Often it is the latter. The most idealistic code of ethics is of little effect if compliance is voluntary;

[94] Data from various news releases by National Citizens Committee for Educational Television (Ring Building, Washington 6, D.C.)

the comic-book industry is accused of having one of the most highly praised and rarely followed codes in existence.[95] On the other hand, a self-regulation system with penalties and machinery for enforcement of the code upon violators is easily subject to abuse and is rarely popular within the industry. The only highly effective program of industry self-regulation has been in the motion-picture industry, which established the "Hays office" [96] to stem the rising tide of legal censorship.[97] Its Production Code Administration (now headed by Joseph Breen) inspects scripts before filming and may recommend changes or disapprove the entire script. Lack of approval makes distribution of the completed film difficult, and practically all producers abide by the Breen office's recommendations. This movie self-regulation has eliminated many offensive features and enabled the industry to avoid the further spread of legal censorship. The existing censorship laws have remained in effect, however, and the Legion of Decency and other private groups keep the movies under careful scrutiny.

Experience seems to indicate that self-regulation is effective only when an industry feels the public breath hot upon its collective neck. Whether purely voluntary codes without machinery for enforcement accomplish anything is debatable. They may persuade an industry towards a greater sense of social responsibility, or they may retard this development by lending an implied sanction to certain dubious but widespread practices within the industry. It may be unrealistic to expect that self-regulation can elevate standards of performance much above the level of bare public toleration.

5. Advisory Councils and Citizens Organizations

Nearly every survey recommends the assembling of readers, listeners, viewers, and movie-goers into organizations, to report periodically on the levels of performance and exert pressure on the industry for improvement. The Commission on the Freedom of the Press recommends a "new and independent agency to appraise and report annually upon the performance of the press." [98] This commission also recommends local citizens' committees to urge better film fare upon local theater operators and to encourage patronage of good films when presented, and a "national advisory board to review and propose changes from time to time in the Motion Picture Production and Advertising Codes." [99]

[95] See "Reform of Comic Books Is Spurred by Hearings," *New York Times,* June 13, 1954, IV, p. 6.

[96] Officially the Motion Picture Producers and Distributors of America, later shortened to the Motion Picture Association of America, and first headed by prominent churchman and public official, Will H. Hays, Jr.

[97] Inglis, *op. cit.,* Ch. 3.

[98] *Op. cit.,* p. 100.

[99] Inglis, *op. cit.,* pp. vii-viii.

The Radio Council of Greater Cleveland and the Wisconsin Association for Better Radio Listening are operating examples of consumer organization. They seek to improve radio content by praising good programs, encouraging discriminative listening, exerting pressure upon stations, promoting discussion and publicity about programs, carrying members' views to the FCC, and through other activities.[100]

Where tried, such organizations seem to work—to have a real effect upon performance. If nationally organized, their local effect would be far greater. But are many citizens interested enough to bother? This is doubtful. And may such a citizens group become another pressure group, seeking to impose its own narrow views upon the public? Unless broadly democratic in structure and operation, this is a possibility.

SUMMARY

Changes in the technology and business organization of communication have revolutionized the interchange of ideas and the formation of the public opinion by which democracy operates. To many responsible critics, the performance of the media and the vitality of democracy are threatened (1) by tendencies toward monopoly and concentration of control of the media, (2) by their biases and occasional irresponsibility, (3) by the limited variety and low cultural level of their content, and (4) by threats of censorship. Critics also feel that the public, due to its indirect investments in and subsidies to the media, has a legitimate right to a voice in shaping their policies. The numerous suggestions for improvement include: (1) action to reduce the degree of concentration, (2) censorship, (3) development of noncommercial facilities to supplement commercial media, (4) industry self-regulation, and (5) citizens advisory councils and organizations.

To maintain the opportunity for all groups to be heard on vital issues in a period of mechanized, large-scale communication will require a steadily expanding sense of social responsibility from the owners of the media, a changing concept of the role of government in protecting freedom of expression, and an enlarged interest and activity from the public.

This chapter may give to the student an unjustifiably critical impression of the over-all operation of our media of communication. Since it is only the alleged defects of the media that arouse discussion and concern, any presentation of "communications problems" will be mainly a recital of these criticisms. Yet even these critics readily concede that they see much improvement. The press is greatly more accurate, impartial, and responsible than in earlier decades. Movies have become more artistically

---

[100] See Siepman, *Radio, Television and Society, op. cit.*, pp. 77-80; R. J. Blakely, in *Mass Media and Education*, Fifty-third Yearbook, Part II, of the National Society for the Study of Education (Chicago, University of Chicago Press, 1954), pp. 284-285.

produced, and now offend the moral sensibilities of fewer people. Radio has admitted certain groups which it formerly barred, and noncommercial radio and television are helping to provide greater diversity than ever before. Owing in large part to the mass media, no other nation of similar size and ethnic heterogeneity is as well informed as we. The mass media have helped to elevate the level of popular taste, so that by 1951 we were buying more admissions to symphonic concerts than to baseball games.

There is a present tendency throughout the media to avoid controversial issues and curtail minority viewpoints, in deference to the present anxiety over subversion. Whether this tendency continues will depend upon what happens to the general intellectual atmosphere of our society. If this atmosphere grows steadily more repressive and authoritarian—as it appears to have been growing in recent years—all discussions of press freedom will become purely academic. But if such curbs are avoided, there is reasonable prospect that the performance of the media will grow steadily more satisfactory to public and critics alike.

SUGGESTED READINGS

BIRD, George L. and MERWIN, Frederic E., *The Press and Society* (New York, Prentice-Hall, Inc., 1951). A collection of readings dealing with many phases of the press in America.

CALLAHAN, Jennie W., *Television in School, College and Community* (New York, McGraw-Hill Book Company, Inc., 1953). A handbook on the organization and operation of an educational television station.

Commission on the Freedom of the Press, *A Free and Responsible Press* (Chicago, University of Chicago Press, 1947). An authoritative report on the performance of the press, with recommendations for improvement.

ERNST, Morris L., *The First Freedom* (New York, The Macmillan Company, 1946). A critical survey of the problem of monopoly in the mass media of communication, with recommendations for preserving competition and diversity.

Federal Communications Commission, *Public Service Responsibility of Broadcast Licensees* (Washington, Government Printing Office, 1946). A statement of standards of public service for radio, with data on the industry's degree of fulfillment.

INGLIS, Ruth A., *Freedom of the Movies* (Chicago, University of Chicago Press, 1947). A report on movies for the Commission on Freedom of the Press. The history and operation of self-regulation in the movie industry, with recommendations for improvement.

JACOBSON, David J., *The Affairs of Dame Rumor* (New York, Rinehart and Company, 1948). A popularly written, highly entertaining account of how rumors arise and circulate.

LAZARSFELD, Paul F., and STANTON, Frank N., *Communications Research, 1948-1949* (New York, Harper and Brothers, 1949). A collection of research into various aspects of mass media. The section, "The Children Talk About Comics," pp. 3-50, is of especial interest

SIEPMAN, Charles A., *The Radio Listener's Bill of Rights* (New York, Anti-Defamation League of B'nai B'rith, 1948). A brief pamphlet outlining the "rights" of radio listeners and means of securing them.

SIEPMAN, Charles A., *Radio, Television, and Society* (New York, Oxford University Press, 1950). A critical evaluation of the history, structure, and operation of the broadcast industry and means for protecting the public interest.

WHITE, Llewellyn, *The American Radio* (Chicago, University of Chicago Press, 1947). A report on radio for the Commission on Freedom of the Press.

AUDIO-VISUAL AIDS

Freedom of the Press (United World Films, Inc., 1445 Park Ave., New York), 17 minutes, sound, black and white. A historical review of freedom of the press in America from Zinger's weekly journal to today's newspapers. Prepared for use in occupied areas in Europe.

Freedom to Read (Columbia University, Center for Mass Communications, New York), 14 minutes, sound, black and white. Dramatizes the issue of whether a library should remove "controversial" books from circulation.

Rumor (Columbia University, Center for Mass Communications, New York), 8 minutes, sound, black and white. A case-history of a rumor, showing its origin, spread, and consequences. Poses the question of how to deal with rumors.

QUESTIONS AND PROJECTS

1. Why is modern society more dependent upon mass media than ever before?

2. Our founding fathers apparently felt that the only serious threat to freedom of speech and press came from government. Is this view sound today?

3. Should newspapers suppress news which is "harmful" to the community? What further questions are raised by this issue?

4. Should the mass media give the public what it *wants* or what it *needs?* What are the difficulties in trying to give the public what it "needs"?

5. Why does the commercial broadcast industry make relatively little effort to cater to minority tastes? Why is it easier for noncommercial broadcasting to do so?

6. What explains the generally conservative bias of the mass media?

7. What are the "advantages" and "disadvantages" of mass media which have a generally conservative bias?

8. How does the avoidance of controversial issues result in bias? What kind of bias?

9. What would be the effects upon society if the mass media generally reflected a liberal bias?

10. Why has self-regulation been more effective for the movies than for the other media?

11. What is meant by the "least-common-denominator" approach to programming? What are its results?

12. Why is broadcasting the only medium which is subject to much government regulation?

CHAPTER 16

The Personal Pathologies

People don't understand how slot machines can be illegal in Illinois while the Federal government collects a tax of $150 per year on each machine. The lawyer can explain the difference between the gambling laws of Illinois and the revenue laws of the United States. The average citizen, however, naturally assumes that when a machine has been properly registered with the Collector of Internal Revenue and the tax has been paid, the owner is entitled to use it. The owner is indignant when gambling devices on which he has paid the Federal tax are confiscated and destroyed under state law.[1]

... there is little question that the number of alcoholics (by any definition) runs into millions; that annual fatalities in automobile accidents alone, where alcohol is involved, exceed our annual deaths in the Korean war; and that our jails and work houses the country over exist primarily for the temporary restraint of those found guilty of drunkenness.[2]

Arrested by the vice squad of the first precinct, 9-20-40, in a large northern industrial city.... The charge was pandering. The complainant was Simone Potter, 26 years, white, separated from husband. Simone claimed that she prostituted for Helen Bleeker about nine months. She met her when defendant [Helen Bleeker] came to a beer garden where she was employed. On 9-4-40 she passed the defendant's home and defendant called to her. During the conversation the complainant told defendant she was looking for work. Defendant said "Come and work for me. I need a girl."[3]

EACH of the above illustrates a social malady—and a personal affliction. Each may be considered in the abstract—drug addiction, mental illness, prostitution—just as with urbanization, social class, and population. But when one speaks of drug addicts, the insane, or streetwalkers, there is an added implication. There is "something wrong" with such people. Social class, urbanization, and population problems do not depend upon indi-

[1] Governor Adlai E. Stevenson, "Who Runs the Gambling Machines?" *Atlantic Monthly*, 189 (February, 1952), p. 35.
[2] Robert Straus and Selden D. Bacon, *Drinking in College* (New Haven, Yale University Press, 1953), p. 16.
[3] Walter C. Reckless, *The Crime Problem* (New York, Appleton-Century-Crofts, Inc., 1950), p. 241.

vidual "wrongdoing"; nor are they matters of the individual succumbing to forces which many think "should have been resisted." One may be born in an urban slum but ordinarily he is not born a drug addict or a "pimp." He may *become* one of these in subsequent years. The problem inheres both in the *conditions* which lead people into such pathological patterns and in the *persons* who become involved. Those who yield need to be rehabilitated. Even more basic is the need to *prevent* as well as to *cure.*

MENTAL ILLNESS

Magnitude of the Problem

Although we know that the need is great, there are no reliable statistics on the number of people who need hospitalization for emotional problems. The available statistics tell us more about existing facilities for dealing with the mentally ill than about the magnitude of the problem. Commitment rates to mental institutions, for example, vary directly with the adequacy of hospital facilities. States with the fewest hospitals tend to have the lowest commitment rates and states with the most hospitals per unit of population have the highest rates. All but the expensive private sanitaria are tremendously overcrowded. The number of people admitted depends not upon how many people need treatment but upon how much room is available.

Year	Number in Thousands
1923	268
1936	420
1951	584

FIG. 16-1. The Increasing Number of Persons in Hospitals for Mental Diseases. (Data from U. S. Bureau of the Census, *Statistical Abstract of the United States: 1952* [Washington, Government Printing Office], p. 83; and *ibid.,* 1954, p. 92)

In 1951 there were 584,000 people in hospitals for mental disease in the United States.[4] Approximately 150,000 new patients are admitted each year. Mental patients occupy over half of all hospital beds—more than are required for the treatment of all physical illnesses and injuries combined. About one out of every twenty persons in the United States spends at least part of his life in a mental institution. Yet these appallingly high figures still reflect available facilities more than they do actual need. A more accurate picture of the incidence of emotional illness among a re-

[4] U. S. Bureau of the Census, *Statistical Abstract of the United States: 1954* (Washington, 1954), p. 92.

stricted age and sex group is provided by the draft rejection rates during World War II. Over one and one-half million men were rejected for military service because of personality disorders—12 per cent of all men called up.[5] In addition, during the three and one-half years from January, 1942, to June 30, 1945, over 550,000 men were discharged from the army and navy for neuropsychiatric causes.[6] Perhaps one-third of all man power lost to the armed services was due to mental-emotional problems.

The total burden of mental illness is almost beyond belief. In states with better hospital programs, such as New York, nearly one person out of ten encounters hospitalization during his lifetime. That one person out of five in the entire country could substantially profit from psychotherapy, at one time or another, is a conservative estimate.

Nature of Mental Illness

Not long ago a beyond-middle-aged lady remarked to this writer, in the course of a casual conversation, that her husband was "crazy as a loon." And she meant it. She said it as casually as if she had said "my husband has a clubfoot"! She meant to convey only the facts that she could not expect very much from her husband and that in many ways he was a nuisance. It did not occur to her, apparently, that he was "ill" or that anything might be done about his condition. Her ignorance of the true nature of mental illness is quite typical; her blasé acceptance of it, quite atypical. Most people are frightened into near-silence by any mention of mental illness. They are ashamed of its presence in themselves, their families, or their friends, almost as they would be of syphilis. They feel, somehow, that one is to be blamed for becoming ill, and that it is a mark of depravity and inferiority. These definitions are not unexplainable since they reflect directly the accumulated ignorance of the past. They are, however, grossly unrealistic and bear little relation to the true facts.

All of us are potential victims of mental illness. Undoubtedly some persons are more susceptible than others, but no one is immune. It is rather well established that most types of mental illness are not directly hereditary, though a hereditary tendency toward mental illness has not been ruled out. Equally important, mental illness develops through experience just as more normal behavior does. Moreover, normality shades off into illness by almost imperceptible degrees. Checking two or three times to make sure that the door is locked or that the gas is turned off, blaming others for our own failures, and wondering if we are not being

[5] Carl Binger, M.D., "What Is the Psychiatrist's Job?" *McCall's Magazine* (October, 1946), p. 211.

[6] Daniel Blaine, M.D., and John H. Baird, M.D., "The Neuropsychiatric Program of the Veteran's Administration," *American Journal of Psychiatry,* 103 (January, 1947), pp. 463-466.

talked about, are all behaviors which in slightly more exaggerated form would be regarded as pathological. Illness is frequently a matter of degree rather than of kind. Temporary conditions of great stress such as the death of a loved one, a divorce, the marriage of one's child, losing one's job, getting a big promotion, or moving to another city may bring on temporary or even permanent signs of illness in persons who otherwise seem to be reasonably well adjusted. In the light of these facts, the usual distinction between those people who are "crazy" and those who are not is not very useful. We need definitions that will cover the whole range of behavior from the very normal to the most bizarre and dangerous.

Psychotherapists generally use the terms *neurosis* and *psychosis* to indicate both varying *degrees* and *types* of emotional illness. Neurotic behavior ordinarily is less disabling and less serious, covering the whole range from almost normal to that which is serious enough (and possibly incurable) to warrant institutionalization. Psychotic behavior is usually characterized by a more complete break with reality. The psychotic person may have delusions, that is, believe himself to be another person, believe that he has some kind of sacred mission to perform, or that he is being persecuted by other people; or he may suffer hallucinations, that is, hear voices or see visions.

Psychotics may be declared by courts of law to be insane, insanity being a legal status and not a type of illness. Persons defined as insane may be forcibly committed to mental institutions, and thus it is primarily psychotics who populate our mental hospitals and who provide most of the statistics offered at the beginning of this discussion. Not all psychotics, however, are in institutions. Most of us come into occasional contact with one or more of them during our daily activities.

Treatment Facilities and Methods

Rapid progress in the cure and prevention of mental illness is rendered impossible by the shortage of well-qualified, trained personnel. There are approximately 4000 psychiatrists in the United States, when it would take three to four times that many to handle the potential case load recognized at the present time. Moreover, the prospects for rapidly increasing the number of psychiatrists in the near future seem dim indeed. Our medical schools are set up to provide for the training of only a relatively few psychiatrists at a time, and their training is exorbitantly expensive. Both the medical schools and the medical associations oppose rapid expansion of training facilities, presumably upon the grounds that the quality of training would thereby be lowered. That much of conventional medical training is largely irrelevant to the successful practice of psychiatry does not swerve them from their stand. From the standpoint of the prospective psychiatric trainee, psychiatrists even after their long period of training often earn less than general practitioners with good practices. Moreover, the medical associations vigorously oppose the right of any group other than psychiatrists to do psychotherapy. At the present time training facilities are slowly and haltingly being expanded and numerous groups are challenging the medical profession's self-declared monopoly on the treatment of emotional problems, but it will be many years under the most ideal conditions before even a minimum adequate number of therapists can be trained.

The inadequacy of hospital facilities already has been suggested. Most mental hospitals now hold at least 25 to 50 per cent more patients than they were designed to accommodate. Conditions are frequently unsanitary and personally degrading. Patients are quartered in hallways and corridors, sitting on the floors for lack of adequate furniture, and occasionally are even without clothing. And there is constantly pressure on the staff to make room for more. Persons for whom commitment orders have been obtained are denied admittance because there is no room. Even more serious, patients who are not cured are often discharged upon the "hope" that they will not "get into trouble again." [7]

The state governments (especially legislators) which generally administer and finance the hospitals are frequently unaware of and insensitive to their needs. Mental patients cannot complain effectively when they are denied adequate care. The salaries provided for staff members are so low that it is practically impossible to obtain and to hold competent personnel. Attendants, particularly, include large numbers of unintelligent, sadistic, and otherwise maladjusted persons. When a state does decide to put more money into its mental institutions, it is likely to insist that the funds be put into buildings or something that is "tangible," for the public to see. The very rare multimillion-dollar buildings provide a shiny new front for the same old barbarously inadequate care—custodial care by an underpaid, frequently disgruntled, skeleton staff.

Hospitals are supposed to be treatment centers. But overcrowding and understaffing combine to make effective treatment the exception rather than the rule. "Treatment" often consists of administering a battery of tests to the patient when he is admitted to the hospital in order to "classify" him, and then of incarcerating him with a group of similarly classified patients. Psychotherapy, which offers the greatest possibility for actual rehabilitation, is rarely used. Occupational therapy *may be* available to one patient out of twenty. Only the least effective and most drastic treatments are at all widely used. Hydrotherapy, which consists of soaking the patient in a tub of warm water or swathing him in wet blankets,

---

[7] For an authoritative account of the deplorable conditions prevalent in state mental hospitals, see Albert Deutsch, *The Shame of the States* (New York, Harcourt, Brace & Company, Inc., 1948).

makes him easier to handle for a few hours but does little more. Electric- or chemical-shock treatments are widely used and widely condemned. Certainly patients hate and fear them. The most debatable of all is the wide use made of surgical operations that sever some of the higher brain centers. Advocates of such methods insist that following the operation, patients are generally less violent, less inclined to bizarre thoughts and behavior, and thereby "better adjusted." Critics claim that, by destroying part of the patients' affective capacity, they are rendered less capable of any kind of thought or emotion.

It should be noted that there exists an extremely wide gap between the usual standards of care and treatment of the mentally ill and those which are theoretically possible in terms of the best modern knowledge. Considerable progress has been made both in the accumulation of knowledge and in improving standards of treatment. In a book of this sort it is not possible to do more than to "scratch the surface" and to indicate some of the conflicts which are currently raging. Students who are interested in pursuing the problem would do well to consult a thorough analysis such as that contained in Albert Deutsch's *The Mentally Ill in America* (Columbia University Press, 1949).

MENTAL DEFICIENCY

Mental illness and mental deficiency are often confused. Properly, mental illness refers to *disorder* or *disorganization* of the personal life, whereas mental deficiency refers to *subnormal learning ability*, a *lack of* ability rather than disorganization. Psychologists use the term *dements* (down) to designate the mentally ill and the term *aments* (without) to designate the mentally deficient. The two conditions, however, may be closely associated. When the mentally ill person "withdraws" from participation in the social world around him, he often seems to be, and for all practical purposes he is, mentally deficient. His biological capacity to learn may be quite normal, but his illness prevents the effective use of that capacity. In still other cases the same person may be both mentally ill and mentally deficient because of some injury to or deformity of the brain. The important difference between these two types of cases is in the prognosis—the possibility of doing something about the substandard performance. In the former case, cure of the illness releases the capacity to learn; in the latter the condition is generally irreversible.

Estimates of the number of mental defectives generally range from 2 to 3 per cent of the total population, thus from a little over three million to almost five million people in the United States. These figures include all defectives from the almost totally helpless to the almost normal. Generally defectives are classified by I.Q., that is, by their performance upon standardized intelligence tests. An I.Q. of 100 is considered normal or average, I.Q.'s of above 100 indicate superior intelligence, and I.Q.'s much below 100 indicate mental deficiency. A common scheme of classification is:

I.Q.	Classification
90-110	Normal
80- 90	Dull Normal
70- 80	Borderline
50- 70	Moron
20- 50	Imbecile
0- 20	Idiot

The idiot and imbecile groups are the smallest, probably including less than half a million persons in the United States. The vast majority of deficients fall within the moron and borderline categories.

The extreme lack of capacity in idiots and imbeciles is generally accompanied by other complications. The abnormality extends into the structure of the body at large, producing severe physical disability and often bringing death at an early age. Included in this group are the microcephalics, hydrocephalics, cretins, mongolian idiots, and amaurotic idiots. With the possible exception of hydrocephaly these conditions are all congenital, that is, they are present at birth. In most cases both hereditary and intra-uterine environmental factors seem to be involved. Marked glandular deficiencies in the mother are associated with cretinism, and pregnancies in women who are approaching the menopause are much more likely to produce mongolian idiots than are the pregnancies of younger women. Such conditions do not tend to run in specific family lines but tend to appear almost at random in the general population. Thus wholly normal parents are almost as likely to produce an idiot or imbecile as mentally deficient parents are. Such low-grade deficients seldom reproduce. Their abilities are so limited that they remain continuously dependent upon others for the performance of even the simplest tasks. A large proportion of them are institutionalized from infancy onward and their life spans are generally short. The great tragedy of such extreme deficiency, beyond the plight of the helpless creatures themselves, is the tremendous burden of anguish placed upon parents and other family members. Especially in middle-class society, parents are supposed to love *all* of their children, no matter what. Yet love implies mutual response and admiration. The hopelessly deficient child can seldom respond in meaningful fashion and is not regarded as an object of admiration. Feelings of sorrow are likely to be mixed with feelings of guilt and shame. Parents can hardly help feeling that "we are to blame" or that "we must be grossly deficient ourselves to produce such a deficient child." Such feelings as these are not supported by the findings of genetics and medical science, but few persons are sufficiently familiar with or sufficiently able to accept such rational knowledge.

At least five-sixths of the mentally deficient are somewhat educable. Relatively few of this group are institutionalized but even fewer of them receive the kind of care and guidance which might turn them into really useful citizens. Unlike the extreme deficients, most morons are produced by their own kind. Morons beget morons—in distressingly large numbers. Beyond indicating that subnormal intelligence runs in certain families, however, it is most difficult to determine its basis with any degree of precision. It seems clear that heredity plays a major role in some cases and that social factors are primary in some others. Although it is not surprising that perhaps half of all such deficiency is of genetic origin, it is surprising that the other half could perpetuate itself through generation after generation without there being any hereditary inferiority.

Most of the families involved are to be found among the lowest income and education groups. They exist apart from most of the benefits of modern civilization, living in filth, squalor, and social isolation. Children are trained early and continuously in the incompetence of their parents. Motivation for improvement is absent; even the possibility of improvement remains undiscovered. By the time school age is reached, the pattern is well established in a new generation. Far too frequently such children are placed in special classes for the mentally retarded, where the chief goal is to keep them occupied until they become old enough legally to drop out of school. The educational system has often done as much to reinforce the pattern as to correct it! Adequate programs for rehabilitating such children scarcely exist today. Few teachers are sufficiently well trained and sufficiently skilled to do the job, and even then the necessary funds to run a successful program are generally lacking. Communities by and large are not interested in the mentally retarded. Instead, the incompetents are defined as "worthless," "no-goods," "lazy," "impossible of rehabilitation." Such definitions neatly absolve the community of much responsibility for the deficient (other than to provide food baskets at Thanksgiving and Christmas), but they do little to prevent the appearance of an even larger group of morons in the next generation.

ALCOHOLISM

Magnitude of the Problem

Americans spend more money for alcohol each year than they spend upon the education of their children. An estimated two-thirds of all adults drink, some 60-80 million people in the United States.[8] Most people are *social drinkers,* or at least they start out that way. They begin the drinking pattern as a part of the organized social life in which they participate.

[8] Robert Straus and Selden D. Bacon, *Drinking in College* (New Haven, Yale University Press, 1953), p. 9.

What they drink, where, when, and in what quantities, depends upon the social context. Beer, wine, whiskey, bourbon, scotch, and brandy have different appeals at different social levels. In some groups men drink with men; in other groups men and women drink together. In one situation the goal is to get rapidly and boisterously drunk; in another, two drinks before dinner may be followed by three or four more afterward. Certainly "well-bred" people do not become intoxicated—that is, *too* intoxicated! But in all cases it is the consumption of alcohol which counts. The intoxication may be genteel or crude, but generally it is some degree of intoxication.

Intoxication may be of two sorts—acute or chronic. It may be the temporary result of too much celebration or a too successful party, such incidents being sandwiched between longer or shorter periods of relative sobriety. Or it may be a fairly continual pattern. When the periods of sobriety in between become shorter and the intoxicated state becomes the generally preferred one, the intoxication has become chronic. The amount of drunkenness, both acute and chronic, is exceedingly difficult to measure, as is even the number of people who are drinkers. The best estimates available, however, indicate a pool of probably three million *excessive* drinkers out of the total 60-80 million drinkers. Perhaps 750,000 people in the United States are chronic alcoholics. Approximately 13,500 of them are the victims of alcoholic psychoses.[9] Over 200,000 people are arrested by the police each year and charged either with drunkenness or disorderly conduct—more than five times the number charged with gambling, drug addiction, and prostitution combined.

The Alcoholic Pattern

Drinking is a recognized part of American culture. One need not look for aberrant personality factors or unresolved frustrations to explain why most people begin. A recently completed study of the drinking habits of over 15,000 college students indicated that 80 per cent of the men and approximately 60 per cent of the women engage in some kind of drinking.[10] Moreover the study reveals that knowledge of the students' backgrounds and their present social situation provides some basis for predicting how many of them will be drinkers, what they will drink and how much and how often they will drink. The probability that an individual will imbibe apparently is greater if he attends a private nonsectarian college, if his family has a substantial income, if he does not belong to the Mormon church, if his parents drink, and if his close friends drink. Moreover, most of the students who are drinkers began before they en-

[9] The Research Council on Problems of Alcohol, *The Scientific Approach to the Problem of Chronic Alcoholism* (New York, 1947), pp. 5-6.

[10] Robert Straus and Selden D. Bacon, *op. cit.*, p. 47.

tered college and took their first drinks in their own homes.[11] The study in general, however, does not support the stereotype of widespread *excessive* drinking among college students. Chronic drinking and alcoholism appear to develop somewhat later in life.

Once drinking has begun there is always the risk that it will get out of control. The antisocial chronic alcoholics of tomorrow are to be found, by and large, among the social drinkers of today. One study of chronic alcoholics revealed that only 10 per cent of them began as solitary drinkers.[12] Instead, there is a steady path from moderate, controlled drinking to uncontrollable alcoholism. It is a path of demoralization and decay, involving loss of self-respect as a minimum and often job, home, and even family as a part of the process.

Acute intoxication appears to be the first step. In the study of college drinking patterns referred to above, 80 per cent of men drinkers and 49 per cent of women drinkers admitted to having been tight at least once.[13] Occasional acute intoxication is almost inevitable if drinking is continued over any period of time. Possibly most drinkers succeed in limiting themselves to this first stage. But for a sizable group, some loss of control over future drinking tends to follow the experience of intoxication. In the aforementioned study of chronic alcoholics, loss of control followed the first intoxication by about two years.[14] The intoxication becomes chronic. The next step is the blackout, where following a drinking spree the individual can remember little or nothing that happened while he was under the influence. Sobriety brings torment. No one approves of such extreme intoxication. It is disgraceful! What did one do and say? How could one have so completely lost control? Intoxication itself comes to afford the only relief from shame and doubt. Sneak drinking sets in. One must always keep a bottle nearby in case it is needed. But the need implies dependence—one cannot get along without it! Such a sorry state must be concealed from the eyes of others. Drinking becomes solitary. Self-protection demands isolation and the individual becomes antisocial. The first drink is taken upon awaking in the morning, and drinking continues. Complete intoxication becomes more frequent and lasts longer. The alcoholic goes on "benders" which last for days at a time and during which his personal life goes to pieces. Demoralization is practically complete. There seems to be no escape and no solution.

[11] *Ibid., passim.*

[12] E. M. Jellinek, "Phases in the Drinking History of Alcoholics," *Quarterly Journal of Studies on Alcohol,* 7 (June 1946), pp. 1-97.

[13] Being "tight" was defined as "suggests unsteadiness in ordinary physical activities, or noticeable aggressiveness, or oversolicitousness, or loss of control over social amenities or of verbal accuracy, or slight nausea." *Op. cit.,* p. 131.

[14] E. M. Jellinek, *op. cit.*

Alcoholics Anonymous

The seemingly hopeless plight of most alcoholics has led many persons to refer to alcoholism as a disease. Although such broad usage of the term *disease* is questionable, it does stress the fact of uncontrollable dependence upon alcohol. Alcoholism parallels drug addiction in that there develops both psychological and physiological dependence. Efforts at cure must break that dependence. One of the most successful efforts to date is the growing movement called Alcoholics Anonymous.

Alcoholics Anonymous makes use of the terror and understanding of alcoholics and former alcoholics themselves. It is, in fact, an organization of former alcoholics committed to aid others to rehabilitation. The movement which began in 1934 stresses unlimited personal aid to the person who is attempting to stop drinking, combined with a kind of nonsectarian religious fellowship shared by all members of the group. The tenets of that fellowship to which each member subscribes are:

1. To admit that one is powerless over alcohol—that he has lost control of his life.
2. To believe in a higher Power who can restore men to sanity.
3. To will to turn one's life over to God, as one understands Him.
4. To make a searching and fearless inventory of himself.
5. To admit to God, to himself, and to another human being the nature of his wrongs.
6. To be ready to have God remove these defects of character.
7. To humbly ask God to remove one's shortcomings.
8. To make a list of all persons one has harmed and to be willing to make amends to them.
9. To make amends wherever possible.
10. To continue to take personal inventory and to admit all wrongs.
11. To seek contact with God, as one understands Him, through prayer and meditation to know His will and to have the power to accept His will.
12. To carry this message to other alcoholics and to practice these principles in all of one's affairs.

Any member who begins to feel that he may succumb to the desire for alcohol in spite of these tenets has only to contact other members who, day or night, will come to his aid and remain with him until the period of danger has passed.

While not a universal solution, Alcoholics Anonymous has proved its usefulness. From its beginning among primarily business and professional groups it has spread into almost all levels of society and by April, 1954, numbered 5401 groups with 128,296 members in the United States and foreign countries.[15] The exact proportion of its successes and failures is not known. One estimate states that probably one-fourth of the "cured"

[15] Correspondence from Alcoholics Anonymous, New York. Cited in Walter C. Reckless, *The Crime Problem*, 2nd ed. (New York, Appleton-Century-Crofts, Inc., 1955), p. 340.

alcoholics have relapses and that with another 25 per cent it fails alto-gether.[16]

GAMBLING

Its Nature and Extent

Probably gambling is the most difficult of the personal pathologies to define and to describe with precision. Basically, gambling involves a de-pendence upon chance—dependence upon the turn of a card, the roll of dice, the appearance of a certain combination of numbers or symbols, or the winner of a race. Uncertainty and the possibility of benefiting or los-ing as the uncertainty is translated into reality are inevitably a part of gambling whatever specific form it may take.

We easily recognize certain forms of gambling which are commercial-ized and which utilize establishments and/or devices arranged specifi-cally for that purpose. These would cover the usual run of "gambling joints," roulette wheels, gaming tables, and so on down to the private card game in the back room of a local tavern or pool hall. Not always recognized as gambling are the policy or numbers rackets, lotteries, and pinball machines which pay off in the form of cash, merchandise, or only "free" games. Even less widely recognized are raffles and bingo games used by church, civic, and charitable groups to raise money for worthy causes. If carried much further, gambling becomes truly indistinguishable from the normal elements of chance that are a part of living itself. Specu-lation on the stock market and commodity or futures markets is now rather widely recognized as gambling, but what about the large or small investor who merely hopes that his securities may undergo a modest in-crease in value in addition to providing dividends or interest? Where does gambling cease and legitimate business investment begin? Consider the man who takes a chance by parking his automobile in a restricted zone, who underinsures his house, or even who crosses a busy street away from the intersection? These are not gambling in the conventional sense but they contain similar elements of chance.

Sociologically, gambling can be differentiated from the normal opera-tion of chance in our lives by two criteria. First, gambling exists when the individual hopes or works for extraordinary gain—gain out of propor-tion to the money invested or to the effort exerted. The gambler typically hopes to "make a killing." Second, gambling serves as an escape—an escape from the predictability or the routine or the frustration of every-day life. At least temporarily the gambler sees the opportunity to be freed from some of the restrictions he ordinarily faces. If he is lucky he may be able to avoid experiencing those restrictions again. Seldom if ever is he

[16] Anonymous, "My Return from the Half-World of Alcoholism," *Reader's Digest*, 48 (January, 1946), p. 34.

that lucky, of course, but even the act of gambling may afford him temporary relief. He may "live beyond himself" for as long as the gambling lasts and may come to depend on the process of gambling as formerly he did upon the hope of winning.

For the very reasons that gambling cannot be precisely defined, the number of gamblers and the money cost of gambling to the society are difficult to estimate. Probably the majority of adults participate in professional gambling of some kind. The risk of being arrested for gambling ordinarily is not great. More arrests are made for gambling than for narcotics violations or prostitution but gambling arrests do not number one-tenth of those for drunkenness. Much gambling, obviously, is done in very private circumstances, but even in public places the police are likely to "look the other way" unless there is general disorderliness or unless too many people complain.

The money costs of some limited forms of gambling have been estimated. Betting the horses, for example, certainly costs the American people more than a billion dollars annually.[17] The numbers or policy rackets have an estimated "take" of approximately a billion dollars each year, and slot machines probably take another billion dollars from the gambling public. Bloch reports an estimate to the effect that gambling profits are greater than the combined profits of the hundred largest manufacturing concerns in the United States, including such giants as General Motors, General Electric, and the United States Steel Corporation.[18] These are merely *some* of the *money* costs of gambling. The personal costs are far greater.

Legal Status

Gambling in the United States ordinarily is illegal. Only one state, Nevada, has legalized gambling and put it under government regulation. The importance of gambling in the Nevada economy is indicated by the fact that an estimated 15 per cent of all state revenue is derived from taxes on the gambling take and from the licensure of gaming establishments and devices.[19] In the other forty-seven states gambling operates without the sanction of law but is frequently unmolested. There are some genuine efforts to stamp out gambling in certain localities, but these rarely meet with any degree of success. For one thing, gambling is profitable and, on the local level at least, gamblers often wield political power far out of proportion to their numbers. Again, gambling is often an adjunct to businesses that are not themselves illegal. The law can attack the

[17] Albert H. Morehead, "What Makes Men Gamble?" *New York Times Magazine,* January 13, 1946, p. 24.

[18] Herbert A. Bloch, *Disorganization, Personal and Social* (New York, Alfred A. Knopf, Inc., 1952), p. 473.

[19] *Ibid.,* p. 474.

gambling but not the businesses that nurture it. Finally, the existence of gambling is tacitly supported by a sizable proportion of the population including some of the very people who are charged with eliminating it. The public sentiment which is translated into antigambling laws simply is not very effective on the enforcement level.

One of the least understood aspects of the problem is the seemingly conflicting policies and authorities of various governmental units in relation to gambling. The division of power between the federal, state, and local governments provides part of the basis for this confusion. Gambling ordinarily is regulated by the separate states, but the Constitution gives to the federal government certain broad powers to raise revenue and to regulate the flow of commerce among the states. Since gambling is so profitable and since it is not prohibited by federal law, the federal government has often seen fit to tax it. The statement by the former governor of Illinois quoted at the beginning of this chapter shows how the federal government thus taxes activities which are illegal in the localities where they operate. Payment of the federal tax does not render the gamblers immune to prosecution under the local laws but instead may render prosecution easier by identifying the gamblers and providing records of their activities. The most recent, and probably the most threatening to professional gamblers, of these taxes is the federal tax of $50 per year upon the gambler himself. If he pays the tax the gambler opens himself to local prosecution; if he does not pay it he may be prosecuted by the federal government for violation of the revenue laws. The two-way squeeze is making professional gambling operations increasingly hazardous.

Personal Demoralization

The gravest cost of gambling cannot be measured in purely monetary terms. The tremendous sums of money wagered represent a loss in productive effort to the society and represent a kind of social parasitism, with the professional gamblers drawing sustenance from but not contributing to the labors of others. But what is more tragic is what happens to the personal lives of many persons who become inveterate gamblers.

It is unlikely that many of the persons who gamble for the first time do so out of purely neurotic inclination or even out of a passionate desire to increase their holdings. Most persons become acquainted with gambling through ordinary daily routine. Many children's games involve the roll of dice or the drawing of cards or otherwise include a large chance element. Family card games, church raffles, and so on, are known to most of us. The excitement of anticipating the unknown and the pleasure of being rewarded for being lucky are common experiences. It is only a short step then to gambling in adult life. Bridge parties, poker games, football pools, playing the numbers, and wagering on the outcome of elections grade into playing the horses and sitting at the gaming tables. For most persons gambling remains, however, a pleasant diversion. Knowledge of "the odds" discourages serious dependence on gambling and occasional small losses strengthen that conviction.

Occasionally, nevertheless, the pattern takes hold. Gambling is much more frequent in some social groups than in others and belonging to such a group increases the probability of extensive participation. With more extensive participation may come more dependence on the excitement of gambling as an escape from frustration of any sort. The more one gambles the greater the tendency for losses to mount, and the less the probability that one can afford or support the pattern. When the individual gets in too deep, the recuperation of losses by any normal means may become well-nigh impossible. A man's total earnings may be plunged at the expense of home, family, job, and respectability. These losses, rather than discourage gambling, may increase dependence upon it. One "streak of luck" may seem to be the only way out and may pull the individual steadily downhill. Inability to pay gambling debts may increase dishonor and lead to evasion or even theft as a means of meeting them. The process once begun is difficult to halt, let alone to be reversed. Herein lies the greatest tragedy in gambling—that what began as pleasant diversion may become the means to complete personal destruction.

DRUG ADDICTION

Nature and Costs

Distortion and misinformation comprise much of the "knowledge" that most people have of narcotic addiction. The specter of innumerable shady characters loafing around street corners and school yards hoping to induce high-school students to become addicts is almost pure fantasy. Not that an occasional high-school student does not become addicted—some do. In fact some forms of addiction, at least, are most common among very young adults. Occasionally these groups may initiate a high-school acquaintance into the use of drugs, but the facts of this situation are a far cry from the supposed exposés luridly detailed in newspapers and magazines.

Again, no one knows exactly how many drug addicts there are in the United States. The available evidence indicates, however, that the number is probably smaller than is generally believed and is decreasing with the passage of time. Many estimates have placed the number of probable addicts at something over a hundred thousand. The Federal Bureau of Narcotics, on the other hand, estimates that there are currently not over 60,000 addicts in the United States.[20] This is less than one-twelfth the

[20] John Gerrity, "The Truth About the Drug Menace," *Harper's*, 204 (February, 1952), p. 28.

number of chronic alcoholics. Moreover, the vast majority of addicts apparently are concentrated in several of our largest cities—New York, Philadelphia, Chicago, Washington, Detroit, Baltimore, New Orleans, and Los Angeles.[21]

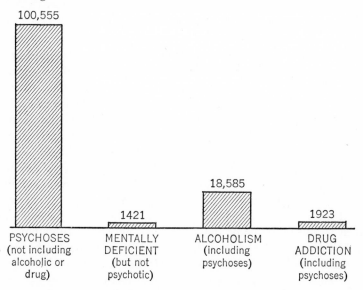

FIG. 16-2. Comparative Hospitalization for Mental Illness, Mental Deficiency, Alcoholism, and Drug Addiction, 1949. (Data from U. S. Bureau of the Census, *Statistical Abstract of the United States: 1954* [Washington, Government Printing Office], p. 91)

That addiction is less common today than formerly is not surprising. Federal regulation has taken narcotics out of general sale, whereas a generation ago many narcotic drugs could be bought by anyone without medical prescription. During the First World War one out of every 1500 draftees was found to be an addict, but the figure dropped to only one out of every 10,000 selectees during World War II.[22] The post-World War II period brought public attention to the problem and Congressional investigation of the drug traffic was begun. There have been sporadic increases in the number of narcotic arrests since the war, but these probably reflect more rigid enforcement of the laws rather than an increase in the use of drugs.

The monetary costs of drug addiction are phenomenally high. Even if we omit the proportion of ordinary police work which goes into suppressing the drug traffic, governmental costs will amount to over $5 million per year. The two federal narcotics hospitals cost $3 million per year to

[21] *Ibid.*
[22] *Ibid.*

run, and the Narcotics Bureau is likely to spend over $2 million each year.[23] Added to these figures, the average addict must spend from $15 to $75 per day to support the habit. Using the minimum figure, 60,000 addicts would spend over $300 million dollars per year for drugs.

Addiction and Demoralization

As with the other personal pathologies, the greatest costs of drug addiction must be measured in terms of broken lives. The path to addiction is the path to demoralization and despair.

Persons apparently begin to use drugs in one of two principal ways. They may use them consciously and deliberately for the intoxicating or euphoric effects the drugs provide. Or drugs may first be used for the relief of pain while under medical treatment. However begun, the use of drugs is habit forming. The user seeks to repeat the "kick" or "jolt" or again to relieve the pain. For some drugs, tolerance develops with use. That is, it begins to require more of the drug to produce the same effect provided by the initial doses. As increased use develops, the body begins to adjust to the presence of the drug and physiologic functioning is altered. At this stage, real withdrawal symptoms appear. As the drug begins to wear off, the body, which has become dependent upon its presence, causes the user to experience great distress. The symptoms may range from excessive perspiration and dilation of the pupils of the eyes to violent trembling and vomiting. As soon as the user connects his distress to withdrawal of the drug and seeks more narcotics to relieve the discomfort, he is "hooked." [24] He is an addict. The lurid conceptions of confirmed addicts, supposedly "high" on narcotics, are far less accurate than those which picture addicts as tormented souls continually on the verge of physical distress and struggling desperately to maintain an adequate supply of drugs.

Once hooked, the addict is likely to have little time or energy for anything other than replenishing his supply of narcotics. Because the trade is illegal, narcotics are expensive. Few addicts can earn the $15 or more per day required to purchase them. Thus the addict is prone to become involved in crime. To support the habit he may turn to "boosting" (shoplifting) and often to forging checks. Since the addict generally secures at least part of his supply through legitimate trade channels, he may steal physicians' prescription forms and forge the prescriptions themselves. His addiction places him in continuing and increasing jeopardy and makes normal living virtually impossible.

[23] Alden Stevens, "Make Dope Legal," *Harper's*, 205 (November, 1952), p. 42.
[24] Alfred R. Lindesmith, *Opiate Addiction* (Bloomington, Ind., Principia Press, 1947).

Treatment

Treatment for addiction is both unpleasant and not very successful. Withdrawal of the drug must be accomplished whether it be sudden or gradual, with or without the temporary assistance of other drugs. The two federal narcotics hospitals, one at Lexington, Kentucky, and the other at Fort Worth, Texas, accept both patients forcibly committed by the courts and those who voluntarily apply for treatment. In either case, recidivism is common and the proportion of permanent cures is low. The key to the whole problem seems to lie not so much in the rehabilitation of known addicts as in a broad educational program combined with increased efforts to make narcotics unavailable.

PROSTITUTION

The Problem

The red-light districts in most American cities are less extensive, less well known, and probably less well organized than they were a generation ago. This does not necessarily mean that prostitution is less common today, though what little evidence is available supports that belief.[25] It does mean that the *pattern* of prostitution has changed.

It would be erroneous to believe that law enforcement has been really effective in controlling prostitution or even that public opinion is solidly behind the efforts at control. Yet, together with the Mann Act that prohibits transporting a female across state lines for immoral purposes and the May Act that prohibits prostitution near military establishments, these forces have at least accomplished some dispersal of the prostitutes. Whereas formerly much of the organized prostitution was concentrated in one area of the city, it is now spread over a much wider area. The development of rapid intracity transportation has permitted the pattern to disperse under "outside" pressure and has yet kept prostitution readily available.

Just how much prostitution exists today is extremely difficult to say. At what point, for example, does promiscuous behavior cease merely to be promiscuous and become prostitution? The courts in most states are prone to interpret any relatively permanent relationship between a man and woman as something other than prostitution. If the couple do not live together and the man only "visits" occasionally, the relationship is apt to be more difficult to define satisfactorily but is still not likely to be regarded

[25] Kinsey and his associates found that though the proportion of males who had patronized prostitutes had not changed over the last generation, the importance of prostitution in their sex patterns had declined somewhat. *Sexual Behavior in the Human Male* (Philadelphia, W. B. Saunders Company, 1948), pp. 410-413.

as prostitution. In other cases the woman may accept gifts from one or more men, which gifts are not-very-well-disguised payment for sexual favors. In still other cases the woman may occasionally prostitute for money but derives most of her income from some legitimate employment. Finally there is the widely recognized prostitute who depends upon prostitution to make her living. One estimate states that there are perhaps 600,000 women in the latter category in the United States.[26] The same writer would add another 600,000 women as occasional prostitutes.[27]

The Pattern

There are several somewhat distinct groups and patterns of operation among habitual prostitutes. In a sense, prostitutes form a kind of hierarchy according to the social class they come from and the class status of their patrons, and according to their age, general attractiveness, and the length of time they have been in "the life." At the base of the pyramid exist the brothel or house prostitutes who are almost employees of the madam or procurer and who accept all comers. They are likely to be physically and personally unattractive and to have a history of arrests, venereal disease, and often alcoholism. The second category, of street-walkers, is very similar to that of brothel prostitute except that this second group often operate alone, making their contacts in bars and on the street and then taking their patrons to their rooms or to rooms that are rented specifically for the purpose. "Call-girls" generally have an arrangement with bellhops or other hotel personnel who summon the prostitute by telephone to the man's room. The call-girl's clientele is somewhat more limited than that of the above categories and generally she must protect herself against extreme demoralization. For when she becomes too degenerate she can no longer be tolerated in or around hotels and she tends to gravitate downward into the streetwalker and brothel categories. Probably the highest prostitute category is composed of professionals who are of middle-class background and who maintain residences or apartments away from the central part of the city. Such women cater to upper-class men who are referred or brought to them by taxi drivers or others who of course receive some payment for their services. Some of these women are able to be rather selective in their patrons, to charge high prices, and to resist the tendency toward complete demoralization. Others of them tend to move downward into the lower categories as they become victims of venereal disease, increasing age, and decreasing attractiveness.

[26] *Encyclopedia Americana,* "Vice, Regulation of," Vol. 28, 1945, p. 58.
[27] *Ibid.*

Demoralization

As implied above, prostitution is a part of and contributes to the process of complete personal demoralization. Prostitutes are likely to have a history of involvement not unlike that of the drug addict, the gambler, and the alcoholic. Probably very few women are initiated into sexual experience through prostitution. Rather, some previous sex experience seems to be almost a prerequisite to entering prostitution. Especially as the woman has some contact with persons who are either involved in prostitution or are exceedingly promiscuous in their behavior, the prospects of her becoming involved are heightened. Following entrance into the profession, she is most in demand before the risks of prostitution have time to exact their toll. Sooner or later she may be arrested, contract venereal disease, have to seek abortion, begin to drink heavily, or even resort to drugs. As she is less in demand, she may begin to steal from her patrons and others. She tends to move downward in the hierarchy of prostitutes themselves until there is no further to go.

The control of prostitution is handled almost exclusively through local police departments. Very occasionally the Mann and May acts permit the federal government to step in, but these cases are numerically not very important. The local police make sporadic arrests, sometimes have the arrested woman examined for venereal disease by the local health department, and less commonly secure convictions which send the women to penal institutions for a period of months or years. Efforts at and facilities for rehabilitation are practically nonexistent. As a first step toward meeting the problem, separate Women's Bureaus are appearing in the police department of some of our larger cities, but even here the orientation tends primarily toward punishment and only secondarily toward rehabilitation.

HOMOSEXUALITY

American society is exceedingly intolerant of sexual variation of any kind. As was indicated in Chapter 7, the fact that the sexual practices of most people vary from those considered acceptable in law and tradition makes little difference. Whenever knowledge of sexual variation comes to public attention the individuals concerned are apt to be subjected to the most ruthless kind of treatment. Nowhere is this more true than in the case of homosexuality. Known homosexuals are likely to be fired from their jobs, divorced by their spouses, beaten and robbed by vandals, arrested by the police, and to be shunned by all others.

Kinsey and his associates found approximately 4 per cent of their male subjects and from 1 to 3 per cent of their female subjects to be true homosexuals.[28] If their statistics were representative of the general population, this would mean some three million male and possibly one and one-half million female homosexuals in the United States. There would have to be added to these figures an undetermined number of persons of both sexes who are *bisexual,* who, under appropriate circumstances, can respond sexually to members of *either* sex. Probably most bisexuals tend to give up their homosexual patterns as regular heterosexual outlets become available. Bisexuals often marry, rear children, and live out their lives without encountering any major difficulties. There is an additional group of persons of both sexes who have the capacity for homosexual attachment but who never become actively involved in overt homosexual relationships. Therapists refer to such persons as latent homosexuals.

More startling than the above statistics are the Kinsey findings that *at one time or another* in their lives approximately 37 per cent of their male respondents and 13 per cent of their female respondents had had a complete homosexual experience.[29] The etiology of homosexuality is not well understood, but it seems for the most part to result from early emotional conditioning. A sizable proportion of all persons have some exploratory homosexual experience, as indicated above, in the process of growing up. Unless the early emotional conditionings have been too unfavorable, however, they go on to make the transition to adult heterosexuality. The role of biological and endocrine factors in causing some cases of homosexuality is still uncertain, but such cases are believed to be definitely in the minority.

Traditionally, homosexuals have been arrested under the law and punished for their misbehavior. This probably still is the majority practice. Recently, however, several states have enacted "sexual psychopath" laws which define homosexuals as victims of illness rather than as criminals. Such laws generally provide for hospitalization and treatment in the hope that the homosexual needs may be eliminated and the individual returned to society as a useful citizen. Though such laws are not yet widespread and though their administration is often crude and uneven, they mark a radical departure from earlier practice.

PERSONAL DEVIATION

Each of the preceding sections has dealt with a specific type of personal deviation. Each describes the problems of a particular group of people who are *different enough* to be regarded by others, and often by themselves, as problems. All members of the society would not agree precisely on what the problems are, but few would deny that something

---

[28] *Sexual Behavior in the Human Male,* p. 651, and *Sexual Behavior in the Human Female,* p. 488.

[29] *Sexual Behavior in the Human Male,* p. 623, and *Sexual Behavior in the Human Female,* p. 493.

needs to be done in relation to each of these pathologies. Before we can evaluate the conflicting policies recommended, we must seek further to understand the nature of these personal deviations.

In most instances, the pathology has a *history* of development. Eventually the drinker may become an alcoholic, the gambler may find that he cannot quit, and the drug user that he is "hooked." Such pathologies develop through experience; they do not spring full-blown from the germ plasm. In a small minority of cases there does seem to be a kind of presocial causation involved. The small proportion of psychotics in whom there are associated physical symptoms, the mentally deficient who are clearly not products of adverse environmental circumstances, and possibly some homosexuals are problems for medical and biological scientists, rather than social scientists, to analyze. Practically all alcoholism, gambling, drug addiction, and prostitution, and most mental illness and homosexuality, are primarily social problems. They must be explained, if at all, in terms of the history or experience through which they develop.

The history of development is one of gradual loss of control and increasing demoralization. In the beginning stages the behaviors seem not to differ significantly from the normal. Rationalizing, blaming others, drinking, gambling, experimenting sexually, and even using drugs are common enough in this culture that almost anyone may be introduced to them. It is not necessary to assume that one must "be different" *to begin with,* in order to be introduced to any of these things. The *probability of becoming involved does vary* with the social groups to which one belongs. Drug addiction, for example, is primarily an urban pattern; the chances that a rural person will become an addict are slim indeed. Nor are betting the horses and prostitution widespread rural patterns. Some types of mental illness, such as schizophrenia, tend to be concentrated in certain family lines and the probability of being committed to an institution, at least, depends upon where one happens to live. The individual is more likely to drink and gamble if drinking and gambling are common among his friends and associates. Once the behaviors are started, the stage for eventual personal destruction has been set. Explaining away one's failures, drinking, gambling, using drugs, and illicit sexual activity are all "escapes." They provide at least temporary satisfaction without the necessity to meet societal expectations. So long as recourse to them is seldom and not extreme, the pattern may not become progressive. But the potential for progressive involvement is always there. It becomes easier and easier to seek the escape. And each time it is more difficult to resist. The individual finds himself caught in a grip he cannot escape, and demoralization begins.

The most important question that remains unanswered is why, when so many are exposed, some persons succumb and some do not. Part of the explanation undoubtedly lies in the conditions under which exposure occurs. Some persons are exposed only occasionally and then temporarily, whereas for others the exposure is relatively constant and continuous. Some persons are exposed before they have had opportunity to develop convictions that would sustain them against involvement. Children who witness these patterns within their families and among their friends may come to accept such behaviors long before they are able critically to evaluate them. Others are exposed at times when they are particularly vulnerable to disorganization. Personal and family crises such as a death or the loss of one's job may reduce temporarily the capacity to resist. If exposure should come immediately following such crises even very resistant persons might yield. Common-sense experience recognizes "the straw that breaks the camel's back"; we must recognize that the capacity to resist is at least partly a function of the actual strain to which one is subjected.

The other part of the equation that cannot be ignored is the individual himself. Some persons resist strains that would crush most others; some persons crumple under the slightest pressure. Why the difference? At least two separate sets of personality factors must be considered. One of these is the extent and character of the moral definitions the individual makes. The more adamant he is in defining drinking, gambling, and prostitution as morally wrong, the less the probability that he will participate in them. Such strong convictions are a source of protection against gradual, unwilling involvement. Moral definitions alone, however, do not provide an adequate explanation, for some persons become involved despite moral proscriptions to the contrary and extreme moral rigidity is occasionally an indication of mental illness—one of the very pathologies being considered. The second important variable is the degree to which the individual has met and successfully conquered past frustrations and problems. "Nothing succeeds like success." And nothing is better preparation for meeting future temptations than past temptations which have been successfully resolved. Persons whose past experiences have taught them to feel quite secure in themselves and in relation to others have little need for the relief provided by "escapes." On the other hand, insecure and anxiety-ridden people are prone to any behavior which affords temporary well-being, even though the consequences of that behavior may be disastrous. These two factors of moral definitions and general adjustment in the individual, combined with the nature of the stresses to which he is subjected, hold the key to whether discernible deviance develops.

VALUE-CONFLICTS

In any area, major conflicts may develop over whether or not a problem exists, over what the nature of the problem is, and, finally, over what should be done about it. There is fairly general agreement that what we have called personal pathologies *are* social problems. But beyond this point agreement tends to break down. When it comes to *in what way* gambling, prostitution, and so on, are social problems and to *how* to deal with the problems, major value-differences appear. How should society view the alcoholic or the psychotic? Is he to be scorned, pitied, punished, or helped? What can be done to stamp out drug addiction and prostitution? Or *can* they be eliminated?

Legalization versus Extermination

Many people believe that vices such as gambling, prostitution, and narcotic addiction are inevitable; that no matter how much we try to eliminate them, they will continue to exist. Some people, of course, do not want them eliminated. Millions of Americans enjoy gambling and millions more take part in, or profit from, the other pathologies. Many in these groups, along with others who thoroughly disapprove of them, will proclaim that much of the harm which attends these practices derives not from the practices themselves but from the fact that they are illegal.

Prostitution and gambling, they declare, are even socially somewhat useful. Both act as "safety valves," draining off tensions which might otherwise be expressed in antisocial behavior. They may insist, generally without evidence, that if the houses of prostitution are closed the number of "Peeping Toms" will increase. Furthermore, they continue, one of the chief evils of prostitution, venereal disease, could be made less common if prostitution were made legal and the registration and frequent medical examination of prostitutes were required. Gambling, it is pointed out, is a tremendously profitable business—so profitable, in fact, that in most localities organized criminal gangs seek to monopolize it. Once the monopoly is established it is a simple matter to "rig" the odds so that gamblers have little chance of winning. And, because gambling is illegal, the government is denied one of its most lucrative possibilities for taxation. The same kind of reasoning is used to argue for the legalized sale of drugs. Since drugs cannot be obtained legally, their cost is many times higher than it would be on the open market and the addict virtually is forced into forgery and thievery. Moreover, if drugs could be obtained legally from physicians, many more addicts could be induced to break the habit through medical treatment. Additional evidence could be mustered, but by now the viewpoint is probably clear. It states: these pathologies are inevitable; they are mixed blessings; they would be less harmful, and in some cases would even be quite useful, were they made legal and subject to strict governmental regulation.

Other powerful and articulate groups are violently opposed to giving legal sanction to any of these practices. Such vices are, it is pointed out, both morally wrong and personally degrading. To legalize them would be to encourage their practice and to increase the toll of human misery which they already exact. The arguments of those who favor legalization are merely rationalizations; the not-too-plausible rationalizations of people who in reality do not want to see such vices eliminated. Effective regulation, they say, is virtually impossible. The examination of prostitutes to control venereal disease would have to be done every day, and even then it would not work. To make cheap narcotics available would tremendously increase the number of users. To legalize gambling would only multiply the opportunities for graft and corruption as well as to sanction the robbery of countless people of money needed to feed, clothe, and house their families. The logical solution to these problems in the eyes of most of those who oppose legalization is unrelenting enforcement of the laws until the practices are completely eliminated. That elimination may be difficult is no excuse for compromising human dignity.

That these opposing philosophies can be completely reconciled is doubtful. That either one will soon completely win out over the others is similarly unlikely. The law, except in Nevada, now reflects the views of those who favor vigorous suppression. Though the zeal with which the laws are enforced varies widely from one location to another, the past few decades probably have seen enforcement in general become somewhat more effective. There are no signs, however, that any of the pathologies are nearing extinction.

Punishment versus Rehabilitation

Perhaps more significant than the trend toward more effective law enforcement has been the appearance of a relatively new and controversial philosophy of treatment for deviant persons of many sorts—the mentally ill, sex deviants, alcoholics, gamblers, and addicts.

Traditionally the aim has been to punish those who were guilty of "wrongdoing." Theoretically, if the punishments were made severe enough, offenders would be forced to give up their deviant practices. Heavy fines and long jail sentences were relied upon to accomplish this end. In the case of the mentally ill, the aim was not so much to punish as to remove such persons from the society. As indicated earlier, the concept of mental *illness* with prospects for curing that illness is of very recent origin. As long as the mentally ill were defined as *abnormal* and generally incurable, they were treated very much like criminals. Much of the American population even today considers institutionalization to be the most satisfactory answer to such problems. Deviants should be jailed until such time as they are willing to conform to societal expectations; and if they show no inclination to reform, then institutionalization should be permanent.

An increasing number of people attack this philosophy as being barbaric and medieval. Advancements in knowledge, they claim, have long since invalidated the simple pain-pleasure principle upon which the philosophy is based. Deviants, it is pointed out, are frequently *unable* as much as *unwilling* to change. Punishment alone will do little good and, moreover, the very institutions to which deviants are committed tend as much to produce deviancy as to eliminate it. Deviants should be *helped* rather than punished. In many cases some temporary institutionalization may still be necessary to protect society and the deviant himself while treatment is carried out. But most importantly, the emphasis should be on treatment. The aim should be to return the individual to a useful life as soon as there is reasonable probability that he will be able to adjust satisfactorily.

The present trend in the United States is toward the latter philosophy, but majority practice probably is still in terms of the former. People are slow to give up vindictiveness where social codes have been violated. The rehabilitation philosophy gradually is coming to be mirrored in law and administrative procedure, but public and private opinion often demand vengeance. Even where the new philosophy is accepted in principle it is often virtually inoperative because of the lack of trained personnel and general unwillingness to appropriate funds for their hire.

SOCIAL DISORGANIZATION

Personal deviation is measured by either social or biological standards. No matter what the accepted standards are, there are always some persons who are inadequate. But the amount and kind of inadequacy derives from the nature of the accepted standards as well as from individual differences. What the society demands, and the help it provides in meeting those demands, have much to do with the nature and amount of personal deviancy.

Increasing Demands?

By former standards, modern life is tremendously complex. The youth of today participate in a variety of groups and manipulate an array of machines unknown to previous generations. The period of formal training required to prepare youth for adult life has lengthened considerably and new levels of intellectual, social, and mechanical competence constantly are being attained. There were always some persons who were inadequate even under the old standards of behavior—some who did not have sufficient mental capacity and some who broke down under the strain, resorting to one or another pathological pattern. Logically, one might expect increasing standards to result in increased numbers of inadequate persons. The greater complexity of modern life might be a major factor in raising the incidence of the personal pathologies.

Indeed, many persons have assumed such a causal relationship. The constantly increasing numbers of persons committed to mental institutions are pointed out as evidence. More people presumably are succumbing to the increased demands placed upon them. Unfortunately for the theory, the commitment rate is not a good index of the rate of mental illness. It is impossible to say whether more people are ill or merely whether more of the ill are being committed. Nor is there adequate evidence that other of the personal pathologies are increasing. In the case of narcotic addiction and prostitution there is even some evidence that law enforcement has succeeded in reducing the size of the problem somewhat.

The relative strain placed upon people from one time period to another is not a simple thing to measure. Certainly the requirements of farm life and a machine technology are different. But by what objective standards can the one be said to be more difficult than the other? A common assumption is that there are limits to the amount of adjustment and learning of which man is capable and that the limits rapidly are being approached. The assumption remains unproved, however. The same assumption, in fact, has been made for many centuries past. On the other hand, such limits undoubtedly do exist, and if and when they are approached, the rate of personal breakdown probably will increase. The present rate of increase in personal breakdown remains a matter for speculation.

Breakdown of Controls

Personal pathologies indicate individual inabilities to adjust but they also indicate failure of the social structure to protect the individual against disorganization. Ideally, each person should be so indoctrinated with the prevailing group values that he will not be tempted to engage in disapproved behavior, and the social structure should provide sufficiently adequate interpersonal relationships that he will not be driven to disapproved behaviors as compensation or escape. Traditionally, family and other intimate group ties have performed these functions. The family is the primary agency entrusted with the indoctrination of the young and is also their primary source of refuge throughout life. Community institutions, particularly the church and school, play strong supporting roles. Occasionally these agencies fail in their respective tasks, but it is quite significant that the incidence of personal pathologies is lowest where family and community life are most satisfactory. Conversely, personal pathologies are most common in areas and situations where family and community life are not well organized.

It has already been pointed out in earlier chapters that community life functions most smoothly in rural areas, where there is not much mobility, and that the anonymous, heterogeneous, mobile character of urban life is disruptive of many of the more traditional kinds of human relationships. Institutional commitments and arrests for gambling, drunkenness, prostitution, and homosexuality are all unusually high in urban "blight" areas, around military installations, and in communities which undergo "boomtown" conditions. Social isolation and extreme mobility of the population are statistically associated with increased evidence of personality disorganization.

The exact extent to which the breakdown of close interpersonal relationships produces personal pathology is not known. Certainly arrest and commitment rates mushroom under such conditions but, again, such rates may not perfectly reflect increased incidences of pathology. One alternative explanation is that the pathology, when it does appear, is less tolerable when family and friends are not available to close ranks and protect both the afflicted one and society at large from its manifestations. Persons living in deteriorated areas probably are more subject to arrest *as well as* to pathological involvement itself. An additional complicating factor exists in the high mobility rates in such areas. Deviants may be *drawn* to deteriorated areas because of the slight protection which their anonymity affords. The most reasonable conclusion seems to be that the recognized tendency for social isolation to foster personal pathology is augmented both by decreased ability to care for deviant persons under these conditions and by a tendency for already deviant persons to gravitate to areas where isolation is possible.

SUMMARY

Mental illness is the greatest single health problem in the United States today. Over half of all hospital beds are occupied by mental patients and there are more mentally ill people outside than inside the hospitals. Not all mental illness requires hospitalization, of course, but the number of trained personnel and treatment facilities are woefully inadequate at all levels. Because of their psychological withdrawal from the world around them, mentally ill people are often mistakenly believed to be mentally deficient.

Mental deficiency differs from the other personal pathologies in that it is less a matter of "escape" from trial and frustration. Deficiency is generally a product of adverse hereditary factors or of environmental factors so unfavorable that they take their toll either before birth or during the first few years of life. Perhaps half of all the mentally deficient are potentially somewhat educable, but proper facilities are almost nonexistent.

Alcoholism, gambling, drug addiction, prostitution, and homosexuality are all escapes from the demands of normal social living. The less extreme patterns which open the way for the individual to succumb to these pathologies are not in themselves pathological, however. They are to be found in one form or another as common elements of American culture. These personal pathologies have a history of development. Involvement tends to become progressive and eventually the individual finds that he has lost control. Continued participation leads to complete personal demoralization.

The probability of becoming involved in pathological behavior varies from one social group to another. The more prevalent such patterns among one's associates, the greater the likelihood of becoming involved. Some persons, however, are able to resist involvement; some are not. Persons who have not learned to handle other problem situations successfully are especially prone. Moral definitions which prohibit any participation in such patterns are ordinarily a protection against involvement, and crisis situations tend to render individuals temporarily more vulnerable.

At least two major conflicts rage over how to deal with the pathologies. One faction argues that they are inevitable and that, in the long run, less harm would result if the practices were legalized and subjected to strict government regulation. The opposing faction clamors for vigorous suppression and eventual elimination. The second dispute concerns whether the individuals involved should be defined as wrongdoers and be punished for their actions, or whether they should be defined as ill and aided to recover their capacity to resist. There is, at present, a tendency toward the latter definition.

Certain factors in the society at large contribute to the existence of the personal pathologies. The complexity of modern life subjects individuals to great strain and perhaps heightens the tendency to seek escape measures. The relative strains to which people are subjected in two different time periods is extremely difficult to measure, however, and caution is suggested. The incidence of pathology is greater under conditions of social isolation and mobility. Probably such conditions also attract deviants and render their presence more apparent.

SUGGESTED READINGS

BEERS, Clifford W., *A Mind That Found Itself* (New York, Doubleday, Doran & Co., 1948). The fascinating autobiography of a man restored to sanity. Constitutes an indictment of methods of dealing with the mentally ill.

BLOCH, Herbert A., *Disorganization, Personal and Social* (New York, Alfred A. Knopf, Inc., 1952), Chs. 13-16, 18, 20-22. Excellent chapters on sexual pathologies, drug addiction and gambling, mental deficiency, mental illness, and suicide.

DEUTSCH, Albert, *The Mentally Ill in America,* 2nd ed. (New York, Columbia University Press, 1949). One of the best treatments of the whole problem of treatment for the mentally ill. Discusses history, trends, and problems.

LINDESMITH, Alfred R., *Opiate Addiction* (Bloomington, Ind., Principia Press, 1947). Contains the most satisfactory schema yet devised for explaining the phenomenon of opiate addiction.

RECKLESS, Walter C., *The Crime Problem*, 2nd ed. (New York, Appleton-Century-Crofts, Inc., 1955), Part III, "Affiliated Problems." A series of chapters on various personal pathologies. Brief, clear, and to the point.

STRAUS, Robert, and BACON, Selden D., *Drinking in College* (New Haven, Yale University Press, 1953). A study of the drinking histories and drinking patterns of approximately 16,000 college students in 27 colleges and universities.

WARD, Mary Jane, *The Snake Pit* (New York, Random House, Inc., 1946). A best-selling novel which highlights the anti-therapeutic aspects of the environment of mental hospitals. Fascinating reading.

AUDIO-VISUAL AIDS

Howard Street (Kinesis, Inc., 566 Commercial, San Francisco), 10 minutes, sound, black and white. A documentation of life on the street which is the home of the personal dregs—the alcoholics, the unemployables, the lost individuals. There is no editorial comment. The sound employed was recorded directly on the scene.

Mental Hospital (International Film Bureau, Suite 308-316, 57 E. Jackson Blvd., Chicago), 20 minutes, sound, black and white. Sponsored by Oklahoma State Department of Health and Oklahoma State Department of Mental Health. The day-to-day story of the treatment received by a mental patient from the time of admission to the hospital until he is discharged.

The Lonesome Road (Columbia University, Center for Mass Communications, New York), eight 15-minute, 16-inch, 33⅓ rpm transcriptions. Transcriptions prepared especially for sale to radio stations. The series uses, dramatically, the actual voices of alcoholics from Skid Row and the shaded lawns of residential areas, as well as voices of law enforcement officers, doctors, and psychologists. A complete, compelling exposition of the alcoholism problem.

This Is the United Nations, No. 6, U.N. Laboratory Aids Fight on Opium Smuggling (United Nations, Films and Visual Information Division, New York), black and white.

QUESTIONS AND PROJECTS

1. Explain the difficulties inherent in estimating the amount of mental illness in American society.

2. How generally adequate are facilities for the treatment of mental illness?

3. Approximately what proportion of all mental deficiency cases are strictly hereditary in origin? How can you account for the cases which are not hereditary?

4. Trace the route from moderate social drinking to confirmed alcoholism.

5. Give an adequate sociological definition of gambling. Is there a gambling parallel to the pattern referred to in the previous question?

6. How widespread is drug addiction in the United States? Does the evidence indicate that the number of addicts is increasing rapidly?

7. Describe the process of demoralization experienced by a typical prostitute.

8. Explain the statement that "most cases of personal pathology have a history of development."

9. Give as many arguments as you can in favor of the legalization of gambling and the sale of narcotics. Give contrary arguments in favor of exterminating gambling and narcotic addiction.

10. Assess, critically, the argument that the rate of personal breakdown is increasing in modern society.

11. Take a field trip to one of the state hospitals for the mentally ill. How many persons was it designed to accommodate? How many persons are located there? What techniques of therapy are used to aid the patients? Ask one of the officials there to give you a brief history of the institution, citing the improvements that have been made both in the care and treatment of patients. What plans have been made for further improvement?

12. Contact the local police department to see what facilities exist for the control of narcotic addiction in your community. Do the police believe that there is much of a problem? Does any other evidence exist to indicate that there is or is not a problem? If a problem exists, to what extent does it approximate the lurid accounts of drug addiction detailed in our newspapers and magazines?

CHAPTER 17

Health and Medical Care

With five children to support, Michael D., 42, a telephone operator, had to mortgage his home to pay doctor's bills during his wife's long illness. Last year, when Mrs. D. died, Mr. D.'s aged mother moved in to run the household and his oldest daughter, Florence, now 18, went to work to help meet expenses. Despite her financial aid, the D.'s lost their home and had to move to an apartment. Three months ago Mr. D.'s mother died.

But this loyal family is still undefeated. Trudy, 14, and Philip, 13, have taken over much of the housework and marketing under their father's direction and try to look after Bobby, 9, and Anne, 6. Bobby, however, requires special attention. Grieving for his mother, he has grown apathetic in school and complains of deafness. Several times lately he has barely escaped being run down in traffic because of his apparent inability to hear cars approaching.

Unable to afford private medical care for Bobby, harassed Mr. D. has appealed to the [social casework] agency. The counselor will arrange clinic tests for Bobby and psychiatric treatment, if that proves necessary, but in the coming year Mr. D. will need continued guidance in handling all of the heavy family responsibilities alone.[1]

When the very life of a man, or the lives of his family, may depend upon his receiving adequate medical services, society must make every effort to provide them. When this man knows that such health services exist, available to some and denied to him, a free society will find the way to comply with the demand that he will surely make. These benefits sometimes can be obtained by the individual's own effort; but when these efforts fail, other means must be found. And democracy requires that the same high quality of service be made available to all men equally.[2]

We readily admit that under . . . [the present system of medical practice] a certain number of cases of early tuberculosis and cancer, for instance, may go undetected. Is it not better that a few such should perish than that the majority of the population should be encouraged on every occasion to run sniveling to the doctor?[3]

[1] Case 38, "New York's Hundred Neediest Cases," *New York Times*, December 7, 1952.

[2] President's Commission on the Health Needs of the Nation, *Building America's Health* (Washington, Government Printing Office, 1953), Vol. I, p. 1.

[3] Editorial, *New York State Journal of Medicine* (August 15, 1949).

Undue reverence for authority as such, a serene satisfaction with the status quo, and a fatuous objection to change have often retarded the progress of medicine. In every generation, in every country, there have been, and ever will be ... men in high places who lent the weight of a complacent conservatism to bolster up an ineffectual attempt to stay the progress of a new idea.[4]

ILL health is probably the greatest single cause of human suffering in modern society. It is doubtful if any other single circumstance produces so much poverty and dependency, so much family disruption, or so much economic inefficiency as illness. In an average day in the United States, nearly two million persons of working age have no jobs because of disability, nearly another million with jobs are absent because of illness, and roughly one-fourth of the rest are working at less than full efficiency because of nondisabling illness. We are now spending nearly $15 billion a year for medical care and health services, and wages lost through ill health add another $5 billion to our health bill. Although by no means can all illness be prevented or cured, our present mores define *any* ill health as undesirable and as a problem to command our concern.

AMERICA'S HEALTH—HOW GOOD IS IT?

Many Americans have comfortably assumed that as the wealthiest and admittedly the most "progressive" nation on earth, we must also be the healthiest. Whether we actually are the world's healthiest nation is debatable. We have many more doctors and hospital beds per 1000 people than any other country [5] and, according to the American Medical Association (AMA), our doctors are better trained and more competent than those of any other country. Yet health statistics for the leading nations are so close together, and so imperfectly comparable, that it is impossible to say any one nation is the "healthiest" in the world. We certainly do not lead the world in health by the margin that our greater wealth and technical resources make easily possible.

Our country's health standing has, however, been rapidly improving. A half century ago, we were far behind other modern nations. Even in 1938, we were eighth from the top in infant mortality, twenty-second in maternal mortality, fifth in tuberculosis deaths, seventh in diphtheria deaths, and ninth in deaths from all causes.[6] Recent reductions, however, have been spectacular. Between 1933 and 1950, our maternal mortality rate fell from 6.2 to 0.8 deaths per 1000 live births, our infant mortality

---

[4] Sir William Osler, Bt., M.D., *F.R.S. Aequanimitas with other addresses* (Philadelphia, P. Blakiston's Sons, 1932).

[5] Except Israel, with a large number of refugee doctors, mainly from Germany.

[6] Carl Malmberg, *140 Million Patients* (New York, Reynal & Hitchcock, 1947), pp. 4-7. This ranking should be viewed in the light of the fact that differences in population composition and in methods of reporting make exact comparisons more or less misleading.

rate fell from 58.1 to 29.1 deaths per 1000 live births, while the expectation of life rose from 59.7 years in 1930 to 62.9 in 1940 and 67.6 in 1949.[7]

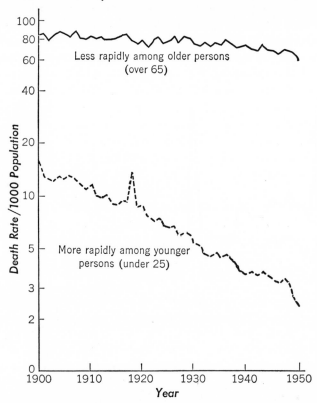

FIG. 17-1. Death Rates Have Fallen at All Ages. (From President's Commission on the Health Needs of the Nation, op. cit., Vol. I, p. 10)

Although these are remarkable accomplishments, it is notable that New Mexico had in 1949 nearly three times as many infant deaths as Connecticut, and a mother in Mississippi was four times as likely to die in childbirth as a mother in Delaware.[8] The President's Commission on the Health Needs of the Nation asserts that two-thirds of the 4122 maternal deaths in 1948 were preventable, and that 2700 deaths "would not have occurred if something like ideal care had been available for all expectant

---

[7] President's Commission on the Health Needs of the Nation, *op. cit.*, Vol. IV, pp. 20-21. (This was a group of prominent physicians and citizens appointed by President Truman to study the health problem and make recommendations for its improvement.)

[8] Unless otherwise documented, all statistics hereafter quoted in this chapter are taken from the five volumes of the President's Commission on the Health Needs of the Nation's report, *Building America's Health,* the most comprehensive recent compilation of health information available.

mothers." [9] In 1947, the Federal Security Administrator, Oscar Ewing, estimated that 23 per cent of all deaths were preventable, and that 325,000 people died needlessly each year.[10] During World War II the armed services inducted 1,500,000 men with correctable deficiencies but found it necessary to "rehabilitate" them before they were considered fit for service, and the medical director of Selective Service estimated that one-sixth of the remaining 4-F's had defects which "could easily have

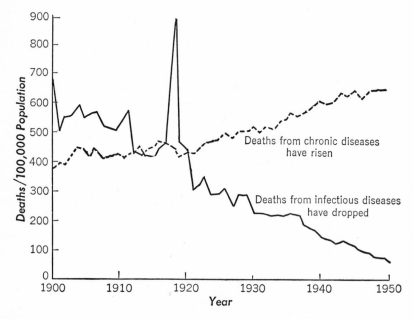

FIG. 17-2. Deaths per 100,000 Population from Chronic and Infectious Diseases, 1900-1950. (From President's Commission on the Health Needs of the Nation, op. cit., Vol. I, p. 8)

been remedied." [11] Five orphanages in North Carolina found that only 1.4 per cent of their 1138 former students called in the draft had been rejected, while the rejection rate for the entire state was 56.8 per cent at the time of the study. This spectacular contrast was explained by Dr. Clarence Poe, of the North Carolina Hospital and Medical Care Commission, as a result of "sound nutrition and reasonably adequate medical and hospital care." [12] Data such as these show that America's health,

[9] *Ibid.*, Vol. II, p. 68.

[10] U. S. Federal Security Agency, *The Nation's Health* (Washington, Government Printing Office, 1948), p. 9. This estimate has been sharply attacked for including 40,000 accidental deaths in the figure and may be an exaggeration of the possibilities of prevention through "health and medical services."

[11] Cf. Malmberg, *op. cit.*, p. 12.

[12] *Ibid.*, p. 27.

while it compares very favorably with that of the rest of the world, could be greatly improved.

AMERICAN MEDICAL CARE—HOW ADEQUATE?

Health is a product of several variables. Heredity, diet, living conditions, personal habits, and medical care are all important. To assume that all variations in health levels are due entirely to variations in medical care is a common error. Yet with almost no exceptions, low health levels are accompanied by low levels of medical care. Although by no means the sole factor, medical care is an important factor in the health level, and the one to which this chapter is devoted.

1. Is There a Shortage of Medical Care in America?

Is there a serious shortage of physicians in the United States? Organized medicine (officers of the AMA and of state and local medical societies) says "no." [13] Many other students of the health problem say "yes." The President's Commission on the Health Needs of the Nation estimates that it would take 30,000 more physicians than we shall have by 1960 to give "reasonably comprehensive medical care to the whole civilian population" and to supply the armed services and other employers of medical personnel. Recent expansions in medical school enrollments are just about large enough to maintain the present ratio of one physician for each 750 persons.

The shortage of nurses is not disputed. Every city and every region in the country reports a shortage of trained nurses, and many of the more remote hospitals are operating at part-capacity because of nursing shortages. Although the percentage of girls entering nursing has doubled since 1920, the number of active nurses is rising less rapidly than the demand, and the President's Commission predicts a national shortage of 50,000 by 1960.

In every kind of auxiliary or "para-medical" personnel—nurses aides, laboratory technicians, x-ray technicians, dieticians, physical and occupa-

---

[13] Volume V of the report of the President's Commission on the Health Needs of the Nation, *op. cit.,* quotes numerous medical spokesmen, who are almost unanimous in denying any important physician shortage. Dr. Charles Hudson, President, Cleveland Academy of Medicine, says, "... it is our belief that in general the ratio of physicians to population is adequate." (p. 198.) Dr. C. E. Umphrey, Past President Michigan State Medical Society, claims that statisticians predict "... that we shall have an oversupply of doctors of medicine within ten years." (p. 202.) Dr. John C. McDonald, President, Oklahoma Medical Society, blames the government and the armed services for a temporary shortage and chides the public for complaining, saying, "Should not the average American be willing to make some sacrifice so that the health personnel now serving in the military forces can hope to return to reasonable prospects of employment, rather than return to find the health care field so completely overexpanded that they can only hope to face possible unemployment?" (p. 215.)

tional therapists, and medical social workers—similar shortages exist. Hospitals recently reported 18,000 vacant positions for workers in seven para-medical fields, with 35,000 additional positions expected to develop within five more years. Taken as a whole, the health-services field shows severe personnel shortages that are likely to become still greater within the next decade.

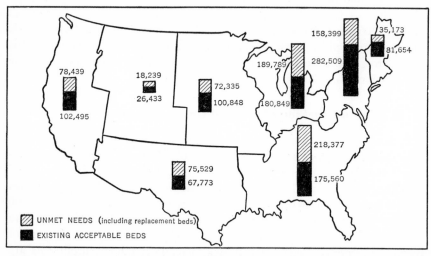

FIG. 17-3. Existing and Needed Hospital Beds by Region, June, 1952. (From President's Commission on the Health Needs of the Nation, *op. cit.,* **Vol. I, p. 23)**

2. Does Anyone Lack Medical Care?

The medical profession takes pride in the fact that, with relatively few exceptions, medical services are given to everyone who reaches the doctor or hospital and asks for treatment. This record is a generous one, but it overlooks these important facts: (1) some people are unable to reach or locate a physician or hospital bed when needed; and (2) many people, for one reason or another, do not ask for the medical services their health requires. There are at least three major groups whose medical needs are only partly filled.

a. Those living in medical shortage areas get less and poorer medical care. Although some concentration of medical facilities in the larger cities is efficient, the present urban concentration goes far beyond considerations of medical efficiency. The greater metropolitan centers have nearly four times as many physicians per 1000 people as the isolated rural areas. Furthermore, these rural small-town physicians are older, less well trained, and work longer hours; nearly one-third of the physicians in rural areas are semiactive physicians over 65 years of age, contrasted with only 12 per cent of the urban physicians. Of the 757 "medical service areas" into which the AMA divides the country, the number of physicians in 1950 varied from one for each 380 persons to one for each 5100 persons. There were 75 areas with more than 2000 persons per physician, and 262 areas with more than 1500 persons per physician.[14]

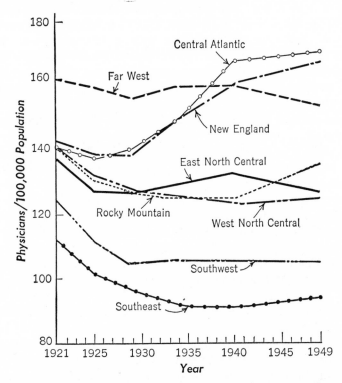

FIG. 17-4. Regional Differences in the Supply of Physicians Have Increased. (From President's Commission on the Health Needs of the Nation, *op. cit.*, Vol. II, p. 116)

The Central Atlantic states as a group have nearly twice as many physicians per 100,000 people as the Southeastern states (161 to 86 in 1949). While the state of New York had one active civilian physician for each 503 persons in 1949, Mississippi had one for each 1441 persons. The seriousness of the uneven distribution of physicians is a subject of dispute. AMA spokesmen term the present distribution of physicians "excellent but not perfect," [15] whereas the President's Commission on the Health Needs of the Nation takes a serious view of the growing disparity in the medical resources of different areas of the country.[16]

[14] Frank G. Dickinson, Director, Bureau of Medical Economic Research, AMA, *How Bad Is the Distribution of Physicians?* Bulletin 94B (Chicago, American Medical Association, 1954).

[15] *Ibid.*, p. 11.

[16] *Op. cit.*, Vol. II, pp. 116-117.

Other medical facilities show similar geographic variations—hospital beds, nurses, para-medical personnel, and public-health facilities. The most obvious reasons are economic. The number of physicians and hospital beds per 100,000 people corresponds quite closely to the per capita income of each region. But other important reasons include: (a) physicians' dislike for practice in isolation from their fellow-practitioners; (b) physicians' dislike for practice where hospital, laboratory, and specialist services are limited or inferior; (c) medical graduates' tendency to establish practice either in their home towns or in the area where they attended medical school. All these factors favor the urbanized areas and the prosperous regions, and those areas which are already medically well-equipped attract a disproportionate number of each year's medical graduates.

b. Low-income groups. Medical care is costly. The "average" American family in 1953 spent either $110 or $207 for personal medical services, depending upon whether the median or mean is taken as an "average." [17] The proportion of all families who see no physician during the year is three times as high for families whose income is under $1200 a year than for those whose income is $10,000 or more (20.2 per cent to 7.2 per cent). A Michigan survey found positive symptoms untreated by any physician over four times as prevalent among persons in families under $1000 in annual income as among persons in families over $3500 in annual income.[18] A few years ago one study showed that families with incomes over $5000 consult medical specialists ten times as often as families under $1200 a year.[19] Literally hundreds of similar statistics can easily be cited to show that low-income persons receive only a fraction of the medical services received by more prosperous people.

Some of this disparity may be due to a lack of effort by low-income people who are not educated to seek medical treatment, but to "blame" *all* untreated illness among low-income folk on lack of effort would be a crude evasion of facts. For while the amount spent for medical care rises with income, the *proportion* of income spent for medical care is larger for the lower incomes. Although some of this money is unwisely spent on "quack" practitioners and self-medication, it is a reasonable measure of the *effort* of low-income people to get treatment for their illness.

Low-income people also receive free medical care from various sources. Local public-health departments provide some free health services to many low-income people; but 30 million people live in areas with no full-time local health department, and only 5 per cent of the full-time health

[17] Odin N. Anderson, *National Family Survey of Medical Costs and Voluntary Health Insurance* (New York, Health Information Foundation, 1954), p. 25.

[18] Charles R. Hoffer, *Health and Health Services for Michigan Farm Families,* Special Bulletin 352 (Lansing, Michigan State College, 1948), p. 17.

[19] M. M. Davis, *America Organizes Medicine* (New York, Harper and Brothers, 1941), p. 58.

departments in 1947 offered general medical care services.[20] Medical-school hospitals and clinics provide many free services to low-income persons within the surrounding area. Federal, state, and local government provide certain services for certain groups of people or for certain categories of illness. Physicians give a great deal of service with no expecta-

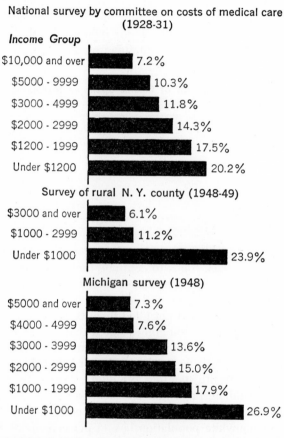

National survey by committee on costs of medical care
(1928-31)

Income Group

$10,000 and over — 7.2%
$5000 - 9999 — 10.3%
$3000 - 4999 — 11.8%
$2000 - 2999 — 14.3%
$1200 - 1999 — 17.5%
Under $1200 — 20.2%

Survey of rural N. Y. county (1948-49)

$3000 and over — 6.1%
$1000 - 2999 — 11.2%
Under $1000 — 23.9%

Michigan survey (1948)

$5000 and over — 7.3%
$4000 - 4999 — 7.6%
$3000 - 3999 — 13.6%
$2000 - 2999 — 15.0%
$1000 - 1999 — 17.9%
Under $1000 — 26.9%

FIG. 17-5. Several Studies Show That Many Americans Receive No Medical Care. (From President's Commission on the Health Needs of the Nation, *op. cit.,* Vol. II, p. 229)

tion of payment. A number of voluntary health organizations provide treatment for certain illnesses, and private social agencies provide some medical services. Out of this confusing patchwork of agencies, a good deal of free medical care appears. *Some* of the low-income people have *some* of their medical care needs fulfilled. Many others are missed, either because the services they need are not locally available to them or be-

[20] Oscar N. Serbein, Sr., *Paying for Medical Care in the United States* (New York, Columbia University Press, 1953), p. 297.

cause their pride prevents them from accepting "charity" medical care. A few years ago, two different national surveys showed 29 and 31 per cent of the population reporting that they "put off going to a doctor because of cost." [21] And much free medical service is wasted because of lack of co-ordination and continuity. In many areas, a person who is self-supporting is ineligible for free services and can obtain them only by waiting until he becomes unemployable and goes "on relief," whereupon he becomes an eligible "indigent." Those who are barely self-supporting usually have greater difficulty in obtaining medical care than those who are indigent.

**TABLE 17-1. Per Cent of Income Spent on Medical Care,
Families and Single Persons, 1944**

Annual Income After Taxation	Average Expenditure	Per Cent of Income
Less than $500	$ 48	17.0
501-999	76	8.8
2,500-2,999	119	4.3
5,000 or more	260	3.4

President's Commission on the Health Needs of the Nation, *op. cit.*, Vol. IV, p. 10.

Some of the medical care purchased by low-income people is also wasted because they lack funds to continue the treatment to its completion. One small pilot study of persons who felt that their medical needs were not met revealed that one-fifth of them had seen a physician and received prescriptions but had not filled them because of lack of funds. [22]

c. Racial minorities. It is sometimes stated that America's *white* population is more healthy than the population of any other country on earth —that it is the low health level of our Negroes, Indians, and Mexicans that pulls down our health standing. No doubt a very rosy picture of our nation's health could be presented by excluding sickly groups, but the amount of illness is not thereby reduced. As compared with our white population, our nonwhite population has 43 per cent more disabling illness and has a death rate higher by 50 per cent. The disparity is greatest for precisely those diseases which medical care can prevent or cure. Nonwhite death rates are five times as high for typhoid and syphilis, four times as high for whooping cough and dysentery, three times as high for diphtheria, tuberculosis, and diseases of pregnancy, twice as high for pneumonia and diarrhea, and ten times as high for "unknown or unspecified causes" (a term which usually indicates a lack of medical attention

[21] Clarence A. Peters, *Free Medical Care* (New York, H. W. Wilson Company, 1946), pp. 94-95.

[22] Neilie N. Reid, *Survey of Doctor Service, Hospital, and Medication Needs in the City of Kalamazoo* (Kalamazoo, Michigan, County Health Department, 1953), pp. 30-33.

either before or after death!). For the less easily preventable diseases, such as cancer, diabetes, or arteriosclerosis, the white population's death rate is higher than that of the nonwhites—more of whom don't live long enough to develop these diseases!

Most of our nonwhite population is in the lower income brackets, and much of it lives in those areas where medical facilities are least adequate. Discrimination reduces further the medical facilities available to minorities. In the St. Louis area, to cite only one of dozens of examples, three-fifths of the tuberculosis victims are Negroes, but only one-third of the tuberculosis hospital beds are available to Negroes. Health-insurance premiums are usually higher for minority groups, if they are eligible at all. There are many localities, even fair-sized cities, where no dentist will accept Negro patients. Negroes report great difficulty in getting physicians to make after-hours house calls. Although one-tenth of our people are Negroes, fewer than one-fiftieth of the physicians are Negroes, and the proportion has been declining for a quarter century. Negro entrance into the medical profession is limited by the inadequacy of the high-school education available to Negroes in many areas, by the high cost of medical education, by the lack of medical schools accepting Negroes in some parts of the country, and by many discriminatory practices in granting hospital interneships and appointments, and medical and specialty society memberships. Considering all these factors, it is not surprising that tuberculosis kills proportionately twice as many Negroes and ten times as many Indians as whites.

3. How Good Is the Quality of Medical Care?

Many discussions of health problems, while granting that distribution might be imperfect, have assumed that the *quality* of medical care in the United States is entirely satisfactory and needs only to be protected from dangerous meddling. It may be true, as organized medicine claims, that the quality of medical care in the United States is the highest in the world. Even so, there are a number of situations and organizational imperfections which limit the effectiveness of the medical services which our people receive.

a. Isolation of practitioners. According to a Subcommittee on Medical Care of the American Public Health Association, "The greatest single deterrent to good service is the isolation of the individual practitioner from his colleagues." [23] Modern medical science is exceedingly complex and rapidly changing. The highest levels of medical care require the close co-operation of general practitioners, specialists, hospitals, laboratory

[23] Subcommittee on Medical Care of the American Public Health Association, "Quality of Medical Care in a National Health Program," *American Journal of Public Health,* 39, No. 7 (July, 1949), pp. 700 ff.

technicians, and all other medical and para-medical personnel. Solo practitioners, practicing in scattered private offices, cannot make efficient use of many kinds of expensive and highly specialized equipment. It is more inconvenient to arrange consultations with other practitioners or to arrange for laboratory tests, and the patient's time is wasted as he trots from place to place. Most important of all, the physician loses the exchange of knowledge and the stimulus toward professional excellence that comes from a close working association with his fellows. A widespread recognition of these facts by the medical profession is partly responsible for the current spread of the group practice of medicine, and for the growing tendency to organize medical services around hospitals and clinics rather than independent offices.

b. The fee-for-service system of payment is widely accused of increasing costs while lowering the quality of medical services. Under this method, the patient pays a separate fee for each item of service he receives; under the *capitation* method, the physician receives a stated fee for each person to whom he provides whatever services are needed over a period of time; or the physician may be paid on a *salary* basis. According to the above subcommittee of the American Public Health Association,[24]

The fee-for-service method puts emphasis upon sickness rather than health and upon quantity rather than quality. It hinders appropriate referral of patients because it provides an economic incentive for the physician to retain his patient [rather than referring him to another physician better qualified to treat his particular disorder]. This factor, in addition, seriously limits the effectiveness of regional centers for necessary consultant services. . . . By removing or minimizing the incentive for quantity inherent in fee-for-service, the [ideal] program could make careful, deliberate work, rather than the multiplication of services, the principal motivation for a physician to improve his professional and economic status.

The fee-for-service system is also said to discourage early diagnosis and treatment, and to provide little incentive for preventative medicine or health education.[25]

c. Fee-splitting and ghost-surgery are two additional abuses which the fee-for-service system encourages. "Ghost-surgery" exists when the patient pays for the services of a highly-regarded surgeon but, without his knowledge, is operated upon by another surgeon who receives only a part of the fee the patient has paid. "Fee-splitting" exists when the specialist or surgeon shares part of his fee with the physician who referred the patient to him. Both practices are classed as "unethical" by the AMA

[24] *Ibid.* (This report was published for discussion only and is not an official pronouncement of the American Public Health Association.)

[25] Cf. President's Commission on the Health Needs of the Nation, *op. cit.,* Vol. IV, pp. 104-105.

and nearly all state and local medical societies because they tempt the physician to refer his patients to the specialist or surgeon who gives the largest "split" rather than the one who is most competent. Although less widespread than it used to be, fee-splitting is still a common practice in some areas, and an official of the American College of Surgeons writes, "... in some areas of the middle west [fee-splitting] is practiced by the great majority of general practitioners and general surgeons...." [26] The American College of Surgeons has been campaigning against fee-splitting,[27] and one official charges the medical societies with failing to co-operate in its elimination.[28] Although twenty-three states have laws forbidding fee-splitting, there is no record of a prosecution.

d. Limitation of hospital privileges reduces the effectiveness of many physicians and surgeons. In some instances the denial of hospital appointments is based upon a physician's incompetence or unethical behavior, but this does not explain why in some large cities as many as 56 per cent of all general physicians do not have hospital affiliation. Dr. Russel V. Lee, of the President's Commission on the Health Needs of the Nation, says, "A lot of doctors complain that they cannot get on a hospital staff and cannot practice proper medicine unless they do." [29] In many areas, Negro physicians have extreme difficulty in securing hospital affiliation, without which they cannot treat their patients within the hospital. Some excellently-trained young physicians and surgeons are barred from hospital affiliation by less-well-trained older physicians who fear their competition.[30]

e. High cost of medical services prevents some paying patients from getting all the services that might aid them. As Paul De Kruif writes,[31]

The cost of really complete medical care is ... bearable only by the rich. For all others ... the doctor must be on the watch to avoid sending his sick patient from the frying pan of disease into the fire of subsequent worry about unbearable medical debt. This is medicine's tragedy: where doctors are individual business men dealing with the average individual sick man, they dare not sell all the science they have to offer. Their regard for the average indi-

[26] Greer Williams, "Unjustified Surgery," *Harper's,* 208 (February, 1954), pp. 35-41.

[27] *Bulletin of the American College of Surgeons,* 37 (September-October, 1952), p. 233.

[28] Dr. Fred W. Rankin, former AMA president and incoming president of the American College of Surgeons has "accused the AMA of subtly opposing the efforts of surgeons to root out exhorbitant fees, kickbacks and unnecessary operations." ("Surgeon Questions AMA's Sincerity," *Chicago Sun-Times,* October 10, 1953, p. 7.) See also Albert Q. Maisel, "Medical Kickbacks Can be Ended," *Reader's Digest,* 52 (May, 1948), pp. 58-61.

[29] *Op. cit.,* Vol. V, p. 204.

[30] See J. D. Ratcliff, "Give Young Doctors a Break," *Woman's Home Companion,* LXXV (October, 1948), pp. 32-33.

[31] Paul De Kruif, *Kaiser Wakes the Doctors* (New York, Harcourt, Brace & Company, Inc., 1943), pp. 36-37.

vidual's pocketbook makes it necessary for them to withhold the full power of that science. They must go easy on X-rays, blood chemistry, special nursing, new chemical treatment, complicated operations—expensive procedures that, limitless, may make the difference between life and death.

When a patient of modest means is ineligible for "free" medical care or his pride will not let him accept it, the physician often must find a compromise between giving him everything that might help him and giving him what he can afford.

f. Lack of continuity and of co-ordination reduces the effectiveness of much medical care. Because of the costs, many prescriptions remain unfilled and many courses of treatment are not carried through to completion. Many medical services are ineffective because of lack of co-ordination with the services of a medical or psychiatric social worker, who works with the patient and his family on living conditions, health habits, diet, and emotional understanding. The fact that from one-half to three-fourths of all physical illnesses involve emotional causes calls for a co-ordination of medical and psychiatric practice which is largely lacking in our health-service organization.

g. Overwork in the medical profession is a constant drain on its effectiveness. Physicians in general practice work an *average* of about 60 hours a week—meaning that some work far longer—and their hours are irregular and their rest broken. Physicians have an expectation of life several years shorter than other professional groups. Their heavy duties make it difficult to find time for vacations, for periodic advanced study, or even to keep up with a changing field. A distinguished surgeon and medical educator writes that of the thirty doctors he knew intimately, only five kept abreast of medical progress, while the other twenty-five read little or no scientific material and merely treated symptoms instead of making diagnoses.[32] A large publisher of medical books reports that less than 15 per cent of the practitioners buy new medical books with any regularity.[33] The occasional tragic errors of even the best practitioners can often be attributed to sheer exhaustion. It is simply an impossibility for an overworked profession to maintain the highest level of professional service.

The over-all quality of American medical care is somewhat lower than it might be if these several limitations were removed. It is not suggested that any person or group is necessarily "to blame" for them; they are perhaps better interpreted as a *culture lag in the organization of health services.* For, as the President's Commission on the Health Needs of the Nation states, "The genius for organization, so characteristic of American life in general, is conspicuous in health services by its absence. By organi-

[32] Caleb Smith, "How Good Is Your Family Doctor?" *Atlantic Monthly*, 186 (August, 1950), pp. 43-48.

[33] Quoted in Dr. James Peter Warbasse, "Doctors and Dollars," *The Progressive*, 14 (November, 1950), pp. 12-14.

zation is meant the process of putting together people and facilities, and utilizing them in the most efficient manner." [34] It is clear that a more efficient organization of medical services could measurably improve the quality of medical care in the United States.

DEFINITION OF THE PROBLEM

As with all social problems, people disagree upon whether there is a "problem" of medical care, upon its exact nature, and upon its seriousness. At least four levels of definition can be recognized.

1. Some feel that there is *no serious health-services problem;* that while there may be certain small imperfections, these are now being taken care of by the medical profession. This is the attitude of most of the spokesmen for organized medicine.[35] To these persons, the problem is mainly one of protecting an "excellent" system of medical care from "dangerous" attempts to modify it. The membership of the medical profession is divided; a significant minority feels that there *is* a serious medical care problem and is active in promoting changes in medical organization.

2. Some view the problem as mainly one of *providing for catastrophic illness.* American families pay an average of 4 or 5 per cent of their incomes for medical care—enough to cover ordinary illnesses. But 7 per cent spend over $500 a year; each year a million families pay over 50 per cent of their income for medical care and a half-million families pay out more than their entire year's income.[36] About one-fifth of the nation's families were in debt to doctors, dentists, or hospitals in 1952, and small loan companies make more loans to pay medical bills than for any other purpose. Some people define the problem as one of providing insurance protection against these unbearable costs of catastrophic illness, assuming that most people can meet purely routine medical needs without assistance.

3. Others see the problem as one of *insuring medical care for all,* since it is clear that many who need medical care do not get it. Some feel that the problem is met if medical services are available to all who *ask for them.* Others, noting that ignorance and pride keep many from asking for free medical services, believe that the problem includes the need for an educational and promotional campaign to encourage these people to ask for the medical care they need.

4. The most inclusive definition of the problem includes all these objectives in demanding a sweeping *reorganization of the administration of*

[34] *Op. cit.,* Vol. I, p. 29.

[35] See President's Commission on the Health Needs of the Nation, *op. cit.,* "Doctors Speak," Vol. V, pp. 193-256.

[36] Odin W. Anderson, *National Family Survey of Medical Costs and Voluntary Health Insurance* (New York, Health Insurance Foundation, 1954), p. 25.

health services. Some critics believe that the quality of medical care could be improved and its cost lowered through a rational reorganization of health services administration. They define the problem as partly one of promoting such a reorganization.

APPROACHES TO THE PROBLEM

The Social-Disorganization Approach

The genial country doctor with his familiar black bag was fairly adequate for the medical needs of our great-grandparents. He didn't know much medicine, because there was not much medical knowledge for him to learn. But most of the patients got well anyway, and his earnest efforts and his long nightly vigils earned him the respect and affection of his neighbors.

The spectacular growth of medical knowledge is revolutionizing the arrangements of medical practice. With the discovery of how disease is transmitted has come the realization that disease anywhere in the community is a threat to the health of all of the community.[37] This realization leads to the demand that health services be made equally available to all. Modern medical care involves many specialized fields and skills, and the traditional method of solo fee-for-service practice comes under fire as a major obstacle to high-quality medical care. The constant stream of new medical discoveries and treatments enables us to save many today who yesterday would have died—and also makes good medical care so costly that traditional methods of payment became unsatisfactory and new ones are appearing.

Changes in the society also disorganize the traditional administration of health services. The growth of large-scale industry has led to industrial health-service plans that sometimes "infringe" upon private practice. The changing age distribution of our population, due mainly to our lower birth rate, calls for changes in medical emphasis and organization. The tendency to offer public assistance to practically all who fail to support themselves makes those who are unemployable because of illness a heavier economic burden on the entire society than they once were. In many ways, current experiments in the organization of health services are reflecting the familiar "change-disorganization-reorganization" cycle.

The Value-Conflict Approach

Most of the value-conflicts in this problem are found lurking behind the opposing statements of the alleged "facts." Defenders of the medical

[37] E.g., the AMA recently announced that the major source of infection for tuberculosis is found among the "skid-row" bums, who often work as cooks and dishwashers in restaurants. (See "AMA Sees Top Source of TB in 'Skid-Rows'," *Chicago Sun-Times,* July 10, 1954, p. 15.)

status quo point out that few who ask for free treatment are denied. Critics point out that the medical status quo discourages many from asking for the treatment they need but feel they cannot afford. Both facts are true, and each implies a different value-judgment. *How important is it that all should be offered complete medical care under conditions that strongly encourage all to ask freely for it? How important is it to preserve the system of practice which a majority of the doctors seem to prefer?* These value-questions lie at the heart of current medical controversy.

Is ill health among those too ignorant or too indolent to seek treatment a problem? Some say, "No, it is their own fault!" Some say, "Yes, they must be educated to recognize their need and to demand treatment." These answers imply several value-judgments about personal versus public responsibility, about taxes and public expenditure, and about the degree to which we should be "our brothers' keeper."

Not all health "problems" stem from value-*conflicts.* Even among those who agree upon objectives, there are disagreements upon the best programs for reaching them. But all health problems stem from a value-*judgment*—a feeling that a "bad" situation needs correcting.

The Personal-Deviation Approach

Of the many persons who follow poor health habits and are unaccustomed to seek medical services, only a few are deviant persons. The rest are merely reflecting the normal behavior of persons in their social environment. The members of some groups or cults raise religious objections to medical services, and these persons are perhaps deviant to some degree.

When the deviant person is also an emotionally disturbed person, as he frequently is, he is less likely to remain physically healthy for any long period. Various medical estimates define from one-half to three-fourths of all physical disorders as being wholly or partly caused by emotional disturbances. Today there is scarcely any disorder—not even cancer—from which emotional factors are definitely excluded as being of no importance. Of course, not all deviants are disorganized or emotionally disturbed. But deviation often carries emotional tensions, anxieties, confusions, and resentments that become active causes of a long list of physical ailments.[38] Much chronic illness is emotional in origin, and an endless succession of ailments strongly suggests emotional causation. When one is unconsciously using illness for an escape from responsibility, an appeal for affection, or a means of revenge, the "curing" of one ailment merely forces the patient to develop another. In this way, personal deviation is responsible for a certain proportion of our ill health. And, as with

[38] Cf. Helen Flanders Dunbar, *Mind and Body: Psychosomatic Medicine* (New York, Random House, Inc., 1947).

all social problems, some deviant persons approach health problems with a bitter and vindictive irrationality that makes a rational "solution" of the problem more difficult.

PROPOSALS FOR IMPROVING THE ADMINISTRATION OF HEALTH SERVICES

Whether a particular proposal is "good" or "bad" depends upon whose values are used in measuring it. In 1948 the National Health Assembly, some 800 representatives of professional organizations and public and private agencies concerned with health matters, adopted the following criteria for evaluating the effectiveness of prepayment plans (whose members pay a weekly or monthly premium to become eligible for certain services) in meeting the medical care needs of the people: [39]

1. The extent to which a prepayment plan makes available to those it serves the whole range of scientific medicine for prevention of disease and for treatment of all types of illness or injury.
2. The proportion of the population of its area—local, state, or national, as the case may be—covered by a plan (cost in relation to ability to pay, restrictions on enrollment imposed by actuarial considerations, income level, age, conditions of employment, means of securing enrollment and collecting premiums).
3. The degree to which a plan makes use of and encourages the development of a high quality of medical care for its subscribers (standards of personnel and facilities, organization of services, emphasis on prevention of disease, promotion of health, health education).
4. The degree to which freedom and willingness to experiment with methods of payment and operation are encouraged in a plan.
5. The degree to which a plan succeeds in arranging amounts and methods of payment and conditions of participation that are satisfactory to physicians, hospitals, and others serving the plan's subscribers.
6. The extent to which sound financing, efficiency, and economy in the operation of a plan are achieved and encouraged by its basic policies and its administrative techniques.
7. The extent to which the individuals or board members who carry the ultimate responsibility for a plan represent the interest of those entitled to service and those who are paying the cost, as well as of the physicians, hospitals or others who are providing the services.

These tests of "adequacy" might be abbreviated as (1) comprehensive medical care, (2) universal enrollment, (3) high quality, (4) freedom to experiment, (5) satisfactory methods of payments, (6) costs and efficiency, and (7) consumer participation in control. This is not the only set of criteria which might be used, and this one is not entirely acceptable to organized medicine, but it may serve as a useful guide for comparing the several alternative proposals which follow.

[39] National Health Assembly, *America's Health* (New York, Harper and Brothers, 1949), pp. 222-223.

1. *Group Practice*

Although group practice is not a method of prepayment, it has attracted wide support as a pattern of organization. In group practice,[40]

A number of physicians combine their practice, utilize the same offices and other facilities, which are owned in common, refer patients to one another according to the patient's needs, and share by agreement in the expenses and the net income. The group includes specialists and, if it plans to extend complete medical care, general practitioners.

Advocates of group practice claim that it offers a higher quality of service at lower costs than traditional practice. The New York Academy of Medicine stated in 1947: [41]

There are obvious scientific, financial, and professional advantages in well-organized group practice. . . . Besides offering more inclusive service the group can extend medical care quantitatively by lowering charges and distributing them more evenly. Overhead expenses are relatively low. . . . Close association with colleagues in such groups tends to maintain both ethical and technical standards. Solo practitioners, on the other hand, are "on their own" in these matters. It is one of the weaknesses of prevailing general practice that there is no means for maintaining standards, save within the broad limits set by licensure and the laws against malpractice. . . . But . . . outside pressure is not likely to prove effective and would certainly be resisted by physicians as being coercive. The merit of group practice is that it provides for some control of standards within the professional family. . . . Close association with colleagues also proves stimulating to the individual members.

To sum up, group practice . . . affords a better quality of care to patients and improved professional conditions for physicians. Most important, it is more adaptable than solo practice to comprehensive voluntary prepayment plans, and so facilitates a wider extension of medical care.

The President's Commission on the Health Needs of the Nation comments that with group practice: [42]

The patient benefits through having his entire health service concentrated in one place. This gives greater unity and continuity to his care, encourages consultation whenever it is needed and minimizes travel. The patient also gets more service per dollar spent through the economy of group practice.

Physicians working together in a group continue the best features of their training period throughout their professional lives—the stimulation to keep up with medical progress through constant appraisal by informed colleagues and ready access to consultations and technical assistance. On the personal side the physician in group practice has greater opportunity to take time off for study and vacation in addition to a more stable income throughout his years of practice.

[40] New York Academy of Medicine, *Medicine in the Changing Order* (New York, The Commonwealth Fund and Harvard University Press, 1947), p. 137.
[41] *Ibid.*, pp. 137-139.
[42] *Op. cit.*, Vol. I, pp. 33-34.

These advantages of group practice account for its steadily growing popularity within the medical profession, with over 5000 physicians engaged in group practice by 1950. Group practice appears to have no inherent disadvantages, yet certain problems have limited its expansion. Some physicians are too individualistic to enjoy group practice. The large cash investment required for offices and equipment has been an obstacle. Some groups failed because the controlling physicians sought to exploit the underpaid, younger physicians in the group. And, "in many parts of the country, organized medical bodies have been distinctly hostile to group practice" [43] and have greatly impeded its growth.

Advocates of group practice do not claim that it is a "solution" to the entire problem of medical care. They merely claim that group practice is a more efficient way of organizing medical practice. Problems of financing, of providing care for low-income groups, and of shortages in isolated areas would still remain. But because group practice is considered more efficient and economical, its expansion is a central feature of practically every proposed plan for comprehensive health services.

2. Voluntary Health Insurance (Limited)

Over 98 million people, or about two-thirds of the civilian population, had some form of health-insurance protection by the end of 1953.[44] Nearly half of these were insured with Blue Cross plans, and the rest divided among industrial and union programs, independent plans, and commercial insurance company policies. *Comprehensive* health-service plans, covering most of a family's medical costs, were held by about three-and-a-half million persons, or less than 3 per cent of the people. Most persons with health insurance receive *limited* services, mostly hospital services and perhaps certain surgical and medical services while in the hospital. There is sharp disagreement upon what services should be covered by health insurance. Most medical society spokesmen and Blue Cross officials contend that routine medical expenses—house calls, office calls, occasional treatment of minor ailments—are certain to be needed by everyone, and for this reason are noninsurable; they state that health insurance should seek to cover only the heavier costs of the catastrophic illness.[45]

There is a wide variety of health insurance plans in operation. Commercial insurance companies have long sold "health and accident" poli-

---

[43] *Ibid.*, Vol. I, p. 34.

[44] *The Extent of Voluntary Health Insurance Coverage in the United States* (New York, Health Insurance Council, 1954), p. 2.

[45] See statements of George W. Cooley, Secretary of the Council on Medical Service, AMA, and of Charles G. Hayden, Executive Director of Massachusetts Medical Service, in President's Commission on the Health Needs of the Nation, *op. cit.*, Vol. IV, pp. 77, 79; 50.

cies which pay specified cash benefits to individual policyholders. As a means of meeting medical costs, these policies are costly and inefficient; administrative costs consume nearly half of each dollar, and the size of the cash benefit bears no necessary relation to the costs of treatment. Commercial insurance companies are now promoting the sale of group health-insurance policies, where administrative costs are somewhat lower (averaging 26 per cent) and sometimes providing medical service benefits rather than paying cash benefits.

The Blue Cross plans are the most popular. These are operated by nonprofit organizations largely controlled by hospital administrators. Blue Cross hospitalization plans cost an average of about $45 a year for a family in 1951, and covered the cost of a ward bed or semiprivate room for varying periods ranging from 30 to 120 days per illness. Certain other hospital expenses, such as drugs and dressings, operating room use, laboratory services, and other items are often included. Maternity care is usually provided only after the family has been enrolled for nine to twelve months or longer, and coverage for certain causes, such as tuberculosis or nervous and mental disorders, is usually restricted to shorter periods of care.

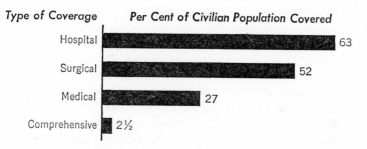

FIG. 17-6. Health Insurance Coverage in the United States, 1953. (Data from Health Insurance Council, *The Extent of Voluntary Health Insurance Coverage in the United States*, 1953; and President's Commission on the Health Needs of the Nation, *op. cit.*, Vol. IV, p. 327)

The Blue Shield Medical-Surgical Care plans are organized and controlled by the medical profession. At a family cost which averaged $35 a year in 1951, these plans pay to the physician specified sums for certain services to the member while a bed patient in a hospital. For nearly all surgery in the hospital, the physician receives payment according to a schedule of fees, although he may bill the patient for additional fees unless the patient is in a specified low-income bracket. Charges for doctor's visits to a hospital bed-patient are covered up to specified amounts. Certain other services are usually included, such as maternity services (after nine months' membership), diagnostic x-ray, anesthesia, and emergency treatment in hospital or doctor's office up to a specified sum for accidental injuries.

Many other voluntary insurance plans offering coverages roughly comparable to Blue Cross and Blue Shield are operated by industries, unions, and commercial insurance companies. All have many limitations and exclusions and do not attempt to cover *all* of a family's expense. Their purpose is to cover that part of one's medical costs which is most likely to come in a sudden, unbearable flood.

If the limited voluntary health plans are evaluated according to the National Health Assembly's criteria, their achievements and limitations become evident.

a. Comprehensive medical care is not provided by Blue Cross plus Blue Shield or other comparable plans (except in the states of Washington, Oregon, and California). The home and office calls that comprise the bulk of the average family's ordinary medical expenses are defined as "noninsurable." Either a time limit or a dollar limit is placed on practically every kind of service provided. Blue Cross plus Blue Shield defrays an average of about 40 per cent of the *total* cost of those illnesses which involve hospitalization under the contract, and virtually none of the costs of other illnesses. In 1951, only 15 per cent of all consumer expenditures for medical services were covered by any form of health insurance.

b. Universal enrollment—the insuring of all people—is unattainable under purely voluntary health insurance. Most plans have an upper age limit, and only 15 per cent of the persons over 75 years old have any sort of health insurance. Most plans insure only *groups* of people, or accept *individual* insureds only at a considerably higher premium. This is done because group enrollment cuts administrative costs and secures a more normal distribution of health risks, whereas individual enrollment loads the plan with members who expect heavy medical expenses. Low-income groups cannot afford to carry health insurance. Unemployed persons cannot easily continue their protection at the higher individual rate. Most migratory and seasonal workers are ineligible, even if they could afford the premiums—which they cannot. It is doubtful if a purely voluntary insurance program can ever reach more than three-fourths of the population, which would still leave 40 million people with no prepaid medical services. Even though voluntary health insurance is now supplemented by free medical care for the indigent (non-self-supporting), millions of people who are not eligible for free medical services will continue to find it impractical to attempt to purchase health insurance.

c. The *quality* of medical services secured through limited voluntary health insurance is neither better nor poorer than that generally available under private medical practice. Group practice is not particularly encouraged and its special advantages are not secured. Health education and preventive medicine are not included. Most of the kinds of services involved in early detection and diagnosis are not covered, although the coverages do aid in prompt treatment of some disorders when they are discovered.

d. Freedom to experiment is present to some degree in voluntary health insurance. Different plans vary somewhat in coverage and charges. There has been very little experimentation in methods of remuneration or organization of medical practice, largely because organized medicine disapproves of such experimentation.

e. Methods of payment and conditions of participation have been quite satisfactory to physicians and hospitals, since they control the plans. The hospitalization plans were largely developed by hospitals, partly to stabilize their income during the depression, and are largely controlled by hospital representatives.[46] The Blue Shield plans are controlled by the medical profession and use the fee-for-service system of payment.[47]

f. Costs remain high and *efficiency* of practice is not greatly improved under limited voluntary health insurance, since there are no important changes in the organization of practice. Inasmuch as the fee-for-service system is retained, the tendency may be to *increase* costs rather than reduce them. The physician is tempted to recommend unnecessary services, since the patient does not himself pay for them. There is evidence that much unnecessary surgery takes place, partly from mistaken diagnosis but partly for mercenary reasons.[48] The schedule of *maximum* fees which the insurance plan will pay for specified operations tends to become the *minimum* which surgeons charge, and sometimes the surgeon adds an additional fee for the patient himself to pay, a practice which the AMA discourages.[49] There are even instances of physicians billing the insurance plan for services never performed. The California Physicians' Service re-

[46] Of Blue Cross directors in 1947, 55 per cent are hospital representatives, 17 per cent represent the medical profession, and 38 per cent represent the public, and to use the name "Blue Cross," a plan must be approved by the American Hospital Association. Louis S. Reed, *Blue Cross and Medical Service Plans,* United States Public Health Service (Washington, Government Printing Office, 1947), pp. 81-85.

[47] Two-thirds of the directors of Blue Shield plans are physicians, and a plan may use the name "Blue Shield" only if it meets certain standards of the Blue Shield Commission, including approval by the local, county or state medical societies. Serbein, *op. cit.,* p. 134.

[48] Dr. Paul R. Hawley, Executive Director of the American College of Surgeons, says, "Unjustifiable surgery goes on in many parts of the country and we run into it every day.... Some of these are performed because of bad judgment, and some for mercenary reasons." (*Time* [February 15, 1954], p. 72.) Dr. Hawley also says, "When the rate [of "normal" appendixes removed] gets over 15 per cent, then there is something wrong. Yet I can show you places where 60 and 70 per cent of the appendixes removed are normal...," and adds, "The normal rate [of Caesarian deliveries] ought to be three or four per cent, and there are hospitals where it runs to 15 per cent. That is unnecessary surgery." ("Needless Surgery—Doctors, Good and Bad," *Reader's Digest,* 62 [May, 1953], pp. 53-57.) An editorial in the *Journal of the AMA* states that 37 per cent of pelvis operations were unnecessary. (Cited in *Chicago Sun-Times,* June 15, 1951.)

[49] *Journal of the American Medical Association,* 148 (March 22, 1952), p. 1036.

cently announced that it had been paying 200 or more dishonest physicians over $1 million a year—about 6 per cent of its benefits—for services they never had rendered.[50] Patients sometimes seek hospitalization for services which could easily be performed outside the hospital, but which are covered by insurance only if performed in the hospital. For this and other reasons, "almost 20 per cent of the Blue Cross dollar is spent on unnecessary hospitalization," according to a survey by the Michigan State Medical Society.[51] One critic states,[52]

> As long as there is no consumer representation on these programs, there can be no effective control over the problem of cost. This applies particularly to the medical society plans which play up their "non-profit" character and yet are exclusively controlled by the very doctors who give the service at fees which they establish. However honest, no one can be entrusted with spending another person's money economically when it is primarily a matter of paying himself.

In many ways, limited voluntary health insurance using fee-for-service payment tends to maintain and even increase the high cost of medical service and the somewhat inefficient organization of medical practice.

g. *Consumer participation* is largely lacking in the control of these plans. In 1933 the House of Delegates of the AMA approved the organization of voluntary health plans under the control of the medical profession. The medical societies sponsored legislation, since passed in about half the states, insuring that control of voluntary health organizations would remain with the medical profession. Some laws permit no such agencies to operate without official approval by the state or local medical societies; some require that all or most of the directors be nominated, appointed, or approved by the medical societies; some permit none but medical societies to organize and operate health-insurance programs. Even in states without such legislation, pressure and intimidation by medical societies has largely prevented the organization of consumer-controlled health-insurance organizations. Consequently, there is very little effective consumer representation at the policy-making level in voluntary health-insurance organizations—which may or may not be a defect, according to one's values.

In summary, limited voluntary health insurance provides the majority of the American people some protection against unbearable medical expense. It has undoubtedly made good medical care more easily available to a great many people than it used to be In the view of most medical society spokesmen, "the people are now being taken care of"; [53] and lim-

[50] "Doctors' Chisel," *Time* (March 24, 1952), pp. 80 ff.

[51] "Open Campaign to Halt 'Abuse' of Blue Cross Hospital Plan," *Kalamazoo Gazette*, December 20, 1953, p. 46.

[52] Nelson Cruikshank, Labor Advisor, Mutual Security Agency, in President's Commission on the Health Needs of the Nation, *op. cit.*, Vol. IV, p. 119.

[53] Dr. J. W. Thompson, President, Missouri Medical Association, quoted in President's Commission on the Health Needs of the Nation, *op. cit.*, Vol. IV, p. 243.

ited voluntary health insurance, plus public-health services, free medical care for the indigent, and certain other grants and programs, provides a satisfactory solution for any medical-care problem which may exist in the United States. In the view of its critics, however, voluntary health insurance with limited coverage and fee-for-service payments is inadequate and basically unsound, because,[54]

Voluntary insurance plans not only fail to provide adequate insurance protection but they do not, and apparently can not, provide needed additional financial support for personnel and facilities and for educational and related resources. They hinder at least as much as they help the development of group practice arrangements required for advancement of quality of care. They encourage segmented and categorical services, with excesses in various directions, rather than coordinated care. They impede as much as they support modern preventative medicine. They are inherently more expensive than comprehensive insurance can and should be. And some of them encourage financial exploitation by practitioners and progressive commercialization of health services.

3. Comprehensive Medical-Care Plans

In 1946, the Co-operative Health Federation of America was organized to become "the national voice and spokesman for democratically controlled co-operative and group health plans throughout the country." It has grown steadily and now numbers about 20 organizations caring for over 750,000 people. Its basic principles are: (a) prepayment, budgeting the costs of medical care, (b) comprehensive medical and health care—preventive and curative, (c) group medical practice, (d) management of facilities by members, and (e) democratic control. Most of the comprehensive plans are sponsored by consumer co-operatives (such as Group Health, Washington, D.C., or Elk City, Oklahoma), or by community nonprofit organizations (such as Health Insurance Plan, New York) or by labor unions and employee mutual-benefit associations. The Permanente Health Plan and the Ross-Loos Clinic in California are similar in coverage and operation but are controlled by doctors rather than by consumers.

The Permanente Health Plan provides 111 days of full hospital care for each illness or injury, all services of physicians and surgeons without charge while hospitalized, all office visits at $1.00 per visit, and all necessary home calls by doctors and by nurses. A $2.00 charge is made for the first home call of each illness. It provides all drugs and medicines without charge while hospitalized, and at a reasonable charge when not hospitalized, and all x-ray therapy, physical therapy, and certain other services. Membership fees (1952) were $114 a year for a member and two or more dependents.[55]

[54] I. S. Falk, Director of Research and Statistics, Social Security Administration, quoted in *ibid.*, Vol. IV, p. 67.
[55] *Ibid.*, Vol. V, pp. 408-409.

The Community Health Association of Two Harbors, Minnesota, provides a ward hospital bed for up to 90 days, laboratory services, drugs, and all other hospital facilities without charge except $1.00 per x-ray film and charge for blood plasma. All medical, surgical, and specialist services are provided in hospital, office, or home without charge except $2.00 for the first home call for each illness. A family of three or more paid $81 a year for these services in 1952.[56]

An evaluation of comprehensive medical-care plans according to the National Health Assembly's criteria reveals characteristics quite different from limited health-insurance plans.

a. Comprehensive health care is provided as the main function of such plans. Some exclusions are necessary, but the coverage is far more extensive. Office calls are covered at little or no charge and home calls at nominal charge. There are no dollar limits on coverage for surgery or for medical service in office or hospital. The average family would probably find 80 to 90 per cent of its total medical costs covered by the comprehensive plans.

b. Universal membership has not been approached by comprehensive care plans, with only about 2.5 per cent of the people having any kind of comprehensive coverage. The growth of comprehensive plans has been retarded by the difficulty of financing the necessary facilities, by restrictive legislation, and by the opposition of organized medicine. Furthermore, *no* form of voluntary health insurance will reach *all* people, for the unemployed, the low-income groups, the migratory workers, and many of the aged would never be covered unless someone else paid their premiums.

c. The *quality* of medical care provided by comprehensive plans is, according to its advocates, *higher* than that ordinarily obtained by most other people. Group practice is used to provide the continuity of care, ease of consultation, and stimulus towards professional excellence that are claimed to inhere in group practice. The comprehensive plans usually set exacting standards for personnel; in most plans, all specialist and surgical services are rendered or supervised by physicians who either hold or are obtaining certification from their appropriate board of specialty, whereas for the entire country, nearly half the specialists, including two-thirds of the surgeons, are not certified by their American Specialty Board.[57] Preventive measures such as health examinations and immunizations are usually covered, and health education is actively promoted. Members appear to be generally well satisfied and complaints are few.[58]

[56] *Ibid.*, Vol. IV, pp. 124-125

[57] *Ibid.*, Vol. III, p. 165.

[58] The Brooklyn branch of Health Insurance Plan of New York reports that, from persons to whom 72,586 medical services were rendered, the office received 104 written and 200 verbal complaints, equal to four-tenths of 1 per cent, and fewer than the 400 unsolicited letters of commendation received. Of all members who left the

d. Freedom and willingness to experiment are usually encouraged in the charters of the plans, but restrictive legislation and the opposition of organized medicine sharply limits the range of experimentation that is possible. The earlier plans faced bitter opposition from medical societies. Physicians serving the plans were denied membership in the local medical societies, barred from hospitals, denied referrals of patients, and generally classed as medical outlaws—exceedingly grave penalties for any physician to face. Several celebrated court battles ended with the Supreme Court ruling that such medical boycotts were a violation of law, and the AMA adopted in 1949 a set of 20 principles for lay-sponsored cooperative health plans.[59] But initial approval rests with state and local societies, where opposition has continued.

e. Methods of payment and conditions of participation have been relatively satisfactory to the participating physicians. The comprehensive health plans report that resignations by staff physicians have been remarkably few, and the Co-operative Health Federation of America now receives more applications from physicians seeking positions than it can place.[60] Physicians like the regular hours (they take turns on night duty), opportunities for advanced study, and relief from office chores. Payment is usually by salary for full or part time, a method apparently agreeable to the employed physicians but disliked by organized medicine, since it departs from the fee-for-service system.

f. Efficiency is high and costs are greatly lowered under these plans. Group practice raises efficiency in the use of facilities, in arranging consultations and in use of the physician's time. The medical services received at a cost of $118 by the average family of four under the Permanente Health Plan would cost $167 at private rates.[61] Costs are further reduced by the removal of the incentive for unnecessary services. "Overutilization," or the demanding of unnecessary services by neurotic or malingering patients, has not been a serious problem.[62]

g. Consumer participation in control is provided by most of the comprehensive medical-care plans, although some are physician-controlled or employer-controlled. In all cases physicians retain complete control

---

group, only 9 per cent expressed dissatisfaction. (Robert A. Rothenberg, Karl Pickard, and Joel E. Rothenberg, *Group Medicine and Health Insurance in Action* [New York, Crown Publishers, 1949], p. 212.)

[59] See James Howard Means, *Doctors, People, and Government* (Boston, Little, Brown & Company, 1953), Ch. X, "Legislation and Litigation."

[60] *Ibid.*, p. 135.

[61] President's Commission on the Health Needs of the Nation, *op. cit.*, Vol. IV, pp. 360-363.

[62] Cf. Rothenberg and others, *op. cit.*, Ch. X, "Utilization of Services." In the Windsor Medical Service, "Removal of the economic barrier to the receipt of comprehensive physicians' services has not resulted in excessive utilization of physicians...." (President's Commission on the Health Needs of the Nation, *op. cit.*, Vol. III, p. 268.)

over all *medical* matters—what treatment to give, what drugs to prescribe, when to operate, and so on. It is the *administrative* matters—coverage, charges, methods of payment, and the like—which laymen control in many of the plans.

In summary, the comprehensive medical-care plans present a means whereby a majority of the people could get better medical care at considerably less cost than is now available to them. These plans have been opposed by organized medicine because they were often controlled by laymen, abandoned fee-for-service payment, and offered a comprehensive service which organized medicine considered impractical. Largely because of determined opposition from medical societies, these plans are now available to only a few people, and are showing little growth at present. And even if fully expanded, these plans would still be unavailable to millions of people because of mobility, unemployment, and low income.

4. National Health Insurance

Many countries, including England, France, Germany, Norway, and New Zealand, have some form of comprehensive medical care financed by taxation. Compulsory health insurance has twice been seriously considered in the United States, once just before and after the First World War, and again during the Truman administration. The more recent proposal calls for a national system of compulsory health insurance, built on the framework of the Social Security administration and covering all persons who now make payments into or receive benefits from federal insurance systems, together with their dependents—about 85 per cent of the people. Other persons might join voluntarily. Payments equal to 3 per cent of income would be collected, using the same machinery that now collects social security payments. Benefits would include all necessary services of dentists and physicians, including specialists, hospital care, home nursing care, laboratory and related services, and the more expensive appliances and medicines. All practitioners and facilities would be free to participate if they desired. Special measures would deal with shortage areas and annual grants would be made to medical schools, with maintenance grants to medical students and grants for medical research. National administration would be vested in a national board and advisory council which would determine policy and allocate funds; local administration would be handled by local boards composed of laymen and physicians. The recommendations and proposed bills have included many specific guarantees, including: [63]

[63] I. S. Falk, Director, Division of Research and Statistics, Social Security Administration, in President's Commission on the Health Needs of the Nation, *op. cit.*, Vol. IV, pp. 68-69.

... the right of all qualified practitioners, hospitals and other facilities to participate and be paid for services to insured persons; the right of ... voluntary health service insurance plans to participate; free choice of doctor, hospital, etc., by the insured persons; freedom of the doctor, dentist or nurse to practice where he chooses; no intrusion into the management of hospitals; payments to practitioners by the methods of their choice, at rates sufficient to yield adequate annual incomes; full-cost reimbursement to hospitals; and preservation of the confidentiality of personal records.

Since national health insurance is a *proposal* rather than a plan in operation in the United States, it is difficult to be certain what it would accomplish. An attempted evaluation according to the National Health Assembly's criteria might describe it as follows:

a. *Comprehensive* care is promised, somewhat limited at first, but expanded as rapidly as personnel and facilities could be provided.

b. Expected *enrollment* of 85 per cent of the people does not include everyone but is more extensive than any other single plan is likely to reach. The remaining 15 per cent, some of whom would be migratory workers and other low-income people, would need other provisions if their medical needs were to be met.

c. *Quality* of care is heatedly debated. Advocates point out that in many ways—better distribution of personnel and facilities, elimination of financial barriers to treatment, co-ordination and continuity of care, and others—the quality of care *might be improved* by national health insurance. Dissent comes from two groups. (1) Opponents of "socialized medicine," as they term it, insist that quality of care would deteriorate terribly because of political interference and corruption, bureaucratic incompetence, patient malingering, and other abuses.[64] (2) Some supporters of the national health-insurance principle object that the present proposals do not go far enough in promoting group practice and the salary method of payment to secure possible gains in quality of care.

d. *Freedom to experiment* would be substantial, as administration would be decentralized with state and local units retaining considerable freedom of action.

e. *Payment methods and conditions of participation* satisfactory to medical personnel are specifically guaranteed in the proposal. Whether they would be realized is a matter of dispute. The medical societies and hospital associations are guaranteed a major voice in these matters, but not the sole control which organized medicine feels it should have.

f. *Costs and efficiency* levels are also disputed. Costs of collection, using the existing social security machinery, should be extremely low, but

[64] E.g., an AMA pamphlet, "The Voluntary Way is the American Way," published about 1950 (no date given), states, "... the historical record of every great country to try politically-controlled medicine, is a record of: deterioration of medical education, training, and research; degeneration of medical standards, and of medical care; steady decline of the people's health." (p. 9.)

other costs are not accurately predictable. Most plans, both public and private, have found that costs exceeded original estimates. Opponents of "socialized medicine" predict astronomical costs and disgraceful inefficiency.[65] Some supporters of the national health-insurance principle claim that, since this particular proposal permits solo practice and fee-for-service payment, costs would be unnecessarily high, and the present alleged inefficiencies of medical practice would only be continued and compounded.

g. *Consumer participation* in all levels of policy-making is provided through membership in the various administrative boards.

5. Special Grants and Categorical Services

Governmental and private philanthropic agencies promote many kinds of *categorical* programs, meaning that each deals only with certain specified disorders or only with a specified group of people. Voluntary private agencies like the National Tuberculosis Association and the National Foundation for Infantile Paralysis provide treatment and promote research in certain diseases. Federal, state and local governments spent $3¼ billion for civilian health services in 1951, nearly one-fourth of our nation's $14 billion medical bill. Services are offered to a wide variety of specific groups—Indians, drug addicts, crippled children and adults, the indigent, tuberculosis victims, and others. Federal grants are made for numerous definite purposes: to aid state and local governments in conducting certain programs, for hospital construction, for research, and many others.[66] It is clear that we already have a partly "socialized" system of medical care, and that it has been a major factor in the health gains we have already accomplished. If government financing of health services is "socialized medicine," then the issue is not *whether* to "socialize" medicine in the United States, but *how much further* to "socialize" medicine in the United States.

Whether grants and categorical services are a more practical approach to health problems than a wholesale reorganization of medical practice is a debatable issue. Grants and categorical services result in a medical patchwork with many gaps, considerable overlapping, and little co-ordination. On the other hand, such programs can be started cheaply and expanded gradually, and excite less opposition than sweeping reorganization proposals.

[65] An AMA pamphlet states, "The medical bill of the average family would be doubled, if not trebled." "America would require a million and a half non-medical employees ... siphoning off medical funds...." (*Ibid.*, pp. 4, 5.)

[66] See Oscar N. Serbein, *op. cit.*, Part V, "Governmental Programs," for a detailed outline of governmental health activities.

TABLE 17-2. Governmental Expenditures for Civilian Health, 1951
(millions of dollars)

Type of Program	Federal	State and Local	Total
Hospital and medical care	642.7	1,120.6	1,763.3
New hospital construction	254.0	317.0	571.9
Community and related health services ° ..	61.2	740.2	810.2
Maternal health and child care	23.1	11.3	34.4
Medical rehabilitation	3.3	3.3	6.5
Medical and public health research	56.7	2.0	58.7
Health personnel, in service training	5.0	2.6	7.6
Total	1,046.9	2,179.0	3,243.8

President's Commission on the Health Needs of the Nation, *op. cit.*, Vol. IV, p. 153.
* Includes U. S. Public Health Service, Food and Drug Administration, and state and local expenditures on community health and sanitation.

In 1952, the President's Commission on the Health Needs of the Nation recommended that federal grants be increased by an additional $1 billion a year, distributed as follows: [67]

Training of health personnel; grants to schools, scholarships to students	$ 100,000,000
Hospital construction	77,000,000
Local health services; support of general operations, chronic disease, maternal and child health activities, and environmental health activities	60,000,000
Medical research	20,000,000
Assistance in developing regional coordination of health services	10,000,000
Grants-in-aid to States to assist in provision of personal health services, including loans to establish voluntary prepaid comprehensive health care plans	750,000,000
Other, including industrial health and migratory workers ..	1,000,000
Total	$1,018,000,000

Since these grants would in many cases be matched by state and local funds, a susbtantial increase in medical expenditures was implied. Through these grants, *together with encouragement of voluntary, prepaid, comprehensive health-care plans using group practice,* the Commission hoped that the supply of facilities would be increased, the quality and availability of medical care improved, and the general health level advanced.[68]

Leaders of the AMA sharply attacked the President's Commission and

[67] *Op. cit.*, Vol. I, p. 79.
[68] *Ibid.*, Vol. I, *Findings and Recommendations.*

its recommendations as "Creeping Socialism." [69] AMA officials charged that the federal aid to medical education features carried the "danger of bureaucratic control" [70] and denounced the prepayment proposal as outright "compulsory health insurance." [71] Few of the Commission's recommendations have been adopted.

THE "SOCIALIZED-MEDICINE" CONTROVERSY

With the aggressive support of President Truman and various health officers of the federal government, the proposal for national health insurance aroused one of the most bitter political battles in decades. Supporters included most labor organizations and co-operatives, consumer organizations, and a number of physicians organized into Physicians Forum. Opponents included the medical and hospital associations, the American Legion, the D.A.R., national business and commercial associations, and many other politically conservative groups and organizations. A "Committee for the Nation's Health" [72] was formed to unite the promotional efforts of the proposal's advocates, who painted a rosily optimistic picture of the nation's health under national health insurance. The AMA launched its "National Educational Campaign" [73] to publish publicity and organize opposition.

In addition to the above charges that costs would be staggering and quality of care poor, the AMA and its supporters lodged charges that doctors would be regimented, destroying their freedom of practice and their incentives for improvement; medical careers would become unattractive and medical school enrollments would decline; private practice would be destroyed; the medical privacy of the patient would be invaded; the patient's "free choice of physician" would be limited; the patient-doctor relationship would suffer; politicians might threaten to withhold medical services from persons who did not support the party in power; health insurance would be socialistic and communistic, and merely a first step to the regimentation of all the professions and the destruction of free enterprise. Lenin was widely—and incorrectly—quoted as having said that "socialized medicine is the keystone to the arch of the socialist state," [74] and the motives of the supporters of national health

[69] See editorial, "Creeping Socialism by Commission," *Journal of the American Medical Association,* 151 (March 21, 1953), p. 1003; also articles by Director of the Bureau of Medical Economics Research of the AMA, Frank G. Dickinson, "Building Health by Commission," *Journal of the American Medical Association,* 151 (March 21, 1953), pp. 1032-1039; and "Appendix—Specific Comments on Volumes 2 and 3," 151 (April 4, 1953), pp. 1225-1226.

[70] *Chicago Sun-Times,* June 10, 1952, p. 18.

[71] *New York Times,* Dec. 2, 1952, IV, p. 2.

[72] 1416 F Street, N.W., Washington 4, D.C.

[73] One LaSalle Building, Chicago, Illinois.

[74] This alleged Lenin quotation, extensively circulated in AMA campaign material, was first "quoted" by Lawrence Sullivan in *The Case Against Socialized Medicine*

insurance were liberally impugned. The British National Health Service was depicted as an alarming example of what national health insurance would bring to the United States.[75]

Some of these charges no doubt expressed real possibilities and dangers. The possibilities of political manipulation, of graft and corruption, and of red-tape entangled bureaucracy are too real to be ignored. Others among the charges have been quite unrealistic, in view of the provisions and specific guarantees in the proposed bills. In particular, the flagrant misrepresentation and distortion of the British National Health Service presents a remarkable study in irresponsible propaganda. Many pamphlets, paid advertisements, and articles in mass magazines have pictured medical care in Britain as disgraceful and British health as rapidly deteriorating. British medical journals have protested repeatedly against the misleading caricatures drawn by Americans who study Britain's Health Service "with the idea of finding out everything bad about it so they can make their compatriots' flesh creep when they go home."[76] The facts appear to be that the sudden expansion of their National Health Service in 1948 overloaded it for a time, and that some initial errors were made, but by 1952 public-opinion polls were showing 85 to 90 per cent of the public well satisfied with the health service. As for the British medical profession, "the people who work it, having started as bitter opponents, are now ready to fight all attempts to destroy it," according to an editor of *The Lancet,* a British medical journal.[77] A recent official survey conducted by prominent British physicians reports that "the relationship between doctor and patient is as good as ever, and in many ways has improved.[78] Nearly everyone in Britain approves the principle of national compulsory health insurance, although both doctors and laymen often complain about certain details of its operation.[79] The general success of Britain's National Health Service is now an established fact—which does not, of course, imply that we should necessarily copy it, for our needs and traditions may be different.

Several public-opinion polls between 1942 and 1946 revealed that some system of national health insurance was acceptable to a majority of our

(Washington, Statesman Press, 1949), but neither Mr. Sullivan nor anyone else has given an exact reference to this "quotation" in any of Lenin's recorded writings or utterances. Although there is no doubt that Lenin favored a system of state medicine, there is no evidence that he ever made this particular statement.

[75] See such AMA pamphlets as "The Voluntary Way Is the American Way," "Compulsory Health Insurance," and "Pickpocket Medicine," and see Melchior Palyi, *Compulsory Medical Care and the Welfare State* (Chicago, National Institute of Professional Services, 1949), for detailed statements of these charges.

[76] Sir Heneage Ogilvie, M.D., in *British Medical Journal* (March 25, 1950), pp. 714-715.

[77] Stephen Taylor, "I Was Sick and Ye Comforted Me," *United Nations World* (June, 1952), pp. 48-51.

[78] *Time* (July 12, 1954), p. 44.

[79] Means, *op. cit.*, "Britain's Venture in Government Medicine," Ch. VI.

people.[80] In 1946, a poll of the Medical Society of the County of New York found these physicians voting 502 to 154—over three to one—against the compulsory health-insurance bill then before Congress.[81] In the ensuing socialized medicine controversy, public support apparently declined and the bill was easily defeated. Public discussion has largely disappeared, and it appears highly improbable that any such legislation will be passed in the near future.

The Eisenhower administration presented its health program in 1954 and again in 1955. It consisted of (1) modest increases in federal grants for public-health services, hospital construction, and medical research; (2) grants to the states for medical services to the indigent; and (3) a federal "reinsurance" fund to help voluntary health insurance agencies to extend their coverage.[82] Even these modest proposals aroused AMA opposition.[83] Administrators of voluntary health insurance agencies have shown little enthusiasm for the "reinsurance" proposal, which would neither reduce costs nor increase the total amount of funds available. Proponents of comprehensive health-care plans view the proposals as timid and ineffectual,[84] and it appears unlikely that Congress will enact them.

SOME ISSUES—REAL AND UNREAL—IN THE HEALTH PROBLEM

Attempts to meet the health problem have been greatly confused by several "phony" or unreal "issues"—unreal because they incorrectly state the choices open to us.

1. The "socialist" issue is an unreal issue. None of the medical-care proposals—not even national health insurance—would either create a socialist state or require a socialist government for its operation. Like public schools, highways, and postal systems—all once denounced as "socialistic"—a health service plan can be operated by any form of government.

---

[80] A poll in *Fortune*, 26 (July, 1942), reported 74 per cent agreeing that the federal government should "collect enough taxes after the war for medical care for everyone who needs it"; the American Institute of Public Opinion (Gallup) Poll (August, 1943) found 59 per cent favoring an expansion of the social security system to cover medical care; the National Opinion Research Center (August, 1944) found 68 per cent thinking it a "good idea" if "the social security law also provided paying for the doctor and hospital care"; a poll conducted by an advertising agency for the California Medical Association found 50 per cent answering "yes" to the somewhat "loaded" question, "Do you think we should have some sort of a socialized government-controlled medical plan?" In each case, from 9 to 16 per cent were undecided, while only from 19 to 34 per cent voiced opposition. Polls are summarized in Malmberg, *op. cit.*, pp. 230-232, and Peters, *op. cit.*, pp. 93-104.

[81] Malmberg, *op. cit.*, p. 232.

[82] *New York Times*, January 24, 1954, p. 1; February 6, 1955, IV, p. 6.

[83] *New York Times*, January 24, 1954, IV, p. 2; January 30, 1954, p. 8.

[84] *New York Times*, February 6, 1955, IV, p. 6.

Nor would government-financed health services necessarily promote socialist philosophy. During the past quarter-century of expanding governmental services, public-opinion polls have shown a steady decline in popular support for nationalization of banks, mines, and railroads—the heart of the real socialist program.[85] The interjection of the bogeyman of "socialism" and "communism" into the health discussion serves only in an effort to replace rational with emotional thinking and to shift the basis of decision from a practical to a theoretical or doctrinaire level.

2. The "free-enterprise" issue—whether to retain or destroy "the free-enterprise system of medical care" is no real issue. Medical practice in America is not a "free enterprise" in any normal use of the term. Doctors are prevented by law or by professional ethics from doing many of the things which a competitive business may properly do—enter and leave the business at will, advertise, entice away customers from one another, criticize competitors' products, cut prices and hold "sales," and so on. Medical practice has privileges and obligations quite different from those of the businessman. To invoke the terminology of the market place in discussing medical practice is only confusing.

There are, however, some real issues—vital questions upon which the future direction of health organization will hinge.

1. How Much Shall We Sacrifice to Gain Full Health Care for All?

How much shall we spend? We are currently spending about as much, individual and government, for medical services as we spend for alcohol and tobacco, and individuals spend for health services a trifle more than they spend for alcohol. Shall we increase taxes—for any major increase would need to be through taxation—in order to spend more for medical care? Shall we determine to spend *whatever is required* to provide high-quality medical services to everyone? The cost might be considerable. A recent survey in Michigan—a relatively healthy and prosperous state—found "that there were more persons in rural areas who had none of their medical needs met than those who had all of them cared for."[86] In 1953, after a long decline, the number of new cases of syphilis turned upward, largely because "federal and state funds for detecting and treating the disease have been cut back too fast."[87] National health cannot be bought at bargain prices!

Should low-income persons be *encouraged* or *discouraged* from asking for free medical care? Should those too ignorant to recognize their medi-

[85] Four Gallup polls, taken in 1936, 1945, 1949, and 1953, show popular support for these propositions steadily declining to less than half its 1936 level. (*Time* [October 19, 1953], p. 28.)

[86] President's Commission on the Health Needs of the Nation, *op. cit.*, Vol. III, p. 273.

[87] *Time* (December 21, 1953), p. 71.

cal needs be encouraged to seek services for which they cannot pay, or should we be grateful that they do not clamor for free attention? These questions are important, both for health and for government finance.

There are *some* health expenditures which eventually pay for themselves in reduced dependency. At a cost to federal and state governments of $32.6 million in 1952, some 63,682 vocationally handicapped persons were rehabilitated; their annual earnings increased by $100 million after rehabilitation, and the federal government collected an additional $9.2 millions in income taxes in the first year.[88] Vocational rehabilitation more than pays for itself. Whether all increases in government health increases would also pay for themselves is not certain.

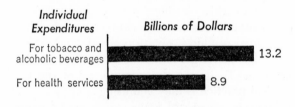

Individual
Expenditures   Billions of Dollars

For tobacco and
alcoholic beverages   13.2

For health services   8.9

FIG. 17-7. Individual Expenditures for Health Services, Tobacco, and Alcoholic Beverages in the United States, 1951. (From President's Commission on the Health Needs of the Nation, *op. cit.*, Vol. IV, p. 135)

Health is also a matter of diet, of housing, of health habits. Shall we make the determined (and costly) attack upon poverty, substandard housing, and ignorance which would be needed to reach the highest health level? Or shall we use these conditions to excuse and justify the continuation of widespread unmet medical needs in the United States? All these questions are important; all involve major value choices, and each answer imposes sacrifices upon some of us.

2. Who Shall Control the Organization of Medical Services?

Organized medicine feels that the profession should control all phases of medical practice—financial and administrative as well as medical—and has obtained laws in about half the states to insure such control. A number of laymen, joined by some physicians, feel that laymen should be permitted to organize medical-care plans in which they control the business and financial management. According to Means, a former president of the American College of Surgeons, "This is the chief bone of contention between the doctors and the people." [89]

[88] President's Commission on the Health Needs of the Nation, *op. cit.*, Vol. IV, pp. 196-197.
[89] *Op cit.*, p. 168.

3. To What Extent Shall the Reorganization of Medical Practice Be Forced?

A great many members of the medical profession feel that the present system is a good one and are rather resentful that it is under attack. But the growing trend toward group practice and salary payment and the successful operation of the comprehensive health-care plans suggest that an eventual reorganization along such lines is perhaps inevitable. Meanwhile, should only plans fully acceptable to organized medicine be promoted, or should other plans be demanded despite medical opposition? [90]

4. What Should Be the Role of Government in Health Services?

There is no serious proposal that government should assume *direct control* of medical practice. The real issues include: (*a*) How actively should the government promote medical reorganization (such as the President's Commission's recommendation for federal grants to encourage voluntary, comprehensive, group-practice medical-care plans)? Should the government, perhaps, grant medical leadership a veto power in deciding what to promote? (*b*) How much shall the government spend on health services, and should it try to discover unmet medical needs in order to meet them? (*c*) What health grants and services shall the government provide, and what should it leave to individual initiative and private philanthropy?

As the American people seek to grapple with the health problem, issues such as these arise, are partly answered, and then are redefined in different form to be considered again. Such is the process of policy formation in a democracy. Meanwhile, medical knowledge continues to grow, the health level continues to rise, and American medical practice continues its sometimes painful process of adapting itself to serve the changing needs of a dynamic society.

SUMMARY

Americans are as healthy as any people in the world, but less healthy than they might be. Health is a product of many factors—diet, housing and living conditions, health habits, sanitation, preventive medicine and medical care. All of these factors tend to go hand in hand, in close association with income. Health facilities are at present insufficient to provide all of the people with full medical care and are unevenly distributed over

[90] See David R. Hyde and Payson Wolff, with Ann Gross and Elliot Lee Hoffman, "The American Medical Association: Power, Purpose, and Politics in Organized Medicine," *Yale Law Review,* 63 (May, 1954), pp. 938-1022, for an objective, elaborately documented account of the political activities and pressure operations of organized medicine.

the country. People in rural and isolated areas, low-income persons, and racial minorities receive far less medical care and have far higher illness and death rates than the national average.

The quality of medical care, while higher than in most—possibly all—other countries, is still impaired by a number of limitations: isolation of practitioners in solo practice, the fee-for-service system, fee-splitting, exclusion of some physicians from hospital privileges, high cost of medical services, lack of continuity and co-ordination, and overworking of medical personnel. Proposed improvements include group practice, voluntary health insurance, voluntary comprehensive health-care plans, compulsory national health insurance, governmental grants, and categorical services. All but one of these proposals are being increasingly applied in the United States. Compulsory national health insurance has been decisively rejected, at least for the present.

The health problem can be analyzed in terms of the inability of traditional methods of medical organization and finance to handle efficiently the growing body of medical knowledge and meet changing medical needs—a social-disorganization approach. The problem can be analyzed in terms of differing value-judgments concerning the extent of medical "needs" and of "desirable" ways of meeting them—a value-conflict approach. The problem can be analyzed in terms of the manner in which deviant personality organization contributes both to ill health and to debate about the problem—a personal-deviation approach. Each approach contributes to a complete understanding of the problem.

No single proposal will "solve" the health problem, because a number of "causes" are involved. Among the major issues to be decided by the American people are these: How extensive an attack upon *all* the causes of ill health—poverty, housing, ignorance, and medical care—should be mounted? How much tax money should be spent for health purposes? Should health services be provided, without cost if necessary, to all who *need* them or only to all who *request* them? How extensive a reorganization of medical administration should be encouraged, or even demanded? How should control of medical administration be divided between the medical profession and the public? What should be the role of government in the financing and control of medical services? These are not questions of fact, but of value and social policy.

There are many other aspects of health problems—dental health services, mental health, chronic illness, the health needs of the aged, the migrant-labor health problem, and others—which this chapter does not discuss. But to present at all adequately the entire health problem would require not a chapter but a bookshelf.

SUGGESTED READINGS

EWING, Oscar R., *The Nation's Health: a Ten Year Program* (Washington, Government Printing Office, 1948). A report to the President by the director of the Federal Security Agency A detailed outline of the proposal for National Health Insurance sought during the Truman administration.

DEKRUIF, Paul, *Kaiser Wakes the Doctors* (New York, Harcourt, Brace and Company, Inc., 1943). A brief, highly readable account of the organization and early operation of Kaiser's comprehensive health-care plan for Kaiser employees.

"A Game of Wild Indians," *New Yorker* (April 5, 1952), pp. 74 ff. A true medical detective story; a highly readable account of how Department of Health officers prevented a typhoid outbreak from becoming an epidemic by tracking down and eliminating the source of the infection.

MEANS, James Howard, *Doctors, People, and Government* (Boston, Little, Brown & Company, 1953). A former president of the American College of Surgeons and leading medical educator in a semi-popular discussion of the problem of securing better medical care for all the American people. Includes a chapter describing the history and operation of Britain's National Health Service.

National Health Assembly, *America's Health* (New York, Harper and Brothers, 1949). An authoritative survey of American health needs by a group of 800 prominent physicians and laymen, asked by the President to formulate a health program for the nation.

New York Academy of Medicine, *Medicine in the Changing Order* (New York, The Commonwealth Fund, 1947). A study of the implications of social change for medical practice by the Committee on Medicine and the Changing Order of the largest, and one of the most "progressive" local medical societies in the country. Includes recommendations less conservative than those of organized medicine in general.

PALYI, Melchior, *Compulsory Medical Care and the Welfare State* (Chicago, National Institute of Professional Services, 1949). A strong condemnation of compulsory health insurance and the "welfare state" in general, with critical description of compulsory health insurance systems in European countries.

President's Commission on the Health Needs of the Nation, *Building America's Health* (Washington, Government Printing Office, 1953). A five-volume report by a committee of distinguished physicians and citizens appointed by Dr. Paul B. Magnuson at the request of President Truman. This is the most comprehensive recent compilation of statistical data on American health needs and resources that is available. A brief Volume I, "Findings and Recommendations," summarizes both the statistical data and the recommendations of the Commission, and is highly recommended to the student for supplementary reading.

ROTHENBERG, Robert E., PICKARD, Karl, and ROTHENBERG, Joel E., *Group Medicine and Health Insurance in Action* (New York, Crown Publishers, 1949). An account of actual experience in a prepaid comprehensive medical care plan, the Health Insurance Plan of Greater New York, written by two physicians and an attorney active in its operation. An interesting report of what actually goes on in such plans, with detailed suggestions on how to establish one. The final chapter outlines an interesting plan for a National Voluntary Health Insurance system.

Serbein, Oscar N., Jr. *Paying for Medical Care in the United States* (New York, Columbia University Press, 1953). A source book of statistical and descriptive data on medical costs, prepayment plans, and governmental activities and expenditures for health services.

AUDIO-VISUAL AIDS

Both Ends of Locust Street (Association Films, Inc., 347 Madison Ave., New York), 28 minutes, sound, black and white. Describes a case in which the doctor and the local medical society work out a plan whereby a low-income person can obtain a costly operation.

QUESTIONS AND PROJECTS

1. Why, in spite of medical progress, is the death rate from chronic diseases higher than a half-century ago?

2. Why has the death rate for young people fallen so much faster than the death rate for older people?

3. Can the death rate of an area be interpreted as a fairly accurate measure of the quality and adequacy of medical care received by the people of that area? Why or why not?

4. Why is the "mean" family expenditure for medical services nearly twice as high as the "median"? What does this fact show about the kind of distribution curve which family medical expenditure would show on a graph?

5. Why do graduating doctors prefer to settle in urban areas? What would be necessary to attract more doctors to small towns and rural areas?

6. Why are there so few Negro physicians? Is this a "problem" or merely a statistical fact?

7. Do you think that, if you were a physician, you would prefer to practice under group practice or individual practice? Why?

8. Distinguish between the *need* for medical care and the *demand* for medical care. Which largely determines the distribution of facilities and medical personnel? Which term is evaluative and which is merely descriptive?

9. Discuss the proposition: "The main issue in the health field is whether medicine in America shall be socialized."

10. What is your position on each of the "issues" stated at the end of the chapter? What *evidence* can you cite to support your position? What value-judgments do you make in taking your position?

11. Dr. James Means, in the final chapter of *Doctors, People, and Government,* proposes a plan he believes would insure good medical care for all, without using compulsory national health insurance. Read this chapter and evaluate his proposal.

12. Evaluate the National Voluntary Health Insurance proposal in the final chapter of Dr. Robert Rothenberg and others, *Group Medicine and Health Insurance in Action.* Which aspects of the health problem would this plan "solve"? What opposition might be expected?

CHAPTER 18

War and International Organization

A dying man, supporting himself on crutches, made his way to the rostrum of the National Assembly and told of his experience in Buchenwald—he had been a cripple ever since, and now, very soon, was going to die. 'We Frenchmen who survived Buchenwald swore that never again should Germany be allowed to build up its military power. I have come here to renew that oath. I am going to die, Mr. President. I am going to die because of what the Germans did to me. I warn you, do not trust the Germans!' Deeply moved, the whole Assembly rose and cheered. Men had tears in their eyes as they watched George Heuillard, a Radical deputy, painfully make his way down the steps and start back to the hospital.[1]

A "THERMONUCLEAR device" was detonated on a small island in the mid-Pacific; that is, there was an island there before the explosion. Following the blast, a number of Japanese fishing boats returned to port bearing various degrees of radioactive contamination. All were well outside the specified danger zone—men 80 miles away were showered by atomic ash and were hospitalized with radiation burns, and one boat which claims to have been no nearer than 1200 miles from the site showed definite evidence of contamination. Many Japanese feared that fish from the contaminated boats had reached the market and the price of tuna plummeted. All shipments received at western United States ports had to be checked carefully, lest the American people be exposed.

The total damage wrought by this more-powerful-than-expected hydrogen explosion is not yet known. Fortunately we are not formally at war and the target was an uninhabited island. But these are preparations for war. Even the most naive person could not imagine a legitimate peaceful use for bombs of such destructive power. A "war to end all wars" was fought from 1914-1918, and a second one lasted from 1939-1945. A minor war—there were perhaps only 250,000 casualties—has ended, temporarily at least, in Korea. A far more costly but still local war almost destroyed French Indo-China. The threat of another world-wide war is the most immediate threat to humankind today. Unless the problem of war can be

[1] *The Nation*, 174 (March 1, 1952), p. 202.

met and solved there may not be the opportunity—or the need—to solve any of the other problems treated in this book.

WAR AS A CULTURE PATTERN

A wit once said, "We are such a peace-loving people that we go to war every twenty years to prove it." He was being facetious. Or *was* he? That one remark expresses an unpleasant fact that is true of Western European culture generally. Most people fervently desire peace, but wars occur with distressing frequency. There are literally dozens of organizations devoted to the cause of national and world peace, countless man-hours are consumed, and huge sums of money are spent for the prevention of war. But these same nations express pride over never having lost a war, build countless statues of military heroes, describe history in terms of battles and wars, and form nonintervention pacts with other nations— strange behaviors for peaceful peoples. We struggle valiantly to preserve the peace, but there is a point beyond which we will not go. "National honor" will not be sacrificed. We will go to war if necessary, and "necessary" it has often been!

War goes far back into our cultural history. The Greeks and Romans, who are among our remote cultural ancestors, were warlike peoples; eventually both succumbed to the strains of war. Intermittent wars continued to spot history as the great nation-states developed in Europe, and the United States itself was born in war. The American Revolution was followed by the War of 1812, by a series of battles against the indigenous Indian population, by the Mexican War, by the Civil War, by the Spanish-American War, by World War I, by World War II, and then by the undeclared Korean conflict (only 10,000 Americans killed). Historically, warfare is a major feature of our culture pattern.

The present American scene cannot help but reflect these past wars. It also reflects the current state of international tension and the possibility of future wars. Figure 18-1 shows the estimated proportion of each tax dollar spent for various military and nonmilitary purposes in the fiscal year 1954. Current military expenditures take nearly 60 cents out of every tax dollar and another 6 cents is being paid to veterans of past wars. The interest on the national debt, contracted largely to finance our various wars, takes another 8 cents, and most of the 10 cents allotted to international expenditure goes directly or indirectly to strengthen our potential wartime allies. Only 17 cents is allotted to all other governmental services combined. *Over four-fifths of the national budget is a war budget!* Whether we like it or not, the American economy is overwhelmingly tied to war.

To suggest that war is in any sense normal or to be expected is almost heresy. Most persons continue to define it as an inexcusable aberration of the relations between nations, as an evil event which somehow must be the creature of the evil intent of a few evil minds. War must be associated with villainy—Hitler, Mussolini, and Tojo being some of the most recent villains. It is a curious fact that the villains are always leaders of the nations which *lose* the wars. Such leaders do play an important part in the initiation and conduct of wars, but to identify them as *the cause* of war is to indulge in wishful thinking. Though it is comforting to think that if we can eliminate the "bad" men we will have eliminated war, history should have taught us either that there is an inexhaustible supply of bad men or that war is more than an aberration of culture! The frightening prospect is that war is deeply rooted in the culture of modern nations and that only major alterations in that culture offer much hope for its elimination.

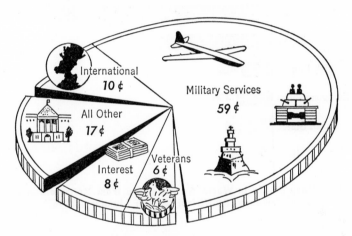

Fig. 18-1. The Tax Cost of Warfare. (Data from Executive Office of the President, Bureau of the Budget)

THE DESTRUCTIVENESS OF MODERN WAR

Literature is replete with imaginary accounts of wars among preliterate peoples. Hence it is not difficult to conjure up visions of screaming hordes of savages busily impaling one another upon poison-tipped spears. Modern anthropology, however, has shown us the inaccuracy of these impressions. War is found in many preliterate societies, as among ourselves, but "savages" generally fight a remarkably civilized kind of war. Total casualties in these encounters seldom reach a hundred, and to have half a dozen people killed is often sufficient reason to bring the war to an end. Modern man has no monopoly upon war but here, as elsewhere, he is wondrously efficient. In a single war he kills more people and destroys more property than could be accomplished in a thousand preliterate wars.

The history of war is one of continually increasing destructiveness. Originally our wars probably were not much more terrible than those of preliterates, but the technology of war developed apace with technology in general. Firearms were more efficient than thrown or hurled weapons, then automatic firearms, artillery, armored vehicles, aircraft, and finally nuclear weapons revolutionized warfare. In one sense the difference seems to be only a difference of degree, but in another sense it is at least a difference in kind.

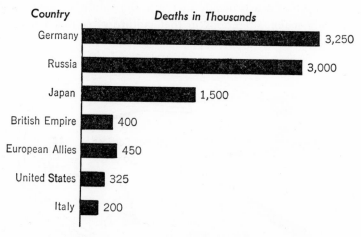

FIG. 18-2. Military Deaths in World War II. (Data from Metropolitan Life Insurance Company, *Statistical Bulletin* [January, 1946])

The destructiveness attained in war over the past few decades almost defies imagination. One measure of the destructiveness, of course, is the number of men killed in battle. Americans are not likely to be aware of the awful toll of human life because, relatively speaking, American casualties have not been heavy. In World War II the United States suffered approximately 325,000 men killed. The individual families involved have some idea of what war means, but the majority of American families have suffered no overwhelming personal loss. The total number of military deaths in World War II, however, numbered nearly ten million! Germany and Russia lost over three million men apiece—each one ten times the American figure. Japan lost 1,500,000 men, the British lost 400,000, and our other European allies lost approximately 450,000. As if the misery and suffering caused by this mass slaughter were not enough, it will be at least a full generation before the economic life of the separate nations will recover from the loss of vigorous young man power.

TABLE 18-1. What an H-Bomb Would Do to Some Major U. S. Cities

Washington. Aiming point: the Lincoln Memorial. The perimeter of total destruction would include the entire District of Columbia and Arlington County, Va. (The Pentagon, National Airport), the suburbs of Chevy Chase, Bethesda, Silver Springs, Hyattsville, Alexandria.

New York. Aiming point: Rockefeller Center. The circle of complete destruction would extend from Spuyten Duyvil to the Statue of Liberty, cover all Manhattan, Hoboken, Weehawken, large parts of The Bronx, Queens, Brooklyn and Jersey City.

Philadelphia. Aiming point: City Hall. All of the midtown and South Philadelphia areas, the Navy Yard, Germantown, Upper Darby and Camden destroyed; Chestnut Hill, Bryn Mawr, Chester severely damaged.

Boston. Aiming point: the State House. The heart of the city, Cambridge, Watertown, Brookline, most of the Newtons would be destroyed. Severely damaged: Concord, Lexington, Lynn and Quincy.

Detroit. Aiming point: Cadillac Square. Wiped out: downtown Detroit, Hamtramck, River Rouge, Highland Park, Windsor. Major blast damage: Dearborn, Grosse Pointe, Royal Oak.

Los Angeles. Aiming point: the Hollywood Race Track. Totally destroyed: much of the business district, several major aircraft factories, Dow Chemical, M-G-M, El Segundo Oilfield and part of Santa Monica.

Chicago. Aiming point: the International Amphitheater in the stockyards. Destroyed: the Loop, the Gold Coast, the University of Chicago, Municipal Airport, Cicero. Badly blasted: South Side steel mills and the North Shore.

Reprinted from *Time;* Copyright Time, Inc., 1954.

In World War II, for the first time, whole civilian populations came under attack. Up until that time the folkways of warfare had permitted the fine young men from each nation to slaughter one another without too seriously disrupting life in the society at large. Mass aerial bombing ended all that. Saturation raids on the city of Dresden, Germany, killed 200,000 people in a single night. In 1945, a single atomic bomb from a single airplane killed between 70,000 and 80,000 people in Hiroshima and a few days later a similar bomb killed from 35,000 to 40,000 people in Nagasaki. One estimate places the total number of civilians killed at approximately twelve million—more than the number of soldiers killed in combat! [2] Major wars will no longer be fought by armies but by nations, with the wholesale extermination of civilian populations as an inevitable result. Any nation on earth can now be almost completely destroyed in a matter of days!

The destruction of property and the wastage of resources during World

[2] Mabel Elliott and Francis Merrill, *Social Disorganization,* 3rd ed. (New York, Harper and Brothers, 1950), p. 713.

War II are impossible to estimate accurately. One index of such destruction is pure monetary cost. Most of the war probably cost the American people in excess of $250 million per day. The United States entered the war with a national debt of $50 billion and emerged "victorious" with a debt of $260 billion. The total cost to the United States may have been as much as $400 billion. World costs are even harder to determine, but one estimate places the total monetary cost of the war at $1¼ trillion and the total economic cost, including property destruction, at $4 trillion.[3]

The day has passed when any nation could "win" a major war. A third world war would so deplete the earth's natural resources as to lower living standards everywhere. The financial costs would probably bankrupt the participants. And nuclear weapons undoubtedly would be used. If World War III is fought with nuclear weapons, World War IV will have to be fought with clubs!

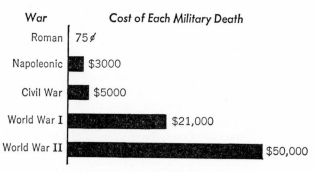

FIG. 18-3. The High Cost of Killing a Man. (Data from J. H. S. Bossard, "War and the Family," *American Sociological Review,* 6 [June, 1941], p. 339)

INTERNATIONAL ORGANIZATION

Like war itself, various attempts to prevent war go far back into history. Treaties have been signed, declarations made, and conferences held—but without any long-term effects. Most such efforts have involved only a few nations who were attempting to cope with a particular set of tensions or conflicting interests. Naturally these agreements provided no basis for resolving other tensions not included in the agreements, and even such limited pacts as were made contained no real provisions for enforcement. They depended upon the continued good will of the signatories. When the good will disappeared, so did the effectiveness of the pacts.

Efforts to prevent war are not new, but attempts to prevent war through large-scale international organization are relatively new. An important first step was taken with the establishment of the first Permanent Court of Arbitration in 1901, as an outgrowth of the Hague Conference

[3] Harry E. Barnes and Oreen M. Ruedi, *The American Way of Life* (New York, Prentice-Hall, Inc., 1950), p. 435.

of 1899. The Court was never very successful in its operation: the nations of the world simply were not ready to submit their grievances to arbitration by an international body. The Court was powerless to prevent World War I from occurring. Yet the Court was important for it carried the *idea* of peaceful settlement of differences via an international organization through the First World War to the peace conference of 1919.

The League of Nations

The plan for the League of Nations was taken to the peace conference by President Woodrow Wilson. The League was to be an instrument of international good will, providing a variety of social services and constituting a forum, aided by the World Court, for settling disputes between nations. But the League of Nations, as finally established, was ill-designed to preserve world peace.

The failure of the League cannot be laid in any one place. Instead, a series of unforeseen developments conspired to destroy it. One of the first and one of the most important of these was the unwillingness of the United States government to participate in it. President Wilson and his internationalist philosophy lost favor very rapidly as the war came to a close. By the time the peace treaty was signed the isolationist United States refused to be a party to it. Since America had emerged from the war as the world's greatest economic and military power, her unwillingness to join was a blow from which the League never recovered.

Unfortunately, too, the League was not conceived in a spirit of international co-operation but was made a part of the very harsh Treaty of Versailles. The sanctions taken against Germany and the Soviet Union included denial, for a time, of membership in the League. Thus, in addition to the United States, two of the most powerful nations in Europe were left outside its orbit. By the time they were eventually admitted the damage had already been done.

Membership in the League included approximately sixty nations. From the very beginning it proved itself most effective in dealing with many social issues; problems pertaining to world health, regulation of the narcotics trade, improvement of agricultural practices, and others, were attacked most successfully. But in the crucial area of settling international disputes and preventing armed aggression the League proved impotent. A few minor disputes were settled amicably, but the League's death knell began to sound when it was unable to cope with the Japanese invasion of Manchuria in 1931. Japan's open defiance of the League was repeated with Mussolini's seizure of Ethiopia in 1935. It was only a matter of time then until World War II should begin. The League continued to function in its ineffectual way until the end of the war. It then dissolved in favor of the new United Nations Organization.

The United Nations

Plans for a new and more adequate world organization were under way well before the end of World War II. The Dumbarton Oaks Conference was followed by an organizational meeting in San Francisco in 1945. This time the United States played a major role in the formation of the organization and became a charter member.

The United Nations is composed of four main bodies, plus an administrative organization called the Secretariat. The hub of the organization is the Security Council. This executive organ is composed of representatives from eleven nations. There are five permanent members, the United States, the U.S.S.R., Great Britain, France, and China, and six additional members elected on a yearly basis by the General Assembly. The General Assembly is the legislative body, the Economic and Social Council is charged with continuing and improving the social services begun by the League of Nations, and the Trusteeship Council is responsible for the administration of territories under United Nations jurisdiction.

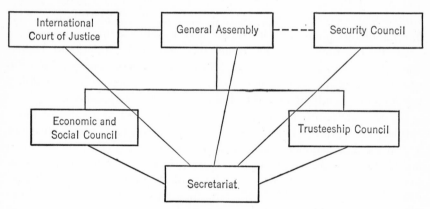

FIG. 18-4. The United Nations Organization. Only the Security Council can take military action.

The UN had no sooner been organized in 1946 than major difficulties appeared. Although it has a basically democratic structure, most of the UN's real power centers in the Security Council, and there *the major powers including the United States* had insisted that they must have the right of veto. Any one of the "Big Five" could prevent the Council from taking action, and the assumption that the veto power would be used responsibly proved fallacious. The wartime harmony among the Allies did not carry over into the peace. American opinion repudiated the wartime agreements reached at Yalta, Teheran, and Potsdam; and the United States was launched upon a policy of "containing" the Soviet Union. The Russians, on the other hand, proved determined to consolidate their gains and seemed to demand even more. Soviet diplomacy proved aggressive, obstinate, and bewildering. Russia had used the veto forty times by December of 1949.

The conflict was heightened when the China government supported by the United States was defeated in civil war and driven into exile by the Chinese communists. The communists, supported by Russia, demanded China's seat on the Security Council. The United States refused to recognize even the validity of the Chinese communist government. Clearly the UN was not off to a good start, and many observers forecast an early grave for it beside that of the League of Nations.

A series of otherwise tragic events in 1950 helped give the United Nations a new lease on life. When the communist-dominated northern half of Korea launched a military attack upon the Republic of South Korea the United States acted swiftly. Rushing troops to the battlefront, she called upon the UN to support the action and to condemn the communist aggression. The Soviets, who had petulantly walked out of the UN, were unable to prevent the action and seventeen nations eventually served under the UN flag. Never before in history had there been such swift concerted resistance to armed attack. The Soviet Union had no choice but to return to the UN, which by now had taken on new importance. The Korean issue is not yet settled but the action taken there is an unprecedented step in international relations. Whereas formerly attacks upon small nations could be made with relative impunity, future aggressors will always have to weigh the threat of possible retaliation by other groups of nations.

The fate of the United Nations is still uncertain. Although it has proved to be a limited deterrent to war, the resistance in Korea was made possible by an unusual combination of circumstances that might not occur again. Moreover, there is ample evidence that most nations are prepared to give the UN only qualified support. The traditional distrusts of supra-national organizations still exist and there are important obstacles to effective international organization which may yet prove to be the UN's undoing.

Obstacles to International Organization

Men have long sought, without complete success, to locate *the causes* of war. Explanations have ranged through supposed "instincts" for war and "man's natural combativeness" to the theory that war results from unbridled economic competition. Of these, the first two have been rather completely discredited and the third shown to be an inadequate explanation by itself. On the other hand, when war is recognized as a part of culture it becomes possible to locate other elements within the culture that contribute to war and make effective international organization difficult. Four such elements in modern culture are: historical enmities; colonialism; power pacts; and the concept of sovereignty.

Historical Enmities. The strength of the hates and fears between nations is illustrated vividly by the passage which begins this chapter. Though the French-German hostility is one of the most widely publicized, it is but one of many. Created by past wars, defeats, humiliations, and exploitations, animosities are slow to be forgotten. Each country vents its anxieties in bitter condemnation of the other; each strives to be militarily strong while vigorously opposing the arming of the other. Since neither country will willingly face possible annihilation by a traditional enemy, efforts toward disarmament tend to give way to an armaments race instead.

The military aspects of these continuing conflicts are fairly well known. What is not widely recognized, however, is how the military patterns are supported and reinforced in the cultures at large. Government pronouncements, news reports, editorial comment, and even the history taught in the schools are pervaded by subtle, and sometimes not so subtle, distortions which provoke one nation to antagonism toward the other. French and German children each learn that the other is a usurper in the Saar, American youth learn that England was a despotic mother country, English youth learn that the American colonies were impetuous and ungrateful, and even within the United States the terms *dam-yankee* and *rebel* persist. War has produced many terrible weapons, but of all the weapons which civilized nations have used against one another, probably none has been quite so insidious in creating an atmosphere conducive to war as has the biased history textbook!

The almost complete disappearance of hostility between the North and the South, and the strong friendship between this country and Great Britain are proof enough that such enmities *may* be overcome. Yet many nations today—Jordan and Israel, Pakistan and India, the U.S.S.R. and the United States, Egypt and England, France and Germany—are engaged in the most intense kind of psychological warfare. Most of these countries are members of the United Nations, but there are among them distrusts so deeply rooted that much of the diplomacy of each is designed merely to counter the proposals of others. That process continued is one of the most direct routes to open war. Only the most pervasive of re-education programs offers much hope to reverse it.

Colonialism. A large part of Africa, much of southeast Asia, parts of the Middle East, and even some of Central America are seething with discontent. Riots are easily provoked, hidden weapons abound, and lives are often in danger. The fury generally is directed at one or more of the great world powers and against local governments supported by those powers. The great powers are on the defensive against a widespread and unreasoning hatred—a hatred they helped to create

World-wide colonialism followed the period of sixteenth-century international exploration. Aided by the fruits of the Industrial Revolution, western Europe was able to dominate economically, and often politically, much of the world. In many ways it was a beneficent domination; mineral resources were tapped, production was increased, and living standards were raised. Understandably, however, much of the wealth was drained off by the mother countries so that the domination was also exploitative. Moreover, in many areas the local European population set itself up as a caste apart, maintaining itself by prejudice and discrimination against the native peoples. Thus the very processes which increased native wealth sowed the seeds of discontent and paved the way for ultimate rebellion.

From the beginning colonialism was bathed in war. Not only did some of the native peoples resist intrusion, but the major powers fought among themselves for the right to colonize many areas. Most of the major wars of the past three centuries have included colonial struggles. Even the two world wars have been described as wars between the "have" and "have-not" nations—between those who had colonies and those who wanted them.

The past decade has accented still another element in the colonial struggle. A long-smoldering nationalism among the native peoples has burst into flame. Compromise, in the form of quasi-independence or eventual independence, offered by the major powers frequently is not enough. Yet refusal to compromise may be met with naked force. The U.S.S.R., a relative newcomer among the major powers and without established colonies herself, apparently has seen fit to encourage violent rebellion both as a means of weakening the Western powers and as a means of establishing communist-dominated governments friendly to herself.

Colonialism, in the traditional sense, is dying. As world opinion becomes more and more hostile, the great powers gradually are being forced to give up many of their prerogatives. If they likewise give up the *philosophy* of colonialism, one major obstacle to peace will have been removed. But the traditional powers will not give up their advantages easily; they will continue to struggle with native peoples and with new powers which seek to gain advantages for themselves.

Power Pacts. Formal and informal alliances among nations far outdate the relatively recent attempts at world organization. By banding together nations could make an attack on any one of them more hazardous and thus be somewhat protected against threats of war. England with her "balance of power" formula probably was the chief architect of this pattern. Throughout the nineteenth century she was able, by a judicious array of alliances, to make herself the crucial factor in almost any power struggle between nations. According to the formula the threat of such massed power is the most effective deterrent to war, but should war develop, it also provides the means to win it.

Such "defense pacts," however, present something of a paradox. Presumably designed to help preserve the peace, their existence is a major stimulant toward war. Inevitably they array groups of nations against one another. A pact designed to resist aggression by one power poses a threat to that country and encourages it to seek compensatory alliances with other nations who are then rendered parties to the conflict, and so the spiral continues. Threats mount up, and either side may decide to precipitate a crisis whenever it feels that to delay might cause it to lose the advantage. Thus the means to prevent war becomes a factor in causing war.

Both the League of Nations and the United Nations have been plagued by the existence of power pacts. The League was unable to supersede them and was, itself, destroyed in World War II. Since 1945 the Soviet Union has ringed herself with a group of satellites extending from the Baltic countries to North Korea and communist China while the west has formed the North Atlantic Treaty Organization and the Southeast Asia Treaty Organization. These preparations for defense are also preparations for war. If they continue unchecked, the United Nations is probably doomed.

Sovereignty. One of the most formidable obstacles to effective international organization is the reluctance of individual nations to give up any of their sovereign power. To yield any real authority to an international body often seems to threaten the very independence of the separate nations, and recommendations in that direction are fiercely resisted. The decisions of international courts and of arbitration bodies have been widely rejected upon the grounds that the decisions were infringements upon the sovereignty of one or more of the disputants. The League of Nations was a weak organization precisely because it had no sovereign power itself but had to deal with sovereign nations. The United Nations again lacks any large measure of sovereign power because the permanent members of the Security Council have the power to veto any concerted action. Should a major crisis involving one of the Big Five arise today there is little question but what the UN could not handle it. The UN could not legally take action over a veto.

There is considerable evidence, however, that in some quarters, at least, the resistance to yielding sovereignty is weakening. The UN has machinery for action which was never granted to the League, and there is talk of an effort to seek to remove the obstructionist use of the veto power at the forthcoming UN conference for charter revision. Such revision is not likely to pass during the current state of international tension, but the mere fact that the possibility is being considered is some indication of progress.

On still another front, negotiations among several European nations since World War II concerning both defense and the pooling of natural resources have seen those nations yielding some sovereignty under conditions that were obviously for the common good. A similar approach to the UN would immeasurably improve its chances to preserve the peace, but it must be recognized that the jealous guardianship of sovereignty is still a major fact and a major obstacle to lasting world organization.

WAR AND DISORGANIZATION

War Under Rules

Since the hate and destruction of war are so completely contrary to the professed beliefs of Western society, war is often considered to be the perfect example of social disorganization. Yet war is not, as is often believed, completely unregulated conflict. It is in fact the final step in the breakdown of efforts to achieve national goals through more acceptable channels. Warfare is conducted not *without* rules but under *another set* of rules.

The roots of war are to be found in the conflicting values and interests of nations and in the occasional inability to find peaceful means whereby those differences may be reconciled. Nations are in fairly continuous competition to achieve various economic and political goals. They struggle for raw materials and markets, for favored trade relationships, for land, for additional human resources, and for the right to dominate the economic and political life of other peoples. The means of competition range from offering advantageous trade relationships to manipulating currencies, infiltrating governments, and making a show of military force. Alliances with other nations and military build-up are a part of the pattern. The use of force is the ultimate means of seeking a redress of power. Whenever an impasse is reached, the use of military force becomes more and more probable. Experience has shown that higher government echelons are generally aware of an impending conflict and commit themselves to it long before hostilities actually begin. Military preparations are rushed, efforts are made to create a favorable climate of opinion in the populace at large, and the maneuvering begins. The incident which finally sets it off is, by this time, almost inevitable. The beginning of hostilities is a signal to all that the old rules are no longer in effect and that from now on the rules are the rules of war.

For the Western world, at least, the rules of war are symbolized by the Geneva Convention. Among other things the convention outlawed the use of poison gas, guaranteed unarmed medical corpsmen, marked ambulances, and hospitals freedom from attack, and set up standards for the care and treatment of prisoners of war. Nations that commit mayhem upon one another are urged to do it *by the rules!* Generally the provisions of the convention have been adhered to, and even nations which have not ratified the agreement have permitted themselves to be bound by it. Consequently, war per se, as terrible as it is, is not the ultimate in social disorganization.

Breakdown of the War Rules

Although war is conducted under rules, there is a strong tendency for those rules to break down. Then, perhaps, do we get the extreme of social disorganization; when the rules of war collapse, so also does human dignity and human worth.

It is not surprising that the rules of war are unstable. Rather, it is surprising that they are adhered to as conscientiously as they are, for if ever a human institution were designed to force breakdown in its own rules war is that institution. Two factors which encourage breakdown are: (1) the absolute need to win the war; and (2) the loss of control over individual behavior which is an inevitable accompaniment of combat conditions.

Need to Win. The consequences of war may be much more grave than those of any other form of conflict among nations. A diplomatic defeat or the disruption of an espionage ring does not seriously interfere with a nation's ability to continue the conflict. To lose minor skirmishes does not preclude ultimate victory. With the outbreak of open warfare, however, much more is at stake. To lose the war may mean to lose one's independence or even one's existence. Consequently, nations often feel that they must win at *any* cost.

Observance of the rules, frankly, makes it more difficult to win. There is some protection in observance of the rules, for then one can expect the enemy to adhere to them also, but the impairment of efficiency that accompanies observance may be the difference between victory and defeat. It is costly both in man power and material to take and care for prisoners of war; medics and hospitals save human lives but they also return those lives to battle. Prisoners shot on the spot require no further care, and destroyed hospitals demoralize rather than aid the enemy. The temptation to ignore the rules is so strong that some violation is almost inescapable. Undoubtedly armies vary in the kinds and amount of atrocities they commit and the atrocities that receive public attention are seldom the violations committed by one's own forces. But the conditions of warfare, including hates, fears, and desperations, produce some breakdown irrespective of the identification of the combatants.

Loss of Control. In most instances of violation it is exceedingly difficult to determine the extent to which the atrocities are matters of deliberate policy and the degree to which they result from inability to regulate the behavior of small groups of soldiers. The circumstances of war differ from those of peace, where there are many controls upon individual behavior. Small groups of soldiers operate in virtual isolation from their fellows. The restraining influences of families, friends, business associates and the like which normally induce the individual to suppress, redirect, or limit his antisocial impulses are largely absent. Much has been written about the supposed comradeship of men in arms but little has been written about the quasi-isolation which most of them actually experience. The combined forces of isolation from any permanent relationships, the institutional encouragement of aggression toward the enemy, and the physical isolation of the battlefront permit men to easily overstep the restrictions only half-heartedly enforced by the military itself. Large numbers of men of both sides commit many heinous acts that are contrary both to the rules of war and to their own moral codes. The cumulative effect of such individual atrocities is to produce a condition of widespread disregard for human life and human welfare that results in almost unbelievably wanton destruction of life and property. No other condition on earth so effectively brutalizes human behavior.

VALUE-CONFLICTS

War and the relations among nations provide almost unlimited opportunity for the study of value-conflicts. A book the size of this one might well deal with this aspect of international relations alone. Here we shall deal with just two conflicts important in the American scene and involved in the effort to prevent future wars.

Internationalism versus Isolationism

The United States perhaps more than any other major nation has vacillated between active participation in and withdrawal from international affairs. Following war and in peacetime she has sought to avoid entanglement in European and Asian affairs only to be drawn into the fray again in time to participate in the next war. From these facts are drawn diametrically opposing conclusions. One group claims that our mistakes lay in ever permitting ourselves to be drawn into the conflict again, whereas the opposing faction maintains that future wars may be prevented only if the United States takes an active role in world affairs.

Isolationism. Isolationists look to the past to buttress their position. They cite Washington's farewell address warning of foreign entanglements and the Monroe Doctrine which sought to protect the western hemisphere against foreign interference. Internationalism, they assert, is contrary to the principles laid down in the Constitution and adhered to by the founding fathers. In short, it is both immoral and unworkable. The isolationist position also makes two important assumptions about the modern world: first, that power struggles in the rest of the world need not concern the United States; and second, that the United States is capable of defending itself against all external forces.

Isolationists point out that all our foreign wars have been fought on alien soil, that the United States has seldom been a direct party to the underlying disputes, and that the United States has borne the major cost of such wars. Europe and Asia, they claim, with their illogically drawn boundaries, border disputes, surplus populations, currency problems, trade barriers, and power struggles, are natural trouble areas. If America persists in becoming involved in such foreign wars, the continued strain upon her natural resources, her population, and her economy will eventually lead to national bankruptcy and domestic chaos.

The corollary argument is that America is capable of meeting any threat that might develop from foreign sources. First of all, the American continent is surrounded by vast oceans which provide a formidable barrier to potential invaders. Secondly, we could ring the nation with impenetrable defenses and warn possible enemies of complete destruction of their countries by air power should an attack be made upon us. Not even totalitarian governments bent upon world domination could successfully wage war upon the United States, so armed, and thus there is nothing to fear and no reason to become involved in foreign wars of attrition. The tremendous productive capacity of the American system, freed of the necessity to wage and support constant wars, would raise the domestic living standard considerably and would be the most powerful inducement to other nations to imitate the American economic and political system.

Internationalism. The isolationist arguments have periodically gained and waned in popularity, giving way increasingly to internationalist philosophy. The prime tenet of the internationalist position is that no major country can isolate itself from world affairs; that interdependence among nations is so great that both the foreign and domestic policies of each nation affect, and hence are the concern of, all the others.

Apart from war, it is asserted that the United States cannot afford to curtail relationships with other areas of the world. The American economy is a production economy, producing far more goods than it consumes directly and deriving part of its high standard of living by favorable trade relationships with other countries. The United States exports manufactured goods and farm products. She must import large quantities of raw materials—rubber, oil, fissionable materials, and many basic metals. These commercial needs, alone, indicate the unworkability of isolationism. Satisfactory trade relationships depend upon friendly governments; it does make a difference what faction is in power in a country which is 5000 miles away. Under these circumstances, it is unrealistic to talk about not becoming involved in foreign affairs.

When the possibility of war is brought into the picture the internationalists become even more insistent. They deny the possibility of physical isolation in a world characterized by speeds faster than sound and non-stop flights around the earth. The next war, if there is one, will be fought along great circle routes over the North Pole so that the United States may be attacked without ever crossing the Atlantic or the Pacific. By these new routes no American city is out of bombing range by the other major powers. Moreover, military experts agree that even the magnificent American technology could not prevent enemy bombers from getting through in the event of a mass attack. Atom and hydrogen bombs would be sure to hit American cities. The best defense, it is claimed, lies in a ring of bases thousands of miles from America so that aggression might be met very near its source. The United States must therefore band together with other free nations, pooling both resources and man power to stave off the twin threats posed by the prospect of having to maintain continuous full mobilization and being subject to overwhelming attack.

The long-run trend in American affairs appears to be away from the isolationist view and toward the internationalist one. It is not a clear and unswerving trend, however. The climate of public opinion and official policy both continue to vacillate back and forth so that, to date, the United States has had no really *consistent* policy regarding the conduct of foreign affairs.

Sovereignty and Human Rights

An earlier section detailed the role of sovereignty as an obstacle to world organization and also indicated that awareness of this situation is becoming evident in some quarters. The United States as a nation is not in the forefront of the movement to yield sovereignty and the implied necessity for such action has aroused bitter controversy.

Sovereignty, of course, implies "national rights," and the urge to preserve sovereignty is often associated with a presumed or actual threat to a particular right rather than with sovereignty in a more general and abstract sense. For example, the military alliances of World War II and the Korean conflict established important precedents in the relinquishment of sovereign power, but these events passed virtually unnoticed because they obviously were an aid in the attainment of United States military goals. No direct threat to our national rights seemed to be involved. In another area, however, where the requirements of national security are not so pressing, a seemingly minor matter has become a major issue.

As a part of its program of general social and economic betterment the UN is attempting to construct a Universal Declaration of Human Rights. This declaration would put all member nations on record as advocating at least minimum standards of living, health, and leisure for all the world's peoples. At first glance the resolution seems harmless enough, and unquestionably it is in accord with many of our professed democratic and Judeo-Christian values. Many Americans, acting in terms of those values, have come out strongly in favor of the resolution. Other groups of Americans, powerful and articulate, vigorously oppose it.

Opposition to the declaration stems not so much from failure to sympathize with its goals but from fear of what its implementation would entail. Most everyone favors higher living standards *provided* they are not achieved at his expense. That is the crux of the problem. Opponents of the declaration insist, with some logic (see pp. 192-195), that the means do not exist simply to raise the standards in underdeveloped areas. The underdeveloped areas contain the bulk of the world's people and cannot begin to raise their standards by themselves: consequently, if standards are raised the Western nations and particularly the United States must bear the burden. The United States could not carry such a tremendous burden of support without making drastic sacrifices in her own living standards. Objection to the declaration then becomes objection to sacrificing domestic standards in order to raise the lower common denominator.

If the declaration should pass, the way will have been opened for demands that the United States meet its share of the obligation. From that point, opponents claim, it is merely a series of short steps to complete dictation of American policy by a foreign body. All the labors of the American people to build a superior way of life will have been sacrificed to the lesser ambitions and lesser accomplishments of backward nations. The 1953-1954 session of Congress saw the introduction of an amendment to the Constitution which would prevent the government from entering into agreements which might result in curtailment of American sovereign power. Though the amendment failed to pass, it is likely to be an issue for years to come.

Advocates of the Universal Declaration of Human Rights generally do not dispute the difficulty of raising world standards without some sacrifice of standards at home. They deny the proposition that the declaration is merely a means to granting complete control to an international body, but they do tend to feel that *some* relinquishment of sovereignty and some general raising of world standards is essential to peaceful international relations. Further, they attack the assumption that property rights are inviolable even in the face of human suffering. They conclude, again with some logic, that sovereignty, when it is obviously related to the tax rate, will be protected to the last ditch!

PERSONAL DEVIATION

Throughout this book we have paid special attention to the ways in which deviant persons are involved in social problem situations. Generally we have centered upon the roles which deviants play in helping to create problems. Certainly deviant personalities are not difficult to find operating in war situations, and here again we shall briefly explore their function. In addition, we shall consider the reverse part of this process, namely, how war helps to produce or at least to give prominence to deviant persons.

Accounts of past wars devote considerable space to analysis of the personalities of various civilian and military leaders. From Hannibal down through Caesar and Charlemagne to Hitler and Mussolini, the motives and needs of dictators and generals have influenced their conduct of foreign affairs. A steadily recurrent pattern in the reported personalities of such leaders combines haunting feelings of personal inferiority and a thirst for power. Modern psychology suggests that the acquisition of power in such cases may be a means of compensation for the feelings of inadequacy.

The power needs of the ruler strike fertile ground in the frustrations and hostilities of many of his subjects and the trappings of war help satisfy the needs of both. The period of preparation for war generally sees the emergence of some kind of "divine destiny" concept around which the nation unites. The *particular* destiny may be "to rule the world," "to create or perpetuate a super-race," or "to rid the world of a despot bent upon one of the preceding 'destinies'." Gross distortions of fact are espoused by leaders and populace alike. In more extreme cases, the fanatic adherence to these slogans is not unlike the delusions experienced by mentally ill people. Feelings of personal importance are supported by the creation of gaudy uniforms and the employment of symbols, such as the swastika of Nazi Germany. The process of war involves the manipulation of powerful machines and an orgy of mass destruction. Conquests give great power over conquered peoples, and the frequency of atrocities committed on such helpless persons provides evidence of the needs of soldiers and of armies to abuse that power. These and many other facets of war support the broad pattern of assuaging personal and group doubts at the expense of other populations.

Unfortunately for purposes of precise observation, social scientists have not yet been able to subject any of these noted personages to detailed study. We must depend instead upon the accounts of biographers and upon the observations of associates whose accounts of their former leader's behavior may be influenced both by their personal relationship to him and by the biases implicit in the demands of the conquering audience. We cannot be certain whether or not psychometric testing would show such leaders to differ significantly on inferiority feelings and power-striving from the general run of the population. The subtle interplay between the leader's personality and the influences of his position as wartime leader are difficult to disentwine.

A final important question which remains to be considered is whether the personalities of war leaders differ significantly from those of peacetime leaders. Certainly wartime leaders receive more public attention and are longer remembered. Most of the students who read this book probably can name most of the United States war presidents, but how many of the peacetime presidents can they name? How many of the peacetime presidents would be remembered had it been their misfortune to be chief executive during a war? Thus we come to the disturbing question of whether a leader comes to be defined as a "great leader" because he is intrinsically a great leader or because of the characteristics of the period during which he holds office. The role played by societal factors is unquestionably great: the special personality characteristics of wartime leaders, if they are ever definitely established, may be both cause and effect of the war.

SUMMARY

War is not simply a product of modern culture but has its roots deeply in the history of that culture. Though widely condemned, it is one recognized means of resolving conflicts among nations. It will not just "go away," and it will only be eliminated through drastic changes in the culture of which it is a part. With the prospect that a third world war would destroy entire nations, war has ceased to be merely an academic problem. The very existence of human civilization depends upon the discovery of a solution.

The most immediate hope for the elimination of war is through international organization. The League of Nations was never adequate, and perished in World War II. Its successor, the United Nations, is now on trial. The UN has shown some capacity for limiting aggression, but serious obstacles stand in the way of complete success.

War for all its terrible destructive power generally is conducted under rules. The conditions of war, however, conduce to breakdown in those rules. The overpowering need to win the war and the loss of effective control over individual behavior combine to produce a disregard for human life and welfare not matched in any other human endeavor.

The United States stands divided on two major issues where continued division is an invitation to blundering into another war. The first is dispute over the role America should play in world affairs and the second is division over "national" versus "human" rights.

Feelings of inadequacy and consequent strivings for power, both in national leaders and in the general population, provide fertile ground for embarking upon war. Whether testing would show wartime leaders to differ significantly on these traits has not yet been determined.

SUGGESTED READINGS

BURCH, Guy I., and PENDELL, Elmer, *Human Breeding and Survival, Population Roads to Peace or War* (New York, Penguin Books, Inc., 1948). A neo-Malthusian monograph on the role of population factors in causing war. Useful as an illustration of particularistic theories of warfare.

DOLIVET, Louis, *The United Nations: A Handbook on the New World Organization* (New York, Farrar, Straus, and Co., 1952). A brief treatment of the structure and functioning of the United Nations.

DUVALL, Sylvanus M., *War and Human Nature*, Public Affairs Pamphlet No. 125 (New York, Public Affairs Committee, Inc., 1947). Refutes the notion that human beings are inherently warlike, and includes a section on education for world peace.

NEHRU, Pandit J., "The Pursuit of Peace Armaments Will Not Solve Basic Problems," *Vital Speeches of the Day*, Vol. 16, No. 2 (November 1, 1949); reprinted in Nordskog, John E., McDonagh, Edward C., and Vincent, Melvin J., *Analyzing Social Problems* (New York, The Dryden Press, 1950), pp. 718-723. A speech by the Prime Minister of India in which he opposes the militant preparations for war which are common among Western nations.

ORWELL, George, *1984* (New York, Harcourt, Brace & Company, Inc., 1949). An anti-utopian novel. Paints a frightening picture based upon extension of present patterns of warfare and totalitarian trends.

WALLER, Willard, *War in the Twentieth Century* (New York, The Dryden Press, 1940). Contains an excellent account of various modern theories of warfare. Can be readily appreciated by the intelligent layman.

AUDIO-VISUAL AIDS

Guilty or Not Guilty—The Nuremberg Trials (Film Forum Foundation, 924 W. 18th, Spokane), 29½ minutes, sound, black and white. Shows pictures of the atrocities presented as evidence at the trials and raises questions regarding the moral foundations of international justice.

Man in the Twentieth Century (McGraw-Hill Book Company, Inc., Text-Film Dept., 330 W. 42nd, New York), 17 minutes, sound, black and white. Sets forth the idea that although man has reached a high peak of material progress in the twentieth century, his daily routine is often one of boredom and dissatisfaction. Stresses man's desire for peace in a world split by conflicting philosophies. Presents public education and the mechanism of the United Nations as means for securing peace and happiness for future generations.

Social Revolution (Encyclopaedia Britannica Films, Inc., 1150 Wilmette Ave., Wilmette, Ill.), 17 minutes, sound, black and white. Traces social changes during the past two hundred years. Contrasts constructive or peaceful methods of change with destructive or violent methods.

A Time for Greatness (Association Films, Inc., 347 Madison Ave., New York), 27 minutes, sound, black and white. Sponsored by the American Friends Service Committee. Expresses moral concern over the use of military force as the chief instrument of foreign policy. Surveys what the Quakers have learned about securing peace and understanding between peoples of other nations, derived from the work of the American Friends Service Committee.

QUESTIONS AND PROJECTS

1. Explain the phrase, "war as a culture pattern."

2. What proportion of the men killed in World War II were Americans? Evaluate the statement that "the United States does not really know what war means."

3. Will any nation "win" the next major war? Why or why not?

4. What crucial weakness was common to all of the peace pacts made prior to the present era of international organization?

5. What role did the United States play in the League of Nations?

6. Name the major organs of the United Nations. Describe the general functions of each.

7. Evaluate the statement that "biased history textbooks are a major obstacle to the prevention of future wars."

8. List and discuss at least three major obstacles to the prevention of war.

9. Is war ordinarily fought without rules? What important factors encourage breakdown in the rules?

10. What are the arguments used by both "nationalist" and "internationalist" groups in the United States?

11. How does warfare help give prominence to deviant persons?

12. Read George Orwell's *1984* and relate its message to the continued use of war as an instrument of national and international policy. Evaluate the proposition that increased tendencies toward totalitarianism are inevitable for all major nations involved in warfare.

13. Arrange a panel discussion, in class, upon the United Nations. What bases do the panelists use in their evaluation of the UN? How much of the evaluation derives from objective consideration of the UN's successes and failures and how much of it is a function of the individual's nationalist-internationalist bias?

CHAPTER 19

Civil Liberties and Subversion

Every idea is an incitement. It offers itself for belief and if believed it is acted on unless some other belief outweighs it or some failure of energy stifles the movement at its birth.[1]

Communism can be defeated by the truth—and only by the truth. Vigilante attacks, irrational tirades, and forceful suppression are instruments which increase and do not decrease the menace.[2]

Risk for risk, for myself I had rather take my chance that some traitors will escape detection than spread abroad a spirit of general suspicion and distrust which accepts rumor and gossip in place of undismayed and unintimidated inquiry.[3]

. . . guard against those who pretend to defend freedom with weapons from the arsenal of the tyrant, for to defend freedom in ways that destroy freedom is suicide.[4]

FREEDOM has been a rare flower in world history. In nearly all times and places, the dungeon, torture chamber, and gallows awaited all who dared to question the accepted authorities and values. Today, many Americans fear that our liberties are in danger. At no time since perhaps the early days of the republic have so many books and articles been devoted to a searching analysis of freedom and the conditions of its survival. What is the American heritage of freedom, and what are the developments which seem to place it in jeopardy?

THE AMERICAN HERITAGE OF FREEDOM

We hold these truths to be self-evident, that all men are created equal, that they are endowed by their Creator with certain inalienable rights, that among these are Life, Liberty, and the pursuit of Happiness—That to secure these

---

[1] Oliver Wendell Holmes, Jr., Associate Justice, Supreme Court of the United States.
[2] J. Edgar Hoover, Director, Federal Bureau of Investigation, quoted in *The Progressive*, 17 (January, 1953), p. 5.
[3] Judge Learned Hand, address before sixty-eighth convention of the University of the State of New York, Albany, October 24, 1952.
[4] President Dwight D. Eisenhower, at Mount Rushmore.

TABLE 19-1. How Much Civil Liberty Do Americans Favor?

	ANSWERS OF NATIONAL SAMPLE OF INFORMANTS		
	Yes %	No opinion %	No %
If a person wanted to make a speech in your community favoring government ownership of all the railroads and big industries, should he be allowed to speak, or not?	58	11	31
If some people in your community suggested that a book he wrote favoring government ownership should be taken out of your public library, would you favor removing the book, or not?	35	13	52
If a person wanted to make a speech in your community against churches and religion, should he be allowed to speak, or not?	37	3	60
Consider a man whose loyalty has been questioned before a Congressional committee, but who swears under oath he has never been a Communist. Should he be allowed to make a speech in your community, or not?	70	9	21
Suppose he is teaching in a college or university. Should he be fired, or not?	22	9	69
Suppose an admitted Communist wants to make a speech in your community. Should he be allowed to speak, or not?	27	5	68
Suppose he is a clerk in a store. Should he be fired, or not?	68	6	26
Should an admitted Communist have his American citizenship taken away from him, or not?	77	10	13
Should an admitted Communist be put in jail, or not?	51	15	34

Adapted from *Communism, Conformity, and Civil Liberties,* by Samuel A. Stouffer. Copyright, 1955, by Samuel A. Stouffer, reprinted by permission of Doubleday & Company, Inc.

rights, Governments are instituted among Men, deriving their just powers from the consent of the governed—That when any Form of Government becomes destructive of these ends, it is the Right of the People to alter or to abolish it, and to institute new Government. . . .

The Declaration of Independence and the Constitution were the work of men who were classical scholars. (Today, they would be called "egg-heads.") They were acquainted with the history and literature of ancient Rome and Greece and fully familiar with the rationalist philosophy of the eighteenth century. They firmly believed in *natural rights,* that governments were man-made (not divinely ordained) institutions for securing these rights, and that when governments fail to do this they should be altered or overthrown. They firmly believed that freedom of thought and expression were as inseparable parts of a divinely-ordained natural order of things as was the law of gravity, and that any society which curtails freedom of thought and expression must suffer as surely as the person who violates the law of gravity.

In framing the Constitution, and especially the Bill of Rights, these men sought to devise a government with the power to govern but without the power to oppress. These men were highly aware of social change and of the need for adapting governmental institutions to a changing society. But remembering the bitter costs of change by revolution, they attempted to devise a government with built-in provisions for peaceful change— an experiment which much of the world regarded as highly impractical. These provisions for peaceful change included not only a system of elections, but guarantees of freedom of speech, press, and religion, of peaceful assembly and freedom of political activity. In this way, the people could secure government of their choice at all times, and resort to armed revolt would be unnecessary.

The Basic Assumptions of American Democracy

This attempt to harmonize orderly government with a free society rests upon two fundamental assumptions. First is *the faith that truth defeats error,* that in the market place of free competition in ideas, truth will eventually triumph. Unless truth can win out over error in open contest, then it follows that we must protect truth by suppressing error. Democratic government must rest upon the assumption that the majority of the people, given free access to the facts and unlimited opportunity to discuss them freely, will arrive at the right answers most of the time. Any attempt to prevent the expression of "wrong" ideas is a confession of doubt in the ability of the people to arrive at the right conclusions. If the majority of the people are "too dumb" to arrive at the right conclusions, then democratic government cannot endure and we may as well start considering what kind of dictatorship we prefer.

A second fundamental basis of democratic government is an implicit social contract in which *the majority gives up the persecution of the minority providing the minority gives up the practice of revolution.* The majority agrees to tolerate the criticism and dissent of the minority (or minorities), while the minority agrees to seek power only through persuasion and political activity, not through violence. Such an unspoken agreement is necessary for orderly representative government. If the governing officials representing the majority seek to outlaw opposing political parties, jail critics, suppress critical newspapers, and so on, then it is no longer a free government, and the minority feels justified in organizing a revolution. Conversely, if any members of the minority are unwilling to rely upon persuasion, but use force and violence in attempting to gain power, they have sacrificed their claim to political freedom. Revolution, to our founding fathers, was justifiable in a republic only when the ruling powers interfered with the efforts of the minority to gain power through criticism, persuasion, and political activity; *if the government did so interfere, then revolution became a duty* ("it is their right, it is their duty, to throw off such Government. . . ."). This is the real meaning of freedom— freedom for the idea one hates as well for the idea he shares. Unless people are free to express unpopular opinions and to support "dangerous" ideas without sacrifice of liberty, property, or employment, then freedom is an empty word and free government an illusion.

It cannot be too strongly emphasized that our ancestors erected these constitutional guarantees of freedom, not from any fondness for radicalism, but because they wanted *order.* Having lived through the chaos of revolution, they wanted a social order in which revolution would be unnecessary. They felt that free speech and unrestricted political agitation, even for the ideas they loathed, were less of a threat to orderly government than the seething intrigues and secret conspiracies which the denial of freedom will provoke. Such a belief, together with a confidence in the people's wisdom, is reflected in Jefferson's statement in his First Inaugural address,

If there be any among us who wish to dissolve this union, or change its republican form, let them stand undisturbed, as monuments of the safety with which error of opinion may be tolerated, where reason is left free to combat it.

It is true that not all of our ancestors shared the faiths that lie behind our constitutional guarantees of freedom. Hamilton's famous retort, "Your people, sir, is a great beast," expressed the views of a great many of the colonial aristocracy. Aaron Burr's revolutionary conspiracies received much support from persons who disliked the notion of popular government. At no time in our history has everyone agreed that the people could be trusted with intellectual and political freedom.

Historic Violations of Freedom in America

At no time in our history has our practice of freedom fully measured up to our ideals. Racial minorities have not enjoyed the full rights of citizenship or the full protection of the law. Scores of dissenters have been tarred and feathered, and to burn the plant of an unpopular newspaper is an old American custom. Both radical political movements and efforts to organize labor unions have been opposed with injunction, intimidation, and violence. Even movements which today seem quite innocuous, such as the feminist movement, brought public ridicule and even physical danger to their promoters. Although American society has been far more tolerant of unorthodoxy and dissent than most other nations, the record shows considerably less than complete toleration.

There have been several periods in our history when waves of suppression swept over the country. The first brought the Alien and Sedition Laws, which sound strangely up-to-date. The French Revolution had released revolutionary ideas of equality and democracy which the upper classes throughout the civilized world correctly viewed as a dangerous threat to their power and privilege. The excesses of the Jacobin "reign of terror" added an emotional intensity to their intellectual distaste for the ideals of the French Revolution. The union of a revolutionary ideology with an aggressive military power under Napoleon filled the world's wellborn with an anxious foreboding.

In the United States the Democratic-Republican Party of Jefferson, Madison, and Monroe included many who, while objecting to the excesses of the French Revolution, shared many of its ideals and tended to be "French sympathizers" in the wars of the French Revolution. The Federalist party of Hamilton, Adams, and Marshall, with many members who felt that the American Revolution had gone entirely "too far," tended to sympathize with the British who led the aristocratic opposition to the equalitarian ideals of the French Revolution. Leading members of both parties in America were deeply involved with foreign agents, to whom state secrets were handed with an abandon which, today, would put dozens of them in jail. Each group accused the other of disloyalty and treason, and name-calling ("royalist," "Jacobin," "anarchist," "atheist"), guilt-by-association, and all the other propaganda techniques had a liberal workout.

In this tense situation, the Federalists were trying to retain power in the face of growing Democratic-Republican popularity. The Federalists used the foreign danger as an excuse for passing the Alien and Sedition Laws, which were intended to silence domestic political opponents, to discourage the spread of "dangerous" ideas, and to prevent disloyalty during the expected war with France. Under these laws, practically any criticism of the Federalist administration became a crime, and a number of editors, teachers, preachers, and other citizens were jailed for "proFrench" and other "seditious" utterances. Jefferson and the Democratic-Republicans won the election in spite of (or perhaps because of) these suppressions; those imprisoned for "sedition" were freed, and all the Alien and Sedition Laws either lapsed or were repealed. With the defeat of Napoleon and the establishment of conservative régimes in Europe, anxiety over "dangerous" ideas declined. This first great assault upon American civil liberties proved ineffectual both as a means of maintaining Federalist power and protecting conservative values, for it was followed by a forty-year reign of the Democratic-Republican (later known as the Democratic) party, during which many "radical" ideas became firmly established. And as a means of protecting against treason and subversion, the Alien and Sedition Laws now appear in historical retrospect to have been both ineffectual and unnecessary.

Another serious curtailment of civil liberties accompanied the slavery issue preceding the Civil War. In the early nineteenth century there was a vigorous public discussion in the South over the merits of slavery. But with the increased economic value of slaves following the invention of the cotton gin, and with the increasingly bitter political rivalry with the North over control of the West, the middle decades brought a crystallization of Southern opinion to the point where no doubts about slavery might safely be expressed in print, pulpit, classroom, or even street corner. After the Nat Turner insurrection (1831) abolitionist meetings were suppressed, the mails closed to abolitionist books and newspapers, and abolitionists threatened with death if they crossed Southern soil. The North, meanwhile, sought to avoid conflict by preventing discussion of the slavery question. Abolitionists were viewed as dangerous trouble-makers, and, besides, they were often obnoxious radicals about other things. Abolitionist meeting places and printing presses were burned. William Lloyd Garrison and James C. Birney narrowly escaped death and Elijah Lovejoy met death at the hands of angry mobs. Hundreds of teachers, college professors, and ministers were dismissed in both North and South for expressing views that deviated from the local moral imperatives. This suppression of civil liberties, too, was a failure, for it neither preserved slavery nor prevented conflict.

Still another wave of suppression came after the close of World War I. Disillusionment with the peace settlements encouraged a return to traditional isolationism, with overtones of disdain for "foreigners" and "foreign ideas." The success of the Russian Revolution stimulated radical agitation, while both the communist ideology and the bloody extremes of the Russian Revolution aroused in some Americans an intense fear of revolutionary outbreak. Although the possibility of revolution in the United States was remote, the fear was real, and radical propaganda of any sort aroused disproportionate anxieties. In this situation, the ill and ailing President Wilson's Attorney General, A. Mitchell Palmer, ordered the arrest of hundreds of labor organizers, radicals, and agitators of all sorts. Most were arrested without proper warrants, jailed in violation of the "due process of law" specified in the Constitution, and eventually released without trial or even any specific charges. About this time, Sacco and Vanzetti, two obscure anarchists, were convicted and eventually executed in one of the most celebrated cases in American history. The charge was murder, but the evidence was so unconvincing and the trial so prejudicial that many prominent citizens believed Sacco and Vanzetti were victims of a legal lynching because they were radicals who could easily be "framed" for a conventional crime.[5] The effectiveness of such methods of

[5] Cf. Felix Frankfurter, *The Case of Sacco and Vanzetti* (Boston, Little, Brown & Company, 1927).

suppressing radicalism may be deduced from Vanzetti's final statement to the court: [6]

If it had not been for these things I might have lived out my life talking at street corners to scorning men. I might have died, unmarked, unknown, a failure. Now we are not a failure. This is our career and our triumph. Never in our full life could we hope to do such work for tolerance, for justice, for man's understanding of man, as now we do by accident. Our words, our lives, our pains—nothing. The taking of our lives—lives of a good shoemaker and a poor fish peddler—all. The last moment belongs to us—that agony is our triumph.

It is to be expected that the approved values of a culture will never be fully attained. It is not surprising that the ideal of civil liberty has often been violated in practice. Throughout our history, those who sharply challenged the status quo have been persecuted for their opinions. "Republicans," "anarchists," "abolitionists," "feminists," "socialists," "bolsheviks," "communists"—the names change but the reaction against the disbeliever and the critic remains fundamentally unchanged. In tranquil periods, suppression of dissent is largely unorganized and sporadic. In periods of national anxiety, suppression may become the rule and civil liberties may go into a temporary eclipse. America is today in such a period of national anxiety and is again debating the perennial question of whether some curtailment of civil liberties is necessary.

THE COMMUNIST CHALLENGE

Communists are noisy champions of the cause of civil liberty wherever they are seeking power, but allow few civil liberties wherever they succeed. Their raucous demand for social reform is matched only by the venom of their hatred for liberals and reformers. A brief summary of communist ideology and practice may explain these inconsistences.[7]

The Communist Ideology

There have been many versions of the communist gospel, but all share several basic propositions. (The paragraphs which follow are *not* the

[6] Quoted in Fred Hamlin, *Land of Liberty* (New York, Thomas Y. Crowell Company, 1947), p. 281.

[7] See Karl Marx and Friedrich Engels, *The Communist Manifesto,* published in 1848 and available in various editions in any good library, for a concise statement of orthodox communist ideology. See Nikolai Lenin, *The State and Revolution* (New York, The Vanguard Press, 1927) for a classic statement of the communist technique of action. See *Communism in Action,* House Document No. 754, 79th Congress, 2nd Session (Washington, Government Printing Office, 1946), for an authoritative account of communism as it actually operates in the Soviet Union. For a competent summary and critique of present-day communism, see Chapter I of William Ebenstein, *Today's Isms* (New York, Prentice-Hall, Inc., 1954).

opinions held by the authors of this textbook, but a summary of the beliefs held by communists.)

1. The *labor theory of value,* a respectable classical economic theory, held that all value was created by labor, whereas trade and distribution were "nonproductive." Communism interprets this to mean that all profits are stolen from the workers, and private capital is but an accumulation of past thievery. In "expropriating" private capital, the working class would merely be returning stolen property to its rightful owners.

2. The *class-conflict* theory holds that the interests of the capitalist class and the working class are unalterably opposed, and that all history is but the record of class warfare.

3. The doctrine of *economic determinism* states that all other aspects of the culture are determined by its economic aspects. The methods of economic production and the system of ownership of the means of production (land, machines, resources) are said to shape and mold all other aspects of the culture into harmony with these economic aspects. Thus, communism teaches that under capitalistic ownership and operation of the economy, the family takes the forms and functions most profitable to capitalists; law, government, and the police are only devices for protecting the capitalists; warfare is only the effort of opposing groups of capitalists to steal resources and markets from one another; religion is but an "opiate of the people" promising them a "pie in the sky" in exchange for earthly servitude; "bourgeois" morality is merely a body of superstitions to keep the working classes servile, while occasional crumbs of charity induce the poor to kiss the hands which rob them.

4. The *progressive misery of the proletariat,* the working class, is claimed to be inevitable under capitalism, where the rich allegedly grow richer and the poor grow poorer. Monopoly destroys small business, and the independent middle class of small business and professional men becomes "proletarized," or converted into hired servants of the capitalists. Eventually, the workers become aware of their misery, and this proletarized middle class comes to identify its interest with that of the workers, and capitalist rule is overthrown.

5. The *inevitability of violent revolution* stems from the refusal of the capitalist class to surrender its privileges. Political parties, elections, and the other trappings of representative government are said to be only a pretense which disguises the rule of the capitalists. As soon as the people show signs of a serious challenge to capitalistic rule, civil liberties are promptly withdrawn, and the people may vote only as long as most of them support candidates and policies acceptable to the capitalists. Communism cannot be voted gradually or peacefully into power, for the capitalists will resort to force to prevent it. Therefore, communism will eventually gain power through a violent revolution provoked by capitalist repression.

6. Following the revolution, there is to be a temporary *dictatorship of the proletariat* which must ruthlessly exterminate all capitalist or bourgeois elements lest they sabotage the régime or promote a counterrevolution.

7. After a generation or so of this dictatorship, the *classless society* is supposed to emerge. The state, since it is only an instrument of capitalist oppression, would be unnecessary and should gradually "wither away." The planning of production and other administration problems would be handled by local, regional, and national organizations of workers, and liberty and abundance would be enjoyed by all!

Evaluation of Communist Ideology

Although many details are omitted, these are the basic ideas of communist ideology. To what extent are they true? This question is both difficult and dangerous to answer, for many will be unable or unwilling to accept an unemotional appraisal. But could a doctrine which is entirely false have the world effects which communism has produced? An unemotional answer is necessary if the growth of communism is to be understood.

The labor theory of value and the doctrines of economic determinism and class conflict are half-truths. The economic institutions have tremendous influence upon the rest of a culture, but are far from the sole determinant. Class conflict has played a major role in nearly every great social controversy, but not the sole role. Although the interests of the different classes often conflict, it is also true that their interests often coincide.

The "progressive misery of the proletariat" has not materialized. Instead of growing more miserable during the past century, the workers in Western Europe and the United States have grown more prosperous and less radical. Marx believed that capitalist industrialism must inevitably produce a growing exploitation of the working classes, with revolt as the final consequence of completed industrialization. Instead, the most fully industrialized nations have the most comfortable workers and the least successful revolutionary movements, while communism has a mass following only in the undeveloped areas and impoverished countries.

Only the communists (and some extreme anti-communists) believe that violent revolution is inevitable. It is possible that a growing communist movement would not be permitted to come into power peacefully but would be forced into revolutionary activity by the suppression of their political freedom. It is even more likely that communists would attempt a violent revolution at any time they thought it might succeed. But it is most unlikely that communism can gain power through either channel in the more prosperous democracies.

The dictatorship of the proletariat and the transition to a classless society are completely unrealistic concepts. In no communist-dominated country have workers much control over their individual actions or an effective voice in national policy. Communist rule is not a dictatorship by the proletariat, but dictatorship by a small ruling élite which claims to represent the proletariat, while the proletariat is about as completely controlled as it is possible to be. Sociologists doubt that a classless society is possible, except among the simplest primitive cultures. Instead of creating a classless society, communism appears to replace the aristocracy of property owners with an aristocracy of party officialdom. The state shows no signs of "withering away" in communist countries, and it is unrealistic to expect that any complex society could function without both the bureaucracy and the police power of the state. In short, communist ideology as outlined by Marx contains a passably accurate description of the misery of European workers a hundred years ago but a misery which workers have been steadily escaping in most democratic countries. The communist interpretation of history and social dynamics is a half-truth, and its blueprint for Utopia is unrealistic and unattainable.

Communist Techniques of Action

From the basic principles of communist ideology, certain principles of communist action emerge.

1. *Communism Is Nonmoral.* All conventional laws and moral codes are denounced as only tricks to protect the wealthy. Anything is "right" if it serves the interests of the party.

2. *Communists Seek Revolution, Not Reform.*[8] Communists are both contemptuous of and infuriated at the reformers who try to improve a status quo which the communists wish to overthrow, for successful social reforms reduce social discontent and postpone the revolution. For example, the communists in Italy long clamored for land reform, but when the de Gasperi government finally produced a real program of land reform, the communists opposed it; they didn't wish their favorite propaganda theme to be destroyed. The communists hate social reforms, yet dare not oppose them openly lest their concern for the people sound insincere. Therefore, *the basic communist strategy is to "support" social reforms in ways which discourage their adoption.* They insistently demand reforms of all sorts—fair employment practices legislation, free medical care, federal aid to education, civil rights legislation, and so on—in a raucous and offensive way that alienates possible supporters. They call attention to their communist "support" of reforms and thereby give them

[8] The official *History of the Communist Party in the Soviet Union* states, "The transition from capitalism to Socialism and the liberation of the working class from the yoke of capitalism cannot be effected by slow changes, by reforms, but only by a qualitative change of the capitalist system by revolution. Hence, in order not to err in policy, one must be a revolutionist, not a reformist." (Quoted in Herbert A. Philbrick, *I Led Three Lives* [New York, McGraw-Hill Book Company, Inc., 1952], p. 292.)

the "kiss of death" and alienate many of the supporters. They reject modest reforms, to insist upon sweeping reforms which have no chance of adoption. In discussion of reforms, they are preoccupied with the "social injustices" and have little interest in planning out the details of a workable reform program. They infiltrate liberal organizations, seeking either to convert them into sounding boards for communist propaganda, or to disrupt and destroy them. All this is an effort to (a) discourage the adoption of reforms, while (b) maintaining a public pose as the champion of social reform and true friend of the masses. Therefore, the communists do not mind when conservatives accuse liberals of "pro-communism" and attack moderate reforms as "communist ideas," for this helps the communists to achieve both their objectives.

This helps explain why the *public* position of the Communist party, as expressed by the *Daily Worker,* is often at complete variance from the real position of the party's leaders. As an FBI undercover agent with nine years' experience in the party reports,[9]

Publicly, the party gave lip service to [price] controls, urging them as necessary to the saving of the nation's economy and in the interests of justice. This appeal drew a huge popular response. But it did not represent the party's true objective. . . .
The termination of controls over the economy, the party blueprint said, would encourage inflation through runaway prices, and bring on the depression even more quickly. The National Association of Manufacturers, the party whispered in private, was in this respect a strong ally of the communist movement. The most rabid reactionaries are invariably the Communists' best friends.

Communists have occasionally formed a "popular front" or temporary working alliance with liberals, socialists, and other reform-minded groups when they felt it expedient to do so. During these brief alliances, their vitriolic denunciations of liberals, reformers, and socialists are suspended, but they never cease to regard the liberals and socialists as their real enemy and the capitalists as their unwitting allies. As Lenin, who directed the Russian Revolution, wrote some years ago,[10]

The millionaires of all countries are now behaving on an international scale in a way that deserves our heartiest thanks. They are hunting Bolshevism [as

[9] Philbrick, *op. cit.,* pp. 202-203, 210. Philbrick also quotes a party leader as saying "that it doesn't make much difference whether price controls as they are now proposed are on or off. Capitalism is caught in a trap of contradictions which the economy cannot shake loose." (p. 202.) Because of these "contradictions" in capitalism, the communists felt that the price control issue would aid them, no matter which way it ended. They felt that termination of price controls would promote inflation and increase popular discontent, whereas continuation of price controls would promote bureaucracy, which also undermines capitalism. Therefore, as Philbrick states, ". . . Communists are pro-bureaucratic, in that they recognize bureaucracy as one of the 'creeping diseases of capitalism'." (p. 202.)
[10] Nikolai Lenin, "Left-Wing Communism, an Infantile Disorder," *Little Lenin Library,* Vol. 20 (New York, International Publishers Co. Inc., 1934), p. 81.

communism was then termed] with the same zeal as did Kerensky and Company; they are, moreover, "overdoing" it and helping us just as Kerensky did.

When the French bourgeoisie [capitalist class] makes Bolshevism the central issue at the elections, and abuses the comparatively moderate or vacillating Socialists for being Bolsheviks; when the American bourgeoisie, having completely lost its head, seizes thousands and thousands of people on suspicion of Bolshevism, creates an atmosphere of panic and broadcasts stories of Bolshevik plots; when the British bourgeoisie—the most "solid" in the world—despite all its wisdom and experience, commits acts of incredible stupidity, founds richly endowed "anti-Bolshevik societies," creates a special literature on Bolshevism, and hires an extra number of scientists, agitators, and priests to combat it— we must bow and thank the capitalist gentlemen. They are working for us. . . .

3. *Communists Prefer That Capitalist Governments Be Reactionary.* They wish the masses to feel oppressed by a "rich man's government," utterly indifferent to the welfare of the masses. It is the communist's dream to manipulate the situation so that the oppressed and resentful masses see no possible hope for a better life except by supporting the communists. To create such a situation, the communists need (1) a period of genuine economic distress, (2) a government which is unable or unwilling to do anything effective to relieve their distress, and (3) an atmosphere in which all reform movements have been destroyed, so that the people must choose between enduring their misery or supporting the communists. So, while communists may publicly call for liberal government, they privately consider a reactionary government most helpful to their effort to gain power.

4. *Communists Seek Martyrdom and Invite Persecution.* Like Br'er Rabbit, who kept begging "Don't throw me into that briar patch" until the fox finally did so, the communists keep defending civil liberties in the hope that liberties will be attacked. Communists eagerly seek the martyr's crown, feeling that a moderate degree of persecution is helpful to them. They publicly demand an end to Congressional investigations of "un-American activities," but fervently hope that the investigations will continue to afford the communists an opportunity to magnify their importance, discredit liberals, and parade their "martyrdom." [11] They love to see police beating up strikers,[12] and consider each suppression of the

[11] Philbrick quotes one party leader as saying, "The House [Un-American Activities] Committee? Bah! How much more are we helped than we are harmed? What can they do? They call us before the committee. So we put on a suitable performance. . . . Going before the House Committee is a chance for winning as many friends as we can to the party, and creating as many enemies of the American Congress as possible." Philbrick states that among the professional party workers, "there was no genuine concern that the United States was, as we told the rank-and-filers, heading straight for the fascist state! It was to the interest of the party that the country become more fascist, not less. And yet, outside of its secret councils, the Communist party posed with its own membership as the champion of antifascism." (Philbrick, *ibid.*, p. 186.)

[12] Philbrick states that the trusted party members were instructed to arrange to have new members beaten up, if possible: " 'Work them into the most precarious

civil liberties of a communist (or if he is only an "alleged" communist, so much the better) to be the very best advertising obtainable. There may be some kinds of legislation which communist leaders genuinely fear, but most "anti-communist" legislation to date has been greeted by the party leaders with loud hoots of derision.[13]

These are only a few of the many subtleties of communist strategy. It is not implied that *all* one-time members of the Communist party have held the cynically opportunistic views described above. Many well-meaning persons with humanitarian sentiments joined the party briefly, especially during the 1930's and early 1940's, but left upon finding its humanitarianism was insincere. But the hard-core veterans of many years' membership are likely to reflect the cynical duplicity described above.

THE CURRENT AMERICAN REACTION

It would seem that a prosperous and democratic nation like the United States would have little fear of a communist movement which never, even during the depression, was able to poll over 100,000 votes in the entire country and whose present membership is rapidly shrinking. But American fears of communism are nourished by several conditions: (1) the genuine possibilities of espionage and sabotage by a conspiratorial organization that specializes in these arts; (2) the possibility of a war with Russia or China, during which the dangers of communist espionage and sabotage would be even greater; (3) the fact that there *is* a conspiracy, directed from Moscow, whose declared purpose is to infiltrate free societies, discredit their institutions, and disrupt their efforts to deal rationally with their social problems; (4) a greatly exaggerated popular impression of the size and power of the communist movement in the United States. This exaggeration is encouraged by certain politicians who build their political careers upon "fighting communism," and by conservative groups who find an exaggerated fear of communism a useful weapon in fighting liberalism.

There is a sound factual basis for fear of communist espionage and sabotage and for the extensive counterespionage program which the FBI is conducting. While the Communist party works openly, espionage must be done secretly by persons who are not suspected of communist sympathies. Therefore, communist espionage is conducted by "underground" organizations entirely separate from, and unknown to, the public Communist party members. A person who "talks like a radical" is almost certain *not* to be a communist spy, for a real spy seeks to remain unnoticed by

---

positions, and hope that trouble will brew,' we were told. Once a grubber [a small-fry member] gets cracked over the head with a police club, we don't have to argue with him about the existence or nonexistence of police brutality." (*Ibid.*, p. 187.)
   [13] *Ibid.*, p. 258.

avoiding political discussions and acting like a completely conventional person.[14] The problem of communist espionage and sabotage is, therefore, quite separate and distinct from the problem of dealing with communism as a political movement. And communist espionage and sabotage are a police problem, not a sociological problem.

The Communist Party in the U.S.A.—How Powerful?

It is with communism as a political movement that sociologists are concerned. Although organized radical activity has a long history in the United States, it is only since the Russian Revolution that we have had an active Communist party. Fully controlled from Moscow, the Communist party in the United States has never been able to attract a genuine mass membership. Its program was designed to serve the changing interests of Russian domestic and foreign policy. Whenever Russian policy changed, the American Communist party had to reverse itself, even when this alienated its American membership. For example, when Russia and Germany signed a nonaggression pact in 1939, the Communist party in the United States ceased overnight its denunciations of fascism, a switch which lost several thousand members to the party. When Russia denounced the Marshall Plan in 1947, all national communist parties were forced to join the chorus of condemnation, and more thousands left the party both in the United States and in the countries receiving Marshall Plan aid.

Furthermore, a communist philosophy which originated in the anticlerical, class-conscious intellectual atmosphere of a rigidly-stratified European society has limited appeal in a country with individualistic traditions, a relatively open-class system, and an optimistic expectation of personal advancement and social progress. The "party line" in America has been dictated by persons who had little understanding of the American character, and were unable or unwilling to fit the party program to American political needs and interests.

In over thirty years of intense activity, the Communist party in the United States has had an average membership of about 40,000, reaching a peak of over 100,000 during our wartime alliance with Russia and declining to less than one-fourth that number at present, according to the FBI, which also estimates that over 700,000 people are ex-members. The hard core of leaders and long-time members is estimated at 5000 to 8000.[15]

[14] For example, Harry Gold, who carried Klaus Fuchs' atomic information to his Soviet contacts, reports: "I was told by my superior to stay away from the Communist Party, never to read the *Daily Worker,* and never to read liberal literature or express liberal thoughts." Quoted in Clair Wilcox, ed., *Civil Liberties Under Attack* (Philadelphia, University of Pennsylvania Press, 1951), pp. 94-95.

[15] Cf. Morris L. Ernst and David Loth, *Report on the American Communist* (New York, Henry Holt & Company, Inc., 1952), p. 33.

This constant turnover of party membership shows a highly significant inability to "hold" its converts, who soon become disillusioned and leave the party. When compared with even such momentarily successful social movements as populism or the prohibition movement, or with the well-established labor movement, the communist movement in America is revealed as a spectacular flop!

At no time in thirty years has the communist movement been as weak and as discredited as it is today. Yet at no time have "anti-communist" investigations and activities (some would say "hysteria") been as intense as in the two or three years preceding the writing (1955) of this chapter. The grim reality of a world power struggle with Russia makes even a small communist movement appear as a major menace and has led many to feel that vigorous anti-communist measures are necessary. These measures have been of several forms.

FORMS OF AMERICAN ANTI-COMMUNIST EFFORT

1. Congressional Investigations

Ever since the birth of the House Committee on Un-American Activities in 1938, one or more Congressional committees have been investigating communism. Their main procedure has been to hear and publish testimony from witnesses who tell what they know (or claim to know) of communist operations, organizations, and membership. "Friendly" witnesses, usually ex-communists, name their former communist associates, who are then subpoenaed and questioned, required to name *their* associates, and so on. The files of the Un-American Activities Committee are said to contain dossiers on over 1,000,000 persons who have been "named" by a witness, or whose names have been found as contributors or members of organizations which have been "named" as communist organizations, or who have been seen at an allegedly communist-sponsored meeting, or something of the sort.

If a citizen ignores a subpoena or refuses to answer questions put by a Congressional committee, he can be imprisoned for contempt of Congress, unless he bases his refusal upon the Fifth Amendment, which states that one may not be compelled to give evidence against himself which might be used against him in a criminal prosecution. In the present atmosphere, one who invokes the Fifth Amendment becomes a "Fifth-Amendment Communist," and faces almost certain professional ruin and social ostracism. The witness is under oath, so if he lies, he can be imprisoned for perjury.

Violent controversy has raged over the methods of the various Congressional committees investigating communism. Since a Congressional committee is not a court, the witness has none of the legal rights of an accused in a court trial. Since the supposed purpose of a Congressional committee is not to "try" prisoners but to collect information, there are practically no limits upon what questions they may ask or what statements they may publish (with immunity from libel actions). In practice, however, committees have sometimes functioned much like courts, but courts in which the "accused" is charged on a basis of secret charges, is not permitted to face or cross-examine his accusers, or to call witnesses in his own behalf, and not always permitted to be represented by counsel. Although a committee has no power to issue sentences like a court, the power to destroy career and reputation gives them a very real power to punish. Many critics of such procedures, including the National Council of Churches and the American Bar Association, have suggested that committees either cease acting as courts, or adopt rules that protect the rights of the accused as in the legitimate courts.[16]

Committees have frequently received testimony from witnesses of doubtful reliability and, without verifying this "evidence," have made public charges against the loyalty of private citizens. Such charges make sensational newspaper headlines, whereas the accused's denial often appears later on the inside pages. The technique of public accusations based upon secret evidence places the burden of proof on the accused—a reversal of the American judicial doctrine that one is presumed innocent until proven guilty. The charges are often worded with a vagueness which makes it almost impossible for the accused to establish his innocence. For example, the House Un-American Activities Committee in 1947 accused Dr. Edward U. Condon, director of the U. S. Bureau of Standards, of having been "one of the weakest links in our atomic security"—a type of charge not easy to disprove, even if it should be false. In Dr. Condon's case, the committee repeated its attacks upon him, while refusing for four years his repeated requests for an opportunity to refute the charges in a public hearing.[17] Following widespread criticism of such refusals, the Un-American Activities Committee under Chairman Velde, in 1953, announced a policy of granting hearings to persons who felt themselves injured by the committee.

---

[16] Cf. Jacob K. Javits, "Some Queensbury Rules for Congressional Investigations," *Reporter,* 9 (September 1, 1953), pp. 23-25. (Mr. Javits, a Republican, is a former U. S. Representative and present Attorney-General of the State of New York.) Cf. also, *New York Times,* March 12, 1953, p. 1; August 12, 1954, p. 10; August 18, 1954, p. 15.

[17] Cf. *Time* (October 8, 1951), pp. 54-56. Finally in 1952 Dr. Condon was granted a hearing, but only after a change of committee membership, and after Dr. Condon, one of the nations leading scientists, had resigned to take a better-paying position as research director of the Corning Glass Company. He eventually resigned this job because cancellation of his security clearance, apparently in a political campaign maneuver, limited his usefulness. His standing among scientists is indicated by his election as 1954 president of the American Association for the Advancement of Science, and scientists are bitter about his treatment. See *Time* (January 10, 1955), p. 58.

The evidence which committees receive often includes rumor, hearsay, opinion, speculation, and other material which would not be admitted into a court of law. As a part of its proper function of collecting information, all agree that it is entirely proper for a committee to *receive* such evidence. But whether a committee should *publish* such "evidence," without first verifying it, is another matter. Such evidence is sometimes the result of faulty recollection, of mistaken identity, or even of malice and deliberate falsehood. In every large office or bureau, there are disgruntled employees and frustrated neurotics who are happy to make grave charges against their superiors before an appreciative committee. The use of unverified hearsay evidence ("lots of people told me he was a communist") for public attacks upon individuals has been a severely criticized practice of the Congressional committees.

The committee has relied heavily on the guilt-by-association test of loyalty. If one's name is on a letterhead along with names of any communists, or any "named as" communist by some witness; if one published an article in a magazine which later becomes "identified" as having been a "subversive" magazine; if one signed a petition which was also signed by some communists; if one delivered a lecture at a meeting sponsored, however secretly, by a communist organization; if one delivered a lecture at a church whose minister is "named as" a communist some years later; these may be listed as "evidence" of one's communist sympathies.[18] Incredible as it may sound, all of these were cited as "evidence" that Bishop G. Bromley Oxnam "served God on Sunday and the communist front for the balance of the week. . . ." [19] Even to have joined an organization when unaware of its communist domination, and to have withdrawn upon discovering its communist domination, is no defense against the charge of "serving" the communists, for committee members have stated that the accused should have known that there were communists active in the organization.[20] If this test were generally applied, it would paralyze the voluntary organizational activity which has been traditional in America, for it is obviously impractical to check the secret purposes of the members of every organization one joins or supports. And anyone who was highly

[18] See *Testimony of Bishop G. Bromley Oxnam,* Hearing before the Committee on Un-American Activities, House of Representatives, Eighty-Third Congress, First Session, July 21, 1953 (Washington, Government Printing Office, 1954), especially exhibit No. 5, and pp. 3629, 3661, 3791.

[19] *Ibid.,* p. 3588.

[20] Chairman Velde stated to Bishop Oxnam, "Bishop, I am just a little bit puzzled as to how you could belong to such an organization, having stated that you had been anti-communist all your life, and not realize that the Communist Party was infiltrating these particular organizations." (*Ibid.,* p. 3671.) "It has puzzled members of the committee as to how you could be listed as a sponsor for these various organizations, how you could be listed as a member of these various organizations, without some knowledge that they were Communist organizations or Communist-inspired organizations. . . ." (*Ibid.,* p. 3698.)

active in liberal, humanitarian, or reform movements during the 1930's or 1940's is certain to be vulnerable to attack as a "pro-communist," for he is practically certain to have belonged to some organizations which were communist-inspired.

The methods of the Congressional committees have varied considerably, depending upon the personnel and upon the witnesses they were questioning. Many examples of both scrupulous fairness and callous disregard for decency can be found. Many witnesses have been arrogant, provocative, and insulting. Communist witnesses have deliberately sought to exasperate or "bait" the committee members, who sometimes have had some excuse for losing their tempers and abusing witnesses. It may be remembered, however, that there are other persons—teachers, physicians and nurses, social workers, police officers, salespersons—who sometimes must deal with obnoxious people, but are not excused for unprofessional conduct.

An objective appraisal will recognize that the communist movement has received both aid and injury from the Congressional investigating committees.[21] These committees have uncovered some facts which might have been overlooked. They have made people aware of the communist conspiracy and of the danger of giving undiscriminating support to organizations. On the other hand, they have played into the hands of the communists by exaggerating their power and influence, by helping them claim martyrdom, and by discrediting liberals and liberal organizations so that communists have less reason to fear that a vigorous progressive movement will weaken their propaganda.

Perhaps the greatest single weakness of the Congressional investigations has been their failure to provide any real insight into the communist movement. Why do its converts join it? What kind of personalities are attracted? What are they really seeking when they become communist members or fellow-travelers? Why do most of them become disillusioned? How may communism's attraction best be neutralized? Congressional committees, in over fifteen years of investigation, have produced far less insight into these questions than is found in a single small volume by Ernst and Loth.[22]

---

[21] See Robert K. Carr, *The House Committee on Un-American Activities, 1945-50* (Ithaca, N. Y., Cornell University Press, 1952), for a scholarly appraisal by a Professor of Law and Political Science at Dartmouth College. See also Telford Taylor, *Grand Inquest, The Story of Congressional Investigations* (New York, Simon and Schuster, 1955); Alan Barth, *Government by Investigation* (New York, The Viking Press, 1955).

[22] *Op. cit.*, based on interviews with 300 ex-communists. Ernst and Loth state, "In 109 thick volumes of Congressional testimony studied in preparation for this book, we could find virtually nothing elicited except by accident or inadvertence, to establish the fundamental facts about the types of people who join the party, their family backgrounds, why they leave, the amount and kind of education they received."

"The Congressional inquiries often have been called "witch hunts." While it would

2. Antisubversive Legislation

Laws against treason and espionage have existed for generations. These offences must be overt actions, with two witnesses or documentary evidence thereof, done with the intention of injuring the United States. A number of new laws have been passed recently to deal with subversion. The Voorhis Act of 1940 requires the registration of persons and organizations who act as agents for foreign powers or organizations. The Smith Act of 1940 forbids the advocacy by speech, printed matter, or conspiracy, of the forceful overthrow of the government. Both these acts were originally aimed mainly at the Nazis, but were later applied to the communists. As this is written, over one hundred communists have been convicted and sentenced under the Smith Act.

The Internal Security Act of 1950, known as the McCarran Act, strengthens the espionage laws, tightens immigration and naturalization laws, provides for detention in time of national emergency of anyone considered a potential spy or saboteur, and requires both "communist-action" and "communist front" organizations to register with the Attorney General.[23] This law has been hotly debated, and its constitutionality is still in process of being determined by the courts as this is written.

The Communist Control Act of 1954 outlaws the Communist party or any successor of like purpose and, if upheld by the courts, will presumably prevent the party from placing candidates on the ballot, using the mails, holding bank accounts, suing in court, or engaging in any corporate activity. Anyone who becomes or remains a member "with knowledge of the purpose or objective of such organization" must register with the Attorney General or face $10,000 fine and ten years imprisonment. The law adds a third category of communist organization—the "communist-infiltrated" organization—which is any group which the Attorney-General determines is communist-controlled, and subjects it to the same penalties as the communist-action group. This hastily-drawn and vaguely-

---

be dangerous to carry the parallel between these investigations and the Salem witchcraft trials to extremes (e.g., witches were imaginary while Communists *do* exist), there is a useful analogy. The Salem trials developed as little truth about witches as the Congressional investigations have about Communists. The hysterical courts of Salem seemed to desire only a confession, and immunity was promised to those who confessed. All of the accused preferred to burn. The Congressional committees also have been mainly concerned with confessions. They have obtained some, but the chief result has been that ... the witness burned anyway at the bar of public opinion. In Salem no one bothered to ask how these people were drawn into witchcraft, any more than Congress has tried to learn how Communists are drawn into the party." (pp. 2, 227-228.)

[23] A "communist-action" group is defined as one under the domination of a foreign power and aimed at the forcible overthrow of the government. A "communist front" group is one which communists secretly dominate and use deceptively for communist purposes.

worded act was opposed by President Eisenhower, Attorney-General Brownell, and FBI director Hoover on the grounds that it was probably unconstitutional and certain to interfere with efforts to enforce the Internal Security Act of 1950.[24] This law was promoted by senators and representatives who apparently were seeking to protect themselves against campaign charges of "softness" on communism. Its passing illustrates what sort of laws may be passed when there is a national atmosphere in which it is politically dangerous for a legislator to vote against any bill which is called "anti-communist." It is very possible that this law will have been either repealed or amended by the time this book gets into print.[25]

Congress also passed legislation in 1954 which permits the Attorney-General to grant witnesses immunity from prosecution as a result of any of their confessions, so that they may no longer use the Fifth Amendment to justify refusal to answer questions of an investigating committee. Congress also appears likely to pass legislation authorizing the practice of wiretapping (of private telephone conversations) by federal officials and the use of wiretap evidence in federal courts, and legislation to bar subversives from civilian facilities that are indirectly related to national defense.[26]

A wide variety of state laws and local ordinances have also been passed, many of them far more stringent than the federal laws, and many of which are probably unconstitutional. *It is difficult to pass laws "against communism" which will also be consistent with a Constitution which was intended to protect the freedom to hold and advocate unpopular and even revolutionary ideas.*

How much the communists are injured by "anti-communist" legislation is difficult to determine. The more wild proposals (such as one Congressman's bill requiring the Librarian of Congress to mark all "subversive" matter in the 9,000,000 volumes in the library) aid the communists by making the anti-communists look either ridiculous or oppressive. The laws requiring registration have probably hurt the communists by making it more difficult for them to work undetected. Yet it is significant that *the most rapid drop in communist membership occurred between 1945 and 1948, before the legislative attack on communism got under way.* It is likely that political and economic conditions have affected the communist movement more than the laws under which it has operated. It is also interesting to note that every nation which has voluntarily "gone communist" was well-furnished with anti-communist legislation far more stringent than ours.

[24] See "Communist Control Law a Riddle for Courts," *New York Times,* August 29, 1954, IV, p. 6.
[25] *Time* (August 23, 1954), p. 10.
[26] *New York Times,* May 16, 1954, IV, p. 10.

3. Loyalty and Security Procedures

In response to charges that the Democratic administration was infiltrated by communists, President Truman established in 1947 a government loyalty program designed to eliminate "potentially disloyal" persons from federal employment. Under this program, the FBI made "loyalty checks" on all federal employees, transmitting its information to the heads of government departments for action. Each government department had a loyalty board which ruled whether there were "reasonable grounds for belief that the person involved is disloyal." A dismissed person might appeal an adverse decision to the Loyalty Review Board for review if he wished. During the first three years of this program, loyalty checks on about 2,500,000 federal employees were completed, of whom only 202 were dismissed for disloyalty, while about 2400 resigned during investigation, and not a single act of espionage or any other disloyal *act* was discovered by the loyalty program.[27] The failure of the loyalty program to find any large number of subversives was interpreted by some to mean that there were only a few subversives in the government, whereas others insisted that the administration was simply "covering up" for them.

In 1951, the basis for dismissal was changed from "reasonable grounds for belief" that the person is disloyal to "reasonable doubt as to the loyalty of the person involved," thereby placing the burden of proof largely upon the accused and resolving all doubtful cases against him. In 1953, President Eisenhower made further changes, abolishing the Loyalty Review Board and the employee's right of appeal and telescoping "loyalty" and "security" risk classifications into a single category of "security risk." A "security risk" may be a person of doubtful loyalty or may be one whose reliability is uncertain for any of several reasons: he may talk too freely or drink too much to be trusted with important information; he may be vulnerable to blackmail because of drug addiction, sex deviations, past indiscretions, or because he has relatives living in communist-dominated lands, or has relatives or friends who are or once were communists or radicals. Although some unscrupulous politicians of both parties have sought to equate "security risk" with "subversive," every responsible official in the security program has pointed out that not all security risks are suspected of disloyalty.

During the first two years of the Eisenhower administration, from over 2,500,000 employees, some 8008 "security separations" were made, of whom 5006 resigned while their cases were under consideration (and sometimes without knowing they were under suspicion), while 3002 were dismissals. Only 2096 were said to have in their files "information indicat-

[27] According to Seth Richardson, Chairman, Loyalty Review Board, cited in John C. Wahlke, ed., *Loyalty in a Democratic State* (Boston, D. C. Heath & Company, 1952), p. 54.

ing varying degrees of subversive activities." [28] All this phrase actually says, however, is that each of these security files contained one or more charges that some unknown person claims to have seen the suspect at a communist-front meeting many years ago, or claims to have known him as a fellow-communist, or says he once had a reputation for being communistic, or used to read a communist magazine, or had some communist friends, or something of the sort. Obviously, this is far from *proof* of subversion. Although many such charges are doubtlessly true, it is also well established that cases of mistaken identity, faulty recollection, or even malicious misrepresentation are common in such charges. Consequently, there is no way of knowing how many of these 2096 cases were actually subversives. Among the entire 8008 "security risks," *not one is officially alleged to be an actual, active communist, spy, or traitor.* Obviously, loose charges to the effect that "thousands of communists, subversives, and fellow-travelers have been thrown out of the government" are grossly misleading, since the present box-score of the security program would appear to read: no communists, some probable subversives, an unknown number of fellow-travelers, and a large number of persons who were considered fully loyal but not fully dependable.

Some Difficulties Inherent in a Security Program. The government's loyalty and security programs appear to have been, for the most part, carefully administered by conscientious, judicious, fair-minded men, but the nature of its task is such that the issue of civil liberties inevitably arises. For a security program is not an effort to locate people who *have been* disloyal, but to locate those who *may become* disloyal or untrustworthy at some time in the future. How can one's *potential* disloyalty be measured? Only by probing his past associations, his beliefs, his opinions, his convictions. Only by making certain that he is so thoroughly and unquestioningly wedded to the conventional order of things that he is psychologically incapable of seeking to change it! This means that a complete loyalty investigation inevitably becomes an investigation into opinions and values, with any kind of independence or unconventionality a symptom of undependability, for independent thinkers may arrive at unconventional conclusions.

This means that one's *lack* of intellectual interests becomes a recommendation, whereas an active interest in social issues becomes a basis for

---

[28] *New York Times,* January 9, 1955, IV, p. 2. For an analysis of the security program see Cabell Phillips, "Security System Is Again Under Sharpest Scrutiny," *New York Times,* October 14, 1954, IV, p. 5. Phillips reports that under the present security program, security panels and agency heads "are under dual pressure to resolve every doubt in favor of the Government and against the 'defendant.' First, the wording and intent of the present security order make this virtually mandatory. Second, there is an emotional pressure on them not to be caught on the wrong side of a security question themselves; not to run the risk of having to justify a favorable finding before some Congressional inquisitor who thinks it should have gone the other way."

suspicion. Some of the questions asked in loyalty board hearings are revealing: [29]

> Have you ever had Negroes in your home?
> There is a suspicion in the record that you are in sympathy
>   with the underprivileged. Is this true?
> In your recollection, do you recall ever discussing any topic which might be
>   sympathetic to Communist doctrine?
> Are your friends and associates intelligent, clever?
> Are you in favor of the Marshall Plan?
> Did you ever hear any political discussions at X's home?
> If you are, as you say, a loyal American, why do you persist in denying that
>   you were a member of the Communist Party?

Although these questions are quoted out of context, they show how a security investigation becomes an inquiry into the basic mental outlook of the subject, an attempt to see whether he has the kind of interests and values which might ever lead to an unconventional judgment. To one subject who had stated that he was not a communist and did not believe in revolution but did believe that people should be allowed to *advocate* revolution, as long as there was no probability of violence, a loyalty board chairman said,[30]

> What causes us concern is your basic philosophy, which seems to go so far as to defend the right of advocacy even to overthrow the government of the United States, unless the conditions at the time are such that they would prob- ably incite a dangerous upheaval. It is not all of these marginal things that con- cerns me; it's your basic philosophy that concerns me!

A loyalty or security hearing *must* become an inquiry into one's basic philosophy because it seeks to determine not what one *has done* but what he *might do*. Unlike a court trial, the burden of proof is on the suspect, who is not accused of any specific wrongdoing, but vaguely accused of "associating with communists" or "expressing agreement with communist viewpoints" at some unspecified time or place, or of being "unreliable," or of "having had a reputation as a radical." Not even the security board knows who makes the accusation, for the FBI must keep secret the iden- tity of its informants if they are to collect further information. This makes it possible for anyone who dislikes a federal employee to denounce and possibly ruin him with false accusations, and in some celebrated in- stances, this has very nearly happened.[31] In another celebrated case, after a government employee spent four years and $10,000 defending himself against charges of disloyalty and perjury, it developed that the only firm evidence against him was a joking inference, nineteen years earlier, to

[29] Quoted from transcripts of loyalty board hearings, as quoted in Wahlke, *op. cit.,* p. 55.

[30] Quoted in Alan Barth, *The Loyalty of Free Men* (New York, Viking Press, Inc., 1951), pp. 121-122.

[31] See *Time* (May 10, 1954), p. 22; (September 13, 1954), p. 25.

some callers as a "communist-cell meeting"—a costly bit of humor.[32] Such cases are unusual, but the basic task of a security program makes such cases inevitable.

Whether a security program does more good than harm to American security is a debatable question.[33] It is perhaps impossible to have a loyalty program unless we are prepared to limit government employment to those who are thoroughly conventional and timidly conformist, with the intellectually curious and those with unconventional interests excluded. What effects this may have on government service is problematic. In hiring research scientists, for example, it is becoming difficult to get good scientists—intellectually critical, inquiring, and exploratory—who are also good security risks, safely conventional and conformist. Many of the nation's leading scientists, as well as the American Scientists Federation, have protested that the visa curbs of the McCarran Act and the government security program are a threat to scientific freedom and a hindrance to scientific progress—at a time when Russia is apparently overtaking America in atomic research.[34] It is said that Einstein, Szilard, Urey, and Fermi, who launched our atomic energy program, would probably have difficulty in getting a security clearance if they were being "cleared" today.[35]

4. Blacklists, Official and Unofficial

President Truman, in 1947, instructed the Attorney General to prepare and publish a list of subversive organizations. This list of about 200 organizations, revised occasionally, has been widely used by loyalty boards, the armed services, and the FBI as a measure of loyalty, with one's membership in any organization on the "Attorney General's list" a damning bit of evidence.

The Attorney General may list as "subversive" any organization he considers subversive, and not until 1953 were the organizations involved given a hearing in which they might protest such designation. The Attorneys General entrusted with this responsibility have, thus far, exercised it with restraint and have not indiscriminately branded organizations as subversive without some cause. What a less moderate Attorney General

[32] *Time* (June 7, 1954), pp. 20-21.
[33] Cf. L. A. Nikoloric, "The Government Loyalty Program," in Wahlke, *op. cit.,* pp. 50-58; Morris L. Ernst, "Some Affirmative Suggestions for a Loyalty Program," in Wahlke, *op. cit.,* pp. 59-64; Sidney Hook, "Fallacies in Our Thinking About Security," *New York Times Magazine,* January 30, 1955, pp. 15 ff.
[34] Cf. *New York Times,* October 15, 1952, p. 1; April 15, 1954, p. 1; April 18, 1954, p. 1; June 4, 1954, p. 1; June 13, 1954, VI, p. 9. See also "Secrecy, Security, and Loyalty," a special issue of the *Bulletin of the Atomic Scientists,* IX, No. 4 (April, 1955).
[35] Cf. Walter Gellhorn, "Security, Secrecy, and the Advancement of Science," in Clair Wilson, *op. cit.,* pp. 85-106.

might do with this authority in a period of national unrest, is interesting to ponder. In nondemocratic countries it has been a common practice for the state to designate what "loyal" citizens may believe and join, but this is the first time in American history that a government official has been granted authority to determine what organizations loyal citizens may not join. That such a fundamental extension of federal authority should be accepted with so little public discussion, especially from the long-time opponents of "federal controls," is a striking illustration of how readily people will surrender their freedoms in the name of anti-communism.

Perhaps the most famous privately-sponsored black-list is a list of 151 writers, actors, singers, dancers, producers and network executives in a book *Red Channels*, published in 1950 by three former FBI agents.[36] This book listed the allegedly subversive activities and associations of each person, quoting mainly from the reports of the various un-American activities investigating committees, especially from the notoriously inaccurate California Un-American Activities Committee.[37] Public interest was aroused when a radio contract for actress Jean Muir was abruptly cancelled because her name appeared in *Red Channels*. Many of those listed in *Red Channels* have had their careers ruined, at least temporarily, since movie, radio and television executives simply avoid them as "controversial." Many of those listed have protested their loyalty, but as there is no court, loyalty board, or tribunal to which they can appeal for "clearance," they are helpless to defend themselves.

Many feel that the private black-list, with no guarantee of accuracy and no opportunity for effective defense by those listed, is intolerable in a free and just society. Yet, as long as the social atmosphere is so tense that advertising and entertainment executives fear to hire anyone who is "controversial," the private black-lists are likely to circulate.

5. McCarthyism

The term *McCarthyism* has recently entered the language to describe the use of certain techniques of anti-communism. The 1955 edition of the *American College Dictionary* includes a new listing, "McCarthyism,"

[36] American Business Consultants, *Red Channels* (New York, Counterattack, 1950). See Merle Miller, *The Judges and the Judged* (Garden City, Doubleday & Company, Inc., 1952) for an American Civil Liberties Union-sponsored study of this blacklisting operation.

[37] Of this committee's chairman, Senator Jack B. Tenney, the *San Francisco Chronicle*, considered to be a conservative Republican newspaper, commented, "Anyone who was in favor of overthrowing Tenney, as distinguished from overthrowing the government, was likely to be hauled up and smeared by inquisition and innuendo. His methods have done more damage to the cause of intelligently combating Communism than almost any other influence in California." (Quoted in Miller, *op. cit.*, p. 129.) See Edward L. Barrett, Jr., *The Tenney Committee, Legislative Investigation of Subversive Activities in California* (Ithaca, N. Y., Cornell University Press, 1951) for a scholarly study of this committee.

with three definitions: "1—Public accusation of disloyalty, especially of pro-Communist activity, in many instances unsupported by proof or based on slight, doubtful, or irrelevant evidence; 2—Unfairness in investigative technique; 3—Persistent search for and exposure of disloyalty, especially in government offices." [38] These definitions parallel the contrasting evaluations of Senator McCarthy; to some he has been a great patriot and the relentless scourge of the communists,[39] whereas to others he has been their unwitting ally and a hindrance to an effective anti-communist program.[40] It is doubtful if any senator in decades has aroused such intense loyalties or such bitter hostilities, received as much newspaper attention, or inspired such a rapid succession of books about him.[41] As this is written, McCarthy's influence appears to have declined. But McCarthyism—however the term may be defined—was not invented by McCarthy, nor will it disappear if his influence fades. It is the anxieties and fears of a people which create McCarthyism, and its practitioners arise when there is a social appetite. For McCarthy to have successfully remained the nation's most prominent communist-hunter for four years while failing to uncover even *one* authenticated communist would be impossible unless the social atmosphere were tense, uncritical, and neurotic.

6. And Still Others...

To describe completely the changes in American thought and action in the name of anti-communism would fill a book, not a chapter. In hundreds of little-noticed newspaper items these subtle changes are revealed. A Canadian symphony orchestra cancels its American tour because six members cannot get entry visas under the McCarran Act. International scientific, religious, and cultural organizations find it so difficult, under

[38] *American College Dictionary* (New York, Random House, 1955), p. 754.

[39] E.g., John T. Flynn writes, "McCarthy's objective is to rid our government of that [communist] conspiracy. For the life of me, I cannot see why any loyal American should not approve of this." (John T. Flynn, "What Is Joe McCarthy Really Trying to Do?" *American Mercury*, 78 [March, 1954], pp. 69-72.) Hugh Roy Cullen, millionaire philanthropist, says, "Senator McCarthy is...a great patriotic American," and "the greatest man in America." (Quoted in *Fortune*, 49 [May, 1954], p. 100.)

[40] E.g., Herbert Philbrick, the FBI undercover agent who rose higher in Communist party circles than any other counterspy whose work has been revealed, is quoted as saying, "According to the leaders of the Communist Party, McCarthy has helped them a great deal. The kind of attacks he has made do three things that the comrades like: 1—They add greatly to the confusion, putting up a smoke screen for the party and making it more difficult than ever for people to discern just who is a Communist and who is not. 2—They make the party appear to be a lot stronger than it is. 3—They do considerable damage to some of the 'stupid liberals' whom the party hates." (Quoted in *The Progressive*, 16 [March, 1952], p. 5.)

[41] See William F. Buckley, *McCarthy and His Enemies* (Chicago, Henry Regnery Company, 1954), for a sympathetic appraisal of McCarthy. See James Rorty and Moshe Decter, *McCarthy and the Communists* (Boston, Beacon Press, 1954) for a critical evaluation. See also *Time* (October 22, 1951), pp. 21-24; (October 4, 1954), pp. 21-25 for concise appraisals.

the visa requirements of the McCarran Act, to meet in the United States that many such organizations—the International Red Cross, for one—have refused to meet in the United States.[42] Mezzo-soprano Jennie Tourel, to satisfy a group of Legionnaires in Dallas, edits the word "Russian" out of the cantata, *Alexander Nevsky,* a eulogy to a thirteenth-century Russian patriot.[43] Cartoonist Al Capp marries off Li'l Abner with the explanation that satire has become unpopular in America.[44] Playwright James Thurber states that "it isn't possible to write a comedy like that [*The Male Animal*] any more because we're living in the most frightened country in the world." [45] Poet-humorist Ogden Nash states that "there are many more prohibitions than there used to be, taboos, things you can't say." [46] People attending a meeting of World Federalists at Baltimore note that police are busily recording their licence numbers.[47] Experimenters in Madison, Wisconsin, find only one person out of 112 approached who was willing to sign a statement composed of parts of the Bill of Rights and the Declaration of Independence.[48] Radicalism among college students, once a powerful stimulus to campus thought and discussion, has almost completely disappeared; student organizations are now described as "conservative and resigned," [49] and the burning social issue which most excites many students today is where to park their cars. An urge toward conformity has reached the point where controversy itself is undesirable, as witness Samuel French, Inc.'s recent announcement of a playwriting contest in which it "reserves the right at any time to declare ineligible any author who is, or becomes publicly involved, in a scholastic, literary, political, or moral controversy." [50] As far back as 1950, the *New York Times* was noting that the intelligentsia had become wary of political campaign activity, especially if in behalf of liberal candidates.[51] Science Service reports that "very quietly but effectively, scientists who have been liberals and subject to political gossip are being cut off from subsidies for scientific research." [52] The great philanthropic foundations have recently been "investigated" by a special Congressional committee which attacked them for, among other things, supporting "empirical methods of research"

[42] *Chicago Sun-Times,* April 11, 1952.
[43] *Time* (December 11, 1950), p. 40.
[44] Cf. *Time* (March 31, 1952), p. 53.
[45] *New York Times Magazine,* June 29, 1952, p. 19.
[46] *New York Times Book Review,* April 21, 1953, p. 10.
[47] American Civil Liberties Union, *Report on Civil Liberties (January, 1951-June, 1953),* p. 34.
[48] *Time* (August 13, 1951), p. 17.
[49] Cf. *Time* (September 13, 1954), p. 91.
[50] Quoted in *New Yorker* (March 7, 1953), p. 19, whose editors comment, "To us the emaciated condition of controversy and the rising tide of conformity and docility are a national emergency eclipsing even the large emergency that was, and is, the root of the trouble."
[51] *New York Times,* November 2, 1950, p. 23.
[52] *Kalamazoo Gazette,* May 16, 1954, p. 17.

—the first time a committee of Congress has ventured to judge the research methods scientists may employ, or suggested that foundations' grants in the arts and sciences should be conditioned upon the political views of the recipients.[53] The number of jobs in industry which require a security clearance grows steadily, and some labor leaders fear that certain employers use the security check as a device for eliminating aggressive union members.[54] In addition to the other penalties imposed upon those who invoke the Fifth Amendment in refusing to answer questions put by Congressional committees, a few workers have recently been "roughed up" and barred from their jobs by fellow workers, while the chairman of the Congressional sub-committee involved applauded this vigilante development as "the best kind of reaction there could have been to our hearings." [55] Quotations from prominent Americans expressing concern over the pressures toward conformity and widespread fears of dissent appear by the dozen, and the Ford Foundation sets up the Fund for the Republic with a $15 million grant, to "support activities directed toward the elimination of restrictions on freedom of thought, inquiry, and expression in the United States, and the development of policies and procedures best adapted to protect those rights in the face of persistent international tension." [56] A public-opinion poll a few years ago showed that one-third of the American people apparently believe that there are certain groups in America whose civil rights should be curtailed.[57] And many European scholars and statesmen who lived through the rise and fall of German Nazism comment on current American developments in an uneasy "this-is-where-I-came-in" manner.[58] These are but a few of the hundreds of similar items which might be cited. *It is difficult to escape the conclusion that during the last decade or two, American civil, political, and intellectual liberties have been substantially narrowed, qualified, hemmed in, and restricted.*

THE BALANCE SHEET—FREEDOM IN AMERICAN AND RUSSIAN SOCIETY

A comparison of civil liberties in America with those of a totalitarian society may indicate how civil liberties are changing in America today.

1. *Absolute conformity* in belief and behavior is demanded in a totali-

[53] Cf. Sumner H. Slichter, "Undermining the Foundations," *Atlantic Monthly,* 154 (September, 1954), pp. 50-54.

[54] Cf. John Warner, "Labor Unions and 'Security Risks'," *Reporter,* 11 (July 6, 1954), pp. 14-19.

[55] *New York Times,* May 15, 1954, p. 9; *Kalamazoo Gazette,* May 15, 1954, p. 1; May 16, 1954, p. 24.

[56] *New York Times,* February 26, 1953, p. 1.

[57] "The Roper Poll," *Detroit Free Press,* May 23, 1948, A, p. 6.

[58] Cf. C. L. Sulzberger, "Europe Fears Effects of McCarthyism on U. S.," *New York Times,* March 29, 1953, IV, p. 3.

tarian society. Disbelief is disloyalty, and controversy is suspicious, since it is an indication of doubt. Under communism, history, literature, and art must all support the official orthodoxy.

No such sweeping demands for conformity are enforced in America, but there is little doubt that nonconformity is far more heavily penalized than it was a few years ago. No one is likely to be jailed for unconventional ideas alone, but one's job and reputation may depend upon avoiding all signs of independent thought or action.

2. *Loyalty* in a totalitarian state is measured, not by one's *motives*, but by the *effects* of one's actions. If a Soviet commissar makes a miscalculation, if an engineering project fails to work out, if a tactic of foreign policy backfires, the official responsible faces charges of disloyalty or sabotage. The striking rarity of *live* retired officials in communist lands is eloquent testimony to the condition of "freedom" therein.

The American tradition measures loyalty according to the intention of one's actions and judgments, not according to their consequences. There have always been some, however, who sought to read disloyalty into the failures or errors of their opponents. The present demand of some Americans to know "who was responsible for the policies which resulted in communist gain in China, etc. . . ." suggests a tendency to equate error or failure with treason. A typical illustration is this statement of one newspaper columnist that "the total disarmament of Japan and Germany, the vicious Morgenthau Plan, the terrible blunders in China, and countless other destructive policies . . . came from a network of individuals working, not for the welfare of their own country, but for that of Soviet Russia. Doubts no longer remain." [59] The efficiency and morale of our diplomatic service has apparently been seriously damaged by the practice [60]

. . . of equating subversive intent with faulty judgment with respect to any government official left holding the bag for a policy that happens to turn sour.

If these [foreign service] officers are made to feel—as many of them do—that their honest judgments of trends and conditions in their distant posts are liable to be turned against them later, they will be bound to put caution before objectivity in their reports.

3. A totalitarian state often measures loyalty by *past* actions, evaluated in the light of *present* attitudes and knowledge. If one strongly expresses a view or joins a group which, at some later date, becomes condemned, he too is condemned. The only way to be safe in such a climate is to join no groups and express no views.

The American tradition measures loyalty according to *present* views and actions and evaluates past actions according to the knowledge and

---

[59] Syndicated newspaper column by Louis Bromfield, December 13, 1953.
[60] Cabell Phillips, in *New York Times,* December 21, 1952, IV, p. 3.

attitudes which prevailed at that time. Not all Americans are careful to observe this tradition, for some delight in evaluating the past actions of their victims according to the knowledge and attitudes which have developed in later years. As one government official remarks,[61]

> It is very difficult for a liberal who was active in the Thirties to survive political life in the Fifties. Take my case. As soon as I became convinced there was any evidence of communist control in liberal organizations I belonged to, I dropped my membership—formally and completely. But do you think that explanation would do me much good in the atmosphere of today against political opponents who wouldn't scruple to cite my "guilty record" against me?

4. A *dual system of justice* prevails in communist lands, where political offenders are dealt with differently than conventional criminals. Although conventional criminals in Russia, at least before the war, received rather mild treatment, political offenders were severely punished, with "trials" designed as a public display of guilt rather than a means of determining guilt.

In America our courts have perhaps been less affected by current anxieties than most other institutions. Persons tried for violation of any law receive trials in which injustice is the exception rather than the rule. But most "subversive" cases are "tried," not by a court but before a Congressional committee or a security board, where the accused has none of the rights of a criminal defendant. He has no right to be represented by counsel, to know the evidence against him, to confront and cross-examine his accusers, to present witnesses on his own behalf, or even to demand an appearance and hearing before a committee, although some of these privileges have sometimes been granted. This use of security boards and Congressional committees as agencies of prosecution and punishment raises grave questions of justice and protection against abuse which cannot easily be settled. Another symptom of a double standard of justice is seen in the alacrity with which the accused who lies in his defense is prosecuted for perjury, in contrast to the relative immunity from perjury prosecutions thus far enjoyed by "friendly" witnesses who may have lied under oath.[62] Furthermore, persons accused of disloyalty have increasing difficulty in securing an attorney to defend them, for few attorneys wish to face the inevitable attack upon their own loyalty as "defenders of communists." [63]

5. The *use of secret police in intimidating and destroying political opponents* is a characteristic feature of the totalitarian state. The secret police compile files of information on all important persons, including

[61] Quoted in *New York Times Magazine,* April 12, 1953, p. 28.

[62] See syndicated newspaper columns by Joseph and Stewart Alsop, September 13, 1951; February 7, 1952; July 2, 1954; July 12, 1954.

[63] Cf. *Time* (September 7, 1953), p. 19.

youthful indiscretions, past associations with persons and groups now officially suspect, accusations collected from various secret informants, and any other damaging information. These secret files can be used to blackmail the subject into any desired co-operation, perhaps in informing on still others. The ruling party can dip into the secret files and publish such material as will destroy the public reputation of the subject and his associates and discredit the policies he advocates. It is this feature of the totalitarian state—the "conviction" of citizens on a basis of secret evidence supplied by anonymous informers, and not subject to public examination or judicial cross-examination—which makes the individual utterly helpless before his rulers and makes the totalitarian state so terrifying to believers in human freedom.

America has a secret police (the FBI plus perhaps the Central Intelligence Agency) which collects dossiers on individuals and uses secret informers—as any modern state must in order to protect itself against espionage, sabotage, and treason. But herein lies a dilemma: the collection of secret files on many individuals is probably necessary to national security, yet their existence creates for the administration in power a constant temptation to use these files in attacking its opponents. Only a few instances of the political use of the secret files have already occurred at the time this is written.[64] If it should become a common practice, political life in America would soon acquire a distinctly totalitarian flavor.

This partial list of contrasts shows both that there are fundamental differences between American and communistic "freedoms," and that the differences may be smaller than we sometimes imagine. It is not true, as is sometimes wildly announced, that we have "lost our freedom" or "become a fascist" state. To speak of a "national hysteria" is an exaggeration. Yet there *is* fear, as many bits of evidence attest. And we have in America *all the machinery necessary* to develop a state with little more freedom than the communist states we fear. All we would need to do would be to continue for a generation or two the trends of the past decade, for freedom can be extinguished by almost imperceptible degrees. Most college students are not old enough to recognize any trend or to realize that the civil liberties "issues" of six or eight years ago (such as "should *past* membership in communist organizations bar one from all government employment," or "should communists be permitted to teach school, provided they do not propagandize") have now been firmly decided, whereas the present "issues" (such as "should the Communist party be outlawed," or "should all active communists be jailed,") were not even issues because they seemed dangerously extreme only a few years ago.

[64] See Francis Biddle, " 'Ethics in Government' and the Use of FBI Files," *Reporter*, 10 (January 5, 1954), pp. 13-16.

DEFINITION OF THE PROBLEM

To some, the problem is, How can we protect America against a cynical conspiracy to subvert it without destroying civil and intellectual freedom in the process? This definition is implicit in most of the recent literature on civil liberties. People who accept this definition consider many recent anti-communist activities a greater danger than the communist menace at which they are supposedly directed. As a Catholic missionary with firsthand experience with communism states,[65]

I would rather return to my Chinese communist prison cell than avail myself of Senator McCarthy's protection. He is as great—if not a greater—threat to American freedom than the military might of the Kremlin, and believe me, I do not under-estimate either the Kremlin's might or its cleverness. My missionary career in China ended in a communist court in which accusations were taken as facts and charges as proofs.... As a result of that experience, I cling desperately to the principle that ... man is innocent until he is proven guilty.... If you must betray democracy in order to save it, why bother?

There are many people, however, who see no fundamental difference between communism and socialism, liberalism, New-Dealism and other varieties of reformism, all of which they consider merely stepping-stones to communism. Although some of those who denounce liberals and reformers as "communistic" are consciously and cynically trying to neutralize them, there are many who firmly believe that liberals *are* communistic, and that federal aid to education for example, *would* bring communism closer to power. The facts that communists often pose as liberals and reformers and that liberals have sometimes been naively uncritical of communism both help reinforce the notion that communism and liberalism differ only in degree. People who believe this merely nod in agreement when liberals are incorrectly accused of communism and are undisturbed when liberals' jobs and reputations are destroyed. Although many of these people believe in civil liberties as an abstract value, they are easily convinced that the civil liberties of communists and "pro-communists" should be curtailed. To these people the only threat to civil liberties comes from the communists, and the problem of civil liberties is purely one of keeping the communists from power.

This group fades imperceptibly into another group of those who realize the difference between communism and social reform, but willingly use charges of communism as a means of defeating social reforms and discrediting social reformers. It is impossible to understand some kinds of "anti-communist" activity unless it is realized that *liberalism is its real target*. This may explain why some professional "anti-communists" show

[65] The Reverend Leon Sullivan, O.F.M., quoted in *Commonweal*, 57 (November 14, 1952), p. 143.

no interest in developing accurate knowledge about communism and why it attracts certain people. First, their real fight is with liberalism. Second, accurate public knowledge about communism would impair the value of their brand of "anti-communism" as a weapon against liberalism. To destroy completely the communist movement would deprive many conservative groups of their favorite weapon against liberals.

There are some who really do not believe in civil liberties at all. They doubt the ability of "the people" to make wise decisions, and feel that if communists and other "radicals" are permitted to agitate freely, too many people will be beguiled by them. They view civil liberties as a dangerous idea, and are contemptuous of the "bleeding hearts" and "sentimentalists" who are concerned about civil liberties.

Finally, there are the communists themselves, to whom civil liberties are valuable while they seek power, especially if accompanied by occasional suppressions of civil liberties, giving them an issue to dramatize. A *complete* suppression of civil liberties checks the communists for as long as the suppression can be maintained, but creates an atmosphere of conspiracy and repression which communists believe helpful to their long-run objectives. *Complete freedom* of speech, press, and political activity is not particularly helpful to communists in a prosperously contented society, as they cannot strike a heroic pose as martyrs and defenders of liberty. But a tradition of civil liberty coupled with occasional conspicuous denials of these liberties gives communists an ideal "issue." For the communists, then, the "problem" of civil liberties in a country like the United States is one of how to "bait" the society into a partial denial of its professed liberties so that they may exploit this inconsistency.

Some of these definitions overlap with one another, and some persons may vacillate back and forth between them. Possibly the largest group of people do not recognize any problem at all. In a recent national survey asking nearly 5000 people the question, "What kinds of things do you worry about most?", not over 20 people volunteered a worry over civil liberties.[66] Few people seem to get much aroused over civil liberties until they feel that *their* freedom to act or speak as they wish is impaired. In this fact, lies freedom's greatest danger.

APPROACHES TO THE PROBLEM

The Social-Disorganization Approach

Like Godliness and chastity, civil liberty in the American republic has been a value approved in theory but often ignored in practice. Throughout our history, legal and extralegal penalties have been exacted from

[66] Samuel A. Stouffer, *Communism, Conformity, and Civil Liberties* (Garden City, N. Y., Doubleday & Company, Inc., 1955), p. 69.

the dissenter and the nonconformist. Although it is inconsistent with the ideal of civil liberty, vigilante action against nonconformists has been an integral part of the *organization* of American society. Suppression of civil liberties, therefore, cannot be accurately described as "disorganization."

But the disorganization of any aspect of the culture arouses anxieties, jeopardizes vested interests, inspires the questioning of established institutions, and stimulates many a forceful effort to silence these questionings and protect the status quo. Periods of disturbing change normally bring a crisis in civil liberties, whereas periods of relative cultural stability show fewer suppressions of liberty. The crisis of laissez-faire capitalism and the trend to a partially managed economy during the 1930's and 1940's was a change profoundly disturbing to many Americans, and the assumption of world responsibility by an America which must remain permanently mobilized for war is another disturbing change. If tension with Russia were to subside, many civil liberties issues would dissolve overnight.

Changing technology, too, creates civil liberties problems. George Orwell's disturbing picture of a television camera policing every living room [67] seems improbable, yet the question of how widely the television camera may be used to "watch" people has already arisen. Wiretapping is a growing practice and may soon be legalized. The increasing portability of atomic bombs multiplies the potential destructiveness of the spy or saboteur, and stimulates increased security precautions. The problem of preserving genuine freedom of speech in an age of mass communications, discussed in another chapter of this textbook, has attracted much attention. Any society will need to deal in some manner with the civil liberties question, while the organization and disorganization of that society helps constantly to redefine the problem.

The Value-Conflict Approach

The term *subversion* implies a value-conflict. If all shared the same values, there could be no subversion. But people differ in the values they wish to preserve and in the means they think proper in preserving them. As indicated earlier, some wish to check communism while promoting liberalism, some wish to check both communism and liberalism, and a tiny few wish to promote communism while confusing and paralyzing liberalism. Some believe in civil liberties; some do not. At one extreme are those who follow Holmes' "clear and present danger" doctrine [68]—that we should allow any *ideas* to be expressed and advocated, however

[67] George Orwell, *1984* (New York, Harcourt, Brace & Company, Inc., 1949).

[68] Mr. Justice Holmes stated, and the full Supreme Court accepted the principle, that "The question in every case is whether the words used are used in such circumstances and are of such a nature as to create a clear and present danger that will bring about the substantive evils that [the State] has a right to prevent." (Schenck *v.* United States, 249 U. S. 47, 52.)

repugnant, so long as there is no "clear and present danger" that violence will result. These people are likely to join the American Civil Liberties Union [69] and defend the right of all Americans, even those they despise, to express any views, even those they detest. At the opposite extreme are those who believe—as do the communists—that only the "safe," "right," or "American" ideas are entitled to freedom of expression. When Vishinsky writes, "In our state, naturally there can be no place for freedom of speech, press, and so on for the foes of socialism," [70] these Americans need change only the last word to be in complete agreement. Between these two extremes fall many people with a vague general belief in civil liberty except when they are afraid, and who can sometimes be panicked into a suppression of liberty during a period of national anxiety.

The Personal-Deviation Approach

Most extremists are deviants. Most extremists show a fanatical preoccupation with their "cause," a suspicious distrust of other people in general, a disinterest in normal pursuits, recreations, and "small talk," and a strong tendency to divide other people into enemies and allies. These are symptoms of an unhappy, neurotic personality. Ernst and Loth's study of American ex-communists [71] finds that most of them were young people who were not yet settled in adult life, from comfortable but unhappy homes, intelligent and well-educated, but frequently unpopular folk who had never really "belonged" until they found the party. Most suffered strong feelings of personal inadequacy and harbored hostilities or resentments against their domineering parents. Many of the rank-and-file were idealistic, self-sacrificing, submissive and unselfish. The total pic-

[69] The American Civil Liberties Union is a private organization of persons who strongly believe in the right of all Americans to enjoy all the rights and immunities guaranteed by our Constitution and our laws, even to those Americans they dislike and whose values they detest. The ACLU offers legal assistance to persons whose legal rights have been violated, and carries on publicity defending civil liberties. Those whom it aids include racial and religious minorities, political radicals, labor organizers—anyone, regardless of his views, whose rights of expression are being curtailed. This has meant that the ACLU often found itself defending the constitutional rights of unpopular and obnoxious persons, including communists, which has led some persons to the mistaken conclusion that the ACLU was a pro-communist organization. This mistaken belief, which a reading of any ACLU report will easily dispel, shows how difficult it is for some to understand that a person can detest another's views, yet defend his right to express them. The *New York Times* said editorially on August 28, 1952, "The American Civil Liberties Union [is a] useful and thoroughly patriotic organization...," while the *St. Louis Post-Dispatch* stated editorially on August 29, 1952, "The ACLU has established its fearlessness by independent reputation, and particularly its freedom from Communist control, by 32 years of evenhanded defense of a principle—the freedom principle of the Bill of Rights...."

[70] In *The Law of the Soviet Union,* 1948; quoted in Wahlke, *op. cit.,* p. 45.

[71] *Op. cit.,* especially pp. 1-15. See also Dean Brelis, "The Making of a Spy" [Harry Gold], *Life* (June 12, 1950), pp. 7-15; Walter White, "Portrait of a Communist," [Benjamin J. Davis, Jr.], *The Progressive,* 14 (November, 1950) p. 17.

ture is that of an unhappy, insecure person who needs a "cause" in which to lose himself and gain a sense of personal worth. The members were not much changed by their experience, retaining much the same personalities they possessed before and during their membership.

The Ernst and Loth study is largely confined to short-term young members. A similar study by Almond shows the hard-core party professionals to be more cynical, ruthless, and opportunistic.[72] They, too, remain much the same kind of personalities when they become ex-communists. As a communist, Whittaker Chambers viewed the world as a hostile conspiracy in which the liberals, the reformers, much of the church and school, and all moderates were unwitting allies of the capitalistic oppression; he now sees these same groups as unwitting allies of the communists. As a communist, he saw social reform as an obstacle to revolution; he now sees reform as a bridge to revolution. As a communist, he saw conspiracy and wicked scheming against him on every side; he still does. As a communist, he foresaw an eventual titanic struggle between communism and its enemies in which one must inevitably destroy the other; he still does.[73] It is this inability of the extremists—whether of the right or of the left—to see a reasonable "middle way" which causes so many ex-communists, when they abandon one set of undemocratic absolutes, to embrace another. The ease with which German communists turned Nazi, and, later, Nazis turned communists, further shows how a certain type of personality can be equally at home with either totalitarianism.

How reliable is the information provided by ex-communist informants? It varies widely. Some informants are stable and dependable; some are neurotics who cannot tell fact from fancy; some are publicity-seekers; some are pathological liars. At one extreme are highly reliable informants such as Herbert Philbrick, who joined the party at FBI request and served as an undercover agent at considerable personal hardship, and was always careful not to smear innocent people. At the opposite extreme are informants such as Harvey Matusow, an unstable, restless young man who, by his own admission, made quite a racket of false accusation.[74] A number of ex-communist informers have been repeatedly caught in contradictions and inaccuracies.[75] Some have received pay as government "consultants"

[72] Gabriel A. Almond and others, *The Appeals of Communism* (Princeton, N. J., Princeton University Press, 1954), based on intimate studies of 221 former American, British, French, and Italian communists.

[73] Cf. Whittaker Chambers, *Witness* (New York, Random House, Inc., 1952). See also Arthur Schlesinger, Jr., John Dos Passos, Charles Alan Wright, Richard M. Nixon, Richard B. Morris (symposium), "Whittaker Chambers and His Witness," *Saturday Review*, 35 (May 24, 1952), pp. 8-13 ff.; also Elmer Davis, "History in Doublethink," *Saturday Review*, 35 (June 28, 1952), pp. 8-9.

[74] See Harvey Matusow, *False Witness* (New York, Cameron and Kahn, 1955).

[75] See Joseph W. Alsop, "The Strange Case of Louis Budenz," *Atlantic Monthly*, 189 (April, 1952), pp. 29-33; also syndicated newspaper column by the Alsops, July 12, 1954.

or as government witnesses in court trials, a practice which carries certain dangers, since they get paid only as long as they can recall incriminating evidence.

The Department of Justice and some other government agencies appear to have willingly used unreliable informers and dubious testimony in their efforts to identify "security risks" or get convictions of suspected subversives. And upon learning that an informant has been untruthful, the Department of Justice has, as yet, made little effort to restore the reputations which its unreliable informants have besmirched.[76] It would appear that at the time of this writing, the Department of Justice has, in its efforts to convict those it considered guilty, forgotten its duty to protect the innocent! And its willingness to use unreliable informants may have done more to undermine public confidence in the Department of Justice than thirty years of communist attacks upon it could accomplish.

The personal-deviation approach is highly suggestive. If more "experts" on communism had studied communism as a refuge for maladjusted personalities instead of viewing it as a contagious disease, fatal upon exposure, many of our difficulties with communism as an internal social movement would have been avoided.

RATIONAL PROPOSALS FOR PRESERVING LIBERTY AND SECURITY

If it be assumed that our objective is to preserve both civil liberty and American security, then several courses of action are indicated.

1. *Accurate knowledge of communism* is necessary if it is to be opposed intelligently. This includes distinguishing between communism and liberalism, and between the genuine and the professed objectives of communism. People who do not fully understand communism often fall into the communist's trap by doing just what the communists want them to do. Conservatives do this when they smear liberals as "communistic," or when they cry, "Wolf!", "Communist Wolf!" so often that moderate men get into the habit of disregarding *all* charges of communism as unfounded "smears." Liberals fall into the communist's trap when they denounce *all* anti-communist efforts as "red-baiting," and when they are reluctant to admit that there *is* a ruthless communist conspiracy directed against American democracy.

2. *Understanding of the American heritage of liberty* is also necessary if it is to be continued. A study of past civil liberties crises is reassuring, for it shows that the present problem is not so greatly different from those of the past. Communism—and certain modes of opposing it—are

---

[76] Although according to *Time* (February 14, 1955, p. 22), "The FBI has known for years that Matusow was a squalid liar," he was not repudiated by the government until he had publicly proclaimed himself a liar.

the present threat to civil liberties, but the basic issue is constantly the same old question of *whether to trust the people to reach their own decisions, or to make their decisions for them.* This question is always with us, to be reargued each generation.

3. *An adequate national defense* is, needless to say, necessary in a world where an international revolutionary movement is joined to an aggressive major power. This is a military problem, not a sociological problem, and is not discussed here.

4. *Counterespionage is essential.* Highly trained professional agencies such as the FBI and the Central Intelligence Agency can do this efficiently and without endangering personal liberties of citizens. If headline-hunting congressmen, Legion officials, or other amateurs turn G-man, they merely scare off any real spies and destroy the counterespionage efforts of the professionals.[77]

5. *Reform of Congressional committee procedures* is necessary if civil liberties are to be protected. Unless committees either cease acting as courts "trying" people for disloyalty or allow the accused the safeguards long since adopted by courts to protect the accused from injustice, it is inevitable that injustice will be done to many citizens. Furthermore, it is at least debatable whether the Congressional committees have done the communist movement more harm than good, and it is clear that the major defense against subversion lies elsewhere.

6. *A more forgiving attitude towards ex-communists* and ex-fellow-travelers might help undermine the party. Our social and economic ostracism of the former communist or fellow-traveler discourages members from leaving the party, encourages former members to try to conceal their past, and encourages the former member to try to redeem himself by an orgy of denunciation. Ernst and Loth suggest that a "Communists Anonymous" organization, patterned after Alcoholics Anonymous, would help in the social and economic rehabilitation of ex-communists.[78] This would weaken one of the most powerful forces which keep people in the party.

7. *A prosperous, progressive society* is the best defense against communism or any other kind of subversion. Although there will probably be a few who are communists for reasons of emotion and personality, there is no prospect of communists gaining a mass following as long as our society is prosperous and free. The greatest tragedy recently to befall the American communists was our failure to go into an economic tailspin after the recent war. No prosperous, progressive country in the world has ever had a strong communist movement. In America the communist "menace," insofar as it concerns communism as an *internal revolutionary*

---

[77] See statement of J. Edgar Hoover, FBI Director, in *New York Times,* May 11, 1954, p. 18.

[78] *Op. cit.,* pp. 230-235.

movement, is little more than a bogey-man for unscrupulous politicians and reactionaries to exploit in misleading the gullible. If America remains a free and prosperous society, no other defense against communism as an ideology and revolutionary movement will be necessary.

A list of proposed laws is conspicuously missing from this series of proposals. The omission is deliberate. Although national security requires a vigorous enforcement of existing laws against espionage and sabotage, it is difficult to find any social scientist of repute who feels that national security requires additional *antisubversive* legislation. Laws passed "against communism" are likely to curtail the liberties of non-communists while not greatly bothering the communists. Laws compelling *disclosure* of sponsorship of propaganda and of sources and uses of funds of the party (and other propagandistic organizations) might help prevent the party (and other organizations) from deceptively misleading people.[79] But in controlling or defeating communism as a social and political movement, laws are largely irrelevant. If we have a strong, prosperous, and free society, antisubversive legislation is unnecessary; if our society does not remain prosperous and free, antisubversive legislation will probably be ineffective.

SUMMARY

America is now experiencing one of its recurrent attacks of anxiety over its liberties. These liberties were written into our constitutional system at a time when our nation was weak and divided and menaced by powerful enemies within and without—written by men who believed that good government must protect civil liberties if it is to survive.

Communism provides the current occasion for a variety of laws and activities, some honestly directed at communism, and some apparently intended to achieve other political or ideological objectives under the pretext of opposing communism. Some of these measures may actually aid the communists; at least the communists seem to think so. Many of the existing and proposed laws pose a great *potential* danger to civil liberties. If administered by moderate and judicious men, civil liberties may not be impaired; if administered by frightened or bigoted men during a period of national anxiety, our present legal machinery could easily become an instrument of widespread oppression.

It is perhaps impossible, in the modern world, to grant a government the power to govern effectively and protect the national security adequately without also granting it the power to curtail the liberties of its citizens. It is also impossible, in modern life, to prevent private organizations and communications media from possessing a great power to intimidate and punish individuals, to penalize and inhibit independent thinking, to promote a timidly conforming population.

[79] *Ibid.,* pp. 223-226.

Whether these powers are used to achieve these ends depends upon several factors. A frightened people is unlikely to remain free, and a hungry man treasures freedom less than bread. An American people intelligently informed about the genuine purposes and techniques of communism will be neither greatly attracted nor greatly frightened by communism. The possibilities of war, of sabotage, and of espionage are the continuing threats to our national security which it would be unrealistic to ignore, but ineffective to "treat" by curbing the speech, thought, and associations of our citizens. The menace of communism as an ideology and political movement is a largely imaginary danger in any country which remains prosperous and free. And, in the long run, the communist movement in America may be far more greatly affected by what we do to ourselves in the process of opposing communism than by anything we can do to the communists.

SUGGESTED READINGS

ALMOND, Gabriel A., and others, *The Appeals of Communism* (Princeton, N. J., Princeton University Press, 1954). A study of 221 former American, British, French, and Italian Communists, to see what attracted them to communism, and why they eventually left it.

American Civil Liberties Union, *America's Need: A New Birth of Freedom, 34th Annual Report, 1953-1954* (New York, American Ciivl Liberties Union, 1954). A survey of the current state of civil liberties in the United States.

COOK, Thomas L., *Democratic Rights and Communist Activity* (Garden City, N. Y., Doubleday & Company, Inc., 1954). One of the Doubleday short studies in Political Science, presenting reasonably and concisely the case for increased anti-communist legislation and legal penalties for communist activity.

ERNST, Morris L. and LOTH, David, *Report on the American Communist* (New York, Henry Holt & Company, Inc., 1952). A highly readable description of the sorts of people who become communists in America, why they join, why they leave, and suggestions for effectively opposing communism. Based on interviews with 300 ex-communists.

LASSWELL, Harold D., *National Security and Individual Freedom* (New York, McGraw-Hill Book Company, Inc., 1950). Seeks to outline a detailed policy for safeguarding national security against both military and ideological dangers without destroying our civil liberties in the process.

Legislative Reference Service of the Library of Congress, *Communism in Action,* House Document No. 754, 79th Congress, 2nd Session (Washington, Government Printing Office, 1946). A documented study and analysis of communism in operation in the Soviet Union.

Legislative Reference Service of the Library of Congress, *Fascism in Action,* House Document No. 401, 80th Congress, 1st Session (Washington, Government Printing Office, 1947). A documented study and analysis of fascism as it operated in European countries.

MARX, Karl, and ENGELS, Friedrich, *The Communist Manifesto.* A brief authoritative statement of the ideology and objectives of communism. Available in various editions and collections in any good library.

MAXWELL, Allen, ed., *The Present Danger* (Dallas, Southern Methodist University Press, 1953). Four short essays on American freedom as it involves business, the press, the law, and education, by four prominent public citizens.

PHILBRICK, Herbert, *I Led 3 Lives* (New York, McGraw-Hill Book Company, Inc., 1952). The fascinating account of an FBI counterspy's nine years within the Communist party. Gives many insights into the character and techniques and secret purposes of the communist leadership in America.

STOUFFER, Samuel A., *Communism, Conformity, and Civil Liberties* (Garden City, N. Y., Doubleday and Company, Inc., 1955). A comprehensive study of American attitudes upon communism and civil liberties.

WAHLKE, John C., ed., *Loyalty in a Democratic State* (Boston, D. C. Heath & Company, 1952). A collection of essays on loyalty and security problems by a number of prominent citizens, scholars, and public officials.

AUDIO-VISUAL AIDS

Action Against the Law (Teaching Films Custodians, Inc., 25 West 43rd, New York), 28 minutes, sound, black and white. An excerpt from a Paramount Pictures feature film, *The Lawless;* an incident between the citizens of a California town and the migrant fruit-pickers shows how intergroup frictions may be aggravated to a point where some citizens take the law into their own hands.

Friday Is a Great Day (American Civil Liberties Union, 170 Fifth Ave., New York), 26 minutes, 33⅓ rpm transcription. An NBC broadcast to commemorate "Bill of Rights" day; dramatizes civil-liberties incidents and issues.

Is Fighting Communism Periling Civil Rights? (American Film Forum, Inc., 516 Fifth Ave., New York), 15 minutes, sound, black and white. A discussion film; opposing points of view presented by two members of Congress.

Social Revolution (Encyclopedia Britannica Films, Inc., 1150 Wilmette Ave., Wilmette, Ill.), 17 minutes, sound, black and white. Traces social changes during the past two hundred years; contrasts constructive or peaceful methods of change with destructive or violent methods.

QUESTIONS AND PROJECTS

1. If Jefferson were living today, holding the same values he did hold when living, what do you suppose he would approve and disapprove in our current situation? What would he say about communism? About McCarthyism? Would he be a "security risk"?

2. What did the framers of our Constitution and Bill of Rights rely upon to prevent revolution in America?

3. Are the dangers of subversion greater now than they were in 1801 when Jefferson obtained repeal (or nonrenewal) of the Alien and Sedition Laws?

4. Why do communists desire revolution rather than social reform?

5. Why do communists support social reforms, if they really don't want reform?

6. Whom do the communist leaders consider to be their major enemies? Why?

7. How have conservatives or reactionaries sometimes given unintentional assistance to the communists? How have liberals sometimes given unintentional assistance to the communists?

8. How can those persons and organizations which are honestly seeking social reforms be distinguished from those who seek to exploit popular interest in reform as a means of promoting communist propaganda?

9. How would the behavior of a communist spy in our government differ from the behavior of a pro-communist or "fellow-traveler?" Which would be more likely to express the "Communist party line"?

10. How does the problem of dealing with possible espionage and sabotage differ from the problem of dealing with subversive social movements?

11. What value-conflicts are involved in defining the problem of civil liberties?

12. Will there ever be a time when civil liberty ceases to be a problem in the United States?

13. During a period of prosperity, communism appears to attract only those who are somewhat emotionally maladjusted. Would this still be true during a long period of depression and hardship?

14. What jobs should admitted communists be permitted to hold? If none, then what should be done with communists? Should any distinction be made between communists who admire Russia and communists (such as Titoists) who hate the Russian communists?

Part III

CONCLUSIONS

CHAPTER 20

The Three Approaches Reassessed: I

PART I of this book provided a definition of and a body of understand‚ings about social problems in general. Three approaches to the study of social problems were formulated and the student received some guidance in the interpretation of data. In Part II, a variety of important problems were analyzed and interpreted in terms of the three approaches. The task of this final section is that of synthesis. The three approaches need to be reassessed in terms of their application to the concrete data of Part II. Recurrent threads—factors causing disorganization, pervasive value-conflicts, and personality influences—must be organized into patterns and the patterns related to one another. The final chapter of this section will attempt to foreshadow the course of history—to hazard predictions about the course of things to come.

SOCIAL DISORGANIZATION: RETROSPECT AND PROSPECT

Social problems are in large measure products of change. The change may be a major revolution in human civilization or the slightest alteration in local conditions. Its effects may be felt for centuries after, or months and years before, the change occurs. The change may be of attitude or knowledge. But whatever the specific case, the fact of change is fundamental to the emergence of social problems.

The Effects of Change

Regardless of its nature, change requires persons, and/or groups, and/or institutions to make adjustments. Change (1) threatens vested interests, (2) interrupts habits, (3) creates distress, and (4) eventually results in the development of new patterns.

1. *Threatens Vested Interests.* Inevitably some groups in a society create for themselves, or are the recipients of, positions of special advantage. In a theocracy they might be priests; in a bureaucracy, politicians or civil

servants; in a society dominated by pecuniary values, businessmen and merchants; in a gerontocracy, the aged; and so on. The prevailing values determine which group reaps what special benefits; and not one but, ordinarily, numerous groups soon come to have a special interest in maintaining the status quo. Change, unless they themselves initiate it, vested interest groups view with suspicion or with open hostility. With the multiplicity of interest groups, most any change will prove threatening to some of them. At the first suggestion of change, interested groups mobilize their resources to do battle. The ensuing conflict increases awareness, sharpens differences, and furthers antagonism. These are the conditions of social problem situations.

2. *Interrupts Habits.* The various interest groups curry favor with whomsoever will give them an audience and possibly support. Many persons take sides but the majority of persons ordinarily have no clear vested interest in a particular change. They stand neither to reap great profit nor to suffer great loss. But when the change occurs, they suffer for it nevertheless. For men are creatures of habit, and change disturbs habits. A new traffic light at an intersection where one is accustomed to passing through or a new filing system at the office disturbs personal habits as surely, though perhaps not as drastically, as do major wars and depressions. Routines which had long ago become so automatic as to become unconscious and attitudes so familiar as to seem almost sacred are suddenly called back into consciousness. The individual must "work at" what formerly was routine. Not only must time and energy be devoted to the changing situation but such effort interferes with the smooth operation of other habits. The automobile driver cannot plan tonight's dinner or reminisce about last night but must concentrate on seeing if the light turns red. The office-worker cannot daydream about his upcoming vacation for having to cope with this "pesky" new filing system. Change, because it disturbs old habits, is uncomfortable. Because it is uncomfortable it tends to be resisted. To many otherwise disinterested persons, change itself becomes the problem. If only all this nonsense were stopped, one could go back to the comfortable routines of before.

3. *Creates Distress.* Because habits are so persistent the adjustment to change is often difficult. Attitudes and values in particular are slow to change and are frequently held long after the conditions to which they were appropriate have disappeared. The average person does not see that his failure to adjust is an important factor in the disorganization caused by change. He knows that something is wrong, but his definition of what is wrong centers upon the breakdown of the familiar and what are to him "the right" ways of doing things. His feelings are apt to be expressed in such phrases as, "Remember the good old days?", "What is the world coming to?", "Such things would never have happened back in...," and

so on. The emphasis is upon the breakdown of the old patterns and upon the resulting chaos and confusion. And obviously many of the persons who think and feel this way are in dire distress. For no reason at all, things seem to have gone wrong and there is little that one can do about it. The husband and wife caught up in divorce procedure, the Southern white man who must send his children to a school attended by Negroes, and the devoted parishioner who hears her minister talk of the "figures of speech" in the Bible all have this one factor in common. Something seems to be terribly wrong.

4. *Results in New Patterns.* The serious distress of countless people is not always quickly alleviated. Divorce, desegregation, and the modern gospel may be bitterly resisted for years and even for generations. But even as the resistance continues it is gradually being undermined. Some persons cease to venerate the past and seek to understand the present. Soon there appears a whole new generation which never knew of the old conditions and to whom the reminiscences of their elders are a sign of deterioration. Youngsters more quickly see the order in the new patterns, for their vision is uncluttered by the habit-debris of the past. And the order is there, or at least it is in the offing. For much social change is not merely the breakdown of traditional patterns but their replacement by new, unfamiliar, and therefore disturbing ones. In many cases the new and the old exist side by side, with the old gradually relinquishing ground. In still other cases, the old patterns may begin to break down before new patterns appear. Especially when change results from the imposition of elements from outside the culture or from another area of culture, there may be a time lag between the breakdown of the old and the complete development of the new. The period of lag will be a period of widespread dissatisfaction, and the dissatisfaction will continue until such time as the new patterns become established.

Major Changes in Western Culture

A truly comprehensive discussion of the changes that underlie current symptoms of disorganization would have to include a complete history of Western culture as well as substantial amounts of world history. There are, however, a relatively few pervasive historical developments in the Western world, an understanding of which will aid immeasurably in putting the present scene into proper perspective. Four of these developments are: (1) the rise of science and "scientism"; (2) the Industrial Revolution; (3) urbanization; (4) and the rise of secularism.

1. *Science and Scientism.* Mastery of the techniques of science is one of the most distinguishing characteristics of Western culture. The West has gained unparalleled control over the physical world and has produced

hitherto undreamed of quantities of material goods. It is not surprising that great pride should be taken in these accomplishments or that the production of more and better goods should be regarded as a hopeful prospect for solution of many current problems. Especially where deprivation and low living standards contribute to the problem, the diffusion of technological "know-how" holds great promise. But there is ample evidence that there are grave shortcomings in this approach.

First, there is a strong tendency to confuse the material results of scientific investigation with the process of objective inquiry which made them possible. Many persons who sing the praises of science do not really admire *science* so much as they admire the *technology* that is a product of science. They actually oppose free scientific inquiry at every point where it might threaten some of their other values. Such persons would encourage research, but only under conditions that would prevent new knowledge from interfering with their interests. Scientists, however, have long held—and the history of scientific development supports this view—that such restriction is inimical to scientific progress; that scientists must be free to explore seemingly unpromising avenues and even extremely controversial ones. Many of the greatest scientific discoveries have followed such "impractical" investigation.

A second deficiency frequently found in this approach is the unwitting expectation that the discovery of new knowledge or inventions should make it evident how such inventions should be used and should insure their proper employment. In addition to being grossly unrealistic, such expectations betray great ignorance of the nature of science. Science itself includes no value-system which guarantees that its fruits will be used to provide the greatest benefit for the greatest number of people. Science has helped to *alleviate* and also to *create* problems. It is no panacea but provides great potential for change, which change creates the need for tremendous adjustment as well.

2. *The Industrial Revolution.* Not the least of the accompaniments of scientific development was the Industrial Revolution. Together with the related revolution in agricultural methods, the Industrial Revolution resulted, perhaps, in the most far-reaching changes in Western culture since the development of written language. Within a span of only decades it had uprooted the traditions of centuries and launched the Western world upon a period of unprecedented expansion and development. Simple methods of hand production gave way to mass production and the factory system: the former luxuries of the élite became the necessities of the masses. And still more goods were produced. The resulting trade relationships and military prowess combined to permit the West to dominate much of the world.

At least certain aspects of almost every problem treated in this book have some of their origins in this period. The present pattern of race conflict, the demand for and ability to support universal public education, the quintupling of the world's population, the atomization of the family, and so on, are mingled in a cause-and-effect network with the Industrial Revolution. The significance of the Industrial Revolution, however, goes far beyond the changed production methods and the improved military status of Western nations. It was part of a process of expansion and development which continues even more rapidly at the present time and which is spreading to all corners of the earth. The steam engine, the cotton gin, and the Bessemer process of steel-making were wonderful inventions, but they must be compared with the supersonic air travel and nuclear fission of the present and with the prospects for harnessing solar energy and the possible synthesis of carbohydrates in the near future. The rate of change seems not to be decreasing but to be accelerating at a dizzy rate. According to an early Atomic Energy Commission report, the world progressed as far during the period from 1940 to the dropping of the first atomic bomb on Hiroshima in 1945 as it had traveled during the entire period from the discovery of fire to the building of the first locomotive.

To expect that such radical changes could be rapidly and effectively adjusted to is not very realistic. Those who decry the fact that social problems never seem to be eliminated ignore the fact that change constantly requires new adjustments. Even keeping up with those changes is a major accomplishment. So long as society is characterized by rapid change, there will be the lags and stresses that we call social disorganization.

3. *Urbanization.* Not only has man not always lived in cities but the large cities of modern times are a very recent development. The changes sponsored by the Industrial Revolution made them both possible and necessary. Again urbanization must be seen not as a condition but as a process. The United States has moved from an almost exclusively rural nation to one which is predominantly urban. Up until the third decade of the present century the pattern was one of rapid growth in the largest of cities. Huge populations clustered around single business centers. Skyscrapers appeared to concentrate more people in a given land area—congestion, contamination, slums, and tenements were all by-products. The 1930 census showed the emergence of a new trend—the trend toward suburbanization. The largest cities began to slow down in their rate of growth. Yet the number of metropolitan centers continued to increase. They built outward instead of upward. Low-cost housing developments and shopping centers and industries on the periphery became the order of the day.

The trend still continues. Since World War II, some new notes have appeared. The planned community with its winding streets, its own schools, parks, recreation, and business centers, has appeared in large numbers. "Development" houses now range in price up to $40,000 or more. A whole new highly mobile, managerial class has located in the suburbs and complicated their structure. Highway and traffic problems, taxation, and representation are the 1955 counterparts of the congestion problems of the urban 1920's. How long the present era of suburbanization will continue is impossible to say. Already the hydrogen bomb, bacterial warfare, tax and labor problems, hydroelectric developments, and so on, threaten to alter the pattern. Urban expansion is one of the major characteristics of our time. Whatever the specific direction it takes, future urban development will be much involved in social problem situations ranging from racial discrimination (in housing, schools, and so on) to the detection of criminal behavior.

4. *Secularization.* It is not difficult to see how the processes of scientific development, industrial progress, and urbanization are intertwined. As observable trends they are a part of the more general change in fabric of Western society. At least one additional element needs to be added—the process of secularization.

The trend toward secular thinking is as revolutionary and far-reaching in its effects as any of the others, for it represents a radically new approach to the solution of human problems. Very simply, secular thinking is utilitarian thinking. It assumes that man has broad control over the conditions of his own existence and that when a problem arises he should manipulate those conditions in whatever manner necessary to remove the problem. Secular thinking relates means to ends and judges both means and ends in terms of their usefulness in attaining other goals. Secular thinking in this sense is the polar opposite of sacred thinking, which is oriented to and judges all actions by standards coming out of the past. Sacred thinking is tradition-oriented and discourages change: secular thinking subjects the eternal verities to the withering test of practical application.

Probably no society is either completely sacred or completely secular in orientation. Some societies are more conservative and more tradition-bound than others. Recent centuries have seen drastic changes in the sacred-secular balance of Western society. The development of science and the revolutions in industry and agriculture have given man a degree of power he never before possessed and have encouraged him to seek more control over his own destiny. The schism in organized religion, personified by the Reformation, was both a part of and contributed to the process.Whereas formerly much effort was directed toward explaining *why* given conditions existed and *why* they must be borne, it has become *how* can they be changed to suit man's needs. The trend toward secular thinking is not complete, and a major conflict relating thereto is discussed in a subsequent section. But the past and current change resulting from this trend are dwarfed only by its future potential. Modern society has come not only to accept change but to value it. The rate of social change is not apt to decline in a society which is so oriented.

Recurrent Upheavals

Not all of the major changes in Western culture are continuous and directional as in the case of the alterations discussed above. Instead, some of them are temporary, recurrent, and even periodic. Their significance lies not only in their long-term effects but also in the temporary chaos they produce. Intense and extensive disorganization follows their appearance and subsides again as traditional or modified controls reassert themselves. Such periods of disorganization are often called *crises*. Four types of recurrent crisis familiar in Western culture are war, depression, fluctuations in birth and death rates, and physical catastrophes.

War. It was pointed out in the chapter on war and international organization that the vigorous denunciation of war as an instrument of national policy is belied by the fact that war is often so used. History shows an almost continuous pattern of periods of peace alternating with periods of war. War has been used and continues to be used as a major technique for seeking the redistribution of political and economic power. War is, and has been, expensive: it produces destruction, chaos, tragedy, and suffering. To date, however, the cost of war has not been great enough to bring about its elimination.

Superficially, at least, efforts to eliminate war have been underway now for some time. However well intentioned, such efforts have had little chance of success. They have sought to eliminate war, but without making any of the fundamental changes that might make its elimination possible. National pride, sovereignty, and the fruits of victory all have been deemed more important. And war has not been *too* terrible. Some conflicts, in Latin America for instance, have been almost bloodless. The United States has had more people killed by automobiles in the past fifty years than in all of her wars combined. Were this pattern the only one, and were it to continue, it is very unlikely that war would disappear. War is changing, however—possibly faster than man can be made to realize.

The past decade has seen the development of weapons which in the event of another major conflagration might actually destroy human civilization. The threat of war today is not the same old threat of a few years of hardship and suffering but is a threat to survival itself. There is ample evidence, too, that the full import of this threat is not yet completely realized. International intercourse continues to be carried on according to timeworn and demonstrably unsuccessful patterns. Whether these patterns can be changed and whether the efforts at prevention will become serious enough to be successful cannot be foretold. The future of at least Western culture hangs in the balance.

Depression. Occasional severe economic recessions have been a second plague upon modern Western nations. Every so often the system of distributing goods and services has tended to break down; idleness, unemployment, panic, and wastage being the result. Some recessions have been mild and of short duration, whereas others have been world-wide and lasted for a decade. Inevitably such depressions create and/or intensify social problems. Families suffer when breadwinners lose their jobs and can find no others; manufacturers are unable to sell and hence are unable to produce more goods; an atmosphere of pessimism and insecurity prevails. It is an atmosphere of crisis.

Such a crisis climate is a favorable one for additional social change. The former inertia of habits and the reluctance to alter the status quo give way to despair and even to desperation. Any proposed change that might aid in ending the depression is apt to receive a hearing. Liberal and even radical proposals find favor.

During the last great depression of the 1930's the United States social security program, minimum wage laws, unemployment insurance, large scale deficit financing, and public works programs all got their start. Arguments that these were inevitable do not alter the fact that they at least developed sooner because of the depression. The 1930's also saw the development of widespread interest in the supposedly communist experiment in the Soviet Union. Liberal intellectuals, idealistic dreamers, and discouraged persons of many ilks, hoped to find in communism the way out of depression catastrophes. The purge of communists and communist thinking of the mid-1950's is ample evidence of a shift away from the experiment-oriented thinking of two decades ago. Some depression-sponsored changes may become a permanent part of the cultural heritage and some may be refuted after the crisis has passed, but both can be interpreted in terms of the distress created by economic hardship.

There is a widespread belief at the present time that the United States finally has learned to cope with depressions—that another prolonged depression can be avoided by the government "pump-priming" techniques developed during the 1930's. If so, a major force making for unpredictable social change will have been eliminated. The theory, however, has not been tested as yet. Another major depression might well be more severe than any yet experienced and might render the New Deal reforms and communist fad pale by comparison.

Birth- and Death-Rate Fluctuations. Changes in birth and death rates make themselves felt through the alterations which they bring about in the size and age structure of the population. Unlike wars and depressions, these changes are seldom concentrated over a period of a few years but usually require one or more generations to run their course. Although not so dramatic, their effects may be even more far reaching than those of the more spectacular short-run changes.

During most of the modern era both birth and death rates in Western culture have been in a process of decline. Under the impetus of modern sanitation techniques, death rates began to decline first and continued to decline rapidly until well into the present century. The decline in birth rates began somewhat later, appearing to be a product of modern means of contraception. The combination of high birth rates and high death rates produced a young, vigorous population which accented the virtues of youth and largely ignored the problems of age. By now, however, the death rate has dropped to the point where the aged have become numerous and their problems acute. Gerontology, a term almost unknown twenty years ago, receives a great deal of public attention. The decade of the 1940's saw at least a partial reversal in the downward trend of the birth rate. Larger families are creating the need for more spacious housing, for station wagons in lieu of the old family automobile, and are threatening to swamp our educational system.

How far present trends are projected into the future determines, of course, what some of the *specific* problems of that future will be. Most important, however, neither the continuation nor the modification of present patterns will permit us to *avoid* problems. Whatever the future vital statistics rates, both the short- and long-run changes they bring about will require compensating adjustments in other areas. The effect of change in one area of culture is always some disorganization elsewhere. So long as rates continue to fluctuate and so long as their effects cannot be fully anticipated, they will remain a part of social problem situations.

Physical Catastrophes. Not all of the factors involved in social problems are exclusively social and not all of the many types of change that produce social disorganization are strictly social changes: man is still a physical organism that must function in a physical universe. That universe exhibits fluctuations which disturb his patterns of adjustment and which result in temporary disorganization. Examples of such fluctuations are the many varieties of physical catastrophe: earthquakes, floods, hail, tornadoes, insect plagues, and drought. By destroying property and disrupting the processes of communication and order, such catastrophes create distress. From time immemorial they have cropped up occasionally to complicate the adjustment needs created by man himself.

It seems probable that until fairly recently most such catastrophes would not have fit our definition of social problems. During most of human history these occasional disasters probably were regarded as inevitable and simply to be endured. Over time and especially within the past three or four centuries, man has gradually gained some control over the physical environment, however, so that the prospect of mitigating climatic and geographical factors has become a practical one. Through plowing, grading, seeding, domesticating, and building, man has rendered himself somewhat less directly threatened by the vagaries of nature.

At the same time, his inventions for harnessing nature have rendered man somewhat more vulnerable in certain respects. By plowing and clearing timber he increases the likelihood of floods and increases the hazards of droughts. Through heavy production he wastes the land, and through using insecticides he may inadvertently be breeding hardier varieties of insects.

The unanticipated consequences of human actions are not so relevant here, however, as in the fact that even *physical* disasters become properly *social* problems whenever men begin to consider what changes can be made in order to eliminate them. Once this process begins it may not be long until the original physical problem is dwarfed by the changes wrought by man's efforts to cope with it. As civilization advances, larger portions of such problem areas become social engineering problems somewhat removed from the original physical problem. Yet the divorcement is not complete and man still has to struggle with the forces of nature. Minor changes in nature's pattern bring him back to temporary disorganization in the face of new adjustment needs.

Unsolved Problems in Social Disorganization

To expect that social science, or even that man himself, should succeed in eliminating disorganization from social life is as naive as for the farmer to believe that the insect problem will be eliminated once he has halted a particular invasion of grasshoppers or locusts. There are thousands of varieties of insects all of which cannot be fought at the same time, and even those which he does combat breed new generations from year to year. Our farmer must be ever on the alert, pushing back the hordes, repairing the damage, and shifting his attack to meet new developments. So it is also in society. Not one line of change, but many affect our daily lives—and while one set of adjustments is being worked out, the need for others is developing. Here, too, man needs to learn to anticipate and to control so that the damage in terms of human suffering may be reduced to a minimum. The long-sought *answers* to social disorganization lie not in its elimination—which could occur only if social change were halted—but in the development of continually more efficient techniques of adjustment.

That new techniques of adjustment are constantly appearing is unquestionable. Each of the chapters in Part II of this book discusses some of them. Whether the schisms and lags of today are less numerous and less serious than those of the past, however, is open to question. In many ways it seems that distress and disaster are more prevalent today than ever before. Are we falling behind in our ability to adjust to new demands or does it only seem that way? Are we nearer to ultimate disaster, or do we merely lack perspective on problems that are near at hand? There are in this connection at least two basic problems in social change which remain unsolved. The first problem is the unequal rates of change in different aspects of culture, and the second problem involves the constantly heavier demands made upon individuals by accelerating rates of social change.

1. *Unequal Rates of Change.* This is an era of unprecedented technological expansion. The process of creating material inventions appears to be cumulative. The more inventions that are made, the faster new ones appear and the more complex they become. The past fifty years have seen us move from the "horse and buggy stage" to the stage of jet and rocket propulsion. And just the past two decades have seen the development of nuclear fission, deadly nerve gases, and bacteriological warfare. Man's tools of destruction have reached the point where the annihilation of civilization, if not of all mankind, is a grave possibility.

The danger to mankind, however, does not lie solely in the development of continually more destructive weapons. It also lies in the failure of other aspects of culture to change rapidly enough to meet the challenge presented to them. Particularly, long outmoded political institutions and practices tend to persist. As outlined in the chapter on war and international organization, nations continue to conduct their affairs as though eighteenth-century conditions still prevailed. How long can this gap between material invention and social practice continue to widen? Present prospects are that another major war would result in world-wide disaster, and with each new invention the prospects become even more terrible.

The only possible solution to this dilemma appears to lie in a rapid transformation of world political and, to an extent, all other institutions. Occasionally another solution, a moratorium on further material invention, is proposed, but no competent authorities actually believe that such a "holiday from invention" could be accomplished. Nor does past experience indicate that a rapid overhaul of social institutions is likely. This is the most pressing of the great unsolved problems of our time. The wrong combination of further social change and a lack of social change may eliminate all social problems—permanently!

2. *Increasing Demands.* The gap, outlined above, between the rate of material invention and the rate of institutional change is a function of inertia within the social system. It is not a question of whether human beings can live under political institutions which would render war unnecessary but it is a question as to whether they *will* develop such institutions. That problem does not raise the question of ultimate human capacity to adjust to ever more rapid social change.

It is probable that ever since he became capable of reflecting upon such things, man has questioned his capacity to adjust to the new and unfamiliar. Up to the present, of course, such fears have proved groundless. There has always been, up to now, a kind of reservoir of potential which man has been able to draw upon to adjust to the new complexities that faced him. Thus, there is some justification for believing that apprehensions about the future are at least partly a function of our unfamiliarity with new culture patterns which are appearing. Students in the next century may look back upon the present era with the same feeling of condescension we now experience when we think of the "terrible complexity" of horseless carriages and continuous radio broadcasting.

Yet there undoubtedly are limits to man's capacity to adjust. His brain and nervous system are wonderfully plastic but they are finite. Since the rate of human biological evolution is almost imperceptible and the rate of social change constantly increases, it is logical to assume that sooner or later the limits of man's ability to adjust will be reached. As indicated in the chapter on the personal pathologies, many persons feel that the high rate of mental-emotional breakdown in modern society is proof that the limits have nearly been reached. Unfortunately, there is no way of knowing for certain whether the actual rates of mental illness have increased or only that there is now more awareness of the problem. Present knowledge will not permit a definite answer to the question, but we are now accumulating enough data so that future trends in the rate of personal breakdown will permit some judgment as to whether society is becoming too complex. If illness rates soar and therapeutic measures prove ineffective, then the inference will be that the limits have nearly been reached. If, on the other hand, the rates do not increase appreciably, then our respect for the human organism should grow apace.

VALUE-CONFLICTS: RELATIVITY AND THE SEARCH FOR STANDARDS

Social problems inevitably include value-conflicts. Ordinarily, values are slowly crystallized, over time, in response to established conditions. But the very nature of social problems includes social change. Social problems are not products of static conditions and accepted definitions: they are products of change and the search for new definitions. When established values provide no effective means of coping with a problem, then new and more adequate values must be developed. The search for new values crystallizes differences among groups which formerly had not received so much attention.

Bases for Value-Conflicts

Many groups, when the issues are sharpened, differ fundamentally on important matters. The common assumption that reasonable people "can get together if only they will try" is found to be something less than completely true. A part of the remaining truth is that on social issues there are no universally accepted standards of what is right or wrong, good or bad. At best there are surface conflicts concerning how a particular agreed-upon-solution to a problem may be implemented in practice, and at worst there are fundamental value-differences which make any agreement at all, on whether a problem exists or on what ought to be done about it, virtually impossible.

The key to understanding value-conflicts and their role in social problem situations lies in the recognition of group differences and in the attitudes that people take toward those differences. The range of group differences is almost limitless. For purposes of convenience and illustration, we will mention just four principal sources of value-differences that conduce to conflict.

1. *Several Economic, Political, and Religious Systems.* The terms *Republican* and *Democrat, Protestant, Catholic,* and *Jew, free enterprise* and *government regulation* are all common terms used in everyday speech. Usually in a vague sort of way it is recognized that a man who is labeled as Republican, Protestant, and an advocate of free enterprise feels, thinks, and acts somewhat differently from a man who is labeled Democrat, Catholic, and in favor of more government regulation of the economy. What needs stressing here is that this series of identifications, whatever the specific combination, influences far more than how the man will vote on, say, a proposed public power project. It indicates with some predictability what he conceives to be the nature of man, the relation of man to his God, the role of government in relation to both man and God and what he will define as good or evil in both man and society and all their works. People do differ in these most basic definitions according to their group affiliations. The fact that Catholic and Protestant, Republican and Democrat can work together cordially in the same office, enjoy the same movies, and be equally devoted to their families does not mean that they would make the same changes in society if they had the power to do so. At countless points their preferred changes would go in completely opposite directions. Awareness of problem situations and the possibility that "something might be done" in the problem area brings these customarily glossed-over differences to the fore. Then people who are neighbors, coworkers, and even friends become embroiled in bitter conflict.

2. *Racial and Ethnic Variation.* Ethnic and racial differences are neither so subtle nor so well camouflaged as economic, religious, and political ones. Over fifteen million United States citizens are a group set apart racially, that is, by physical identification, and many millions more are set apart by cultural or ethnic differences. Into the former category fall most Negroes and Orientals, together with some Indians, Mexicans, and Jews. Into the latter category fall most of the European immigrant groups who have retained much of the European traditions and also some small religious sects whose beliefs and patterns render them readily identifiable.

The democratic proscription against group discrimination has been notoriously ineffective in relation to racial and ethnic groups, and conflict is seldom absent in the lives of minority group members. Racial epithets of many sorts are used to express antipathy toward or from these groups. Substantial numbers of each group resent any rights or privileges enjoyed by the others, and feel themselves morally justified in if not obligated to "keep the ———— in their proper place." Social problem situations and the solutions proposed to them often derive from or threaten to change some aspects of the relations between these groups. All of the antipathies, the conflicts of interest, and the desires to exploit are immediately involved in a struggle to determine whose values shall prevail.

3. *Conflicts of Interest.* Social life always involves a balance between those interests which persons and groups have in common and those which they do not share. In simpler societies it is often difficult to determine where the common interest ends and the individual interests begin. Any tendency for an individual to shirk his obligations to others may result in such quick and drastic retaliation that the person soon learns not to attempt it. In fact, if the society's techniques of indoctrination have functioned smoothly, it probably will not even occur to him to try it. Even in complex, modern societies it is sometimes difficult to separate the joint interest from the individual interest. The interests of labor and management, for example, often tend to be opposed, but just as this is being written several thousand workers in one of the nation's major industrial firms have accepted a 15 to 20 per cent wage cut in order to improve their company's competitive position and avoid a shutdown. This does not mean, of course, that the workers are wholeheartedly behind management policies, but it does stress the difficulty of clearly categorizing the separate interests of individuals and groups.

On the other hand, the larger and more complex the society the more clearly can *short-run* interests, at least, be in conflict with one another. At the present time, for instance, express toll highways are being planned in many parts of the nation. Traffic problems mount daily and such thoroughfares seem to be one part of the solution. In the long run such highways will benefit the entire country. Yet, wherever new highway proposals are made the conflicts begin to rage. Many citizens groups in cities and towns would like to rid themselves of through traffic. But many merchants complain that express highways will hurt their businesses. Other businessmen, who hope to gain concession rights along the highway, are all in favor of it. Farmers oppose the highways because they threaten to isolate and hence reduce the value of certain farms. Other "strategically located" farmers see chances for quick profits. Concrete and asphalt manufacturing companies struggle to have their materials used in the construction, politicians vie for the right to fill the new jobs created, and so on. Although the long-run interests in increased flow of traffic, safety, and economic prosperity may be shared by all these groups, the opportunities for short run conflict and temporary advantage are numerous.

The conflicts of interests illustrated here could be duplicated in almost any area of modern life. The number of groups and the special interests they hold almost defy imagination. These conflicting interests are both a part of and are distinct from the religious, racial, ethnic, political, and major economic cleavages discussed above. They help to explain why the inexorable onslaught of social change is always accompanied by emerging and continuing patterns of conflict.

4. *Diversity and Heterogeneity.* Although they are perhaps the more dramatic, not all of the value-differences and incipient value-conflicts in modern society derive from clear-cut clashes of interest. Nor do they all derive from group and ideological differences where prejudice and discrimination are consistently operative. A large part of the value-differences are simply products of slightly different conditions of life. Such differences are far more characteristic of urban than of rural living and the larger and more diversified the city the more evident they become.

There is first the whole range of occupational differences: the bricklayer may have something in common with the stone mason and with certain other members of the building trades, but how much does he have in common with the druggist, the file clerk, the chiropodist, the school teacher, and the tailor? Occupational differences are accompanied by income differences and problems of wages and salaries. Housing conditions, recreational facilities, transportation needs, and so on, vary almost *ad infinitum*. In most of these cases there are no special conflicts of interest so much as there is a lack of *shared* interests. There is no necessary *conflict* between the slum dwellers whose housing problem includes infestation with rats and the suburban-development residents whose problem is a water-filled drainage ditch, but neither group is particularly interested in the specific problem of the other. Without the bond of immediate shared interests, such groups are to a great extent unavailable to one another for aid in achieving their separate goals.

When there is so little communication, either of meaning or feeling, group attempts to realize particular values may be complicated in at least two ways. First, the group may not be able to get any real support for its program. Unless the group is articulate or powerful, this is often the case. Its members often become antagonistic toward those persons who seem to frustrate their program or they become generally hostile toward other groups and their needs. The second and more significant outcome is that in order to put its program across the group must resort to other than purely rational appeals. It must, in effect, become a pressure group and seek to mold opinion by means of propaganda. Pressure-group tactics are, of course, creative of conflict. Conflicts of interest are born where formerly only difference existed.

SUGGESTED READINGS

Since this chapter and the following one are a single unit which is divided for convenience only, the suggested readings for both chapters are located at the end of the next chapter.

AUDIO-VISUAL AIDS

The High Wall (McGraw-Hill Book Company, Inc., Text-Film Department, 330 W. 42nd, New York), 32 minutes, sound, black and white. Produced under the joint sponsorship of the Anti-Defamation League of B'nai B'rith, the State of Illinois Departments of Public Instruction and Welfare, and the Columbia Foundation, San Francisco. When an outbreak between teen-age gangs lands two boys in the hospital, a psychiatrist, with the aid of a social caseworker, reconstructs the background of facts. He finds that fear, frustration, and narrow, bigoted thinking has been fostered in the boys by their home life. Can be used to illustrate both social-disorganization and personal-deviation factors involved in social problems.

Social Revolution (Encyclopaedia Britannica Films, Inc., 1150 Wilmette Ave., Wilmette, Ill.), 17 minutes, sound, black and white. Traces social changes during the past two hundred years. Contrasts constructive or peaceful methods of change with destructive or violent methods.

QUESTIONS AND PROJECTS

1. How does the interruption of established habits help to create social problems?

2. Social breakdown often appears more evident to mature adults than to young adults and youth. Explain. How is this difference related to the appearance of new culture patterns?

3. List four major changes in Western European culture which play major roles in the development of many current social problems.

4. Differentiate between science and scientism.

5. Define "secular thinking" and differentiate it from "sacred thinking."

6. How are crises related to the appearance of social problems?

7. Why is it unrealistic to expect that disorganization should soon be entirely eliminated from social life? Illustrate your answer.

8. Discuss the thesis that unequal rates of change in different aspects of culture pose a grave threat to human civilization.

9. Explain the statement that "major value-differences exist within American society, independent of particular instances of social change."

CHAPTER 21

The Three Approaches Reassessed: II

MAJOR VALUE-ISSUES IN WESTERN SOCIETY

AMONG the myriad conflicts that pervade social problem situations there are occasional recurrent and persistent themes. The broad course of social change in Western society which was outlined in the last chapter has inevitably resulted in the re-examination of values that were formerly uncritically held. New values, themselves part of a larger pattern, begin to appear. In the clash between the traditional and what *may* be the patterns of the future are found the major issues of today and tomorrow.

The depth of the conflicts to be considered here is measured by the amount of emotional heat they engender. Any one of them will send many persons' blood pressures to the boiling point. For these are not mere surface conflicts, with outcomes of limited significance. These conflicts involve the validity of the most basic assumptions upon which people build their lives and upon which they depend for definitions of right and wrong. Regardless of which side of an issue an individual espouses, he is not apt to be easily converted to the point of view of the other.

1. Sacred versus Secular

By what standards should a man, a law, an idea, or an action be judged? Any of these can, in the United States at the present time, be judged as completely praiseworthy or as absolutely reprehensible by different groups of people. Not all, or even most, of the people who make the judgments will be adequately aware of the presuppositions upon which their judgments are based. But whatever the issue, one part of those assumptions is likely to involve *where* the individuals look for standards.

To one group of persons all actions are judged externally by whether or not they conform to the beliefs and practices which come to us from the past. It is not loyalty to the past alone, however, that characterizes sacred thinking and differentiates it from secular thinking. In addition, the sacred orientation assumes that the heritage from the past is not to be questioned, and that not only the ideals of the past but also the forms through which these ideals were met are inherently good. Deviations from past standards are judged not by whether the results of the deviations help satisfy other traditional values but by the fact that they are deviations.

Secular thinking rejects the notion that deviation is inherently bad and claims instead that it is rigidity—the inability to adjust forms and practices to changed conditions—which is bad. The secular orientation would preserve that part of the heritage from the past which is still useful and discard all the rest. It would define man's needs in terms of a set of values which is consistent within itself rather than in terms of any special ties to the past.

As indicated earlier, a marked trend toward secular thinking is a major feature of Western culture. It is too soon to say, however, how far the balance will shift and how permanent the shift will be. Just in the past few years there has developed a "back to the traditional values" emphasis in education, politics, economics, and religion. Whither the balance will swing in a few more years is not certain. In any event, the conflict promises to be a central one for many years to come.

2. Freedom versus Minimum Living Standards

Conflict over the developing philosophy of minimum standards is probably more acute in the United States than elsewhere in the Western world, for the conditions leading to the conflict have operated at very near maximum in this country. The conflict is a product of both rising standards of living and inequalities in standards of living. Only rather recently in the United States have inequalities in living standards come to be regarded as a problem in themselves.

The United States has, and has had, one of the world's highest levels of living. The American economy is a tremendously productive one, and the benefits of that productivity have been widely distributed throughout the population. Certainly the American people as a whole have a stake in the preservation and improvement of that productive capacity. At the same time, the United States has had one of the world's freest economies in the sense that both business and industry have been permitted to develop and to operate with a minimum of regulation by government. This is our philosophy of "free enterprise" or "unrestricted" capitalism. Historically, at least, the two conditions of high living standards and minimum regulation of the economy have been closely associated. In the light of this close historic association many people have asserted a direct causal relationship, for example, "It is the free economy which is responsible for the high living standards and the continuance of the high living standards depends upon the continuance of maximum freedom in the production and distribution of goods and services."

Unquestionably, this statement of the relation between living standards and free enterprise is gross oversimplification. Seldom, if ever, do we find simple, direct cause-and-effect relationships among institutional and other social patterns. High living standards in the United States *are* associated with relatively unhampered business activity but they are *also* associated with such other plausibly causal variables as abundant natural resources, a tremendous land area, a young and vigorous population, a strategic physical location, and democratic political institutions. Just how much each of these has contributed to our high living standards it is impossible to say. We value each of them for itself and for the role it has played in our economic development. At the very minimum, relatively free capitalism is one of these factors and at maximum it might outweigh the others to the point of being indispensable. From the most naive viewpoint to the most sophisticated, it is important to have the maximum amount of personal freedom or the minimum amount of government regulation that is consistent with the achievement of our other societal values.

The same unrestricted distribution of goods and services which has been instrumental in raising living standards has played an important role in crystallizing the minimum-standards values that are part of the present conflict. Although living standards in general were being raised, some groups were profiting hugely and others little if at all. Thus, while economic freedom in this sense meant the freedom to make a fortune, it also meant the freedom to live in abject poverty and to be unable to share in the society's increased productivity. For many decades it was held to be the individual's own responsibility to see that he did share in the benefits, and presumably he could do so, according to his ability, if only he was ambitious and willing to work. More recently, as the competitive advantages of upper economic status and the competitive handicaps of lower economic status have come to be recognized, the philosophy has begun to develop that there are certain minimum benefits to which an individual or a family should be entitled, whether or not they are earned through direct economic competition. This philosophy assumes that society itself has the obligation to provide certain minimum benefits. The essential benefits generally are stated in terms of the right to be gainfully employed, to earn a living wage, to be assured to adequate medical care and to be protected against disability, to have paid vacations, and to be assured of adequate income in retirement. The "minimum standards" tend gradually to be raised as living standards improve and as the philosophy itself gains greater acceptance.

Actually it appears that the *philosophy* of minimum standards has already gained acceptance and is here to stay. The great depression of the

1930's resulted in the passage of minimum wage laws, unemployment compensation, and the social security program which are now permanent aspects of the American scene. The struggle of the present and the near future concerns just *where* the minimum standards should be located. The advocates of business freedom claim that they are already dangerously high and that further increases might stifle business initiative and wreck the economy. Advocates of higher minimum standards contend that business is not afraid of government interference as such, for example, tariffs, fair trade laws, and the like, and that the same forecasts of disaster have been used to oppose every step of progress that has already been made. Neither set of arguments appears to impress the other side and the conflict goes on.

3. *Nationalism versus Internationalism*

War is the ultimate issue here, and much of the debate centers around which philosophy offers more hope for preventing it. War is not the whole issue, however, for there are other "practical" as well as moral issues involved.

The so-called practical issues concern the whole tenor of our relationships with other peoples as well as our political and economic well-being. The nationalist philosophy in approaching these problems states in effect: "We have a superior system in practically all ways. Objective comparison cannot help but confirm that superiority. Therefore, we should encourage other peoples to become familiar with our system in order that they might imitate it. When they have patterned their systems after ours, the majority of the world's problems will have been solved." The internationalist approach on the other hand asserts: "Attempts by one nation to impose its standards on other nations are likely to incur only resentment and hostility. Even if others accept our technological superiority that does not mean that they will wish to copy us, and they are apt to feel strongly that in other areas their way of life is clearly superior to ours. To get along adequately with other nations we must strive to understand their viewpoints and we should be prepared to compromise important differences." The nationalist philosophy sees hope for world progress only as other nations can be induced to follow our lead. The internationalist philosophy stresses the need for mutual understanding and compromise.

There is, too, a moral issue involved: that of our alleged superiority. That superiority is reputed to be a mixture of biology and culture. Since the culture is superior, there is a strong presumption that the biological stock which produced that culture is itself a desirable one. In matters of immigration, for example, this is presumed to be sufficient reason for preserving the basic biological composition of the American people. Opponents of this alleged superiority claim that the biological composition of the people has had little to do with the development of American culture and that the whole philosophy is contradictory to our professed democratic and Judeo-Christian beliefs. The current struggle between those who would continue to drastically restrict the numbers of immigrants who may come to the United States from non-Northwest European countries and those who would eliminate the favored treatment given to just a few nations is a part of the larger conflict over nationalist-internationalist ideologies.

Ultimately the issue becomes one of war and peace. Those who hold to the nationalist position stress the belligerent nature of nations, the conflict of political and economic ideologies, and the likelihood of war when any nondemocratic, noncapitalist nation believes that it has a good chance to win. From these assumptions, it would be folly to relax our guard and thus give a potential enemy his opportunity. Since there is a strong probability of future wars anyway, we must be strong enough to foredoom an attack to failure. Only in such a program of preparedness, according to nationalist philosophy, is there any real possibility of preventing future wars.

Internationalist thinking sees this nationalist rationale as one of the major forces operating to perpetuate the pattern of intermittent warfare. By assuming that war is almost inevitable, they claim, and by acting as though war would come, the efforts to prevent it actually serve to make war more likely. Only by a relatively complete break with past patterns of international diplomacy do they see much hope for breaking the cycle. The co-existence of such antithetical ideologies as capitalism and communism, democracy and dictatorship, require that all of man's resources be put into a supreme effort to discover ways whereby the differences may be either reconciled or accommodated. Past experience has amply demonstrated that armaments and alliances do not prevent wars; an all-out effort to accommodate national differences has not yet been made.

AMELIORATION CONFLICTS

Conflicts rage at each step in the definition, operation, and solution of social problems. The conflict usually begins when it is first asserted that "a condition is bad," for there are always some persons who profit by that condition and some who believe it to be right, proper, or inherent in the scheme of things. Then conflicts are apt to develop over whether anything can be done about the condition and which of several alternative solutions should be tried. Finally the conflict is apt to shift to the way in which the proposed solution should be put into effect. Even when all factions are agreed upon what needs to be done, there generally remains disagreement on how to do it. Thus, conflicts center about the issues themselves and about policies for dealing with the problems. In the "technique" or "policy" area, two disagreements on how to deal with problem situations recur time and again.

1. Regulate or Scourge?

In many different problem situations there is continuing debate over "whether the devils should be exorcised or whether they should be permitted to remain but with their malevolent powers curbed." In matters of family instability, racial segregation, and gambling, for example, one alternative is to strike at the heart of the matter; to forbid divorce, to eliminate segregation, and to stamp out gambling. The other alternative is to permit all three but to remove the elements in each situation which cause hardship. The trauma might be removed from divorce procedures, the separate but *equal* provision might be vigorously enforced, and gambling might be legalized, regulated, and taxed. These are fundamentally different proposals and the proponents of each generally are scornful of the other.

Advocates of vigorous efforts to scourge the undesirable conditions frequently hold that to do otherwise is immoral. When a situation is defined as wrong there should be no compromise with it. Determination and courage are called for; to speak of regulating or controlling vice is either wishy-washy or it amounts to rationalization by those who really wish the evils to continue. The proponents of regulation and control are prone to argue that efforts to stamp out such vices are naive and unrealistic. Prostitution and drug addiction, they remind us, have existed from time immemorial. Since social change cannot be reversed and since the condemned practices *will* continue, the sensible approach is to make them available but under conditions where a minimum of harm will be done and where some incidental public good might result. The traits which are called for, they suggest, are understanding and discretion rather than fanaticism and myopia.

It seems apparent that there are some elements of validity in each of these positions and that many persons hold to each view out of the genuine conviction that it is the correct one. In some cases, however, there is also reason to suspect that the insinuations cast by each group regarding the characters and motivations of some of the other group may bear some scrutiny. Some fanatics, whose motivations are complex, do tend to the former position and some apologists for the status quo do tend to the latter. That problem, however, is reserved for the last part of this chapter.

2. Fast or Slow?

A closely related conflict concerns the method or "rate" at which any proposed solution should be put into effect. The one position is that proposed changes should be instituted as rapidly as possible, whereas the counterposition is that changes should be made as gradually as possible over an extended period of time. Many, though by no means all, of the persons who feel that problem conditions should be completely uprooted also feel that it should be done quickly, and many of those who favor regulation also favor going slowly in whatever is done.

The advocates of rapid change are again prone to emphasize the inconsistency between ideals and practice and to work energetically toward making the ideals a reality. They are inclined to favor change through legislation and to point to instances, such as the whole series of laws and rulings against racial discrimination, as evidence that this "taking-the-bull-by-the-horns" approach does work. The "go-slow" approach of others is again interpreted as evidence of faintheartedness or as reluctance to see the changes made.

Those who favor a cautious approach stress the importance of cultural traditions which are opposed to the anticipated change. "You can't change a whole way of life overnight," they feel, and fundamental alterations in habit and custom may require a generation or more to be accomplished successfully. Efforts to bring them about quickly are sure to meet with evasion and hostility that will make the problem more difficult rather than less difficult to solve.

The charges by each side of unrecognized or unacknowledged motivations on the part of their opponents are again not completely true nor are they without any foundation. Personal interest and personal conviction are not synonymous nor are they wholly separable. The personal elements in such conflicts are discussed in the next section.

PERSONAL DEVIATION: PATHOLOGY AND VARIATION

Both social change and value-conflicts may operate on a grand scale and in seemingly impersonal fashion. Nevertheless, personalities are always involved. Some persons adjust readily to changed conditions whereas others do not; and value-conflicts are products of the divergent values held by individuals and groups. Personality factors intrude into the concepts of social disorganization and value-conflicts, and they play an important role in their own right. The present section re-examines the nature of these personality factors and the mode of their involvement in social problem situations.

The Deviant in Social Problems

One of the first questions to be answered is just how personal deviancy contributes to the development of problem situations. In answer: deviants (1) may play an important causative role, (2) they may help precipitate or aggravate the problem, or (3) they may *be* the problem.

1. *Deviants May Play an Important Causative Role.* Some of the important variables in any social situation are the needs, desires, strengths, weaknesses, and peculiarities of the persons who occupy places of leadership. The positions of leadership are multiple and varied: they include the heads of governments, military leaders, political figures, scholars, literary experts, scientists, the officers and "bosses" of major organizations, and so on. The important consideration is that the person be in such a strategic position that his personal peculiarities have important influence on the behavior of numerous other persons. Marked paranoid tendencies, for example, in the "man on the street" are not apt to have broad repercussions in the behavior of others. People may say, simply, "he's a suspicious cuss," or they may shy away from contacts with him, or if he becomes too troublesome they may institutionalize him. *But* those same feelings of persecution in a major public official, or in the publisher of a large newspaper, may be instrumental in creating a climate of fear and hostility leading to religious persecution, race riots, or even war. The influence of the deviant personality is in direct proportion to the power and influence wielded by the person so afflicted.

One need not assert that dictators and presidents, bishops and popes, physicists and inventors, have *caused* the world's problems. There is always a complex web of cause and effect centering about the personalities of leaders and the social conditions that enabled them to assume leadership. Whether the social climate produces the man or whether the man creates the social climate is a kind of "chicken before the egg" question. Social problems do not have *a* cause, they have *many* causes. Some of those causes may well inhere in the deviant characters of important leaders. History from Hannibal to Hitler illustrates the point.

2. *Deviants May Precipitate or Aggravate the Problem.* Though the personalities of leaders must occupy a conspicuous role and though most ordinary individuals wield but little power and influence, the "little man's" contribution to problem situations cannot be discounted. For one thing, even the exhortations of the famous must fall on receptive ears if they are to be effective. The demagogue thrives not so much because he personally is popular as because he mirrors, heightens, and gives focus to the insecurities and rabid strivings of the masses. Remove his fanatical following and the demagogue is doomed. Thus, in the *aggregate,* the deviancies of individuals assume an importance which separately they could never have.

In still another way neurotic persons, who are not otherwise outstanding, play a limited causative role in the crystallization of problems. They often provide the "incidents" that bring incipient conflicts to the point of explosion, and once the explosion occurs they fan the resulting flames and constantly seek to add new fuel. Such "trouble-makers" can generally be found deeply involved in or loitering on the periphery of any pending dispute. They are extreme and intemperate in the positions they take and they deprecate compromise in favor of a violent, angry crusade to win their ends. They suppress, twist, distort, and magnify. They "use" but do not accept other persons, casting each one aside when he has ceased to be useful. With an attack upon some person or program, they often succeed in "creating" an issue. Drawn by the smell of blood, other deviants join the fray, revising the issue at will in order to keep the struggle alive. The issues would seldom develop, of course, were there not a serious underlying conflict, but neurotic persons may both trigger and intensify the conflict as well as impede its solution.

3. *Deviants May Be the Problem.* Certain types of deviants are themselves defined as problems. Drug addicts, alcoholics, inveterate gamblers, prostitutes, homosexuals, the mentally ill, the mentally deficient—the whole range of personal pathologies—are subjected to public scrutiny and to efforts at reform. The problem is probably never as simple as "here are some errant persons who must be cured," for there are more than personal factors involved. Many of the pathologic behaviors are tolerated and even approved by some groups. Many of them shade off from accepted social behavior by almost imperceptible degrees. Even when the origin of the deviancy is largely hereditary, there are questions of treatment and care which go far beyond the handicapped persons themselves. The deviant persons are not *all* of the problem but they are the *heart* of the problem. Were it not for the tendency of the deviants to "get in trouble," the associated social issues would not be regarded as problems at all.

Among the deviants who are considered problems there are at least two discernible patterns. In one case the deviants appear to be inadequate to meet normal social demands. It is not so much that they defy convention and violate expectations as that they are *unable* to do what is expected of them. In the other case, the deviants seemingly have sufficient intelligence and capability to behave normally but they still do not do so. They rebel *against* established norms. This dichotomy is not wholly satisfactory, for the question arises as to whether the *seemingly* capable deviant is in any better control of his behavior than the deviant who clearly lacks capacity. If this limitation is kept in mind, however, it does provide a useful basis for analyzing the nature of deviancy.

Personal Inadequacy

In some cases of personal deviation it is evident that there is something lacking—that the problem is one of inadequacy. To deal successfully with such cases it is important to know the source of the inadequacy and what, if anything, can be done to relieve it. Given cases of inadequacy may be (1) hereditary, (2) congenital, or (3) social.

1. *Hereditary Inadequacy.* The estimated importance of hereditary

factors in producing behavioral maladjustments has been declining in the face of more extensive knowledge of human behavior. First of all, *behavior* is never inherited. One inherits the biologic and physiologic *structures* through which behavior becomes possible, but not behavior itself. The distinction is important, for practically all of the structures inherited by man are sufficiently flexible to permit alternative patterns of behavior. Hereditary factors assume importance in producing deviant behavior in precisely those instances where individual structures do not have the flexibility which they normally would have. Probably the best single example is that of intelligence. At the extreme levels of idiocy and imbecility, structures are so limited that little learning is possible. If such individuals are able to master a few bodily functions that is about all that can be asked. The vast majority of the mentally deficient, however, are not so severely limited, and some learning and relearning generally are possible. The more rigid and limited the structures, the more the problem is a hereditary and a biological one; the more flexible the structures, the more the problem becomes primarily social.

2. *Congenital Inadequacy.* It is probably true that in most cases where the causes of personal deviation are basically hereditary that the deviation becomes apparent soon after birth. Not all cases of such extreme deviation, however, are hereditary. Environment, though a predominantly biological environment, exists from the moment of conception and affects the fetus throughout the prenatal period. Some types of deviancy apparently are produced by grossly abnormal conditions in that environment. Perhaps the most striking illustrations of congenital inadequacy are linked to endocrine gland malfunctioning in the mother; cretinism, mongoloidism, and amaurotic idiocy all seem to depend in part upon glandular factors. Diseases in the mother, for example, measles and syphilis, and some treatments for disease such as x-rays and quinine may be instrumental in producing conditions ranging from blindness and deafness to mental illness. Finally, accidental injuries during birth, especially to the central nervous system, sometimes result in permanent damage with behavioral manifestations.

Like the hereditary conditions discussed above, congenital abnormalities are generally irreversible. An important difference exists, however, in that the congenital conditions are far more *preventable*. Advances in medical technology are greatly reducing the number of birth injuries, and the undesirable aftereffects of most diseases and treatments therefore can similarly be prevented. Glandular malfunctionings in expectant mothers present a more perplexing problem but even these may yield in the near future. Certainly they offer more hope than do hereditary abnormalities.

3. *Social Inadequacy.* Hereditary and congenital abnormalities combined account for a relatively small fraction of the total burden of incom-

petence in modern society. In terms of the total man power lost to society, if not in terms of the extremity of the afflictions, social inadequacy is the great problem. Because the associated physical symptoms are so striking, hereditary and congenital abnormalities are widely recognized. Social inadequacy, except for the absence of physical stigmata, presents a parallel syndrome and is often confused with biological inadequacy.

Social inadequacy most frequently is a product of deprivation. The individuals involved, because they do not have normal learning *opportunities,* are functionally as handicapped *as if* they were biologically inadequate. Most such persons are to be found in the lower income groups or in groups that in some other way are denied full participation in the culture; for example, Negroes and certain ethnic groups. Even here the inadequacy is not spread at random but tends instead to be concentrated in certain families which are even more isolated from the larger culture than are most of their fellows. The cultural poverty in such families tends to be self-perpetuating. Their isolation prevents them from acquiring normal abilities and their incapacity enhances the probability of their remaining isolated. Probably over half of all cases of personal incapacity are explainable in terms of subnormal learning opportunities.

The importance of distinguishing between social and biological origins of personal inadequacy lies in the possibility of correcting the responsible social conditions. Though some day man may master the distribution of inherited human characteristics, that time is far in the future. However, he has the knowledge *now* to eliminate the sources of most social inadequacy were there sufficient will to do so. As yet, pitifully little has been done. No single public or private agency has either the power or the resources to deal with the problem. Neither the government nor the schools nor private agencies will move forward until there is far greater public awareness.

Personal Variation

Most of the deviant persons involved in social problem situations are not noticeably limited either in intelligence or in general ability. They have sufficient innate capacity to behave as they are expected to behave, but they do not conform. They remain "different." These are the persons who, if they occupy influential positions, may play an important causative role in social problems and who, if they do not have great power or prestige, often help to precipitate or to aggravate problems. It is important to recognize that such individual variation (1) is learned, (2) is partly a product of diverse norms, and (3) derives much of its significance from the social context.

1. *Is Learned.* It cannot be overemphasized that the deviant person is that way because of experiences he has had in the past. He learns to hate,

fear, and mistrust, to aspire, envision, and covet just as less deviant persons learn these same things in more moderate form. Just how and why *some* persons learn *some* things in much more extreme form than most other persons do is a fascinating and complex problem which has not been completely solved. In some cases it seems to be a matter of "overlearning" which interferes with subsequent learning. The boy-grown-to-manhood who still so reveres his mother that he cannot adjust to a wife, and the "completely honest" man who insults his friends and loses his business, are both cases in point. In still other cases persons "block" or resist what seem to be normal learnings for them and acquire deviant and often disapproved patterns instead. The boy from "a nice home" may rebel murderously because, though the home provides all wanted material goods, it fails to meet his emotional needs.

Whatever the variant pattern assumed, the deviant seldom is completely antisocial. More frequently, his rejection of one set of norms is accompanied by acceptance of a different set of norms.

2. *A Product of Diverse Norms.* Sociologically, variation in norms and practices is entirely normal. Though some small, homogeneous societies may possess but a single set of standards which are universally accepted, all large, complex societies have multiple systems of values which are not wholly congruent with one another and which conflict at many points. Among various elements of the society there even exist entire culture patterns which stand opposed to those values accepted by the society as a whole. The codes of delinquent street-corner gangs and the loyalties of subversive groups are illustrations. It is characteristic of many deviants (in fact this is one way in which deviancy is defined) that they have rejected loyalty to certain values of the larger society in favor of the generally disapproved values of minority groups.

The generally disapproved values of deviant groups are sociologically just as much a part of the culture as are universally accepted ones. Widespread condemnation does not necessarily mean that these are elements soon to disappear from the culture. Indeed, some of the widely held values of today may be persecuted in the future, when they are replaced by some of today's radical notions.

3. *Importance of the Social Context.* Intrinsic importance does not attach to the mere fact of deviation. At least equally important is the way in which the deviation fits in, or does not fit in, with the important issues of the day. There are at all times numerous deviant persons whose deviancy brings them no great attention and who never become involved in major public conflicts. Probably most such persons are regarded by their associates as somewhat eccentric or "strange," and there the matter rests. However, when the eccentricity centers in an area of public dispute or perhaps slightly anticipates the direction of social change, the person may be lifted into prominence and even into positions of leadership. Although

the process whereby leadership develops is not well understood, there is abundant evidence that the long-term significance of a particular leadership is determined by the course of history as well as by the personal qualities of the leader himself. From dictators and presidents down through minor leaders of all sorts, the social climate of the period has had much to do with both the rise to power and with the ultimate definition of the man. Deviation is both created and defined by the social milieu.

SUMMARY

Social change is basic to the appearance of social problems. Change inevitably threatens vested interests, interrupts habits, creates distress, and results in the development of new social patterns. Major alterations in Western culture which have contributed much to current problem situations are the rise of science and scientism, the Industrial Revolution, urbanization, and the rise of secularism. Not all social change, however, is directional. Crises such as wars, depressions, periods of rising and falling birth and death rates, and natural catastrophes all contribute to the development and recognition of social problems.

Social change generally sharpens conflicts of values. The bases for conflict exist, independent of change, in the facts of economic, political, and religious differences, in racial and ethnic variation, in conflicts of interest, and in the diversity and heterogeneity which characterize complex societies. Major conflicts in Western society include sacred versus secular thinking, the ideology of business freedom versus the ideology of minimum standards, and nationalist versus internationalist approaches to world affairs. Important conflicts also rage over the proper approach to problem situations; over whether the problems should be attacked directly or whether they should be merely regulated and controlled, and whether all of this should be accomplished rapidly or over extended periods of time.

Personal deviation is a third element found in all social problems. Deviants, when they occupy important positions, often play a causative role in the development of problem situations. Deviants in less critical positions help to precipitate and to aggravate problems. When the deviation is sufficiently great, the deviants may even be a considerable part of the problem. Some personal deviation is clearly a matter of incapacity; hereditary, congenital, or social. In other cases the deviation is more a matter of variation than of basic incapacity. Such social variation is learned, is partly a product of diverse norms, and derives much of its significance from the social context.

SUGGESTED READINGS

BARNES, Harry E., *Society in Transition* (New York, Prentice-Hall, Inc., 1939). Detailed description of the influence of the Industrial Revolution upon modern American society. Includes treatment of urbanization and secularization of modern society.

CUBER, John F., and HARPER, Robert A., *Problems of American Society: Values in Conflict* (New York, Henry Holt & Company, Inc., 1951). A leading social problems textbook, based upon the conflict-of-values approach.

OGBURN, William F., *Social Change* (New York, Viking Press, Inc., 1922). Stresses the disorganizing influences which are felt when some aspects of culture change more rapidly than others. Assigns a determinative role to technology.

SCHEINFELD, Amram, *The New You and Heredity* (Philadelphia, J. B. Lippincott Company, 1950). An excellent nontechnical treatment of the role of hereditary factors in producing personal deviation.

WRIGHT, Richard, *Black Boy* (New York, Harper and Brothers, 1945). Powerful, autobiographical novel which reveals the development of deviant personality characteristics through subjection of the author to racial prejudice and discrimination.

QUESTIONS AND PROJECTS

1. Do you see any connections between the sacred versus secular and the freedom versus minimum standards controversies? Could you predict how most persons would feel on the one issue through knowledge of their feelings on the other issue?

2. What is meant by amelioration conflicts?

3. Defend the policy of attempting to regulate or control problem conditions as opposed to the policy of attempting to stamp them out completely.

4. How may deviant persons play an important causative role in producing social problem situations?

5. What classes of deviants are often considered to *be* the problem?

6. What kind of program would you recommend for attempting to reduce the burden of seriously deficient persons upon society? What assumptions does your program make about the causes of such personal inadequacy?

7. How may deviancy appear through overlearning? Illustrate your answer.

8. Explain the statement that "widely disapproved values are part of the culture."

9. How does the social context influence the definition given to deviant personality characteristics? Give several illustrations.

CHAPTER 22

The Orientation of American Society

WE could easily add a second volume to this textbook without repeating ourselves. Many other problems—housing, immigration, politics, labor relations, poverty, depressions, natural resources,—are among those a second volume might treat. But neither the college term nor the student's patience last forever. At some point, one must simply stop, recapitulate, and attempt to assess prospects for the future.

One cannot accurately predict either the exact nature of future problems or our future action toward them. But, aware of the continuity of culture, we may assume that most of the established trends in American society will continue, and that future social problems and social action will be shaped by these trends.

TRENDS IN AMERICAN SOCIETY

Important trends in American society which are well enough established to need no documentation include the following:

1. *Increasing Productivity and Rising Standards of Living.* Our productivity per man hour has increased by about six times during the past century. If this rate of increase continues for another century, our average worker in 2050 will produce and earn as much in one 7-hour day as he now does in a 40-hour week, and as much as he produced in 1850 by working more than three weeks at 70 hours a week.[1] But productivity per man-hour is now rising even faster than ever before, averaging 3.5 per cent a year, or more than enough to double our real income each 25 years.[2]

This is a tremendously important social fact. Throughout fully 99 per cent of recorded history, most of the world's people lived at or near the level of bare subsistence; most of the world's people still do. At nearly all times and places, high birth rates and low worker productivity made

[1] J. Frederic Dewhurst and associates, *America's Needs and Resources: A New Survey* (New York, The Twentieth Century Fund, 1955), p. 942.
[2] *Ibid.*, p. 920.

poverty normal and inescapable, and "social problems" were so insoluble that such situations were not even defined as "problems." It is only in the United States and a few other nations where we *can produce enough* to make possible such luxuries as public assistance to the indigent, universal education, or widespread health services. This high and rapidly rising productivity and the rising standards of living it makes possible are among the most significant social facts of modern life.

2. *Increasing Leisure.* Most of the people of the world have followed— and still follow—a daily routine of, in the words of Galsworthy, "get up, work, go to bed, sleep." Until very recently in Western civilization, leisure was an upper-class monopoly. Ours is the first civilization in which the masses of the people enjoy leisure in any appreciable amounts. Although the mass enjoyment of leisure may not be an unmixed blessing, its development is a social fact of tremendous significance.

3. *The Democratization of Comforts.* It may be no accident that the most highly productive peoples are those with a comparatively small gap between the living standards of the very rich and of the masses. A social system which produces such stupendous adornments as the Taj Mahal, the Pyramids, or the palace city of Versailles does not reward its workers with the high standard of living that encourages maximum productivity. The democratization of luxuries and comforts also tends to make political conservatives of the masses who have acquired a vested interest in a social system that provides these comforts. It is also a potentially explosive factor, since a population accustomed to a high standard of living will not quietly surrender it.

4. *Increasing Economic Security.* A little over twenty years ago, our society awakened to the fact that the shift from a folk society to an urban-industrial society had greatly reduced the economic security of the individual. It also became clear that in an increasingly interdependent economy, the economic hardship of any major group—business, labor, farmers— had depressing consequences upon the entire economy. It appears that government has abandoned its "neutral" role and that, regardless of political party, government will accept responsibility for maintaining prosperity and protecting each major economic group from severe hardship. Labor now has minimum wage laws, unemployment insurance, and union contracts; business has a wide variety of government aids and subsidies; farmers have price supports. Each group seeks governmental assistance for itself (while deploring this tendency among others). A continuing determination of every group in the United States to seek protection against economic adversity through group action is one of the inescapable social and political facts of modern life.

5. *Growing Power of Pressure Groups.* In a mass society, the individual has no voice except through his group connections. The unorganized mass is inarticulate and politically ineffectual. Even *democratic* decision-

making in a mass society cannot be a mere counting of heads but inevitably becomes a counting of organizations. The number of interest
groups who maintain formal lobbying machinery grows rapidly, and the
pressure group becomes the real center of political power in the United
States.

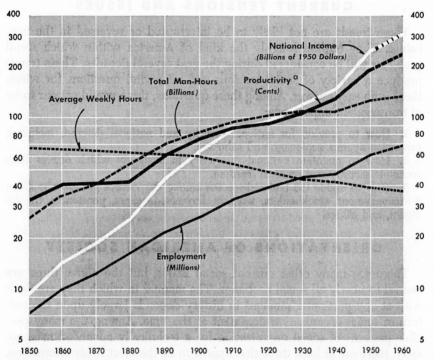

**FIG. 22-1. Estimated Trends in Employment, Working Hours, Productivity, and
National Income, 1850-1960. (From J. Frederic Dewhurst and associates, *America's
Needs and Resources: A New Survey* [New York, Twentieth Century Fund, 1955],
p. 44)**

6. *Growing International Interdependence and Vulnerability.* Economically we grow steadily more dependent upon other nations. Our
high-grade iron ore deposits approach exhaustion, and advancing science
and technology transform one after another of the 101 known chemical
elements from a laboratory curiosity into an industrial raw material. Far
more dramatic, however, is the collapse of geographic defenses in a day
of intercontinental bombers, guided missiles, and atomic weapons. The
knowledge that half our cities and a fourth of our people may be destroyed in a single hour is a Damoclean sword under which we have
learned to live with surprising equanimity. Yet our anxieties over possible wars and revolutions fomented by communist nations now dominate
our social controversy. It is difficult to discuss any social problem without

considerations of national defense, security, and "subversion" arising. Technology is not reversible, and each nation grows steadily more vulnerable to every other technically advanced major nation. This is perhaps the most significant political fact in the world today.

CURRENT TENSIONS AND ISSUES

These trends are not likely to be interrupted or reversed in the near future. They outline roughly the kind of America within which social problems will be considered during the next several decades. These trends produce a variety of social tensions and raise vital questions for which there is no easy answer. Among these questions, three would appear to be of transcendent importance:

1. How to provide for national security and national defense, including protection against espionage and sabotage.
2. How to maintain national prosperity in a society which desires both economic security and political freedom.
3. How to divide the national income among the various groups who claim it—management, stockholders, workers, farmers, teachers, pensioners, the indigent, and others.

ORIENTATIONS OF AMERICAN SOCIETY

There are many other current social issues, but the above three are central to nearly all social problems. The manner in which they are dealt with at any particular moment in history depends largely upon the pattern of social organization dominant at the time. Among the many possible patterns of social organization for a technically advanced mass society, there are at least three that appear to be the most likely alternatives for our society.

1. *The Democratic State.* Despite many imperfections and occasional derelictions, the ethos of American culture has been predominantly democratic. Our history shows an almost unbroken effort to democratize opportunity, to preserve individual dignity, and to diffuse widely among our people the necessities and comforts of life. It can be argued that the process of decision-making is more widely diffused than at any time in our history—one of the consequences of the proliferation of pressure groups.[3] Although these features of American life may or may not be blessings, according to one's values, they are undeniably democratic.

A democratic state is unlikely to be indifferent to social problems.

[3] There is also an opposing point of view—that the organization of the pressure group enables a small leadership clique to impose its views upon the large membership, and that the centralization of industry, finance, and mass communication gives a narrowing group of "decision-makers" a growing power to determine social policy. See Floyd Hunter, *Community Power Structure* (Chapel Hill, University of North Carolina Press, 1953).

Democratic values inevitably define many conditions as "social problems" and encourage action upon them. Democratic traditions encourage voluntary association in order to promote reforms, raise funds, and devise plans for dealing with problems. If democratic social organization persists, our society will probably continue to define and treat social problems much as it has been doing.

Whether democracy will persist is less clear. The development of a pressure-group-activated mass society,[4] the partial lack of a unifying core of universally-held values,[5] the expanding role of government in economic and social life, the development of highly centralized systems of mass communication, and the effort to insure national security in an increasingly insecure world—each carries a potential threat to democracy. It is possible that democracy is a pattern of social organization that can appear and flourish only under certain rare combinations of historic circumstances. If so, its replacement by some other alternative may be expected.

2. *The Garrison State.* When a modern society faces a long military crisis, lasting for decades, its transformation into a garrison-police state becomes more than a theoretical possibility. A long-term military crisis requires that all other interests and values must be subordinated to the requirements of national security. Civil liberties become a nuisance in dealing with suspected traitors and are likely to be curtailed. The pressure for mounting military expenditures requires that other public services—national parks, conservation, civilian education, and all other services not directly related to defense—must be curtailed. The functions and authorities of the government expand in a hundred directions, from the stockpiling of raw materials to the conduct of "psychological warfare." The historic privacy of the individual is steadily narrowed, as his friends, organizational memberships, reading habits, and presumed philosophical views come under security scrutiny; his telephone conversations are tapped and taped, and official guesswork as to his future loyalty becomes a normal function of government. The number of jobs requiring "security clearance" grows, the procedural safeguards in identifying "security risks" are reduced, and the tests of "security" become steadily more stringent. Private intelligence services provide "security" information to employers, and private detective services come to specialize in spying on employees. The industrialist's decisions about factory location, plant layout, raw material utilization, choice of personnel and employees, and many other business matters become increasingly dominated by defense and security needs as each such decision is "cleared" with the proper government official. Passports, scholarships, research grants, and university teaching

[4] Cf. Stuart Chase, *Democracy Under Pressure: Special Interests vs. the Public Welfare* (New York, Twentieth Century Fund, 1945).

[5] Cf. Robert C. Angell, *The Integration of American Society* (New York, McGraw-Hill Book Company, Inc., 1941).

staffs all come under police surveillance and are conditioned upon security considerations. Art, music, and literature cease to be "nonpolitical," and both the political orthodoxy of the production and the alleged political views of the artist, writer, actor, or composer become a basis for determining the acceptability of his work. The atmosphere of suspicion grows and deepens until privacy, independent thinking, and spontaneity of association become, in themselves, suspicious and incriminating.

The government withholds information it feels the people should not know, and the news agencies become dependent upon official "handouts" in many areas of public policy. Political parties join in a "bipartisan" approach that removes certain vital issues from public discussion of alternatives. In numerous areas of public policy, the technical expert states the defense "needs"—a specified radar screen, a certain number of missile platforms, a certain amount of money to develop a uranium mining area, and so on. The legislators and civilian administrators, who cannot be given complete access to the facts upon which such decisions are based, are almost forced to accept and approve these decisions.

In these and many other ways, a prolonged military crisis can transform a democratic society into a garrison state. Some of the more subtle aspects of this transformation are outlined by a distinguished political scientist: [6]

> This transformation would come about gradually as men abandon their former roles and take up new ones, which are thought of as temporary. The owner or active head of a business notes that he is losing able associates to the civil or military services. Sensing that his own activities are becoming more stereotyped, the executive may himself "put on a suit" [join the civil or military service]. A credit manager connects with the political police because of his knowledge of the network of industrial-information contacts across the nation. A trades-unionist joins up [as a secret informer] in order to spy on communists and supposed fellow travelers in the labor movement. It is on the basis of thousands of choices of this kind that the transformation of American society would take place. At any given moment the currents appear to be running as usual in all directions. Closer inspection would show drift away from the activities comparatively untouched by the crisis into operations immediately involved. The garrison-police state is both a "state of mind" and a "state of readiness." It is when the state of mind gets set that the transformation is well along.

The garrison state is not a purely theoretical possibility, as indicated by the fact that many of the tendencies described above are clearly operative to some degree in present American society. It may be that a prolonged military crisis makes the garrison state an inevitability. Whether America becomes a fully developed garrison-police state depends both upon the duration and severity of the crisis in American-Russian relations

[6] By permission from *National Security and Individual Freedom*, pp. 47-48, by Harold D. Lasswell. Copyright, 1950, McGraw-Hill Book Company, Inc., 1950.

and upon the vitality of our democratic value-heritage. There are some countries, such as Finland, which appear to have remained relatively democratic during a fairly long period of national insecurity far greater than ours. Possibly a study of their experience would be revealing.

In a garrison state, social problems are defined largely according to security criteria. Crime, mental illness, and personal pathologies continue to be defined as problems. Ill health and certain kinds of educational deficiency might receive an increased attention; subversion becomes a leading problem while civil liberties become a nuisance, and the "problem" of mass communication becomes one of organizing the media to transmit only the approved propaganda most effectively.

The treatment of social problems in the garrison state emphasizes state action rather than private initiative. Experimentation by voluntary organizations is not encouraged, and agitation for reform is distinctly dangerous. Membership in any but officially approved organizations is highly hazardous, and this would greatly curtail much of the sort of private activity now devoted to social problems. It is likely that well-established voluntary organizations (for example, the Red Cross) would conduct fund drives with semiofficial endorsement and carry on "noncontroversial" activities consistent with defense needs, while all "controversial" voluntary organizational activity would disappear.

The garrison state inevitably becomes a "welfare state" to a degree, as it assumes welfare services that contribute to national strength. These might include free health services, elementary education of the functionally illiterate, support of technical and professional education in certain areas, and perhaps others. The garrison state is highly active with respect to social problems, although both its definitions and its responses differ greatly from those of the democratic state.

3. *The Fascist State.*[7] If America's international tensions could be resolved, a number of problems would be simplified, but others might be aggravated. With the economic props of a large military program removed, the problem of maintaining economic prosperity would probably become *the* great problem. As this is written, our nation has had no "normal" peacetime prosperity for a quarter-century. Certain institutional machinery erected during this period and intended to prevent the recurrence of another great depression has had no real test and its effectiveness is undemonstrated.

A major depression would accentuate many of the tensions and cleavages in American society. Racial antagonisms would probably become

[7] The term *fascist* is not currently fashionable. Communism has replaced fascism as "the enemy," and the communists have so freely applied the term *fascist* to everyone and everything they dislike that others have shied away from its use. But as a term to describe a particular kind of society, it has a certain usefulness. For a concise analysis of fascist states, past and present, see William Ebenstein, *Today's Isms* (New York, Prentice-Hall, Inc., 1954), Ch. 2, "Totalitarian Fascism."

more tense as Negro and white competed for the same scarce jobs. Radical social movements would gain in strength and conservative fears of radicalism would mount accordingly. Since people who are insecure find it easy to blame any plausible scapegoat, every division of class, race, religion, or occupation could become a potential point of antagonism to be exploited by those who crave power.[8]

A major depression, or some other similar set of developments, can create a situation in which the people are divided into hostile, warring camps, lacking common values and unable to agree upon a common course of action. This results in paralysis of effective governmental action. It results in endless talk and interminable legislative bickering but indecisive action, because *no* particular action will please more than a minority of the people. Demagogues flourish, to rouse false hopes by promising the impossible, and to foment dangerous passions by denouncing error as evil and indecision as cowardice. Eventually, people may grow weary of indecision and lend support to the "strong man" or party that promises to bring order out of chaos. Although no two fascist states are exactly alike or come to power in exactly the same way, this is the general manner in which fascism gained power in both Germany and Italy.[9] In each case there was widespread economic distress, an indecisive government in which the people had lost confidence, and a popular craving for prompt, decisive action. In each case, a multiplicity of political parties helped contribute to the parliamentary confusion of which the people grew weary. In each case, recent military defeats and sweeping social changes had reduced and weakened the core of unifying values which all revered in common. In each case, the absence of a firm democratic tradition made it easy for the people to exchange a half-understood freedom for a much-desired order.

A fascist state, having gained power, tends to become a garrison-police state as well. To maintain order and prevent bickering, the suppression of dissent is soon required. Censorship, police surveillance, security certification, outlawing of any real political opposition, demands for political conformity in the arts, removal of "disloyal" teachers and preachers—all these inevitably follow from the attempt to solve social problems by imposing an authoritarian pattern of control upon the society. Whereas the

[8] See Lawrence Dennis, *The Coming American Fascism* (New York, Harper and Brothers, 1936), for an unabashed statement of the thesis that America should, and inevitably will, become fascist.

[9] Cf. Calvin B. Hoover, *Germany Enters the Third Reich* (New York, The Macmillan Company, 1933); Erica Mann, *The Lights Go Down* (New York, Farrar and Rinehart, Inc., 1940); H. R. Knickerbocker, *The German Crisis* (New York, Farrar and Rinehart, Inc., 1932); Robert A. Brady, *The Spirit and Structure of German Fascism* (New York, Viking Press, Inc., 1937); Frederick L. Schumann, *The Nazi Dictatorship* (New York, Alfred A. Knopf, Inc., 1935); John Strachey, *The Menace of Fascism* (New York, Covici Friede, 1933); Giuseppe Borgese, *The March of Fascism* (New York, Viking Press, Inc., 1937).

slogan of the French Revolution—"liberty, equality, fraternity"—eventually helped produce a democratic society, the slogans of fascism—"order, discipline, system"—call for actions and policies which inevitably destroy democracy.

The fascist state emerges from a society's inability or failure to deal effectively with its social problems. No nation has become fascist (or communist) as an end result of too bold or sweeping (or "socialistic") an attack upon social problems. Fascism or communism is more likely to gain power following prolonged attempts to postpone dealing realistically with social problems. Once installed, the fascist state attempts to "solve" social problems in a manner consistent with its authoritarian philosophy. Its definitions of problems reflect the philosophy of the fascist state; the "problem" of "civil liberty" vanishes while the problem of "loyalty" grows, and the problems of "education" and "mass communication" become those of insuring (not of preventing) their conversion into agents of official indoctrination. "Solutions" emerge not from public discussion and agreement but from the counsels of the élite, who then impose these solutions upon the society. Social problems receive a great deal of attention in a fascist state, and the "solutions" sought are often so drastic that they arouse bitter opposition that must then be forcefully suppressed. Many of the "solutions," however, are likely to be showy palliatives rather than fundamental solutions, for the fascist state must constantly dazzle the population with its "accomplishments," to make their surrender of freedom appear as a good bargain.

In this discussion of alternatives, the communist state is absent. Although there are parts of the world where communism has powerful appeal, it would be difficult to find a social scientist who believes that communism, as a political movement, has any prospect of gaining power in the United States. If communism were to gain a considerable following in the United States, the probable result would be not a communist state, but a fascist state established to "save" the country from communism.

WHICH ALTERNATIVE?

Will democracy survive in the United States? Within which framework will social problems be defined and considered? This question cannot be answered positively. Actions of other countries will greatly affect the outcome. Our success in maintaining economic prosperity is a crucial factor; it is unlikely that democracy could survive repeated or prolonged economic crises, for idle and despairing men are not rational social analysts. Unless economic problems are met fairly successfully, there can be no rational atmosphere for consideration of any other problems.

Assuming reasonable success in maintaining prosperity and in avoiding wars or war fevers, the survival of democracy may depend upon the vitality of our value-heritage. There is no doubt that there are powerful currents of antidemocratic thought in America,[10] but there is also a value-heritage highly favorable to democracy. As long as these values survive, our approach to social problems is likely to remain democratic.

THE AMERICAN VALUE-HERITAGE

Among the many values which comprise our value-system, the following are conspicuous:

1. *Pleasure.* Most people appear to feel that life should be pleasant and enjoyable, now, in this world.

2. *Property.* Most people desire property and demand a social order that protects the right to acquire and enjoy it.

3. *Freedom.* Most people resent being "pushed around," insisting upon thinking and acting much as they wish with a minimum of arbitrary restraints.

4. *Fair Play.* Most people feel that people in general should have equal opportunities, that the strong should not "bully" the weak, and that deception, insincerity, and entrapment should be confined to harmless games and rituals.

5. *Education.* Most people consider education desirable and a mark of individual achievement and cultural advance.

6. *Religion.* Most people consider religion necessary for a good society, and many also consider a personal religious faith essential.

7. *Science and Technology.* To most people, applied science and technology hold great prestige as the source of our high standard of living and as the means of national survival in the atomic era. Pure science and the ideals of scientific objectivity and freedom are less widely understood and less highly valued.

8. *Progress.* A desire for "progress" and a belief in its attainability is almost universal in American society. The definition of "progress," however, varies widely and reflects the total value-system of each individual.

9. *Democracy.* For a great many people, "democracy" is a major value. Although the varied meanings they give to the term are a reflection of their individual value-systems, some ideals of freedom, equality, and fair play are nearly always implied.

If this describes correctly the major value-system of most Americans, it is clear that social problems will not disappear. These values inevitably define many situations as social problems, and our rapidly changing (disorganized?) society produces many such situations.

Failure to meet these problems with some degree of success would eventually destroy a democratic society. Totalitarianism, either of the left

[10] Cf. David Spitz, *Patterns of Anti-Democratic Thought* (New York, The Macmillan Company, 1949).

(communism) or of the right (fascism) awaits a democratic society that cannot or will not deal effectively with its social problems. That these totalitarianisms, so much alike in many respects, promise no real "solutions," as defined by democratic values, is perhaps true but irrelevant. Recent history clearly shows that the disorganizing effects of rapid social change inevitably produce social tensions fatal to democracy unless directed into constructive social policy.

KNOWLEDGE FOR WHAT?

If a rapidly changing society can remain reasonably tranquil and orderly only by continuously and consciously reorganizing itself, this calls for high levels of knowledge, rationality, and unselfishness.

The *knowledge* needed to deal effectively with social problems is available to a considerable degree. We do not know all "the answers" about any problem, but *we do know some of "the answers."* We are steadily learning more of them. The use of expert consultants in developing and administering social policy appears to be increasing. Today it is easy to find many examples of both brilliant use of knowledge and spectacular evasions of knowledge in dealing with social problems.

Rationality is needed if knowledge is to be useful. Unless one can consider various alternatives objectively, viewing each proposal on its merits, no rational approach is possible. Where thinking has frozen into rigid, inflexible dogmas, a rational analysis is impossible. On some problems, many people are incapable of thinking rationally. Some vital issues have become so "controversial" that although we *must* decide them, we dare not discuss them.[11] Some people's social thinking today consists largely of a set of conditioned reflexes whereby they mechanically oppose whatever Russia or the communists are said to favor, and favor whatever they oppose. Anti-communism (or anti-fascism, or anti-Catholicism, or anti-Republicanism, or anti-anything) can become a substitute for rational analyses.

Unselfishness is a homely virtue that still plays a leading role in meeting social problems. It is historically true, of course, that action on many problems came only when an interest group was persuaded to redefine its

[11] For example, a number of colleges and universities decided in 1954-1955 that the Speech Association of America's debate topic, "Resolved, That the United States should extend diplomatic recognition to the Communist government of China," was too controversial to debate. One college president objected that students should not be allowed to "spend half their time arguing the Communist side." The commanding officers of Annapolis and West Point cancelled debates, stating that to argue the affirmative would make their students "liable to misrepresentation. . . ." A Duke University debater received a letter from U. S. Rep. Edward Robeson, advising him not to debate the affirmative because "quotations from your statements may embarrass you for the rest of your life." ("Subject for Debate," *Time* [November 29, 1954], p. 43.)

vested interest, that is, persuaded to support a reform or policy by being shown how it would benefit the interest group itself. Corporations contribute to the Community Chest because (among other possible reasons) they consider it "good business" to do so. C.I.O. unions oppose racial discrimination because (among other possible reasons) racial discrimination weakens the union and depresses white wages. Much of the motivation for treating social problems stems from an enlightened self-interest.

But not all motivation is "selfish" in an ordinary sense of the word. *Solutions always cost somebody something!* For each solution, taxes must be collected, contributions offered, profits trimmed, opportunities for exploitation surrendered, power shared, prestige sacrificed, prejudices suspended, cherished values compromised—someone always has to give up something or other. These sacrifices do not always "pay off" financially, at least not soon enough to do the maker any good. The successful treatment of a social problem nearly always requires that a number of persons be willing to make some personal sacrifice in order to achieve some larger public benefit. By whatever name it is called—brotherly love, Christian charity, social consciousness—such a spirit of unselfishness is not a saccharine sentimentality but a major force in social action. Whatever stimulates or inhibits this spirit of unselfishness—religion, education, unique personal experience—becomes an indirect determinant of success in treating social problems.

CONSENSUS UPON VALUES

When people share the same values, even though they may be ignorant and clumsy, they can usually arrive at workable agreements. When their values differ, no amount of technical knowledge and parliamentary finesse can produce better than a tolerable compromise. Most important decisions eventually resolve themselves into a choice between values. How to spend one's life—how to kill oneself, for that is the ultimate price of living—is answered only by one's choices between values.

To this most important of all questions, science has no complete answer. Values are matters of preference, not matters of factual knowledge. Any attempt to say which values people "ought" to hold makes one a philosopher, not a scientist.

Social scientists may, however, guide people in their value-choices in at least three ways.

1. *Science May Show the Implications of Alternative Values.* Science may show what each value-choice involves. If national unity, or equality of opportunity, or "free enterprise" is proposed as the primary value, social scientists may show what social arrangements each choice requires. If one objects (and some do) to "materialism" as a primary value, the social scientist can show some of the institutional rearrangements which

would be needed in order to replace materialism with some other value. It is likely that many who listened approvingly to Hitler in the early 1930's had no clear idea of the kind of society which Hitler's values would *necessarily* produce. If social science can *show people what they are choosing* when they make their value-choices, much social conflict will be avoided.

2. *Science May Show the Relation Between Values.* Certain values, such as "democracy" and "caste," are incompatible and cannot coexist without many cumbersome evasions and compromises. Other values, like "freedom of speech" and "equality of opportunity," are so mutually supporting that it is difficult to have one without the other. Since, in adopting one major value (for example, "democracy," "discipline," or "rugged individualism,") one implicitly accepts the other values and institutional arrangements that go with it, knowledge about the relations between values should reduce confusions and social tensions.

3. *Science Can Indicate Which Values Are Functionally Useful in a Particular Social Setting.* This is as close to "choosing" values for people that scientists, as scientists, can come. For example, the social scientist can point out how certain frontier values do not fit an urbanized, industrialized, interdependent society. A value like "thrift"—spending only the bare minimum and saving all the rest—was useful to a society with a capital shortage but would be economically disastrous if widely followed in a mass-production economy such as ours. A tolerant attitude toward cultural differences, unnecessary in an isolated frontier hamlet, becomes highly useful in an interdependent heterogeneous modern world. Early marriage and high fertility are useful cultural ideals in a frontier society, in a society with a high death rate, or a society organized for warfare; for a peaceful society with an ample population and a low death rate, a far lower birth rate is conducive to an orderly society. To value "retribution" in dealing with criminals is incompatible with scientific knowledge of its consequences. Although this test of functional utility for a given social setting will not resolve all value-choices, it will in some cases indicate which values are likely to "work" to our satisfaction.

Will these contributions of science to the selection of values produce an American consensus upon values and thereby simplify the treatment of social problems? Not necessarily. Values emerge from the social experience of groups of people and are not adopted on a basis of sociological suggestion. But to the extent that people gain insight into their value-choices and are aware of the social significance of their value-judgments, their social experience *is* modified. Social experience has *meaning* only as it is interpreted by individuals and groups, in the light of their knowledge and insight. To some degree, therefore, the scientific study of values may contribute to a rational consensus upon values, and thereby simplify the task of reaching agreements upon social problems and their treatment.

CONCLUSION

There is no way to "finish" a social problems textbook. Each attempt at a conclusion succeeds only in raising additional questions. But this is the way of all science—no field of inquiry is ever exhausted. All scientific truth is tentative and the search is unending; each "conclusion" is an intermission, not a finale.

In the opening chapter of this textbook, the authors expressed the hope that students might be helped to develop an (1) *awareness* of social problems, (2) some *knowledge* about them, (3) some understanding of their *sociological* origins, (4) some awareness of the roles of *theory and practice*, (5) a balanced *perspective* upon social problems, (6) an appreciation of the *role of the expert*, and (7) an intelligent *personal involvement*. Perhaps there is no better way to conclude this volume than to repeat this hope and append to it the further hope that, long after this volume's bits and pieces of data are forgotten, some fragments of these habits of social analysis may be retained.

SUGGESTED READINGS

Bain, Read, "Our Schizoid Culture," *Sociology and Social Research*, 19 (January-February, 1935), pp. 266-276. A classic sociological essay: a pungent statement of many of the value-conflicts and inconsistencies in American social life.

Ebenstein, William, *Today's Isms* (New York, Prentice-Hall, Inc., 1954). A penetrating description and comparison of communism, fascism, socialism, and capitalism. Chapter 3, "Democratic Capitalism," is especially recommended.

Lundberg, George, *Can Science Save Us?* (New York, Longmans, Green & Company, 1947). A somewhat pessimistic view of the prospects for rational guidance of society.

Lynd, Robert, *Knowledge for What?* (Princeton, N. J., Princeton University Press, 1939). An eloquent plea for the use of scientific knowledge in directing society. A vivid contrast to the above Lundberg volume.

Mannheim, Karl, *Freedom, Power and Democratic Planning* (New York, Oxford University Press, 1950). An attempt to show how social planning can reconcile conflicting social forces in a democratic society.

Reimer, Svend, "Social Planning and Social Organization," *American Journal of Sociology*, 52 (May, 1947), pp. 508-517. A stimulating discussion of the prospects for rational control of a society which has not yet accepted the rational ideology of planning.

Riesman, David, with Nathan Glazer and Reuel Denney, *The Lonely Crowd* (New Haven, Yale University Press, 1950); abridged pocket edition (Garden City, N. Y., Doubleday & Company, Inc., 1953). A study of the changing American character in a mass society wherein people are guided by interiorized values and goals rather than by custom and tradition.

QUESTIONS AND PROJECTS

1. When will all social problems be solved? Why?

2. What are the "trends in American society" mentioned in this chapter? Are there any others which should be added? What reason is there to believe that these trends will continue?

3. Criticize this statement: "The easiest way to settle the question of how to divide the national income is simply to give everyone a fair share."

4. Toward what values is the democratic state oriented? The garrison state? The fascist state?

5. Would a transition to a garrison or a fascist state be gradual and imperceptible or abrupt and dramatic? Or are both kinds of transition possible?

6. Why is the communist state not included among the alternatives?

7. Of what importance is the American value-heritage with respect to social problems?

8. To what extent can science guide people in choosing values?

9. Why is value consensus important in dealing with social problems?

10. Social problems can be dealt with either by seeking to solve them, or by redefining the situations so that they are no longer problems. Can the latter course be followed without modifying our value-heritage?

11. What are some possible policies or "solutions" upon which many people have such an inflexible attitude that no rational evaluation is possible?

12. Is "enlightened self-interest" a rational reason for supporting social action? Can support for practical solutions always be secured by appeal to "enlightened self-interest"? If not, what else is sometimes effective?

Author Index

Adorno, T. W., 293
Alinsky, Saul, 140
Allport, Gordon, W., 290, 325
Almond, Gabriel, A., 518, 522
Alsop, Joseph, 512, 518
Alsop, Stewart, 512
Anderson, H. Dewey, 262, 263
Anderson, Odin N., 428, 435
Angell, Robert C., 561
Ash, Ellis, 133
Ashley-Montagu, M. F., 101
Ashmore, Harry S., 317
Atelsek, Frank J., 309
Aurelio, Thomas A., 114
Auster, Donald, 364

Baber, Ray E., 146, 155, 156, 161
Bacon, Selden D., 390, 397, 398, 399, 419
Bain, Read, 570
Baird, John H., 392
Baker, Kenneth, 371
Barer, Naomi, 139
Barnes, Harry E., 101, 102, 122, 127, 129, 132, 466, 556
Barrett, Edward L., Jr., 507
Barth, Alan, 500, 505
Beale, Howard K., 236
Beers, Clifford W., 418
Bell, Daniel, 93
Benedict, Ruth, 276, 325
Bendix, Reinhard, 268
Bernard, Jessie, 188
Berry, Brewton, 288, 294, 295, 301, 325
Bestor, Arthur E., 227
Bettelheim, Bruno, 291
Biddle, Francis, 513
Binger, Carl, 392
Bingham, Robert A., 238
Bird, George L., 369, 388
Blaine, Daniel, 392
Blaisdell, Donald C., 81
Blakely, R. J., 387
Blanshard, Paul, 179, 185
Bloch, Herbert A., 402, 418
Bluemel, C. S., 43

Blumberg, Nathan B., 364, 365
Blumer, Herbert, 355
Bowles, Chester, 282
Boyo, Gene, 91
Brady, Robert A., 362, 564
Brameld, Theodore, 307
Bredemeier, Harry C., 69, 81
Brelis, Dean, 517
Britt, S. H., 290
Brockway, A. F., 134
Bromfield, Louis, 511
Bronner, A., 136
Browder, Earl, 37
Brown, Lawrence G., 33
Bryson, Lyman, 368
Buchanan, W. A., 88
Buckley, William F., 508
Burch, Guy S., 481
Burgess, David S., 188
Burgess, Ernest W., 147, 349
Burkhard, J. Austin, 242
Burma, John H., 317

Callahan, Jennie W., 388
Cantril, Hadley, 47, 357
Carlson, John R., 292, 305
Carr, Robert K., 500
Casey, Roy, 136
Centers, Richard, 272
Chambers, Whittaker, 518
Chappell, Richard A., 135
Chase, Stuart, 37, 561
Chatto, Clarence A., 307
Christensen, Harold T., 162, 165
Churchill, Winston, 40
Clark, William, 377
Collins, Mary E., 309
Conant, James B., 181
Conwell, Chic, 112
Cook, Elaine F., 242, 246, 248, 307
Cook, Lloyd A., 242, 246, 248, 307
Coolidge, Calvin, 47
Cooper, Courtney, 112
Cooper, Eunice, 308
Costello, Frank, 114
Cottrell, Leonard S., 147

573

Subject Index